DEDICATION

To our families, without whose patience
and support there would have been no book.

Director, Programming Books

Allen L. Wyatt, Sr.

Product Manager

Joseph Wikert

Acquisitions Editor

Gregory Croy

Cover and Book Design

Dan Armstrong

Production

Brad Chinn
Don Clemons
T. R. Emrick
Chuck Hutchinson
Betty Kish
Bob LaRoche
Cindy L. Phipps
Joe Ramon
Dennis Sheehan
Louise Shinault
Bruce Steed
Mary Beth Wakefield

Senior Editor

Rebecca Whitney

Editors

Gail S. Burlakoff
Kathy Ewing
Jodi Jensen
Sam Karnick
Andy Saff

Technical Editor

Allen L. Wyatt, Sr.

Editorial Assistants

San Dee Phillips
Ann K. Taylor

Illustrations

Susan Moore

Index

Hilary Adams
Jill Bomaster
Joelynn Gifford

Composed in Garamond and OCRB
by Que Corporation

ABOUT THE AUTHORS ▼

Lee Atkinson

T he senior author Lee Atkinson is a 20-year veteran of the data processing industry. He has written code professionally in C, Pascal, COBOL, Fortran, PL/I, APL, and a number of assembly languages for machines ranging from the smallest microprocessors to IBM's top-of-the-line mainframes. He is currently an MVS systems programmer for a Mississippi-based regional retail company. He was a contributing author of Que's *Turbo C Programming*.

Mark Atkinson

M ark Atkinson was introduced to computer programming in 1959 with a Fortran ballistics program that tracked the Saturn-V rocket and astronauts to the moon. He has been involved with computing continuously since that time, including consulting and contract programming for IBM PCs and mainframes in a variety of languages. He is currently a PC technician for the area's largest vendor of office systems.

CONTENT OVERVIEW ▼

Introduction   1

Part I   Introduction to Standard C

Chapter 1   Getting Started With C   9
Chapter 2   Basic I/O Programming   51
Chapter 3   Building C Programs   103
Chapter 4   A Closer Look at C Programs   151
Chapter 5   Objects, Expressions, Operators,
             and Conversions   191
Chapter 6   More about C Functions   243
Chapter 7   Controlling Program Logic Flow   281
Chapter 8   Programming with Pointers, Arrays,
             and Strings   325
Chapter 9   More about Using Pointers   379
Chapter 10   File I/O Programming   415
Chapter 11   Deriving New Complex Data Types   457
Chapter 12   Portability and Conversion Issues   505

Part II   Using the Standard C Function Library

Chapter 13   Debugging, Error Handling, and
             Character Handling   537
Chapter 14   Math, Numbers, and Conversions   547
Chapter 15   Alternate Transfers of Control and
             Variable Argument Lists   571
Chapter 16   Common Macros and I/O Functions   585
Chapter 17   String, Time, and Miscellaneous Functions   635

Part III   C++ Programming Basics

Chapter 18   Objects and Object-Oriented Programming   685
Chapter 19   Defining Classes and Objects   707
Chapter 20   Controlling Classes and Objects   751
Chapter 21   More on C++ Methods and Objects   793
Appendix A   ASCII Character Set   833
Appendix B   ANSI C Predefined Macros   837
Appendix C   ANSI C Function Library   845
Appendix D   The *finance.c* Program   857
Appendix E   IBM PC Communications Programming   877
Appendix F   B-Spline Derivation   897
Appendix G   Performance-Measurement Software   899
Bibliography   911
Index   915

TABLE OF CONTENTS ▼

Introduction 1

Purpose of This Book 2
Who Should Use This Book? 3
Getting Prepared To Use This Book 3
The Book's Format 4
How To Use This Book 5

▼

I   Introduction to Standard C

1   Getting Started With C 9

Approaching the C Language 9
  A Brief History of C 10
    In the Beginning: Kernighan and Ritchie 10
    The Move from UNIX to DOS 10
    ANSI Gets Interested 11
      Codifying Practice 11
      Conforming to ANSI C 12
      Portability Issues 12
    Looking Toward the Future: C++ 12
      Object-Oriented Programming 13
      Bell Labs Again 13
    Comparing C to Other Languages 13
    Comparing C and Assembly Language 13
    Comparing C and Pascal 14
    Comparing C and COBOL 14
    Comparing C and FORTRAN 15
  A First Look at C and Punctuation 15
    How To Look at a C Program 15
    Noticing the C "Punctuators" 16
Understanding the Parts of a C Program 19
  Including the Header Files 20
    Including Source Files in General 21
    Header Files and Built-In Functions 22
    Placing the Includes 23
    Two Ways to Include 24
    A Note about Multiple Source Files 25

Defining Data to C 26
  Setting Aside Memory for Data 26
  Where Do You Put It? 26
What the *main( )* Function Does 28
  The *main( )* Entry Point 28
  Setting Up the Environment 28
  Normal Program Termination 29
Providing User-defined Functions 29
  Functions Act Like Data 29
  Where Do They Go? 30
Writing a C Program 31
Start with the Right Design 32
A Top-down Approach to Coding 32
Making Programs Readable 33
  Using Indentation and White Space 33
  Using Comments 34
  Aligning Braces and Parentheses 35
Writing Programs in the C Environment 36
Evaluating the Text Editor 36
What's in a Good C Compiler? 38
  Compiler Features 39
  The Linkage Editor and Compatibility 41
  Project-Management Facilities 42
  Compatibility with Other Languages 44
Command-line versus Integrated Environments 45
  What's the Difference? 46
  Why You Need Both 46
Do You Need a Visual Debugger? 46
  What Is a Visual Debugger? 47
  Features of a Good Debugger 48
  Legitimate Uses of a Debugger 49
Summary 49

2   Basic I/O Programming **51**

The Problem with Input and Output 52
Understanding Stream I/O 56
Comparing Streams, Files, and Devices 57
  Interactive Devices 58
  Data Files 60
  Introducing C Streams 60
The Standard Streams 61
  stdin, stdout, and *stderr* 62
  Relating Streams to DOS Handles 64

The Simple I/O Functions 65
  Connecting Files to Streams: *fopen( )* 66
    Declaring the Stream Data Object 66
    Opening the File 68
  Closing the File: *fclose( )* 70
  Character I/O Functions 72
  String I/O Functions 79
  Handling I/O Errors and End-of-File 83
  Converting Data Formats 83
The Formatted I/O Functions 86
  Displaying Data with *printf( )* 87
  Getting Input with *scanf( )* 91
  Putting It All Together 94
Coping with Hardware and System Dependencies 94
  Using Extensions to Standard C 95
    Supporting Extended DOS Streams 95
    Programming IBM PC I/O Ports 97
  The IBM PC Video-Display Controversy 98
    "Glass Teletype" I/O and Standard Streams 98
    Getting Around the Problem 98
Summary 101

3 Building C Programs **103**

Managing Data in a C Program 104
  The Standard C Data Types 104
  Working with Constant Values (Literals) 112
  Declaring Variable Data 115
    Naming Variables 115
    Declarators and Declarator Lists 116
    Initializing Variables 121
    Local and Global Variables 122
Declaring Functions and Passing Parameters 131
  Using Full Function Prototypes 132
    The Prototype Declaration Format 134
    Writing the Function Type Specifier 134
    Writing the Function Name and Formal
      Parameter List 136
    Effects on the Order of Appearance 138
  Coding the Function Definition 138
    Building the Function Body 139
    Writing C Statements 140
      Writing Expression Statements 140
      Writing Flow Control Statements 141

Using Labeled Statements 143
Using Null Statements 144
Writing Compound (Block) Statements 144
Returning Values From a Function 145
Calling the Function 148
Summary 149

4   A Closer Look at C Programs 151

More Detail on Language Conventions 152
The C Character Set 152
Bits, Bytes, and Characters 152
The C "Minimal" Character Set 155
Handling Special Characters 156
Mnemonic Escape Sequences 158
Numeric Escape Sequences 162
Using Trigraphs 163
Multibyte Characters 165
Source and Target Character Sets 166
How C Looks at Your Source Program 166
The Phases of Program Translation 167
Tokens and Translation Units 170
Identifiers in General 171
Using C Reserved Words 172
The C Keywords 172
The Standard Macros and Functions 173
Using Compiler Directives and Macros 174
Revisiting the C Preprocessor 174
The Source File Inclusion Directive 175
Macro Substitution Directives 177
Conditional Compilation Directives 184
Line-control, Error, Pragma, and Null Directives 186
Predefined Macro Names 188
Summary 189

5   Objects, Expressions, Operators, and
Conversions 191

Another Look at Scope and Duration 192
Taking Advantage of Storage Class 192
Determining the Scope of an Object 195
Determining the Linkage of an Object 196
Controlling Initializers for Objects 199
Accessing External Data and Functions 200

Compiling Modules Separately 202
Setting Up the Header Files 206
Coding References to Other Modules 209
Linking the Modules Together 210
Understanding C Expressions 214
Rules Governing C Expressions 214
Primary Expressions 217
rvalue and *lvalue* Expressions 218
Function Designator Expressions 219
void Expressions 220
Controlling the C Operators 220
Classifying the C Operators 220
Postfix Operators 221
Unary Operators 224
Cast Operators 228
Binary Operators 228
The Conditional (Ternary) Operator 232
Simple and Compound Assignment Operators 233
The Comma Operator 234
The Key to C: Operator Precedence 235
Converting Data Types to Other Types 236
Automatic Type Conversions 237
Type Promotion in Expressions 237
Implicit Conversion by Assignment 238
Explicit Conversions With Type Casts 238
Summary 241

6   More about C Functions **243**

Details about Passing Parameters 244
Pass by Value and Pass by Reference 244
Parameters Are Passed on the Stack 244
Passing Parameters by Value 245
Passing Parameters by Reference 245
Function Argument Promotions 247
Function Prototypes with Incomplete Types 248
Variable-length Argument Lists 249
Passing Parameters to *main()* 256
Accessing Command-line Parameters 256
argc and *argv[]* 256
Designing Command-line Formats 258
Functions that Call Themselves 260
Understanding Recursion 260

	Avoiding Open-ended Recursion	262
	Eliminating Recursion	264
	Other Ways To Invoke Functions	266
	Using Pointers to Functions	267
	The *signal( )* and *raise( )* Functions	271
	The *setjmp( )* and *longjmp( )* Functions	274
	Summary	280

7   Controlling Program Logic Flow   281

Designing Program Loops	282
Properties of Program Loops	282
Doing It the Hard Way—Not Recommended	284
Front-End Condition Checking: *while( )*	289
Back-End Condition Checking: *do-while( )*	292
Getting It All: the *for( )* Loop	297
Altering Logic Flow in a Loop	301
goto versus *break*	304
Using *continue* To Loop Early	306
Programming Conditional Logic	308
If-Then-Else Statements	309
More Complex Conditions: *switch( )*	312
The *switch( )* Statement	312
case: Labels	313
Using *break;* and *default:*	317
Terminating the Program Early	318
Invoking the System Command Processor	321
Common Extensions to the ANSI Standard	322
Summary	323

8   Programming with Pointers, Arrays, and Strings   325

Pointers and Composite Data Types	326
Reviewing Indirect Addressing	326
Referring to Pointers and Their Objects	327
Pointer Comparisons and Arithmetic	331
When Do You Need a Pointer?	339
Defining Arrays of Variables	340
Defining One-dimensional Arrays	341
Declaring the Array	341
Referencing Array Elements	343
Defining Multidimensional Arrays	344
Declaring the Array	344

Referencing Array Elements 345
Pointer and Subscript Equivalence 346
Using Arrays for Smoothing Geometric Curves 348
Using Arrays To Represent Shapes 349
Curve-smoothing Methods: *spline.c* 349
Using Arrays To Solve Systems of Equations 356
Using Arrays To Represent Equations 356
Solving the Equations: *gauss.c* 356
Strings Are Arrays of Characters 359
The Internal Representation of Strings 359
Declaring String Variables 360
Initializing String Variables 361
Manipulating Strings 361
Using Strings To Edit Text 363
Inserting and Deleting Characters 365
General-Purpose String Edit: *stredit.c* 367
Arrays and Strings as Function Parameters 368
Strings as Function Parameters 376
Arrays as Function Parameters 377
Summary 378

9   More about Using Pointers 379

Using Pointers to Pointers 379
Using Multiple Indirection 380
Referencing and Dereferencing Multiple Pointers 381
Using Pointers To Scan and Parse Text 382
Creating a Lexical Scanner 382
What a Scanner Does 382
Why `strtok()` Won't Work Here 383
How the Scanner Uses Pointers 384
Creating a Parsing Routine 394
What "Recursive Descent" Means 394
Building the Parser 395
Evaluating Formulas: *formula.c* 396
Mixing Arrays and Pointers 403
Defining Arrays of Pointer 403
Defining a Pointer to Array 405
Improving Program Performance with Pointers 406
Using Pointers To Increase Flexibility 406
Speeding Up Sorting with Pointers 407
Summary 414

10   File I/O Programming **415**

Using C's File-Management Functions 416
    Deleting a File with *remove( )* 416
    Changing the File Name with *rename( )* 417
    Back to the Beginning with *rewind( )* 418
    Creating and Using Temporary Files 420
Buffered I/O Concepts 421
    What Difference Does It Make? 422
    Buffering and *stdin, stdout,* and *stderr* 423
Selecting an I/O Mode for File Streams 425
    Selecting the Access Mode 426
        Open Options for Input Mode 426
        Open Options for Output Mode 427
        Open Options for Update Mode 428
        Summary of Modes 429
    Mixing Reads and Writes in Update Modes 430
    Using Text and Binary File Modes 431
Direct-Access File Programming 434
Direct-Access Concepts 435
    Using *ftell( )* and *fgetpos( )* 439
    Using *fseek( )* and *fsetpos( )* 440
Direct Access with Hashed Keys 441
Writing High-Performance File Routines 450
    Choosing the File Mode 450
    Minimizing I/O Overhead 450
        Using `setbuf( )` and `setvbuf( )` 451
            Reducing I/O Events 453
            Releasing the Buffers at Close 454
        Loading Directly to RAM 454
Common Extensions to the ANSI Standard 455
    Low-Level I/O Practices 455
    Files in a Networking Environment 455
Summary 456

11   Deriving New Complex Data Types **457**

Defining Structures of Items 458
    Basic Structure Declarations 458
        Defining Structured Data Objects 458
        Using Structure Tags 462
    Accessing Structure Members 464
    Using Bit-fields in Structures 467
    Combining Structures and Arrays 469

Defining Unions of Structures 473
   The Overlay Concept of Unions 473
   Declaring a Union 474
   Accessing Members of a Union 474
Deriving Types with *typedef*.. 476
Managing Data in Dynamic Memory 478
   Allocating Memory at Run-time 478
   Keeping Track of Allocations 481
Structures and Unions as Function Parameters 482
Building Linked Lists with Structures 483
Using Enumeration Constants 501
Summary 503

12   **Portability and Conversion Issues** **505**

Keeping the Spirit of C... 506
   The Programmer Is King.. 506
   Keep It Simple 507
   Make It Unique 507
   Performance Is the Rule 507
A Treaty between Vendor and Programmer 507
   A Meeting of the Minds.. 508
   When It Backfires 508
Unspecified Behavior 508
   What It Means 508
   What To Look For 508
Undefined Behavior 510
   What It Means 510
   What To Look For 510
Implementation-Defined Behavior 518
   What It Means 518
   What To Look For 518
      Environment... 518
      Identifiers 518
      Characters.. 519
      Integers 519
      Floating Point 519
      Arrays and Pointers 520
      Registers 520
      Structures, Unions, Enumerations, and Bit-fields........ 520
      Qualifiers 520
      Declarators 521
      Statements 521
      Preprocessing Directives 521

Library Functions 521

Locale-specific Behavior 523

Quiet Changes to K & R C 523

What Is a Quiet Change? 524

Converting K & R C Programs 524

Environmental Considerations 528

Translation Limitations 528

Common Extensions to ANSI Standard C 529

Environment Arguments 530

Specialized Identifiers 530

Length and Case of Identifiers 530

Scope of Identifiers 530

Writable String Literals 531

Other Arithmetic Types 531

Function Pointer Casts 531

Non-*int* Bit-field Types 531

The *fortran* Keyword 531

The *asm* Keyword 531

Multiple External Definitions 531

Empty Macro Arguments 532

Predefined Macro Names 532

Extra Arguments for Signal Handlers 532

Additional Stream Types and File Modes 532

Defined File-position Indicator 532

Summary 533

II   Using the Standard C Function Library

**13   Debugging, Error Handling, and Character
Handling** 537

#include <assert.h> 537

#include <errno.h> 538

#include <ctype.h> 540

Summary 544

14   Math, Numbers, and Conversions 547

#include <float.h> 548

#include <limits.h> 551

#include <locale.h> 554

#include <math.h> 559

Error Conditions 560

Trigonometric Functions 560
Hyperbolic Functions 563
Exponential and Logarithmic Functions 564
Power Functions 567
Closest Integer, Absolute Value,
    and Remainder Functions 568
Summary 569

15   Alternate Transfers of Control and Variable Argument Lists **571**

#include <setjmp.h> 571
#include <signal.h> 575
#include <stdarg.h> 579
Summary 582

16   Common Macros and I/O Functions **585**

#include <stddef.h> 585
    Types 585
    Macros 586
#include <stdio.h> 586
    Types 587
    Macros 587
    File Utilities 589
    Accessing Files 592
    Formatted I/O 599
    Character I/O 615
    Direct I/O 623
    Error-handling Functions 631
Summary 634

17   String, Time, and Miscellaneous Functions **635**

#include <stdlib.h> 635
    Type Declarations 636
    Macro Definitions 636
    Converting Strings to Numbers 637
    Generating Pseudorandom Numbers 642
    Managing Memory 643
    Communicating with The Environment 647
    Searching and Sorting 650
    Arithmetic for Integers 654
    Handling Multibyte Characters 655
    Handling Multibyte Strings 657

#include string.h 658
   Copying 659
   Concatenation 661
   Comparing Strings 662
   String Searching 666
   Other String Functions 671
#include time.h 672
   Macros 673
   Type Definitions 673
   Manipulating Time 674
   Converting Time 678
Summary 682

III   C++ Programming Basics

18   Objects and Object-Oriented Programming 685

Objects Are Working Models 686
   Data Abstraction Is Data Hiding 686
   C Functions as Object Methods 688
Classes Are Abstract Data Types 692
   Going Beyond *typedef* 698
   What Encapsulation Means 699
Class Inheritance Is Type Derivation 699
Definitions of Object-Oriented Systems 700
   Wegner's Definition 700
   Zortech's Definition 702
   Stroustrup's Comments 703
Other Issues in Object-Oriented Systems 704
   Multiple Inheritance 704
   Object Implementations: Functional, Server,
     Autonomous, and Slot-based 705
Summary 706

19   Defining Classes and Objects 707

Defining Classes to C++ 708
   Setting Up the Class Definition 710
   Member Elements: *private:*, *public:*, and *protected:* 715
   What Is *this* 716
Initializing and Destroying Class Objects 720
   Constructors and Destructors 720
   Copy Initializers 726

Using Class Objects 727

    Calling Member Functions 727

    Building a Virtual Screen Class 729

Summary 749

20   **Controlling Classes and Objects** **751**

Understanding C++'s Free Store 752

    Using the Global *new* and *delete* Operators 753

    Defining Your Own *new* and *delete* 758

    What about *this* and *::operator new( )*? 763

Defining Objects to C++ 765

    What Are Static and Dynamic Objects? 765

    Dynamic Objects on the Stack 766

    Global Static Objects 768

    Static Objects on the Free Store 770

Derived Classes and Inheritance 771

    Understanding Code Reusability 772

    Reusing Code by Composition 772

    Reusing Code by Inheritance 778

    Extending Class Capability with Virtual Functions 783

C++ Stream I/O 787

    Reading and Writing with *cin* and *cout* 787

    Mixing Input and Output Streams 791

    I/O Redirection and Streams 791

Summary 792

21   **More on C++ Methods and Objects** **793**

Pointers and References in C++ 794

    The Reference Operator 794

    Defining Pointers to Objects 797

    Passing Objects as Parameters 799

    Referencing Other Objects 801

Overloading Functions 804

    Overloading Member Functions 806

    Overloading Friend Functions 806

Overloading Operators 807

    What Can Be Overloaded? 807

    User-defined Type Conversions 826

Recent Changes to C++ 827

    Multiple Inheritance and Virtual Base Classes 827

    Overloaded Functions and Type-Safe Linkage 828

    Using *const*, *volatile*, and *static* Member Functions 829

Summary 830

A	**ASCII Character Set**	833

B	**ANSI C Predefined Macros**	837
	#include <assert.h>	837
	#include <float.h>	838
	#include <limits.h>	839
	#include <locale.h>	840
	#include <math.h>	840
	#include <setjmp.h>	840
	#include <signal.h>	841
	#include <stdarg.h>	841
	#include <stddef.h>	842
	#include <stdio.h>	842
	#include <stdlib.h>	843
	#include time.h	843

C	**ANSI C Function Library**	845
	#include <ctype.h>	845
	#include <locale.h>	846
	#include <math.h>	846
	#include <setjmp.h>	847
	#include <signal.h>	848
	#include <stdio.h>	848
	#include <stdlib.h>	851
	#include string.h	853
	#include time.h	855

D	**The *finance.c* Program**	857
	Program Structure and Operation	870
	Using *finance.c* Computations	872
	General Business Functions	872
	Interest-Rate Conversion	872
	Time Value of Money	873
	Mortgage Analysis and Amortization	874

E	**IBM PC Communications Programming**	877

F	**B-Spline Derivation**	897

G   **Performance-Measurement Software** 899

Data Areas Used in *timer.c* 902
Reprogramming the Timer Chip 903
Handling the Timer-Tick Interrupts 905
Cleaning Up after High Resolution Timing 906
Separate Compilation of *timer.c* 907
Converting *timer.c* to Turbo C 908
Using the *timer.c* Functions 909

Bibliography 911

Index 915

▼ ACKNOWLEDGMENTS

Grateful acknowledgements is made to the following persons and organizations:

The Que Corporation editorial and production staff—especially Allen L. Wyatt, Sr., Gregory S. Croy, Katherine Stuart Ewing, and Gail Burlakoff—for their guidance, patience, and friendship.

The American National Standards Institute for permission to quote parts of X3.159.

TRADEMARK
ACKNOWLEDGMENTS

Que Corporation has made every attempt to supply trademark information about company names, products, and services mentioned in this book. Trademarks indicated below were derived from various sources. Que Corporation cannot attest to the accuracy of this information.

CompuServe Incorporated is a registered trademark of H&R Block, Inc.

UNIX is a trademark of AT&T.

Turbo C is a registered trademark and Turbo Assembler and TASM are trademarks of Borland International, Inc.

DEC is a registered trademark and PDP-11 and VAX are trademarks of Digital Equipment Corporation.

CP/M is a registered trademark of Digital Research Inc.

IBM and OS/2 are registered trademarks and IBM PC XT and PS/2 are trademarks of International Business Machines Corporation.

Microsoft, MS-DOS, XENIX, and QuickC are registered trademarks and Codeview is a trademark of Microsoft Corporation.

Seagate is a registered trademark of Seagate Technology.

Introduction

The world of C programming is endlessly fascinating, a world in which you can always find something new and profitable. Computer programming, especially in C, is a world in which you go beyond mastering your environment: you create it with each new program.

In this book, you begin (or perhaps continue) the process of learning a language well-suited to creating and manipulating computer environments. C has been characterized as a high-level assembly language, easily capable of controlling your computer's hardware, and has been labeled a particularly powerful high-level language suitable for rapid development of rich, complex programs. In fact, C is both of these things.

C is not *all* things to all people—nothing ever is. It is, however, about as close as you can get to that in computer programming, which explains its booming popularity. You can write just about any kind of program in C, from business and scientific applications to operating systems.

This book contains the material you need in order to comprehend all the fundamentals of the modern C programming language. We designed it to accomplish this goal in one volume—a rather ambitious task, although this book has no pretensions of being encyclopedic. The following tradeoffs therefore were necessary in controlling the development of the book:

❑ *The size had to be controlled, but depth of coverage is important.* The table of contents shows the range of topics that constitutes the fundamentals of modern C. We have tried to cover them in sufficient depth to allow you to write C programs with confidence and enjoyment, and to prepare you to move on to advanced skill levels.

❏ *The sample programs teach the language, not specific applications*. Large, complex projects belong in other books, and would only consume space and confuse the issues here. We have tried to avoid boring examples, however. The powerful techniques in this book are basic building blocks for the larger projects.

❏ *C is not just C anymore*. Beyond K & R C are ANSI C (the basic language) and C++ (ANSI C plus object-oriented extensions). We necessarily place the emphasis on ANSI C, with which you get the basic concepts necessary for an understanding of *all* C programming. Only when you have mastered these concepts are you ready for C++, and we have provided a solid primer for that as well.

Purpose of This Book

The most important purpose of this book is to introduce you to modern standard C programming, and to help you raise your skills from the beginning to the intermediate level. We also hope that this book will be a useful tool that you will not quickly outgrow as you become a more sophisticated C programmer. Three specific purposes are aimed at achieving these goals. They are as follows:

❏ *Present all the fundamentals of modern C programming*. This includes ANSI C and C++ programming. You do not have to buy several books, each covering only part of what you need to know to get a sound start in C programming.

❏ *Teach the C language effectively*. Learning C, when approached incorrectly, can be confusing and difficult. This need not be so. The process can be a fruitful and enjoyable one. We have made every effort to arrange the material in such a way as to hasten your proficiency in C, without leaving you to sink or swim.

❏ *Be a handy reference source*. This book is intended to be a single-volume sourcebook about modern C programming. To serve that purpose, we have included reference and summary information in both tabular and easily found graphic formats, as well as a whole reference section. When you have used this book to learn C, you can use it to quickly refresh your memory, or to look up an obscure point.

Who Should Use This Book?

Using C is aimed specifically at beginning and intermediate-level C programmers. You can use this book to learn C from the beginning, and continue with it to increase your knowledge and skills.

Those who already have experience with C might find it useful also. If you are a longtime C user accustomed to the old-style programming methods, you can use this book to update your knowledge about the latest developments in C programming. All C programmers can profit from the summary and reference information.

This book is *not* intended to promote the product of any particular compiler vendor. It is about *standard C*—those things that make C what it is. This does not mean that specific compilers are never mentioned. For one thing, this would eliminate the possibility of writing sample programs that actually work. The compiler used is noted with each example. The following compilers were used:

Turbo C 2.0	(Borland)
Turbo C++	(Borland)
Microsoft C 6.0	(Microsoft)
QuickC 2.5	(Microsoft)
Zortech C++ 1.7	(Zortech)

There are also occasional notes on features that the different compilers provide as extensions to ANSI C, and on how they differ in implementing some things.

Getting Prepared To Use This Book

To learn C programming, you really need some experience with computers in general, as well as with programming in particular. It *is* possible to learn C as a first language, and this book can help you do that, but it may be a jarring experience. C is a sophisticated language, and seems to embody everything programmers traditionally use to confuse the layman. You should be familiar with the way computers do things, at the very least.

If you are a complete beginner and want to learn C right now anyway, the antidote is simply to get and read some basic computer books as you go along. You can refer to the Bibliography at the end of this book for some suggestions about what to read to get started.

The Book's Format

The material in this book is arranged in three major parts covering ANSI C fundamentals, the ANSI standard library functions, and C++. In the first part, the mechanics of the language are presented and their meaning and use explained. The second part can be used as a reference while mastering the first, and also by itself, later. The third part is a tutorial primer on C++.

Tables, figures, listings, and similar material are set off from the text in Que's standard format, using separating lines and (for listings) a different type style. They are easily visible without disrupting the flow of your reading.

In listings of entire programs, every line is numbered. This makes referring to specific lines easy without having to struggle to find them. Very short code fragments are inserted directly in the text and do not have line numbers.

Throughout the book are boxes of summary and reference information called *C-Notes*. The title line of the C-Note tells you in which of the following four categories it fits and what kind of information it contains. There are four kinds of C-Notes:

❏ *ANSI C Rationale*. These *C-Notes* contain comments about why the ANSI standard was implemented in certain ways rather than others. This helps in your overall understanding of the language.

❏ *Old-Style Coding*. Tremendous numbers of C programs were written before the ANSI standard was published. These notes help you read old-style code and convert it to modern style.

❏ *Compiler Dependency*. Because of the large variety of machines and operating systems C can run with, the precise behavior of a surprisingly large number of features was left up to each compiler manufacturer. You should be aware of them if you deal with more than one compiler.

❑ *Quick-Reference*. Wherever a summary of C rules or technical information is appropriate, you will find one of these notes. They are handy for quick review or for a bird's-eye perspective of the topic being discussed and are the most common type of C-Note.

How To Use This Book

You can use this book as either a learning resource for C or a reference to the language.

The order in which material is presented is designed for C students. It is not the order you would find in a formal definition of the language. This means that you can read through Parts I and III in sequence and cover the whole language. Do not hurry the reading. Follow the explanations of sample programs in detail—doing so takes you a long way toward understanding how C rules work in practice. Most of all, do not try to memorize the rules. Because you can learn C best by *writing C*, begin by duplicating the examples, and then branch out to programs of your own. And keep at it.

You can use this book also as a reference. The table of contents is fairly detailed; you can use it to navigate quickly to a particular topic. If the table of contents does not help you locate what you need, try the index. After you have found the discussion of interest, look for tables of information and Quick-Reference C-Notes. Finally, Part II of the book is mostly reference, covering the standard library functions and predefined macros.

Part II is useful also while you work through Part I. Because C is a complex language, writing sample programs early on that make no use of the extensive library of functions built into C compilers is almost impossible. Yet the early part of the book is not the place to go into detail about how the library functions work. We frequently make use of the `printf()` function, for example, before we discuss it in detail. You can look ahead to the reference information in Part II to get a better idea of what a function is and how to use it in situations like this.

Part I

Introduction to Standard C

Getting Started With C

I f you want to learn the standard C programming language, you will find everything you need in this book. If you are new to C programming, this chapter is the place to start. If you already have some experience with C, you might want to just skim this chapter for a review.

Approaching the C Language

To learn a new language, you need a good overview of the subject as well as the right kind of information. Getting the big picture gives you a context that makes the subject meaningful. This chapter gives you an overview of C. You will learn about the following:

❑ *The history of C, from K & R to C++*

❑ *How C compares to other languages*

❑ *How to read and make sense of a C program*

❑ *The basic ingredients of a C program*

❑ *The process of writing C programs*

❑ *What tools you need to write C programs*

A Brief History of C

Where did C come from? Why was it developed? What is it good for? Knowing the answers to these questions does not affect whether you can learn C but gives you a sense of context and continuity, a sense of knowing what you are dealing with.

In the Beginning: Kernighan and Ritchie

In 1978, Prentice-Hall published *The C Programming Language*, written by Brian W. Kernighan and Dennis M. Ritchie. Thus began the C explosion.

At first, it wasn't really an explosion. C was developed by Dennis Ritchie for use on and with the UNIX operating system, running on DEC PDP-11 computers at the Bell Laboratories in Murray Hill, New Jersey. In addition to the compiler itself, the UNIX operating system and most of its utility programs were written in C.

Several players other than Kernighan and Ritchie were involved. The software that resulted in UNIX and its companion C began with Martin Richards, who developed a language called BCPL. This language in turn strongly influenced the development of the next language, B—yes, really!—by Ken Thompson in 1970 for use with the original UNIX on the DEC PDP-7. By 1972, Dennis Ritchie (working with Ken Thompson) had expanded B into C. The new C added something that B did not have: data types.

For some time, C was considered an esoteric language, difficult to learn, and pretty much confined to DEC machines and UNIX. By the time K & R published their historic book, C was implemented on IBM, Honeywell, and Interdata computers, among others. C was now on the road.

The Move from UNIX to DOS

C did not travel directly from UNIX to DOS in one easy step. It first passed through a phase of implementation on 8-bit microcomputers running the CP/M operating system. Although CP/M, a scaled-down derivation of UNIX developed by Digital Research, was quite popular, the C explosion had not truly begun in this phase. A principal reason for this is that 8-bit systems were typically constrained to 64K RAM sizes—and C doesn't hit its stride until more memory is available.

The microcomputer memory barrier was broken, and the C explosion got moving, with the introduction of the 8088 and 8086 family of 16-bit microprocessors in 1980. Continuity was the rule here, too. The DOS operating system was first designed and marketed (also in 1980) by Seattle Computer Products as 86-DOS. Its author, Tim Paterson, deliberately positioned it to make conversion from CP/M easy.

The entry of Microsoft and IBM into the picture virtually guaranteed that software companies would develop products, including compilers, for the new machine and operating system. The success of the IBM PC and software for it exceeded all expectations; part of that success is the blooming popularity of C compilers for that environment. C has successfully made the transition from ivory tower programmers to the masses of programmers who code because they *like* it.

ANSI Gets Interested

Some early writers on C said that C retained so much purity because it was largely the work of only two men—Ken Thompson and Dennis Ritchie. These writers scorned the committee approach to compiler standardization, noting that a camel is "a horse designed by a committee."

There is some truth to this. ANSI (American National Standards Institute) has been involved in defining criteria for other languages, notably COBOL. A much touted benefit of such standardization is "portability." Our experience with porting COBOL applications from one ANSI standard compiler to another indicates that *complete* portability is a pipe dream. This is true even when dealing with two compilers from the same vendor.

ANSI interest in C, then, does not automatically guarantee a programmer's utopia in which C is just C, no matter what. Yet a cynical attitude toward ANSI standardization is unfair. Adhering to ANSI standard C definitions has several benefits, and ANSI has done a better job with C than with COBOL.

Codifying Practice

ANSI created a committee, X3J11, whose task was to propose what constitutes "standard C." A major concern of the charter given to the committee was that they should *codify common existing practice*. This means that wherever possible the new standard was to leave C alone. They have done that, with good results. C is still largely what K & R defined it to be, with some loopholes closed and inconsistencies corrected.

The application of this principle to the standard has one extremely important consequence: *most existing code still runs* when handled by a compiler conforming to the new standard. A lot of C code exists, and its total commercial value is high. To render that code unusable would have guaranteed that the standard would never have been accepted in the marketplace.

Conforming to ANSI C

No law says that compiler manufacturers *have* to make their product conform to the ANSI C standard. They are free to produce anything they want. Marketing a product that claims to be "ANSI compatible" when it is not, however, would not be wise. Such a violation of programmers' expectations would quickly ruin the product's sales. On the other hand, a compiler that is *only* ANSI conforming would have no practical use at all. Real-world programs frequently must control their host hardware and operating system not only to achieve adequate performance levels, but sometimes even to supply certain functions.

Both ANSI and the compiler vendors realize that *implementation-dependent extensions* to the standard need to be allowed. The trick is not to advertise them as part of the standard. Thus, you will find that C compilers commonly provide routines for interfacing with DOS, accessing I/O ports, controlling the display, and so on. In fact, you *need* a compiler that is rich in extensions, if you want your programs to amount to much.

Portability Issues

Portability means the ability to use a program's source code, without modification, on more than one vendor's compiler. This is where the tire meets the road, as far as a standard is concerned. A standard that does not promote portability is useless.

This is also where the conflicts arise for a powerful language like C. One of the great benefits of C is that it can control much of its environment directly without having to resort to assembler, even though every environment is different. A 100-percent portable compiler unfortunately does not exist.

The ANSI C committee partially solved this problem by deciding that the standard should give the programmer a fighting chance to write portable code, but not force him to do so. What this means to you, the programmer, is a little complex. For a complete discussion of conversion and portability issues, read Chapter 11.

Looking Toward the Future: C++

ANSI standardization will not make the C language popular; rather, C will be standardized because it is becoming popular. Standardization is imminent. The draft work has been done, and the results published by the X3J11 committee. Further, as of December 15, 1989, the ANSI standardization committee X3J16 on C++ has convened in Washington, DC. C is no longer the esoteric tool of research labs and hackers. It's everyone's route to powerful, portable programming. The appearance of C++ (C with object-oriented extensions) may become even more significant than a standard for the language.

Object-oriented Programming

Object-oriented programming systems, or *OOPS* (pronounced as it is spelled) have been around for quite some time. Characterized by their flexibility and power, they are slightly notorious for poor performance. C++ comes to the rescue—it is both object-oriented *and* a hot performer.

C++ buys you more than execution speed. It also buys you programming speed. It allows faster development of larger projects by helping you prevent errors and by supplying some tools that ordinary C does not have.

Bell Labs Again

Somehow, it seems only fitting that this latest marvel of C efficiency should come from Bell Labs. C++ was developed by one man, Bjarne Stroustrup. Aficianados of C++ fondly refer to his book, *The C++ Programming Language*, published by Addison-Wesley in 1986, as "the Book."

C++ is not a complete departure from ANSI C. In fact, ANSI C may be regarded as a subset of C++, because the two borrowed heavily of each other for ideas and methods. However, C++ definitely goes far beyond standard C. It supplies a storehouse of extra tools: encapsulation, data hiding, classes and derived classes, function and operator overloading, and much more.

Comparing C to Other Languages

Like all languages, C has both advantages and disadvantages. Because C's philosophy is to provide straightforward implementation, to commit to fast run-time code, to furnish a mature function library and a rich operator set, C compares well to other languages.

Comparing C and Assembly Language

No high-level language can beat assembly language at producing fast run-time code or code that's highly compact and tuned. Of all high-level languages, however, C probably comes closest to keeping up with assembly language. Originally a language for systems programmers, C remains in touch with low-level components of the system and can be used as a high-level assembler.

In areas in which C is slower than assembly language, C's flexibility and power often more than make up for its lack of speed. The same can be said of code size. C run-time code is always larger than that of a comparable assembly language program, mainly because of the presence of the generalized library functions that make the language so rich and powerful.

Comparing C and Pascal

Originally, Pascal was intended to be a tool used for teaching the fundamentals of programming while masking the more detailed aspects of the hardware and operating system environments. It is therefore more generalized than C and less capable of attaining C's performance levels. Pascal has matured but (unlike C and assembler) is rarely, if ever, used for large development projects such as operating systems, canned packages, etc.

On the flip side, Pascal programmers probably will have less trouble acclimatizing themselves to C syntax than will other programmers. There are many similarities between C and Pascal; much of the punctuation, the general style of block statements, the way arrays are handled, and the packaging of complex data objects are some of the ways the languages resemble one another. Still, there are enough differences to make the process of converting from one to the other a laborious, tedious job.

Comparing C and COBOL

There are almost no similarities of syntax and construction between C and COBOL. C is a much more free and flowing language than COBOL. It knows nothing of the rigid separation of components found in COBOL's Identification, Environment, Data, and Procedure divisions. C programs always result in significantly faster and more compact run-time code than COBOL programs (at least using the compilers with which we are familiar).

For business programming tasks, however, using COBOL has a significant advantage: the built-in availability of decimal data and arithmetic. This advantage may be short-lived, however; Turbo C++ now has built-in classes that support decimal data and arithmetic, too.

Comparing C and FORTRAN

Justly famous for its number-crunching capability, FORTRAN (FORmula TRANslation) was the first language both of us used—it has been around for a *long* time.

FORTRAN is still the undisputed master of number-crunching applications. It is used, for example, in the ballistics programs that run the IBM Federal Systems computers guiding NASA space vehicles. (These systems are based on the old 360 mainframe technology—old, but tried and true.)

Could C ever displace applications like this? Conceivably, it could. C programs running on 80386 processors with a math coprocessor, or on the newest 80486 processors, would *significantly* outperform the older technology. C's formula-translating capability is every bit as good as FORTRAN's, and the advanced math functions could easily be added to the function library. What C can't do is overcome the weight of tradition in this case.

A First Look at C and Punctuation

Reading the sample C programs is one of the most important parts of mastering the material in this book. If you can't read a program, you certainly can't write one. The first step in learning to read C programs is to learn something about how they are put together.

How To Look at a C Program

Suppose that you are sitting at your computer, and that your favorite text editor is running with the source file for a C program on the screen. What do you see? If you are brand new to C programming, the display may look like the result of an explosion at the local dictionary factory. Don't worry. It really does make sense once you get the hang of it.

You very accurately can define a C source program to be a series of declarations. A *declaration* tells the compiler what it needs to know about (like variables and what a function is supposed to do). You can write a declaration to tell the compiler how to do the following:

❏ *Recognize a name you have created*

❏ *Set aside storage (RAM) for data objects such as variables, constants, etc. and (optionally) initialize their values*

❑ *Define the behavior of a function*

❑ *Interpret a particular type of data*

Strictly speaking, *statements* (instructions that *do* something) are only parts of a function declaration; they never appear outside a function and are not declarations. At this level, *functions* are just collections of statements. From the compiler's viewpoint, looking at the whole program, the entire program is just a collection of declarations that tell the compiler *how to generate object code*, not *how to perform the ultimate task* you want the program to perform. For those of us who are not computer scientists, that is a strange way of looking at things—but it makes sense. Compilers don't know what you are thinking—only what you *tell* them.

You can begin reading C programs before you finish this book because C declarations often make intuitive sense. The very terms used tell you something about what is going on. Furthermore, declarations are found mostly in groups of a single kind, and those groups are separated by blank lines (*white space*, in C lingo). By putting these clues together, you get an overview of the program's structure and function.

Noticing the C "Punctuators"

Punctuation in C is extremely important. (If you are not accustomed to it, it is strange, also!) You can use punctuation as another source of clues about what a program is doing, however. You may want to look ahead now to listing 1.1, `first.c`, to see the punctuators in action as they are discussed.

Quick-Reference: The C Punctuators

All the C punctuators are predefined. Only the following punctuators are valid:

`[ ] ( ) { } * , : = ; ... # ##`

You cannot use these characters for anything but punctuation in the manner defined by C except, of course, as data inside a string or character literal.

Both `#` and `##` are actually preprocessing operators; they are not included in the ANSI X3J11 document's list of punctuators. Because they are used only during preprocessing and behave more like punctuators than true operators, we include them here.

Notice first that most lines in listing 1.1 end with a semicolon (;). The semicolon is used to terminate all simple statements and declarations in C. For example, in the following statement:

```
i = i * 2;
```

the value of i is doubled and placed back in the variable's location in storage (RAM).

You can identify a *block statement* by noting that it is composed of one or more simple statements enclosed in curly braces ({}). The body of the function calc() is an example of a block statement:

```
int calc( int i )
{
   i = i * 2;
   i++;
   return i;
}
```

Look carefully at the preceding lines. Although each simple statement is terminated with a semicolon, the block statement *does not* end in a semicolon after the curly brace (}). All this means is that the entire group of simple statements inside the braces is to be considered as a single, undivided entity. Either the whole block is executed, or none of it.

Next, you can easily pick out compiler directives; notice that they all begin with the pound sign (#) in the leftmost column, as in the following example:

```
#include <stdlib.h>
```

Compiler directives are not part of the source code you want translated into object code; they are instructions to the compiler on how to go about the translation process. Because these instructions must be found and interpreted before any real compilation takes place, they are also called *preprocessing directives*. Directives do not need the semicolon to terminate them. If the statement includes a semicolon, it is there for another reason, which is covered in detail in Chapter 4.

Finally, *comments* play an important role in making a C program readable. Comments are delimited by special sequences of characters that are neither punctuation nor C operators. A comment begins with the sequence /* (a slash and an asterisk) and ends with the sequence */ (an asterisk and a slash) (see the first two lines of listing 1.1). Comments also can appear on the same line with legitimate C statements.

The only purpose of a comment is to provide human eyes with some clarification to help make the program comprehensible. The compiler just replaces the whole comment with a single blank before proceeding with translation.

Sneak Preview: Characters, Arrays, and Strings

It is nearly impossible to discuss the C language without some mention of *strings*. In order to understand strings, you must also have some acquaintance with characters and arrays. These three types of data have the following characteristics:

❑ *A character is a data variable that can be printed or displayed, or which can control a display device.* The letters, numbers, and punctuation on this page are *display characters*. *Control characters* have the same internal structure as display characters, but are generally invisible and control the way other characters appear on a display device (such as a screen or printer). Chapter 4 gives much more detail on characters.

❑ *An array is a group of data variables (all of the same kind) which are all stored together in the computer's memory.* Arrays can be formed from any other kind of variables, including characters. An array of integers, for example, is defined by writing:

```
int counts[10];  /* An array of 10 integers */
```

❑ *A string is a special kind of array composed of characters.* You define a string just like any other array. For example, you might define a name string:

```
char name[40]; /* A name string with up to 39
chars */
```

This string can contain only up to 39 display characters, because the last array element (position) must be reserved for a *null character*. A null character is a special character which has a numeric value of zero. The null character signals the end of the string, and is not displayable. When you initialize a string with a literal value, you do not have to code the null character:

```
char name[40] = "John Aloysius Doe";
```

Understanding the Parts of a C Program

Now that you have an idea of how C programs are put together, it is time to look at what is put into them. Listing 1.1 shows the source code for `first.c`, a short program that has all the basic program components.

Listing 1.1. `first.c`.   *Turbo C*

```
 1   /* -----        FIRST.C      ----- */
 2   /* ----- A short C program ----- */
 3
 4   #include <stdio.h>
 5   #include <stdlib.h>
 6
 7   int calc( int i );
 8
 9   main()
10   {
11      char number_in[4], number_out[5];
12      int i,j;
13
14      puts( "Enter up to a two digit integer." );
15      gets( number_in );
16      i = atoi( number_in );
17      j = calc( i );
18      itoa( j, number_out, 10 );
19      puts( "The calculations on the integer yield:" );
20      puts( number_out );
21   }
22
23   int calc( int i )
24   {
25      i = i * 2;
26      i++;
27      return i;
28   }
```

If you are completely new to C programming, take a little time to look over listing 1.1 and get acquainted with a C program's looks. `first.c` gets a string of characters from the keyboard and converts it to a number. Then it calls a function that doubles the number and returns the result. Finally, the new value is converted back to a character string and displayed on the console. Here's how it breaks out by line numbers:

❑ *Lines 1–2* are comments that give some basic information about the program—its name and that it is a short program.

❑ *Line 3* illustrates that you can leave blank lines anywhere in the program to improve its readability.

❑ *Lines 4–5* are *compiler directives*. In this example, they tell the compiler that some very important information (about the built-in library functions to be used in this program) can be found in the files named. These files are called *header files* because they normally appear at the head of the program.

❑ *Line 7* contains a *function prototype*. It tells the compiler that the program later contains a definition for a function called calc. This function receives an integer *parameter* (something to work with or on), and returns an integer value to whatever place in the program called it. Once defined, a function can be called again and again, from many places in the program (but, as you will later see, not from *every* place). Note that we often refer to a function in the body of the text by writing the function's name, followed by a pair of parentheses. The function in line 7 would be referred to as calc(), for example. You are expected to understand that the function may have parameters and return some data type, and to look in the source-code listing or fragment for particulars.

❑ *Lines 9–21* contain the program's main() function. Every program has a main() function; it is the first thing that begins to execute when you run the program. In listing 1.1, main() gets some input data, converts it to a number, passes that number to calc() for processing, receives a result, and displays the result on-screen.

❑ *Lines 23–28* contain the *function definition* for calc(), the function referred to in the function prototype in line 7. calc() performs the task of doubling the number that main() passed to it as a parameter, and returning that result to main().

Including the Header Files

Lines 4 and 5 of listing 1.1 provide an example of the #include preprocessing directive. It is doubtful that you would ever find a useful C program that didn't have at least one #include directive. What is it and why is it so necessary?

Including Source Files in General

The `#include` directive causes the compiler to do what you might reasonably expect—to pull in another source file. At preprocessing time, before translation to object code begins, the compiler locates on disk the source file named between the angle brackets (the less-than and greater-than signs), reads it in, and inserts it in the current source at the position of the `#include` (see fig. 1.1).

Fig. 1.1. *The* `#include` *directive at work.*

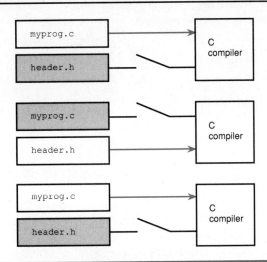

Figure 1.1 implies something else about including other source files: The included file can be anything you want it to be, if it is something the compiler can accept when program translation begins. You could break a long source program into multiple text files and reference them with `#include` statements for compilation. (Note, however, that this is not a very efficient way to handle complex projects.) Building complex projects is mentioned later in this chapter (see "A Note on Multiple Source Files") and discussed in some detail in Chapter 5.

If you have to rekey directives, constants, and similar material every time you want to use them, eventually you will make a typo or some other mistake. C programs normally use `#include` directives to make the use of such things consistent. Ordinarily, you should not place in a header file statements that initialize variables, function definitions (as opposed to declarations, see Chapter 3), or other things that belong in the running code.

Header Files and Built-In Functions

The two #include directives in listing 1.1 are good examples of the way a compiler product makes its library functions and other facilities available to you. These resources are vitally important for writing robust, useful programs.

Quick-Reference: Typical Uses for Header Files

Bjarne Stroustrup, the developer of C++, suggests several uses for header files. Here is a slightly modified list of what a header file should contain:

Type definitions	`struct parts { int stocknum, loc };`
Function declarations	`int area( int length, int width);`
Data declarations	`extern unsigned master_switch;`
Constant definitions	`const int maxsize = 32767;`
Enumerations	`enum toys { top, jacks, slinky };`
Include directives	`#include <graphics.h>`
Macro definitions	`#define TRUE 1`
Comments	`/* This is a header file */`

When you bought your compiler, you got much more than just one compiler program. You got, among other things, a whole library of powerful functions that are not part of the C language. These functions are built into the *package*, but not the *compiler*; they don't change the essence of what constitutes C.

Now that you have them, what can you do with them? The compiler manual tells you all about the functions—what they are, how they work, how to set up a call to them. The significant thing to understand is that, in some ways, functions behave like variables; they return a value that has a certain type. That is why you can use functions on the right side of an assignment statement, as follows:

```
/* What will happen here? */

double x;              /* Define a variable to use */
...
x = sqrt( 3.1415926 ); /* Take the square root of PI */
```

The square root function sqrt() is defined to return a double-length floating-point value, but how does the compiler know that? If you have not declared the function somewhere, but use it anyway, *the compiler assumes that the function returns an integer.* (The integer is the default type in C. Beginning in Chapter 3—and throughout this book—you will see what the acceptable data types are. C can do a *great deal* with data.) Depending on the brand of compiler you use, this error may or may not get by the compiler or linker. If the error does get by, and you try to run the program, things probably will go haywire at this point.

How, if you didn't write the function, are you going to declare it to the compiler? That is what the supplied header files are for. The compiler manual tells you not only how to call the function but also which header file to include in the program so that the function will work correctly. The ANSI standard header file for the square root function is `math.h`; you should correct the code shown in the preceding fragment by adding the `#include` directive for it, as follows:

```
#include <math.h>
...
double x;              /* Define a variable to use */
...
x = sqrt( 3.1415926 ); /* Take the square root of PI */
```

Placing the Includes

Where do you place the `#include` directives in the program? C syntax permits placement just about anywhere. C grammar, however, expects you to declare something before you can use it. (This is as true for supplied library functions as for anything else.)

In the program in listing 1.1, the `#include` directives are preceded only by a couple of comments indicating the program's name and purpose. Placing the directives at or near the top of the source file in every case, so you won't accidentally wait too long, is a good idea.

If you do not use any of the functions (or macros or global variables) a particular header file declares, you don't have to include it—but it normally doesn't hurt to do so. We have the habit, for example, of always including `stdlib.h` and `stdio.h` (just in case). They are used so often that they are easy to forget. If the header files are not needed, this does *not* hurt your program in any way.

What happens if you forget to include a necessary header file? You are quite likely to get some strange error messages at either compile or link edit time. Often, the compiler assumes that the reference is to something in another source file and lets it go by. Then the linker flags the function with a message about having encountered an unresolved external reference. Because this can be confusing, double check the header files for the library functions you use and make sure you included them all.

Two Ways to Include

Listing 1.1 illustrates only one way to write an #include directive. The file to be included was written inside angle brackets (<>)—the same characters you use as greater-than and less-than operators. Be extremely careful not to put any extra blanks inside the brackets; if you do, the compiler cannot find the file. For example:

```
#include <stddef.h>      /* The correct method */
```

is not the same as

```
#include < stddef.h >    /* Wrong! */
```

The ANSI standard says that using angle brackets to write an include causes the compiler to search for the named file in "a sequence of implementation-defined places." Thus, the search takes place *only* in specifically designated directories, which are assumed to contain only header files. This is the kind of #include you should write to include *supplied* header files.

"Implementation-defined" means that the manner of specifying these directories varies from one compiler and operating system to the next. On

Fig. 1.2. *Directories for headers and libraries.*

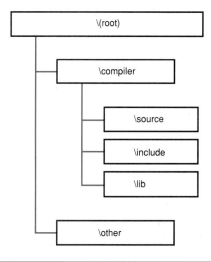

MS-DOS systems, for example, a typical way to identify directories is to put a `SET INCLUDE=d:\dirname` string in the `autoexec.bat` file so that the directory name string becomes part of the environment that the compiler can check. (For details on how to do this, check the manual for *your* compiler.) Figure 1.2 shows a set-up similar to those used by many popular compilers.

As you look at Figure 1.2, remember that normally, the `\source` directory is the current one. You can use the DOS SET command to define PATH, INCLUDE, and LIB specifications for the directories to use for those libraries and files.

The second way to write an `#include` is to enclose the file name within double quotation marks, as follows:

```
#include "myhdr.h"
```

Here, as in the first method, the warning about including extra blanks applies. The ANSI standard says, "The named source file is searched for in an implementation-defined manner." If that fails, the search proceeds as if the first method had been coded. That doesn't say much at all. Every compiler we have used assumes that this syntax means to search *first* in the *current directory* and then, if the file is not there, to go back and search as in the first kind of `#include` (that is, as if angle bracket notation was used).

This is the style you should use for including header files *you have written*. These header files usually are placed in the same directory as the program's source file, not in the directory with the compiler's headers.

A Note about Multiple Source Files

When you begin to write complex programs, you need to learn how to package parts of the program in files that are compiled separately and linked together later. When you compile a group of functions separately, you need to create for them a header file that can be included in other source files, so other functions know how to access your functions and the variables you want to make public (visible to other source files).

In Chapter 5's discussion of "Accessing External Data Items: Setting Up the Header Files," you learn more about building complex programs.

Defining Data to C

All programs (whether written in C or in another language) exist to do one thing: manipulate data. Some of this data exists only within the program; some of it is brought into RAM from different places by the input and output functions. In either case, the compiler has to know how to set up your program's memory to hold that data. A data item is often called an "object" in C documentation.

Setting Aside Memory for Data

Whenever you *declare a variable* or *use a constant*, you cause the compiler to set aside (*allocate*) memory. This kind of memory becomes part of the program—when the compiler writes the run-time code to disk, this kind of data (all constants and variables written outside functions) takes up some space in the file.

By using `malloc()`, `calloc()`, `realloc()`, and related functions, you can allocate memory for data dynamically when you run your program. This group of functions acquires blocks of memory from the operating system, outside the program, at run time, not compile time. (Such methods of allocating memory for data are covered in detail in another chapter.) Dynamically allocated data does *not* take up space in the program file on disk.

For *all* kinds of data, however, the compiler must construct your program so that the run-time program code can keep track of everything. Therefore, certain kinds of data are placed in particular parts of memory. On the 80x86 family of processors, data is placed in the code segment, data segment, or stack segment, according to how the data is used. Figure 1.3 shows how C compilers assign storage for data on 80x86 processors. In the segment layout for the SMALL memory model on an IBM or compatible PC shown in figure 1.3, data is stored in the _DATA, CONST, _BSS, STACK, and Heap segments, all addressed by the DS register. (The *heap* is where C dynamically allocates memory.)

Where Do You Put It?

Look at lines 11 and 12 in `first.c` (listing 1.1). These two lines declare data objects the program will use. Line 11 declares two strings (these are *character arrays*—sequences of displayable characters); line 12 declares two integers.

Fig. 1.3. How data object allocation is handled.

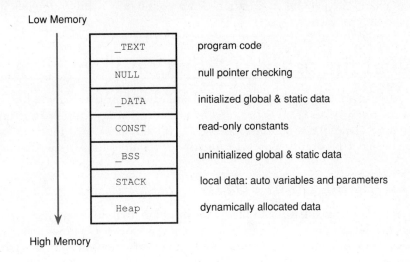

Low Memory

_TEXT	program code
NULL	null pointer checking
_DATA	initialized global & static data
CONST	read-only constants
_BSS	uninitialized global & static data
STACK	local data: auto variables and parameters
Heap	dynamically allocated data

High Memory

Now notice the location of these declarations—they are inside the body of the main() function. Only the main() function can access these variables directly, either to examine them (*fetch* access) or to modify them (*update* access). The main() function is not prevented from passing the values or locations of these variables as parameters to other functions, but only main() can access them directly. You can also declare variables outside a function. Such variables can be accessed by all functions in the source file— they are jointly owned by all (presuming that the variables were declared first, before the functions). This distinction gives rise to an important concept in C: local and global variables.

❑ *Local variables are "visible" only in the block (the function or block statement) in which they are defined.* These variables have *dynamic duration*—they exist only while the block is active (actually running)—unless you override the duration. As you may recall, a block statement is anything surrounded by curly braces; thus, a function body is a block.

❑ *Global variables are "globally visible" in the source file, and can be made visible to other source files as well.* By default, global variables have *static duration*—they remain valid no matter what part of the program is active.

Note that even though you don't enclose the entire source file in curly braces, the whole file is considered a block. This point of view may help you understand the general rule: variables are visible only within the block in which they are defined.

What the *main()* Function Does

You can write any functions you like and call them anything you like—except main(). main() is the only C function that is *required* in every program. (Lines 9 through 21 in listing 1.1 contain the main() function for the first.c program.) A main() function is required for several reasons.

The *main()* Entry Point

Assume that you have compiled your program, that no errors occurred, and that you are ready to run it. Now ask this question—how does the computer know which of the many executable instructions in your program to start with?

One of the primary purposes of the main() function is that it is the primary entry point for the program. The compiler *always* sets up the executable program file, so main() runs first.

Setting Up the Environment

Actually, a little more than this goes on behind the scenes. The compiler creates a program *stub* (short routine) that executes *before* the code you placed in main(). This stub does different things, depending on the machine and operating system being used. Generally, the stub sets up access to the command-line parameters you typed in the system command to execute the program. It also sets up the system environment for the program (determining how interrupt keys are handled, what to do if the program aborts, and so on).

Just because the main() function is required, you do not have to put any particular thing in it. What you supply depends entirely on what you want the program to do. In fact, you don't have to do anything at all. For example, the following is a perfectly legitimate program that compiles correctly and runs without error:

```
main()  /* empty.c */
{
}
```

It just won't do anything!

Normally, main() should perform any set-up tasks that depend on your application—initializing global variables, opening files, calling the first functions to get started, and whatever else may be called for. In a short program, you may even want to put the majority of the statements in main(), just as we did in listing 1.1.

Normal Program Termination

The final major function of main() is to provide a mechanism for ending program execution normally. As you may have noticed in the preceding program fragment (empty.c), no statements are necessary to accomplish this. The effect of allowing the program to "fall through" the bottom of main() is exactly the same as the effect of the following code:

```
main()  /* ending.c */
{
   ... /* Some statements go here */
   exit(0);
}
```

ending.c terminates the program deliberately but normally. The function call exit(0) invokes a library function that cleans up after the program, returns control to the system, and passes a return code of 0 (or whatever you want) to the system.

Providing User-defined Functions

Lines 23 through 28 of listing 1.1 contain a user-defined function: calc(). Such functions are not mandatory, but a C program that had none would be rather strange.

Functions Act Like Data

After you have declared and defined a function, you can invoke it by simply referencing it in an expression as we did, for example, in line 17 of listing 1.1:

```
j = calc( i );
```

The reference to `calc()` occupies a position in this statement in the same way a variable or constant would. That is, the compiler presumes that a function has a value. Within `calc()`, the `return` statement caused the calculated value of `i` to be passed back to the calling routine. Functions behave like data objects in this way.

You can also invoke a function that stands by itself, like this:

```
calc( i );
```

Calling a function without using its result is perfectly legitimate. Any value the function returns is simply thrown away.

Where Do They Go?

Where you place a function in the program depends on where it is declared and on what other parts of the program will call it.

❏ *You can, but should not, reference a function before it has been declared.* As you may recall, doing so causes certain (not always desirable) default actions to take place.

❏ *You can declare a function by defining it, providing the function body as well as the function parameters.* You can now refer to the function anywhere *after* the definition. If you choose this method, you may find yourself positioning functions as if they were Pascal procedures: with the lowest (most detailed) level near the beginning of the program, followed by higher levels, and finishing with `main()` at the very bottom of the program. This is not recommended, because it makes reading the program difficult.

❏ *You can forward declare the function by writing a function prototype early in the program and defining it later.* A *function prototype* is just the header line with no body, as in

```
double do_something( double a_parm );
```

Notice that *in the prototype only*, a semicolon follows the parentheses. In a definition, you would delete this semicolon, and open the function body with a curly brace.

Full function prototyping, the preferred method, has the following distinct advantages:

❏ *You can place `main()` at the top of the program, followed by the next highest-level functions, and so on, in a fashion that resembles the program's logical structure.* This makes the program much easier to read, and therefore easier to debug.

- *You reduce the risk of referencing a library function before it has been declared.* This prevents the accidental return of a data type other than the one you expected (the kind of error that can make your program go crazy!).

- *You can now reference functions in any order, from anywhere in the source file.*

This last point is important to sophisticated programs. If you use the first method, the current function can be invoked correctly only by functions that follow it. For example, consider this arrangement:

```
void function_a( void ) /* wrong.c */
{
  double n;
  n = function_b();
}

double function_b( void )
{
 ... /* Something goes on here */
}
```

At first glance, this code fragment looks fine. Everything is there, and this is not quite the same as forgetting a header file for a library function. The intended return value is a double floating point, and the function that supplies it has that type. So what happens?

Most likely, you won't even get this one through the compile phase. When a program like this is submitted to the QuickC compiler, for example, it stops when the `function_b()` definition is encountered. The resulting error message says that this is a redefinition of the function. This means that, as far as the compiler is concerned, the presumed function type changed suddenly from integer to double float.

In more sophisticated programs, you might even encounter a situation in which `function_a()` may sometimes need to call `function_b()`, whereas at other times `function_b()` calls `function_a()`. For this kind of situation, the modern method of full function prototyping is absolutely necessary.

Writing a C Program

Besides requiring a knowledge of syntax and coding rules, writing a C program needs a good deal of skill and mental preparation. What would happen, for example, if you sat down to write a murder mystery without having considered who did the deed or how? The book would be a haphazard mess. The same is true when you write a C program. You must be prepared first.

Start with the Right Design

For a C program (as for a murder mystery) you need to know the ending before you write the beginning. How else do you know where to start, and how to get there? Thus, decide *exactly* what you want the program to do before you start coding. The structure of most programs can be represented as a *top-down tree structure*. Well-structured programs tend to call functions in layered groups, or levels. The functions become more detailed or "atomic" as you move down the tree structure (see fig. 1.4).

Fig. 1.4. *A typical top-down program structure.*

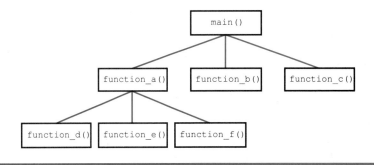

A Top-down Approach to Coding

You don't have to have every line of code in your mind before you approach the keyboard, but you should know how you want the program to behave. You can certainly overlap the program-design and program-coding phases.

An excellent way to do this is to use a top-down approach to both design *and* coding. Begin with the broadest statement of what the program is to do, and break the logic down one level into a series of major tasks needed to do it. Now you have the first level of function calls to write into the `main()`

function. Repeat the process for each function in that second tier, to arrive at a third, more detailed level. At each level, just add to the source code the functions, prototypes, and variables needed (be sure not to put that off—you will forget something).

Program design is a matter of personal style; it can become quite complex if carried out scientifically. A full discussion of it is out of place here. For more information about the process, you may want to read *Turbo C Programming*, published by Que Corporation.

Making Programs Readable

Just as you learned to use breaks in the code and punctuation to read C programs, you can do several things to make your programs readable. They are not difficult to do, and this is the time to start doing them. Later, after you have formed the habit, doing them becomes automatic and painless.

Using Indentation and White Space

C requires only enough blanks to be capable of recognizing keywords and names. Other than that, you can run a program together almost at will. Take another look at wrong.c, written here with no attention paid to coding style:

```
void function_a(void)/* wrong.c */{double
n;n=function_b();}double function_b(void){/*Something
goes on here*/}
```

It looks like garbage, doesn't it? Writing it this way, however, has not introduced any new errors in the code. Perhaps this example is a little dramatic, but it does prove a point. The way you lay out the text in the program makes all the difference in the world to the eye.

All we did to change the first version of wrong.c to this second version was to remove unnecessary blanks and line indentations. Although these blanks and indentations are unnecessary to the compiler, *people* need them desperately. Both the eye and the brain tend to work in units, rather than a continuous, unbroken spectrum. To sum it up:

❏ *Use blanks to separate individual items, wherever suitable and possible*

and

❏ *Indent (to the same level) program statements that belong together.* Some programmers prefer to indent in two-space increments from one level to the next, some prefer to use four spaces, and some prefer other values. The point is that you should pick a style and stick with it. *You* are the most important person who has to read your code.

You should be aware also that most visual debugger products are able to resolve the current position in a program only to the *closest line of code*, not to a single statement or expression. You may therefore want to confine yourself to writing only one statement per line of source code (or perhaps two, if they are very closely related). If you observe this restriction, you do not have to wonder which of several statements on a line actually caused a problem.

Using Comments

Using comments liberally in your programs, especially in those parts where something tricky or difficult is being done, is a good idea. You can clarify your code by using block comments and line comments effectively.

A block comment should introduce a major section of code or a function, and might look something like this:

```
/*
    +---------------------------------------------+
    + Function XYZ.
    +   Input Parameters:   int a      A number
    +                       char q     A character
    +   Returns:            char *     A string "a"
    +                                  bytes long filled
    +                                  with "q"
    +   Purpose:            To illustrate block comments.
    +---------------------------------------------+
*/
```

This is just a suggestion. The style, layout, and contents of such comments are completely up to you, and should suit your own taste. The point is to provide visual separation and to say something useful.

Line comments also can be quite useful. They can help clarify complicated bits of code, so you or someone else does not have to puzzle over the algorithm whenever you look at it. Here is a trivial sample of line comments:

```
int calc( int i )
{
    i = i * 2;      /* First double the value */
    i++;            /* Now increment it by one */
    return i;       /* And send it back */
}
```

Now the function is not so cryptic, is it? Line comments are extremely useful in complicated sections of code. Use them freely where they are needed, but don't clutter the code unnecessarily with them. The need for white space also applies here.

Aligning Braces and Parentheses

You can use the physical alignment of curly braces and parentheses in combination with white space and indentation to make your programs more readable. The compiler *doesn't care* how they are aligned—use a style that reflects your own taste.

We, for example, habitually align braces and parentheses *with each other* when surrounding function bodies (as in the preceding code) or long lists of values (as follows):

```
static char *month_tab[] =
  { "January",
    "February",
    "March",
    "April",
    "May",
    "June",
    "July",
    "August",
    "September",
    "October",
    "November",
    "December",
    "INVALID"
  };
```

Because this requirement would sometimes eat up a lot of vertical space (too many lines) and distract the eye, we tend to align braces and parentheses *with their indentation level* (rather than with each other) when coding conditional and selection statements, like this:

```
if ( a == b ) {
  puts( "Serious error!\n" );
  abort();
}
else {
  puts( "Results OK.\n" );
  a = get_next_thing();
}
```

Notice also the use of white space and indentation, and where the semicolons are and *are not*. Whether you choose an alignment scheme like this is up to you. Again, just pick one and stay with it. Uniformity is important.

Writing Programs in the C Environment

By *C environment*, we mean the tools you need to do productive work in C. The minimum set of tools you need includes the following:

- ❑ *The particular compiler you choose and its features (The choice of compilers and features varies widely.)*

- ❑ *A good text editor.* You need a text editor that at least permits easy insertion and deletion of characters, cutting and pasting, and scrolling the text. Most modern C compilers for the IBM PC provide a built-in editor.

- ❑ *Whether the linker produces code that is compatible with the output of other products*

- ❑ *Project management utilities*

- ❑ *A visual debugging tool*

Evaluating the Text Editor

When you buy a compiler, you may receive a text editor with it. Most compilers' packages do include one, so you can write programs even if you have no other editor. Many programmers prefer to purchase a separate editor, even if the compiler package has one. An editor called BRIEF has developed a large following, as has one called SPF/PC. (IBM mainframe programmers like SPF/PC because they are already accustomed to its "feel.")

In either case, you spend the most time with, and become most intimately acquainted with, the text editor. If your text editor is worthless, you do not get much done. Most text editors have only a subset of the features that we consider either essential or very nice. A few of these features are listed here:

- ❑ *Large edit buffers.* The best editors let you use all the machine's remaining memory. This is important because C programs, at least the impressive, useful ones, tend to run long.

- ❑ *A convenient keyboard layout.* Remembering which key does what shouldn't be difficult. Keystrokes should not be awkward to make. (This can slow you down more than you realize—not to mention the aggravation.) Most popular text editors either support or mimic WordStar's keyboard usage, which although rather awkward, is so universal that most programmers make the keystrokes subconsciously.

❏ *Automatic file backup.* When you begin editing a file, the editor should make a backup copy automatically, for obvious reasons.

❏ *File-merge capability.* Frequently, as you edit a program, you will find it convenient to copy a file from disk into your current edit session. If, as often happens, you find that you have already done something similar to the current project, grab a copy and modify it. There is no need to enter the whole thing again.

❏ *Multiple concurrent edit sessions.* Editing your program in one window while looking at some sample code in another window is just one of the advantages of this feature. Unfortunately, not many editors that come with the popular compilers support this feature.

❏ *An appealing visual interface.* The editor's screens ought to *look* good. It is surprising how quickly you can tire of looking at a poorly designed screen—it can actually disrupt your concentration. Without passing judgment on any of its other features, Microsoft's QuickC editor has an appealing screen (see fig. 1.5).

Fig. 1.5. The QuickC editor screen.

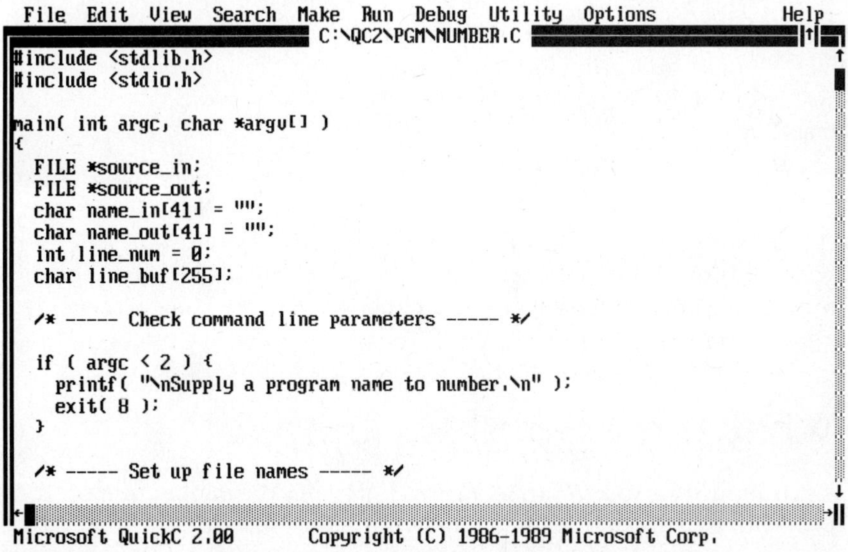

```
  File  Edit  View  Search  Make  Run  Debug  Utility  Options         Help
                         C:\QC2\PGM\NUMBER.C
#include <stdlib.h>
#include <stdio.h>

main( int argc, char *argv[] )
{
  FILE *source_in;
  FILE *source_out;
  char name_in[41] = "";
  char name_out[41] = "";
  int line_num = 0;
  char line_buf[255];

  /* ----- Check command line parameters ----- */

  if ( argc < 2 ) {
    printf( "\nSupply a program name to number.\n" );
    exit( 8 );
  }

  /* ----- Set up file names ----- */

Microsoft QuickC 2.00      Copyright (C) 1986-1989 Microsoft Corp.
```

Most of the more recent compiler products feature an *integrated development environment* (IDE). When you use an IDE, you don't run the compiler, you run the environment. In that environment, the *built-in* text editor is usually the first thing you see. (Microsoft's QuickC editor is a built-in editor, for example.) In a built-in editor, the other functions (compiling, linking, setting options) are just a menu selection or a hot-key away. By contrast, *stand-alone* editors are not part of an IDE. If you choose a stand-alone editor, it should have the same features as an IDE editor (except, obviously, interfaces to compiler and linker).

Editors built into an IDE have two extremely helpful features: *error location* and *advanced project make facilities*. These two features can do more to reduce development time than almost any of the others in the package.

In an IDE, compile-time errors are displayed (in the editor) with the cursor positioned on the first error, ready to correct. The screen typically is divided into two windows, with the edit session in the upper portion of the screen, and a list of error messages in the lower portion. These windows stay synchronized. As you select the next error message in the error window, the cursor is automatically repositioned in the edit window.

Within an IDE, project make facilities (controlling multiple source files is discussed in Chapter 5) can be automated considerably. The Borland products (Turbo C) provide an integrated project make facility as well as a stand-alone make utility. Both integrated project make and stand-alone make facilities require a text file containing make instructions as input. Project files have an extension of .PRJ rather than the usual .MAK (for make files). Project and make files are essentially the same; they differ only in syntax and point of use, not in purpose. The syntax of project files is simpler than that of make files.

The Microsoft integrated environment does much the same thing by using a "program list." Here, too, the syntax is simplified. The list of source files is created within a dialog box and stored in a file with the .MAK extension. When the program list is stored to disk (at your request) that list is converted to make-file format and syntax. Using either vendor's product, you are saved a *great deal* of effort.

What's in a Good C Compiler?

Assuming that your compiler product provides the minimum set of tools in one form or another, how can you tell whether you have a good product?

Again, our answer reflects our opinion—at least, up to a point. Some very popular products we do not like at all; others—not so popular—we feel are top notch. Selecting your C compiler product involves both an element of personal taste—and one of need.

Compiler Features

There is no point in buying a less than robust C compiler, just because you have yet to learn the language. A full-featured package may seem intimidating at first, because there are so many options to control. You probably will find, however, that you will grow quickly into the more sophisticated product.

Choosing between the leading contenders in the C compiler market is difficult, primarily because the best packages are quite similar in what they offer. Yet there are significant differences. When you start thinking about buying a C compiler, you need to investigate at least seven kinds of features:

- *Full ANSI C conformity*
- *Compile-only options*
- *Environment support*
- *Floating-point math support*
- *Support of low-level features*
- *Optimization features*
- *C++ support*

Full ANSI C conformity is crucial, and becomes more so. A compiler that does not conform to the standard, or conforms to only part of it, creates unnecessary problems in manufacturing portable programs. The issue of ANSI conformity, however, applies to your programs as well as to the compiler you use.

The ANSI X3J11 committee wisely allowed for the distinction between strictly conforming (maximally portable) and conforming programs. This distinction was made to permit the presence and legitimate use of extensions to the standard language. Many of these are necessary to produce practical code for a particular machine or system.

ANSI C Rationale

ANSI C allows for extensions to the language in a conforming implementation (compiler), to provide enhanced *functionality* and *performance.* Don't be afraid to use the extensions. They can be the keys to slick, high-performance programs. Low-level I/O and video I/O functions are two areas in which a compiler vendor is likely to provide extensions (in the form of library functions).

You can reduce the impact of using extensions on portability by encapsulating the nonstandard code in a group of user-defined functions and referring to the nonstandard function calls, and so on, only in those functions. When porting the program to another machine or operating system, you then need only convert those functions, leaving the rest of the program alone.

Compile-only options are needed to allow for separate compilation and linkage editing when you construct large, complex projects. This kind of option is so universally available that you are unlikely to find a C compiler that does not support it in some fashion.

Options supporting the host environment make much of the difference between professional-quality compiler tools and lesser products. The compiler should at least provide options for the following:

- ❏ *Generating object-module maps*

- ❏ *Choosing memory models or instruction sets (for IBM 80x86 based machines)*

- ❏ *Selecting the function-calling conventions (to support mixing with other languages, and for performance boost)*

- ❏ *Stack checking at run time*

- ❏ *Controlling the stack and heap size*

- ❏ *Turning on debugging support features*

For systems-programming with C, you might want a compiler that can produce ROMable code (such as the code in a PC extension card). And anyone might want to control the names of files output from the compiler (by using a file extension other than .OBJ, for example).

Floating-point math support obviously is important. Although you can do many things without it, there are equally many things you cannot. The floating-point package should include both floating-point emulation and the capability to use math coprocessor chips directly, without first having to change the source code you write. Control of this feature with a compile time switch is acceptable, but it is much better if the compiler can detect the coprocessor dynamically and build your program accordingly. Dynamic detection of the coprocessor allows your program to run on any machine, with or without the coprocessor, without having to be recompiled.

Support of low-level features is mandatory for systems or commercial-grade work. The compiler should permit access to system I/O ports, low-level I/O functions, system interrupt services, direct DOS calls, and ROM BIOS calls. Why? There are just two reasons: *speed* and *power*. DOS just doesn't do many things very fast—and it doesn't do many other things at all. Nor does the ANSI standard mandate interfaces to such high-performance services. Later in this book, you are introduced to coping with hardware and system dependencies like these. You should be aware that you will mature rapidly as a C programmer and that you will not only want, but also *need* these features.

Optimization features also are key to large, complex projects. Basically, you can optimize code in just two ways. You can optimize for *speed* or for *size*. Sometimes optimizing for one factor contributes to better efficiency for the other, as well. For many of your projects, you do not need to optimize the code. Later, however, you begin to develop polished, high-performance programs that may require wringing the last bit of performance from the machine, or stuffing the greatest possible amount of code into memory.

Finally, *C++ support* rapidly becomes a hallmark of the acceptable compiler. C++ is for neither the beginner nor the faint-hearted. It can be an important tool in the future, however, as more and more software products take advantage of object-oriented features.

The Linkage Editor and Compatibility

Most compilers do not produce *load modules* (executable run-time files) directly. Rather, they produce *object modules* (machine code, but not yet ready to run). A linkage editor then combines the object modules into load modules, performing such tasks as resolving references to data items and function names in separately compiled modules (it links object modules together). The linkage editor is therefore an important part of the compiler product. The catch is that linkage editors are not always interchangeable. The linkage editor is completely dependent on the specific format of the object file produced by the compiler, and some vendors' compilers produce object formats compatible only with their own linkage editors.

In the IBM-compatible and MS-DOS arena, Microsoft naturally sets the standard with object formats acceptable to MS LINK. All MS language products use this linker, and many other products more or less base their formats on this standard. Even if the level of conformity to the MS object format is less rather than more, however, selecting a compiler product with a companion linkage editor is still important, because Microsoft no longer provides MS LINK with the DOS system, but only with their own language products.

Borland supplies TLINK with the Turbo C Professional 2.0 system. This linker is presented as a high-performance subset of MS LINK, with the caveat that code compiled with Microsoft C often cannot be handled because that code has undocumented (proprietary) format object records. The manual does not comment on whether MS LINK can be used with Turbo C object modules.

Zortech C modules, on the other hand, can be linked routinely with MS LINK and, in fact, *should* be if you want to use Microsoft's CodeView debugger with Zortech C programs. Conversely, only the Zortech Link program can perform the fix-ups needed for C++. If you use MS LINK, another utility (BUNCH) is required to perform the necessary patches for C++.

At the other end of the spectrum, Mix Software's Power C doesn't produce MS–format object records at all. Output from this compiler has the .MIX extension (not .OBJ) and can be linked only with the MIX linkage editor. MASM (Microsoft Macro Assembler) modules can be linked in, but only after they have been converted by a special utility program provided by Mix.

No vendor's product is either superior or inferior to any other. You just need to understand which linkage editor you need to use and what its limitations may be. Two things are true, however: the compiler package you choose must have a linkage editor and should at least allow the inclusion of Microsoft assembler modules (or modules produced by the vendor's own assembler). Any package that does not is not suitable for advanced work later.

Project-management Facilities

To continue with the idea that you need a compiler product that allows you to grow in sophistication without having to buy a new compiler, you can see that the package should have some facilities that support *complex projects*. These facilities themselves can be more or less sophisticated, but you really need at least two utilities: MAKE and TOUCH. These utilities, which originated in UNIX systems, have made the transition (with C) to the PC and are indispensable to serious programmers.

MAKE automates and controls the compilation and linkage editing of programs made up of several source files. A single *make file* (a text file describing the compile/link edit steps) can control generation of one or several complex programs. MAKE differs from the integrated project management facilities mentioned earlier, in that it is a separately run utility program. Living without such a utility is possible, but there are some important advantages to having it:

❑ *You don't have to remember which object modules go together to make up a load module.* You record this information once in the make file, and completely eliminate the risk of forgetting anything when regenerating the programs.

❑ *You can record dependencies of one source file on another in the make file.* MAKE notes when changes are made to a module (by comparing dates and times), and automatically recompiles or relinks any modules dependent on the first.

❑ MAKE *saves a great deal of time, because it recompiles or relinks only modules that actually need it.* A DOS batch (.BAT) file, by comparison, can only recompile and relink everything.

❑ *Although you generally can handle much more complex projects with* MAKE *than you can with IDE facilities (as described earlier), this is not always true.* MAKE can be used also in those rare cases when you *must* use the stand-alone compiler rather than the integrated environment.

TOUCH is a companion utility to MAKE. Sometimes you know that you need to force the recompilation or relinking of a module, although the date or time stamps on the files involved have not changed. TOUCH updates the date and time stamps of source or object files, making them more recent than dependent files. Then when MAKE is run again, it rebuilds from the TOUCHed files.

TOUCH may be either a separate utility, as in the Borland and Zortech products, or it may be integrated into the MAKE utility, as in Microsoft's QuickC (called NMAKE in version 2.0). If you find that you are using a package which does not supply any form of TOUCH, you can supply one yourself! Listing 1.2 shows uctouch.c, which is an example of how to write such a program in Turbo C++ (plain C style).

Listing 1.2. `uctouch.c`. *A user-written* TOUCH *utility.*

```
1   #include <dos.h>
2   #include <io.h>
3   #include <string.h>
4   #include <stdio.h>
5
6   void main( int argc, char *argv[] )
7   {
8     struct time t;
9     struct date d;
10    struct ftime f;
11    FILE *tfile;
12
13    if ( argc < 2 ) {
14      puts( "Specify a file name." );
15      abort();
16    }
17    if ( NULL == ( tfile = fopen( argv[1], "r" ) ) ) {
18      puts( "File open error." );
19      abort();
20    }
21    gettime( &t );
22    f.ft_tsec = t.ti_sec;
23    f.ft_min  = t.ti_min;
24    f.ft_hour = t.ti_hour;
25    getdate( &d );
26    f.ft_day   = d.da_day;
27    f.ft_month = d.da_mon;
28    f.ft_year  = d.da_year - 1980;
29
30    setftime( fileno( tfile ), &f );
31    fclose( tfile );
32  }
```

The program in listing 1.2 uses library functions (`gettime()`, `getdate()`, and `setftime()`) that are unique to Turbo C++. They are not part of the ANSI standard library, nor are they necessarily found in the same form in other vendor's compilers. You will need to convert those functions to the forms used by your own compiler.

Compatibility with Other Languages

Earlier in this chapter, you saw a brief comparison of C to other languages. Clearly, some languages are better suited than others to certain tasks. In some cases, building a single program from modules compiled in more than one language is desirable. When that is true, the compilers involved must be able to do several things in compatible ways. One of the most important of these tasks is using the system stack to pass parameters to subroutines.

Suppose, for example, that you have written a fancy new C program, the performance of which could be improved considerably by recoding one of its functions in assembly language. Suppose also that you know the stack is used to pass parameters to the function, and that the part of the stack used to do this is called a *stack frame*. Which parameters are placed at the top of the stack frame and which at the bottom? How do you code the assembler routine to access the individual parameters correctly?

Doing this requires a knowledge of how the C compiler generates code internally, as well as a knowledge of assembler. To make the problem worse, suppose that the other language is not assembler, but some other high-level language—FORTRAN, for instance. Now you have no control over handling the passing of parameters. Both compilers do it in a specific way. Do they match in their parameter passing methods?

Matching dissimilar compilers for use together is a matter of some research. You have to *know*, not guess, their characteristics before you start. We have never seen a C compiler (although there may be one somewhere) that could not interface somehow to an assembler routine. Beyond assembler interfacing, however, the rule is *do your homework*.

The search for compatible compilers can be a deceptive one. You might think, for example, that the Turbo C and Turbo Pascal compilers could be used together, especially because Turbo C allows you to declare functions that use a Pascal calling convention. Can you use them together? No! The Pascal calling convention is a Turbo C feature used to enhance performance, but output from the two compilers is not always compatible and you cannot mix object modules from them.

Command-line versus Integrated Environments

As important as an integrated development environment is to rapid construction of programs, it cannot be used at times. When the integrated development environment can't be used, you must resort to the command-line compiler.

What's the Difference?

The command-line environment is a manual environment. You must edit the program with a stand-alone editor (you can use an IDE editor, but only for editing), execute the compiler, and then execute the linkage editor. Each command must be typed at the system prompt (the DOS `c>` prompt, for example), and each utility must be run to completion before the next can be run.

Obviously, you lose all the advantages of automation when you use a command-line environment. You also lose a corresponding increment of speed in the development process. Why would you ever want to work in the command-line environment? You would only rarely, but there are some good reasons for having it available.

Why You Need Both

First, you would want a command-line version of your compiler because the full range of function frequently is available only there. Most of the compiler's options are available in the integrated environment, but a few may not be. To use these extra options, you need to specify (in the command invoking the compiler) the options you want. Suppose, for example, that you want to use Turbo C to compile a C program, generating only assembly language output, not an object module. The command-line parameters would look like this:

```
tcc -S first
```

This command would compile the `first.c` program, with assembler output. You could then fine tune the resulting assembler source for very high performance and assemble it separately, or simply study it to see how the compiler handles different C source statements.

Sometimes, the command-line compiler is the only way you can compile a sophisticated program. (Just what kind of program this may be depends on the compiler.) Microsoft's QuickC, for example, can handle in-line assembly statements directly, whereas Turbo C must be run from the command line. With Turbo C, you must specify the `-B` option and have available a separate assembler.

Do You Need a Visual Debugger?

You *do* need a visual debugger. Testing the program is an inescapable part of program development. Almost invariably, the result of testing is *debug-*

ging—finding and fixing problems with the code. Doing this without a debugger can be difficult, to say the least.

If the compiler you select does not have an integrated development environment with debugging built in, at least verify that a visual debugger is available as a separate package. If none is available, we strongly suggest that you stay away from that particular package.

What Is a Visual Debugger?

The great advantage of a visual debugger is its interactive nature. It *shows* you what is going on within the program while it allows you to control execution of the program.

As the program is being executed (by you, as slowly as you like), a visual debugger displays the source code on-screen, indicating with a current-position pointer the next statement to be executed. At every step, you can *see* what is about to happen. Figure 1.6 shows the screen displayed by the Turbo C Professional Debugger while first.c is being debugged.

Fig. 1.6. *The Turbo C Professional stand-alone debugger.*

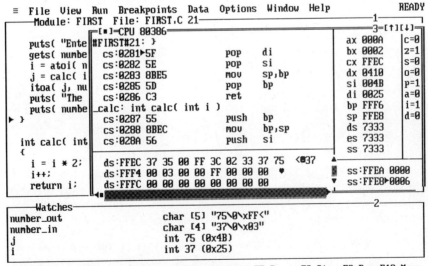

The solid triangular pointer to the left of the source code statements indicates the current position. As you can see, execution of the program has been followed down into the `calc()` function.

Features of a Good Debugger

Figure 1.6 also shows several other things the debugger can track and display. This is just a sampling of the features a good debugger provides. Some of the features you may want in a debugger are described in this section.

Integrated environment and stand-alone versions of the debugger. Debugging in an IDE can be convenient for short programs, whereas a stand-alone debugger is essential for large or extremely complex programs. Although having both kinds of debugger is not absolutely essential, it certainly is helpful.

Step-over and trace-into execution. Stepping over allows you to execute a program one line at a time. If a line contains a function call, the call is treated like a *black box* (the function is executed, but the display continues to show the calling line of code). *Tracing into* also executes one line at a time, but when a function call is encountered, the visual display follows execution down into the called function. Both methods of debugging are appropriate at different times.

Multiple display windows. Being able to track several things simultaneously on-screen and to switch easily and rapidly to another kind of display is important to quick, efficient debugging.

Breakpoint and variable watch support. You can execute the program one line or statement at a time. Sometimes this is necessary, but it can be extremely time consuming. By setting breakpoints, you can speed up debugging considerably. You can flag as a breakpoint the last statement or line you know to be working correctly, and let the program execute at full speed until the breakpoint is reached. Setting up a variable watch window, telling the debugger which variables to "watch" (continuously), is also very helpful. Again, you can let the program execute at full speed while you observe how the selected variables are being changed.

System and environment displays. To find errors in complex programs, debugging occasionally must get *extremely* detailed. When this need arises, you may want to look, for example, into the system hardware registers or the condition of the program stack. A good debugger allows you to do so.

Interactive modification of the program. Interactive modification does not mean rewriting the source code on the fly. However, you may want to observe the effects of *changing the value* of a variable that has been corrupted by some part of the program. If, by correcting such a value, you cause the program to run correctly, you have isolated the problem to a narrow range of possible causes.

Support multiple source files. Many programs (of any complexity and consequent usefulness) are composed of several independent source files. A good visual debugger loads and displays the different source files at the correct times. Debugging large programs would be nearly impossible without this feature.

The features listed here, although by no means all that a full-featured visual debugger provides, cover the most important features that go beyond following source code during execution.

Legitimate Uses of a Debugger

The purpose of a debugger is to locate the cause of problems in a program, or to verify that a *specific* section of code is working correctly. Surprisingly, debugging tools, especially the more sophisticated ones, are easy to abuse. That is, you can easily confuse *debugging* with *testing*, and use the debugger as a testing tool.

This kind of mistake is subtle and can lead to a lot of trouble. The temptation is to assume that because you have "gotten inside" the program while it executes, you have also verified every aspect of its execution. *That is not automatically true.*

Using a debugger does not guarantee that you have successfully predicted every situation that might arise while running the program. There is no substitute for adequately designing a program, nor for taking the time to design thoroughly the test cases for it. After you have done this, you can use a debugger to verify correct operation of the program under all the circumstances it might encounter.

Summary

This chapter introduced you to the world of C programming, with only a broad overview of what goes into building a C program. The purpose of the chapter is to give you a sense of context, a foundation of the concepts that guide and control writing C programs. This chapter discussed the following:

❑ *Where C came from, and the context in which it was developed.* You learned something about the flavor of the language.

❑ *A comparison of C to several other languages, painted in broad strokes.* C compares well to other languages but does not replace all other languages. (They wouldn't exist if there were no need for them.)

❑ *An introductory to C form and punctuation.* You must understand them to learn to read—and later write—C programs. They are also the first things that confuse new students of C programming.

❑ *The basic parts of a C program: header-file inclusion directives, data definitions, the* `main( )` *function, and user-defined functions.* All but the most simple C programs contain all these parts.

❑ *The first steps in writing a C program.* Here, you not only learned the basics of how to design a C program, but also how to make it readable for later correction or modification.

❑ *What tools a C programmer needs.* The text editor is important, because you interface with it more often than with any other part of a C compiler package. The compiler, to be useful to you, must have the right features. You also saw the difference between integrated development environments and command-line environments—and why both must be available. Finally, you learned that a visual debugger is a crucial item in the C programmer's tool bag.

Now you have a platform to work from. In the next chapter, we launch right into the nuts and bolts of C programming, examining the basics of C input and output functions.

Basic I/O Programming

Because a computer program that does no input or output probably is a program that doesn't do much of anything, this chapter has been placed early in the book so that you can begin to write meaningful programs as soon as possible.

The purpose of this chapter is twofold: to introduce you to the basics of I/O programming in C, and to introduce you to the philosophy behind I/O programming in general. In this chapter you do the following:

❏ *See some of the reasons that new programmers often have trouble with I/O programming.* Understanding what you are trying to do is the best way to begin understanding how to do it.

❏ *Learn about the C I/O environment.* This environment includes C data streams, the kinds of I/O devices, and file handling.

❏ *See how to deal with C's predefined, or standard, data streams.*

❏ *Learn how to write programs using both the simple and formatted I/O library functions, as well as how to convert data formats after inputting items.*

❏ *See what it costs to do I/O programming without using the library functions.* Doing this gives you the following:
1) an appreciation for the library I/O functions; 2) knowledge

of how I/O is implemented on an IBM-compatible PC; and 3) two useful utilities: a working communications program to build on later, and a high performance version of the DOS MORE utility.

The Problem with Input and Output

I/O programming often presents the programmer-in-training with unexpected difficulties. The answers to the following three questions unravel much of the mystery of I/O operations and prepare the way for a discussion of C's stream I/O functions.

❏ *What precisely is I/O?*

❏ *How far do the operating system and other components go in masking the complexity of I/O?*

❏ *What built-in facilities does my C compiler provide for interfacing with the I/O system?*

I/O is nothing more than moving data from secondary storage into main storage (*input*, or *read* operations) and out of main storage to secondary storage (*output*, or *write* operations). In the process, one or more kinds of cache (high-speed buffer) memory may be used.

Each kind of memory is characterized by its *speed* (how fast the CPU can access it) and *persistence* (how long it retains data). The block diagram in figure 2.1 shows how the components of a digital computer system relate to one another.

Main storage is the memory inside your PC's system unit. This is where your programs reside while they are run, and where they manipulate data. Main storage is often called RAM, or *random access memory*. It has fast access time (typically around 100 nanoseconds, or billionths of a second), and short-term persistence (only as long as the machine is powered on).

Secondary storage is a collective term signifying a group of objects called simply *I/O devices*, or *peripheral devices* (which means *outside the computer*). In this book, we use the term *I/O device* because it implies the read-write operations the devices perform.

I/O devices differ drastically from main memory in both speed and memory persistence. A fast hard disk drive may have an access time of 28 milliseconds (about 280,000 times slower than main memory). Comparisons to instruction execution speed are similarly disproportionate. The original IBM PC, running at 4.77 MHz, could execute its fastest instructions

Fig. 2.1. *Memory in relation to system components.*

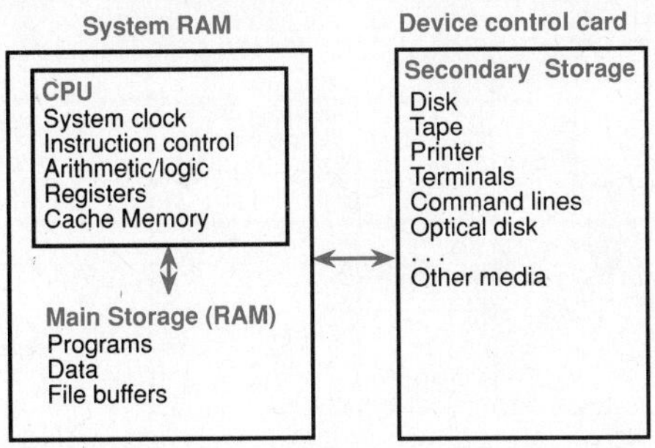

in 210 nanoseconds, or about 133,333 times faster than the previously mentioned hard disk can set up for an I/O operation (without actually performing it).

This is why I/O is the single greatest roadblock to high-performance programs. On the other hand, some I/O devices (like disks and tapes) have long-term persistence; they can retain recorded data for many years, even when the machine is switched off.

There are only two basic ways to perform an I/O operation (read or write): *memory-mapped I/O*, and channel or *port I/O*. Although the exact manner of implementation of these methods may vary from one machine to another, all I/O operations fall into one of these categories. Later in this chapter, you see examples of both of these methods of handling I/O on the IBM PC.

A program performs memory-mapped I/O by moving data bytes into and out of an area of RAM designated for a particular device. The area of RAM is the same as, and is part of, the system's normal RAM used by programs and data. The instructions used are those used to move data bytes around elsewhere in RAM. Figure 2.2 shows how memory-mapped I/O is used for controlling a PC display terminal.

High-performance disk drives (both floppy and fixed disks) use an even more sophisticated method of memory-mapped I/O called *direct memory access* (DMA) in which a peripheral device can read and write directly to RAM. DMA involves complicated programming, as well as special support circuitry.

Port I/O is more complex for several reasons. A program maintains data in RAM, but only for its own use. The data must be fetched from the RAM areas (buffers) and sent to the I/O device via a special machine instruction that

Fig. 2.2. *Memory-mapped I/O implemented for PC display.*

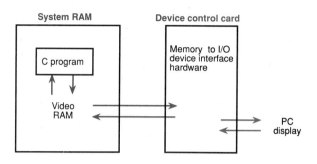

writes to the port. Similarly, input operations read data from the port, leaving it to the program to dispose of the data in some way. When doing direct port I/O, the software must be concerned with the input and output of control information as well as data. Figure 2.3 illustrates these operations.

Fig. 2.3. *Port I/O to and from a communications interface.*

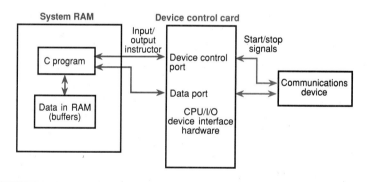

The complexity of port I/O doesn't stop with data transfer. As you can see from figure 2.3, there is a *device control port* as well as a data I/O port. Control ports are used to inform the device whether the next operation is input or output, how to set up for it, whether to clear and reset, and so forth. Disks also use control ports as well as DMA—an extremely complicated, but necessary, arrangement.

Fortunately for programmers, this kind of overhead programming does not have to be written directly into every program. Responsibility for such control functions is divided among several pieces of code:

❏ *The device controller circuitry handles the most time-sensitive and delicate activities, such as timing disk rotation and actually stepping the read/write head into position.* These functions are built into the controller card at the factory; you do not need to worry about them.

❏ *The system BIOS (Basic I/O System) sends requests to and receives status information from the device controller circuitry by reading and writing the control ports assigned to a particular device.* It also reads and writes data through the assigned data ports.

❏ *The operating system (DOS, OS/2, UNIX, etc.) converts your program's logical I/O requests into physical I/O requests and passes them to the BIOS.* A logical request might involve requesting a particular record number from a file. Converting it to a physical request would involve calculating the sector number on disk where the data resides. The operating system also receives *status information* about the operation from the BIOS and passes it back to your program.

❏ *The compiler's built-in I/O functions do a variety of things that are covered in our discussion of I/O.* Typical functions do such things as keeping track of the next available record number, noting whether I/O operations were successful, and converting I/O requests into the operating system's format. Standard C I/O functions make all I/O appear to the program as if the data flows in and out of the program as a continuous stream of characters (bytes).

❏ *It remains for your code to use the built-in I/O functions.* You request that the next character or block of characters be read or written. You will begin to see how to do that in the following sections of this chapter.

A lot goes on behind the scenes. From the programmer's point of view, most of the complexity is hidden behind the services provided by the compiler's built-in functions and the operating system services. Figure 2.4 summarizes the division of responsibility for I/O among the different components.

Fig. 2.4. *Division of I/O responsibilities.*

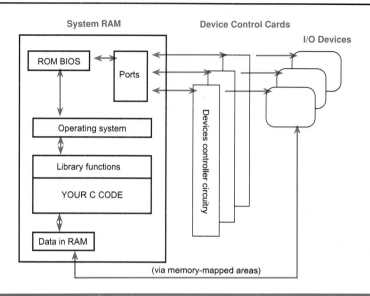

Understanding Stream I/O

In ANSI standard C, all I/O appears to the program as a continuous stream of characters or perhaps groups of characters. Stream I/O was adopted as the standard method for several reasons, of which the following are prominent:

❏ *Stream I/O provides device independence; the C programmer does not have to write I/O functions for each specific kind of device.* With stream I/O, a C program sees a file as a continuous stream of text characters, even if they are stored in widely separated chunks (blocks) scattered over a disk.

❏ *Stream I/O permits a C program to access files in a standard way, independent of its physical format on an external storage medium.* An important side effect of device independence is that file access is the same from one compiler to another.

❏ *Stream I/O not only provides for buffering of input and output data, whenever the devices used permit that, in a uniform way, but also allows the programmer to tune I/O performance by controlling buffer size.*

Comparing Streams, Files, and Devices

Streams, files, and devices are all related; they make up a hierarchy of concepts.

❏   *Streams always are associated with an external file.*

❏   *A file may be a collection of related data that resides on a storage device, or it may be an interactive device.*

Although you, the programmer, may not be directly aware of it, the way files are buffered differs from one device type to another. The specific differences are described in the discussions of specific device types.

Buffering is an important part of I/O, and streams are buffered whenever possible (depending on the I/O device being used). What is a buffer, and why is it important?

A *buffer* is a block of RAM into or from which the I/O functions read or write a large chunk of data. This may be going on behind the scenes even if your program is requesting only one character at a time.

Standard C provides three kinds of buffering for streams:

❏   *Unbuffered I/O starts a new I/O operation for every character of data transferred.*

❏   *Line buffered I/O collects characters into lines of text, with a newline character at the end of each line, before making them available to the program.*

❏   *Fully buffered I/O reads or writes an arbitrary, but usually fairly large number of characters at a time.*

Controlling buffers may seem like a lot of trouble. You probably wonder "Why do it?"

Buffers perform a *speed-matching function*. If your program read or wrote only one character, there would be no problem; but a typical program reads and writes many thousands of bytes. Without a speed-matching mechanism, the program would spend most of its time waiting for I/O and would take an intolerable amount of time to run.

Remember that I/O devices are several orders of magnitude slower than the computer itself due, in large part, to *set-up overhead time*. This is particularly true for devices like disks, which maintain relatively large amounts of data. Several factors contribute to overhead time for disk I/O operations:

❏ *The library functions must translate your request into a form acceptable to the operating system.* They must also update control information about the stream kept within the C program.

❏ *The operating system must translate the request into a form acceptable to the BIOS.* Control information kept within the operating system is updated also.

❏ *The BIOS then outputs the request to the disk controller.* Provisions must be made for handling the physical transfer of data to or from RAM, and for recognizing when I/O activity is complete.

❏ *The disk controller activates the particular drive, steps the read/write head to the correct track (seek time), notes the head's position on the track, and waits for the correct sector to rotate under the head (rotational delay, or latency).*

Whenever this overhead can be avoided (or at least worked around), program performance increases. On single-user systems (such as PCs running DOS), your program must come to a complete halt while it waits for I/O. The only way to reduce that overhead is to reduce the number of I/O "starts" by providing efficient buffering of data.

To illustrate this point, we set up a test file and program. The program read the file (18,738 bytes of text) repetitively, significantly increasing the buffer size on each pass. The unrealistically small initial buffer size of 16 bytes was multiplied by 8 for each repetition, resulting in a final buffer size of 8K bytes (not nearly as large as it might be). Read time for the file decreased rapidly as buffer size increases. The point of diminishing returns will be reached eventually, however, when no increase helps. Figure 2.5 graphically illustrates the results of that test.

Even though the test system was already running an intelligent disk-buffering package, read time dropped from 0.6913 to 0.1479 seconds, nearly a five-fold improvement. (See Appendix F for a description of the timing software used.)

Interactive Devices

Interactive devices differ from other I/O devices in that they don't provide long-term storage of data and are designed to interact directly with a user of the system. Common examples of interactive devices are video displays, keyboards, and communications ports. Figure 2.6 shows how interactive devices relate to the computer system.

Fig. 2.5. *The effects of buffer size on read time.*

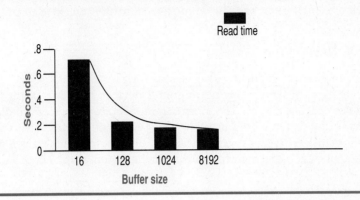

Fig. 2.6. *Interactive devices.*

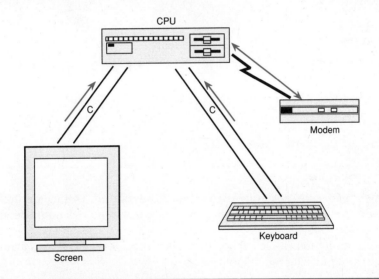

Interactive devices may be either completely unbuffered or only line buffered. In *unbuffered files*, as the term implies, each byte or character is read or written immediately. The library functions do not place the byte in an intermediate RAM area. Some of the simple keyboard input library functions, for example, use unbuffered I/O.

The keyboard may also be *line buffered*. Characters are received and stored in RAM until you press the Enter (Return) key. Then the newline character is added to the buffer, and the whole line of text is sent to your program.

Data Files

Data files are not themselves devices, as are interactive "files." Rather, they are collections of data that reside on storage devices. Files on a storage device share the space available. The most common storage devices are diskettes and hard disk drives. A volume directory keeps track of where everything is. Tracks on disk are closer together than the eye can see. Each track is divided into sectors, each of which contains a fixed amount of data (see fig. 2.7).

Fig. 2.7. Files on storage devices..

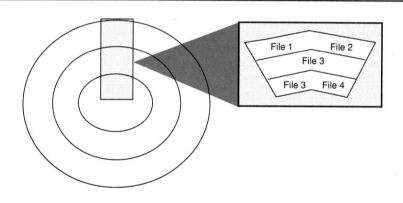

Data files are, in the nature of the case, fully buffered. This means that the buffer is made large enough to be efficient, but that it does not necessarily correspond to logical lines of text. You can still read lines of text from data files, but doing so involves having the library routines retrieve data from the buffers and building the line of text.

Even when you seem to be reading a fully buffered file, one character at a time, the buffers are in action behind the scenes. This was the case, for example, in the test run illustrated in figure 2.5.

Introducing C Streams

Is it buffered? Is it not buffered? If it is buffered, how large is the buffer? Is that efficient? With C streams as implemented by the standard C library functions, you can write reasonably efficient file-handling programs and never worry about the details of buffering. In Chapter 10, we show you how to plan for and implement procedures for high-performance I/O code—but you need not do that for many of the tasks for which you write C programs.

Streams may be classified as *text* or *binary* streams. Although the file associated with the stream is the same in either case, there is an important distinction in the way the library functions handle I/O for text and binary streams.

Text streams (files) can be understood in an intuitive way—they are files that contain text data which people can read immediately. The stream of characters in text files is organized into lines, which also are understood in the ordinary way. Each line is terminated by an end-of-line character (or characters). According to the standard, the lines in a text file must be capable of containing at least 254 characters. A text file can be read and written also as a binary file.

The library functions perform some translation of some special characters when reading or writing text files. The characters that physically indicate end-of-line (usually a carriage return and linefeed pair of characters) are transformed into a single newline character. Certain other characters also are recognized. A tab character, for instance, causes the display position on-screen to be changed when it is written to the video display.

Binary streams (files) are so named because they are read and written bit-for-bit exactly as found in the physical file, with no translation of characters. Characters (unsigned characters) are still being handled, but now the program must determine what to do with special characters.

Facilities for handling binary files are provided so that you can work with any data that does not fall into the category of text. There are quite a few of these files—the .EXE and .COM files that compilers and linkers must produce, data files that contain numeric information in internal formats (to save disk space, for example), and many others.

The Standard Streams

Standard C provides three streams that always are associated with input or output files. These are the *standard input* (stdin), *standard output* (stdout), and *standard error* (stderr) streams.

The standard streams are text streams; you normally do not have the option of treating them as binary files.

The standard streams always are available for immediate use, and require no preparatory action on your part. In fact, some of the library functions assume the presence of standard streams, so that you do not have to name them explicitly.

stdin, stdout, and stderr

The standard I/O files are prepared for use by the C initialization code in a process normally hidden from the programmer. The associated files are *opened* at program start-up, and *closed* at program termination (unless the program is aborted). Shortly, you will learn how to open and close files to associate them with streams.

One feature of standard I/O is that *I/O redirection* can be used to vary the actual places the input and output go. stdin usually gets its input from, and stdout usually sends output to, the system console. This can be changed with redirection. Incidentally, I/O redirection is supported almost identically in DOS, UNIX, and OS/2. The manuals for these systems document how to use redirection at the command-line level. All you have to do in your program is use the standard streams.

In standard C, the list of library functions for I/O is reasonably rich. Any of the stream functions can refer to the standard streams (except purely control functions), and eight functions assume that a standard stream is meant so that you do not have to specify a stream name in the function call. Table 2.1 summarizes these eight functions. It also shows their more general counterparts, which can refer to any stream.

Table 2.1. *I/O functions assuming standard I/O.*

Implies stdxxx	*Requires Stream Name*	*Action of Function*
printf()	fprintf()	Formatted output
scanf()	fscanf()	Formatted input
vprintf()	vfprintf()	Formatted output, variable argument list
getchar()	getc(), fgetc()	Character input
gets()	fgets()	String input
putchar()	putc(), fputc()	Character output
puts()	fputs()	String output
perror()	---	Send error message to stderr only

With these eight I/O functions, you can do just about any file I/O you want to without having to name a stream explicitly. With I/O redirection available, it can also be disk file text I/O.

Listing 2.1 is a short program, `stream.c`. It illustrates the equivalence of `getc()`/`getchar()`, and `putc()`/`putchar()`. It also illustrates a couple of interesting points about standard stream I/O that you need to see in action before we explain them. Take the time now to type listing 2.1 into your C editor, then compile and run it. After you have done that, read the following discussion.

Listing 2.1. `stream.c` *(Character I/O).*   *Turbo C 2.0*

```
1   /*+---------------------------------------------------------
2    +                         STREAM.C
3    + This short demo shows how getchar() and putchar()
4    + relate to getc() and putc().
5    +---------------------------------------------------------
6   */
7
8   #include <stdlib.h>
9   #include <stdio.h>
10
11  main()
12  {
13    char char_buffer;
14
15    /* Do it the easy way first. */
16
17    printf( "\nType in a line, up to 80 characters, and " );
18    printf( "the computer will repeat\n" );
19    printf( "it using getchar() and putchar().\n" );
20    while ( ( char_buffer = getchar() ) != '\n' )
21      putchar( char_buffer );
22
23    /* Now do it the hard way. */
24
25    printf( "\n\nPlease type another line. This time the " );
26    printf( "computer will use the\n" );
27    printf( "functions getc() and putc().\n" );
28    while ( ( char_buffer = getc( stdin ) ) != '\n' )
29      putc( char_buffer, stdout );
30  }
```

Even though the listing header indicates that this is a Turbo C program, it contains only code that conforms to standard C. It compiles and runs in the same way on all compilers available to us, including Microsoft compilers (MS C and QuickC).

The presence of the `printf()` function calls is only incidental to the program. (That function is covered a little later in this chapter.) Right now, the calls to `getchar()` and `putchar()` in lines 20 and 21, and `getc()` and `putc()` in lines 28 and 29 are of interest.

Did you notice that they are used without preamble of any kind? These function calls either imply, or explicitly name, only `stdin` and `stdout` streams. No preparation is needed—they were already open (see "Connecting Files to Streams," a little later in this chapter) and ready when the `main()` function began to execute.

Secondly, you should reflect on how the program behaved when run, compared to the function calls in the `while` loops. Think about those loops for just a moment. The way the program is written, a character is read, and the same character is immediately written to `stdout`.

That is not the way the screen looked when it was run, however. You were able to type the entire string and press Enter before the string as a whole was echoed on the screen. For example, suppose that you typed the letters *abc*. They would have appeared on the screen as follows:

```
abc
abc
```

But if each character is output *immediately* after it is read, why did it not appear as follows instead?

```
aabbcc
```

The reason is line buffering. The ANSI C standard requires only that the `stderr` not be fully buffered, and that the `stdin` and `stdout` streams be fully buffered, but *not if* they are associated with interactive devices.

On an IBM or compatible PC, the system console is actually *two* interactive devices—the keyboard and the video display. Therefore the `stdin` and `stdout` streams are not fully buffered—they are *line* buffered in most C compilers (this is not a guarantee, by the way).

This explains the program's behavior. Characters *are* read and immediately output—to the `stdout` *buffer*. They are not sent physically to the display until the whole line has arrived, signalled by the end-of-line character (pressing Enter). Hence, the input and output characters remain unmingled.

Relating Streams to DOS Handles

DOS relates files (either interactive or data files) with integer numbers called file *handles*. It also has standard input and output handles (as well as error, auxiliary, and print handles) to which C relates its standard streams. Table 2.2 relates the standard C streams to the DOS handles for standard I/O.

Table 2.2. *C streams and DOS handles.*

C Stream	DOS Handle	I/O Type
stdin	0	Standard input
stdout	1	Standard output
stderr	2	Standard error message
stdaux	3	Standard asynch communications
stdprn	4	Standard printer output

There are five standard streams in DOS, and most C compilers for this environment extend the support for standard streams to support them all. The last two streams shown are not part of ANSI standard C, however.

The Simple I/O Functions

In the following sections, you learn the specific I/O functions and ways to implement I/O in your programs. The simple I/O functions are presented first because, being relatively uncluttered in both syntax and operation, they are easiest to learn.

The simple stream I/O functions are those that do not separate and interpret data content, except to supply newline characters at the ends of strings in text mode I/O. A character is just a character, and a string just a string to the simple I/O functions. They are not concerned with which character, or with what is in the string. One important exception to this rule is the class of characters called *control characters*, which make the I/O behave in certain ways. We will point them out as we go along here; they are discussed in detail in Chapter 4.

A small, easy-to-remember group of four simple I/O functions— getchar(), putchar(), gets(), and puts()—helps you remember their more explicit counterparts listed in table 2.1. The remaining simple I/O functions are getc(), fgetc(), putc(), fputc(), fgets(), and fputs().

Connecting Files to Streams: *fopen( )*

The names you assign to streams in your program are different from the file names stored on disk. *Stream names* are C identifiers, whereas *file names* are string data values. Thus, in normal I/O function calls you can use a short but meaningful name that does not have to be a long, quoted string.

The `fopen()` function brings the stream name and file name together. It associates the string value (the file name on disk) with the stream name you choose. It asks DOS (or other operating system) to open the file identified by the string value, and to return the numeric file handle.

When the file handle is successfully received, it is stored (with other information about the state of the stream, such as where in the file the next I/O takes place, buffer location, error and end-of-file conditions, and so forth) in a control block—usually called the `_iob`. Figure 2.8 illustrates the relationship between your program, the operating system, and the `_iob`.

Fig. 2.8. *The relation of streams to handles.*

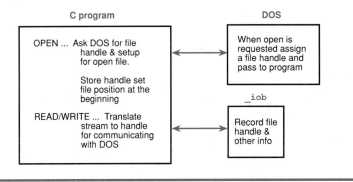

Declaring the Stream Data Object

Before opening the stream, you must declare it to be a data object. It is not a simple data object, such as `int`, but its complexity is hidden in the `#include` file. You declare the stream as follows:

```
#include <stdio.h>
...

main()
{
   FILE *input_file;
```

```
... open and use input_file,
... then close it when done.

}
```

Here the stream `input_file` is declared to be a *pointer*—a variable that contains the address of another variable—to a data object of type `FILE`. The definition of the `FILE` is in the `stdio.h` header file; don't forget to include it. You *must* type the word `FILE` in *uppercase letters*.

Sneak Preview: C Pointers

A *pointer* is a variable whose contents are the *memory address of another variable* rather than a data value directly. Use an asterisk (*, the *indirection operator*) to define a pointer:

```
int a;   /* a plain integer */
int *b;  /* a pointer to int */
```

To get an address value into the pointer, use an ampersand (&, the *address-of operator*) to extract the address of another variable:

```
b = &a; /* address of a placed in pointer b */
```

To get to the data in a variable being pointed to, use the indirection operator in an expression or statement (as opposed to the original pointer definition):

```
int c;
c = a;  /* assign a data value to c */
c = *b; /* assign the same data value to c */
```

Using the indirection operator to extract a data value being pointed to is called *dereferencing the pointer*. If you refer to a pointer *without* the asterisk, you are dealing with an address value:

```
int a;  /* an integer */
int *b; /* a pointer to an int */
int *c; /* another pointer to int */
...
b = &a; /* get an address into the first pointer */
c = b;  /* the value of b is an address ! */
```

> A pointer has an *indeterminate* value before it is initialized: It cannot yet be used. A pointer may also have a *zero value* even when initialized, in which case it should be understood to point to nothing at all. Such a pointer is called a *null pointer*. Most compilers supply a predefined macro name—NULL—that defines a zero pointer value. The main idea, however, is that *the value of a pointer is the address of another variable* or another area of memory.

This stream object is declared inside the main() function. This means that the stream can be used directly only with this function. In order for another function to use it to do I/O, a pointer to the stream object would have to be passed to it as a parameter. You will do that anyway, when you call the open function.

Opening the File

Once you have defined a stream object—also called a stream variable or file variable, but it is always a pointer type variable—you must open the stream (file) before you can use it for reading and writing data. The stdio.h header declares the fopen() function like this:

```
FILE *fopen( const char *filename, const char *mode );
```

but it is more instructive to illustrate how you use the fopen() like this:

```
FILE *input_file;
...
char filename[40]; /* 40 byte string holds name */
...
input_file = fopen( filename, "r" );
```

This means, first, that the function returns a pointer to an object of type FILE. You assign that pointer to the stream variable name. The value of this pointer is also the means of determining whether the open function was successful. If it was not successful, fopen() returns a null (empty) pointer. Most C compilers have already defined a macro with the name NULL (in uppercase letters) that you can use to check this result.

The first parameter inside the parentheses of a call to fopen() is a pointer to a string containing the name of the file (as it exists on the disk) that you want opened. The const type modifier means that the fopen() function does not intend to change this name string. The file name can be either a string variable or a string constant:

```
fname[40] = "c:\usr\check.dat";
/* Define 40-byte string */
...
input_file = fopen( fname, "r" );
```

is entirely equivalent to

```
input_file = fopen( "c:\usr\check.dat", "r" );
```

because either method opens the file in exactly the same way. Now the general procedure to open a file looks like this, including error checking to see whether the fopen() call worked.

```
#include <stdio.h>
...

main()
{
  FILE *input_file;

  input_file = fopen( "c:\usr\check.dat", "r" );
  if ( NULL == input_file ) abort();
  ... use input_file,
  ... then close it when done.
}
```

Now the stream has been opened, and the result of the operation verified. If the pointer returned to the program was NULL, there was an error and the program was *aborted* (abnormally terminated using the standard library function abort()).

The second parameter inside the parentheses of the function call is the *file mode parameter*. The mode determines exactly how reads and writes to the file take place. There are three basic modes:

❏   "r" *indicates that the stream is to be opened in read-only mode.* You cannot write into a read-mode file. If the file does not exist, or any other problem occurs, the open fails and returns a null pointer.

❏   "w" *indicates that the file is to be opened in write-only mode.* You cannot read from a write-mode file. If the file does not exist, an attempt is made to create it; if it does exist, its length is truncated to zero, and it is written over (old contents destroyed) from the beginning. If either action cannot be carried out, the open fails and a null pointer is returned.

❏   "a" *indicates that the file is to be opened in append mode.*
Append mode means that you can only write in the file, and
only at the end of the data already present. New information is
appended at the end, even if you use the fseek() function to
reset the current position elsewhere, such as at the beginning
of the file. If the file does not exist, it is created. If it cannot be
created or otherwise accessed, the open fails and a null pointer
is returned.

Using any one of these modes opens a file as a *text file*. You can add a 'b'
to the end of the mode strings to open a file in binary mode: "rb", "wb", and
"ab" are all valid modes. These and other advanced file modes are covered
in detail in Chapter 10.

The ANSI standard for C has one loophole that can affect append
processing in binary mode. When a binary file is created, the standard allows
an implementation of C to append any number of null characters to the end
of that file (to fill out a sector or block). If the binary file is then opened for
append-mode processing, the current position may be *beyond* the actual
end-of-file because of the padding characters. Because DOS takes care of
such padding, this normally is not a problem for DOS-based compilers. You
should, however, know whether your particular compiler can be so affected.

The preceding file-open facilities are all you need to read, write, and
append data to files. Figure 2.9 summarizes the effects of the modes of
opening files, including direction of data flow and positioning within the file.

Closing the File: *fclose( )*

After you have opened and used the file, you should close it. Closing the
file performs two important tasks. First, it releases the stream from the file
so that the stream can be reused. Even more important, it ensures the
accuracy of write-mode files. It does this by physically writing to the storage
device any tag-end data in output buffers.

The ANSI standard for C specifies that you can count on having the buffers
flushed (cleared, with a write, if needed) like this only if you actually perform
the close. Many compilers have a feature that closes all open files properly
when a program terminates *normally*. If, however, you forgot to close a file,
and your program crashes, you lose the data.

The function prototype for fclose() is also in stdio.h. It has the following syntax:

```
int fclose(FILE *stream);
```

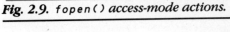

Fig. 2.9. `fopen()` *access-mode actions.*

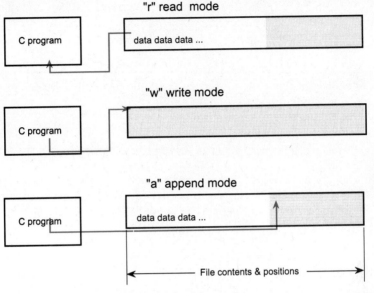

The `fclose()` function returns an integer to the program, indicating the outcome of the operation. This integer is zero if the close was successful; a negative integer (usually –1) is returned if the close was not successful. This negative integer is represented by an ANSI-required macro name, `EOF` (for "End Of File").

The entire sequence of events, as developed so far, results in a program that looks like this:

```
#include <stdio.h>
...

main()
{
  FILE *input_file;

  input_file = fopen( "c:\usr\check.dat", "r" );
  if ( NULL == input_file ) abort();
  ... use input_file,
  fclose( input_file );
}
```

Even though `fclose()` returns an integer result, it was not checked in this code fragment—it was simply thrown away.

For an output (write-mode) file, ignoring the results of `fclose()` would not be a good idea. Instead, you should take some action, such as that shown in the following example:

```
if ( fclose( output_file ) == EOF ) {
  printf( "Error closing %s.\n", filename );
  abort();
}
```

This would at least give the person running the program a chance to know there was a problem and to do something about it.

Character I/O Functions

In C, characters frequently are handled as if they were integers. This is especially true when characters are passed to functions as parameters. As you can see from the following C-Note (Character I/O Function Prototypes), they are passed as integers.

Quick-Reference: Character I/O Function Prototypes

```
#include <stdio.h>

...

int getchar(void);
int getc(FILE *stream);
int fgetc(FILE *stream);
int putchar(int c);
int putc(int c, FILE *stream);
int fputc(int c, FILE *stream);
```

You can pass an unsigned character (one byte) to the library functions. It is converted (*cast*) to an integer before use by the function.

It's time to put all this knowledge to work. Let's begin by using the simple character I/O functions to write a program you can use—one that protects the data in your private files. The program (`cipher.c`) encrypts your text files according to a key that only you know.

Because this program is significantly longer (128 lines) than any of those earlier in this book, we will take a moment to define what we want it to do, and how it will work.

`cipher.c` should be able to both encrypt a file for security, and decrypt it again so that you can use it. Therefore, it needs to accept a command-line parameter that indicates which action is to be taken. If we use the lowercase letter *n* to mean e*n*crypt the file and the lowercase letter *d* to mean *d*ecrypt it, the command to execute the program (so far) looks like this:

```
cipher n ... or
cipher d ...
```

Next, we should be able to tell the program which file to use. Because we don't want to use redirection or piping in this case, another command-line parameter is in order.

For simplicity's sake, so the user of the program does not have to type a file extension when running the program, let's assume that the extension of the *plaintext file* (the unencoded file) is always `.TXT`, and that the extension of the encrypted file is always `.ENC`. Now the command-line information looks like this:

```
cipher n filename ...
```

or like this:

```
cipher d filename ...
```

An encryption key, definable by the user, also must be available. This key is the third and last command-line parameter. The complete command looks like this:

```
cipher n filename string

cipher d filename string
```

This string is used internally to generate an unsigned character (byte field), which, in turn, is used to encrypt (or decrypt) every character in the text file. If this string contains no blanks, it can appear without punctuation. However, because this is C, the string can also be quoted if you want to use something difficult to guess. For example, you could encrypt a file named `acctdata.txt` with the command:

```
cipher n acctdata "phone plug 123"
```

Note that the *exact* same key string must be used to decrypt the file; otherwise, the result will be garbage.

If the user types the command `cipher`, without using any command-line arguments, the program should respond by displaying basic instructions for use, and then terminate normally.

Now that you know the requirements for the program, take a few minutes to examine the program's structure, as shown in listing 2.2.

Listing 2.2. `cipher.c` *(Data encryption).*   *Turbo C 2.0*

```
1   /*+-----------------------------------------------------------
2    +                        CIPHER.C
3    + This program uses basic character I/O to support a
4    + binary transformation data encryption scheme.
5    +-----------------------------------------------------------
6   */
7
8   #include <stdlib.h>
9   #include <stdio.h>
10
11  FILE *normal_file, *cipher_file;
12
13  static char *help[] =
14    {
15      "- - - - - CIPHER.C - - - - -",
16      " ",
17      "CIPHER.C requires that you enter\
18  three arguments on the",
19      "command line when you start the program:",
20      " ",
21      "       encrypt:       cipher n name string",
22      "       decrypt:       cipher d name string",
23      " ",
24      "You enter the file name without an extension. CIPHER",
25      "appends an extension of \".txt\" to the normal text",
26      "file and \".enc\" to the encrypted file.",
27      " ",
28      "The third argument generates an encryption key. This",
29      "argument can be any string. If it contains blanks,",
30      "enclose it in double quotes.",
31      ""
32    };
33
34  int open_file( char *process_type, char *file_name );
35  unsigned char generate_key( char *key_string );
36  void encode_file( unsigned char key_value );
37  void decode_file( unsigned char key_value );
38
39  main( int argc, char *argv[] )
40  {
41
42    int hold_char;
43    int i;
44    unsigned char key_value;
45
46    if ( argc < 4 )
47      {
48        clrscr();
```

```
49        for ( i=0; *help[i]; i++ ) puts( help[i] );
50    }
51    else
52      switch ( *argv[1] ) {
53        case 'n':
54            printf( "File encoding started\n" );
55            if ( ! open_file( argv[1],argv[2] ) ) {
56               printf( "\n\nCan't open file.\n" );
57               exit( 8 );
58            }
59            key_value = generate_key( argv[3] );
60            encode_file( key_value );
61            fcloseall();
62            break;
63        case 'd':
64            printf( "File decoding started\n" );
65            if ( ! open_file( argv[1], argv[2] ) ) {
66               printf( "\n\nCan't open file.\n" );
67               exit( 8 );
68            }
69            key_value = generate_key( argv[3] );
70            decode_file( key_value );
71            fcloseall();
72            break;
73        default:
74            printf( "Invalid option, try again.\n" );
75      }
76 }
77
78 int open_file( char *process_type, char *file_name )
79 {
80    char name1[25], name2[25];
81
82    printf("Opening files.\n");
83    strcpy( name1, file_name );
84    strcpy( name2, file_name );
85    strcat( name1, ".txt" );
86    strcat( name2, ".enc" );
87
88    if ( process_type[0] == 'n' ) {
89      normal_file = fopen( name1, "rb" );
90      cipher_file = fopen( name2, "wb" );
91    }
92    else {
93      cipher_file = fopen(name2, "rb" );
94      normal_file = fopen(name1, "wb" );
95    }
96
97    if ( ( normal_file == NULL ) || ( cipher_file == NULL ) )
98      return 0;
```

Listing 2.2. continues

Listing 2.2. *continued*

```
 99    else
100       return 1;
101  }
102
103  unsigned char generate_key( char *key_string )
104  {
105    int i = 0, j = 0;
106    unsigned char key_value = 0;
107
108    while ( ( j = key_string[i++] ) != '\0' ) key_value += j;
109    return key_value;
110  }
111
112  void encode_file( unsigned char key_value )
113  {
114    int temp_char;
115
116    while ( ( temp_char = fgetc( normal_file ) ) != EOF ) {
117        fputc( temp_char ^ key_value, cipher_file );
118    }
119  }
120
121  void decode_file( unsigned char key_value )
122  {
123    int temp_char;
124
125    while ( ( temp_char = fgetc( cipher_file ) ) != EOF ) {
126        fputc( temp_char ^ key_value, normal_file );
127    }
128  }
```

The first point of interest in listing 2.2 is line 11. Two streams (`normal_file` and `cipher_file`) are declared. Notice again that they are actually declared as pointers to objects of type `FILE`.

Lines 13 through 32 contain the definitions of the help text. The following declaration:

```
static char *help[] = { ... };
```

indicates that `help` is an *array of pointers to* strings. From the overview in Chapter 1, you already know that a string is an array of characters. The square brackets `[]` indicate an array of some kind. In this case, it is an array of `char *`, or pointer to character, which is how you point to (not define) a string. Finally, the token `static` is a storage class modifier. (Chapter 5 has details on storage class.) Its purpose here is to supply a syntax that allows the array of pointers to strings to be initialized directly in the declaration. This is done by the series of string literals inside the {} braces. Notice that the strings in the list are separated by commas.

Because this is an *initializer list*, not a block statement of the kind described in Chapter 1, the whole thing is followed by a semicolon, even though curly braces ({ }) are used. The very last string in the help text is a *null string* (one with nothing in it). This string acts as a "fence," so that the program can detect the end of the array of strings (see line 31).

Lines 34–37 contain function prototypes for the user-defined functions defined later in the program. You could define the user functions before `main()`, and before they were referenced anywhere, but the method used here is preferred. If nothing else, it prevents inadvertently calling a function that has not been defined.

The `main()` function is contained in lines 39–76. This time—instead of just empty parentheses—some parameters are declared for `main()`:

```
main( int argc, char *argv[] ) ...
```

This method of declaring `main()` is how C programs can access the command-line parameters typed by the user to execute the program. The first, `argc`, is an integer that has the count of parameters present in the command line. This count *includes the program name*. For instance, because `cipher` requires the program name plus three parameters to run correctly, `argc` has a value of *four*.

`char *argv[]` is another array of pointers to string (as was `help`). Because arrays are indexed from zero, the program name from the command line is pointed to by `argv[0]`, the action parameter (n or d) is pointed to by `argv[1]`, and so on.

On entry to `main()`, the number of command-line arguments is checked in line 46. If it is less than 4, something was left out, and the help text must be displayed. This is one of those places where the marvelous compactness of C code can be seen. The entire logic for doing this is found in one line (49), in the following single `for` loop:

```
for ( i=0; *help[i]; i++ ) puts( help[i] );
```

The integer `i` is used to step through the array of pointers. Look at the parts of the `for`-loop control structure in the following three paragraphs.

`i=0` sets the index variable to its initial value.

The cryptic *help[i] notation checks to see whether the end of the array has been reached. *help[i] refers to the *value* of the first character in the i th string in the list. Because the last string is null, this expression evaluates to zero (false), ending the loop.

The i++ expression uses the *postfix* increment operator (named for obvious reasons) to update the value of the index variable. This is done *after* the logic for each pass of the loop is performed.

The main part of the work is done in the switch statement (lines 52–75). This is just a fancy if-then-else arrangement. Look at the switch statement—you can see its intent. If the value of *argv[1] is an n, encoding is requested; if a d, decoding. The default keyword is a special case that indicates what to do if none of the indicated values were matched in one of the case statements.

In both of the case statements, there is a function call to fcloseall(). This is not an ANSI standard function. It is an extension that the compiler (Turbo C, in this instance) provides for convenience.

The user-defined function open_file() is found in lines 78–101. It returns an integer, as does the fopen() function it calls. The purpose of this function is to associate the file with the .TXT extension to the stream named normal_file, and the file with the extension .ENC with the stream named cipher_file. (The arrangement of if statements does this.)

A word also needs to be said about the generate_key() function. generate_key() converts the cipher key *string* into the cipher *key*, a single unsigned character—one byte. The method, known as a *checksum*, is simply to step down the string, adding the value of each character to the cipher key. When you develop a checksum, any carries or overflows from the addition are thrown away. The one-byte checksum is used to encode the plaintext file by exclusive-ORing its value with each character of the input file. This is why you need to use exactly the same key string for encryption and decryption.

The meat of the program is in the two simple functions encode_file() and decode_file(), found in lines 112–128 of listing 2.2. The process is the same in both cases. Only the direction of translation differs.

The fgetc() library function is used for inputting characters, and fputc() is used for outputting characters. The entire encryption/decryption process can be accomplished in a single short while loop, as in the following example:

```
while ( ( temp_char = fgetc( normal_file ) ) != EOF ){
   fputc( temp_char ^ key_value, cipher_file );
}
```

The `while` statement contains a conditional expression within the parentheses—positioned almost like parameters in a function call—that determines when the loop is finished. Here, the conditional expression is being used not only to read characters, but also to check for the end-of-file condition. First, the character is read, using `fgetc()`, and placed in the variable `temp_char`. The next level of parentheses means that the result of that read is to be compared to `EOF`. If EOF is *not* true (`!=`), the `while` continues.

In a fashion similar to the open and close functions, `fgetc()` *returns* an integer/character, while the character is *passed to* `fputc()` as a parameter. The character actually passed is the exclusive-OR of the input character and the cipher key.

Suppose that the bit pattern of the input byte is 11001010 and that of the cipher key is 01110111. Encoding the input byte yields the following:

```
    11001010
XOR 01110111
    _____
    10111101
```

To decode, just take the ciphertext (encoded) character and XOR it again, with *exactly the same key*:

```
    10111101
XOR 01110111
    _____
    11001010
```

String I/O Functions

Frequently, dealing with text files as collections of lines of text (as opposed to collections of simple characters) is convenient or necessary. The string I/O functions provide for this need. Strictly speaking, the ANSI document classifies the string I/O functions as character functions with the others, because they also do no particular data formatting. The string I/O functions are summarized in the following Quick-Reference C-Note.

`gets()` and `puts()`, of course, assume that a standard stream is being used. `fgets()` and `fputs()` streams must be opened and associated with a file before use. All four of the functions require a pointer to a string as a parameter, to or from which the I/O will take place.

Quick-Reference: String I/O Function Prototypes

```
#include <stdio.h>
...
char *gets(char *s);
char *fgets(char *s, int n, FILE *stream);
int puts(char *s);
int fputs(const char *s, FILE *stream);
```

In contrast to what you have seen so far, both string input functions return a pointer to a string. If the input function was successful, this will be a pointer to the same string that was passed as a parameter. If the function was not successful, it will be a null pointer. You can test for this condition with a statement like this:

```
char line_in[81];
...
if ( NULL == gets( line_in )) ... /* do something */
```

The puts() and fputs() functions return integers to the caller. These integers have the same meaning as before—zero means successful I/O, and EOF means either that the end-of-file was reached or that there was an error.

fgets() introduces something new. Its second parameter is an integer that specifies the maximum number of characters that can be input so that the I/O operation does not overrun the area allotted for it. In this example:

```
char in_stuff[80];
...
fgets( in_stuff, 80, in_file );
```

the integer is 80. Actually, this integer is *one more than the number of allowed characters*, because C strings are terminated by a null (binary zero) character, which takes up one of the array positions. In this fragment, then, only 79 characters could be input. If the end of the text line has not been reached by that time, the library function clips the string short, reserving the rest of the line for the next input request.

If the end of the line *is* reached, the physical end-of-line indicator(s) is converted to a newline character, and this character is placed in the receiving string. In most cases, this is what you want. If it is not, you have to write the code to remove the newline character from the string (see fmore.c in listing 2.8, later in this chapter).

Listing 2.3 puts this new knowledge to work. The purpose of program number.c is to read a text file, prefix each line with its corresponding line number, and write a new, numbered, text file.

Listing 2.3. number.c *Number text files.*   *QuickC 2.0*

```
1   #include <stdlib.h>
2   #include <stdio.h>
3
4   main( int argc, char *argv[] )
5   {
6     FILE *source_in;
7     FILE *source_out;
8     char name_in[41] = "";
9     char name_out[41] = "";
10    int line_num = 0;
11    char line_buf[255];
12
13    /* ----- Check command line parameters ----- */
14
15    if ( argc < 2 ) {
16      printf( "\nSupply a program name to number.\n" );
17      exit( 8 );
18    }
19
20    /* ----- Set up file names ----- */
21
22    strcpy( name_in, argv[1] );
23    strcpy( name_out, name_in );
24    if ( !strchr( name_in, '.' ) ) {
25      strcat( name_in, ".C" );
26      strcat( name_out, ".NUM" );
27    }
28    else {
29      char *p = name_out;
30      while( *p != '.' ) p++;
31      *p = '\0';
32      strcat( name_out, ".NUM" );
33    }
34
35    /* ----- Open input and output files ----- */
36
37    if ( NULL == ( source_in = fopen( name_in, "r" ) ) ) {
38      printf( "\nCan't locate %s, exiting.\n", name_in );
39      exit( 8 );
40    }
41    if ( NULL == ( source_out = fopen( name_out, "w" ) ) ) {
42      printf( "\nCan't locate %s, exiting.\n", name_out );
43      exit( 8 );
44    }
```

Listing 2.3. continues

Listing 2.3. continued

```
45
46      /* ----- NUMBER THE FILE ----- */
47
48      while ( fgets( line_buf, 255, source_in ) )
49        fprintf( source_out, "%3d  %s", ++line_num, line_buf );
50
51      /* ----- Close input and output file ----- */
52
53      fclose( source_in );
54      fclose( source_out );
55    }
```

Like cipher.c (listing 2.2), number.c (listing 2.3) expects a command-line parameter—the name of the file to be numbered. The code is designed to accept a file name, with or without an extension. If you supply the file extension, it can be anything you want it to be. If you do not supply one, it is assumed to be .C. (There is a good reason for this—this is the program we used to number the sample programs for this book.) In either case, the output file is forced to have the extension .NUM.

The logic to handle the file extensions is in lines 23–33. The code uses the strcpy() (string copy) function to move the strings around, the strcat() (string concatenate) function to splice the pieces together, and the strchr() (string character search) function to look for a period and thus determine whether the name has an extension.

If there is an extension, and the output file name must be forced to .NUM, lines 29–32 handle the situation. The code uses a temporary pointer variable p to step through the string to the period, and then overlay it with a null character, effectively truncating the string there. Then the proper extension can be concatenated to it. You might want to adapt this logic for cipher.c in listing 2.2 to generalize its file-name-handling logic.

The while loop in lines 48 and 49 is the workhorse of the program. It provides another example of the compactness possible with C syntax. The conditional expression for the while is nothing more than the call to fgets(). Because a (nonnull) pointer is returned for each successful read, the loop continues (nonzero = true). When end-of-file is reached, fgets() returns a null pointer, and the loop ends (null = 0 = false).

Handling I/O Errors and End-of-File

Clearly, some means is needed to separate end-of-file conditions from error conditions. These conditions are not at all the same, and you frequently must know which is which (instead of just assuming something). There are four standard functions for handling these conditions:

❏ `void clearerr(FILE *stream);`

`clearerr()` clears the end-of-file condition, an error condition, or both for the named stream. It returns nothing.

❏ `int feof(FILE *stream);`

`feof()` tests the named stream for the end-of-file condition. If end-of-file has been reached, the function returns 1, or true; if not, it returns 0, or false.

❏ `int ferror(FILE *stream);`

`ferror()` tests for an error indicator for the named stream. If an error has occurred, the function returns 1 or true. If not, it returns 0, or false.

❏ `void perror(const char *s);`

`perror()` prints a text error message. If an error has occurred, the library function detecting it will have set an internal variable `errno`. `perror()` uses *errno* to index into an array of strings (like the `help` text array in listing 2.2) to locate a message describing the problem. `perror()` first prints the string s, which was passed to it as a parameter, followed by a colon and a blank, followed by the system error text. You provide the string s, which can be anything informative you want to use.

The following is an example of the use of `ferror()` and `perror()`:

```
if ( ferror( some_stream ) )
  perror( "C detected file error" );
```

Converting Data Formats

Later in this chapter, you will learn how to use formatted I/O functions to extract specific fields from input text, how to use library functions to break a string into tokens, and even how to construct your own text-scanning and parsing routines. Sometimes, even then, simply converting a string to a numeric internal format is useful. The six standard functions converting data formats are

```
atof()     atoi()
atol()     strtod()
strol()    stroul()
```

The header file to include for these functions is `stdlib.h`. The following paragraphs summarize how the data format conversion functions are used.

```
double atof(const char *nptr);
int atoi(const char *nptr);
long int atol(const char *nptr);
```

The `ato...()` functions convert ASCII text strings, pointed to by `nptr`, to double-float, integer, and long-integer numbers, respectively. These functions, which have been around since K & R introduced C, are still so useful that they have been incorporated into the ANSI standard. These three functions do not have any error-recognition mechanism; what happens if an error occurs is strictly up to the specific implementation.

```
double strtod(const char *nptr, char **endptr);
```

`strtod()` converts a string pointed to by `nptr` to a double-precision float. White space in front of the number is skipped, the number converted, and conversion stopped at the first character that cannot be converted. `endptr` points to the first character that was *not* converted. Calling this function is a little different. Here is how it works:

```
char *where;
char numstring[20] = "   3.1415926*";
double numval;
...
numval = strtod( numstring, &where );
```

When this statement is executed, the value of *pi* is converted from the string and placed in `numval`. Because the asterisk cannot be converted to a number, conversion stops, and `where` is made to point to the asterisk. Notice especially that the parameter `endptr` is a *pointer to a pointer*, and the *address-of* operator (&) was used in the function call to make sure the argument passed to the function matched the formal parameter requirement (pointer to pointer). Don't forget this tricky little point when you use the `strto...()` functions.

The `strto...()` group of functions does detect and report errors. If no conversion can be performed, 0 is returned. If successful conversion would cause overflow, either the plus or minus `HUGE_VAL` macro value is returned, and the system variable `errno` is set to the predefined value `ERANGE`.

```
long int strol(const char *nptr, char **endptr,
    int base);
unsigned long int stroul(const char *nptr,
    char **endptr, int base);
```

These two functions perform the conversion for long and unsigned long integers, respectively. Error detection works the same way. Overflow in strol() returns LONG_MAX or LONG_MIN; overflow in stroul() returns ULONG_MAX. In both cases, errno is set to ERANGE.

These functions have the added option of providing a way to specify the base number system in which the input string number is written. If the base is given as 0, an ordinary decimal constant for these data types is expected. Otherwise, the base can be from 2 to 36. (For a more detailed explanation of this option, see Part II, Chapter 17 of this book.)

The program (strtox.c) in listing 2.4 illustrates the use of these functions. Look at the code, and we will then get right to the subject of formatted I/O.

Listing 2.4. strtox.c.   *Turbo C++*

```
1   #include <stdlib.h>
2   #include <stdio.h>
3   #include <ctype.h>
4   #include <limits.h>
5
6   #define long_const(x) #x " is an unsigned long integer."
7
8   main()
9   {
10     char double_string[] =
11       "+2.9979250e8 is the speed of light.";
12     char long_string[] =
13       "2341, 2347, 2351, and 2357"
14       " are consecutive prime numbers.";
15     char ulong_string[] = long_const( ULONG_MAX );
16     char *pointer;
17     long i = 0;
18     int count;
19
20     clrscr();
21     printf( "%s\n", double_string );
22     pointer = double_string;
23     printf( "Half the speed of light is: %f\n\n",
24         strtod( pointer, &pointer ) / 2 );
25
26     printf( "%s\n", long_string );
27     pointer = long_string;
```

Listing 2.4. continues

Listing 2.4. continued

```
28    for ( count = 1; count <=4; count ++ ) {
29       i += strtol( pointer, &pointer, 0 );
30       while ( !isdigit( *pointer ) ) pointer++;
31    }
32    printf( "The sum of the prime numbers is: %ld\n\n", i );
33
34    printf( "%s\n", ulong_string );
35    pointer = ulong_string;
36    printf( "%lu is the decimal value"
37            " of this unsigned long int.\n",
38            strtoul( pointer, &pointer, 0 ) );
39  }
```

The Formatted I/O Functions

The formatted I/O library functions are perhaps the most commonly used functions in ordinary C programming. They are without a doubt handy routines to have around.

The purpose of the formatted I/O routines is to format text data found in continuous strings into discrete data objects (fields), and vice versa. Each formatted I/O function accepts as one of its parameters a *format string* that controls the conversion process. The format string can contain both text and *conversion specifiers*, which state the precise manner of conversion of one of the data parameters being processed. The format string and conversion specifiers differ slightly for input and output function types.

Quick-Reference:
Formatted I/O Function Prototypes

```
int printf(const char *format, arg1, ..., argn);
int fprintf(FILE *stream, const char *format,
arg1, ..., argn);
int sprintf(const char *s, const char *format,
arg1, ..., argn);
int scanf(const char *format, arg1, ..., argn);
int fscanf(FILE *stream, const char *format, arg1,
..., argn);
int sscanf(const char *s, const char *format,
arg1, ..., argn);
```

Displaying Data with *printf()*

The formatted I/O functions for output, which we call the `printf()` family, create a continuous output string from a collection of *arguments* (variables, expressions, constants) under the control of a *format string*, and send it to the `stdout` stream, to the named stream, or to another string. To explain the process, we use `printf()`, which sends output to `stdout`, and then mention the variations on that theme. (Any data types that have not yet been discussed are covered in Chapter 3.)

Compare the following use of `printf()`:

```
printf( "The value of PI is %6.4f\n", 3.1415926 );
```

to the function prototype shown in the "Formatted I/O Function Prototypes" C-Note. The output from this function call appears on `stdout` as follows:

```
The value of PI is 3.1416
```

The first parameter passed to `printf()` is the *format string*, which controls the entire operation. `printf()` immediately sends normal text in the format string to `stdout` immediately, until it encounters a *conversion specification*, which gives instructions on how to convert and format one of the subsequent arguments. In the sample `printf()` line, `%6.4f` is the conversion specifier; the constant `3.1415926` is its corresponding argument.

Because `printf()` processes the conversion specifiers in the format string from left to right, as it encounters them, the arguments that match each specifier must also be in the correct order from left to right. The ANSI standard says that if the number of conversion specifiers and actual arguments don't match, the "behavior is undefined." This means that you had better check the manual to see what it will do in *your* case.

In the format string, normal text and conversion specifiers can be mixed freely, if the specifiers are recognizable and coded correctly. For example:

```
char c1[10] = "dog";
char c2[10] = "cat";
...
printf( "The first critter is a %s and the second is a %s",
        c1, c2 );
```

results in the output:

```
The first critter is a dog and the second is a cat
```

The principle is pretty simple. All you need to know now is how to form the conversion specifiers. Figure 2.10 summarizes the structure of conversion specifiers. (For complete details of the specifier parts and their meanings, see Part II.)

Fig. 2.10. *Using* `printf()` *conversion specifiers.*

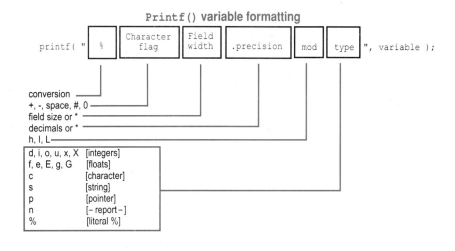

❑   *The conversion character % begins the conversion of the next argument, moving left to right.*

❑   *The optimal flag character can control field justification, the addition of numeric signs, use of an alternate form, or whether to use leading zeros.*

❑   *The optimal field width states the minimum number of characters the field contains. It is a minimum because this specifier never causes truncation—if the output requires more room than stated here, more room is used.* If field width is not specified, as many characters as needed are used.

❑   *The optional precision specifier, if present, means different things for different argument types.* For strings, it is the *maximum* number of character positions to be used (truncation *will* occur). For floating point and double floating point, it is the number of decimal digits to format to the right of the decimal place. For integer types, it is the *minimum* number of positions to use—the technique used in `number.c` (listing 2.3) to achieve a uniform field width for the line numbers. In all cases, a period must be written before the precision specifier.

❑ *An optimal modifier character can cause the conversion of appropriate types to short integer (h), to long integer (l—ell), or to long double (L) format.*

❑ *The required type character states the type of argument and what basic conversion is to take place.* All the basic types can be converted, as can strings and pointers. The most common types are

d	(decimal) integers
f	(double) floating point
s	string
c	character

The width and precision fields have an interesting feature that allows for very flexible output formats. Instead of a number, you can specify an asterisk in either or both parts (%*.*x). Each asterisk instructs the formatting routines to look for an argument in the list and to use its value for this specifier. Scanning is, as always, from left to right—just place these special-use arguments in sequence with the others. The program printit.c (see listing 2.5) uses this handy feature to create an on-screen "printer plot" of a sine wave.

Listing 2.5. printit.c.   *QuickC 2.0*

```
1   #include <stdlib.h>
2   #include <stdio.h>
3   #include <math.h>
4
5   main()
6   {
7     char ch;
8     double x;
9     int i;
10
11    printf( "A sine wave, from 0 to 2 PI radians:\n" );
12    x = 0;
13    for ( i=0; i<21; i++ ) {
14      printf( "%*c\n", 30 + (int)( 30.0 * sin( x ) ), '*' );
15      x += 0.314;
16    }
17  }
```

The construction (int) in line 14 is called a *type cast*. Its purpose is to force the floating-point value of the subsequent expression to an integer value that the %c conversion can handle.

The two other forms of the `printf()` function—`sprintf()` and `fprintf()`—behave like `printf()`, only the destination of the output differs.

If you refer to the C-Note that shows the formatted I/O function prototypes, you can see that `sprintf()` has an extra parameter, a string pointer (`*s`). The string pointed to is the destination for the formatted output rather than a stream.

You can use the combination of capabilities to format flexibly and to output the results into a string to do certain chores. In listing 2.6, for example, the function `center_text()` centers a title within a given line width:

Listing 2.6. `center c.`   *All Compilers*

```
 1   #include <stdlib.h>
 2   #include <stdio.h>
 3   #include <string.h>
 4
 5   int center_text( char *s, char *t, int width );
 6
 7   main()
 8   {
 9     char lineout[81];
10
11     if ( center_text( "A centered title!", lineout, 80 ) )
12       printf( "%s\n", lineout );
13   }
14
15   int center_text( char *s, char *t, int width )
16   {
17     int l;
18
19     l = strlen( s );
20     if ( l > width ) return 0;
21     sprintf( t, "%*s", ( ( width-l ) / 2 ) + l, s );
22     return 1;
23   }
```

Don't forget to `#include <string.h>` in programs that will use `center_text`. The `strlen()` function is declared in `string.h`.

The effect of the `center_text()` function is to supply enough blanks on the left end of the output string t to center the input string s in a field *width* characters wide. If the string fits in the output field, the operation is performed and a nonzero value is returned; if not, a zero is returned.

fprintf() also has an extra first parameter. This parameter is the name of a stream (which you should have opened). The behavior is once more the same as printf(), but the destination for the output string is now the file associated with the named stream. There are advantages and disadvantages with specifying a destination stream. Although fprintf() certainly allows you to write formatted text to a disk file, for example, you cannot redirect output to any other stream. Here is a short example using printf():

```
FILE *hfile;
if ( NULL == ( hfile = fopen( "c:history.txt", "w" ) ) )
   exit( 8 );
fprintf( hfile, "%s\n", "Dear diary ... " );
```

Getting Input with *scanf( )*

Input can be formatted with the scanf() family of functions that, like the printf() family, has three forms: scanf() receives and formats input from stdin; fscanf(), from a user-defined stream; and sscanf(), from a string in RAM.

As you can see from figure 2.11, the two families are similar in several ways. Both use conversion specifiers, many of the conversion types and all the type modifiers are the same, and conversion specifiers are processed from left to right with their corresponding arguments.

Fig. 2.11. scanf() *input data conversion.*

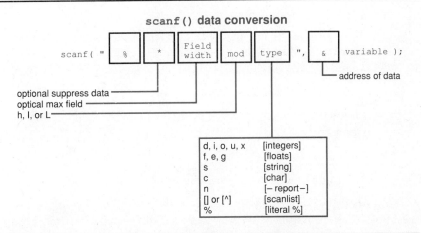

There are also some important *differences* between the two families. The details of scanf() are completely documented in Part II, but you should be aware of the following peculiarities:

❑ *The arguments are all pointers.* The printf() functions accept *values* as parameters (except for arrays, which are always passed as pointers), because the conversion routines do not alter the variables (when variables are used). But scanf() *does* alter the parameter variables—that is the whole point of scanning out an input string. To specify an argument that is a pointer to a variable, you do nothing extra for strings and arrays because their names alone constitute a pointer name. For other data objects, however, you must precede the variable name with an ampersand *address-of* operator, as in the following example:

```
address_of_item  = &item;
```

❑ scanf() *expects any text in the format string that is not part of a conversion specifier to be matched, character for character, in the string being scanned (except spaces, which are skipped).* This feature allows scanf() to skip any input text that should not be part of a converted input field.

❑ *Double floating-point data types are not supported by* scanf(). When you use the %f, %e, or %g conversion specifiers, their corresponding argument variable (it had better be a variable) must be a type float.

❑ *The field width part of a conversion specifier is used a little differently.* scanf() uses width to split out similar fields that are run together in the input string. For example, the scanf() call

```
scanf( "%2d%3d", &num1, &num2 );
```

can be used to split out two numbers from the following input string:

```
12345
```

The value of num1 is 12, and the value of num2 is 345.

Traditionally, scanf() has not been widely used for extensive input operations because in spite of its complexity, it is stiff-necked and unforgiving. When used correctly, however, scanf() can do some pretty amazing things. (It probably is not as widely appreciated as it should be.) The program readit.c, shown in listing 2.7, uses scanf() to gather information on the way to some interesting conclusions:

Listing 2.7. `readit.c`.   *All Compilers*

```
1    #include <stdlib.h>
2    #include <stdio.h>
3    #include <math.h>
4
5    double SPFV( double apr, double freq, double periods );
6    double USFV( double apr, double freq, double periods );
7
8    main()
9    {
10      char firstname[20];
11      char lastname[20];
12      int age;
13      float salary;
14
15      printf( "Enter your first and last names, your age, "
16          "and your annual salary:\n" );
17
18      scanf( "%s%s%d%f", firstname, lastname, &age, &salary );
19
20      printf( "\nIf %s %s, who is %d years old and "
21              "earns %10.2f,\n"
22              "were to save only 10%% of every monthly\n"
23              "paycheck, drawing only 6%% interest, after a 30\n"
24              "year career, you would have %10.2f dollars!\n",
25              firstname, lastname, age, salary,
26              ( salary / 120.0 ) * USFV( 6.0, 12.0, 360 )
27          );
28   }
29
30   double SPFV( double apr, double freq, double periods )
31   {
32      return( pow(1.0+(apr/freq)/100.0,periods) );
33   }
34
35   double USFV( double apr, double freq, double periods )
36   {
37      return( ( SPFV(apr,freq,periods) - 1.0)
38              / (apr/freq/100.0) );
39   }
```

The `scanf()` function call is in line 18. Notice that because the string arguments imply a pointer, they are *not* prefixed with &. The integer and float variables *are* prefixed with the address-of operator.

The `scanf()` call in line 18 prompts you for four pieces of information. Just type them, in the order requested, with as many blanks as you want between the items. (You can also press Return after typing each item, but you cannot use commas between them, *unless* you code them directly in the format string as explained previously.) You may be surprised to learn what regularly saving a little money can buy you later. And if you want to learn how to use those time value of money routines in lines 30–39, just hang on one minute.

Putting It All Together

Everyone likes money—no doubt about it. How would you like a program (one that uses both the simple and formatted I/O functions) that can calculate the payout on your home mortgage, analyze and convert interest rates, display or print a mortgage amortization table, and a few other interesting things?

Did you say you don't know enough C yet? Yes, you do. You just may not have seen a longer program put together. The program `finance.c` (listing C.1 in Appendix C) does all these things, with very few features that you either have not yet seen or cannot understand intuitively.

In fact, the only reason we put `finance.c` in Appendix C, instead of including it here, is that we didn't want this chapter to be too long. (The program is long, and its use requires explanation.) This is a good time for you to turn to Appendix C and study the code and usage instructions.

Coping with Hardware and System Dependencies

The ANSI standard for C states that the purpose of codifying the language is not to stifle its utility, but to enhance portability across compilers and systems. There is therefore no reason that a compiler manufacturer should not provide extensions to the ANSI standard features—and many reasons that they should. All of these reasons have to do with the fact that a compiler lacking them is unusable in a real environment.

There is just no getting around the fact that to do something useful with a program, to do it fast and with a certain flair and style, you must at least get a little close to the machine and operating system. This situation pops up most often in *I/O programming*.

Disk I/O programming can mostly be done with standard C library functions. The C library functions for files and streams do the job well, especially when some of the more advanced features are used. But standard C doesn't even pretend to do the job for situations such as printer support (except by I/O redirection), video display I/O that is fast enough not to bore the user to death, and communications I/O programming.

Using Extensions to Standard C

Printers, video displays, and communications lines require programming support that can be found only in extensions to the standard C language.

This presents you, the programmer, with a dilemma. Do you use these extensions? If you do, the programs you write will not always be portable—the specific machines and systems on which the program runs are by definition a limited group. To move the source code over, you will not only have to recompile it, but also rewrite parts of it.

To answer the question directly, yes, you do use the extensions. You will find it impossible not to in the long run. If you don't, your programs will lack critical capabilities and performance. In a word, users will not stand for it—they won't use the programs. The trick is to isolate that part of the code which has to be rewritten in order to port it to another environment. You can do this, mainly, by hiding dependent code in separate (and thus isolated) source files and functions.

Now, having answered the question, let's take a look at the cost of using some of those extended features.

Supporting Extended DOS Streams

Readers of this book are most likely to encounter the MS-DOS environment. This environment provides a good example of the operating system services, and access to them through C extensions, that you need in order to construct full-featured programs.

You already have seen that DOS has more standard streams than standard C allows for. The program `cprint.c`, in listing 2.8, shows how to send a text file to a printer by using a predefined stream (in this compiler) named `stdprn`. The `cprint.c` program counts lines, ejects, or pages to avoid overprinting the perforations, and places a header line on each page.

Listing 2.8. `cprint.c` *(Printing text files).*   *QuickC 2.0*

```
1   #include <stdlib.h>
2   #include <stdio.h>
3
4   struct rep_type {
5     int lines_page;
6     int line_count;
7     int page_count;
8   } report;
9   char file_name[41] = "";
10
11  void print_file( char *fname, struct rep_type *rep );
12
13  main( int argc, char *argv[] )
14  {
15    if ( argc < 2 ) {
16      puts( "Command format: "
17            "cprint [d:][\path\]file[.ext]\n" );
18      exit( 0 );
19    }
20    strcpy( file_name, argv[1] );
21    report.lines_page = 57;
22    report.line_count = 0;
23    report.page_count = 0;
24    print_file( file_name, &report );
25    printf( "Printed %d lines on %d pages from %s\n",
26            report.line_count, report.page_count, file_name );
27  }
28
29  void print_file( char *fname, struct rep_type *rep )
30  {
31    char *print_line;
32    FILE *filein;
33    int cur_line = 1;
34
35    if ( NULL == ( filein = fopen( fname, "r" ) ) ) {
36      printf( "Could not open %s\n", fname );
37      exit( 0 );
38    }
39    print_line = malloc( 255 );
40    while ( NULL != fgets( print_line, 255, filein ) ) {
41      if ( cur_line == 1 ) {
42        fprintf( stdprn, "Listing of: %s\n\n", file_name );
43        cur_line = 3;
44        rep->page_count++;
45      }
46      fputs( print_line, stdprn );
47      cur_line++;
48      rep->line_count++;
```

```
49        if ( cur_line > rep->lines_page ) {
50           cur_line = 1;
51           fputc( '\f', stdprn );
52        }
53     }
54     free( print_line );
55  }
```

Notice that stdprn is handled like one of the true standard streams. You don't have to open or close the stream, although you do have to name the stream in the fprintf() and fputs() function calls.

You may want to try modifying the program to supply page numbers in the header line, line numbers at the left, to handle margin and line count control—or just about any other customizing feature you want. Don't be bashful about remolding it to suit *your* purposes. And don't delay practicing what you are learning about C. *Everyone* who learns C occasionally gets into deep water and has to start over.

Programming IBM PC I/O Ports

When neither DOS nor the system BIOS provides adequate services for a task, you have to get down to cases and do it yourself. This is the case with I/O support for communications programs on the PC and compatibles. In this section, we introduce you to a program that gives you a close look at what is involved in doing I/O directly, through the system I/O ports. This was the method used—along with a good deal of other technique—to write ccom.c (listing D.1 in Appendix D).

To say it briefly, ccom.c is an interrupt-driven, port I/O-oriented C communications program. Its purpose is not only to illustrate what you are getting into when you descend to the hardware level in controlling your machine, but also to give you a working program you can use if you want to dial CompuServe. Before you attempt to modify ccom.c, you need to learn a good deal more about C, and particularly about communications.

Because ccom.c is rather long, we put its source code listing in Appendix D, along with instructions for use. By all means, type it and compile it. Have your Turbo C manual handy when you do, however, and be careful to get it *exactly* as you see it. Then spend some time reflecting on portability issues. We think you will find that you *really* appreciate all those lovely built-in library functions.

The IBM PC Video-Display Controversy

There has been a great deal of discussion, in print and otherwise, about whether to write portable (and truly blase) or nonportable (and really peppy and attractive) video-display support routines for the PC. In the main, commercial packages and good home-grown programs tend to opt for the nonportable, but really useful, methods.

"Glass Teletype" I/O and Standard Streams

The problem with video I/O can be summed up in one word—*slow*! Most computer users do not appreciate programs that force them to watch text crawl sluggishly across and down the screen.

Even worse, screen output generally looks like a glass Teletype. Lines of text scroll up from the bottom of the screen—exactly as they do on a real Teletype machine. There is little or no color support, no full-screen formatting of displays, and no *speed*. This tends to be true even when BIOS services are used. They, in fact, are the reason DOS services are so slow: BIOS calls are how DOS gets to the screen, too. Because of this, C's standard streams for the video display (stdout) are relatively slow also.

Getting Around the Problem

Most users of IBM and compatible PCs are aware that the video display is a memory-mapped I/O device (even if they don't know the term). They are aware that the screen can be programmed by using screen RAM.

Whether or not to use screen RAM is the focus of the glass Teletype controversy. It is said that if the screen RAM address changes, all those programs that poke characters directly into screen RAM will no longer run. But in all these years, the original addresses haven't changed, even though newer devices sometimes require *additional* screen RAM. Direct screen RAM access is the *only* method that has acceptable speed for displaying large amounts of text quickly.

Slow display speed and the methods used to get around it are so common that it is worth presenting an example of it. The program fmore.c is faster than the DOS-supplied MORE program. fmore.c displays a text file, one screen at a time, and waits for you to press a key for the next screen. Listing 2.9 contains the source for fmore.c.

Listing 2.9. `fmore.c` *(A faster MORE display).*   *QuickC 2.0*

```
1    #include <stdio.h>
2    #include <conio.h>
3    #include <dos.h>
4    #include <string.h>
5    #include <graph.h>
6
7    int x, y;
8    char far *scrseg;
9    struct videoconfig screen_state;
10
11   void find_screen(void)
12   {
13     _getvideoconfig( &screen_state );
14     switch( screen_state.mode ) {
15       case 0:
16       case 1:
17       case 2:
18       case 3:
19       case 4:
20       case 5:
21       case 6:    scrseg = (char far *)0xB8000000L; break;
22       case 7:    scrseg = (char far *)0xb0000000L; break;
23       case 13:
24       case 14:
25       case 15:
26       case 16:
27       case 17:
28       case 18:
29       case 19:   scrseg = (char far *)0xA0000000L; break;
30       default:   printf( "\nCan't locate screen RAM.\n" );
31              exit(0);
32     }
33   }
34
35   void show_line( char *ostring )
36   {
37     char far *screen;
38     int hold = y - 1;
39
40     x = 1;
41     screen = (char far *)( scrseg +
42            ( hold << 7 ) + ( hold << 5 ) );
43     while ( *ostring && *ostring != '\n') {
44       if ( *ostring == '\t' ) {
45         do {
46           x++;
```

Listing 2.9. continues

Listing 2.9. continued

```
47            screen += 2;
48          } while ( x % 8 != 1 );
49          ostring++;
50          continue;
51        }
52        *screen = *ostring++;
53        x++;
54        screen += 2;
55        if ( x > 79 ) break;
56    }
57  }
58
59  main(argc,argv)
60    int argc;
61    char *argv[];
62  {
63    FILE *pix;
64    char pline[83];
65    char ch;
66
67    if ( argc < 2 ) exit(0);
68    if ( NULL == (pix = fopen(argv[1],"rt")) ) exit(0);
69    find_screen();
70    y = 1;
71    for ( ;; ) {
72      _clearscreen( _GCLEARSCREEN ); _settextposition(1,1);
73      while ( y <= screen_state.numtextrows - 1 ) {
74        if ( NULL == (fgets( pline,83,pix ) ) ) {
75          fclose(pix);
76          show_line( "... Press Any Key To End ..." );
77          ch = getch(); if ( ch == 0 ) getch();
78          _clearscreen( _GCLEARSCREEN );
79          exit( 0 );
80        }
81        show_line( pline );
82        y++;
83      }
84      show_line( "... Press Any Key For More ..." );
85      ch = getch(); if ( ch == 0 ) getch();
86      y = 1;
87    }
88  }
```

To get started, this program uses extensions to standard C that are peculiar to the Microsoft QuickC compiler. (Other compilers have similar, but slightly different, features.) The _getvideoconfig() function, declared in `graph.h`, detects the video mode. Although this can be done with direct calls to BIOS functions, why not use the *easier* nonportable method?

Then the video mode is used in a `switch` statement, to determine the screen RAM address, and a pointer is formed. This type of pointer is not standard C but is required by the PC's hardware characteristics.

The `main()` function handles the gross logic of reading input text lines, detecting when to pause and wait for a keystroke, when to close the file, and when to get out. It also has a nonstandard technique that waits for the keystroke:

```
ch = getch(); if ( ch == 0 ) getch();
```

`getch()` is a nonstandard but common function. It gets a keystroke, waiting for it if necessary, and does *not* echo that keystroke to the screen.

But there is more. Why should you compare the input character to a zero? Because doing that is how you can detect when an *extended ASCII key* (function keys, as well as arrow and paging keys) has been pressed. If one of these keys has been pressed, the character code is zero and another code, indicating which extended key it was, will be sent. We are not concerned with extended keys here, except that we don't want the program to get confused when one is used. (It does say "Press *Any* Key.")

The `show_line()` function (lines 35–57 of listing 2.9) does the real work. It uses shift techniques for fast multiplication in calculating an offset into screen RAM; detects and handles newline and tab characters (you don't want to poke them directly into RAM as data bytes); and uses pointers to change position very quickly.

There is a moral to these examples of very low-level I/O. They provide blazing performance. *But sophisticated techniques require sophisticated code*. If you are going to take this route to I/O programming, get ready. You have to work to get the results you want.

Summary

This chapter covered quite a bit of ground. But the price of using a powerful language like C is that its users must be knowledgeable. In this chapter, you have gained a good deal of the knowledge you need for most common I/O functions, and you have laid the foundations for advanced work in a later chapter. You have learned:

❏ *What I/O is, and the fundamental methods of getting it done.* Now you know why I/O can be one of the greatest roadblocks to high-performance code: it requires a great deal of overhead processing. Buffering is an important tool for avoiding some of that overhead work.

❏ *The classification of interactive and storage devices, files, and C streams.* You know what the standard C streams are, and which other streams commonly are provided by operating systems. You also know the difference between text and binary streams.

❏ *How to define your own streams, and how to associate them with files by opening them.* You know that when you are finished with a stream you should close it. This is true especially with output streams (to prevent loss of the last bufferful of data).

❏ *How to use both standard and user-defined streams to get simple character and string text data.* You can control the formatting of text data, get discrete variable values from string input, and convert formats at will by using the `printf()`, `scanf()`, and `strto...()` families of library functions.

❏ *How to take over I/O processes close to the hardware and do it yourself.* Perhaps the most important point here is to know when and why you should do this, and what it will cost you down the road.

This chapter showed clearly that there is a great deal to the C language. It is neither a toy to be trifled with nor an ogre that cannot be controlled. C is just a powerful tool for serious programmers.

3

Building C Programs

N ow that you are familiar with the basic I/O functions, you are ready to build the foundation of your knowledge of C. This chapter and Chapter 4 supply the bricks for that foundation.

Learning the language effectively dictates that you begin by sketching the broadest outlines of what is involved in writing a C program, and that you continue by progressively refining and pinpointing that knowledge. This chapter deals with two of the largest classes of elements that go into a C program: data and functions. Specifically, you will learn the following:

❏ *How to define variables for the basic C data types.* Data can be packaged in several ways, all of which—surprisingly—are variations either on integers or floating-point numbers (real numbers with fractional parts).

❏ *How to write constant (literal) values for the basic data types.* You use these constants to *initialize* (give a starting value to) the variables you define or to compare against or manipulate the variables. You will discover what the maximum and minimum values for each type of constant or variable can be.

❏ *How to declare variable data, and combine variables with constants to initialize the variables.* C provides some fairly flexible ways to go about this, including lists of variables with optional initializers.

❑ *How to decide where to declare a variable.* Its location in the program determines what other parts of the program can "know" about the variable. This will be the first discussion on C *scope*. Pay attention, because scope is an important consideration in C programming.

❑ *How to declare and define your own functions within your programs.* This involves both function *declarations*, which let the compiler know what you intend to do, and function *definitions*, which provide the statements that do the work.

❑ *How to pass to a function the data with which that function works (function parameters), and how the function can pass the results of the operation back to the part of the program that called it.* You will also see how to call the function.

❑ *How to write the statements that do the work within a function definition.* There are several kinds of statements suited to different tasks in C. This is the real meat of C programming.

Managing Data in a C Program

A primary goal of any program, C or otherwise, is to manipulate, transform, and transfer data. To fulfill this goal, the program must "know" how the data will be presented to it, and how it must be handled. This in turn requires that data be represented in a fixed, well-defined format, or *type*. The type of a data object determines and limits what can be done with it. You can add two floating-point numbers, for instance, but they must be converted to a format you can read before you display them on the screen.

In the next few sections, you will learn the fundamentals of managing data within your C programs. You will see how to declare variables with specific types, use constants and literal values to initialize them, and decide where they can be used properly.

The Standard C Data Types

The notion of *type* is used everywhere in C. The value stored in a variable or returned by a function is partially determined by its type. An integer, for instance, cannot by definition have fractional parts, but a floating-point number can. Everything has a type in C.

❏ *Object types describe the characteristics of data objects (variables, constants, etc.).* An object's type determines its internal format, what operations can be performed on it, and how those operations behave (for example, see the discussion of signed and unsigned integers later in this section). The notion of objects will be expanded considerably (and take on a more technical meaning) in Part III, when C++ objects are introduced. For now, the meaning is restricted to variables and constants.

❏ *Function types describe the values returned by a function, just as object types describe data values.* Thus you can speak of an integer function, a floating-point function, and so on, when you mean functions that return integer or floating-point values.

❏ *Incomplete types describe particular objects but lack the information necessary to determine an object's size.* You can determine the address of an object with incomplete type, but you cannot access an object with incomplete type.

Data types are further classified according to whether they are simple (*basic* or elementary types) or complex (*derived* types).

The basic types include *characters*, *signed* and *unsigned integers*, and the *floating-point numbers*. The signed integers and floating-point types can have negative values; unsigned types have only positive or zero values.

Quick-Reference: ANSI C Basic Data Types

The basic data types are displayed here by group and listed using the incomplete type declaration syntax. The left column holds the *type specifiers* which you saw several times in the sample programs in Chapters 1 and 2. After reading this, you might want to look at those programs again, identifying type characteristics.

Elementary Characters

`char`   Stored in one byte. Characters from the minimal set (see Chapter 4) are guaranteed to be positive; all others may be either positive or negative.

(continues)

(Quick Reference continued)

Signed Integers

`signed char`	Stored in one byte, as are plain `char` types. In most implementations, `char` and `signed char` are equivalent in use but classified differently, because equivalence is not mandatory.
`short int` `int`	`short int` and `int` are listed together because, no matter how many bytes are used, the value ranges required by ANSI are identical (see the Quick-Reference C-Note "Limiting Values For Constants" in the next section).
`long int`	The value range for `long int` is much more than double that of `int`. Its physical size is left up to the implementation.

Unsigned Integers   Alternative Specification:

`unsigned char`	(none)
`unsigned short`	(unsigned short int)
`unsigned`	(unsigned int)
`unsigned long`	(unsigned long int)

Floating Point

`float` `double` `long double`	The floating point types have varying degrees of value ranges for both the fractional part (the *mantissa*) and the exponent part (the *characteristic*).

Integers occupy several bytes, the number of which is natural to the machine on which the implementation of C is running. This normally is the same as the machine *word*, which is 2 bytes on 80x86 machines, and may be 4 bytes on other machines. A `short int` may occupy a *halfword* or a *fullword*, provided that the value range requirements are met. Borland products (Turbo C) and Microsoft products (QuickC and MS C) assign the same physical size (2 bytes) to both `int` and `short int` types. A `long int` typically requires 4 bytes on 80x86 processor implementations.

Typical sizes for the `float`, `double`, and `long double` types as implemented on an 80x86 CPU are 4, 8, and 10 bytes, respectively. These sizes are used on such machines because they match the physical sizes required by the 80x87 math coprocessor chips. Other machines may use different sizes (as well as different internal formats).

The `char`, `signed char`, and `unsigned char` types are those which have *external* data formats—they can be sent to an interactive or display device (the screen or printer), and produce readable data. They can be used internally in computations, but only to a limited extent. All the other type formats are *internal* to the CPU. They are used in computations, but are not readable directly.

To examine the contents of internal variables, you must convert from internal format (numeric data) to external format (a character string). The formatted I/O functions covered in Chapter 2 do this—but it is not the only way to convert data. A *dump program* typically converts internal data formats to two kinds of display data (usually hexadecimal characters and ordinary display characters), as shown in figure 3.1.

The program (`sdump.c`) that produced this hex-dump output is shown in listing 3.1. Its purpose is to retrieve characters (single bytes, regardless of any data type a byte is a part of) from a file, display it first as a two-character hex representation (text string), and also display it on the right side of the line (if it is, in fact, a displayable character).

Before you read over the program, note that in addition to our faithful standby, `printf()`, a new library function is used. `memset()`—the "memory set" function used in lines 19 and 34—initializes an area of RAM memory to whatever value you give it. In this case, a text line 80 characters long is being initialized to blanks, preparatory to building a line of dump output text. You can go to Part II reference material on the `memset()` function now and get the full details if you want.

Fig. 3.1. Sample hex dump output.

```
======== SDUMP Output for: sdump.c ========
23696E63 6C756465 203C7374 64696F2E 683E0D0A    |#include.<stdio.h>..
23696E63 6C756465 203C6374 7970652E 683E0D0A    |#include.<ctype.h>..
0D0A6368 6172202A 6865785F 63686172 2820696E    |..char.*hex_char(.in
74206320 293B0D0A 0D0A6D61 696E2820 696E7420    |t.c.);....main(.int.
61726763 2C206368 6172202A 61726776 5B5D2029    |argc,.char.*argv[],)
0D0A7B0D 0A202020 696E7420 632C693B 0D0A2020    |..{....int.c,i;....
2046494C 45202A66 703B0D0A 20202063 68617220    |.FILE.*fp;....char.
6C696E65 5F6F7574 5B38305D 3B0D0A20 20206368    |line_out[80];.....ch
6172202A 6C703B0D 0A0D0A20 20206966 20282061    |ar.*lp;......if.(.a
72676320 3C203220 29206578 69742820 3820293B    |rgc.<.2.).exit(.8.);
0D0A2020 20696628 20667020 3D20666F 70656E28    |....if(.fp.=.fopen(
20617267 765B315D 2C202272 62222C29 20290D0A    |.argv[1],."rb",).)..
2020207B 0D0A2020 20202070 72696E74 66282022    |...{......printf(."
3D3D3D3D 3D3D3D3D 20534455 4D50204F 75747075    |========.SDUMP.Outpu
7420666F 723A2025 73203D3D 3D3D3D3D 3D3D5C6E    |t.for:.%s.========\n
222C0D0A 09202020 20206172 67765B31 5D20293B    |"........argv[1].);
0D0A2020 20206920 3D2031 3B0D0A20 20202020    |....i.=.1;......
6D656D73 65742820 6C696E65 5F6F7574 2C20272720    |memset(.line_out,.'.'
272C2038 3020293B 0D0A2020 2020206C 696E655F    |',.80.);......line_
6F75745B 35325D20 3D2027BA 273B206C 696E655F    |out[52],=,'.';.line_
6F75745B 37335D20 3D2027BA 273B0D0A 20202020    |out[73],=,'.';......
206C696E 655F6F75 745B3738 5D203D20 275C6E27    |.line_out[78],=,'\n'
3B0D0A20 20202020 6C696E65 5F6F7574 5B37395D    |;......line_out[79]
203D2027 5C30273B 0D0A2020 2020206C 70203D20    |,=,'\0';......lp.=.
```

Listing 3.1. sdump.c *(Hex dump program).*   *All compilers*

```c
 1   #include <stdio.h>
 2   #include <ctype.h>
 3
 4   char *hex_char( int c );
 5
 6   main( int argc, char *argv[] )
 7   {
 8      int c,i;
 9      FILE *fp;
10      char line_out[80];
11      char *lp;
12
13      if ( argc < 2 ) exit( 8 );
14      if( fp = fopen( argv[1], "rb" ) )
15      {
16        printf( "======== SDUMP Output for: %s ========\n",
17                argv[1] );
18        i = 1;
19        memset( line_out, ' ', 80 );
20        line_out[52] = '‖'; line_out[73] = '‖';
```

```
21        line_out[78] = '\n';
22        line_out[79] = '\0';
23        lp = line_out;
24        while( (c = fgetc( fp )) != EOF ) {
25           strncpy( lp, hex_char(c), 2 );
26           if ( isgraph( c ) ) line_out[i+52]
27              = (unsigned char)c;
28           else line_out[i+52] = '.';
29           i++; lp += 2;
30           if ( i % 4 == 1 ) lp++;
31           if ( i % 20 == 1 ) {
32              i = 1;
33              printf( "%s", line_out );
34              memset( line_out, ' ', 80 );
35              line_out[52] = ' '; line_out[73] = ' ';
36              line_out[78] = '\n';
37              line_out[79] = '\0';
38              lp = line_out;
39           }
40        }
41        if ( *line_out != ' ' ) printf( "%s", line_out );
42        fclose( fp );
43     }
44     else
45        printf( "Error in opening file\n" );
46  }
47
48  char *hex_char( int c )
49  {
50     static unsigned char hex_out[3];
51
52     hex_out[0] = (unsigned char)( (c & 0x00F0) >> 4 );
53     hex_out[0] += ( hex_out[0] > 9 ) ? 55 : 48 ;
54     hex_out[1] = (unsigned char)( c & 0x000F );
55     hex_out[1] += ( hex_out[1] > 9 ) ? 55 : 48 ;
56     hex_out[2] = '\0';
57     return( hex_out );
58  }
```

You may have noticed that the input file was opened in binary ("rb") mode. As you learned in Chapter 2, using binary mode thus prevents the I/O library functions from performing any conversion whatever on the data. Data is presented to the program bit for bit, exactly as it was recorded in the file—just what you need for a dump program.

The program first reads the input file in a loop (lines 24–39), passing each byte to hex_char() for conversion to a two-byte string of hex characters—hex_char() is invoked in line 25 by being used as an argument to strncpy()—and then places the results in the output line. When the output line is complete, it is sent to the display device via printf() and reinitialized (lines 31–39).

The real meat of the program is in the hex_char() function (lines 48–58). To understand how this routine works, recall that a character is composed of 1 byte, which is 8 bits. Now think of a byte as 2 pieces of 4 bits each (a *nybble*—who says programmers have no sense of humor?). Four bits can hold a maximum numeric value of 15—the same as a hexadecimal F. Hold that thought for a moment.

Next, look at the chart of ASCII characters in Appendix A. You will see that the *decimal values* for the *display characters* 0 through 9 are 48–57, and that the *decimal values* for the display characters A through F (valid hex digits) are 65–70.

hex_char() separates out each group of 4 bits and *scales it up* to a legitimate display character. For example, if the value of a nybble is 10 (hex A), the character *A* has the value 65. Add 55 to the separated nybble and *voila*—the letter *A* results.

Display-character generation is achieved by using some C operators you have not seen yet. Line 52 isolates the left-hand (high-order) nybble with this statement:

```
hex_out[0] = (unsigned char)( (c & 0x00F0) >> 4 );
```

By using the *bitwise* AND *operator* &, the expression (c & 0x00F0) turns off all the bits except those in the high-order nybble of what will become the output character. (Be careful here—remember that in other contexts & can be the address-of operator.) The constant hex value 0x00F0 is called the AND *mask*; if one of its bits is on, the other operand's corresponding bit will remain on; other bits are set to zero.

You can see also that this line deals with the input "character" as if it were an integer. At this point, it *is* an integer. As you may recall, the character I/O libarary functions return input characters as integers. The mask has two leading zeros to emphasize and document this fact, but 0xF0 would have worked just as well—the compiler would have kept everything aligned properly.

After all the unnecessary bits have been turned off, the high-order nybble must be aligned to the right so that a complete display character can be developed from the bits. This is done with the *shift-right operator* (>>). Because the shift-right operator has higher precedence (would be evaluated first) than the bitwise AND, the previous expression had to be surrounded by parentheses to force the correct grouping.

Line 53 now constructs the final display character:

```
hex_out[0] += ( hex_out[0] > 9 ) ? 55 : 48 ;
```

The purpose of this statement is to add the correct scaling factor to the isolated nybble. Working from the left, the first operator you encounter is the *add assign operator* (+=). This operator combines the addition and assignment operations, and is completely equivalent to:

```
hex_out[0] = hex_out[0] + ...
```

You can form complex assignment operators like this one from any of the other operators. Just write the other operator first, followed immediately by the equals sign (-=, *=, /=, &=, and so on).

The process of deciding exactly what to add to the initial value is performed by the *conditional* or *ternary operator*. Its symbols and operands have the following format:

```
expression ? a : b;
```

The expression will be evaluated for a true or false condition. If true, the *a* operand will be used. If false, the *b* operand will be used.

As you can see from this brief discussion, you could have written line 53 in the following equivalent but longer form:

```
if ( hex_out[0] > 9 ) hex_out[0] = hex_out[0] + 55;
else hex_out[0] = hex_out[0] + 48;
```

Line 53 in the listing is just a sample of the compact code possible when you use C's powerful operator set and notation.

Be careful with conversion methods like this. This one is based *solely* on the ASCII collating sequence. ANSI standard C is *not* tied to ASCII-based systems, and such methods may or may not work on other systems without conversion. C running on an IBM mainframe, for example, must cope with the EBCDIC collating sequence. In that case, the scaling values used in listing 3.1 would have to be changed, and you would have to take into account that EBCDIC display characters are not grouped contiguously in the sequence.

C also allows you to specify in an object's declaration two *type qualifiers* —const and volatile.

const indicates that although the object is defined like a variable, it ordinarily should be regarded as a constant:

```
const char inline[21] = "This is a string.";
```

Notice that a const-qualified object can be initialized (and this doesn't have to be directly in the declaration), but then should be used as a read-only object.

`volatile` means that the object is modified in unpredictable ways, perhaps by the operating system or by an interrupt service routine. This subject is best left to an advanced book on C (although we do present an interrupt service routine in Appendix F). You declare a `volatile`-qualified object as follows:

```
volatile int counter;
```

Working with Constant Values (Literals)

In providing data grist for the C mill, using constant values (also called *literals*) is more important than you initially might think. Constants are very important. They are involved somewhere along the line for every data object used: to initialize it, to compare it with, to operate on it.

Then what values can you use in a constant? The answer varies from compiler to compiler, but ANSI has now provided a minimum range of possible values that you can count on from one product or system to another. These values are shown in the following C-Note. Notice how the suffixes U and L are used, either alone or together, in forming the unsigned and long integer constants. (Although these suffixes can be either upper- or lower-case, uppercase tends to show up better when you read a program.)

You already know from observing the character I/O functions that the character types fit into 1 byte. The integer types have assigned value ranges that reflect a 2-byte physical size (which, on most microcomputers, is a *word* field, containing 16 bits). Thus the maximum value for an unsigned int is $2^{16} - 1$, or 65535.

The signed integers behave a little differently, because the high-order bit is used as the *sign bit*. If this bit is 0, the number is positive; if it is 1, the number is negative. An interesting side effect of this usage is that a positive sign bit cannot by definition contribute to (participate in) the value of the number—it must be 0. A negative sign bit, however, can be interpreted as contributing to the magnitude of the number. Thus you will find that, in most implementations, the maximum negative integer value is −32768 (-2^{15}) rather than −32767. This is true of both Borland and Microsoft products for 80x86 machines.

Floating-point numbers are another, more complicated story. Although the ANSI min-max values for all three float types specify an exponent range of −38 to +38, they differ in the number of *required significant digits*. A `float` type requires the equivalent of 6 decimal digits of precision, whereas `double` and `long double` both require 10 decimal digits of precision. Typical min-

Quick-Reference: Limiting Values for Constants

The numerical values you can express in a constant (or in a variable, for that matter) are assigned a *minimum range* that they can assume. The minimum and maximum points in the range have also been assigned macro names as found in `limits.h`. (See Part II of this book for those names and their interpretation.) The ranges are

Bits per `char`	8
`signed char`	–128 through 127
`unsigned char`	0U through 255U
`char`	Usually –128 through 127
Bytes per Multibyte Character	1, at least
`short int`	–32768 through 32767
`unsigned short int`	0U through 65535U
`int`	–32768 through 32767
`unsigned int`	0U through 65535U
`long int`	–2147483647L through 2147483648L
`unsigned long`	0UL through 4294967295UL
`float`	
`double`	
`long-double`	–1E–38 through +1E–38 and 0 and –1E+38 through +1E+38

max values for actual implementations of the fraction part exceed the ANSI standard, and exponent range requirements are much more than satisfied.

Floating-point numbers can be expressed in two ways: as a pure *fractional number*, or in engineering (*exponent*) notation. You should already be familiar with the fractional notation—the decimal-point method of writing numbers (123.0567, 3.1415926, and so on). Exponent notation includes both a fractional part (*mantissa*) and an exponent part (*characteristic*). The first of the preceding numbers, for example, could be written `1.230567E+2`. The exponent (2) effectively "moves" the decimal point two places to the right, preserving the correct value of the number. The "E," meaning exponent, can be either upper- or lowercase. You can also write a floating-point number with a negative characteristic. For example, the notation `1.234E-2` is valid, and is the same as 0.01234.

Notice that when you write a floating-point number in source code, or as part of a text string to be converted to internal format, you write it in decimal notation—not binary, not hex. The conversion routines convert this to the proper internal number system base (*radix*).

Now, how do you use these facts in the context of an actual program? One of the first things for which you will want to use literals is to initialize the value of variables. Listing 3.2 shows the code for literal.c, which illustrates the use of literals for this purpose. Literals *used directly in the variable declaration* are called *initializers*.

Listing 3.2. literal.c *(Using literal values).*   *All compilers*

```
 1    /*+-------------------------------------------------
 2     +                        LITERAL.C
 3     + Assign a literal value to a variable and then print
 4     + it with formatted print function.
 5     +-------------------------------------------------
 6    */
 7
 8    #include <stdio.h>
 9    #include <stdlib.h>
10
11    main()
12    {
13        short int          i =   158;
14        int                j =   999;
15        unsigned int       k =   61489U;
16        long int           l =   -365L;
17        float              x =   2.6736;
18        double             y =   598.342;
19        char               ch = 'A';
20        char          name[8] = "Charles";
21
22        printf( "Short integer, decimal .... i = %d\n", i );
23        printf( "Integer, hex format ....... j = %x\n", j );
24        printf( "Unsigned int has no sign .. k = %u\n", k );
25        printf( "Long int has a sign ....... l = %ld\n\n", l );
26        printf( "Floating point fixed ...... x = %1.4f\n", x);
27        printf( "          or exponential ...... y = %1.4e\n\n", y);
28        printf( "Characters are 1 byte ..... ch = %c\n", ch );
29        printf( "Strings are many bytes .... name = %s\n", name);
30    }
```

The output from `literal.c` appears on the display screen like this:

```
Short integer, decimal .... i = 158
Integer, hex format ....... j = 3e7
Unsigned int has no sign .. k = 61489
Long int has a sign ....... l = -365

Floating point fixed ...... x = 2.6736
        or exponential ...... y = 5.9834e+002

Characters are 1 byte ..... ch = A
Strings are many bytes .... name = Charles
```

This program illustrates how to use literals to initialize variables for most of the basic types. The variables are declared in lines 13–20 within the `main()` function (meaning that they are valid only within this function. More on this later.). A string literal initializer is thrown in for good measure, just to show how it works.

As you can see, initializing most variables at the time you first declare them is quite simple. This is a good practice, because it prevents using an uninitialized variable (which could do more than just produce wrong output; it could terminate your program abnormally).

Declaring Variable Data

`literal.c` (listing 3.2) is also a good jumping-off point for a discussion of declaring, initializing, and controlling variable data within your program.

Clearly, a variable must be both declared and initialized before it can be used. The declarations in lines 13–20 of listing 3.2 accomplish both of these tasks at the same time. Shortly, you will see that it does not always have to be done this way.

Naming Variables

The first task you face is that of naming your variables. When doing this, you should consider the following:

❑ *C identifiers can have no more than 31 significant characters.* This applies to variables as to everything else. Names can be longer than 31 characters, but to be considered different, names must vary within the first 31.

❏ *Make the names long enough to mean something to you.* You will thank yourself later when you debug your program. For instance, which of the following declarations tells you more about the variable being defined?

```
int ss;
int shift_status;
```

The second at least tells you that something about shift status is being recorded. Falling prey to the temptation to make names *too* long is easy, however, and leads to another kind of trouble—too much typing, and a cluttered-looking program. Make it long enough, and then stop.

❏ *Make the name easier to read by using the underscore character to separate parts of the name.* For example:

```
double high_water_mark;
```

is much easier to read than:

```
double highwatermark;
```

Do not, however, use the underscore as the *leading character* in your names. The leading underscore should be reserved for C's predefined macro names and internal function names. It is legal for you to do this, but dangerous.

❏ *Never duplicate one of C's predefined names.* Naturally, you need to be familiar enough with them to avoid the error. If you accidentally duplicate one of these names, what happens next depends on the original predefined object. Most likely you will receive a compiler error saying that the object is being redefined improperly.

Declarators and Declarator Lists

So far, you have seen only simple declarations for individual objects. As you might expect, C provides for a compact notation allowing the declaration of several similar objects in one source line. In the first of the following examples, you write a *declarator*; in the second, you write a declarator *list*. Instead of writing:

```
int a;    /* Three individual declarators */
int b;
int c;
```

you can declare all three variables on one line of code, like this:

```
int a, b, c;    /* A declarator list */
```

You can also provide initializers in a declarator list, like this:

```
#include <stdio.h>

main()
{
  int a = 1, b = 2, c = 3, x;

  x = a + b + c;
  printf( "%d\n", x );
}
```

Naturally, you can add a number of bells and whistles to your declarations to make them more flexible and powerful. The complete general form of a C declaration is

```
[storage-class] type-specifier declarator [initializer];
```

The square brackets here are not meant to be coded, nor do they indicate array subscripts as in a true C declaration. Their purpose here is to show what part of the declaration can be considered optional.

The optional storage-class specifier can be used to modify the default scope (visibility) and lifetime (duration) of a variable within the current block of code. The storage class determines exactly when a variable exists and where in memory it will be kept. There are five storage-class specifier keywords: typedef, extern, static, auto, and register. These keywords will be completely explained in Chapter 5 in the section "Taking Adavantage of Storage Class."

The *type-specifier* (int, float, etc.) and at least one *declarator* name (the variable, or perhaps function) must be present. The type-specifier should name one of the keywords shown in the following C-Note, or perhaps a pointer to one of them. Here are some examples of valid type-specifiers:

```
int count;              /* a simple integer */
unsigned int data;      /* an unsigned integer */
int *age;               /* a pointer to an integer */
char c;                 /* a simple character */
char *s;                /* a pointer to character or string */
```

A declarator is required. The declarator is simply the name you wish to give to the variable. The name must follow the rules for valid C identifiers. These rules are covered in Chapter 4 in the section "Identifiers in General," and in Chapter 12 in the section "Translation Limitations." Right now you need to know that identifiers must begin with a letter or underscore, may contain numbers other than at the beginning, and that current compilers support names at least 31 characters long.

The optional initializer is a starting value for the variable. If you supply an initializer value, it must be either a constant or an expression which has the correct type for the variable being declared. The methods of forming valid constants for all the basic data types were shown earlier in this chapter. Here are some examples of valid initializers:

```
int a = 37;
unsigned int b = 32768U;
double length = 4.0132;
const char name[] = "John Doe";
```

You can use some of the type-specifier keywords to modify others. The combinations allowed are exactly those allowed for basic data types (see the Quick-Reference C-Note "ANSI C Basic Data Types" earlier in this chapter).

As we mentioned at the beginning of this section, what is being declared can be either an individual identifier (*declarator*) or a list of identifiers, separated by commas (*declarator list*). In either case, a declarator can be followed by an equals sign and some initializing value. By using several variations on the basic theme of specifying declarators, you can accomplish different goals when you declare objects. The various kinds of declaration include:

❑ The simple identifier. You have already seen this method several times, whether using one identifier or a list of identifiers. Example:

   `unsigned char ch;` The character variable ch

❑ An *identifier in parentheses*. This method is most often used to specify a pointer to a function but it can be used with simple identifiers *not* in lists. Examples:

```
int ( a );                 Valid.
int ( a ) = 3;             Valid.
int ( a = 3 );             Invalid.Initializer goes
                           outside parentheses.
int ( a ), ( b );          Valid.
int ( a ) = 1, ( b ) = 2;  Valid.
int ( a, b, c );           Invalid. Only 1 identifier
                           allowed inside parentheses.
```

Quick-Reference: C Declaration Type-Specifiers

Keyword	Description
`void`	Unspecified type. Used with generic pointers or to indicate the complete absence of an object.
`char`	One of the character types.
`int`	One of the integer types.
`long`	Used only to modify a type. Either specifies `long int`, or modifies `double`. `long float` is the same as `double`. `long double` is a separate type.
`float`	Short floating point.
`double`	Double-length floating point. This can be modified to `long double`.
`signed`	Used alone, or modifies `char` or `int`. If used in conjunction with `long`, it must be first (as in `signed long int`).
`unsigned`	Used alone, or modifies `char` or `int`. If used in conjunction with `long`, it must be first (as in `unsigned long int`).
struct- or union-specifier	Structures and unions are composite data types that are discussed in Chapter 11.
`enum` *-specifier*	Enumerations are a special type composed of a named set of integer constant values. They are discussed in detail in Chapter 11.
`type`-*def name*	You can derive your own customized data types using `typedef`. This, too, is covered in a later chapter.

❏   An *array identifier*. The identifier name is followed by a constant expression surrounded by square brackets giving the number of elements in the array. Each element in the array has the same basic type as given in the type-specifier. Examples:

```
int p[5];                An array of 5 integers.
double x[20];            An array of 20 double
                         floats.
int s[6][6];             A two-dimensional array of
                         integers.
char text[81];           A string with 80 bytes for
                         text data plus one for the
                         '\0' terminator.
```

Arrays and strings are not basic data types and require special handling that is discussed later in this book.

❏   A *pointer to an identifier*. To declare an object to be a pointer to an object rather than the object itself, precede the identifier with the indirection operator. Examples:

```
int *sflag;              Pointer to integer sflag.
float *rate;             Pointer to float rate.
```

❏   A *function identifier*. The identifier name is followed by a list of parameters or identifiers surrounded by parentheses. The difference between the two kinds of lists should become clear in the section "Declaring Functions and Passing Parameters." Examples:

```
void myfunc( void );     A function with no
                         parameters and returning
                         nothing.
int myfunc( int a );     Function accepts an integer
                         parameter, returns an
                         integer.
myfunc( int a );         Same as above; int is
                         always default type.
double mycalc( a, b, c ); Function accepts 3
                         parameters whose types are
                         unknown; returns a double
                         float.
```

❏   A *pointer to a function*. This form uses both the parentheses around the identifier and the indirection operator *. The grouping of the tokens is dictated by the assumed operator precedence of the parentheses and the indirection operator. Examples:

```
int (*myfunc)();          Pointer to a function
                          returning an
                          integer.

int *(*myfunc)();         Pointer to a function
                          returning a pointer to an
                          integer.
```

Some of this may look strange to you at the moment. The only cure for that is experience. You will see many of these forms throughout the book. They are explained many times, but don't hesitate to return to these pages and review the different forms of declaration syntax. A great way to get their effects firmly in mind is to write test programs using the different combinations, and then watch the results.

Initializing Variables

At this point, you have learned what the basic C data types are, how to form constant values of the various types, and how to declare data objects, or variables, for them. Possibly without realizing it, you also have already learned several ways to initialize variables in your program. Those methods can be summarized and organized as follows:

❏   *Use an initializer at declaration time*. When you declare a variable you can follow it with an assignment of a particular value, as in the following example:

```
double pi = 3.1415926;
```

You can use this technique with strings as well, but there are some limitations on string initialization in other circumstances.

❏   *Assign a constant value to the variable*. A statement of the form:

```
population = 15762385L;
```

can appear in `main()` or any of your other functions to set up a variable. Deciding when to do this depends on when you need the variable in the program, and on when the variable is valid in the program. This last point is discussed in the next section.

❏ *Assign one variable to another*. This is similar to the preceding method, except that a variable, not a constant, is used, as follows:

```
population = prev_count;
```

It is assumed in this example, of course, that `prev_count` has already been initialized by some other method.

❏ *Input data into the variable*. You can use the I/O library functions to read data into the data objects in your program from somewhere else (such as a file or the keyboard). Normally, the bulk of the data your program deals with will come from this source, whereas data initialized internally will serve as work areas and hold temporary results.

Local and Global Variables

In this section, we discuss the issue of *variable scope*. This is part of the larger issue of *storage class*, which is concerned with both the scope *and* duration of a variable.

The *scope* of an object is its visibility to other parts of the program (other than the place it is defined). Just because a variable has been defined *somewhere* within a program (or source file), it is not necessarily visible *everywhere* in the program (or source file).

The *duration* of an object is its lifetime. Duration involves not only how long a variable exists, but when it is created and first becomes available (within the limitations of scope).

The scope of an object in C depends on where you placc its definition, and possibly on modifiers present in the definition which alter its characteristics. Briefly, you can define an object *inside a function*, in which case it has *local scope*; or you can define it *outside any function*, in which case it has *global scope*. Figure 3.2 summarizes how scope is affected by position in the source file.

The intent here is to focus on scope, but it is impossible to discuss scope without having some knowledge of storage class to provide a frame of reference. There are only two kinds of storage class in C: `auto` and `static`. These terms are used to describe an object during discussion; they are also the modifiers mentioned in the preceding paragraph. Note that a storage class is associated with *all* objects, including functions.

Fig. 3.2. Local and global variable scope.

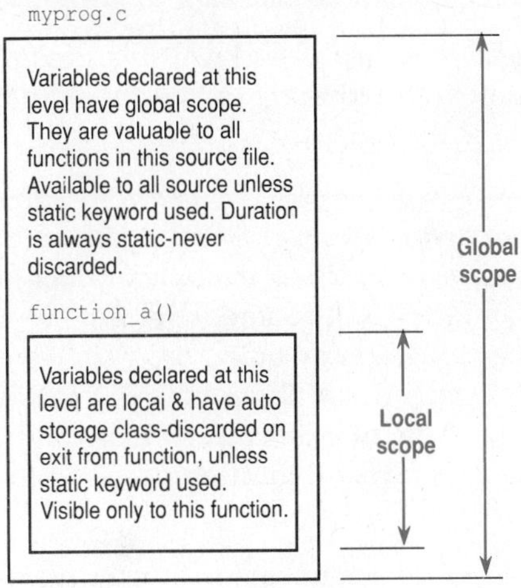

An `auto` variable is one that has dynamic or *automatic duration*. It does not exist when the program begins execution; it is created at some point during the run and discarded at some point before the program finishes running.

A `static` variable is one that has *fixed duration*. Room for the object is set aside at compile time (incidentally, this takes up space in your `.OBJ` files on disk). It already exists at execution time (although not necessarily initialized), exists throughout the run, and is "discarded" only when the program itself is purged from memory at termination time.

Every object has a specific mix of default storage class and scope, depending on the definition's location in the source file. Some combinations of attributes cannot occur; others that can occur can also lead you into confusion and error.

Variables with global scope, called *global variables*, are those defined outside the boundaries of any function. (This is called an *outer declaration*.) Global variables have the following behavior and attributes:

❑ *Global variables have static duration by default.* Storage for them is set aside at compile time, and never discarded. By definition, a global variable cannot also be an `auto` variable.

❑ *Global variables are globally visible within the source file.* They can be referred to by any function *following* the point of definition of the object.

❑ *Objects declared in outer declarations can appear anywhere in the source file.* You can declare data objects at the top of the file, write a few functions, declare another group of global objects, and then write some more functions. This is why the preceding paragraph qualified the visibility of global objects as being the remainder of the source file, beyond the point of declaration. Note that this means that visibility is determined by a declaration's physical location in the source file, not by the logical order of execution.

❑ *Global variables are by default available to other source files in the program.* This is called *external linkage*. You define the object in the normal way in its "home" source file. To refer to it in another source file, declare it again; do not use any initializer (it was initialized by the first source file code) and be sure to qualify the declaration with the `extern` keyword, as in the following example:

Source file A   *Source file B*

```
int count = 0;     extern int count;
```

❑ *Global variables can be hidden from other source files by using the* `static` *storage class specifier.* For example:

```
#define OFF 0
#define ON 1
...
static unsigned char master_switch = OFF;
...
function_a()
{
   ... /* function_a processing */
}
...
main()
{
   ... /* main processing */
}
```

allows `master_switch` to be used both by `function_a()` and `main()` in *this* source file, but it cannot be declared as an `extern` in another source. Global variables have static *duration* in any event. This is just a mechanism for hiding objects from other source modules.

Local variables, in contrast, are those defined *inside a function body*. Even more restrictively, a variable may be local to a particular block statement within a function body (this is discussed a little later in this chapter). This kind of declaration is called an *inner declaration*.

❑ *Local variables have automatic duration.* A local variable, defined within the boundaries of a function body, does not exist until the function is called and run. When the function is entered, setup code generated by the compiler is executed to allocate and initialize the function's `auto` variables (synonymous in this sense with local variables). They exist in, and are used by, only the function in which they are defined. When the function returns to the caller, `auto` variables are discarded and their storage released.

❑ *Local variables can also be defined inside a compound or block statement, as in the following example:*

```
char *string_function( char *input_string )
{
  if ( *input_string == "X" ) {
    int cnt = 0;
    cnt = strlen( input_string );
    /* do something with cnt */
  }
  /* other processing outside the if */
}
```

The integer `cnt` is not valid for the entire duration of `string_function`. It is valid only inside the braces that contain the statements associated with the `if` (in other words, the block statement conditionally executed if the `if` evaluates to true). If the `if` is executed more than once in the function, it is created and destroyed each and every time the `if` condition is true, even though the function is executed only once.

❑ *Local variables are visible only in the block in which they are defined.* Nothing outside that block (or function) is aware of them, or can use them. An interesting but potentially confusing result is that you can define *different* variables, with the *same* name, provided that they are defined in *different* scopes:

```
#include <stdlib.h>
#include <stdio.h>

int cnt = 1;
void function_a( void )
{
  int cnt = 2;
  printf( "%d\n", cnt );
}

main()
{
  printf( "%d\n", cnt );
}
```

In this short program fragment, both `main()` and `function_a()` display the value of a variable named `cnt`. Yet `main()` displays a value of 1, whereas `function_a()` shows 2. In spite of the identical labels for the variables, *two different objects are being used*. The potential for confusion is rather obvious; this practice should be avoided whenever possible (which is almost always). If you define a variable locally to a function, and it has the same name as a global variable, only the local version of it can be used in the function. The global version is temporarily unavailable.

❏ *The declarations for objects defined in an inner declaration must appear at the top of the block.* This is in distinct contrast to the "mobility" of global objects defined in outer declarations, which can appear anywhere in the source file (except within a function, of course). Coding an inner declaration after beginning to write the expression statements of the function body (see the latter part of this chapter, "Building the Function Body") results in a syntax error at compile time.

❏ *Local variables use the static keyword to modify duration, not visibility.* Writing the `static` storage class specifier with a local variable's declaration causes storage to be set aside for the variable (as though it were a global variable) and assigns it static duration, but does not make it globally visible. This usage is more common than you might think. You can use the static keyword to prevent the loss of an otherwise `auto` class variable, when one call to a function may depend on the state of affairs left from a previous call. For example, to "remember" whether a file is open or not, you could write:

```
int file_server( char *buffer, int bufsize )
{
  static int is_open = 0;

  if ( !is_open ) {
    /*open the file, and say so */
    fopen( ... );
    is_open = 1;
  }
  /* service various file requests */
}
```

Clearly, you don't want to open the file whenever `file_server` is entered—it may already be open. The goal is to "remember" that fact.

The terms *local* and *global* make it easy to remember which is which, and where they can go. Why would you want to choose one or the other? Wouldn't it be just as easy to define everything as a global variable and let it go at that? That approach ignores the trade-offs involved.

Global variables are available to every function below them. They should be used when several different functions need a single copy of a particular object. Some functions need to know what others have been doing. You should be aware, however, that such circumstances often can be satisfied by passing a *copy* of the variable as a parameter to the function.

Local variables reduce clutter in the global data declarations. If there is no need to communicate the value of an object to other parts of the program, use an `auto` variable. There is no chance of another function altering its contents unexpectedly, and because it is discarded when not needed, it saves on long-term storage space. The copy of a variable passed as a parameter to a function also has local scope: it is valid only while the function executes, and is discarded when the function returns. Global variables can be used to improve the performance of a program. Because they have static duration, allocating them fresh for every call to a function entails no overhead. However, this practice increases the size of your program, both in memory and on disk.

Alternatively, local variables can help reduce the size of your program. This may be especially critical in long and complex programs. Wherever absolute blinding speed is not required (or the overhead can be otherwise hidden), use a local variable. The program `cvtjul.c`, in listing 3.3, illustrates how some of these features are used (including the use of the `static` storage class specifier in a local scope). `cvtjul.c` has some useful dateformat conversion routines for Julian and six-dates. (You can do math on Julian dates much more easily than with six-dates—dates having a format like mmddyy.)

Listing 3.3. `cvtjul.c` *(Date conversions).*   ***All compilers***

```
 1   #include <stdlib.h>
 2   #include <stdio.h>
 3
 4   #define FALSE 0
 5   #define TRUE 1
 6
 7   int leapyear;
 8
 9   char *getmon( int monum );
10   int getday( unsigned long julday );
11   int isleap( int year );
12   int modays( int monum );
13   unsigned long getjul( int month, int day, int year );
14
15   main()
16   {
17      int i, j, month, day, year;
18      unsigned long julday;
19
20      for ( i=1; i<26; i++ ) printf( "\n" );
21      printf( "Enter julian ddd, a blank, and year yyyy: " );
22      scanf( "%ld%d", &julday, &year );
23
24      leapyear = isleap( year );   /* Do this before invoking */
25                                   /* other routines, sets Feb */
26
27                      /* Let i count down the month */
28      j = julday;          /* But do not destroy julday */
29      for( i=1; j>modays(i); j-=modays(i), i++ );
30      printf( "The six-date is %s %d.\n",
31              getmon( i ), getday( julday ) );
32
33      printf( "Enter mm dd yyyy: " );
34      scanf( "%d%d%d", &month, &day, &year );
35      leapyear = isleap( year );
36      printf( "The Julian date is %ld.",
37              getjul( month, day, year ) );
38   }
39
40   char *getmon( int monum )
41   {
42      static char *moname[] =
43      {
```

```
44       "January",
45       "February",
46       "March",
47       "April",
48       "May",
49       "June",
50       "July",
51       "August",
52       "September",
53       "October",
54       "November",
55       "December",
56       "INVALID MONTH"
57     };
58
59     if ( monum > 0 && monum < 13 ) return( moname[monum-1] );
60     else return( moname[12] );
61   }
62
63   int getday( unsigned long julday )
64   {
65     int i;
66
67     for( i=1; julday>modays(i); julday-=modays(i), i++ );
68     return( (int)julday );
69   }
70
71   int isleap( int year )
72   {
73     if ( 0 == ( year % 1000 ) )      return( FALSE );
74     else if ( 0 == ( year % 400 ) )  return( TRUE );
75     else if ( 0 == ( year % 100 ) )  return( FALSE );
76     else if ( 0 == ( year % 4 )  )   return( TRUE );
77     else                             return( FALSE );
78   }
79
80   int modays( int monum )
81   {
82     static int motab[] = { 31,28,31,30,31,30,
83                            31,31,30,31,30,31 };
84
85     if ( leapyear ) motab[1] = 29; else motab[1] = 28;
86     if ( monum > 0 && monum < 13 )
87       return( motab[monum-1] );
88     else return( 0 );
89   }
90
91   unsigned long getjul( int month, int day, int year )
92   {
93     int i;
94     unsigned long julday = 0;
```

Listing 3.3. continues

Listing 3.3. continued

```
95
96    for ( i=1; i<month; i++ ) julday += modays(i);
97    julday += day;
98    julday = ( julday * 100 ) + ( year % 100 );
99    return( julday );
100  }
```

The algorithms for date conversion are easy, with just a little study. As a good exercise, you may want to go over them in detail and pick out the techniques used here.

The way this program handles variables illustrates some of the points made about local and global scope. The only global variable in the program is `leapyear`. This integer is set once by the `isleap()` function so that other functions, notably `modays()`, do not have to determine repeatedly whether it is a leap year. All other variables are local to a function.

The `static` keyword is used in `getmon()` to qualify the array of month names `moname[]`. Especially since ANSI C allows you to initialize directly *any* variable, `auto` or otherwise, in its first definition, why should you do this?

Analyze what will happen if you don't use the `static` specifier. Because this array is inside the bounds of a function, it has local scope. By default, it is an object with *automatic duration*—it will be rebuilt at *each* call to `getmon()`, and discarded when the function returns to its caller. With an object this size, used in a program that calls a function repeatedly (say, once per record in a database-processing program), the setup overhead would be enormous. The `static` specifier modifies the attributes of the object, giving it static duration—it is set up once only, and left in place. This enhances the program's performance.

You might also reflect on the fact that `main()`, `getday()`, and `getjul()` all declare the integer `i`. Because a local variable is visible only in its scope, these three declarations refer to different variables. When `main()` calls either of these functions, what happens to its copy of `i`? You probably guess intuitively—and correctly—that while `getday()`, for example, is running, it uses it own variable `i`. The variable `i` in `main()` is not used, because its scope has been temporarily suspended while the subordinate function runs.

A final word about terminology. The terms *local* and *global* are borrowed from computer science. Although used only incidentally in the ANSI document, these extremely descriptive terms are used extensively in the literature (even the compiler manuals) in exactly the sense we use them here.

> ### Old-Style Coding: Initializing Local Variables
>
> K & R C did not permit the use of initializers in the declarations of `auto` objects (local variables) that have type `struct`, `union`, or an array. For these derived (complex) objects, you had to use the `static` specifier to change their duration to static. In fact, the original routines used to compose `cvtjul.c` (listing 3.3) were K&R routines, and used the `static` keyword for just this reason—so that the arrays of month names and day counts could be set up with initializers in the declaration.
>
> With ANSI-conforming compilers, this reason no longer applies; using static storage-class is only a performance modification. With recent conforming compilers, you can remove the `static` keyword entirely from the program. The program still works—we verified this—it just works a little more slowly. In general, you can place initializers directly in the declaration of any data object, `auto` or `static`, when using an ANSI-conforming compiler.

Declaring Functions and Passing Parameters

Designing and coding the function declarations and definitions is the glamorous part of writing C programs. Coding data definitions is every bit as necessary and useful, but they don't *do* anything—they just sit there. Functions *do things*.

Learning to write function declarations involves, first of all, understanding that from the larger perspective C regards its functions as objects, much like data objects. How so? Functions, like data objects, all have a *type* and, when accessed, render some *value*.

ANSI has introduced the `void` type, so that a function may have a `void` type and return a `void` value (return nothing at all). Conceptually, `void` is still a type of object—somewhat like the null set in mathematics. The *default* type for functions is `int`. That is, if you don't say anything about a function's type, it is assumed to be integer.

As you probably have noticed from the previous sample programs, you can communicate information to a function by passing it parameters—data objects that not only give the function something to work with but may also tell it how to go about its work. These objects, naturally, also have types.

The types involved can be any of those discussed earlier in this chapter, *except arrays. Only pointers to arrays can be passed as parameters.* The C compiler does quite a bit of work keeping track of types and deciding whether they are matched properly. This process is called *type checking*. The ANSI standard for C promotes (but it does not absolutely require) code that enforces *strong type checking*, meaning that the compiler catches most of the goofs made (instead of having your spiffy new program blow up when you are demonstrating it to the boss).

To write ANSI C code, you need to know how to assign a type to your functions, how to set up parameters for it, where to place both the function prototype and the function definition, and finally, how to actually call the function and get to the returned results.

Using Full Function Prototypes

An abiding principle of all computer programming is that you can't use an object you haven't yet declared. In some languages, you may be able to declare and use an object in the same statement, but it must be declared. The declaration is what tells the compiler or interpreter what it needs to know about the object.

In C, you can declare a function in two ways: by actually defining and writing the function; or by forward declaring it with a function prototype statement, and defining it later.

In the following C-Note, the first of these methods was used. The function process() was declared by defining it. This means that a function has to be declared in the source code before any calls are made to that function. Hence, process() was written before main(), which called it. This order was required even though main() first begins executing when the program is run. The *physical order* here is the reverse of the *logical order*.

Because this tends to be confusing and awkward for longer programs, the second method is the preferred one—use a *function prototype* statement early in the source file, and define the function body later. The first method is used in this book for short programs because it is very convenient for quick development of small projects.

Old-Style Coding: Function Declarations

The original K&R C featured weak typing. Programmers could, and did, take advantage of this to manipulate data in some fairly strange and esoteric ways. Weak typing was, in fact, considered one of the strengths of the language, so that the new ANSI emphasis on strong typing constitutes a major design difference. Weak typing manifested itself precisely in passing parameters to functions. The original function-definition sequence was like this:

```
process( a, b, c )
int a;
int b;
int c;
{
... /* do something with a, b, and c */
}
```

The catch is that there was no way to check and see whether the type of the parameters actually used in a function call matched the type of those given in the function definition.

You could call the function with the wrong type and number of arguments, provided that the number of bytes expected matched. You could do strange things like this:

```
1   #include <stdlib.h>
2   #include <stdio.h>
3
4   process( a, b, c )
5     int a,b,c;
6   {
7     printf( "%d %d %d\n", a, b, c );
8   }
9
10  main()
11  {
12    process( 0xFFFFFFFFUL, 0 );
13  }
```

This strange program actually runs, producing a display of –1, –1, and 0. This is because an `unsigned long int` has the same number of bytes as do two `int`s. This is exactly the sort of thing strong type checking prevents.

The Prototype Declaration Format

A function *definition* has two parts: the function declarator, and the function body. A function *prototype*, on the other hand, has only the declarator, followed immediately by a semicolon. A function prototype declaration has the following general syntax:

```
type-specifiers function-identifier( declaration-list );
```

In K&R C, you could also forward declare a function, but there was less information available for the compiler to use in type checking. For example, compare these two lines of code:

```
double circle_area( double radius );  /* ANSI style */
double circle_area( radius );          /* K&R style */
```

Now let's look in detail at the parts of a full function-prototype declaration.

Writing the Function Type Specifier

Functions have types (just like data objects) because they are expected, in general, to return to the function's caller a data value of the given type. Here are a few examples of function prototype declarations:

```
int is_it_there( char *text, char *search );
char *get_a_line( FILE *infile );
double avg_value( double stuff[20] );
void do_something( void );
here_it_is( int a );
```

The function is_it_there() searches for the string search in the string text, and returns an integer value that can be used to determine the success or failure of the function. get_a_line() has a type of char *, or pointer to character (string), because it returns the address of the last line of text read (this one probably has a static local data object it uses for a line buffer!). And avg_value() computes the average value of all the elements in the double floating-point array stuff[], and returns the result as a double.

The last two examples are a bit more subtle. To even guess what do_something() might actually do is impossible. It receives no parameters, and returns no value—but it still fits the conceptual model, because void is a type specifier. here_it_is(), by way of contrast, does get a parameter and, by default, returns a value—an integer.

We can boil down the rules for coding the function's type specifier into two points:

1. Every function must return a value to its caller. The type of the value can be one of the basic or derived (compound) data types you learned earlier in this chapter or, if it returns nothing, must specify the `void` type. Basic types and some derived types (structures, enumerated types, and `typedefs` you defined) can be returned directly as data values. Only pointers are returned for arrays and strings—generally, their "values" are very large objects requiring too much memory to move around directly (which would cause the function to run slowly—even if there were enough space). You can declare a function type specifier of pointer to anything—it depends only on what you are doing with the function.

    In some cases, using pointers is a good idea even if, technically, you don't have to. Structures, for instance, tend to be too large to do anything else—indiscriminately passing and returning structure "values" directly would degrade your program's performance severely.

2. A function prototype declaration (or a function definition, for that matter) is assumed to return a value of type `int` if you do not code a type specifier. There has to be *some* default—this `int` is it in C. This default can prove to be a subtle trap for programmers new to C. Take our word for it! While you're learning C, the tendency is to forget to code the specifier, when you actually want the type to be something other than `int`. Using ANSI function proto-typing prevents many of the problems that this formerly caused. Failure to code a type specifier shouldn't get past the compiler, unless you insist on using the old-style formats.

You might wonder whether a function—because it has a type—also has storage class like other objects. It does indeed. By default, a function has *external linkage*, so that functions in other source files can call it, if the source file containing the function has an appropriate function prototype (this is the sort of thing you use header files for). You can explicitly code this by using the `extern` keyword, as in the following example:

```
extern int my_function( void );
```

This declaration describes a function that has no parameters, returns an integer, and *is defined in another source file*.

The ANSI document specificaton that an object with external linkage and no stated storage-class specifier shall have *static duration* is true for functions. Functions *always* have static duration.

Furthermore, you can use the `static` keyword to modify the visibility of a function. The function has static duration naturally, but otherwise this keyword affects functions as it does any other global object with this specifier. It forces the function to be visible only to other functions in the same source file (this is called *internal linkage*). This usage allows you to have, without confusion, functions with the same name in different source files.

Writing the Function Name and Formal Parameter List

The function name is like any other name in C. The only thing that sets it apart is that it belongs to a function rather than to something else. The name part of the function declaration should follow at least one blank after the type specifier. This name is the *identifier* by which the function is known to the rest of the program; you use it to call (*invoke*) the function.

There is little magic about a function's name, provided that you observe a few rules in forming it. It should begin with a letter (system reserved names sometimes begin with an underscore); only the first 31 characters are considered significant (although you can write a longer name); and it can contain embedded underscores and numbers. Clearly, the name should mean something to you, but you should be careful not to duplicate C keywords or library function names. That's about it for now. (Chapter 4 provides details on C identifier conventions.)

The *formal parameter list* immediately follows the function name. The parameter list begins with an opening (left) parenthesis, lists the parameters (synonymous with *arguments*), separated by commas, and ends with a closing (right) parenthesis, followed by a semicolon. (The semicolon is used only to delimit the prototype declaration, not the function *definition*.)

You need to know about the following important characteristics of formal parameter lists:

❑ *The argument names in a parameter list are purely formal; they can (but do not have to) duplicate any identifier.* In the following code fragment, for example:

```
void display_time( int hh, int mm, int ss ); /*Prototype*/
...
main()
{
   int hours, minutes, second;
   ...
   display_time( hours, minutes, seconds );
}
```

the parameter names are different in the function prototype and actual function call. What is significant is the relative position and order in the list. Of course, the types of the actual and formal parameters must match; the compiler flags an error if they do not. It *is* acceptable if the actual and formal parameter names are identical—there is no conflict between formal parameters and "physical" variables.

But calling the function like this:

```
display_time( seconds, minutes, hours );
```

is not acceptable. In this case, the function would interpret its actual arguments as if they appeared in the order specified in the prototype (or complete definition, if there were no prototype). The program runs, but not with the desired results.

❑ *Each parameter in the list should have a type specifier, just as ordinary variable declarations do.* However, a formal parameter list does not permit a declaration list. For example:

```
/* THE WRONG WAY */
int sort_table( int *table,entries,status );

/* AND THE RIGHT WAY */
int sort_table( int *table, int entries, int status );
```

Each parameter declarator should have its own type specifier.

❑ *In the function prototype only, it is possible to use only type specifiers in the formal parameter list, with no variable names, as in the following line:*

```
int sort_table( int, int, int ); /* OK for prototype */
```

Again, this is permissible only in the prototype declaration, *never* in the function definition (when the function body is given).

Several references have been made to the fact that arrays (including strings, which are arrays of character) are never passed to a function as parameters. *Only pointers to arrays are passed to a function.* This ought to tell you two things:

1. *It is important.* You will have no end of confusion if you do not keep this fact firmly in mind.

2. There is more than one way to pass parameter information to a function. You can send a *copy* of the actual value of the object (*pass by value*), or you can send a value that is the address of the object—a pointer (*pass by reference*).

Figure 3.3 illustrates how parameters are passed to a function on stack-oriented machines. Begin to watch the sample code for instances of this distinction, and also watch for the manner in which arrays and strings are handled.

Effects on the Order of Appearance

The purpose of using function prototype declarations is to *forward declare* a function—to describe its characteristics before the complete definition appears so that the compiler knows how to handle references to the function in the meantime.

Function prototyping is the feature that allows you to write `main()` first, which in turn calls functions that physically appear later in the source file to handle more detailed tasks. This physical arrangement parallels the top-down design process, in which the major tasks are sketched in first, and fleshed out at deeper level of detail. It also seems to suit the human mind, which is accustomed to reading from the top down.

A side benefit of full function prototyping is that it provides the strongest possible type checking at compile time. There is a much better chance that the compiler will be able to catch and flag inconsistencies, instead of leaving them for you to find later, when the program fails.

Coding the Function Definition

The function definition differs from the function prototype in two ways: the declaration part does *not* end with a semicolon; and the declaration part is followed directly by the *function body*. Here is an example of a function prototype declaration followed by its corresponding function definition:

```
int x = 7, y = 4;
int maxval( int, int );
...
main()
{
   printf( "The greatest number is %d\n",
         maxval( x, y ) );
}
...
int maxval( int a, int b )
{
   return a > b ? a : b;
}
```

The function prototype shown here uses type names without identifiers to describe the formal parameters (remember—you can specify the formal

Fig. 3.3. Passing parameters using the system stack.

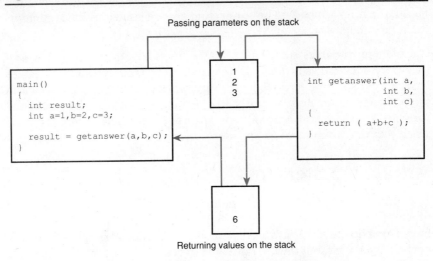

parameter names). The parameter list in the function definition is formal also, but you must use both type and identifier names here—the names of the formal parameters are about to be used in the function body.

The ANSI standard still allows the original style of declaring and defining functions. The formats for the declaration and definition of `max_val()` would look like this:

```
int maxval( a, b );
...
int maxval( a, b )
   int a;
   int b;
{
   return a > b ? a : b;
}
```

Building the Function Body

The function body is just an ordinary C block statement, enclosed by curly braces. The opening brace can be on the same line as the function declaration part, or on the next, and no semicolon follows the closing curly brace. Look for these features in the preceding fragment and reinforce these features in your mind.

Before we move on to the subject of writing statements for the function body, it is important that you understand the transition from the declaration part to the function body. The connecting link, of course, is the arguments in the parameter list.

Parameter variables are used within the bounds of the function just as if they were declared as ordinary local variables. In fact, parameter variables have automatic scope, as do the auto variables declared within the function body. They are created on entry to the function—copies of the actual variables used in the call are made and given to the function—and discarded when the function returns to its caller.

Writing C Statements

Within the bounds of the braces delimiting the block statement that is the function body, you place simple statements, or subordinate block statements, that do the function's work. The different kinds of simple statements are discussed next, but they all have at least one thing in common: they are terminated with a semicolon. To verify this, just glance through the sample programs and code fragments presented so far.

Everything defined and discussed in the book so far has had the characteristics of an *object*—they have all been *things* (including functions considered as a whole)—and they have all had a *value* associated with them (even if it were only the void attribute).

Statements differ from C objects in two ways. They appear only within the confines of function bodies; and they have an effect, not a value. Statements are executed by the computer. They operate on objects.

You should know about five kinds of statements: expression statements, flow control statements, labeled statements, null statements, and compound or block statements.

Writing Expression Statements

The expression statement is the workhorse of C. It is the statement that operates directly on data objects or causes I/O to be done. The two most common expression statements are the assignment statement:

```
a = ( b + c * d ) / e;
```

and the function call:

```
printf( "%d\n", a );
```

C expression statements are much like algebraic statements. They are a sequence of terms and factors, joined together in a specific way by certain operators. One significant difference is that C can have a statement that is not a complete assignment statement; in the preceding line of code, for instance, `printf()` returns an integer value that is thrown away.

C is outstanding in its capability of supporting complex, compact, and efficient expressions. The topic is so important that much of Chapter 5 is devoted to it.

Writing Flow Control Statements

The term *flow control* covers three more precisely named groups of statements: *selection*, *iteration*, and *jump* statements. Look at the following C-Note and notice which statements belong to each of these groups.

Quick-Reference: C Flow Control Summary

In the following specifications for the flow control statements, the tokens shown in italics are expressions, statements, or identifiers that you code to suit your purposes. Punctuation and tokens not shown in italics must be written as shown. Wherever the placeholder statement appears, you may write either a simple statement followed by a semicolon, or a block statement that is not followed by a semicolon. Writing block statements is discussed in detail shortly.

Selection:
　　　　　　　if (*expression*) *statement*
　　　　　　　if (*expression*) *statement* else *statement*
　　　　　　　switch (*expression*) *statement*

Iteration:
　　　　　　　while (*expression*) *statement*
　　　　　　　do *statement* while (*expression*);
　　　　　　　for (*expr1*; *expr2*; *expr3*) *statement*

Jump:
　　　　　　　goto *identifier*;
　　　　　　　continue;
　　　　　　　break;
　　　　　　　return *expression*;

These three classes of statements have been grouped together into one conceptual framework because they all alter the sequence of execution.

Normally, instructions are executed in a sequential fashion. The next instruction to be executed is the next physically sequential instruction after the current one. The presence of a flow control statement changes this; the next instruction to be executed is somewhere else in the function.

That last phrase also is an important one. The flow control instructions shown here can cause execution to continue only somewhere within the current function. Furthermore, all flow control statements (except `goto`, `break`, and `return`) cause a statement within the current block to execute next.

When using selection and iteration statements, be especially careful not to cause any unwanted side effects. The expression parts of the selection and iteration statements are normally meant to be *conditional expressions*, which test the truth or falsehood of some condition. Therefore, in forming these expressions, specific conditional operators normally are used. Here is an example:

```
if ( a == b ) return 0;
```

If you look closely at this statement, you see that the *equality operator* (==), not the assignment operator (=), is being used.

What is the difference? The equality operator does *not* cause the value of b to be placed in a; the assignment operator *does*. Side effects arise when you write a statement like this:

```
if ( a = b ) return 0;
```

This perfectly legitimate C statement first assigns the value of b to a, then examines the value of a (the most elementary value of the expression), and decides whether the condition is false or true (0 or nonzero, respectively). The side effect lies in the fact that an object's value was changed, above and beyond the primary purpose of testing a condition.

Clearly, just by making a typing error, you can easily introduce unwanted side effects into your program in expressions like this one. At times, however, you deliberately want to introduce side effects. You probably can recall one from an earlier sample program. For example, you often see this kind of statement:

```
if ( NULL == (infile = fopen( "myfile.txt", "r" ) ) )
{
   puts( "I can't open the input file." );
   abort();
}
```

This very common statement has an interesting structure, based on the deliberate use of expression side effects. From the preceding C-Note, you know that the if statement has a "simple" conditional expression which is tested, and an accompanying statement (a block statement with no semicolon following here) which is executed only if the condition is true (not 0).

Working from the inside out, the intent obviously is to open the file and check at the same time for a successful open. The fopen() function is called, and the resulting pointer placed in the FILE pointer object infile using the assignment operator. Next the result of that operation (a pointer) is compared against a NULL value (zero value) using the conditional equality operator.

Here is the tricky part: if the file does not open successfully, a null pointer is returned, and compared to another null pointer, *yielding a true condition*. Thus, the result of the conditional expression is *not* zero, and the if's block statement *is* executed—aborting the program. Whew!

This is only a taste of the tangles you can get into by not paying attention to side effects. The subject of flow control is so important that Chapter 7 is devoted to it.

Using Labeled Statements

Inherently, C is a well-structured language that does not promote the use of direct jumps. But the direct jump is supported, in the form of the goto statement (refer to the preceding C-Note).

Every goto must have a target location *within the current function*, although it can be outside the current block. This target is provided in C by the *label statement*, as illustrated by the following code fragment:

```
int some_function( void )
{
  goto pointa ;
  ...
  pointa: a = b;
}
```

The object of a goto is a label that prefixes some other statement. The label is noted by the presence of the full colon. Note also that *the label must be followed by a statement*. That was not formerly the case, but ANSI has standardized around its required presence. (You can get around that by using the null statement, coming up next.)

Two other kinds of labeled statement—the case and default statements —are both associated with the *switch* statement. These statements are discussed in Chapter 7.

Using Null Statements

Null statements are the easiest statements in all of C. Remember that a simple statement is always formed from an expression followed by a semicolon. Now just leave the expression out!

```
;      /* A NULL STATEMENT */
```

You may want to know why in the world you would ever need such a statement. First, you can circumvent the need to follow a label with a complete statement:

```
goto label1;
... /* do some things here */
label1: ;
... /* do other things here */
```

This usage breaks up the continuous flow of statements, enhancing readability.

The other reason for using a null statement is to provide a placeholder when syntax requires a statement but you don't really need one. The while statement, for example, can be used with deliberate side effects to copy one string into another:

```
char a[32];
char b[32] = "This string has something in it";
...
while ( *a++ = *b++ ) ; /* Don't need a statement here */
```

The conditional expression does all the work: it assigns each character of the sending string to the corresponding character of the receiving string, updates the pointers involved, and (when the terminating null character is copied) finds the false condition required to terminate the loop. A null statement was used because the statement usually associated with the while is completely redundant.

Writing Compound (Block) Statements

You have seen block statements many times by now; they are old friends. A block statement is just a series of simple statements (expression or otherwise), surrounded by curly braces. The closing curly brace is *not* followed by a semicolon, although all the internal *simple* statements are. A block statement also may be *nested* inside another block statement, as in the following example:

```
if ( a != b ) { /* if a is not equal to b */
  /* ------ begin a block statement for the if ------ */
  a = b;            /* make it equal */
  for ( i=a; i<100; i++ ) {
    /* ------ begin another for the for ------ */
    ...
  }
}
```

The purpose of the block statement is to provide a means of writing many statements where syntax requires only one. You can see several examples of block statements in the program listings in the closing sections of this chapter.

Returning Values From a Function

If a function has some type other than `void`, it is expected to return a value to its caller. This is done with the `return` statement. An expression (which can be just a simple variable of the correct type) associated with the `return` statement is evaluated, and its result is passed back to the calling routine. On stack-oriented machines, this is accomplished by using the program's stack area (refer to fig. 3.3).

Use of the `return` statement is illustrated in listing 3.4, which shows how to develop the CRC-16 block-checking code used by communications programs to implement error-free file-transfer programs. If you are interested in communications programming, you will find this routine useful.

The `calc_crc16()` function receives a pointer to an array of unsigned characters (the incoming message), together with a length parameter, because the array is not assumed to be a null-terminated string. The array is processed by the `while` loop, and the unsigned integer (16-bit) CRC-16 block-checking code is returned.

Listing 3.4. `crc16.c` *(A function returning a value).*   *All compilers*

```
 1   #include <stdlib.h>
 2
 3   unsigned calc_crc16( char *msgpoly, int bytes )
 4   {
 5     static unsigned crc16 = 0;
 6     static int i;
 7
 8     while ( 0 < bytes-- ) {
 9       crc16 = crc16 ^ ( int )*msgpoly++ << 8;
10       for ( i=0; i<8; i++ ) {
11          if ( crc16 & 0x8000 ) crc16 = crc16 << 1 ^ 0x1021;
12          else crc16 = crc16 << 1;
13       }
14     }
15     return( crc16 );
16   }
17
18   main()
19   {
20      printf( "%X\n", calc_crc16( "Test string.", 12 ) );
21   }
```

If you wanted to develop a CRC-16 checking code for a whole file (noncommunications application), you would have to alter the logic of the function. In the version shown, the next character is fetched by simply updating the array pointer (`msgpoly++`). To process a file (as some compression programs do), you could replace lines 3, 8, and 9 with the following:

```
 3   unsigned calc_crc16( FILE *infile )
       . . .
 8     while ( !feof(infile) ) {
 9        crc16 = crc16 ^ ( int )fgetc( infile ) << 8;
```

presuming that `FILE *infile` has been opened elsewhere.

Because functions that have type `void` are expected to return nothing, the `return` statement must either be omitted, or its expression deleted (code a semicolon only, with no expression). Listing 3.5 contains an interesting function with `void` type. It exchanges the contents of *any* two variables (or areas of RAM) without using temporary work space of any kind:

Listing 3.5. exchange.c *(A function returning nothing).*   *Turbo C++*

```
 1   #include <stddef.h>
 2   #include <stdlib.h>
 3   #include <stdio.h>
 4   #include <string.h>
 5
 6   /* +-----------------------------------------------------+
 7      + Exchange two areas of memory with no auxiliary
 8      +    storage used.
 9      +
10      + Calling Sequence:
11      +
12      + mem_exchange( void *s1, void *s2, size_t n );
13      +
14      +    where s1 and s2 can be of any type (using
15      +    the appropriate casts). Two areas of
16      +    storage each "n" bytes long are exchanged in
17      +    place.
18      +-----------------------------------------------------+
19   */
20   void mem_exchange( void *s1, void *s2, size_t n )
21   {
22      for ( ; n>0; n-- ) {
23        *(unsigned char *)s1 ^= *(unsigned char *)s2;
24        *(unsigned char *)s2 ^= *(unsigned char *)s1;
25        *(unsigned char *)s1 ^= *(unsigned char *)s2;
26        (unsigncd char *)s1 += 1;
27        (unsigned char *)s2 += 1;
28      }
29   }
30
31   main()
32   {
33      char s1[40] = "This is the FIRST string. ";
34      char s2[40] = "This is the SECOND string.";
35      int i1 = 255;
36      int i2 = 127;
37
38      clrscr();
39      printf( "%s\n%s\n", s1, s2 );
40      mem_exchange( (void *)s1, (void *)s2, strlen( s1 ) );
41      printf( "%s\n%s\n\n", s1, s2 );
42
43      printf( "%d\n%d\n", i1, i2 );
44      mem_exchange( (void *)i1, (void *)i2, sizeof( int ) );
45      printf( "%d\n%d\n\n", i1, i2 );
46   }
```

This odd little function is based on a result from Boolean algebra which states that you can exchange the contents of two fields, *a* and *b*, with the following sequence of exclusive-OR instructions:

```
a XOR b
b XOR a
a XOR b
```

where the first operand always receives the result of the operation. Suppose, for example, that you wanted to exchange two fields containing the binary numbers 11110000 and 00001111.

The sequence of operations, moving from left to right, is:

```
      a:11110000           b:00001111             a:11111111
XOR   b:00001111     XOR   a:11111111       XOR   b:11110000
      --------                 --------                 --------
new a:  11111111     new b:11110000         new a:00001111
```

As you can see, *b* has received its new value by the second exclusive-OR; *a*, by the third. On the PC, this method is almost as quick as moving one of the variables to a hold area while swapping; on some other machines, it is actually faster.

Calling the Function

You call the function whenever you want it to yield a result value, much like accessing a variable—you just *state* it. That is, you code the function name, open parentheses, list the *actual* parameter variables (or expressions), close parentheses, and write a semicolon. Remember that the actual argument names do not have to be the same as the formal declaration names, only the same *type*. (They don't *have* to be different, either.)

You can think of the function call as producing its returned value in the exact "spot" at which the call is placed. In the case of mem_exchange(), the type was void; thus, the function call stood alone on a single line. In the case of calc_crc16(), an integer was returned and used directly as an argument in the printf() call. You just call the function wherever you normally would write a variable in an expression.

Summary

This chapter presented some extremely important material. Having read it, you should know the following:

❏ *What C's basic data types are, how to declare them, and how to write literal values for all the types*

❏ *What the limiting values for the basic types are*

❏ *The various ways to declare and initialize variables*

❏ *What local and global variables are, and how scope and duration of variables affect what you can do with them*

❏ *How to declare function prototypes and formal parameter lists, and how this affects where you can reference and place the functions you define*

❏ *How to write the function definition.* You should understand how the various types of C statements are used in the function body, and how to return a value of the appropriate type to the caller.

❏ *How to call (invoke) a function, including where you can place the call, and how to use the returned value*

In the next chapter, we again move closer to the elemental building blocks of a C program, to get all the detail you need to control the programming process. Then the real fun starts, when we begin to look at how to put it all to use.

4

A Closer Look at C Programs

In Chapter 3, you were presented with the broadest classes of elements that make up a C program. The detail developed as the discussion of data and functions unfolded serves as the foundation for this and later chapters.

This chapter expands, in greater and deeper detail, on what goes into a C program—now you will see the irreducible elements of C source code. In particular, you will find the following:

❏ *What characters you can use to write C programs, and how to handle special requirements for them*

❏ *How the compiler works, how you define for it the names you want to use, and how you can avoid misusing the names C reserves for itself*

❏ *How to write and use C macros and other preprocessing directives*

More Detail on Language Conventions

A *language convention* is nothing more than the "legal" way to do something. You have already seen some of C's conventions in its punctuation and general format. Now it's time to get down to details and define just what can go into a valid C program.

The C Character Set

The idea of a *character set* is not as strange as you might think. The Greek alphabet (character set) is different from the English, as are the Russian and Hebrew alphabets. Everyone—even those of us who are not masters of those languages—is familiar with that fact.

The C character set is a subset of English characters and Arabic numerals, plus some other special characters. You need to know two things about C characters: what ANSI considers to be a character, and which characters comprise the ANSI C required character set.

Bits, Bytes, and Characters

The ANSI standard for C considers a *character* to be something that fits in one byte and is a member of the basic character set of either the source environment or the target environment. Source and target character sets are discussed a little later in this chapter. The other terms are more important just now.

The way information is stored in the memory of a digital computer controls what ANSI defines to be bits, bytes, and characters. At the lowest level, information is stored in a *bit*, or *binary digit*. Electronically, a bit can be either off or on; thus, it can store the values zero and one—nothing else. Normally, individual bits are not used to store significant amounts of information however. Bits are used in groups.

A *byte* is a collection of bits that can store some recognizable datum: a number or a character code. Almost universally, eight bits make up a byte, although the ANSI standard leaves the specific number up to the hardware and the compiler. In this book, a byte always means a group of eight bits and a character also is assumed to occupy eight bits of storage.

The bits in a byte are numbered for handy reference. In this book, the *least significant* bit is considered to be bit 0; the *most significant* bit, bit 7 (see fig. 4.1). Least significant and most significant mean just the least and greatest contribution, respectively, to the value of the complete number.

Fig. 4.1. Bit number, values, and powers of 2.

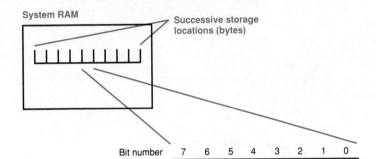

Figure 4.1 is the exploded view of a byte's structure. Moving from low- to-high-order positions, the bits have corresponding decimal values that are successive powers of two. You can convert the binary value of a byte to decimal by noticing which bits are "on" (have a 1 value) and summing all the decimal values. The binary number 00010001, for example, has the decimal value 16 + 1 = 17.

If a byte is composed of 8 bits, it can store 256 different numeric values: 0 through 255. Is each of these values considered a character? Yes, but there are different kinds of characters, depending on their numeric values. In the computer industry, the term character implies two concepts: *display* characters and *control* characters. To express all display and control characters in the English character set, the entire range of byte values is not required. (You will see later how ANSI has provided for languages that require *more* than 256 values.)

Display characters do exactly what the name implies. They can be sent to an output device and displayed in a form that people can read. Naturally, every device attached to a particular computer must assume that the same byte values represent a given character. The numeric values assigned to display characters (as well as to control characters) make up a machine's collating sequence.

Compiler Dependency: The Collating Sequence

Every machine has a character set, and every character set has a collating sequence. A *collating sequence* is the sequence of numerical values assigned to each character in the set. Each C compiler must take into account the character set and collating sequence with which it is intended to be used.

The collating sequence must be chosen so that the characters appear in the correct order when sorted (which is controlled by the numeric values). ANSI requires that the values associated with the numerical display characters (0–9) be not only in order, but also *contiguous*—there must be no gaps in the sequence. Gaps between the values assigned to other characters may possibly exist.

Note that the terms *collating sequence* and *number system* should not be confused. For example, the decimal value for an ASCII blank is 32. This can be expressed equally well by the hexadecimal number 20 or the binary number 100000. Although the IBM PC, its compatibles, and many other computers are ASCII machines, the ANSI standard for C does not presume that the ASCII character set is being used. C is implemented also on IBM mainframes, for example, which use the EBCDIC character set and collating sequence.

Control characters are assigned a common sense significance by the ANSI standard. Primarily, they are *motion-control* characters. The presence of these characters in text is meant to indicate how the text will be formatted and positioned. A horizontal tab character, for example, means that the output device is to move some predetermined number of extra spaces before the next display character. The motion-control characters are meant to control interactive I/O devices that produce output you can see (like displays and printers) but not storage devices (like disks). Storage devices record the control characters, but take no action because of them.

The C "Minimal" Character Set

ANSI standard C is not tied to the ASCII character set, but it is intimately tied to the English language. All the English letters, a selected group of English graphic characters, and the Arabic numerals are all required by the standard.

The required characters comprise the *minimal character set* for C. This does not mean that compiler vendors may not implement additional characters—they can and do, fortunately for the programmers and users of programs.

Characters can be used in two ways: they can be *part of the C source language*, or they can be *elements of the data* the program must work with. Most of the characters in the minimal set are used in C source language; they all can be used as data elements.

Quick-Reference: The C Minimal Character Set

Compilers conforming to the ANSI C standard must support the following letters and characters:

A B C D E F G H I J K L M N O P Q R S T U V W X Y Z

a b c d e f g h i j k l m n o p q r s t u v w x y z

0 1 2 3 4 5 6 7 8 9

! " # % & ' ( ) * + , - . / : ; < = > ? [\ ] ^ _ { | } ~

space(blank), horizontal and vertical tabs, and form feed

end-of-line indicator (a single newline character)

alert, backspace, and carriage return

In addition, the numerical values of the digits 0 through 9 must be successively one greater than the preceding one in the list.

The characters in the minimal C character set can be classified also according to whether they are whitespace, control, upper- or lowercase, printable, hex digit, decimal digit, alphanumeric, punctuation, alphabetic, or graphic in nature. All of these categories can be tested for by the is...() family of functions (see Part II of this book for details). Figure 4.2 shows how these categories break down:

Fig. 4.2. *Minimal C character-set classifications.*

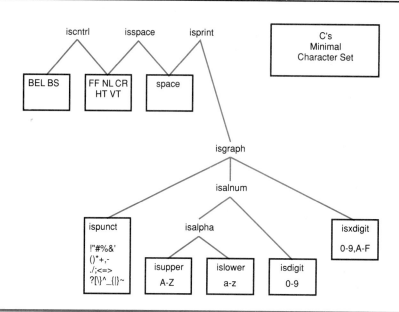

Handling Special Characters

At the end of "The C Minimal Character Set" Quick-Reference C-Note, several of the required C characters are described in words (instead of simply being shown) because they are *control characters*, not display characters. Except for the space character, these special control characters are used in *text data* (like the text you are reading now) to manage its format and position.

If control characters are required but are not display characters (meaning that you normally cannot type them directly), how do you use them in your programs? To write a control character into the source code of your program, you use an escape sequence.

An *escape sequence* is two characters written together. The first of these characters must be a backslash (\), and the second one depends on what you want it to do. Listing 4.1 shows how escape sequences are used in a program. escape.c uses the horizontal tab character ' \ t ' and the newline character ' \n ' to format a simple report with the printf() function.

As you look at the program, notice how the escape sequences are used. Remember that character *strings* are enclosed in double quotation marks ("This is a character string!"). Character *constants* are enclosed in single quotation marks (the character *a* is written 'a'). Character constants are not used in listing 4.1, but the escape sequences would be coded in exactly the same way: '\n' is the newline character.

Listing 4.1. *Using special characters in* printf().

```
 1   /*+-----------------------------------------------------------+
 2       +                              ESCAPE.C
 3       +   An example of the use of special character constants.
 4       +-----------------------------------------------------------+
 5   */
 6
 7   #include <stdio.h>
 8   #include <stdlib.h>
 9
10   main()
11   {
12   /* ----- Setup salespersons' names ----- */
13      char sp1[5] = "John";
14      char sp2[5] = "Joe";
15
16   /* ----- Setup sales amounts for month ----- */
17      float sales1 = 1287.63;
18      float sales2 = 1301.50;
19
20   /* ----- Commission rate ----- */
21      float comm = 0.08;
22
23      printf( "\t*** Sales Report for January ***\n");
24      printf( "Salesman\t\t%s\t\t%s\n", sp1, sp2 );
25      printf( "--------\t\t------\t\t------\n" );
26      printf( "Sales\t\t\t%4.2f\t\t%4.2f\n", sales1, sales2 );
27      printf( "Commission\t\t%4.2f\t\t%4.2f\n",
28         sales1 * comm, sales2 * comm );
29   }
```

The output from this program looks like this:

```
        *** Sales Report for January ***

    Salesman            John            Joe
    --------            ------          ------
    Sales               1287.63         1301.50
    Commission          103.01          104.12
```

Mnemonic Escape Sequences

The letters assigned as the second character of the two-character escape sequences are meant to be *mnemonic* (easy to remember). Be sure to select letters that make sense, such as *a* for alert, *b* for backspace, and so on. You can use these escape sequences in character strings:

```
char stuff[40] = "First sentence.\n";   /* In a string */
```

or in character constants:

```
char m;
...
m = '\r';                                /* In a constant */
```

Quick-Reference: ANSI C Mnemonic Escape Sequences

The ANSI C standard defines these mnemonic escape sequences and their meanings as follows:

Sequence	Meaning
\a	Alert
\b	Backspace
\f	Formfeed
\n	Newline
\r	Carriage return
\t	Horizontal tab
\v	Vertical tab
\'	Single quotation mark
\"	Double quotation mark
\?	Question mark
\\	Backslash

Even though two keystrokes are needed to write these sequences into your program's source code, they occupy (internally) exactly one character—one byte. The numerical values assigned to these characters do not have to be displayable characters (on some output devices, they are).

When sent to an output device, the *alert character* produces an audible or visible alert—a tone, or a graphic message. This is not a motion-control character, because it makes no difference in the formatting or positioning of text. For example,

```
putchar( '\a' );     /* Sound the alert bell */
```

The *backspace character* moves the active position (of the cursor, for example) to the preceding position on the line. This does not necessarily destroy the preceding character. If the active position is already at the beginning of the line, ANSI does not specify what should happen. The following statement would cause the capital letter A to be underlined if output were being directed to a printer:

```
puts( "A\b_\n" );     /* Underline it via Backspace */
```

Formfeed is a motion-control character only for some devices. When a formfeed is sent to a printer, the current page is ejected, and the printer positions the next page for writing. If it is sent to a disk file, its only effect is to take up another byte of disk space. Whether it has any effect on a display screen depends on the software driving the screen. For example,

```
putchar( '\f' );            /* Eject to new page */
```

Standard C regards the *newline character* in a somewhat special light. The ANSI specification requires that text files (see Chapters 2 and 9 for more on text files) " . . . have some way of indicating the end of each line of text . . . " but does not say what that way will be. It then goes on to say that these end-of-line markers will be treated *as if they were a single newline character*. The newline character is a motion-control character that first moves the active position (cursor, and so forth) to the *initial position* of the line (column 1), and then to the next line of text.

The newline character usually is denoted by either of the abbreviations *NL* (for newline) or *LF* (for line feed); on ASCII systems, it has a decimal numerical value of 10. The term line feed ordinarily is used to describe the process of moving the current position down one line but *not* to the first column. The term newline is more accurate when describing C programs. You can demonstrate to yourself that NL has a decimal value of 10 by running this short program:

```
#include <stdio.h>

main()
{
   printf( "%d\n", (int)'\n' );
}
```

This program prints the decimal number 10 (the value for LF as well as for NL). Notice that the \n character is used twice: once between the double quotation marks and once between single quotation marks. The characters between the double quotation marks—the first parameter—are the *format string* for the printf() function. They tell it how to format the output. The number is printed (displayed on-screen) as a decimal number (%d causes this) and then the newline action is taken (\n causes this).

The second parameter:

```
(int)'\n'
```

tells printf() *what* to print. This construction is interpreted to mean that the NL character ('\n') is to be converted to an integer—(int) causes this—and then used as an argument for printing. This kind of conversion is called a *type cast*. You will learn more about type casts in later chapters.

The *carriage-return character* is similar to newline in that it homes the cursor (sets the active position to the initial position) but differs in that it does *not* move the active position to the next line. Carriage return frequently is denoted by the abbreviation *CR*; on ASCII systems, it has a decimal numerical value of 13. To demonstrate this, you can modify the code by substituting \r for each \n.

Compiler Dependency: Terminating Text Lines

ANSI does not specify what the line-terminating characters should be, nor does it tie character-set requirements to the ASCII character set. However, on most ASCII machines you will find that the compiler vendors have chosen the *carriage return* and *line feed* pair of characters to terminate text lines because most text editors store text files using this convention. These are the characters that C interprets as a single newline when dealing with files *in text mode*. Note that *this is not true when performing I/O in binary mode*.

This does not mean that you normally code \r\n in your programs—you should use '\n' for all text mode I/O. C's formatted I/O functions, in particular, expect to translate newline to the CR/LF pair of characters. Writing a short program that uses the following printf() statement:

```
printf( "%d\r\n", (int)'\n' );
```

might be instructive. Run the program both with and without the '\r'—noticing, in each case, where the cursor ends up. There should be no difference. To determine why this is so, use the escape-sequence definitions presented earlier.

The *horizontal tab* (HT) character '\t' is used to set tabs in the same sense that a typewriter sets tabs. When HT is encountered, the current position is moved right (in English systems) to the next tab position. What is the next tab position? Whatever the software you happen to be running decides it is. The Turbo C editor, for example, sets the tabs to every eighth column by default. The implication is that if your program is going to handle tabs, you have to decide where they are in the line. Most ASCII printers can be directed to set tab stops also at user-defined positions.

The *vertical tab* (VT) character has meaning only when sent to the printer. Almost all ASCII printers can handle the VT in some way. VT is recognized also by some PC communications programs that emulate an ASCII terminal.

The remaining escape sequences seem somewhat cryptic until you review what you have learned about writing character constants, character strings, and escape sequences. The compiler recognizes each of these elements by means of certain characters: double or single quotation marks, or a backslash. What if you want to use these special characters as data, not C punctuation?

Whether you need an escape sequence to code a *single quotation* mark as a data element depends on the context. If there can be no confusion about the meaning, an escape sequence is not required. For example,

```
puts( "This isn't an error." );    /* Good, no confusion */
```

However, if you tried to write the code for a single quotation mark as a character constant, like this:

```
putchar( ''' );                    /* Very bad */
```

the compiler flags this as an error. To get around the problem, C provides yet another escape sequence for the single quotation mark character. To display a single quotation mark by itself, you could use this call to putchar():

```
putchar( '\'' );                   /* Very good */
```

Using a double quotation mark as data inside a string is no problem, either. It's done in much the same way:

```
puts( "Jack said, \"Hello!\"" );   /* Quoting a quote! */
```

Getting the compiler to recognize a single or double quotation mark as data is one thing—but what about the backslash character itself? If you want the backslash character to appear as a data character within a string or character constant, you have to introduce it as an escape sequence, like this:

```
puts( "The backslash character \\ is special." );
```

This call to puts() would produce the following output:

```
The backslash character \ is special.
```

Finally, the ANSI C specification allows for the escape sequence \?. This sequence, which is new to C, was developed specifically to accommodate other facilities introduced by the ANSI standard for C. Its purpose is to allow a sequence of two question marks "??" to be coded (as part of a string, for example) without triggering the trigraph escape-sequence mechanism (covered later in this chapter). You would write the string like this:

```
puts( "What's happening, hmm?\?" );
```

to produce the following output:

```
What's happening, hmm??
```

Numeric Escape Sequences

As if all those escape sequences were not enough, ANSI C carries forward the practice of allowing *numeric escape sequences,* in which a backslash character is followed by a numeric—rather than character—constant. By using numeric escape sequences, you can insert *any* of the 256 possible values into a character constant or string. Just as with mnemonic escape sequences, the numeric escapes can be used between single or double quotation marks for constants and strings.

Numeric escape sequences can be a little tricky, because the numeric digits used are always interpreted by the compiler to be either *octal* or *hexadecimal, not decimal.* Octal escape sequences are composed of the backslash and from one to three octal digits (the octal digits are 0–7). Here are some examples of octal escape sequences:

Sequence	Meaning
\0	The null character. Very important in C; terminates all strings.
\123	A single byte, decimal value 83
\779	Two bytes, because 9 is not octal. This would be valid only in a string, such as "AB\779". Octal 77 is decimal 63, the ASCII '?' character. Therefore, this string is equivalent to "AB?9".
\88	An error, because 8 is not a valid octal digit

Notice that octal escape sequences are completed when either three octal digits or a nonoctal digit have been encountered, whichever occurs first.

Hexadecimal escape sequences begin with the backslash followed by an *x* and either one or two digits (0–9, and A–F), as in these examples:

Sequence	Meaning
\x0	The null character. It's not usually coded this way, but would work perfectly.
\x0D	The CR (carriage return) character
\xFF	Value depends on whether the compiler considers characters to be signed or unsigned. If signed, this code has the decimal value −1; if unsigned, the value 255. Be careful of the high-order bit.
\xFG	Valid only in a string, such as "A\xFG\xE". The \xF and \xE characters have values of 15 and 14, respectively, and are the SI (Shift In) and SO (Shift Out) ASCII control characters. You might send such a sequence to a printer, for example.
\ss	Invalid, because *S* is not a valid hexadecimal digit

The hexadecimal escape sequence is terminated only when a nonhex digit is encountered, but the value of the resulting number must not exceed 255 (or hex FF). The hex escape sequences are probably the most useful, because most programmers tend to work with hex rather than binary or octal notations.

Using Trigraphs

The escape sequences discussed so far represent the class of notation called *digraphs*, in which two characters are written to represent one that cannot be typed directly. The escape sequences are used to write character *data* as opposed to C keywords, expressions, or other language elements.

The problem of entering certain symbols directly may extend to the source code itself however. A particular computer's keyboard, for example, may not be able to handle some of the graphic characters that C requires for its normal syntax. ANSI standard C allows for this situation by providing *trigraph escape sequences*. Clearly, trigraphs can be used also to code special characters in constants and strings.

The concept of trigraph sequences flows naturally and intuitively from the escape sequences you just learned. Whereas the escape character for mnemonic and numeric escapes is the backslash (\), the escape character for the trigraphs is a question mark (?), coded twice: for example, ??= is the trigraph for the # character.

Quick-Reference: ANSI C Trigraphs

There are nine trigraphs in the ANSI C specification. They are

Trigraph	Replacement for
??=	#
??(	[
??/	\
??)	]
??'	^
??<	{
??|	|
??>	}
??-	~

The trigraphs listed here are all that exist. Any others produce a compile-time error. In any context other than a trigraph sequence, the meaning of a question mark does not change.

You can use the trigraph sequences anywhere in the source file that the characters they represent would normally appear. For example, the following code fragment:

```
if ( a == b ) {
   a = 1;
   b = a * 3;
}
```

could be written as follows, with the same meaning for the compiler:

```
if ( a == b ) ??<
   a = 1;
   b = a * 3;
??>
```

This second code fragment is not as easy to read as the first, but it is legitimate and, if your keyboard does not have the curly-brace characters ({ and }), is the only way to go. At the time this was being written, none of the compilers we used could support trigraph sequences directly, although Turbo C++ provides a batch utility for converting programs to and from trigraph notation.

Multibyte Characters

All of the character encodings discussed to this point use a single byte of storage, because the character sets do not require all 256 values possible in a byte. This works fine in Western countries with relatively small alphabets. In other countries—notably Japan, China, and other Asian countries—this doesn't work at all.

To be specific, the written Japanese and Chinese languages do not use alphabets. They use *ideograms*, which are highly stylized pictorially based graphic objects. The problem is that tens of thousands of code values are needed to represent all possible "characters."

Multibyte characters are the ANSI C answer to this dilemma. A *multibyte character* is a sequence of one or more bytes that represent a single character. The addition of multibyte characters to the single-byte characters results in an *extended character set*. The following rules govern the use of multibyte characters:

❏ *The extended character set must include the minimal C character set.*

❏ *The use and meaning of any extended characters is considered to be locale specific.* That is, there is no preferred multibyte encoding. You must familiarize yourself with each specific one.

❏ *Multibyte sequences are triggered much like the escape sequences.* When any one of a set of multibyte characters appears in a string or constant, the compiler expects the next single character (or sequence of them) to complete the multibyte sequence. One result of this is that when a multibyte sequence starts in a string, the next character cannot be checked to see whether it is a normal escape character or the closing quote of the string.

❏ *A multibyte sequence may use a state-dependent coding.* The different possible states are called *shift states*. Each multibyte sequence begins in an initial state, in which each byte is considered to be a single normal character, as with the minimal set. Other shift states (which vary with locale and the specific compiler) are entered when certain multibyte character codes are encountered. For example, in "\81a" and "\82a", the *a* might mean two different character representations, if the 0x81 and 0x82 values mean different shift states.

❏ *The null character \0 may not be part of a multibyte encoding.*
That is, the null character is always a single byte code with all
bits zero.

You can deal with multibyte characters in two ways. First, you can deal
with them as a *normal string*. This makes sense, because a multibyte character is a series of several bytes (characters). Second, you can convert
multibyte characters to an internal format called *wide characters*. Wide
characters are just integer types, which can hold much larger values than a
single byte. ANSI C provides a set of conversion functions for translating
between the two formats. For details on how to use these functions, see the
discussion of functions defined in `stdlib.h`, in Part II of this book. The
"Managing Data in a C Program" section in Chapter 3 also discusses how to
define wide character types and constants.

Source and Target Character Sets

Before leaving the topic of C characters, we need to say something about
the distinction between source and target character sets. The *source character set* is the one in which you write the source code for your C program.
It is the character set native to the machine on which you are running the
editor and compiler.

The *target character set*, on the other hand, may be an entirely different
one. It is the character set assumed to be present when the program is *run*
at a later time. If the program will run on the machine on which it was
compiled, the source and target sets will be the same.

If the program will run on a different machine—if a cross-compiler is
being used—the target character set may be completely different. For
example, certain compilers are used on a PC to develop code that will be run
on a mainframe. In that case, the source character set will be ASCII, whereas
the target character set could be EBCDIC.

How C Looks at Your Source Program

Suppose that you have just finished writing a brand new C program—a
statistical analysis program. Think for a moment about what you expect your
program to do. It should do three things: get some data from somewhere,
massage it according to the rules, and produce some significant numerical
results.

Like wheels within wheels, this is exactly the way the C compiler views
your program: *as data*. A C source program—also called a *translation*

unit—is input to the compiler, which transforms that data into machine-executable code. The result of source-file translation is the *object file*. Later, the linkage editor takes this object file, and possibly others, and combines them to produce an executable file, also called a *load module*.

The Phases of Program Translation

Figure 4.3 shows the process by which a C source program is translated into machine code. C compilers, like almost all modern compilers, are *syntax directed*—compilation is controlled by the syntactical structure of the source, which is recognized by the parser. Thus C compilers share the features shown here with many other compilers. You need to have a basic understanding of the terms and processes involved in compilation.

The compiler reads the source file, one character at a time, and feeds each one to the *scanner*. The scanner's function is to recognize, and then feed to the parser, discrete elements of the source code, called *tokens* (keywords, identifiers, constants, punctuation, and so forth).

The *parser* determines how the elements are grouped together. For example, an if keyword must be followed by an opening (left) parenthesis in C. If it is not, the parser flags a syntax error at that point. *Syntax checking* simply means checking the correct grouping of items in the source code.

Fig. 4.3. The C compiler at work.

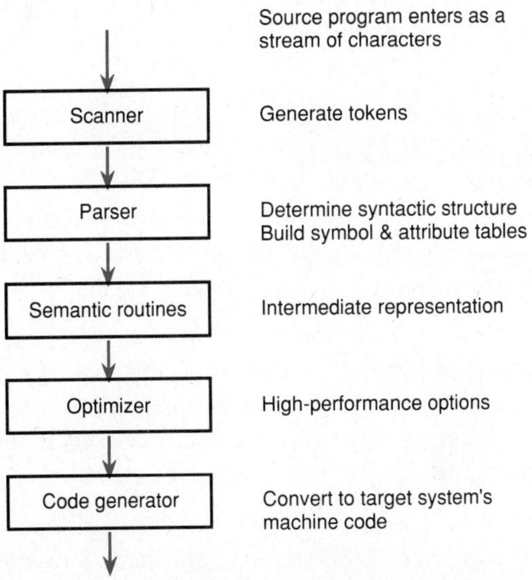

```
                    Source program enters as a
                    stream of characters

    ┌──────────────────┐
    │     Scanner      │   Generate tokens
    └──────────────────┘

    ┌──────────────────┐
    │     Parser       │   Determine syntactic structure
    └──────────────────┘   Build symbol & attribute tables

    ┌──────────────────┐
    │ Semantic routines│   Intermediate representation
    └──────────────────┘

    ┌──────────────────┐
    │    Optimizer     │   High-performance options
    └──────────────────┘

    ┌──────────────────┐
    │  Code generator  │   Convert to target system's
    └──────────────────┘   machine code
```

If the syntactical structure is determined to be correct, the *semantic routines* take over. These routines supply the *meaning* of the program. In the C statement:

```
a = b;
```

for example, the parser notes that equating one variable to another (assigning the value) is legitimate. The semantic routines determine which variables are involved, their location in the program, and what must be done to assign the value of one to the other. The result of all this, called the *intermediate representation*, frequently is stored in a temporary file on disk to make it available to the next phases. All phases so far contribute to information stored in the *symbol table*—a record of the keywords and names used in the program, together with information about how they can be used.

If an optimizer module is present (most good compilers offer one), the intermediate representation of the program is "cleaned up." Unnecessary instructions are removed, loop bodies are made more efficient, and more efficient methods of constructing the machine code in general are implemented. Using an optimizer can be very costly in the time it takes to compile the program. Most compilers that support optimizers allow you to use them as an option, not a default action.

Finally, the code generator takes the intermediate representation and uses it to produce the *target machine code*. This is the object code mentioned earlier, which is used by the linkage editor to produce the final load module. A compiler that uses separate sets of semantic routines and code generators is called a *two-pass compiler*. If these functions are merged, it is called a *one-pass compiler*. One-pass compilers impose some restrictions on the way things must be placed in your source code.

This is only the barest introduction to compiler theory. If you want to go into detail (perhaps to learn how to write a compiler with C), you may want to read *Crafting a Compiler*, by Charles N. Fischer and Richard J. LeBlanc, Jr. This is a good introductory work on compiler theory, but *any* book on this subject requires some knowledge of computer science, or at least a great deal of programming experience.

The ANSI C document specifies that a conforming compiler functions as though eight discrete phases of translation take place consecutively (even if, in practice, the tasks are merged). Actually, only the last two of the phases have to do with actual translation of source code to machine code. The phases of translation are as follows:

❑   *Source-file characters are mapped to the source character set.* Mapping includes converting trigraphs to single-character codes and end-of-line indicators to the newline character.

❑ *Continued lines of source code are spliced together to make single logical lines.* A continued line is indicated by typing a backslash just before pressing Enter. This is especially useful for writing string literals longer than will fit on one line of your display.

❑ *The source file is broken into preprocessing tokens (see the next section) and whitespace sequences (review fig. 2.1's* `isspace` *group).* During this phase, comments also are considered to be whitespace, and each is replaced by a single space.

❑ *Preprocessing directives are executed and macro references expanded.* The `#include` directive causes reading of the current file to be suspended, and processing of the named include file to begin. The included file is processed to this point only, and processing of the previously current file resumes. Includes can be nested (coded inside each other).

❑ *Escape sequences and string literals are converted to the execution character set, which could be a different character set if a cross-compiler is being used.*

❑ *Adjacent character strings are spliced into their internal format.* This means that you can define a string, together with its initializer, like this:

```
char *astring = "This is a str"
                "ing.";
```

This construction is entirely equivalent to the following:

```
char *astring = "This is a string.";
```

This syntax, which was not available with the original K & R C, is extremely convenient. It allows you to define long string literals without having to resort to the line-continuation backslash.

❑ *The first stage of actual translation now begins.* All tokens are now considered ordinary, not preprocessing, tokens. The parser and semantic routines do their work here.

❑ *The final phase is the linkage edit process.* References in one source file to objects and functions in other source files are resolved here (that is, their correct relative addresses are calculated) and the final load module is created. This is also where the C library functions are brought into the program. The load module is packaged together with all information needed for program execution in the target environment.

Tokens and Translation Units

The term *translation units* was introduced to emphasize the fact that what will become a single C program can begin life as separate source files. These source files—the multiple translation units—can be compiled individually and only later linked together into a composite load module. This capability becomes important later, when you begin to design and code large-scale projects.

As you learned earlier in this discussion, tokens are the elements detected by the scanner. To complicate matters, however, there are preprocessing tokens and ordinary tokens. *Preprocessing tokens* are handled during macro expansion (phase 4 of the translation process) and eventually result in ordinary tokens. The ordinary tokens are then handled by the compiler during actual code translation.

There are six kinds of ordinary tokens:

❏ *Keywords*. Special tokens with reserved meanings. You already have seen several keywords, such as if, else, while, int, and double. Keywords are the grammatical basis of the C language.

❏ *Identifiers*. The names you define for your variables and user-defined functions.

❏ *Constants*. A constant is a token that is the value of a variable. You already have seen character constants, as well as several numeric constants. You can change the value of a variable, but not that of a constant. Do not confuse this kind of constant with the const type variable. Such variables are similar to true constants in that you are not allowed to change the value of a const qualified variable.

❏ *String literals*. The string literals you have seen in the sample programs and code fragments are exactly what they seem to be. They are one-dimensional arrays of character. As was mentioned in the discussion of escape characters, all strings are terminated with the \0 null character. Note that you do not have to type the \0 escape when you write a string literal; the compiler adds it internally and automatically.

❏ *Operators*. The symbols used to relate and connect the parts of expressions. You are familiar with many of them (such as =, +, -, *, and /). C has a rich operator set, and there are many more than these. Each operator symbol is a token.

❏ *Punctuators*. The compiler considers the C punctuators you saw in Chapter 1 to be individual tokens.

Identifiers in General

An identifier names an object. That object may be any one of the following:

❏ A *data object*. The name of a data object is just a variable name. If it is defined in another source file, you must declare it as an *external* name. An external object has a *storage-class* of `extern`.

❏ A *user-defined function*. The identifier of a user-defined function cannot be `main`. Note that functions, unlike data objects, are assigned the `extern` storage class automatically.

❏ *One of the following: a structure tag or member, a union tag or member, the name of an enumeration, a* `typedef` *(type definition) name, a statement label, a macro name, or a macro parameter.*

Although an identifier can be almost anything you want it to be, you must observe the following rules in forming identifiers:

❏ *It cannot be one of the C keywords.* The keywords are reserved exclusively for use as part of C's basic grammar.

❏ *An identifier is an alphanumeric token that must begin with a pure alphabetic character.* This means that it can be composed of upper- and lowercase letters, the decimal digits, and the underscore character, and the first character must be either an upper- or lowercase letter or the underscore character.

❏ *If the underscore is used as the first character of an identifier, some caution is needed because this character is reserved for the compiler's internal naming scheme for external identifiers.* Generally, to avoid duplicating an identifier in one of the standard header files, you should not use the underscore as the initial character. It is common practice, however, to use the underscore in the middle of names to give some visual cues in reading the program. For example, it is much easier to read the following line:

```
a = calc_std_dev( table );
```

than it is to read this line:

```
a = calcstddev( table );
```

❏ *Internal identifiers (as opposed to externals) have names significant to 31 characters.* Names can be longer than this, but they must differ within 31 characters to be considered different by the compiler. In K & R C, names had only 8 significant characters.

❏ *External identifiers have names significant to only 6 characters.* Although a particular compiler *may* provide more significance than this, you can't count on it if you want to port your program to several different compilers.

❏ *Names within C source code are case sensitive: it makes a difference whether the character is upper- or lowercase.* ANSI allows a compiler to ignore case sensitivity for external names, however; it depends on the particular C compiler *and* on the compiler used to process the external routine (which may not be C).

Using C Reserved Words

ANSI C reserves a total of 32 tokens for use as *keywords*. The reserved words are the backbone of C grammar. You *may not* duplicate any of the reserved words as you develop your own identifiers. You *should not* duplicate several reserved function and macro names, although you can.

The C Keywords

A keyword means only one thing to a C compiler. The ANSI standard for C defines as keywords the 32 tokens shown in the C-Note "ANSI C Keywords."

Quick-Reference: ANSI C Keywords

auto	double	int	struct
break	else	long	switch
case	enum	register	typedef
char	extern	return	union
const	float	short	unsigned
continue	for	signed	void
default	goto	sizeof	volatile
do	if	static	while

What happens if you accidentally use one of the keywords in a way other than the one C expects? The program does not compile successfully, so this error can't slip by unnoticed. This error is not as dangerous as it might otherwise be.

Such a small number of keywords may seem inconsistent with the claim that C is a rich and complex language. It would be, if the complexity of C depended only on keywords. But the full power of C derives from its set of keywords *plus* its rich operator set *plus* its extensive function library.

The Standard Macros and Functions

C has always had a fairly uniform set of library functions, although different compilers provided some interesting variations. ANSI C has now defined the contents of the truly *standard* function library: the functions and their respective types and parameters, as well as a large number of standardized macro names and constant values. Compiler manufacturers are free to add functions and macros beyond these, but may not claim ANSI conformity unless the full set is present in the prescribed way. Part II of this book provides detailed specifications for the standard functions and macros, and Appendixes A and B provide a summary of their names (and associated header libraries).

The standard function and macro names also are considered reserved— but there is a difference between those names and C keywords. You should not duplicate the standard names, but doing so *may not* produce an error at compile time (or any other time). What it does is (at least) prevent you from using the standard function—your function is the only function by that name available in that program (it doesn't damage the library in any way). You already have seen the `printf()` function used frequently in the code samples, for example. `printf()` is one of the standard library functions, but it is perfectly legal (in a sense) to write your own `printf()` function, as shown in the following code fragment:

```
#include <stdio.h>

void printf( void )
{
   putchar( 'f' );
}

main()
{
   printf();
}
```

There is some protection from inadvertently redefining library functions, though. As we said—this program is legal *in a sense*. In fact, `printf()` is declared in `stdio.h` as having a certain type and certain parameters. Because this new definition doesn't match that declaration, there is a compile-time error. The danger is that you may duplicate name, type, and parameters accidentally. In that case, your version of the function is the only one available for the duration of the program.

Using Compiler Directives and Macros

By using *compiler directives*, you can control how the compiler is to go about translating source code. You can control what that source code is to be by using *macro substitution*. And you can control the way compile-time errors are handled, set up line-number controls for debugging, and control the environment in which the compiler is to work. All this is done by the C preprocessor.

Revisiting the C Preprocessor

The C preprocessor, which was mentioned in the discussion of C tokens and the translation process, does its work before the compilation process begins. The preprocessor may be bundled in with the compiler or it may be a separate utility. In some compilers, such as Turbo C, the preprocessor is available both ways to give you maximum control over the compilation process. Either way, the source code passes first through the preprocessor and is transformed in some way before the compiler is ready to generate machine code. The next few sections outline the preprocessor directives and how they work.

Before you continue reading, take a moment to review what you learned about preprocessor directives in Chapter 1. Remember the following:

❏ *All preprocessor directives begin with the # character, which signals that this line is not part of the ordinary source code.*

❏ *The semicolon character is handled differently in preprocessor directives.* Don't code one in a macro definition unless you want it to appear in the resulting source code.

❏ *Don't mix preprocessing directives and C source code on the same line.* The directives must be on a line by themselves, terminated by a physical end-of-line character (that is, by pressing the Enter key, not by coding the \n escape sequence).

❏ *Additionally, preprocessing tokens nested within a preprocessing directive are not expanded as macros, except in the cases noted in the next few sections.*

Other restrictions on how you can code a directive depend on which one it is; these restrictions are covered in the discussions of specific directives.

The Source File Inclusion Directive

Source file inclusion directives were discussed in Chapter 1 because of their almost universal presence. The format used to include the standard headers is just a specific application of a more generalized facility. In this section, you will see how to include both header files and source text files in general.

Quick-Reference: ANSI C Include Directives

Include Format	Meaning/Use
`#include` *<std-header-file>*	Standard/provided header files
`#include` *"user-header-file"*	User-defined header files
`#include` *macro-name*	A previously defined macro specifies the header file name.

The name used for a header file is assumed to be of the format *xxxxxx.x*, where the *x*'s to the left of the period are the name of the header file, and the single *x* to the right of the period is the file extension. The following rules govern the included names:

❏ *The ANSI C standard allows (but does not require) a compiler implementation to ignore upper- and lowercase distinctions.* Most implementations ignore case.

❏ *An implementation is allowed to limit (to six significant characters) the name to the left of the period.* (Again, this is not required.) For maximum portability, imposing this restriction on yourself for actual header files might be wise. Most implementations do not impose this restriction; they allow you to include any file in your program.

❑   *Normally, you should not use path overrides in the file names for includes that use the standard header inclusion format (<name>).* Although you can use path overrides for the user-defined format ("name"), you ordinarily shouldn't have to if you have set up directories correctly.

❑   *The single character extension most often used for header files is* h. This is not a requirement, however. You can use any character you want. You are not required to limit yourself to one character, either, but doing so maximizes the program's portability.

❑   *The third format's name field is a macro name, not a file name.* You could use this feature to write programs, such as the following, that are intended to be run in several different environments:

```
#define SYS OS2
...
#if SYS == DOS
    #define INC "dosenv.h"
#elif SYS == OS2
    #define INC "os2env.h"
#else
    #define INC "all.h"
#endif
...
#include INC
```

The first line tells the preprocessor to substitute OS2 wherever the macro name SYS is encountered. Next, the value of SYS is tested by the #if directives (see "Conditional Compilation Directives," later in this chapter). Because SYS is equal to OS2, the macro name INC is set to "os2env.h" by the #elif directive (see "Macro Substitution Directives," in the next section). Finally, the #include directive is expanded to #include "os2env.h". Writing the directives for such an arrangement takes some time and trouble. The advantage is that when the environment of the program changes, you need to make only one change to a macro instead of making many changes throughout the program.

A file that has been included may itself contain one or more `#include` directives, as well as the other types of directives. You can nest includes like this up to a limit that the standard leaves up to the implementation.

Macro Substitution Directives

A *macro* is a shorthand notation for something else. That "something else" may be something much longer than the macro name, something difficult to type, or something that can be made more readable by using a macro name for it.

When you think about C macros, remember that the C preprocessor is the program handling your program's code, and that it is treating the code as if it is data. It is treating your code as a sequence of characters and strings of characters. Thus, *macro substitution* or *replacement* is a process of substituting one string of characters for another—the macro name is replaced by its defined substitution string, called the *replacement list*. Refer to the Quick-Reference C-Note "ANSI C Preprocessor Macros" for a summary of macro formats.

Quick-Reference: ANSI C Preprocessor Macros

You can define a macro either as an *object-like* macro with a simple substitution string, or as a *function-like* macro with arguments. And you can undefine a macro when it is no longer needed, or when you want to redefine it for some other use.

```
#define identifier replacement-list
#define identifier(identifier-list) replacement-list
#undef identifier
```

The identifier immediately following the `#define` or `#undef` is the macro name. In object-like macros, the macro name is followed by the replacement list. The replacement list is called a "list" because it should be composed of valid C-language tokens. From the point of view of the preprocessor, the replacement list is just a character string used to replace the macro name wherever it appears. Whitespace *surrounding* the substitution string is not part of the substitution string; whitespace within it is.

Typical uses for object-like macros include the definition of common constants in a readable form (called *manifest constants*). For example, you frequently will see the constants for true and false Boolean conditions coded like this:

```
#define FALSE 0
#define TRUE 1
int table_sorted = FALSE;
void sort_table( void);
...
sort_table();
table_sorted = TRUE;
...
if ( table_sorted ) {
  /* Do something to the table */
}
```

Notice that the substitution string should not be surrounded by quotation marks (like a normal string literal) unless you intend the quotation marks to be part of the expanded text. The substitution string is assumed to begin with the first nonwhite space character following the macro name. For example, the macro definition:

```
#define TSTRING "Text stuff."
```

does not result in the code you expected if you *invoke* the macro this way:

```
char output[20];     /* Define 20-character string */
...
strcpy( output, "TSTRING" );   /* Now initialize it */
```

Because the second argument for `strcpy()` is inside a string literal, it will not be expanded—the preprocessor will not look for macro names inside the quotation marks of string literals or character constants. You could correct this by deleting the double quotation marks in the function call, but not those in the `#define` directive (because this would again require a search for macro names inside the quotation marks in the function call).

This illustrates the fact that *everything* in the substitution string (including any comments you may code in the macro definition) is used to replace the macro name when the macro is invoked. The substitution string is terminated only by the end-of-line character that also terminates the macro definition. Semicolons are handled the same way—don't code one unless you intend it to appear in the expanded source text.

Function-like macros are a little more complex than object-like macros. They have a *formal argument list* that is used to modify and control the substitution text. The formal arguments are placed inside parentheses immediately following the macro name. You don't have to use the same identifier for an argument when *invoking* the macro as when *defining* it. That is why it is called a *formal* argument. Here is an example of a function-like macro and its use:

```
#define CTOF(t) 9.0 / 5.0 * t + 32.0
double fahrenheit, centigrade;
...
centigrade = 15.0;
fahrenheit = CTOF(centigrade);
```

When the preprocessor spots the CTOF invocation in the last line of this example, it will expand that macro name, substituting *actual* arguments; the following line of code results:

```
fahrenheit = 9.0 / 5.0 * centigrade + 32.0;
```

You can have as many arguments as you like, but must use as many as you declare—don't put something in the argument list that is not referenced somewhere in the substitution string. Multiple arguments should be separated by commas in the formal parameter list. Also, when you invoke the macro, be sure that the number of arguments matches the number in the definition (see the following examples):

```
#define DIV(a,b) a / b          /* This is OK */
#define AVG3(a,b,c) (a+b+c)/3 /* This is OK, too */
#define COMP(a,b,c) a + b       /* Invalid, doesn't use c */
...
x = AVG3(m,n);                  /* Invalid, too few arguments */
```

The use of white space should be carefully controlled in function-like macros. In the #define directive, the combination of the macro name followed immediately by the opening (left) parenthesis *with no space in between* identifies the macro as function-like. Why? If a space is there, the syntax seems to declare an object-like macro: there is no way for the preprocessor to determine that you did *not* intend the free-standing parenthesis to be part of the substitution string. With this one exception, you can use white space wherever you please.

The same caveat about quotation marks and semicolons applies also to function-like macros. Don't put them there unless you intend that they should appear in the macro expansion.

You can refer to a macro argument in the substitution string in not just one—but three—ways. You can refer to an argument:

❏ *By itself.* This way has already been illustrated. The macro name is replaced by the substitution string *in toto*, with *actual* arguments replacing *formal* arguments, but no other modifications to the replacement tokens.

❑ *Following the # operator.* In the context of macro argument substitution only, # is the *string literal operator.* If x is a macro argument, the appearance of #x in the substitution string causes "x" to appear in the expansion. That is, the string operator creates a *data* string in the expansion, with the expanded argument x as its contents. Clarifying examples follow shortly.

❑ *Preceding or following the ## operator.* Again in the context of macro argument substitution only, this is the *string concatenation operator.* The concatenation operator cannot appear by itself at the beginning or end of the substitution string, because its whole purpose is to *join* the expanded argument with another C language token, forming a larger *language* string (not a data string). Unlike the string operator, the concatenation operator does not generate double quotation marks around the argument.

The string operator # can be used to create data strings enclosed in double quotation marks, as follows:

```
/*  +----------------------------------------------------+
    +  STROP.C
    +  Test the preprocessor's # string literal operator
    +----------------------------------------------------+
*/
#include <stdlib.h>
#include <stdio.h>

#define STR(x) # x

main()
{
   printf( "%s\n", "This is " STR("Wednesday") "." );
}
```

The program's output looks like this on the screen:

```
This is "Wednesday".
```

This example illustrates several interesting things about the preprocessor string operator. First, notice the use of whitespace in the macro definition of STR(x). There is a space between the # operator and the argument x in the substitution string. This is perfectly legitimate, and does not affect the manner of argument substitution. If there had been multiple arguments with whitespace between them, each instance of whitespace would have been reduced to a single space in the final substitution string. Extra whitespace before and after the substitution string as a whole would have been deleted.

Second, when `STR(x)` is invoked within the `printf()` function call, the argument used is `"Wednesday"` (not just `Wednesday`). The string operator causes the preprocessor not only to surround the argument with double quotation marks, which would produce this erroneous code:

```
printf( "%s\n", "This is " ""Wednesday"" "." );
```

but also to generate backslashes in order to protect the `"` and `\` characters encountered in the invocation, or actual, argument. The expanded macro results in the following:

```
printf( "%s\n", "This is " "\"Wednesday\"" "." );
```

As you may recall, the `\"` characters form the legitimate escape sequence for the double quotation marks. The final output, then, will contain the properly quoted word `"Wednesday"`.

Third, you can use concatenated *data* strings wherever you would define an ordinary quoted string literal. The preceding partially expanded `printf()` shows the format of concatenated string literals. The compiler (not the preprocessor) converts this to a single string literal definition that is completely equivalent to the following:

```
"This is \"Wednesday\"."
```

Concatenated string literals can be used anywhere in C source text, not just in macros. Take special note of the fact that these substrings, because they are *not* arguments or parameters as such, are *not* separated by commas. They are not the same as the expanded C source tokens generated by the `##` preprocessor concatenation operator (discussed next).

With the `##` preprocessing concatenation operator, you can flexibly create sequences of C source code, as well as data strings. The concatenation operator "pastes" together pairs of substrings; it does not supply quotation marks or protecting backslashes. If one of the substrings is also a macro, it is expanded before pasting occurs. For example, in the following macro call, the argument x is replaced with "2" before the substrings are pasted:

```
#define WHICH(x) sub_ ## x
result = WHICH(2)( 37 );
```

The second statement is expanded to

```
result = sub_2 ( 37 );
```

A few more questions about macro expansions need to be answered: Can one macro generate another? How are comments handled in macros? How do you code long macros? What are some of the pitfalls to watch out for in coding C macros? The answers to these questions can be found in the following final points about macro expansion.

❏ *Macros are rescanned.* After all the macro parameters have been located and expanded when a macro is invoked, the preprocessor rescans the result to see whether any macro names (new invocations) were generated. Thus, you can code

```
#define vers 2
#define which(x) sub_ ## x
...
result = which(vers)( 37 );
```

The macro call to `which` is first expanded to `sub_vers ( 37 )` and then finally to `sub_2 ( 37 )`. Be careful, however, to *avoid generating the same name as the macro in the process of being replaced.* This would cause a recursive, and infinite, expansion of the macro, so the preprocessor rescans and replaces any *other* macro name, but not *this* one.

Notice carefully that rescanning for macro *names* does not imply that preprocessor *directives* may be generated by macro expansions, nor may you generally embed directives within directives and rely on proper expansion of the embedded directives.

❏ *Comments are permissible in macros, as long as you understand how they will be handled.* Comments that appear in macro *definitions* also appear in later expansions of the macro. Remember that a macro definition ends only when a physical end-of-line character is found in scanning. Conversely, comments that appear in macro *invocations* do *not* appear in the expansion.

❏ *Long macro definitions are possible, using the backslash continuation character to get around the end-of-line condition*

```
#define longmac "Fourscore and seven  years ago, our \
forefathers brought forth on this continent a new \
tax office to replace the old one."
```

The backslash characters do not become part of the expansion when `longmac` is invoked; you just get the very long string of characters. This is one place where the string concatenation syntax mentioned previously won't work—the macro must be contained in *one* logical line (the first newline character terminates the macro).

❏ *Macros are not expanded inside string literals and character constants.* By the time parameter replacement begins during preprocessing, strings and character constants are already being considered as tokens, not as possible macro names or objects that might contain macro names. The `longmac` macro has its quotes embedded in the macro *definition*, so this macro call is valid:

```
printf( "%s\n", longmac );
```

If the macro did *not* have embedded quotes, a reference to `longmac` would have produced a series of tokens—one for every word in `longmac`'s sentence—which the compiler would try to interpret as variable names or other tokens. Moreover, if you tried to get around that restriction by coding

```
printf( "%s\n", "longmac" );
```

you would still have a problem, because `longmac` now is not to be scanned as a possible macro name.

❑   *Macros and complex arithmetic expressions don't mix well.* The reason is operator precedence. This subject will be covered in detail in Chapter 5, but you already probably know from algebra class that multiplications have higher precedence—they occur first—than additions. If you are not careful, this can cause insidious bugs in your program. For example,

```
#define SQUARE(x) x * x
```

looks deceptively simple. But what if you invoked the macro with an argument like this:

```
y = SQUARE( x + 2 );
```

This does not expand in the way that you probably intended. What you will get is

```
y = x + 2 * x + 2;
```

This expression actually reduces algebraically to $3x + 2$, not the intended $(x + 2) * (x + 2) = x^2 + 4x + 4$. You can use parentheses to force the proper grouping, either in the macro definition or its invocation. The definition is by far the best place to do it, just in case you forget later. You could rewrite the `SQUARE` macro like this, for example,

```
#define SQUARE(x) (x) * (x)
```

This looks a little strange, but it works. And if you write parentheses in both places, that won't hurt, either.

Conditional Compilation Directives

The *conditional compilation directives* are called the *conditional inclusion directives* in the ANSI document. Either description of these directives is apt, because their purpose is to determine whether a section of source code is to be compiled. These directives commonly are used in the standard header files to determine whether the header has already been included. The mechanism works like this:

```
/* Contents of MYHDR.H File */

#if !defined ( MYHDR )
#define MYHDR
extern int a;
extern int b;
#endif
```

This code fragment first checks whether the macro name MYHDR has already been defined. If it has not (!defined), the next three lines define the macro name (an object-like macro—no function-like parameters in the substitution string) and declare two external variable identifiers (these two lines are now compiled). The last line (#endif) tells the preprocessor that this conditional directive is complete.

This construction prevents multiple declarations of a and b, while allowing you to include MYHDR.H whenever and wherever you feel you need to. It doesn't really matter what macro name you choose for such a construction, but it clearly should be descriptive. Now study the Quick-Reference C-Note summary of conditional directives, before reading about their syntax.

Quick-Reference: ANSI C Conditional Directives

In the following list of conditional preprocessing directives, the notation [!] indicates that the logical-NOT symbol ! may optionally be present:

```
#if [!]constant-expression
#elif [!]constant-expression
#else
#if [!]defined identifier
#if [!]defined ( identifier )
#ifdef identifier
#ifndef identifier
#endif
```

The expression `constant-expression` found in the `#if` and `#elif` directives is a numeric expression that must reduce to an integer value. It may contain arithmetic and logical operators, and *it may contain macro names* as described in the following paragraphs. When `constant-expression` is evaluated, macro names are first replaced by their corresponding strings.

After preliminary macro substitution, the resulting integer expression is evaluated as a *Boolean expression* (the result is either true or false). If the expression evaluates to 0 (false), the group of lines that the `#if` precedes is not included as part of the source code. If it evaluates to nonzero (true), the group of lines is included. The lines selected to be processed may contain other directives (such as `#define` or `#include`) or ordinary C source code. This does not violate the rule that prohibits embedding directives within directives.

For example, suppose that you want to determine whether to compile code that invokes a delay loop if the central processor is an 80386 chip. You could write a sequence of directives and code like this:

```
#define CPU 286 /* Define cpu being used */
...
#if CPU == 386
#include "wait.h"   /* These two lines are not used */
wait_msec( 100 );   /* since CPU is == 286 */
#endif
```

All the conditional directives have two things in common: they all end with the `#endif` directive, and they all control the inclusion (use or nonuse) of one or more groups of code lines. A group of code lines is fittingly called a *line-group*.

The `#if`, `#elif`, and `#else` directives work together. You can have an `#if`–`#endif` standing alone, but never an `#elif` or `#else`. They group together like this:

```
#if expression
     ... main line-group
#elif expression
     ... first alternate line-group
#elif expression
     ... next alternate line-group
... other #elif's
#else
     ... default line-group if nothing else selected
#endif
```

The presence of the `#elif` and `#else` is completely optional. If you do not code them, only the initial line-group is available for selection. The `#endif`, of course, is mandatory.

However complex the #if construction may be, only one of the line-groups is selected for inclusion in compilation. The preprocessor performs its test from the top down. If the initial if condition is true, only its line-group is retained, and so on down the list. Notice that the #else has *no* conditional expression attached. If an #else directive is present, and none of the other line-groups are selected, this one unconditionally will be.

In the strictest sense, the #if defined ... and #ifdef forms are equivalent. They mean exactly the same thing. However, the newer #if defined form is preferred, because it yields a clean, unmixed notation, as in the following example:

```
#include <stdio.h>

#define TEST3

main()
{
  #if defined TEST1
    puts( "Test ** 1 ** Selected.\n" );
  #elif defined TEST2
    puts( "Test ** 2 ** Selected.\n" );
  #elif defined TEST3
    puts( "Test ** 3 ** Selected.\n" );
  #else
    puts( "Don't know what was selected!\n" );
  #endif
}
```

When you run this program, it displays the message:

```
Test ** 3 ** Selected.
```

Line-control, Error, Pragma, and Null Directives

Four other directives are seldom used, or are used in a way not completely visible to the programmer. They are the #line, the #error, the #pragma, and the # (or *null*) directives.

❑   The #line directive is used for debugging and error reporting at compile time. Ordinarily, the line number of the line being processed by the compiler is equal to one more than the number of end-of-line (newline) characters encountered so far. You can change what line number the compiler will assign to the *next* line encountered by writing the directive:

```
#line number
```

where *number* is an integer number that will be used to report the source code line number (for example, when the compiler flags a line as containing an error). This does not change the source file in any way. It only affects the way line numbers are reported. This form of the directive modifies the assigned value of the __LINE__ predefined macro (see the next section).

You can also change the *presumed* name of the source file being compiled with this form of the #line directive:

```
#line number "newname"
```

In this case, the value of __LINE__ is modified as before. In addition, the predefined macro __FILE__ is modified to reflect the value of the string literal *"newname"*, which must be enclosed in quotes as shown.

The new line number or the new filename or both can be specified as macro names that you have previously defined somewhere. You can if you wish, use the predefined macros __LINE__ and __FILE__ in your program for your own purposes, as long as you do not change them other than with the #line directive. For example, a short program whose source file name is temp.c,

```
#include <stdio.h>

main()
{
   printf( "This is line %d of file %s.\n",
__LINE__, __FILE__ );
}
```

produces this output on the display:

```
This is line 5 of file TEMP.C.
```

❑ The #error directive is used to force the compiler to issue an error diagnostic message of your choosing. Its format is

```
#error error message
```

The error message is like a string literal in that it contains text more than a character in length, but it is *not* surrounded by quotes. Code the message text just like you would write the replacement string for an object-like macro definition. For example:

```
#define MAGIC
...
#if defined( MAGIC )
#error There is no such thing as MAGIC!
#endif
```

❑   The #pragma directive is supplied to allow the compiler manufacturers to provide directives not otherwise defined by the ANSI standard. Its Format is

```
#pragma tokens
```

where *tokens* can be anything the compiler manual says it can be. Turbo C 2.0 Professional, for example, uses the #pragma directive to signal that the program contains in-line assembler code.

❑   The # or null directive is essentially just another way to introduce white space into the source program. You can use these lines to write comments or whatever you wish:

```
#
# /* This is a comment */
#
```

Predefined Macro Names

ANSI C defines a great many standard macro names that you should be aware of. Appendix A contains a complete list of these macros. Five of them are of interest with regard to preprocessing. They are intended to give the programmer, at *compile time*, access to information that he or she can use to document, debug, and develop programs.

Quick-Reference:
Preprocessing Predefined Macro Names

Macro Name	Meaning
`__LINE__`	Decimal value of the current line number
`__FILE__`	The presumed name of the current source file
`__DATE__`	The date the compiler processed the source file. This is a string literal with the format `"Mmm dd yyyy"`—the same format as the output of the `asctime()` library function (see Part II of this book).
`__TIME__`	The time the source file was compiled. This is a string literal with the format `"hh:mm:ss"`—the format of output from `asctime()`.
`__STDC__`	The decimal value 1. This is just a Boolean "true" constant indicating that the compiler being used conforms to the ANSI standard C specifications.

The values of `__LINE__` and `__FILE__` can change during compilation; `__DATE__`, `__TIME__`, and `__STDC__` remain fixed. These names should never be made the subject of a `#define` or `#undef` directive, although they are always available for interrogation.

Summary

A lot of ground was covered in this chapter. Admittedly, some of it was tedious, but all of it was important for developing powerful C programming skills. Now the fun is about to begin.

Before leaving this chapter, review the list of topics covered here. Be sure at least that you know where to look up a tricky point later. The following seven major topics of importance were covered here:

- ❏ *The C notion of bits, bytes, and characters in general.* These concepts are basic to all understanding of data as recognized and handled by C.

- ❏ *The C minimal source and target character sets, together with the distinction between source and target environments.*

- ❏ *The difference between display and control characters, and the notion of collating sequence.* You never write a program that does not use these concepts.

- ❏ *How C handles special characters.* You should know something about mnemonic and numeric escape sequences, trigraphs, and at least recall what a multibyte character can be used for.

- ❏ *The basic parts of a compiler and how it handles your source program.* Some of these concepts are brought to bear later when we get really fancy with string handling. You should also be familiar with ANSI C required phases of program translation and how this affects the compilation of your program.

- ❏ *The concepts of tokens, translation units, C identifiers, C reserved words, standard macros, and standard functions.* These are the bottom-line building blocks of your program.

- ❏ *C compiler directives and macros.* It is no mistake that a very large part of this chapter was spent discussing these. You can get by without much knowledge here if you only want to tinker with C. But if you want to do some really serious coding, you will spend a great deal of time planning and writing directives and macros.

CHAPTER **5**

Objects, Expressions, Operators, and Conversions

I n Chapter 3, you learned how to design, position, and declare the basic
data types, plus something about initializing them. That's half the game
in controlling and manipulating data in a C program. The other half is
learning how to manipulate data objects to get the results you want.

This chapter deals with topics that begin to reveal C's inner power—those
things that give it that compactness of notation and elegance of style.
Specifically, you will learn the following:

❑ *How to harness the complexity of C's storage classes to control
completely the way your data is handled.* You get full details
on the scope and duration of objects, plus what C does and
does not do when initializing variables for you, and how to
control that.

❑ *How to use separate compilation to build large programs.* You
will see how to package the program modules and what this
means in terms of accessing data objects in multiple source-file
programs.

191

❑ *How to put the full power of C expressions to work.* The C operator set is just about the most powerful general-purpose operator set available. You can do some surprising things when you understand it fully.

❑ *How C controls the conversion of one data type to another, and how you control C.* Conversions can occur implicitly, or you can perform them explicitly.

Another Look at Scope and Duration

Even though you already have the broad outlines of C's handling of variable scope and duration, you need a more detailed understanding because of the initialization rules for C and because of access to data in multiple source-file programs. We revisit this topic and go a little deeper into the ways C deals with these things.

Taking Advantage of Storage Class

In the discussion of scope in Chapter 3, we talked about *local* and *global* variables. Although these common terms describe the concept well in an intuitive way, they can be misleading; something more is needed to fully and effectively implement data objects in your programs. Do not underestimate the importance of this need. If your program's logic is the engine you use for problem solving, data objects—the simple and complex variables you define—are the fuel for the engine. (Note that the term "data" object is used to distinguish these variables from the C++ "class" objects.)

The concept of C *storage class* centers around the idea of *duration,* both automatic and static duration. In terms of basic storage class, just two kinds of objects exist—auto and static—the storage-class specifier keywords. All objects fall into one of these classes by default, and explicit use of the keywords can override the default. Figure 5.1 summarizes the characteristics of the two storage classes.

Fig. 5.1. *Storage class defaults, overrides, and characteristics.*

auto storage class

```
default for objects inside a block
 - function parameters
 - inner-declared objects

keywords used only inside a block
 - auto
 - register

created on entry to block, deleted
on exit

can have only no linkage
```

static storage class

```
default for objects outside any block

keywords used inside or outside of blocks
 - static
 - extern

objects created at compile time, and
never discarded

inner-declared objects:
 - have no linkage even if static
    unless extern specified

outer-declared objects:
 - have internal linkage if static
    specified
 - have external linkage if extern
     specified
```

auto storage class is the default for objects defined *inside a block*. This applies to both inner-declared objects and to function parameters (which are used only within the function body block). auto class objects are created on entry to the block and discarded on exit. Remember also that objects declared within a block must be declared at the top of the block—they cannot be scattered throughout the block, in contrast to objects declared outside a block.

The two keywords associated with `auto` variables can be used *only* within a block. Notice that the storage-class specifier comes before the type specifier in the examples that follow.

`auto` gives an object `auto` storage class. Because this is the default, and this keyword can be used only within a block, it seems to have been included as a keyword for the sake of completeness. The `auto` keyword is used in a declaration as follows:

```
auto int count;
```

`register` also gives an object `auto` storage class, but it does more. It informs the compiler that this object is used frequently and should be held in a system register whenever possible. You should use this keyword sparingly. On most machines, many registers are not available and those that are available are used also when operating on all other objects. Thus, there is no guarantee that this keyword causes an object always to be resident in a register—it may or may not.

Registers are restricted in size (usually a machine word) so that only a limited number of data types are candidates for the `register` keyword. Technically, the selection of possible types is implementation-defined, but it is normally the integers. In the majority of cases, you will use a `register` variable when there is a need for extremely fast integer arithmetic. The following lines of code show how to use `register` in a declaration:

```
register int i;
...
for ( i=0, i<256; ++i ) printf ( "%d\n", i );
```

`static` storage class is the default for objects defined *outside any block*. Space for `static` objects is reserved at compile time and becomes a permanent part of the program—including the record of it on disk. `static` objects are never discarded and are available throughout program execution.

Two storage-class specifier keywords are associated with `static` objects. These keywords may be used in either outer declarations *or* inner declarations, but they have a different effect on *linkage* (visibility), depending on location. Figure 5.1 shows the different kinds of linkage assigned. The next two sections develop the concept of linkage more fully. The keywords are `static` and `extern`.

`static` gives an object static duration, regardless of the declaration's location. For outer (global) declarations, this keyword makes the object invisible to other source files. For inner (local) declarations, it has no effect on visibility but can affect the program's performance. For example,

```
static int project_status; /* Now visible only in this file */
```

`extern` indicates that the *original declaration* of the object (the one that actually reserves storage for the object) is found either in *another source file*, or in a *different scope in the same source file*. External objects always have static duration. In the following line of code, for example, the integer `project_status` should be understood to have been defined in another source file and made available to the current one:

```
extern int project_status; /* Visible in all files */
```

The ANSI specifications group one keyword here that is not actually a storage-class keyword. The `typedef` keyword indicates that what follows is a "dummy layout" for a derived object. It is listed with the storage-class specifiers for "syntactic convenience" only.

Determining the Scope of an Object

The visibility, or *linkage*, of an object depends on the combination of the object's storage class and scope. Therefore, to understand linkage, you must understand *scope* clearly.

ANSI defines four kinds of scope—not just the two classes (local and global) we have been using so far. The four kinds of scope are *file, function, function prototype,* and *block.* The following paragraphs describe the kinds of scope.

File scope refers to an object appearing in an outer declaration (not in a function). This corresponds to the global object of previous discussions.

Function scope is a strange classification that does not mean exactly what it sounds like. It refers to labels used within a function (see Chapter 3). The only practical significance of this kind of scope is that you can reuse a label name in a different function without confusion.

Function prototype scope applies only to the identifiers used in the formal parameter declarations in function prototypes. These names are in scope only during the prototype declaration itself. Identifiers with function proto-types are different from the names used to identify arguments in a function *call.* Those objects have *block* scope.

New C programmers sometimes think that variables or objects declared within the `main()` function have file scope. Not true. Objects declared within `main()` are being *declared within a function body*, just like any other function's `auto` variables. They therefore have only block scope. Objects may also be declared within a block interior to the function body. These objects are in scope only inside that block.

File and block scope are the two most important classes in determining linkage. They have the most effect on combining separately compiled modules and some effect on object initialization.

In certain instances concerning object initialization and loop control, the surrounding scope (of an object or a block, respectively) becomes important. *Surrounding scope* can be viewed as the context in which something is defined. A function, for example, has block scope and is surrounded by file scope. A subordinate block (block within a block) is surrounded by a larger block scope.

Determining the Linkage of an Object

The *linkage* of an object is its visibility to other parts of the program. When the program is contained within a single source file, linkage is a subject of only minor concern, because it is obvious which parts of the program can get to which other parts. When a program resides in several source files, however, each compiled separately and linked together, linkage becomes a more important issue.

The linkage of an object is tied closely to both its scope and storage class and can be modified by changing one or the other of them. That means that linkage, like scope, is partially determined by the location of the object's declaration. Figure 5.2 graphically summarizes the different combinations of attributes affecting linkage.

As you can see from the legend in figure 5.2, three kinds of linkage exist: *internal*, *external*, and *no* linkage.

Internal linkage means visibility to all functions in the *same source file*. Objects with internal linkage have *file scope*; they are found in outer declarations.

External linkage means visibility to functions in *other source files*. Objects defined in outer declarations have external linkage by default. They have *file scope* also, because they are by definition outside any block.

Fig. 5.2. *Internal, external, and no linkage.*

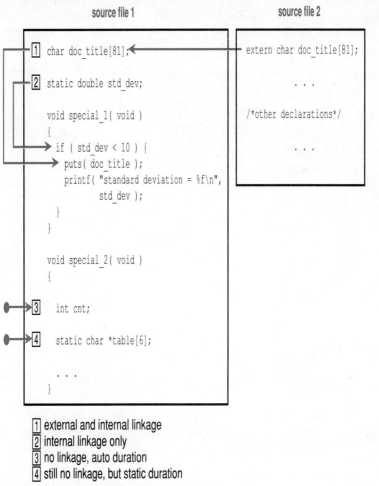

```
                source file 1                              source file 2

        1  char doc_title[81];                   extern char doc_title[81];

        2  static double std_dev;                        . . .

           void special_1( void )                /*other declarations*/
           {
             if ( std_dev < 10 ) {                      . . .
               puts( doc_title );
               printf( "standard deviation = %f\n",
                       std_dev );
             }
           }

           void special_2( void )
           {

        3    int cnt;

        4    static char *table[6];


             . . .
           }
```

1 external and internal linkage
2 internal linkage only
3 no linkage, auto duration
4 still no linkage, but static duration

No linkage means that an object is visible only *within the block* in which it is declared. These are unique objects, not used by other parts of the program. No linkage is the default for objects defined in inner declarations. Objects that have no linkage include the auto variables already mentioned, function parameters, and incomplete types. (Incomplete types are dealt with as they appear, later in the book.)

You should understand that an object's linkage *extends to all subordinate contexts*. This means that objects with file scope are visible to all functions in the source file and to all blocks interior to those functions. An object declared at the top of a block has block scope and is visible within that block and all blocks defined within it. For example, the following code fragment shows how the variable b is visible within an interior block:

```
void test_function( void )
{
  int a = 0;

  if ( a == 0 ) {
    int b = 0;
    a = 1;
    if ( a == 5 ) {
      a *= 2;
      b = a + 3; /* b is visible in interior block */
    }
  }
}
```

The linkage of an object is controlled by the presence or absence of the static and extern storage-class specifiers. The effect of these keywords depends on the location of the declaration.

Outer declarations with no storage-class specifier have both internal and external linkage by default. They can be accessed by functions in both the current, and other, source files.

Outer declarations with the static storage-class specifier have internal linkage only. This keyword effectively makes objects invisible to other source files, although not to the one in which they are defined.

Outer declarations with the extern storage-class *specifier have both internal and external linkage*. This is similar to an outer-declared object with no overriding specifier. However, the presence of the extern specifier means that the current declaration is *not* the original definition of the object.

When the original declaration of an object is in another source file, the *compiler* does not know its address while processing *this* source file—this is resolved only when the *linkage editor* processes all the separately compiled modules.

Inner declarations with no storage-class specifier have no linkage. This is the default auto class variable and is unique to the function or block in which it is defined. No other parts of the program can access it.

Inner declarations with the static storage-class specifier have no linkage. The object is still unique, invisible to other parts of the program. However, it now has static rather than automatic duration. This can give a performance boost to the function (or block) containing it, because it does not need to be allocated and initialized every time the block is entered. Allocation of space for the object occurs at compile time.

Inner declarations with the `extern` storage-class specifier have linkage that depends on the location of the original definition of the object. Regardless of the original definition's location, such an object has static duration, like all other `extern` objects. The actual linkage of the object depends on whether there is another declaration in the same source file for the object having *file scope*.

If there is such a declaration, the object has the *same linkage as the outer object*. The inner declaration also *refers to* the outer object. The following code fragment shows how several of the rules work. (The comments explain each case.)

```
#include <stdlib.h>
#include <stdio.h>
...
static double a; /* a has internal linkage only */
double b;        /* b has internal and external linkage */
extern double c; /* c has internal and external linkage, */
...              /* but refers to an object in another    */
                 /* source file. */
void some_function( void )
{
  extern double a; /* has internal linkage like outer a */
  extern double b; /* internal & external like outer b  */
  extern double c; /* internal & external like outer c  */
...
  /* Both a and b here refer to the actual objects in    */
  /* outer declarations in this file */
  /* c still refers to an object in another source file.*/
}
```

If there is no outer declaration with file scope for the same object, it has *external linkage* and refers to an object originally defined in another source file.

Controlling Initializers for Objects

Initializing data objects is much easier with ANSI-conforming compilers than it was with older K&R compilers. The reason is simply that you can code an initializer directly into a declaration anywhere, regardless of the scope or duration of the object. K&R C did not allow initializers for array, structure, or union objects that had automatic duration. That restriction is now removed. Naturally, you should not write an initializer for objects with *file scope* that also have the extern storage-class specifier; their original definitions (the ones reserving storage for the objects) are in another source file.

In one case specifically mentioned by the ANSI document, however, you may not write an initializer for an object, even if its original definition is in the same source file. If the declaration of an identifier has *block* scope, and the identifier has *internal or external linkage, no initializer* may be written for the identifier.

An object with block scope can occur only within a function or within a subordinate block in a function. The only way such an object can have internal or external linkage is to specify the extern keyword, as was done in the last sample code fragment in the preceding section.

In that fragment are three *outer* declarations for double type variables a, b, and c. The variables a and b *could* have initializers, because a has the static, and b has no storage-class specifier at all. The variable c cannot have an initializer, because it is extern.

There are *inner declarations* also for all three variables in the function some_function(), all having the extern keyword. Because all three of these variables have either internal, external, or both kinds of linkage, the declarations in some_function() may not carry initializers.

How often will you run into this situation? Admittedly, almost never. But because it is still possible, particularly when you begin to write longer, more complex programs, you should be aware of the rule.

Accessing External Data and Functions

We have mentioned *external objects* and *separate compilation* frequently. You know what an external object is and have at least a conceptual understanding of separate compilation. What you need now is concrete information on how to build a program in such a modular fashion.

To illustrate the process, a program named testcstr.c, shown in listing 5.1, is developed over the next few sections. This program calls numeric-to-string conversion functions located in a second source file and calls high-precision timing routines located in a third source file to benchmark one of the conversion functions.

Listing 5.1. `testcstr.c` *(Test numeric-to-string conversion).*   *QuickC 2.5*

```
1   #include <stdlib.h>
2   #include <stdio.h>
3
4   #include "cvtstr.h"
5   #include "timer.h"
6
7   main()
8   {
9      double pi = 3.1415926;
10     int count = -486;
11     long population = 250000000;
12
13     printf( "There were %s items counted.\n", cvtitos( count ) );
14     printf( "The population is currently %s.\n",
15             cvtltos( population ) );
16
17     start_bench();
18     printf( "The value of PI is %s.\n", cvtdtos( pi, 3 ) );
19     stop_bench();
20     printf( "CVTDTOS required %.4f seconds.\n", duration() );
21
22     start_bench();
23     printf( "PI again is %.4f.\n", pi );
24     stop_bench();
25     printf( "PRINTF required %.4f seconds.\n", duration() );
26  }
```

The program in listing 5.1 is short and simple, because all the work is being done by functions located in other source files. The object code from these functions was linked together with this program's object file to make the complete executable program file. Lines 4 and 5 of listing 5.1 contain #include directives to read in the headers for the other source files, and to tell the compiler what to expect from those functions.

Initially, the discussion of building complex programs proceeds as if you were going to perform the process completely manually—compiling each of the source files, one at a time, and then running the linkage editor to build the finished executable program file. This gives you some background on how the parts of a complex program work together and on how to use the basic tools in a C compiler package. After that, we show you a better way.

Compiling Modules Separately

The first step in designing a multiple source file program is to decide what should be placed in which source file.

One of the source files must contain one and only one `main()` function. Normally, the name of this file should be the same as the program name you want to use later for execution—but this is not absolutely required. In the program we are building here, for example, the source file `testcstr.c` is the main file, and the finished executable program resides eventually in file `testcstr.exe`.

In many cases, the main source file contains only a `main()` function, which calls the support functions in other modules as needed. Although this is common, it is by no means universal. You may write any functions you want into the main source file.

Each secondary source file should contain related data objects and functions. This is an instinctive thing to do, not something you have to force yourself into. The `#includes` in lines 4 and 5 of listing 5.1 imply that two secondary source files exist for this sample project. They are `cvtstr.c`, shown in listing 5.2, and `timer.c`, which is documented in Appendix F (see listing F.1).

Listing 5.2. `cvtstr.c` *(Separate source for numeric-to-string conversion functions).*   *QuickC 2.5*

```
 1   #include <stdlib.h>
 2   #include <stdio.h>
 3   #include <string.h>
 4   #include <math.h>
 5
 6   static char outstr[21];
 7
 8   char *cvtitos( int x );
 9   char *cvtltos( long x );
10   char *cvtdtos( double x, int precision );
11   void str_invert( char *s );
12
13   char *cvtitos( int x )
14   {
15      static int i;
16      static div_t ans;
17
18      ans.quot = 0; /* Get everything initialized */
19      ans.rem = 0;
20      i = 0;
```

```
21     if ( x < 0 ) {                    /* If negative, */
22       *( outstr + i++ ) = '-';   /*   set sign in output, */
23       x = 0 - x;                  /*   and make positive */
24     }
25     ans.quot = x;
26
27     /* --- Put the digits out backwards --- */
28     do {
29       ans = div( ans.quot, 10 );
30       *( outstr + i++ ) = ans.rem + 48; /* Make display char */
31     } while ( ans.quot >= 10 );
32     if ( ans.quot > 0 ) *( outstr + i++ ) = ans.quot + 48;
33
34     *( outstr + i ) = '\0'; /* Terminate the string */
35     if ( *outstr == '-' ) str_invert( (outstr + 1 ) );
36     else str_invert( outstr );
37     return( outstr );
38  }
39
40  char *cvtltos( long x )
41  {
42     static int i;
43     static ldiv_t ans;
44
45     ans.quot = 0; /* Get everything initialized */
46     ans.rem = 0;
47     i = 0;
48     if ( x < 0 ) {                    /* If negative, */
49       *( outstr + i++ ) = '-';   /*   set sign in output, */
50       x = 0 - x;                  /*   and make positive */
51     }
52     ans.quot = x;
53
54     /* --- Put the digits out backwards --- */
55     do {
56       ans = ldiv( ans.quot, 10L );
57       *( outstr + i++ ) = ans.rem + 48; /* Make display char */
58     } while ( ans.quot >= 10 );
59     if ( ans.quot > 0 ) *( outstr + i++ ) = ans.quot + 48;
60
61     *( outstr + i ) = '\0'; /* Terminate the string */
62     if ( *outstr == '-' ) str_invert( (outstr + 1 ) );
63     else str_invert( outstr );
64     return( outstr );
65  }
66
67  char *cvtdtos( double x, int precision )
```

Listing 5.2. continues

Listing 5.2. continued

```
68   {
69      static char hold[21];
70      static double dint, dfrac;
71      static long integer, fraction;
72      static char *p, *q;
73
74      dfrac = modf( x, &dint );      /* Separate the parts */
75      integer = (long)dint;         /* Cast the integer part */
76      if ( dfrac < 0.0 ) dfrac *= -1.0; /* Discard extra sign */
77      for ( ; precision > 0; precision-- )
78         dfrac *= 10;                          /* Scale */
79      dfrac += 0.5;                             /* Round */
80      fraction = (long)dfrac;    /* Cast the fraction part */
81      p = hold;
82      cvtltos( integer );
83      q = outstr;
84      while ( *p++ = *q++ ) ;         /* Copy integer part */
85      p--;
86      *p++ = '.';                    /* Splice in a period */
87      cvtltos( fraction );
88      q = outstr;
89      while ( *p++ = *q++ ) ;        /* Copy fraction part */
90      return( hold );
91   }
92
93   void str_invert( char *s )
94   {
95      static char *p;
96
97      if ( !*s ) return;        /* Null string, no work */
98      p = s;
99      while ( *p ) p++; p--; /* Position to end of string */
100     while ( s < p ) *s ^= *p, *p ^= *s, *s++ ^= *p-- ;
101  }
```

Look at cvtstr.c, listing 5.2 as we review some of what you just learned about linkage and external objects. A brief explanation of its functions also is in order.

First, this source file has only one variable with file scope—one global variable. This variable is outstr, in line 6. It's an array of characters—a string—with room for 20 characters plus the null-terminator byte required for C strings. The most interesting thing about it is that it clearly is meant to be used only by the cvtstr.c source file code; it has the static storage-class specifier. Thus outstr has file scope, but only internal linkage. Less technically, it has global scope for this source file only.

Next, the function prototypes are in lines 8–11. Four functions reside in this source file: `cvtitos()`, `cvtltos()`, and `cvtdtos()` convert integers, long integers, and double floating-point types, respectively, to strings, and `str_invert()` reverses the order of characters in a string. `str_invert()` is called by the other functions during the conversion process.

The processes for converting integers and long integers are quite similar, and converting doubles to strings basically works by calling the long integer conversion services. Therefore, we describe only how any integer can be converted to a string. This is followed with comments on the `modf()` function and an explanation of `str_invert()`.

Conceptually, converting integers to strings of display characters is very much like the methods used in hex dumping data (refer to Chapter 3 and the `sdump.c` program in listing 3.1). The process is one of *scaling* partial results as they are developed.

Chapter 4 mentioned that the ANSI standard for C requires that the numeric values for the display characters 0 through 9 be *contiguous;* there must be no gaps in value. The ASCII collating sequence observes this rule. The values are decimal 48 through 57. Therefore, you can add decimal 48 to the integer partial results to get the display characters. You can see this being done in lines 30 and 32 of `cvtitos()`, for example.

How are the partial results calculated? Consider the value used in the test program. Line 10 of listing 5.1 (the main program, `testcstr.c`) shows that –486 is to be converted to a string. Just ignore the minus sign for a moment and think about what happens if you successively divide this number by 10. On the first pass, you get 48, remainder 6—and 6 is the first partial result. Add 6 + 48 = 54, and you have the numeric value for display `'6'`. Apply this process again to 48 to obtain 4, remainder 8, and scale again. On the last pass, you have 4 < 10; you stop and scale the quotient rather than the remainder. This is all done in lines 25–32.

Two techniques used in this process may need some explanation. First, notice that the `div()` function is used to develop quotients and remainders for integers and that `ldiv()` is used for long integers. Full details on these functions are found in Part II, Chapter 17; you may want to look them up now. These functions return a complex object—a *structure*—rather than a simple variable.

The second technique used in these functions also seems peculiar on the surface, but makes sense when you think about it. Both the integer and long-integer conversion routines store the display characters *backwards* in the output string `outstr`. They do so because the partial results are derived backwards (486 yields 6, then 8, then 4) but the output string is accessed from left to right—the most natural way—because the routine needs only to increment an index variable on each pass. Thus, the number 486 is stored in the string as "684". This is why str_invert() is necessary.

A couple of things need to be said about str_invert(). Most compilers supply a library function, strrev(), which performs exactly this function—reversing a string. Because this is *not* an ANSI standard library function, however, we supplied our own version. You may find it useful or informative.

You may notice also that the code in str_invert() (lines 93–101, listing 5.2) is *extremely* cryptic. This is so because full advantage has been taken of C's operator set and compact notation to achieve two goals:

1. To perform the reversal of order in place, using no extra storage to temporarily hold a character

2. To achieve the absolute maximum speed, short of rewriting the function in assembler

Avoiding the use of holding storage should not be new to you. You saw how that was done in Chapter 3 (exchange.c, listing 3.5). You might want to review that sample program to refresh your memory on using the *exclusive-OR* for this purpose. As for the advanced use of pointers for the sake of speed, frankly, we are deferring that discussion until Chapter 8, "Programming with Pointers, Arrays, and Strings." The use of the comma operator is discussed a little later in this chapter.

Finally, the modf() function, line 74 in listing 5.2, is something you have not yet seen. Its purpose is to separate the whole number part and the fraction part of a double floating-point number, making them separately available—as double floats, not integers. Refer to Part II, Chapter 14, for details on this function.

timer.c is not listed here. Its internals are far beyond the scope of this chapter and are fully documented in Appendix F. The names of its functions are given in the next section, but for now, let's focus on how to build programs from multiple source files.

Setting Up the Header Files

Turn back to figure 5.2 for a moment. It contains two boxes, representing two source files, both of which declare a string named doc_title. The original definition (the one that actually reserves storage for the object) is in source file 1; the declaration having the extern specifier is in source file 2.

Now suppose that you have a set of functions and data objects in a source file which is used by many of your programs. If you make no other provision for it, you have to code the external references for *every external object and function* in *each new program* (that is, for every object and function you intend to be visible across source files), but that is what header files are for!

When you write the code for a source file like this, you should create (at that time) the header file for the data objects and functions it contains. Figure 5.3 shows the process of developing such a header file.

Fig. 5.3. *Header files for separate compilation.*

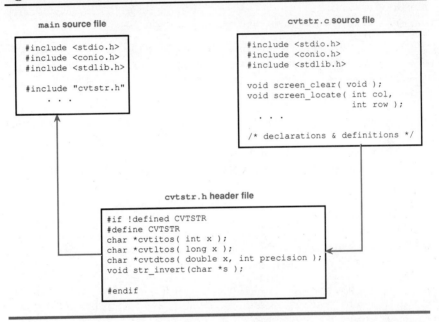

main **source file**

```
#include <stdio.h>
#include <conio.h>
#include <stdlib.h>

#include "cvtstr.h"
    . . .
```

`cvtstr.c` **source file**

```
#include <stdio.h>
#include <conio.h>
#include <stdlib.h>

void screen_clear( void );
void screen_locate( int col,
                     int row );

    . . .

/* declarations & definitions */
```

`cvtstr.h` **header file**

```
#if !defined CVTSTR
#define CVTSTR
char *cvtitos( int x );
char *cvtltos( long x );
char *cvtdtos( double x, int precision );
void str_invert(char *s );

#endif
```

Figure 5.3 highlights an important consideration about header files. In long and complex programs, you may find that the #include for a given header file appears more than once in a source file. You can use the conditional compilation and substitution macros to prevent the inadvertent redeclaration of external objects and functions. For example, cvtstr.h appears as follows:

```
#if !defined CVTSTR
#define CVTSTR
char *cvtitos( int x );
char *cvtltos( long x );
```

```
char *cvtdtos( double x, int precision );
void str_invert( char *s );
#endif
```

The preprocessing string CVTSTR can be anything you want it to be; it does not have to match the program name. Because it does match here, notice that it was coded in uppercase letters to avoid confusion but still convey which header file it is. Because C is a case-sensitive language, remember that all references to CVTSTR (the macro name, that is) must use only uppercase characters.

The extern storage-class specifier is noticeably missing from the declarations in cvtstr.h. This header file contains only function prototypes, and functions are always assumed to have external linkage (if they do not carry the static keyword—those that do are not in the header).

Leaving out the extern keyword is fine for function prototypes, because they do not *define* functions, they only declare them. What about data objects? Do they require the extern keyword in a header? They do if you want them to indicate linkage to external objects.

As you should recall, an #include directive can be used to pull *anything* into the source file. After the included text has been merged, it is compiled just like everything else. If you therefore neglect to specify extern when it *should* be present, the compiler reacts to the declarations as if they were the original declarations for the objects, reserving space for them, but this has already been done in the *other* module, as well. Treating external objects as if they are not external does two things to your program: it prevents access to the objects in the other source file; and it confuses the linkage editor, which is now presented with the dilemma of dealing with two *different* objects that have the same name.

Thus, you can omit the extern keyword for function prototypes for functions in other source files, but should use it for external *data objects*. The timer.h header file, for example, contains

```
#if !defined TIMER
#define TIMER
extern unsigned long ticks;
extern unsigned long begin_time;
extern unsigned long end_time;
extern unsigned long far *clock;

extern void (interrupt far *oldint8)();

void start_bench( void );
void stop_bench( void );
double duration( void );
#endif
```

A final situation has not been mentioned. In the project we are developing here, `testcstr.c` refers to functions in `cvtstr.c`, but not the other way around. Therefore a `cvtstr.h` header is included in `testcstr.c`, but there is no `testcstr.h`. What if two source files refer to external objects or functions in *each other*? Then you may need two header files.

Suppose that you have two hypothetical source files, `one.c` and `two.c`. `one.c` is the main program source file, and `two.c` contains a collection of support and service functions. But *both* of them have objects referred to by the other. You need two header files, arranged like this:

```
/* one.c - main program */    /* two.c - support functions */
#include "twoc.h"                 #include "onec.h"
```

Coding References to Other Modules

When referring to external data and functions, you have only a few rules to go by, all of which make good common sense. These rules follow:

1. Refer to (call) functions from any source file as you would in the source file in which the function definition resides. All source files calling a function should have a function *prototype* for it (a header file is a good way to provide this), but only one source file should have the function *definition*. Secondary declarations of a function in prototypes do not need the `extern` keyword, because it is a prototype and `extern` is the default.

2. All data objects with file scope that are to be shared across source files should have the `extern` keyword, *except* the original definition, which actually reserves storage for the object. It is possible to supply the `extern` keyword for *all* declarations of the object—the one with an initializer is considered the original definition of the object. Because this is confusing, the practice of not using `extern` with the original declaration is recommended.

3. A corollary to the preceding rule is that you should write an initializer for a data object only with the original definition, not redeclarations in other source files. The source file would compile correctly, but the linker would produce an error to the effect that the object already exists in another source file.

4. Having properly identified external references (again, in a header file), refer to external data objects (fetch and store values) as you would in the source file in which the original definition resides.

Now all the source files for your program presumably exist, with all external references properly coded. According to the game plan, this is the time to compile the source files separately, resulting in an object file for each one.

How this is done varies from compiler to compiler. For products with integrated development environments, compilation is just a keystroke away. For other products, a command invocation must be used (products with integrated environments supply command-line access, as well). The following three commands, for example, could have been used to compile the source files separately:

```
C>QCL -c testcstr.c

C>QCL -c cvtstr.c

C>QCL -c timer.c
```

In these commands, QCL is the name of the compiler program (because QuickC was used for this project) and the -c *option flag* tells the compiler to compile only (stop after generating the .OBJ file—QuickC can compile and automatically invoke the linker).

Linking the Modules Together

The linkage editor (linker) performs two vital functions in the program building process:

1. It packages all the object modules (files) together in one executable file. On any machine, but especially on PC-based machines, this is not just a matter of copying several files into one file, one after the other. The compiler has generated code, data, and stack *segments* (discrete areas of storage) for *each* module separately. These must all be collated and grouped correctly in the executable file (or *load module*, which on PCs, is the .EXE file). This part of the process, however, is highly dependent on the machine and operating system.

2. It resolves in the load module the *relative* addresses of objects and functions, as well as external type references to them. The relative address is just the *offset* (number of bytes) from the

beginning of the load module to the location of the actual definition of the object. An offset is used because the program may not be loaded at the same place in RAM every time the program is run (at run time, the operating system's program loader performs the final resolution into absolute addresses).

Figure 5.4 shows the linkage editor performing this process to build a load module for the `testcstr.exe` program.

Fig. 5.4. *Linking the program modules.*

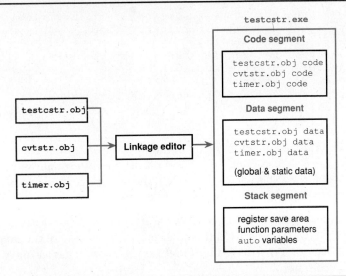

The command line used to start the process shown in figure 5.4 was

```
C>link testcstr.obj+cvtstr.obj+timer.obj,testcstr.exe;
```

Again, the particular command varies from package to package. In this case, the Microsoft linker was used because QuickC is a Microsoft product. Whatever the compiler package, however, having to key such a command frequently—as you certainly do when you develop a complex project—could quickly become irritating. The process is tedious, time consuming, and invites keystroke errors (in which case, you get to retype it!).

This is where the MAKE utility mentioned in Chapter 1 can save a great deal of time (the Microsoft version is called NMAKE). Suppose that, after making a small correction to only one source file, you could rebuild the whole .EXE file with just one short command, as follows:

```
C>nmake -ftestcstr.mak
```

Wouldn't that be better than having to retype both the compile and link commands whenever you make a correction? Experience answers, "You *bet!*" All you have to do is use the text editor *once* to create a file (called a *makefile*) named testcstr.mak, such as this one:

```
# ----- Dependency and link command for .EXE file -----
testcstr.exe: testcstr.obj cvtstr.obj timer.obj
     link testcstr.obj+cvtstr.obj+timer.obj,testcstr.exe;
# ----- Dep. and compile command for testcstr.obj -----
testcstr.obj: testcstr.c cvtstr.h timer.h
     QCL -c testcstr.c
# ----- Dep. and compile for cvtstr.obj -----
cvtstr.obj: cvtstr.c cvtstr.h
     QCL -c cvtstr.c
# ----- Dep. and compile for timer.obj -----
timer.obj: timer.c timer.h
     QCL -c timer.c
```

This file contains all four of the commands given earlier for building testcstr.exe. It also contains a good bit of other information, which is used by MAKE/NMAKE to determine when these commands are to be used. We analyze these statements one piece at a time.

MAKE statements beginning with the # sign are comments. A comment can appear between lines, as in this example, or at the end of the line after a MAKE statement. Everything after the # sign is ignored; it is assumed to be part of the comment.

MAKE statements come in pairs. In the basic form of makefile shown here (there are lots of bells and whistles we don't cover because your manual does it better), such a pair of lines is called a *description block*. The first line in the description block contains a *dependency condition*. For example, the first line of the first dependency block in testcstr.mak contains the following:

```
testcstr.exe: testcstr.obj cvtstr.obj timer.obj
```

This line indicates that testcstr.exe (the *target field*) is dependent on the state of three object files (the *dependent fields*). Dependent in what way? If the files listed in the dependent fields are *newer* than the target (based on the files' date and time stamps on disk), the target file must be updated. But how is the target file to be updated?

The second line of the pair handles this process. This second line:

```
link testcstr.obj+cvtstr.obj+timer.obj,testcstr.exe;
```

should be a valid *command* (in this case, the link command) and is executed if the dependent conditions require it.

The command line should begin with either a *tab* or a *blank*. In summary, the first description block here specifies that if any one of the object files is newer than `testcstr.exe`, relink `testcstr.exe`.

Description blocks can appear in any order, but some orders are better than others. The order in which the description blocks appear doesn't matter to MAKE—it checks them *all* and executes any of the necessary commands to get everything updated. MAKE notes (and takes into account) which dependent fields are also targets in other description blocks. All you have to worry about is getting the description blocks in there. For instance, omitting the `testcstr.exe` dependency, or writing it twice, wouldn't make much sense.

Even though MAKE doesn't care about the order, we think that using the order shown in this example is easier on the eye. It begins with the desired outcome at the top of the makefile and works backward in a logical order, until every possible module has been included.

As you can see, using MAKE to control complex projects makes a great deal of sense. It saves you the administrative work of keeping up with whether the modules are up to date. MAKE doesn't do extra work either. It processes only those files detected as being out of date. This is much more efficient, for example, than using a DOS batch file (which would recompile and relink everything every time).

When the program has been link edited, you can run `testcstr.exe` to produce the following report on screen:

```
There were -486 items counted.
The population is currently 250000000.
The value of PI is 3.142.
CVTDTOS required 0.0025 seconds.
PI again is 3.1416.
PRINTF required 0.0009 seconds.
```

Now you know how to declare, define, and access both functions and data anywhere, whether in a simple or complex program. Next, you see what you can do with them.

Understanding C Expressions

The fundamental vehicle for manipulating data in a C program is the *expression*. The ANSI document defines an expression as a sequence of operators and operands that specifies computation of a value, that designates an object or a function, that generates side effects, or that performs some combination of these.

It is pretty clear what goes between the operators—objects do. What happens to the objects depends entirely on the operators, and there are operators that affect every object in some way—even functions are treated as objects in some respects.

Rules Governing C Expressions

Clearly, there must be rules that govern how operands and operators can be put together; otherwise, the compiler would not be able to sort it all out. To grasp the rules, you need to understand three terms: *side effects*, *sequence points*, and *subexpressions*.

You first saw side effects in Chapter 3, where they were defined as modifying an object's value in a way that is not part of the statement's primary purpose. Now a more accurate definition is needed. ANSI defines a side effect as *any change in the program's execution environment* and in particular, as the act of *accessing a volatile object*, *modifying an object*, *modifying a file*, or *calling a function* that does any of these things.

Sequence points, in contrast to side effects, represent points of stability in the execution environment. They occur at those times during execution of a program when everything is temporarily complete; the effects of all previous expressions are complete, and evaluation of the next expression has not yet begun. Nothing, at that instant, is changing. Sequence points occur at three major places:

1. At the call to a function, after the arguments have been evaluated. That is, evaluation of the call arguments is complete, but the current scope has not been suspended nor has the scope of the called function been entered.

2. At the end of the first operand of: logical AND (&&), logical OR (||), the conditional operator (?), and the comma operator (,). Sequence points are defined in these places to guarantee a particular order of evaluation. In the following example

   ```
   if ( a < b && c < d ) { /* do something here */ }
   ```

the `if` statement says that both `a < b` and `c < d` must be true before the target statement can be executed. To perform the test correctly, `a < b` must be evaluated completely and a sequence point reached before logical AND processing can occur.

3. At the end of a full expression. This includes expressions in an initializer, to the right of an expression statement, in the controlling conditional expression in an `if` or `switch` statement, in the controlling conditional statement in a `do` or `do-while` statement, and in all three conditional expressions in a `for` statement.

A subexpression is a sequence of operators and operands that could stand by itself as a complete expression, syntactically. Thus, the assignment expression `a = c + b` contains four subexpressions: all three identifiers standing alone, as well as `c + b` (but not `a =`).

The rules for forming valid C expressions fall into five major points:

1. Between the preceding and next sequence points, an object's stored value may be *modified once, at most*, by the evaluation of an expression. Additionally, the prior value (the one before evaluation began) of an object may be fetched (retrieved) only for the purpose of determining the value to be stored. For example, the assignment expression:

```
i = i + 1;
```

is perfectly legitimate, whereas the expression

```
i = ++i + 1;
```

is not—the value of `i` is not only fetched twice, it is also updated before the evaluation of the expression is complete. The syntax of the second expression is considered "undefined" (but most compilers evaluate it correctly).

2. The order of evaluation of subexpressions and the order in which side effects take place are undefined, except as indicated by the syntax or otherwise specified by the standard. However, no matter how the expression is *actually* handled internally, it is evaluated in a manner consistent with the syntax specified in the expression. Floating-point operations, for example, are not computationally commutative, even though they may be so mathematically. ANSI specifies a guaranteed no-regrouping rule that prevents subtleties like this from destroying expression results.

3. All operators *except* the bitwise operators (˜, <<, >>, &, ^, and |), can have operands of any legitimate arithmetic type. You can add double floats, integers, characters, and so on, for example. Because the bitwise operators depend on the internal sequence of bit values in an integer, however, their operands *must* be integer types.

4. If an *exception* occurs during the evaluation of an expression, the outcome is undefined—left to the particular compiler to do something. It may do nothing. An exception is considered to be a result that is not mathematically defined or cannot be represented correctly by the object type.

5. Finally, the *stored value* of an object can be accessed only by an identifier with *compatible type*. The rule deals with alternate means of accessing a *single* object (called *aliasing*). The compatible types are as follows:

   a. The same type as the object

   b. A qualified version of the same type (one that has either the `const` or `volatile` type qualifier)

   c. A signed or unsigned version of the same basic type

   d. A signed or unsigned and qualified version of the same basic type

   e. A member object of a structure or union that is compatible in the ways already described

   f. A character type

All but the last of these compatible types are permitted because the variations in declaring such aliased objects do not result in any expected differences in the internal structure of the object. Signed and unsigned integers, for instance, have a common range of values, the representation of which is exactly the same for both types. The following code fragment illustrates using compatible integer types:

```
signed first_val;   /* Here is the signed integer */
unsigned *some_val; /* A pointer to any unsigned integer */
...
some_val = &first_val; /* Use address-of to point to int */
*some_val = 37U;       /* Store a value in the object */

/* ---- This printf() displays a value of 37 ---- */

printf( "The value is: %d\n", first_val );
```

The stipulation that a character type—or more precisely, a pointer to type character—can be used to access *any* object is an important one. This allows the C programmer a means of manipulating any object, however structured internally, one byte at a time. The following code fragment shows how to use a pointer to char to access the individual bytes of an unsigned long variable:

```
#include <stdlib.h>
#include <stdio.h>

main()
{
  unsigned long big_value = 1193180UL;
  char *byte;
  int i;

  byte = (char *)&big_value;
  for ( i=3; i>=0; i-- )
    printf( "%.2X ", (unsigned char)byte[i] );
}
```

The preceding sample code produces the following output:

```
00 12 34 DC
```

Primary Expressions

All the definitions and rules in the preceding section might lead you to believe that there are many possible types of expressions. In fact, there are just four: *primary* expressions, *lvalue and rvalue* expressions, *function designator* expressions, and void expressions.

Primary expressions are the simplest of all expressions. They are expressions with *no operators*, though one primary expression is a bit more complicated than that. Primary expressions can include the following:

Identifiers. An identifier is a primary expression if it has been declared as designating an object (making it an *lvalue*) or a function (making it a function designator). These two further classes are covered in more detail in the next two sections.

Constants. A constant is a primary expression that has a type, as described earlier in the book, which can include floating, integer, enumeration, or character types (and their variations).

String literals. A string literal is a primary expression having type array of char or perhaps array of wchar_t (wide character). A string literal always has static duration and is considered an *lvalue* also.

Parenthesized expressions. This is the one that stretches our definition just a bit. A parenthetical expression, such as (a + b + c), forces the parsing routines to consider it as a single entity. If the interior expression denotes an object—as opposed to a value—it is considered an *lvalue*; if a function, it is a function designator; and if void, it is a void expression. Of course, it could just be a plain expression yielding a value, in which case, it has a type depending on the mix of operands. This is covered later in the chapter in the discussion of type conversions.

rvalue and *lvalue* Expressions

An intuitive understanding of the terms *rvalue* and *lvalue* usually is sufficient: an *rvalue* is anything that can appear to the right of an assignment, and an *lvalue* is anything that can appear to the left of an assignment. In an assignment statement such as this

identifier1 = identifier2;

either identifier could stand in either position, *lvalue* or *rvalue*. But in an assignment statement such as the following:

identifier1 = expression;

the expression on the right cannot be used as an *lvalue* (unless it is also an object identifier).

This leads directly to the more accurate definition of an *lvalue* found in the ANSI standard: An *lvalue* is an expression (with an *object* type or an incomplete type other than void) that *designates an object*.

The more precise ANSI definition of an *lvalue* presents an opportunity to reexamine the concept of an identifier as a primary expression *that is also an lvalue*. How many different kinds of expressions exist that designate an object (again, as opposed to simply yielding a value) and may be an *lvalue*? Just these three:

❑ *A simple identifier is by definition both a simple expression and a primary expression.* A simple identifier can be an *lvalue*.

❑ *A pointer identifier is itself an object and can be an lvalue.* That is, a pointer, but not necessarily the thing it points to, can be an *lvalue*. Therefore, you can write the following kind of statement:

```
char *s;    /* Define a pointer to a string */
...
s = s + 1;  /* Update the pointer */
```

In this example, the pointer—not the object being pointed to—is being manipulated.

❏ *A dereferenced pointer may or may not be an lvalue, depending on what is being pointed to.* Remember that everything in C has one of three generic types: *object* type, *function* type, or *incomplete* type. According to the definition, only object types and incomplete types other than void may qualify as an *lvalue*. The following code illustrates the difference:

```
unsigned char ch;                   /* Declare an object */
unsigned char (*input)( void ); /* Declare function pointer */
...
input = fgetc;   /* OK, gets address of fgetc() */
ch = (*input)(); /* OK, ch is object and lvalue */
ch += 1;         /* OK, ch still lvalue */
(*input) += 1;   /* WRONG, (*input) is a function */
```

Because *lvalue* now essentially means *object locator*, the interesting possibility arises of having an *lvalue* that cannot appear on the left side of an assignment. This can occur if the object has array type, an incomplete type, or a const-qualified type or if it is a structure or union possessing a member variable with a const-qualified type. An *lvalue* that does not suffer from any of these shortcomings is now called a *modifiable lvalue*.

The new ANSI definition of *rvalue* makes little difference, compared to its old usage. (The old meaning of rvalue was simply anything that could legally appear on the right side of an assignment statement.) An *rvalue* is just the *value of an expression*. This definition still permits the observation that anything that is an *lvalue* may also be an *rvalue*, but not necessarily the other way around.

Function Designator Expressions

A *function designator* expression has *function type*—not object or incomplete type. The only way to form a function designator expression is by using the function's identifier, as follows:

```
char *gets( char *s );
char *(*instring)( char *s );
```

The first line simply declares a function that returns a pointer to char (a string). The function designator is gets, which is one of the standard I/O functions.

The second line declares a *pointer* to a function that returns a pointer to char. In this case, instring is both the function designator and the pointer. How function designator expressions are used to call functions is explained shortly, in the "Postfix Operators" section.

void Expressions

A void expression has no type at all—not function, not object, not incomplete. The only one way to form a void expression is to call a function that has void type, as in the following example:

```
void no_function( void );
...
no_function(); /* A void expression */
```

This makes perfect sense when you recall that a function may return a void type, but a void *object* is a contradiction in terms.

Controlling the C Operators

In the next few sections, you learn how to classify and group the operators, their exact effect in expressions, and perhaps most important of all, how they control the *order of evaluation* of an expression.

C has a particularly rich operator set; a great deal of the language's power comes from it. If you don't learn anything else about C, then learn *this* subject.

Classifying the C Operators

In this book, we group the C operators into seven types, or kinds, of usage (the *postfix, unary, cast, binary*, simple and compound *assignment, conditional*, and *comma* operators).

This arrangement follows but does not quite duplicate the ANSI order of presentation. In particular, the binary operator groups and the simple and compound operator group, contain several of the ANSI groupings.

The operators, however classified, are *presented in the order of their precedence* in expression evaluation, with the highest precedence first. The operands of operators having *higher precedence* are *evaluated first* in an expression. Operators have equal precedence within each section. Where our arrangement differs from ANSI's, precedence is stated explicitly. Remember that a subexpression in parentheses is considered a primary expression—it has higher precedence than all the operators about to be discussed. Parentheses frequently are used to force a particular order of evaluation (as they are in algebraic formulae).

The *associativity* of the operators also is discussed. This property of an operator determines the order in which the operands are "associated" with it and not the strictly mathematical associative property. Associativity makes a great difference in evaluation. Consider an assignment statement like this:

```
a = ( b / 3 ) + 37;
```

The equality operators (including simple assignment as in this example) cause the right side of the assignment to be evaluated first. Then the result is made the value of the left operand (*lvalue*). Clearly, the evaluation of this expression could not proceed in any other way.

After operator precedence, associativity is the most important factor determining the order of evaluation of an expression. Although the standard allows either operand to be evaluated first, they are *applied to the operator* in the stated order. This is also called *grouping*: operators are said to *group* left to right, or right to left.

Postfix Operators

Postfix operators are appended to the identifier or expression on which they operate. The expressions involved, called *postfix expressions*, can consist of primary expressions, primary expressions followed by a postfix operator, or a postfix expression (which may already be more than just a primary expression) followed by a postfix operator. The postfix operators group left to right; the object to the left of the postfix operator is its target.

The postfix operators are array subscript `[ ]`, function call `( )`, structure or union member `.`, pointer to structure or union member `->`, postfix increment `++`, and postfix decrement `--`. The name, symbol, and general syntax for each operator is given before its discussion in the following text.

❑   `Array subscript [ ]` *postfix expression [expression]*

The postfix expression must have the type "pointer to object *type*"; the expression within the square brackets must have one of the integral types.

This notation is used both to declare arrays and to reference array elements. The following declaration

```
double points[256];
```

defines an array with 256 elements, each of which has type `double`. All the elements of an array are contiguous—kept together in storage. The integer number within the square brackets in the declaration is the subscript *bound*, because it indicates how many elements there can be.

To refer to an individual element of an array in an expression, you can use an integer constant, an identifier (variable), or an expression in the square brackets, provided that it evaluates to a number greater than or equal to zero (the first element) and less than the subscript bound. For example, using the `points` array, here are some samples of correct and incorrect subscripts:

```
int item = 122;
double hold;
...
hold = points[0];      /* OK, first element */
hold = points[item]    /* OK, 123rd element */
hold = points[item+7]; /* OK, 130th element */
hold = points[-3];     /* WRONG, must be positive */
hold = points[256]     /* WRONG, out of bounds */
```

Because the syntax allows a postfix expression to have an array operator, you can define multidimensional arrays. Because `points[256]` is a postfix expression, you could also define the following:

```
double points[256][3];
```

You can interpret this intuitively to mean a set of 256 three-dimensional points. Chapter 8 covers multidimensional arrays in detail.

❏   `Function call ()` *postfix expression (arg-expr-list)*

To call a function in an expression, use the function designator or a pointer to the function, followed by a pair of parentheses which may optionally contain the arguments to be used for that call. The argument list is optional only in the sense that the *prototype* may have declared a `void` parameter list so that the *call* should not specify any arguments. Here are some examples of function calls:

```
/* ----- declare variables and function prototypes ----- */
int results;
char *new_string;
char longstr[60] = "This is a longer string than the other one";
char shortstr[10] = "Really short";
char *longest_string( char *s1, char *s2 );
void kill_string( char *s1 );
int rand( void );
```

```
/* ----- use the functions ----- */
new_string = longest_string( longstr, shortstr );
kill_string( longstr );    /* a void expression */
results = rand();          /* no arguments allowed */
```

❏   struct (union) member . *postfix expression . identifier*

You can define not only the basic data types and arrays, but also structures—aggregate data types that can contain both basic type objects and other structures. The `struct` keyword defines a type, just as `int`, `double`, and others do. The most useful way to define a structure object looks like the following example:

```
struct circle {
  double center_x, center_y, radius;
};

struct circle circle1;
```

The object `circle1` does not have type `double`; it has type `struct`. Its *member variables*, however, *do* have type `double`. The structure member operator allows you to reference a member variable directly, as in the following:

```
circle1.radius = 25;
```

❏   Struct (union) member pointer ->
    postfix expression -> identifier

Suppose that you have defined an object you want to pass as a parameter to a function. Suppose also that you want to pass only its address, because the object may be too large to pass by value. Using the `circle1` object again, you might code something like the following:

```
struct circle {
  double center_x, center_y, radius;
};
void draw_circle( struct circle *anycircle )
{
... /* draw the circle here */
}
...
main()
{
  struct circle circle1;
  draw_circle( &circle1 );
}
```

`draw_circle()` is expecting a pointer to a structure, not a copy of the whole structure. How do you refer to member objects now? The structure member operator won't do; you must use the member pointer operator, as follows:

```
circle1->radius = 25; /* Dereference struct and get member */
```

The *member pointer operator* is composed of a minus sign and greater than sign. There can be blanks on either side of, but not between, the two characters.

❑　　Postfix increment ++ *postfix expression* ++

The postfix increment operator updates the stored value of the object to its left. *When* it updates it is something else. For instance, in this fragment

```
int a = 1, b;
...
b = a++ + 1;
```

the result placed in b is not 3, but only 2. The value of a is fetched first for purposes of evaluating the expression. This value is not tampered with again—it is 1 here. Next, the + 1 part of the expression is evaluated, yielding 2. The result is placed in b. *Sometime* during that process a is again fetched, incremented (1 is added to it), and replaced in a. The only guarantee for timing the side effect is that it occurs anywhere between the preceding and next sequence points. Of course, if you write

```
a++;
```

as the entire statement, you have guaranteed the timing by isolating the side effect.

❑　　Postfix decrement — *postfix expression*—

The postfix decrement operator reduces by one the value of the object to its left. Timing considerations are the same as for postfix ++.

Unary Operators

Just as the most basic form of postfix expression is the primary expression, so the most basic form of the *unary expression* is the postfix expression. This is not as surprising as you might think. Consider the following expression:

```
-point[i];
```

This expression is very similar to writing −1. It just happens to be an array element (a postfix expression, remember) rather than a constant.

All of the unary operators are prefixed to the object they work on and group right to left. The unary operators include prefix ++ and -- (increment and decrement), the sizeof operator, address-of &, indirection *, unary + and −, one's complement ~, and the logical not !.

Constraints are associated with some of the unary operators. The object of unary + and - must have an arithmetic type (not just integers), the one's complement ~ operates only on an integral type, and logical not ! only on a scalar type (a simple numeric type—this disallows structures and arrays, but permits character objects).

❑   Prefix increment ++ ++*unary expression*

The prefix increment differs greatly from the postfix increment—there is no delayed reaction. The value of the object is fetched, updated, and stored in the object location *immediately*. Only then is the updated value used in evaluating the expression, for example,

```
int a = 1, b;

b = ++a + 1;
printf( "%d\n", b );
```

This code fragment causes the number 3 to be displayed, not 2 as for the postfix increment operator.

❑   Prefix decrement ----*unary expression*

Works the same as prefix increment, except that the object is reduced by 1. Prefix increment and decrement are the only unary operators that modify an object's value (have side effects).

❑   Unary + +*expression*

The unary + operator results in just the value of its operand—it does *not* force the value to be positive, as you might (mistakenly) think when looking at this code fragment:

```
int a = -1;

printf( "%d\n", +a );
```

This code fragment displays –1, not +1. The value of a is not changed by this code.

❑   Unary - -*expression*

This operator causes the negative of its operand to be used in evaluating an expression. It forces a sign change but does not affect the stored value of the object (as does —). If a == 1, then b = b + -a is equivalent to b = b - a. Here is an interesting thought experiment: What is the final result of the following fragment?

```
int a = -1;

b = a - -a;
```

❏   One's Complement   *expression*

The one's complement operator inverts all the bits in its integral operand (which can include character types). Because the operand can be an expression, clearly no stored value is affected.

Inverting the bits means that the result's bit is on if and only if the operand's bit was off. For example, the following line

```
int data = ~0xxFFFF;
```

results in the object data having a value of zero; because every bit was a 1, every result bit is a zero.

❏   Logical not ! *!expression*

Logical not is used to reverse the sense of a conditional expression, that is, in an if statement's conditional expression, for example, you could write

```
int a = 0, b = 0;

if ( !a ) b = 1;
```

Remember that a result of 0 means false, and a result of nonzero means true. Thus, the expression statement b = 1 is executed only if !a evaluates to a true condition. It does here: Because a == 0, the !a is true and therefore evaluates to nonzero. If a had been initialized to 1, !a would have evaluated false, and the corresponding statement *not* executed. In any event, the stored value of a would not have been changed in this fragment. The moral here is be careful of using inverse logic like this. You can lose track faster than you think.

❏   Size-of sizeof *sizeof unary express sizeof (type-name)*

The sizeof operator produces the size, in bytes, of its operand. The result is an integer constant. If the expression is an identifier, the result is the number of bytes required to store the value of the object; if it is an actual expression, it yields the number of bytes that storing the *resulting value* would require. You may also take the size of a type specifier, which yields the number of bytes required to store such an object, as in the following:

```
int result;
...
result = sizeof result;   /*Integers usually 2 */
result - sizeof( char ); /* Will be 1 */
```

If you take the size of a pointer, a function designator, or an array identifier, the result is the number of bytes required to store the *pointer* to the object, not the object being pointed to.

❏ Address-of **&** *&object or &function*

The address-of operator is used to form a pointer to a previously declared object. You saw it used in the structure member pointer example. You can take (extract) the address of an object or of a function, as shown in the following code fragment:

```
#include <stdlib.h>
#include <stdio.h>

main()
{
   int (*inchar)( FILE *fp );

   inchar = &fgetc; /* take address of lib function */
   printf( "\n%c\n", inchar( stdin ) );
}
```

The method used here in printf() to call a function with a function pointer is new with ANSI C. In K & R C, you would have had to call inchar() like this:

```
printf( "\n%c\n", (*inchar)( stdin ) );
```

The older method is still valid. You can use either one.

❏ Indirection ***** **pointer expression*

The indirection operator uses the same source character as the multiplication operator. These operators should not be confused. The compiler keeps them separate by noting the context in which they are used.

The indirection operator is used to both declare a pointer and to dereference one. To declare a pointer to an integer, for example, you would write

```
int *count;
```

The parameter list entry in a function prototype would be similar:

```
int update( int *count );
```

Outside a declaration, the indirection operator is used to dereference the pointer—to access the object pointed to, not the pointer itself, as in the following example:

```
(*count)++; /* postfix incr the count object */
count++;    /* postfix incr the pointer to count */
```

Here, the first line updates the value of `count` by 1. Note that parentheses had to be used to overcome the fact that a postfix increment has higher precedence than indirection. Without the parentheses, only the pointer would have been updated. The second line updates the pointer to count by the `sizeof` an integer—two bytes, on most systems.

Cast Operators

Cast operators are unary operators also, but are handled separately by the ANSI document. The purpose of the cast operator is to change the type of the value of an identifier or expression; the cast operator never affects stored values, and cannot produce an *lvalue*. A cast operator groups operands from right to left like the other unary operators. It must have a scalar operand; arrays and aggregate objects are not permitted, but pointers are.

❑   `Type cast` *(type-name) cast expression*

The *cast expression* can be an identifier, or a primary, postfix, or unary expression, as in the following:

```
double pi 3.1415926;
int number;
...
number = (int)pi; /* "number" is now 3 */
```

Pointers can be cast to new types also, but that discussion comes later in this chapter in the section "Explicit Conversions with Type Casts."

Binary Operators

The binary operators form the bulk of the C operator set. These operators require two operands. They group left to right except for the assignment and conditional operators. Operators within each subclass here have equal precedence, and the subclasses are listed in descending order of precedence.

❑   `Multiplicative operators`
        *m-expression * cast expression* (multiply)
        m-expression / cast expression (divide)
        m-expression % cast expression (modulus)

where *m-expression* means "multiplicative expression" and can be either a cast expression as defined in the preceding section or an expression that already contains multiplicative operators. All these operators require arithmetic type operands; the % modulus (remainder) operator requires integral operands beyond that.

* multiplies two operands together (this is *not* the indirection operator). / divides the left operand by the right; the result is the quotient (truncated to a whole number if integer types). % also performs a division of the operands, but the result is the *remainder* (also a whole number if integer operands). Algebraic signs are preserved in the operations, except perhaps for a modulus, in which case, the sign of the result is implementation-defined.

❏   Additive operators

> *a-expression* + *m-expression* (add)
> *a-expression* – *m-expression* (subtract)

where *a-expression* means "additive expression" and *m-expression* means multiplicative expression. Specifying *m-expression* as the right operand is important. It guarantees that addition (or subtraction) proceeds from left to right. Because, by definition, an *m-expression* does not contain additive operators, an expression such as

```
a = b + c + d;
```

is guaranteed to evaluate *as if* you had written the following:

```
a = ( b + c ) + d;
```

Either both operands must have arithmetic type or one of the operands can be a pointer and the other an integer. When subtracting, *both* operands could be pointers. That is, you can do arithmetic on pointers (within limits discussed in Chapter 8).

❏   Bitwise shift operators

> *shift expression* << *a-expression* (shift left)
> *shift expression* >> *a-expression* (shift right)

All operands of the bitwise shift operators must be integral types. The operations are meant to shift bit patterns to the left or to the right. The left operand expression value (which does not have to be an *lvalue*) is shifted left or right by the number of bits specified by the additive expression on the left. Bits "shifted out" are lost. For example,

```
int n = 0xFFFF;
...
n = n << 8;
printf( "%.4X\n", n );
```

causes FF00 to be displayed on-screen. The syntax implies that shift operations can be compounded by nesting in parentheses. To clear some of the bits and realign them in the integer, you might want to do this:

```
int n = 0xFFFF;
...
n = ( n << 8 ) >> 4;
printf( "%.4X\n", n );
```

The integer n begins with all bits set: 1111111111111111. The left-shift produces 1111111100000000, (0xFF00 as before). Finally, the right-shift of 4 bits centers them in the integer: 0000111111110000 (or 0x0FF0). Note that shifting left *1 bit* is the equivalent of multiplying by 2; shifting right *1 bit* divides by 2. Successive shifts are equal to successive powers of 2.

❑   Relational operators

> *expression* < *expression* (less than)
> *expression* > *expression* (greater than)
> *expression* <= *expression* (less than or equal)
> *expression* >= *expression* (greater than or equal)

The relational operators yield 1 if the specified comparison is true and 0 if false. Because grouping is still left to right, the left operand is compared to the right operand. In the following example

```
if ( a < b ) do_something();
```

a < b means that if a is less than b, do_something() is called. The operands of a relational operator must be either both arithmetic or both pointers to compatible object type (or compatible incomplete object type). ANSI leaves undefined a comparison of pointers to different objects, except that a pointer value one beyond the end of an array is valid for comparison only (to detect the end of the array).

❑   Equality operators

> *expression* == *expression* (equal)
> *expression* != *expression* (not equal)

These operators are similar in use and syntax to the relational operators, except that they have lower precedence. They are not assignment operators, and care should be taken to avoid confusing them. Pointers compare equal when they point to the same point in an object.

You can use the equality operators to compare arithmetic objects, pointers to compatible objects, a pointer to an object and a void pointer, and a pointer and a null pointer constant (integer 0). Equality operators already have been used several times in the examples, particularly in testing the result of stream I/O functions. The following code fragment uses the equality operator to test the results of opening a file:

```
FILE *infile;          /* Read and display a file */
char ch;
..
```

```
if ( NULL == ( infile = fopen( "file.dat", "r" ) ) ) {
   puts( "Can't open the file." );
   abort();
}
while ( EOF != ( ch = fgetc( infile ) ) ) fputc( ch, stdout );
fclose( infile );
```

❏   Bitwise AND & *AND-expression & equality expression*

Binary & accepts only integral type operands. The result is the bitwise AND of the operators. The syntax guarantees left to right grouping of operands by specifying the more inclusive expression class on the left (in other words, associativity is guaranteed; either operand may be evaluated first, because the outcome is the same *as if* it were done left to right).

The bitwise AND sets a result bit on if—and only if—*both* corresponding operand bits are on. You can use this operator to turn off selected bits, as follows:

```
int a = 0xFF, b = 0xFE, c;
...
c = a & b; /* c now == 0xFE */
```

❏   Bitwise exclusive OR ^
     exclusive-OR-expression ^ AND-expression

Binary ^ accepts only integral type operands. The exclusive OR sets a result bit on if—and only if—one or the other corresponding operand bits, *but not both*, are on.

An interesting and useful application of the exclusive OR operator is to clear (turn off) all bits in an integer by exclusive ORing it with itself, as follows:

```
unsigned char flags = 0xAA;
...
flags = flags ^ flags; /* all bits off */
```

❏   Bitwise inclusive OR |
     inclusive-OR-expression | exclusive-OR-expression

Binary | accepts only integral operands. A result bit is set on if either corresponding operand bit, *or both of them*, is on.

You can use inclusive OR to turn on selected bits, like this:

```
unsigned char flags = 0; /* bit pattern 00000000 */
...
flags = flags | 0x80; /* bit pattern 10000000 */
```

❏   Logical AND &&
     logical-AND-expression && inclusive-OR-expression

Logical AND can accept any scalar operands (not just integers). The operands of && are *conditional expressions*; no stored value is affected. In a statement such as

```
if ( a && b ) statement;
```

the associated *statement* (which can be a block statement) is executed if— and only if—both the a *and* b expressions are true (evaluate to nonzero). A null pointer evaluates to false; an uninitialized pointer is not necessarily null.

Unlike the bitwise AND, logical AND guarantees both left to right associativity *and* left to right order of evaluation. If the left operand is false, the right operand is *not* evaluated, and the entire expression evaluates to *false*. This is handy when the state of some variables depends on the value of others. Suppose, for example, that your database program uses a flag field to record whether a stream has been opened. You might code a test statement like this:

```
FILE *database; /* stream pointer */
int flags; /* stream state flags */
...
if ( flags & 0x80 && database ) ... /* go ahead */
```

The left operand is the expression flags & 0x80. The bitwise AND has higher precedence and is to the left of the logical AND; if the high-order bit is on, the remainder of the expression is evaluated. If *database has been opened successfully, this pointer is not null. In other words, if the flag is set, the data base is open; if the data base is open, determine whether it opened correctly.

❏   Logical OR ||
     logical-OR-expression || *logical-AND-expression*

Logical OR accepts scalar operands and guarantees both left-to-right associativity and order of evaluation. The operation evaluates true if *either* operand expression or *both* of them evaluate true. If the first operand expression is false, the remainder of the operation is not done. It works like this:

```
if ( a || b ) { /* if you got here, at least one was true */ }
```

The Conditional (Ternary) Operator

Of all the C operators, the ternary operator is perhaps the strangest in appearance. Several other operators have two characters placed together, but the operator characters in the ternary operator are separated by expressions. These operand expressions associate right to left.

❏ Conditional ?:
logical-OR-expression ? expression : expression

The conditional operator is nothing but a crazy (and extremely useful) `if` statement. The classic example of its use is the function-like `maxval` macro:

```
#define maxval(a,b) (a>b) ? (a) : (b)
...
int a, b, c;
...
c = maxval(a,b); /* get largest number into c */
```

If the logical-OR-expression is *true*, the operand expression to the left of the colon is evaluated and this is the result of the whole expression. If it is false, the operand expression to the right of the colon is evaluated, and that is the result of the whole expression. This operator also guarantees both left to right associativity and order of evaluation.

Simple and Compound Assignment Operators

These operators are the means provided by C for modifying the value of an object (other than by side effects, such as using postfix ++). The compound operators provide an extremely powerful variation on this theme—they modify the object on the left *based on* the value of the expression on the right in certain ways. All the assignment operators associate right to left.

❏ Simple assignment =
modifiable lvalue = expression

The value of the expression is placed in the indicated object's storage location (hence the requirement for a modifiable *lvalue*). Type conversions can occur implicitly here. This is discussed later in the section "Implicit Conversion By Assignment."

❏ Compound assignment
modifiable lvalue op= expression
op == a binary operator

One of the binary operators (except relational, logical, or equality operators) is followed immediately by the assignment operator. The effects of this arrangement are shown in table 5.1.

Table 5.1. *Compound assignment actions.*

Compound Operator	Equivalent Statement
a += b;	a = a + b;
a -= b;	a = a - b;
a *= b;	a = a * b;
a /= b;	a = a / b;
a %= b;	a = a % b;
a &= b;	a = a & b;
a ^= b;	a = a ^ b;
a |= b;	a = a | b;
a <<= b;	a = a << b;
a >>= b;	a = a >> b;

The Comma Operator

The comma operator is used in C to separate *statements* when you are coding several where only one is required—or perhaps where only one is permitted. The different statements are evaluated from left to right. This is exactly what we did in the function `str_invert()` in line 100 of listing 5.2:

```
while ( s < p ) *s ^= *p, *p ^= *s, *s++ ^= *p-- ;
```

When you use the comma operator for this purpose, do it *conservatively*. The best practice is to do this only for *very* closely related groups of statements. One instance in which this is justified is in the controlling expression of a `for` statement. Suppose, for example, that you want to reverse the order of an array of `doubles`. The following code does just that. Notice how the third expression controlling the `for` loop uses a comma to pack *two* expressions in the place of one:

```
double a[64];
double hold;
int i, j;
... /* initialize the array in here, somehow */
for ( i=0,j=63; i<j; i++,j-- ) {
  hold = a[i];
  a[i] = a[j];
  a[j] = hold;
}
```

You should realize that the commas separating arguments in a function call are *not* comma *operators*, but are *punctuation*. Therefore they can do nothing to guarantee a particular order of evaluation of function-call arguments. In fact, the ANSI standard specifically states that such order of evaluation is unspecified. You cannot count on any two compilers doing it the same way.

The Key to C: Operator Precedence

Turn your attention once more to the fact that because an expression enclosed within parentheses is a primary expression, *grouping parentheses have the highest precedence of all*.

When you begin writing more complex programs, you frequently need to use grouping parentheses. In fact, you have already seen a need for it in at least two places. First, you saw it in the statements that opened a file and tested the outcome of the open in one statement:

```
FILE *infile;
...
if ( NULL != ( infile = fopen( ..., ... ) ) ) {
  /* open OK if you got here */
}
```

Why were the parentheses necessary here? Looking back over the operators you just learned, you will find that the equality operator ! = has higher precedence than assignment =. If the parentheses had *not* been there, the expression would have evaluated as if grouped like this:

```
if ( ( NULL != infile ) = fopen( ... ) ) ...
```

This wouldn't even get past the compile process. The result of this expression would be an attempt to assign a pointer to a constant—the results of fopen() into NULL. The compiler diagnostic message would tell you politely that an *lvalue* is required on the left side of an assignment operator.

Second, you saw that careless placement of the arguments in a *function-like macro* can lead to disaster. The best practice is to always surround macro arguments with parentheses to ensure that precedence does not produce some off-the-wall expression—one that may even get by the compiler.

There really is no substitute for knowing operator precedence, but it is not the easiest thing in the world to remember. Table 5.2 summarizes both operator precedence (highest at the top) and operator associativity. Study the table thoroughly and refer to it often.

Table 5.2. *C operator precedence, from highest to lowest.*

Operator(s)	Associativity
POSTFIX	
`function() array[] member-> member. ++ --`	*left to right*
UNARY/PREFIX	
`! ~ ++ -- + - * &` (*type*) `sizeof`	*right to left*
BINARY	
`* / %`	*left to right*
`+ -`	*left to right*
`<< >>`	*left to right*
`< <= > >=`	*left to right*
`== !=`	*left to right*
`&`	*left to right*
`^`	*left to right*
`|`	*left to right*
`&&`	*left to right*
`||`	*left to right*
CONDITIONAL	
`?:`	*right to left*
ASSIGNMENT	
`= += -= *= /= %= &= ^= |= <<= >>=`	*right to left*
COMMA	
`,`	*left to right*

Converting Data Types to Other Types

The conversion of one type of object to another adds a new level of complexity to understanding expression evaluation. You can mix several object types together in one expression, making it necessary to determine what type the final result will have; you can assign the value of one type into another, and you can use the cast operator to convert object types deliberately.

Automatic Type Conversions

Because type conversions can occur automatically, without your requesting them, you would be well advised to know when and how this happens. There are two kinds of automatic type conversion: operand *promotion* in expression evaluation and *implicit conversion* across an assignment operator.

Type Promotion in Expressions

You frequently need to mix operands of differing types in one expression. What is the type of the value resulting from evaluation? In a word, an expression has the same type as the most comprehensive basic object type in the expression. If you mix integers and double floating-point numbers, the expression's type is `double`.

Operands are converted in pairs, for each operator encountered. Naturally, the intermediate result from a subexpression may itself become an operand and be converted again. This process is called *promotion*. The sequence of promotions proceeds according to the rules of *usual arithmetic conversion*. These rules are listed from the most complex basic types to the simplest:

❑ *If either operand of the pair has type* `long double`, *the other operand is converted to* `long double`. It does not matter *which* operand: Either one causes the conversion.

❑ *Otherwise, if either operand has type* `double`, *the other is converted to* `double`.

❑ *Otherwise, if either operand has type* `float`, *the other is converted to* `float`.

❑ *Otherwise, any integral types are converted to a signed or unsigned version, whichever one can preserve the value including the sign bit.*

These rules are called the *integral promotions*.

Following the integral promotions, the following rules are applied:

❑ *If either operand has type* `unsigned long int`, *the other is converted to* `unsigned long int`.

❑ *Otherwise, if either operand has type* `long int`, *and the other has* `unsigned int`, *the* `unsigned int` *is converted to* `long`

> `int` *if that contains the value including the sign; otherwise, both operands are converted to* `unsigned long int`.

❑ *Otherwise, if either operand has type* `long int`, *the other is converted to* `long int`.

❑ *Otherwise, if either operand has type* `unsigned int`, *the other is converted to* `unsigned int`.

❑ *Otherwise, both operands have type* `int`, *and no conversion is needed.*

Notice that the sign of an operand is preserved during conversion, even if the significance of the sign bit is changed. A –1 value held in an `int`, for example, has a bit pattern on most machines of `0xFFFF`. If converted to `unsigned`, the bit pattern is still `0xFFFF`, but the number is no longer considered negative.

When a floating-point number is converted to an integral type, the fraction part is discarded (truncated). The value of the integral type is the next lowest whole number.

When an integral type is converted to a floating-point type, the resulting value may or may not be exactly the same as the original integer. Even if the number is in the proper range, floating-point numbers cannot represent exactly every possible number. If the representation cannot be exact, the result is the nearest representable value. Whether it is chosen to be higher or lower than the original number is implementation-defined.

Implicit Conversion by Assignment

Clearly, type conversion in an expression can lead to some unexpected results if you do not understand the process. You may encounter difficulties resulting from the truncation of fractional parts, bit patterns produced by preserving the sign, or even loss of significant digits if the target type cannot hold the value.

The fact that the same conversions can occur "across an equals sign" often escapes a programmer's notice (even a seasoned one!). This should not be surprising because assignment, like every other part of an expression, involves an operator. The same conversion rules also apply here.

Explicit Conversions With Type Casts

You may want to take control of the conversion process by using the cast operator. Any of the conversions belonging to the usual arithmetic conversions can be done also with the cast operator.

A cast is sometimes needed to keep things straight. A code fragment earlier in the chapter illustrated how to use a pointer to character to access the bytes of an `unsigned long int`. You need to look at the following two lines from that fragment:

```
char *byte;
...
printf( "%.2X ", (unsigned char)byte[i] );
```

Did you notice the `(unsigned char)` cast in the `printf()`? Why do you suppose it is there? It is there to control the usual arithmetic conversions, specifically to *prevent an inadvertent propagation of a sign*. Three things come together here to make this necessary:

1. The `%X` conversion sequence in `printf()` expects an integer type.

2. By default, the `byte` pointer points to a signed character *that is passed as a 2-byte integer* parameter to `printf()`.

3. The arithmetic conversions preserve the sign bit.

Things work fine provided that the character being implicitly converted to an integer is positive—because the sign bit is 0, the conversion to a physically larger type just propagates 0 bits in the high-order positions. But when the sign bit is on (that is, when the number is negative), a 1 bit is propagated to the high-order bit positions.

Therefore, when a negative character such as 0xDC is encountered, an extremely large negative integer emerges from the implicit conversion. Figure 5.5 shows the propagation of the sign bit when converting a 1-byte to a 2-byte field.

The cast to `unsigned char` preserved the sign bit *in place*, but prevents its propagation in conversion to an integer; in an unsigned type, there is no sign to propagate. Of course, we could have defined the pointer as `unsigned char *byte` in the first place, but that would have ruined the example!

Type casts are probably used most often in pointer conversions. Two kinds of pointer conversion are implicit and need no cast: the assignment or comparison of a zero integral value to a pointer (creating or testing a NULL pointer) and direct assignment of values from *any* pointer type to a `void` pointer. `void` pointers can *by definition* point to anything whatever. (Some compilers may nevertheless issue a warning message about this.) Other kinds of pointer conversion require an explicit cast.

A pointer may be cast to an integral type large enough to hold it. Both the size of the integral type required and the mapping algorithm are implementation-dependent. This emphasizes that *pointers are not integers* and should not be used as if they were.

Fig. 5.5. *Sign bit propagation during conversion.*

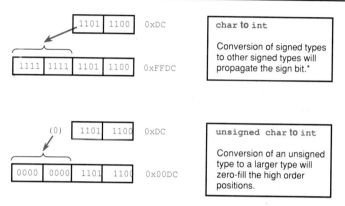

* This is true on CPUs that use 2's complement arithmetic.
Some other method may be used on machines that don't.

An integer of sufficient size may be cast to a pointer. Before you attempt this, be *sure* that you understand the internal structure of the pointer type *on your system* .

One pointer type may be cast to another pointer type. You have seen this already in the example of conversion of a pointer to an unsigned long int to a pointer to char. You possibly could encounter *alignment* problems when you do this. Some systems require an int to be *word-aligned*, for example (placed at a RAM address evenly divisible by the number of bytes in a word). This kind of cast could involve conversion to the same pointer type, except for qualifiers (unsigned int * cast to int *, for example).

To restore an object pointer from a void pointer, you must use the (void *) cast.

A pointer to a function type may be cast to a pointer to another function type. Using pointers to functions is covered in detail in Chapter 6.

The cast operator won't do one thing in particular. You may not cast a pointer to an *object* type to a pointer to a *function* type, or vice versa. The reasons for this are quite obvious.

Summary

Again, a great deal of material has been covered. All of this material is necessary background. In fact, having read this far, you are a more competent C programmer than you may suspect. Experience builds your confidence. Keep writing code!

In the next chapter, we go beyond background to examine some powerful techniques. Before you approach that material, be sure that you have gleaned the following from this chapter:

❏ *The essentials of scope, linkage, and duration.* These things must become second nature to you, because from this point on, you should be writing ever more complex code.

❏ *How to build multiple source-file programs.* Don't stop with just the general concepts that were all we were able to present here. Use *your* compiler and utilities and build some of these programs. Practice these techniques *before* you need them.

❏ *The rules and techniques for writing C expressions.* If any one thing can be labeled the heart of C programming, this is it.

❏ *How to convert object types to other types.* You should understand how to control type promotions during expression evaluation, conversion across the assignment operator, and explicit casts of types.

6

More about C Functions

This chapter deals with some of the more involved aspects of defining and calling functions. C handles functions with a great deal of power and flexibility, and this capability is not difficult to harness. In this chapter, you learn more about the following:

❏ *Passing parameters to functions.* You can pass by value and by reference, pass incomplete types, pass a variable number of arguments, pass a function (pointer) to the function, and even pass arguments to `main()`.

❏ *Recursive functions.* These are functions that call *themselves*. You will see how to avoid open-ended recursion and how to eliminate recursion altogether (and why you should or should not do so).

❏ *Alternative ways to invoke functions.* These methods are relatively simple to implement, but can result in very powerful code.

Details about Passing Parameters

C is implemented on a number of different machine types. Some of them are stack-oriented machines (most personal computers and minicomputers, for example) and some, such as the IBM 370 architecture mainframes, are not.

The physical method of passing parameters may vary, therefore, from one machine and implementation to the next. In this chapter we assume a hypothetical stack-oriented machine for purposes of illustration.

Pass by Value and Pass by Reference

The default method of passing parameters to a function is by *value*. An argument expression (which may be a simple object identifier or a more complex expression) is evaluated, and the result is passed to the function to work with. Passing arguments by value therefore prevents the function from modifying an object's stored value—this is the purpose of the default method.

All the basic data types, plus structures and unions, can be passed by value. Array types, however, cannot. (Remember that this includes strings, which are arrays of char.) Only a *pointer* to an array, taken as a whole, may be passed to the function. This is called passing parameters *by reference*. Of course, you can declare the function prototype so that a pointer must be used for any type.

Parameters Are Passed on the Stack

C is quite common on the stack-oriented machines assumed for this discussion. Parameters are passed to a function by placing the argument *on the stack* on such machines.

You saw an example of this in Chapter 3 and may want to review that figure now (refer to fig. 3.3). The figure shows that arguments usually are placed on the stack from right to left. This is not true for every compiler, nor does it have anything to do with the way the arguments are evaluated. For example, given the following declarations:

```
int sum( int a, int b, int c );
int x = 37, y = 47, z = 57;
```

```
int result;
...
main()
{
   result = sum( x, y, z );
}
```

the value of z usually is placed on the stack first, then y, and finally x. Understanding the order in which arguments are placed on the stack becomes important a little later, when you consider the techniques for passing a variable number of arguments.

Passing Parameters by Value

When parameters are passed by value, only a copy of stored objects is placed on the stack, and the function's code should reference the passed argument values *as though* they were defined within the function body. The following code fragment illustrates both of these points:

```
void reset_it( int p )
{
   p = 99; /* Does not affect main's version of p */
}
...
main()
{
   int p = 44;
   reset_it( p ); /* Pass a copy of p */
}
```

As you may remember, it does not matter that the formal parameter name p in the parameter list for reset_it() happens to be the same as the object name of the actual argument passed to it. They are not the same object. You may recall also that the int object p in main() has *block scope* and *no linkage*. Unless you do something more than is present in this example, reset_it() has access only to the *copy* of p located on the system stack.

Passing Parameters by Reference

Pointers passed as parameters to a function have an entirely different effect on the way objects are handled. We have rewritten the previous code fragment just a little, and see what happens:

```
void reset_it( int *p ) /* Now expecting a pointer */
{
   *p = 99; /* DOES affect main's version of p */
```

```
}
...
main()
{
   int p = 44;

   reset_it( &p );
   /* Stored value of p now 99 */
}
```

In this version of reset_it(), a *reference* to p is passed—a pointer, not a copy of the object's value. This is indicated by the use of the indirection operator in the parameter declaration part of reset_it().

Notice that the *object* p is now accessed within the function by again using the indirection operator. If that operator were missing, the function would sct the *pointer value*, not the object's stored value, to 99. The assignment expression would not compile correctly, anyway. The conversion rules require that an explicit cast be used for converting an integer to a pointer.

The function call also is a little different. Now the call requires that the address-of operator (unary &) be used to take the address of the object during argument evaluation—because this is not an array or a string. If p were an array or a string, the address-of operator would not be required. References to arrays and strings as a whole (as opposed to elements within them) always produce a pointer. If ? were an array, for example, you could write

```
void reset_it( int p[32] ) /* Still expecting a pointer */
{
   int i;

 /* Still affects the original object's stored values */
   for ( i=0, i<32, i++ ) p[i] *= 2; /* Double elements */
}
...
main()
{
   int p[64];

...
/* initialize the array in here */
...
   reset_it( p ); /* p is the address of the array */
}
```

If p were a string, the declarations would be similar:

```
   void reset_it( char *p ) { ... }
   ...
   main()
```

```
{
    char p[64] = "This is a string, now.";
    ...
    reset_it( p );
}
```

Function Argument Promotions

Chapter 5 covered the conversions and promotions possible for object types during expression evaluation. It should not be surprising that the evaluation of function arguments *can* cause type promotions as well—passing arguments to a function involves their evaluation, and, after all, arguments can be expressions as well as objects. Three things should be considered when passing arguments to functions:

❑   *The comma operator does not guarantee order of evaluation, only associativity*. Function arguments are evaluated *as if* from left to right (associativity), but *in fact* may be evaluated in any order. You should not write function argument expressions with side effects and expect them to alter values passed to the function, either. Remember that a sequence point occurs before argument evaluation begins, and after it is complete, but not in between. Thus a call such as:

```
int a = 1;
...
some_function( a++, a );
```

does not pass the values 1 and 2, but passes the values 1 and 1. The postfix incremented value of the original variable a is available when the function has been entered, but not before that time (and does not affect what the function receives to work with anyway).

❑   *Functions that do not have prototypes are subject to the default promotions of their arguments*. These functions include those declared by being defined (no forward declaration at all) and which do not specify parameter types or that have only old-style forward declarations (which also do not specify types and are not true prototypes). The arguments of such functions first undergo the default integer promotions. This means that arguments with type char, short int, or int *always* are promoted to either int or unsigned int, whichever is required to represent them correctly.

Following the integral promotions, all values with type `float` *always* are promoted to `double`. Such promotions can be potentially confusing, especially if the function contains code that in any way depends on the internal structure of the arguments.

❑ *Functions having prototypes do not experience the default promotions.* Full function prototypes provide the compiler with enough information to evaluate arguments while performing only such *implicit conversions* as are required to make actual arguments match the type of corresponding parameters. For example, the following code fragment is legitimate, even the type of the actual argument passed does not match the type of the corresponding formal parameter in the prototype.

```
int scale_num( int num );  /* prototype for scaling numbers */
char p = '1';                    /* display character 1 */
int value;                       /* holds scaled number */
...
value = scale_num( p );   /* arg has type char in call */
```

Passing a `char` type to a function expecting an integer argument causes the argument value to be converted, *as though by assignment*, to the expected integer. You could even pass a `double` to this function, but its fraction part would be lost when the conversion to `int` occurred.

Function Prototypes with Incomplete Types

You may declare a function prototype that contains parameters having *incomplete type*—a type specification insufficient to provide size or content information. This may help you generalize your program so that a change to the source code in one place does not require changes in others. More detail on incomplete types is provided in Chapters 8 and 11, but a quick look at them may be helpful now.

Two kinds of objects—arrays and structures— may have an incomplete type specification. Of these, only incomplete array declarations is of any real use with function prototypes.

❑ *An array declaration with an omitted subscript bound expression is an incomplete type.* The array subscript postfix operator `[ ]` normally contains an expression that defines and limits the number of elements in an array. If the array is defined elsewhere, it can be declared again without the bounds information, as in the following:

```
extern int points[];
```

This declaration supplies enough information to determine the address of the array, the type of each element, and the size of each element—sizeof(int)—but not the size of the entire array. Unless more information is provided by some other means, this limited information may not be enough to be useful. Then again, it may.

A more common use for incomplete array types is to omit *one* of the subscript bounds in a function prototype declaration containing a multidimensional array, like this:

```
void plot_polygon( int count, int points[][3] );
```

This declaration provides information about the number of points in the count variable. Such a declaration could be used to limit a loop that plots any number of points in a polygon, because the first array subscript bound is missing. Why would you want to write a function declaration like this? Generally, it is part of a separately compiled source file. Defining it like this generalizes the routine so that it can be used by many programs, not just one. Chapter 8 goes into detail on handling array declaration with incomplete type.

❑ *A structure declaration with a tag but no member list is an incomplete type*. A declaration such as:

```
struct record1;
```

tells the compiler nothing except that such a structure will be redeclared later with more information to complete the type. This kind of incomplete type is not very useful for function prototype declarations, but does have other uses. More detail on incomplete structure declarations is presented in Chapter 11, in the discussion of derived types.

Variable-length Argument Lists

Think about the printf() and scanf() functions for a moment. Both of these functions have a format string as the first parameter, followed by *any number of variable arguments*. Now, how do these functions know when to stop processing arguments? More than that, how do they know where those arguments are?

The answer to the first question is that `printf()` and `scanf()` can determine the number of arguments by simply counting the number of conversion specifiers in the format string. You are already familiar with the fact that these functions require the number of conversion specifiers to match exactly the number of following arguments. This leads to the first principle of processing a variable number of function-call arguments: *the function declaration must specify the fixed and predictable arguments first, followed by all the other arguments*.

How would you write a function prototype for a function with a variable number of arguments? Standard C provides a special notation for just this situation. It is called an *ellipsis*, and consists of three consecutive periods. The prototype for `printf()`, for example, is

```
int printf( const char *format, ... );
```

The ellipsis must always be the last thing in the parameter list, because that is where the variable number of arguments must appear.

The answer to the second question—how to locate the unspecified arguments—can be difficult if you make it so, but need not be. Simply remember that function arguments are always passed by the same vehicle. On stack-oriented machines, such as those we are using for the examples here, that vehicle is always the system stack. On other machines it may be another vehicle, but it is always predictable. Figure 6.1 illustrates how arguments can be located on a traditional stack-oriented machine.

Fig. 6.1. Locating unspecified arguments on the stack.

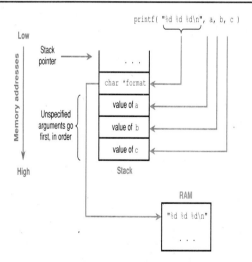

In the model we are using, the system *stack pointer* points just above the fixed, predictable arguments, which are followed in the stack by the variable arguments.

We need to develop some sort of mechanism for accessing the unspecified arguments, one after the other. The mechanism should allow for a mixture of object types.

Because the Turbo C implementation of this feature is very clean and understandable, and closely follows ANSI specifications, we base the discussion on that compiler's declarations. (They can be found in `stdarg.h`.) The Turbo C 2.0 declarations are as follows:

```
typedef void    *va_list;

#define va_start(ap, parmN)   (ap = ...)
#define va_arg(ap, type) (*((type *)(ap))++)
#define va_end(ap)
```

The standard requires that there be one type definition and three macros for advancing through a list or arguments whose type and number are not known at compile time. The preceding declarations follow exactly the required names and operations.

The type definition for `va_list` suits the need for supporting a mixture of argument types, because a `void` pointer can point to anything. The cast to a particular pointer type occurs as each argument value is fetched. You need to declare a pointer object to use for fetching a variable number of arguments in the function that will use it *before* you begin to fetch any arguments. Here is an example of how this is done:

```
#include <stdarg.h>
...
float average( int num, ... )
{
  int i,sum = 0;
  va_list arg_ptr;
  ...
}
```

`arg_ptr` has (derived) type `va_list`. This is entirely equivalent to the following declaration:

```
void *arg_ptr;
```

Next, you must initialize `arg_ptr` so that it points to the first of the unspecified parameters. This is done with the function-like macro `va_start`, as follows:

```
#include <stdarg.h>
...
```

```
float average( int num, ... )
{
  int i,sum = 0;
  va_list arg_ptr;

  va_start( arg_ptr, num );
  ...
}
```

The #define for va_start gives formal parameters of ap for the argument pointer, and parmN for the *last fixed parameter at the beginning of the list*, which in this example is num.

At this point, Turbo C does something that is not specified in the standard. It initializes the argument pointer like this:

```
( ap = ...)
```

as though the ellipsis denoted a pointer variable. This should be considered unique to Turbo C; nowhere does the standard say it's legal. A more compatible way of doing it might look like this:

```
ap = (va_list)&parmN + sizeof(parmN)
```

which is the way QuickC does it. The address of parmN is taken and immediately cast to a pointer of type va_list. When the size of that parameter is added, the first of the unspecified arguments is pointed to. The result is assigned to the argument pointer. In the current example, this would expand to the following:

```
arg_ptr = (va_list)&num + sizeof(num)
```

The process of accessing the arguments in turn is accomplished by writing the va_arg() macro. In this case, the goal is to access a number of integers—how many is to be controlled by num—and sum them, in preparation for calculating their average. Adding a little more code to the function, we get the following:

```
#include <stdarg.h>
...
float average( int num, ... )
{
  int i, sum = 0;
  va_list arg_ptr;

  va_start( arg_ptr, num );
  for ( i = 0; i<num; i++ ) sum += va_arg( arg_ptr, int );
  ...
}
```

va_arg is responsible not only for returning a value of the indicated type, but also for updating the argument pointer to the next argument. The expression used to do this is informative. In this example the statement `sum += va_arg( arg_ptr, int )` expands to the following:

```
sum += (*((int *)(arg_ptr))++)
```

Working from the inside out, you can see that the `void` pointer `arg_ptr` is first cast to a pointer to `int`—`int *)(arg_ptr)`. The macro expansion may yield a different type on subsequent uses of `va_arg()`. The pointer to `int` is next dereferenced to yield a value—`*((int *)(arg_ptr))`. In this case, it yields an integer value.

Finally, the pointer (not the value) is postfix incremented—`(*((int *)(arg_ptr))++)`. The arrangement of parentheses encloses the cast to pointer to `int`, so the pointer is incremented by the size of an integer, maintaining proper addressing. (Only a `char *` pointer is incremented by one byte exactly. All other pointers are updated by an amount equal to the size of the object pointed to.)

To complete the routine, it is necessary only to stop argument-list processing and calculate the average, as follows:

```
#include <stdarg.h>
...
float average( int num, ... )
{
  int i, sum = 0;
  va_list arg_ptr;

  va_start( arg_ptr, num );
  for ( i = 0; i<num; i++ ) sum += va_arg( arg_ptr, int );
  va_end( arg_ptr );
  return( (float)sum / num );
}
```

The ANSI standard states explicitly that the `va_end()` macro must be invoked to terminate argument processing. In the Turbo C implementation, this macro does nothing, because it is not needed. On other machines and systems, however, some action may well be needed to clean up after the function arguments have been accessed.

It should be clear to you that *you* are responsible for determining the number of arguments as well as their type. The macros do not do it for you. `printf()` did it under control of the format string; the preceding example did it by requiring a fixed parameter containing the argument count. Another method you can use when passing an unspecified number of *strings* is to terminate the list with a null string. An example of this method is shown in program listing 6.1.

Listing 6.1. ldisplay.c *(Display a variable-length list of strings).*

Turbo C 2.0

```
 1   #include <stdlib.h>
 2   #include <stdio.h>
 3   #include <stdarg.h>
 4
 5   void display_list( char *title, ... )
 6   {
 7     va_list ap;
 8     char *hold;
 9
10     printf( "%s\n", title );
11     va_start( ap, title );
12     hold = va_arg( ap, char * );   /* Prime the loop */
13     while ( *hold ) {               /* Test the string */
14       printf( "%s\n", hold );
15       hold = va_arg( ap, char * );
16     }
17     va_end( ap );
18   }
19
20   main()
21   {
22     display_list(
23       "This is a list of physical constants ---",
24       "Pi = 3.1415929",
25       "c  = 2.997925E+8 meters per second",
26       "electron mass = 9.109558E-31 kilograms",
27       ""                       /* here is the null string */
28     );
29   }
```

Three standard library functions support the use of variable argument lists. Their prototypes are

```
vfprintf( FILE *stream, const char *format, va_list ap );
vprintf( const char *format, va_list ap );
vsprintf( char *s, const char *format, va_list ap );
```

Because the literature contains any number of examples of how these functions are used to print error messages, we will do something different. The program shown in listing 6.2 uses vsprintf() to clip a message line for a display window. The windowing support itself is not present. The function clip_display() presumes that cursor location has already been set at entry.

Listing 6.2. *c l i p . c (Clip an output message to a window boundary with*
v s p r i n t f ( )).   *Zortech C 1.7*

```
 1   #include <stdlib.h>
 2   #include <stdio.h>
 3   #include <stdarg.h>
 4   #include <string.h>
 5
 6   void clip_display( int offset, int width, char *fmt, ... )
 7   {
 8     char *out;
 9     va_list ap;
10
11     out = malloc( 256U ); /* get an output area */
12     va_start( ap, fmt );
13     vsprintf( out, fmt, ap );                /* format output */
14     va_end( ap );
15     if ( offset < strlen( out ) )      /* offset too far ? */
16       printf( "%.*s", width, out+offset ); /* clip output */
17     free( out );
18   }
19
20   main()
21   {
22     int a = 37, b = 47;
23
24     clip_display( 5, 15,
25       "The value of a is %d and the value of b is %d.\n",
26       a, b );
27   }
```

The input parameters to c l i p_d i s p l a y ( ) are an offset, a window width,
a p r i n t f ( )-compatible format string, and a variable number of arguments.
This function simply provides window-oriented p r i n t f ( ) service.

The input parameter o f f s e t allows for horizontal scrolling. The output
message begins to display o f f s e t characters to the right of the beginning of
the final message string.

To use the v s p r i n t f ( ) function, you must declare a va_l i s t argument
pointer, va_s t a r t ( ), and va_s t o p ( ) exactly as before. v s p r i n t f ( ), line
13, formats the entire message into a dynamically acquired string. va_a r g ( )
is not used—just pass along the argument pointer to v s p r i n t f ( ) or other
v . . . ( ) functions.

After checking to make sure that the offset value does not start printing
beyond the end of the line (line 15), a normal p r i n t f ( ) is used to position

and trim the output message (line 16). As you study this example, you may want to refer to Chapter 2 and review `printf()` conversion specifiers.

Passing Parameters to *main()*

As far as the ANSI standard is concerned, C programs can execute in two environments: *freestanding* environments, in which there is no operating system to support the program (the C program might *be* the operating system); and *hosted* environments, in which a C program runs under the control of an operating system.

Hosted environments usually make available to the guest programs some means of acquiring information about the surrounding environment and the conditions in which they are expected to operate. To support this feature, C provides a mechanism for passing parameters to `main()`.

Accessing Command-line Parameters

In a hosted environment, a C program is executed as a result of a *system command*, which consists of the name of the executable program file, followed by a command tail. The *command tail* is a series of text tokens, separated by blanks, that can have any significance the programmer wants, as follows:

```
C>program parm1 parm2 ... parmn
```

These tokens are called *execution parameters*, or sometimes *command-line parameters*. Command-line parameters are to the program what function parameters are to a function. In Chapter 2, for example, the program `number.c` (refer to listing 2.3) accepted one execution parameter—the name of the text file to be numbered:

```
C>number [drive:][\path\]filename[.ext]
```

Most operating systems consider everything on the command line after the program name to be the command tail. C's set-up routines *divide the command tail into token strings* and pass (to the program) pointers to these strings, so that they can be accessed separately.

argc and *argv[]*

This is all accomplished through the `argc` and `argv[]` parameters, which can be declared only in `main()`. To access execution parameters, you code the declaration for `main()` like this:

```
main( int argc, char *argv[] )
{
...
}
```

The first parameter, int argc, is a count of the number of command parameters available. If your compiler cannot supply such parameters, argc will be zero. If it can supply parameters, the value of argc will be at least 1, because the count *includes the program name*.

The second parameter, char *argv[], is an *array of pointers* to strings. Valid subscript numbers are 0 through argc-1. argv[0] is a pointer to the program name; *argv[0] (dereferencing the pointer), or argv[0][0] (using a subscript), is the first *character* of the program name. Some compilers that can supply command parameters do not have access to the program name. In that case, argv[0] points to a null string; this does not mean that there are no other parameters. Program showarg.c, listing 6.3, illustrates how you can access the command-line parameters, including the program name.

Listing 6.3. showarg.c *(Accessing command-line parameters).*

Zortech C 1.7

```
1   #include <stdlib.h>
2   #include <stdio.h>
3   #include <string.h>
4   #include <ctype.h>
5
6   main( int argc, char *argv[] )
7   {
8     int i;
9
10    /* ----- Display the program name ----- */
11
12    printf( "*** " );
13    for ( i=0; i<strlen( argv[0] ); i++ )
14      printf( "%c ", toupper( argv[0][i] ) );
15    printf( "*** \n" );
16
17    /* ----- Display the command parameters ----- */
18
19    for ( i=1; i<argc; i++ )
20      printf( "Argument %d: %s\n", i, argv[i] );
21  }
```

The output from `showarg.c` in listing 6.3 looks like this:

```
*** C : \ Z O R T E C H \ P G M \ S H O W A R G . E X E ***
Argument 1: 123
Argument 2: abc
Argument 3: another parameter
```

For this example, the program was executed from the `c:\zortech\pgm` directory on the hard drive, running under MS-DOS 4.01. The following command line was used to produce this output:

```
C:\ZORTECH\PGM>showarg 123 abc "another parameter"
```

Note that in this particular host environment, the operating system passes not only the simple program name, but also the path to the executable program file. This may or may not be true on your system.

The double-spaced program name is produced by lines 13 and 14 in listing 6.3. The `for` loop accesses each character from the `argv[0]` string by using a second subscript—`argv[0][i]`—after which it translates the character to uppercase with `toupper()`, and passes the resulting character to `printf()` for display. The format string conveniently adds a blank after the `%c` conversion sequence, causing the double-spacing.

In the `for` loop in lines 19 and 20, the execution parameters are displayed one at a time as strings by `printf()`. Because the parameter string as a whole is being accessed in each case, no second subscript is needed for `argv[i]`.

The third execution parameter in this example is `"another parameter"`. Even though there is a blank in the middle of this substring, it is treated by C—not by the operating system—as a single token. That happens because it is enclosed in parentheses, making it a string literal according to normal C syntax.

Designing Command-line Formats

The number, type, and format of command-line parameters vary from one program to the next. Even if you always design your programs so that the command-line parameters have an extremely uniform appearance, you may forget from time to time exactly what the parameters should be. Whether the format is consistent or not, you should include in your program code that permits a user to get help.

The common method of providing this help was first developed by users of the UNIX operating system, and it has spilled over to other environments as well. The method consists of providing for execution of the program with no parameters at all, which results in a set of messages giving the correct command format. The code for doing this does not need to be extremely complex. Often a simple message will do, such as the one used in `number.c` (refer to listing 2.3 in Chapter 2). The code for generating a help message is in lines 13–18, as follows:

```
13    /* ----- Check command line parameters ----- */
14
15    if ( argc < 2 ) {
16       printf( "\nSupply a program name to number.\n" );
17       exit( 8 );
18    }
```

If the argument count is less than 2, only the program name was typed on the command line. In that case, the program displays a message telling the user to follow the program name with a file name to work with, and terminates execution. The user can try again, with the appropriate parameters.

Although arranging some uniformity in parameter design may not always be possible, it is desirable (if for no other reason than to make running the program easier to remember).

Many programs allow some command-line parameters to be arguments and some to be options. A command-line *argument* is something the program works with: a file name, perhaps. An *option* is a parameter that indicates *how* the program is to do its work. A program designed to print text files in a flexible way, for example, might support a command-line option to control line spacing, as follows:

```
C>toprt myfile.txt -s2
```

The meaning of this command line is clear intuitively—the program sends `myfile.txt` to the system printer, and double-spaces the output.

This same command line shows another practice inherited from UNIX systems. An option parameter is signalled by the presence of a *flag character* (a minus sign here) followed by a letter indicating what the option is, followed (if necessary) by a value to complete the definition.

If you decide to use a format like this, your program ideally should permit the arguments and options to be mixed in any order. The logic to handle separating the arguments and options might look something like this:

```
FILE *infile;
char filename[41];
int spacing;

void handle_option( char *ostring )
{
```

```
   if ( ostring[1] != 's' ) spacing = 1;
     else spacing = atoi( ostring+2 );
}
void handle_arg( char *astring )
{
   strcpy( filename, astring );
}
main( int argc, char *argv[] )
{
   int i;

   for ( i=1; i<argc; i++ ) { /* skip program name */
     if ( *argv[i] == '-' ) handle_option( argv[i] );
       else handle_arg( argv[i] );
   }
   ...
}
```

In this example, the order in which the argument and option are typed doesn't matter; they are handled as they are presented to the program.

Functions That Call Themselves

Whether or not a function has been forward-declared with a prototype, a function designator is in scope for its own function body. Thus a statement within a function body may be a function call—to itself. This is called a *recursive function call*, or more simply, *recursion*.

Handled properly, recursion can be a powerful technique. Some algorithms are well-suited to it. Handled improperly, the technique can be very dangerous. The first step toward correct control of recursion is understanding how it works.

Understanding Recursion

The ANSI document does not define recursion; it says only that recursion is legal. Recursion can be either direct or indirect; both are sanctioned specifically by ANSI. *Direct recursion* is the process of a function calling itself, from within its own function body.

Indirect recursion involves more than one function. Say, for example, that there are two functions, one() and two(). To get things started, main() calls one(), and then one() calls two(). Somewhere in its processing, two()

then calls one()—a *second* call to one(). This is indirect recursion—but it is recursion, because one() has been called twice without ever returning to its caller.

Clearly, unless you do something to stop it, a recursive process can continue forever. That topic is covered in the next section.

Essentially, recursion is an iterative process. A recursive function call presumably is intended to work on call arguments *whose state (value) depends on the preceding recursion*. Thus, when the parameter list is void, recursion is useless and is ignored.

An algorithm that lends itself well to a recursive implementation is Euclid's algorithm for finding the greatest common divisor of two numbers, a and b. The method is to divide one argument into the other until this can no longer be done. Whatever is left is the greatest common divisor. During the computation, the order of the arguments in the recursive call is important, because they swap at every iteration. Using a C-like pseudocode, the algorithm is as follows:

```
long gcd( long a, long b )
{
  if ( b == 0 ) {
    no more division can be done;
    a is the gcd;
    return a;
  }
  get the remainder of a / b;
  set a = b;
  set b = remainder;
  repeat the process;
}
```

Recursion is used at the point in the process where the algorithm "repeats the process." The program euclid.c, shown in listing 6.4, shows how this algorithm can be implemented.

Listing 6.4. euclid.c *(Use recursive function calls to compute the greatest common divisor [GCD]).*   *Turbo C 2.0*

```
1   /*
2       +------------------------------------+
3       +              EUCLID.C              
4       +   Demonstrate Euclid's Algorithm.  
5       +------------------------------------+
6   */
7
8   #include <stdlib.h>
```

Listing 6.4. continues

Listing 6.4. continued

```
 9   #include <stdio.h>
10
11   #define DISPLAY 1
12
13   long int a;
14   long int b;
15
16   /*
17      Euclid's algorithm to find the GREATEST COMMON DIVISOR.
18      This function uses RECURSIVE CALLS to itself. The stack
19      required depends on the size of the numbers.
20   */
21
22   long int gcd( a,b )
23      long int a;
24      long int b;
25   {
26      if ( DISPLAY ) printf( "%ld,%ld\n",a,b );
27      if ( b == 0 ) return( a );
28        else return( gcd( b, a%b ) );
29   }
30
31   main()
32   {
33      a = 19408L;
34      b = 19376L;
35      gcd( a,b );
36   }
```

The macro name DISPLAY in listing 6.4, line 11, is used to determine whether to show intermediate results as the GCD is computed. You can turn off the display by setting DISPLAY to 0, or by deleting lines 11 and 26 from the program.

Lines 27 and 28 show the power of the recursive technique; they contain the *entire* algorithm. If b is zero, a is returned as the GCD. Otherwise, gcd() is called recursively, but now b is the first argument, and a%b is the second. The interior (recursive) call to gcd both computes the remainder and swaps the arguments.

Avoiding Open-ended Recursion

If you consider carefully the code in listing 6.4, you soon realize that gcd() does not return to main() until the complete result has been calculated.

This fact is very significant. It means that call arguments are piled on top of one another in the stack, and that they *accumulate until the last iteration*. Arguments are purged from the stack by returning from the function, but the function may be *called many times without ever returning*, until the bottom layer is reached. Figure 6.2 illustrates how argument values accumulate on the stack during recursive calls.

Fig. 6.2. *Stack growth during recursive function calls.*

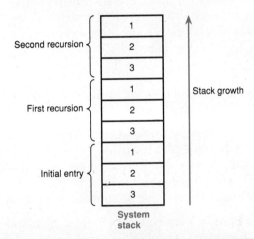

```
void r_function( int a, int b, int c )
{
  r_function( 1, 2, 3 );
  . . .
}
```

The amount of memory available to hold a growing number of argument values is the limiting factor in recursive techniques. After a certain number of recursive calls, that memory (whether stack memory or something else) is exhausted.

This means that you must select very carefully the algorithms you want to implement recursively. An algorithm may be *theoretically* capable of recursive implementation, but your machine (or compiler) may lack the resources to support more than a certain number of iterations.

The only cure for this is to analyze the method, mathematically if necessary, to determine how many recursions can potentially occur. If the answer is "too many," you have to find another way.

Fancy mathematics is not always necessary for analyzing an algorithm. Frequently, all you need is common sense and a clear understanding of what you are trying to do.

Computing the *factorial* of a number is an algorithm suitable for recursive methods. The factorial of any number x is equal to x * x-1 * x-2 * ... *x-x+2 * 1. That is, it is the product of all the numbers from x to 1. You can implement the factorial function recursively like this:

```
long factorial( long a )
{
   if ( a == 1 ) return a;
     else return a * factorial( a - 1 );
}
```

Suppose, for example, that you want to compute the value of factorial 5. A long integer for every number from 5 to 1 must be placed on the stack to pass each lower value to the next recursive call of factorial(). In this case, the memory space needed is not great. If you remember that multiplying by 1 is pointless, you can even tune the function by changing the test to eliminate one iteration of the process, as follows:

```
   if ( a == 2 ) ...
```

For extremely large numbers of iterations, however, this kind of savings is insignificant.

The fact that parameter-passing memory is finite means also that you must take pains to avoid open-ended recursion. *Open-ended recursion* means that the function has no means of detecting when to stop calling itself. The consequences are obvious—the function continues to call itself until all memory is exhausted. Then your program is guaranteed to stop!

There is no hard and fast rule for avoiding open-ended recursion. The method used in every case depends only on the nature of the algorithm itself. In computing the GCD, the second parameter was checked at every pass to make sure that a zero value was detected. In computing the factorial of a number, the parameter was checked to see whether it had reached 1. In any case, adding the logic that detects the terminating condition is up to you.

Eliminating Recursion

If you find that recursion is not a practical way to implement a function with your machine or compiler, yet you must have the function, you have no alternative but to *eliminate the recursion.*

Fortunately, a result of studies in computer science assures us that *any* recursive technique can be rewritten without recursion. It may not have the recursive technique's elegant appearance or slick, tight code, but it works. And it almost invariably runs faster because the overhead of calling functions and passing parameters has been eliminated.

Recursion can be eliminated from the version of gcd() shown in listing 6.4 by the simple expedient of adding a temporary variable to hold the remainder, and using a while loop instead of recursive calls. This is shown in listing 6.5.

Listing 6.5. euclid2.c *(Eliminating recursive calls from GCD calculation).*
Turbo C 2.0

```
1   /*
2       +-------------------------------------+
3       +              EUCLID2.C
4       +  Demonstrate Euclid's Algorithm.
5       +-------------------------------------+
6   */
7
8   #include <stdlib.h>
9   #include <stdio.h>
10
11  #define DISPLAY 1
12
13  long int a;
14  long int b;
15
16  /*
17    Euclid's algorithm to find the GREATEST COMMON DIVISOR.
18    This function REMOVES RECURSIVE CALLS to itself. It is
19    faster, and does not endanger the stack.
20  */
21
22  long int gcd( a,b )
23    long int a;
24    long int b;
25  {
26    long int hold;
27
28    if ( DISPLAY ) printf( "%ld,%ld\n",a,b );
29    while ( b != 0 ) {
30      hold = a % b; a = b; b=hold;
31      if ( DISPLAY ) printf( "%ld,%ld\n",a,b );
32    }
33    return( a );
34  }
35
```

Listing 6.5. continues

Listing 6.5. *continued*

```
36   main()
37   {
38     a = 19408L;
39     b = 19376L;
40     gcd( a,b );
41   }
42
```

This method of eliminating recursion, which should be used when there is only one recursive call at the end of the function, is called *end-recursion removal*. Basically, it consists of resetting parameters and looping, instead of calling the function again with "new" parameters.

This same approach works well also with the `factorial()`. You can rewrite it like this:

```
long new_factorial( long a )
{
  long result;

  result = a--; /* prime arg and decrement a */
  for ( ; a>1; a-- ) result *= a;
  return result;
}
```

Other Ways To Invoke Functions

You access functions most often through ordinary calls. At times, however, this is not possible or just not convenient. C has support also for these circumstances.

Pointers to functions allow you to arrange, very flexibly, the logic of your program. Using function pointers, you can write code that responds to changing conditions, picking the right function *at that time*.

Signal functions permit your program to respond to unexpected conditions. A library function, for example, may detect an abnormal condition and attempt to abort the program. A signal function can intercept this request and do something about it—cleaning up before allowing the abort, or correcting the condition and continuing execution.

Nonlocal jump functions provide a way to circumvent the normal function-call and return protocol. Whereas the `goto` statement can jump anywhere in the same function, the `longjmp()` function can shift execution to anywhere in the *program* that a `setjmp()` function has defined a target location. This facility should be used with great care. It is found most often in conjunction with signal-handling functions, and error-trapping routines.

Using Pointers to Functions

You can define a pointer to a function, and use that pointer to call the function. Being able to do this greatly enhances your control over the logic flow of your program—you can pick a "method" for performing some task, depending on the objects to be manipulated. You can defer that selection until it is time to perform the task. The general syntax for declaring a pointer to a function is as follows:

```
type ( *function-pointer )( parameter-list );
```

The type specifier is the same thing to which you are already accustomed— the type of the value returned by the function. The meaning of the function-pointer identifier is plain enough, as is the indirection operator. Remember that the indirection operator *in a declaration* means that a pointer, not a dereferenced object, is being defined.

Why are there parentheses around **function-pointer*? Operator precedence rules dictate them. Remember that postfix `()` has a higher precedence than the indirection operator. Therefore, without the parentheses you write a declaration for a function *returning a pointer*. To see the difference, compare these two lines of code:

```
int (*f)(...); /* pointer to function returning int */
int *f(...);   /* function returning pointer to int */
```

You can also define an array of pointers to function, all returning the specified *type*. The syntax looks like this:

```
type ( *function-pointer[bound] )( parameter-list );
```

where *bound* is just an integer expression bounding the array—limiting the number of elements, as before.

Getting the parameter list right is important. As at any other time, you need to know what parameters the function-to-be-called expects. If the parameters don't match exactly, all sorts of problems can crop up—most often an abnormally terminated program.

All pointers, including pointers to functions, must be initialized before they can be used. This is just as easy as knowing the names of the functions pointed to, or the name of another pointer to function. Here are some examples of initializing pointers to functions:

```
void first_function( void ); /* a function prototype */
...
void (*functiona)( void );    /* a pointer to function */
void (*methods[16])( void ); /* array of pointers to function*/
...
functiona = first_function;  /* init from designator */
methods[0] = functiona;      /* init from another pointer */
```

Using the function name without the postfix ( ) function-call operator yields a pointer to type function. In fact, C *always* converts a reference to a function designator in an expression to a *pointer* to function. This makes sense, because a function can't be "manipulated" in the sense that an object can; it can only be declared and called.

You call a function through a pointer by dereferencing the pointer, as in the following:

```
double result;
double (*docalc) ( double arg );
double (*methods[8])( double arg1, double arg2 );

docalc = sqrt; /* point to library square root function */
methods[0] = pow;         /* point to power lib function */
result = (*docalc)( 2.0 );            /* square root of 2 */
result = (*methods[0])( 3.0, 2.0 )         /* 3 squared */
```

Old-style Coding: Calling Functions with Pointers

The method of calling a function through a pointer, used in this chapter, originated in K & R C. ANSI permits functions to be called through a pointer by using a syntax that is indistinguishable from a normal function call, as follows:

```
int status;
int (*get_status)( void );
...
status = get_status();
```

This admittedly results in a cleaner appearance. Yet we prefer the old-style invocation, partly because of ingrained habit, but also because the old-style syntax emphasizes the fact that a *pointer*, not a normal function designator, is being used. Further, we sometimes still use compilers that do not support the newer ANSI specifications; backward compatibility is an issue for us. This is not to say that you must do what we do. Pick the method that is comfortable for you, and then be consistent with it.

Now let's put function pointers to work. Suppose that you want to define a general-purpose routine that you can always call to compare two objects—regardless of their type—and that picks the proper comparison method for you. The point is that you have to remember only one function-call format. You have to provide a parameter indicating the objects' type, but that is a small price to pay for the convenience. Such a program, `compares.c`, is shown in listing 6.6.

Listing 6.6. `compares.c` *(Using a pointer to function to invoke a function).*

Zortech C 1.7

```
1   #include <stdlib.h>
2   #include <stdio.h>
3
4   #define INT     0
5   #define CHAR    1
6   #define DOUBLE  2
7   #define LT -1
8   #define EQ  0
9   #define GT  1
10
11  int comp_int( void *obj1, void *obj2 );
12  int comp_char( void *obj1, void *obj2 );
13  int comp_double( void *obj1, void *obj2 );
14  int compares( int type, void *obj1, void *obj2 );
15
16  main()
17  {
18     int a = 64, b = 64;
19     char c = 'z', d = 'a';
20     double e = 1.414, f = 1.732;
21
22     printf( "Returned %d when comparing %d %d\n",
23        compares( INT, &a, &b ), a, b );
24     printf( "Returned %d when comparing %c %c\n",
25        compares( CHAR, &c, &d ), c, d );
26     printf( "Returned %d when comparing %f %f\n",
27        compares( DOUBLE, &e, &f ), e, f );
28  }
29
30  int compares( int type, void *obj1, void *obj2 )
31  {
32     int (*callit)( void *, void * ); /* pointer to function */
33
34     switch( type ) {  /* point to the appropriate function */
35        case INT:    callit = comp_int; break;
36        case CHAR:   callit = comp_char; break;
37        case DOUBLE: callit = comp_double; break;
```

Listing 6.6. continues

Listing 6.6. continued

```
38      default: return 0;   /* just say equal if no match */
39    }
40    return( (*callit)( obj1, obj2 ) ); /* It's this easy ! */
41 }
42
43 int comp_int( void *obj1, void *obj2 )
44 {
45    int result;
46
47    result = *(int *)obj1 - *(int *)obj2;
48    if ( result ) result /= abs( result );
49    return result;
50 }
51
52 int comp_char( void *obj1, void *obj2 )
53 {
54    int result;
55
56    result = *(char *)obj1 - *(char *)obj2;
57    if ( result ) result /= abs( result );
58    return result;
59 }
60
61 int comp_double( void *obj1, void *obj2 )
62 {
63    double result;
64
65    result = *(double *)obj1 - *(double *)obj2;
66    if ( result < 0 ) return -1;
67      else if ( result == 0 ) return 0;
68        else if ( result > 0 ) return 1;
69 }
```

The `compares()` function, lines 30–41 in listing 6.6, is built around the fact that `void` pointers can point to anything. This is first reflected in the call parameters for `compares()`, which consist of an integer identifying the object type (see the `#defines` on lines 4–6), and two `void` pointers. `compares()` does not know the object size and does not care—pointers are always the *same* size.

Within `compares()`, a pointer to a function returning `int` is declared (line 32). All the function has to do now is test the `type` variable and assign to the function pointer a pointer value for the correct comparison routine. This is done in lines 35–37. If the `type` variable is not correct, a value of 0 (indicating "equal") is returned immediately to the caller. Otherwise, the comparison function is called and its result is returned (line 40). After you look at it for a minute, it is really very simple.

`compares()` could have been written in another way. You can pass a function *pointer* as a parameter to a function. The function, and the call to it, would then look like this:

```
int compares( int (*method)( void *, void * ),
              void *obj1, void *obj2 )
{
   return( (*method)( obj1, obj2 ) );
}
...
result = compares( comp_int, &a, &b );
```

The comparison functions also have some interesting points. Look at `comp_int()`, lines 43–50 in listing 6.6. The comparison is made by the simple expedient of subtracting the second object from the first. To do this, the `void` pointer is first cast to the correct type, and then dereferenced to the object (line 47). If `*obj1` is less than `*obj2`, the result is negative; if they are equal, the result is 0; if `*obj1` is greater than `*obj2`, the result is positive.

Line 48, by dividing the result by itself, forces the result to be –1, 0, or 1. The absolute value is used in the denominator so that a negative result will not be forced positive. The method used in `comp_double()` (lines 61–69) is simple brute force. This is done because the division of floating-point numbers frequently does not come out completely exact. When it does not, a cast to `int` might truncate to 0, rather than –1 or 1, giving incorrect results.

The *signal()* and *raise()* Functions

Sometimes, being able to invoke a function on a completely unexpected basis (in response to the break key, or to a math exception, for example) would be convenient. The events triggered by such unexpected conditions are called *asynchronous events*. These events cannot be predicted, and can occur at any time during the program's execution.

Standard C allows for handling these events through the use of *signals*, a reporting mechanism that can invoke your signal-handling routines, based on the kind of event that occurred. Several macros defined in `signal.h` use an integral constant to define the types of signals. Table 6.1 lists macros for the different signal types.

272 Part I: Introduction to Standard C

Table 6.1. *Signal number macro names.*

Macro name	Description
SIGABRT	Abnormal termination; for example, raised by the `abort()` function
SIGFPE	Floating-point arithmetic exceptions; integer divide by 0 and overflow
SIGILL	Illegal instruction exception; for example, a bad pointer caused a function to be overlaid with garbage
SIGINT	Interactive attention signal; on the PC, Ctrl-C and Ctrl-Break
SIGSEGV	Segment violation; invalid memory access (bad segment number, protection exception)
SIGTERM	Program termination request; for example, the `exit()` function was called

You can associate your own signal-handling function with any or all of the signal types by calling the `signal()` function, with the signal type and a pointer-to-the-handler routine as parameters. `signal()` has a prototype in the `signal.h` header. Its syntax is as follows:

```
void (*signal(int sig, void (*func)(int))) (int);
```

This syntax is sufficiently convoluted to warrant dissecting it briefly. The guiding principle in analyzing this declaration is the fact that `signal()` *returns a pointer to a function*—specifically, a pointer to the preceding signal-handling function for the stated signal. How do you return a pointer to a function?

Let's presume that a function `f()` returns a pointer to some object—an integer, for example. Its declaration would then be

```
int *f(...); /* function returns pointer to int */
```

To write a declaration for a plain pointer to a function `f()` that returns `int` and has an `int` parameter, you would specify the following:

```
int (*f)(int); /* pointer to function returning int, parm int */
```

Because this last case is in fact what we want to *return* a pointer to, you would write

```
int (*f(...))(int); /* f() returns pointer, all else is */
                    /* description of pointed-to function */
```

Now apply that syntactical reasoning to the declaration for `signal()`, and recall that `signal()` itself has a parameter that is a function pointer, and you can account for all the parentheses.

You call the signal `function()` to do one of three things for a particular signal number: take the default action, ignore the signal, or invoke your signal-handling routine, as in the following examples:

```
signal( SIGSEGV, SIG_DFL ); /* take the default action */
signal( SIGABRT, SIG_IGN ); /* ignore the signal */
signal( SIGFPE, myfunc );   /* call myfunc() if SIGFPE */
```

Usually, the default action is to terminate the program. If you request that the signal be ignored, nothing at all happens. If you specify a signal-handling function name, what happens is up to you. Don't forget that `signal()` returns a pointer to the preceding handler function. If the request was not successful, it returns a value defined by the macro `SIG_ERR`. Listing 6.7 shows how the signal function and handling routines can be coded.

Listing 6.7. `showsig.c` *(Demonstrate signal handling).*

```
1   #include <stdlib.h>
2   #include <stdio.h>
3   #include <signal.h>
4
5   void handle_term( int sig )
6   {
7     printf( "    The terminate signal was raised.\n" );
8     return;
9   }
10
11  main()
12  {
13    char ch;
14
15    signal( SIGINT, SIG_IGN );
16    puts( "Strike the Control-Break key to see it echoed." );
17    puts( "Then strike Return to continue:" );
18    ch = getchar();
19    puts( "Now let's handle a program termination request." );
20    signal( SIGTERM, handle_term );
21    raise( SIGTERM );
22    puts( "Back in main() again." );
23    puts( "Next, the abort() call allows default action." );
24    signal( SIGABRT, SIG_DFL );
25    abort();
26  }
```

The handler function for SIGTERM is located in lines 5–9 of listing 6.7. The only action taken in this example was to display a message and return. In a "real" program, you might want to close files, notify the user, possibly present the user with alternatives (make a correction and continue, go ahead and terminate, and so forth), or free dynamically allocated memory.

Whenever a signal-handler is entered, the default action for that signal is reset, as though signal(sig, SIG_DFL) had been called. This is not under your control—it always happens. It is important to remember that, if you plan for the signal-handler to be used several times, you must call signal() again to "hook in" your function. You can do this from within the handler function.

The return statement is used in line 8 to leave the signal-handler. Using the return statement to leave a handler function causes the program to resume execution at the point it was interrupted. In general, you can do this, or call abort(), exit(), or longjmp() to get out of a signal handler—*except* when the signal was SIGFPE or an implementation-defined computational error.

When the signal was SIGFPE, you may *not* use the return statement; the subsequent behavior of the program is liable to be unpredictable. Either terminate the program, or use longjmp() to bypass that computation completely. longjmp() and its companion function setjmp() are covered in the next section.

Line 8 in listing 6.7 illustrates the companion function raise(). You use the raise() function to *generate* any of the previously defined signal types. raise() was used in the example, because the exit() function does *not* cause the SIGTERM signal to be sent—it always terminates the program. Some compilers provide an extra parameter to the signal-handling function—beyond the signal number, which is always passed—to identify special conditions. Detecting the fact that the signal resulted from a call to raise() is one such condition.

The ANSI standard allows an implementation to add to the list any signals it wants. The complete list of signals, their semantics, and how default handling is accomplished are all implementation-defined. The only restriction is that all signals (except SIG_ERR) must be positive.

The *setjmp()* and *longjmp()* Functions

The setjmp() function provides a "locator" that is the target of a longjmp() function call. The longjmp() function causes program execution to continue at the associated locator, rather than with the next line of code. `longjmp()` is capable of transferring control *across function boundaries*—you can jump anywhere in the program.

The most common uses for `setjmp()` and `longjmp()` are to return values from deeply nested function calls without having to "percolate" back to the top-level function and to terminate signal-handling routines.

`setjmp()` requires a *jump buffer* within which to store the status information that allows `longjmp()` to transfer control to `setjmp()`. A macro, `jmp_buf`, defines the jump buffer object. Thus the required statements to execute `setjmp()` are:

```
#include <setjmp.h>
jmp_buf env;
setjmp( env );
```

and the function prototype for `setjmp()` is

```
int setjmp( jmp_buf env );
```

`setjmp()` can be "called" in two ways. First, it can execute normally by being invoked directly. In this case, it returns 0, after setting up the environment status in the jump buffer. Note that `setjmp()` *can be executed this way any number of times*—it reestablishes the jump environment each time.

Second, a `longjmp()` can transfer control to the `setjmp()` function internally, passing it a value other than 0. It will seem, to the statement following `setjmp()`, that `setjmp()` was called and returned this other value. These returned values can be used to determine what to do next. You must make very sure of one thing: *the function containing the* `setjmp()` *must not have terminated* when `longjmp()` attempts to reference that location. Here is one possible way to set up for a `longjmp()`:

```
#include <setjmp.h>
jmp_buf main_env; /* notice file scope so everybody can */
                  /* access the jump buffer */
...
void do_calc( void )
{
   ... /* do processing; if error go back to main() */
   long_jmp( main_env, 1 );
   ...
}

main()
{
   int init = 0;
   int return;

   return = setjmp( main_env)
```

```
switch( return ) {        /* longjmp() comes here */
   case 0: init = 1;
           do_calc();     /* jump buffer set, start processing */
           break;
   case 1: /* possibly correct an error */
           do_calc(); /* and restart processing */
   }
}
```

Notice in this code fragment that longjmp() names the jump buffer so that the correct setjmp() location is targeted. This means that setjmp() can be used to initialize any number of jump buffers in different locations, for different purposes.

The other value specified in longjmp() is used to make it appear that setjmp() was called and returned that value. The prototype for longjmp() is as follows:

```
void longjmp( jmp_buf env, int val );
```

longjmp() has type void. It is one of only three functions—together with exit() and abort()—that legitimately never returns. Listing 6.8 illustrates how longjmp() can be used to return to a point from deeply nested function calls.

Listing 6.8. `jmperr.c` (`longjmp()` *out of nested functions*).

All Compilers

```
1    #include <stdlib.h>
2    #include <stdio.h>
3    #include <setjmp.h>
4
5    jmp_buf env1;
6
7    int comp1( void );
8    int comp2( void );
9    int comp3( void );
10
11   main()
12   {
13     int ret;
14     switch( ret = setjmp( env1 ) ) {
15       case 0: puts( "*** Starting computations ***" );
16               comp1(); break;   /* Start the process off */
17         case 1:
18         case 2:
```

```
19        case 3:
20        case 4:
21        case 5: printf( "Process returned code: %d\n", ret );
22                break;
23     }
24  }
25
26  int comp1()
27  {
28     return( comp2() );
29  }
30
31  int comp2()
32  {
33     return( comp3() );
34  }
35
36  int comp3()
37  {
38     char ch[3];
39     int val = 0;
40
41     while( val < 1 || val > 5 ) {
42        printf( "Type in a number from 1 to 5: " );
43        gets( ch );
44        val = atoi( ch );
45     }
46     longjmp( env1, val );
47  }
```

At the time the longjmp() function is called, control has descended down to comp3(), with no intervening returns. When longjmp() is called (line 46), control immediately returns to the point after setjmp(). In this case, that is the first case statement of the switch (line 15). Because this is not the initial call to setjmp(), case 0 is not satisfied.

What happens? Notice in comp3() that you are prompted to enter a number from 1 to 5. That number is used in longjmp() to supply the "simulated return" value. The printf(), line 21, displays which value that was.

The program jmpsig.c (listing 6.9) illustrates the use of longjmp() with more than one setjmp() active, as well as how to use longjmp() to terminate a signal-handler function.

Listing 6.9. `jmpsig.c` (*Terminating signal-handlers with the* `longjmp()` *function*).   *Turbo C 2.0*

```
1   /* +--------------------------------------------------+
2      + JMPSIG.C
3      + Demonstrate the use of longjmp() for terminating
4      + signal-handling functions.
5      +
6      + NOTE: This program does not run under all tested
7      +    compilers. The compilers tested and the results
8      +    are listed below:
9      + TURBO C 2.0 -- Runs successfully. signal() handling
10     +                 includes integer overflow and divide
11     +                 by zero intercept under SIGFPE.
12     +                 longjmp() can cross all function
13     +                 boundaries as per ANSI spec.
14     + QUICKC 2.0  -- Partially successful. longjmp()
15     +                 implementation ANSI conforming,
16     +                 but SIGFPE does not include integer
17     +                 exceptions.
18     + ZORTECH C   -- Unsuccessful. longjmp() not ANSI
19     +                 conforming; Zortech adds restnction
20     +                 that function containing longjmp()
21     +                 must be a DIRECT DESCENDENT of the
22     +                 function containing setjmp(). This
23     +                 prevents compliance with ANSI req.
24     +                 that a signal-handler may terminate
25     +                 via longjmp().
26     +--------------------------------------------------+
27  */
28  #include <stdlib.h>
29  #include <stdio.h>
30  #include <setjmp.h>
31  #include <signal.h>
32  #include <ctype.h>
33
34  jmp_buf break_env;
35  jmp_buf error_env;
36
37  void handle_break( int );
38  void handle_error( int );
39
40  main()
41  {
42     char num[6];
43     int val;
44
45     setjmp( break_env );
46     signal( SIGINT, handle_break );
47     puts( "This program demonstrates the use of longjmp()" );
48     puts( "to terminate signal-handler functions." );
```

```
49    puts( "" );
50    puts( "Enter an integer when the program prompts you." );
51    puts( "(Try a zero and see what happens.)" );
52    puts( "Strike CTRL-BREAK to quit." );
53    puts( "" );
54
55    while ( 1 ) {
56      setjmp( error_env );
57      signal( SIGFPE, handle_error );
58      printf( "Enter a number, up to 5 digits: " );
59      gets( num );
60      val = atoi( num );
61      val = 32767 / val;
62    }
63  }
64
65  void handle_break( int sig )
66  {
67    char ans[4];
68
69    puts( "CTRL-BREAK detected." );
70    puts( "Enter \"y\" or \"yes\" to continue," );
71    puts( " anything else to quit." );
72    gets( ans );
73    if ( 'Y' == toupper( *ans ) ) longjmp( break_env, 1 );
74      else exit( 0 );
75  }
76
77  void handle_error( int sig )
78  {
79    char ans[4];
80
81    puts( "Divide by zero attempted." );
82    puts( "Enter \"y\" or \"yes\" to continue," );
83    puts( " anything else to quit." );
84    gets( ans );
85    if ( 'Y' == toupper( *ans ) ) longjmp( error_env, 1 );
86      else exit( 0 );
87  }
```

As the listing header shows, this particular sample program was written in Turbo C. We used Turbo C because it was the only compiler tested that not only conforms completely to the ANSI standard (for these functions, that is), but that also includes integer arithmetic exceptions in its implementation of SIGFPE handling. The comments in lines 1–26 of the program explain this fully.

Two setjmp() environments are established; one is in line 45, the other in line 56. The setjmp(break_env) in line 45 provides a jump buffer and target location for jumps out of the break-key handler. The `setjmp( error_env )` provides a jump buffer and target location for jumps out of the `SIGFPE` handler. Remember that a function handling `SIGFPE` cannot terminate through `return`.

Both of these jump buffers and targets are active at the same time. They are kept unconfused because the `longjmp()` used to access them *names the jump buffer to use* (see lines 73 and 85).

Line 46, immediately after the `setjmp()` for break-key handling, contains a `signal()` function call that *reestablishes the signal handler for* `SIGINT`. You should recall that entry to a signal-handler resets that signal for default processing.

Line 56 contains a `setjmp()` location for the `SIGFPE` handler. Notice that it is *inside* the `while` loop. The `error_env` jump buffer is reinitialized on every pass through the loop, whether or not a `longjmp()` has targeted the location. This hurts nothing—it only emphasizes the fact that `longjmp()` jumps to the target location defined by the most recent direct call to `setjmp()` specifying that jump buffer name. Line 57 reestablishes the `SIGFPE` handler, as line 46 did the `SIGINT` handler.

Spend some time now to study these examples in detail, thinking about what statement will execute next—and why. Type the programs and run them, observing their behavior. These functions are underrated and not used much, perhaps because they can be confusing at times. But the programming power they make available is well worth the effort.

Summary

In this chapter, you have learned about three important topics:

❏ *Details on passing parameters to functions*

❏ *How to design and control recursive functions*

❏ *Alternative ways to invoke functions*

The concepts and techniques involved give you close to complete control of your C functions, and thus are more important than they may at first seem. Take some time to let this all sink in. Write some code and experiment—get thoroughly familiar with these tools. Later, your programs will be robust, reliable, and a pleasure to write—and to use.

7

Controlling
Program Logic Flow

U nless you do something about it, statements in a computer program
execute one after the other, beginning with the first and continuing
until the end. In fact, if you forget to add code that tells the operating system
when the program is finished, the computer continues merrily to attempt to
execute instructions beyond the end of the code—always with unpleasant
results.

The selection (by the hardware) of the next instruction to execute is called
the *flow of execution*. The flow of execution is inherently *sequential* in
today's computers (although we now have to make an exception for the new
parallel-processing machines). This means that, all other things being equal,
your C program begins running at the first line at the top and keeps going
straight to the last line at the bottom.

Now, if that were all there is to modern computers, saying that they are
useless would not be too harsh a judgement. If you wanted to read every
record from a database containing a million records, for example, you would
have to write a program containing a million input instructions, one after the
other.

Fortunately, this is not the case. Execution flow is *inherently* linear, but
not *necessarily* so. General-purpose digital computers (including your PC)
have special instructions that can cause a *transfer of control*—they cause the

next instruction selected for execution to be one *other than* the next sequential instruction. These special instructions are called *jump* or *branch* instructions, depending on the make of computer.

These instructions can make the hypothetical database input program bearable. The presence of branching instructions raises the possibility of writing just one input instruction and then branching back to it repetitively. This arrangement is called a *loop*. In other circumstances, you might want to skip a particular part of the processing sequence, or pick an alternative sequence by branching to it. This is called *conditional logic*.

In a given program, the particular flow of execution is composed of sequentially executed instructions, program loops, and conditional branches. That is, every program has its own peculiar *logic flow* (some, it might be added, are more peculiar than others!). But in *every* case, it is the ability to loop and perform conditional logic that, more than any other single factor, gives a program its power and flexibility. This is true regardless of whether C or another language is used.

Designing Program Loops

The loop (the repetitive execution of a group of statements) is one of the most omnipresent features of programs that perform useful work. Think back to the sample programs you have seen in this book. They contained all kinds of loops, even though we hadn't yet explained what a loop is: there were loops to read the records of a file, to copy or manipulate the characters of a string, to process all the elements of an array.

Try as we may, it is almost impossible to conceive of sample programs that do anything informative, interesting, or useful that do not contain a loop somewhere. If loops are so much a part of most programs, then, you should take care to write efficient and effective loops. That requires understanding them thoroughly.

Properties of Program Loops

Before writing the code for a loop, plan *how to control it*. It is not enough to be able to branch back to the first statement of a loop—such a loop could go on forever. You need to plan how to determine how often to "pass through" the loop; that implies also planning the means of stopping the loop. There must be some sort of *control variables* to govern the process. And don't forget to plan the task that needs to be accomplished.

Writing a loop entails just four basic steps. *Initialization* is done outside and before the loop structure. This is where you set up control variables for loop control, and initialize any data objects you may need. The *loop body* is the group of statements that are executed repetitively, and that perform useful work. The *adjustment step* occurs within the loop structure; it consists of updating the control variables to keep track of progress. *Condition checking* examines the state of the control variables, and perhaps the data variables also, to determine when the loop is finished. If the loop is finished, it is exited. If it is not finished, a branch is taken back to the first statement in the loop, and the next *iteration* or *pass* begins through the loop body.

These four basic steps are present in some form in all loops, in every source language. Loops in general are characterized by the placement of the condition-checking code. Loops that perform the checking at the end of the loop structure are said to use *back-end condition checking*. This kind of loop structure is illustrated in figure 7.1.

Fig. 7.1. *Back-end loop condition checking.*

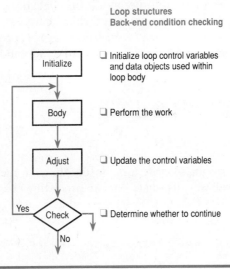

Loop structures
Back-end condition checking

❏ Initialize loop control variables
   and data objects used within
   loop body

❏ Perform the work

❏ Update the control variables

❏ Determine whether to continue

Back-end condition checking is not the only configuration possible. In fact, the most commonly used C loop-control statements feature front-end condition checking, as illustrated in figure 7.2.

Fig. 7.2. *Front-end loop condition checking.*

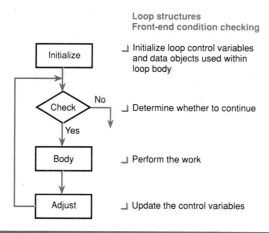

Loop structures
Front-end condition checking

❏ Initialize loop control variables and data objects used within loop body

❏ Determine whether to continue

❏ Perform the work

❏ Update the control variables

You can check control variables more than once in each pass through the loop body. The need for multiple condition checking arises when some condition in the loop body may possibly force an early exit from the loop. In addition to longjmp(), signal(), and raise(), C provides more ordinary means for altering loop flow: the break, continue, and goto statements, all of which are covered in this chapter.

Doing It the Hard Way— Not Recommended

C provides the means to write loops using "brute force" code, if you are so inclined. For example, listing 6.1 in the preceding chapter showed how to use va_arg() in a loop to display an undetermined number of strings passed as arguments to a function. That code looked like this:

```
hold = va_arg( ap, char * );   /* Prime the loop */
while ( *hold ) {              /* Test the string */
   printf( "%s\n", hold );
   hold = va_arg( ap, char * );
}
```

You can use the goto statement together with statement labels to do this the hard way. The resulting code is not nearly as clean or readable as the original example:

```
    hold = va_arg( ap, char * );        /* Prime the loop */
loop1: ;
    if ( *hold != '\0') goto loop2; /* Test the string */
    printf( "%s\n", hold );
    hold = va_arg( ap, char * );
    goto loop1;                                /* loop again */
loop2: ;          /* Null statement with statement label */
```

This construction is not usually recommended; it is almost always better to let the compiler do the detail work of framing the loop structure. Use the statements that C provides expressly for loop control, because they are neater, very efficient, and safer.

Using the C-provided loop syntax is safer because it hides some of the detail work from the programmer. The issue is not at all that programmers are stupid; it is, rather, that using direct goto's and labels *invites* errors. One can easily plant inside the loop statements that don't belong there, or move some that *do* belong there outside, especially when the loop is longer and more complex than the simple examples shown here. It gets even worse when, after some time has elapsed, you come back to a program and modify it—you may have forgotten just what exactly went where in the source code.

The opposite extreme of *never* allowing a goto in your programs may not be wise, however. This philosophy was the rage some years ago, during the initial debates on exactly what structured programming was intended to accomplish. The contention was that a direct jump (goto) *always* introduces confusion into the program. This is simply not true: at times, using a goto is the only sensible thing to do. For example, a goto is used in prime.c, listing 7.1, to reduce confusion.

Listing 7.1. prime.c *(Compute first 350 prime numbers).*   *QuickC 2.5*

```
1   #include <stdlib.h>
2   #include <stdio.h>
3   #include <graph.h>
4   #include <conio.h>
5
6   long *primes;
7   long j, k, n;
8
9   void calc_primes( void );
10  void disp_primes( void );
11
12  main()
13  {
```

Listing 7.1. continues

Listing 7.1. continued

```
14     primes = (long *)calloc( 350, sizeof( long ) );
15     _clearscreen( _GCLEARSCREEN );
16     cputs( "... Calculating table of 350 prime numbers ..." );
17     calc_primes();
18     _clearscreen( _GCLEARSCREEN );
19     disp_primes();
20     free( primes );
21     exit( 0 );
22  }
23
24  /* +-------------------------+
25     +  Calculate the first 350 prime numbers.
26     +  Assumes that the primes{} table was allocated
27     +  in global data.
28     +  Method is Knuth's, 2nd ed., Vol. 1, pp. 143-144
29     +-------------------------+
30  */
31  void calc_primes( void )
32  {
33     ldiv_t ans;
34
35     primes[0] = 2;
36     n = 3;
37     for ( j=1; j<350; j++ ) {
38       primes[j] = n;              /* Store the prime */
39  nextprime: n += 2;
40       k = 1;
41  checkprime: ans = ldiv( n, primes[k] );
42       if ( ans.rem == 0 ) goto nextprime;
43       if ( ans.quot <= primes[k] ) continue;
44       k++;
45       goto checkprime;
46     }
47  }
48
49  void disp_primes( void )
50  {
51     struct rccoord cursor;
52
53     for ( n=0; n<350; n++ ) {
54       cprintf( "%.4ld ", primes[n]  );
55       cursor = _gettextposition();
56       _settextposition( cursor.row, cursor.col+5 );
57       if ( cursor.col > 75 )
58         _settextposition( cursor.row+1, 1 );
59     }
60  }
```

The loop in lines 37–47 calculates the series of prime numbers, and would be quite complex without the `goto` and `continue` statements. Figure 7.3 shows the logic flow of prime-number calculation.

Fig. 7.3. *Prime-number calculation logic.*

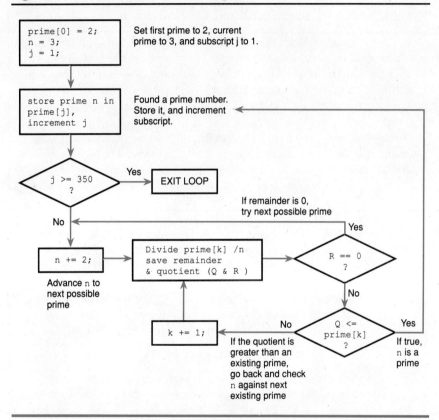

This algorithm is based on two facts. First, given an existing prime number, the next *possible* prime number is n + 2. Second, you can test the possible prime by dividing it into the previously found primes; if any one of these divisions produces a nonzero remainder *and* a quotient that is less than or equal to the prime being used to test, then the candidate also is a prime number.

As you look at figure 7.3, you can see that testing for these conditions involves possible branches in too many directions for the logic to package comfortably in a conventional while or for loop structure. You might be able to examine the logic carefully (and at some length) and find a way to do it—but you would have difficulty finding a way that is this compact and this easily read. Fortunately, the need for this sort of overriding logic is rare.

Quick-Reference: Standard C Loop Control

The standard C language specifications refer to the loop-control statements as *iteration statements*. There are just three of them, but they provide more than enough programming power to accomplish any task you might imagine. All three iteration statements refer to a target *statement* that is the *loop body*. The loop body may be a simple statement, in which case it should be terminated with a semicolon, or it may be a block statement, in which case the group of statements should be surrounded by curly braces ({ }). The syntax and use of the three iteration statements follow:

❑   while (*expression*) *statement*

The loop body *statement* is executed repeatedly, as long as *expression* evaluates to a nonzero integral value (evaluates to true). The while statement features front-end condition checking.

❑   do *statement* while (*expression*) ;

The do statement evaluates *expression* only *after* the loop body has been executed. Thus, do-while features back-end condition checking, and guarantees at least one pass through the loop.

❑   for (*expr1*opt; *expr2*opt; *expr3*opt) *statement*

A for statement combines the initialization, condition-checking, and adjustment steps of loop processing in the three expressions enclosed within the parentheses. All three expressions are optional and may be omitted (which produces a never-ending loop if you do not take other steps), and any of the expressions may be a list of expressions separated by comma operators. The accompanying text explains this more fully. A for loop features front-end condition checking; *expr2* is evaluated before the loop body is executed on each pass.

Front-end Condition Checking: *while()*

The ANSI document refers to loop-controlling statements as *iteration statements*. There are three of them: `while`, `do`, and `for`. Of the three, the `while` has the simplest format. Its syntax is as follows:

```
while ( controlling-expression ) statement
```

This means that while the controlling-expression is *true* (evaluates to a nonzero integral value) the associated statement is executed repetitively. This *target* statement is the loop body. The statement can be a simple statement, terminated with a semicolon, or it can be a block statement enclosed in curly braces.

The `while` statement uses front-end condition checking, as illustrated in figure 7.2. For each pass through the loop, the controlling-expression is evaluated *first* and, when it yields a false integral result, the loop is exited. The `while` statement is shown in the context of a program in listing 7.2. This program uses an array of `double` to represent the coefficients of an algebraic polynomial. Given a particular value for the independent variable x, the polynomial is evaluated for that point.

Listing *7.2.* `poly.c` *(Evaluating a polynomial with* `while`*).*   *Turbo C, 2.0*

```
 1   /* +----------------------------------------------------+
 2       + POLY.C
 3       +  Evaluate a polynomial using Horner's method
 4       +----------------------------------------------------+
 5   */
 6   #include <stdlib.h>
 7   #include <stdio.h>
 8   #include <math.h>
 9
10   #include "timer.h"
11
12   double polynomial( int degree, double var, double *coeff
     );
13
14   main()
15   {
16      double tvalue, cvalue;
17      double x = 2.0;
18      double coeff[4] = { 3, 2, 4, 1 };
19      double coeff2[4] = { 1, 4, 2, 3 };
20
```

Listing **7.2.** *continues*

Listing 7.2. *continued*

```
21   /*
22       Compare our method to Turbo C implementation of poly()
23   */
24      start_bench();
25      tvalue = poly( x, 3, coeff2 );
26      stop_bench();
27      printf( "Turbo C took %8.6f seconds.\n", duration() );
28
29      start_bench();
30      cvalue = polynomial( 3, x, coeff );
31      stop_bench();
32      printf( "Our version took %8.6f seconds.\n", duration() );
33      printf( "The polynomial evaluates to %f\n", cvalue );
34   }
35
36   /* +----------------------------------------------------+
37      + polynomial();
38      + INPUT: degree = highest power of var
39      +          var   = base variable (e.g., "x")
40      +          coeff = array of doubles containing the
41      +                     coefficients. coeff[0] should
42      +                     contain coeff of highest power,
43      +                     coeff[degree+1], coeff of 0 power.
44      +----------------------------------------------------+
45   */
46   double polynomial( int degree, double var, double *coeff )
47   {
48      static double sum;  /* Can't put initializer on static object */
49
50      sum = *coeff++;
51      while ( degree-- > 0 ) sum = sum * var + *coeff++;
52      return sum;
53   }
```

The program `poly.c` in listing 7.2 uses the `timer.c` routines (see Appendix F; remember also that this is a multiple-source file program; don't forget to build a project or MAKE file) to compare the Turbo C implementation of `poly()` with our implementation, called `polynomial()`. Neither implementation is an ANSI standard library function. A similar function is provided by many compilers as a common extension to the language, which is perfectly permissible. Our implementation requires about 0.2 milliseconds longer to run than the compiler-provided library function. There is a moral here: usually, the compiler vendor has taken great pains to provide an extremely efficient function. If the compiler provides the function, you should use it, unless portability to other compilers absolutely prohibits doing so.

This sample program evaluates the polynomial $3x^3 + 4x^2 + 2x + 1$, for the point x = 2. An algorithm known as *Horner's method* is used to implement the code. This algorithm is based on a procedure called *nesting*, which rearranges the formula algebraically for faster machine evaluation. Notice that you can factor out x progressively, like this:

```
3x³ + 4x² + 2x + 1
(3x² + 4x + 2) * x + 1
( (3x + 4 ) * x + 2) * x + 1
```

The function `polynomial()` in lines 46–53 takes advantage of this fact by first initializing the result to the high-order coefficient value (line 50). Thus the routine works even if there is only *one* coefficient.

The complete result is formed by using a `while` statement to compute a running total (line 51). Each pass simply multiplies the preceding sum by x and adds in the next coefficient. This procedure takes advantage of Horner's nesting method to reduce to an absolute minimum the number of multiplications by x.

Notice how the argument-variable `degree` is used to control the loop: deliberate side effects are used in the controlling expression to produce extremely compact code. (As a rule of thumb, you can consider compact code to be faster code—although this is not always true.) Remember that a sequence point is not taken until the complete expression `degree-- > 0` has been evaluated. The correct value of `degree` is used to evaluate the expression; the `degree` object is updated at the sequence point, in time for the next pass.

Side effects are an extremely powerful way to increase the utility of the `while` statement. It is possible to write a `while` loop in which *all* the work is done by the controlling-expression; the target statement may be null. You already have seen this in the code to copy one string to another, using nothing but side effects, as follows:

```
char *s1;
char *s2;
...
while( *s1++ = *s2++ ) ;
```

In each pass through the loop, only front-end checking occurs, but the controlling-expression updates the pointer values to the next location through the use of side effects. This loop copies one string to another, *including the terminating null character*, because the null character is not evaluated as false until *after* it has been "moved across" the assignment operator. The postfix ++ operator does leave both pointers positioned one character beyond the end of each string, however.

Constructing a deliberate never-ending loop with the `while` statement also is possible, as in the following example:

```
while ( 1 ) {
    ... /* something in here had better exit the loop */
}
```

Because the controlling-expression is exactly the integer value 1, it always evaluates to true. The logic contained in the target statement (a block statement, here) is responsible for detecting whatever condition signals the end-of-loop processing and for exiting the loop. Such a construction is sometimes used to handle a keyboard input loop, as follows:

```
char ch;
while ( 1 ) {
    puts( "Enter a selection character or Control-Z "
          "to end the program." );
    ch = getchar();    /* getch() is not standard */
    if ( ch == 26 ) break; /* Ctl-Z ends the loop */
    ...            /* Other processing continues here */
}
```

The `break` statement used here to exit the loop "manually" is covered later in this chapter. (See "Programming Conditional Logic.")

Back-end Condition Checking: *do-while()*

A loop construction using front-end condition checking could, by definition, *possibly never execute the loop body*. The condition check may turn out not to be satisfied on the very first attempt to pass through the loop. Sometimes this is just the protection you want.

At other times, front-end condition checking actually may prevent the successful operation of your program. In certain situations, you want *at least one guaranteed pass through the loop*, no matter what. Loop constructions using back-end condition checking provide this feature (refer to fig. 7.1). C implements back-end condition checking in the `do-while` loop. Its syntax is

```
do statement while ( expression ) ;
```

In a `do-while` loop construction, the target statement that is the loop body appears *before* the controlling-expression. One pass is guaranteed, because the loop body must be executed in order to get to the controlling-expression. Here, as elsewhere, the target statement may be a block statement.

Back-end condition checking is not needed as often as front-end check-ing. But when it is needed, it is indispensable. Consider the task of replacing tab characters in a text file with an appropriate number of blanks for example. Encountering a tab character ' \ t ' in the text always means that the next output position must be increased to the next tab stop—even if the current position is already in a tab-stop location. Therefore, at least one guaranteed pass through the blank-producing loop is required.

The detab.c program in listing 7.3 performs this function. Because this program may be of some long-term use to you, we have provided a fully capable program, rather than a stripped-down example. The program includes command-line options for the input file name and for setting the tab size. It also backs up the input file before modifying it, and takes into account possible I/O errors during processing.

Listing 7.3. detab.c (do-while guarantees at least one pass).

Turbo C 2.0

```
 1   #include <stdlib.h>
 2   #include <stdio.h>
 3   #include <ctype.h>
 4   #include <string.h>
 5
 6   /* +--------------------------------------------------------+
 7      + STRUPR()     String chars to uppercase.
 8      + Turbo C actually has a lib function exactly like
 9      + this one, it is just not standard. Notice that
10      + string.h is included, so the Turbo C version is
11      + replaced by this one (this program only).
12      +--------------------------------------------------------+
13   */
14   char *strupr( char *s )
15   {
16     static char *p; /* Can't return an auto var! */
17
18     p = s;
19     for ( ; *s; *s++ = toupper( *s ) ) ;
20     return( p );
21   }
22
23   main( int argc, char *argv[] )
24   {
25     FILE *tgtfile, *bkupfile;
26     char tgtname[81] = "";
27     char bkupname[81] = "";
28     char ch;
29     int tabsize = 8;
```

Listing 7.3. continues

Listing 7.3. continued

```
30      int i, column = 1;
31
32      /* Show command format if no command line parms */
33
34      if ( argc == 1 ) {
35        puts( "DETAB command line format is:" );
36        puts( "    C:>detab [-tn] -ffilename" );
37        puts( "Tab size is optional, defaults to 8." );
38        puts( "filename is required." );
39        puts( "Type \"-t\" and \"-f\" exactly as shown." );
40        exit( 0 );
41      }
42
43      /* ------ Get command line parameters and options ------ */
44
45      for ( i=1; i<argc; i++ ) {
46        strupr( argv[i] );
47        if ( 0 == strncmp( "-T", argv[i], 2 ) ) {
48          tabsize = (int)strtol( argv[i]+2, NULL, 0 );
49          printf( "Requested tab size of %d characters.\n",
50                  tabsize );
51        }
52        if ( 0 == strncmp( "-F", argv[i], 2 ) ) {
53          strcpy( tgtname, argv[i]+2 );
54          printf( "Detabbing: %s\n", tgtname );
55        }
56      }
57      if ( !*tgtname ) {
58        puts( "No filename given." );
59        exit( 8 );
60      }
61      strcpy( bkupname, tgtname );
62      if ( !strchr( bkupname, '.' ) ) strcat( bkupname, ".BAK" );
63      else {
64        char *p = bkupname;
65        while ( *p != '.' ) p++;
66        *p = '\0';
67        strcat( bkupname, ".BAK" );
68      }
69
70      /* ------ BACK UP the file before touching it! ------ */
71
72      printf( "Copying %s to %s\n", tgtname, bkupname );
73
74      if ( NULL == ( tgtfile = fopen( tgtname, "rb" ) ) ) {
75        puts( "Can't open the input file." );
76        exit( 8 );
77      }
```

```
78      setvbuf( tgtfile, NULL, _IOFBF, 16384 );
79      if ( NULL == ( bkupfile = fopen( bkupname, "wb" ) ) ) {
80        puts( "Can't open the backup file." );
81        exit( 8 );
82      }
83      setvbuf( bkupfile, NULL, _IOFBF, 16384 );
84
85      while ( EOF != ( ch = fgetc( tgtfile ) ) ) {
86        fputc( ch, bkupfile );
87        if ( ferror( bkupfile ) ) {
88          puts( "Error writing backup file." );
89          fclose( tgtfile );
90          fclose( bkupfile );
91          remove( bkupname );
92          exit( 8 );
93        }
94      }
95      if ( ferror( tgtfile ) ) {
96        puts( "Error reading input file." );
97        fclose( tgtfile );
98        fclose( bkupfile );
99        remove( bkupname );
100       exit( 8 );
101     }
102     fclose( tgtfile );
103     fclose( bkupfile );
104
105     /* ------ Finally, detab the target file ------ */
106
107     printf( "Detabbing %s\n", tgtname );
108
109     if ( NULL == ( bkupfile = fopen( bkupname, "rb" ) ) ) {
110       puts( "Can't open the input file." );
111       exit( 8 );
112     }
113     setvbuf( bkupfile, NULL, _IOFBF, 16384 );
114     if ( NULL == ( tgtfile = fopen( tgtname, "wb" ) ) ) {
115       puts( "Can't open the backup file." );
116       exit( 8 );
117     }
118     setvbuf( tgtfile, NULL, _IOFBF, 16384 );
119
120     while ( EOF != ( ch = fgetc( bkupfile ) ) ) {
121       switch( ch ) {
122         case '\t': do {
123                        if ( EOF == fputc( ' ', tgtfile ) ) break;
124                      } while ( ++column % tabsize != 1 );
125                      break;
126         case '\r':
127         case '\n': column = 0;
```

Listing 7.3. continues

Listing 7.3. *continued*

```
128          default:    fputc( ch, tgtfile ); ++column; break;
129        }
130      if ( ferror( tgtfile ) ) {
131        puts( "Error writing target file." );
132        fclose( tgtfile );
133        fclose( bkupfile );
134        exit( 8 );
135      }
136    }
137    if ( ferror( bkupfile ) ) {
138      puts( "Error reading backup file." );
139      fclose( tgtfile );
140      fclose( bkupfile );
141      exit( 8 );
142    }
143    fclose( tgtfile );
144    fclose( bkupfile );
145  }
```

Lines 122–124 of listing 7.3 contain the do-while that substitutes blanks for tab characters. This do-while is written as the action to be taken (as detected by a switch statement, which is discussed shortly) when a tab character is encountered in the input stream. (Notice how much code this program requires to support this one small loop! This is why productive programs are never as short and simple as most sample programs in books.)

The loop body consists of an fputc() that writes blanks to the output file. If an EOF occurs during *output*, the break statement exits the switch statement. Remember that EOF is reported for end-of-file (out of space) *and* error conditions (bad write) occurring in fputc(). Lines 130–135 outside the switch then use the ferror() function to determine whether there was an output error. This error test is always executed; it serves to catch errors from the fputc() in line 128 as well as from tab expansion.

Line 124 contains the controlling-expression for the do-while. It does two things: first it *prefix increments* the column counter, and then it tests whether the remainder of column divided by tabsize is 1. The loop continues to output blanks until the remainder (modulus) is 1.

Why it does this becomes clear when you think of the first character of a text line as column 1. Now suppose that the tabsize is 8 (the default here). The next tab stop is in column 9, then 17, and so on. When the modulus is 1, column represents a tab stop location.

But why is the `column` variable *prefix* incremented? Because the goal is to advance to the *next* tab stop, *no matter what* the current column may be. This is why back-end condition checking is necessary—the current position must be advanced *even if* `column` is already positioned at a tab stop. The prefix increment prevents the modulus from being 1 when the loop *begins* at a tab-stop location. This in turn requires that the loop body be executed beforehand to stay in synch.

We encourage you to try rewriting this loop without using the `do-while` construction. It can be done—but obtaining predictable results in *all* combinations of circumstances won't be easy.

Getting It All: The *for()* Loop

The `for`-loop statement groups the initialization expression, front-end controlling-expression, and loop-variable adjustment expression all together inside a single parenthesized list. The syntax of the `for` statement is as follows:

```
for ( expr1 ; expr2 ; expr3 ) statement
```

Note that this is not a list of parameters (which would be separated by commas). It is a group of expressions, *separated by semicolons*. Keeping this straight is important, because you *can* use the comma operator to write multiple expressions in each expression location. For example:

```
for ( expr1 ; expr2a,expr2b,expr2c ; expr3 ) statement
```

is perfectly legitimate. All three controlling expressions are optional. You can omit any or all of them. When you do use them, their meanings are as follows:

❑ *expr1 is used to initialize the loop-control variable (or variables, if a comma-separated list of expressions is used).*

❑ *expr2 is the front-end controlling expression (or expressions).* The loop continues to execute *statement* (which may be a block statement), as long as the expression, or *all of the comma-separated expressions*, evaluate to true.

❑ *expr3 adjusts the value of the loop-control variable or variables. expr3* may be multiple expressions, separated by commas, also.

Lines 45–56 of listing 7.3 illustrate the normal use of the `for` statement. You may recognize this as the method presented earlier in the book for processing all of the command-line parameters in turn. This use of the `for` statement is the equivalent of a `while` loop constructed like this:

```
expr1;                /* initialize loop variables */
while ( expr2 ) {     /* front-end condition checking */
  statement;
  expr3;              /* update loop variables */
}
```

As in the while loop, the target *statement* of a for can be a null statement. Lines 14–21 of listing 7.3 give a good example of the for loop with one of the expressions omitted, and with a null target statement. The strupr() function shown in these lines converts all the characters of a string to uppercase characters by letting side effects do all the work:

```
char *strupr( char *s )
{
  static char *p; /* Can't return an auto var! */

  p = s;
  for ( ; *s; *s++ = toupper( *s ) ) ;
  return( p );
}
```

Notice in this fragment that expr1 is left out. There is no need for it because the program already "knows" where the target string begins—it begins wherever *s points. The controlling-expression is *s; it evaluates true until the terminating null character is encountered in the string. expr3 performs not only the loop-control variable adjustment (the postfix ++ increment of the pointer) but also the primary work of the loop [= toupper(*s)].

Writing the loop like this:

```
for ( p=s; *s; s++ ) *s = toupper( *s );
```

would have been just as correct. This second method is even easier to read.

Is there any reason, then, to write code as compactly as possible? There are two reasons: writing compact code frequently reduces the size and length of the source file and often allows the compiler to produce more efficient (*faster*) code. The gain in efficiency is small enough to be unproductive, however, if it results in code you cannot read and control. Making this choice is always a judgement call, but remember that *you* are the one who has to live with the result.

What about more complicated situations? Can you, for instance, write loops inside of loops? You certainly can, and often this is exactly the way to do things. Writing loops inside of other loop bodies is called *nesting*. It can produce some very clean logic capable of sophisticated work. Listing 7.4

shows the program a s c i i . c, which produces an ASCII chart on your display by using nested loops. This program uses the Zortech compiler's d i s p_ . . . () group of functions for high-speed screen display. You may have to change the screen output functions if you do not have the Zortech compiler.

Listing 7.4. ascii.c *(Nested* for*-loops increase loop sophistication).*

Zortech C 1.7

```
1    /* +--------------------------------------------------+
2       +   ASCII.C                              ZORTECH C
3       +   Display an ASCII chart for all 256 characters
4       +   in the IBM-PC collating sequence
5       +--------------------------------------------------+
6    */
7    #include <stdlib.h>
8    #include <stdio.h>
9    #include <disp.h>
10
11   main()
12   {
13     int i, j, x, y;
14     char ch;
15
16     disp_open();            /* start Zortech display package */
17     disp_scroll( 0, 0, 0, 42, 79, 0x07 ); /* clear screen */
18     i = 0;
19     for ( j=0; j<2; j++ ) {    /* half the table at a time */
20       for ( x=0; x<80; x+=10 ) {        /* write 8 columns */
21         for ( y=0; y<16; y++ ) {          /* with 16 lines */
22           disp_move( y, x );
23           disp_printf( "(%.3d)", i );
24           disp_pokew( y, x+6, 0x0700 + i++ ); /* char out */
25         }
26       }
27       disp_move( 24, 40 );
28       disp_printf( "Strike a key to continue ..." );
29       ch = '\0'; while( !ch ) ch = getch();
30     }
31     disp_scroll( 0, 0, 0, 42, 79, 0x07 ); /* clear screen */
32     disp_close();
33   }
```

The nested loop structure for producing the ASCII chart is in lines 19–31 of listing 7.4. Notice the comments on lines 19, 20, and 21—these are the successive for statements controlling the nested loops. You can think of these as the loop "tops" (entry points).

The largest, or *outer*, loop comprises all the source lines from 19 to 31. The outer loop produces half the ASCII chart at a time. The next *inner* loop, lines 20–26, produces 8 columns of display. Finally, the innermost loop, lines 21–25, produces the codes and characters for a single column of the display.

Now think about how a loop body is executed repeatedly as long as the controlling-expression is true, and reflect on how a nested loop works. You should think of the flow of execution as *descending into* the nested structure, with the innermost loop being the lowest level. It is the innermost loop that completes first. An inner loop *runs to completion* for *every pass* of the loop in which it is contained.

Now we translate that concept into an analysis of this example. Here again are lines 19–21 from listing 7.4:

```
19      for ( j=0; j<2; j++ ) {     /* half the table at a time */
20        for ( x=0; x<80; x+=10 ) {        /* write 8 columns */
21          for ( y=0; y<16; y++ ) {         /* with 16 lines */
    . . .
```

When line 19 is encountered, the outer loop is initiated. Its target statement here is a block statement that happens to contain other loops. The target statement—the loop body—is executed completely for every pass through the outer loop. This means that each inner loop is completely executed, all the way to loop termination, *for every pass through the outer loop.*

The same applies to the loop defined in line 20. As soon as it is initiated, execution flow descends again and the third, innermost loop, line 21, is initiated also. Execution flow does not "percolate" back up to line 20 again until the entire innermost loop is complete—16 lines of columnar information is written.

At this point, line 20 executes again, and determines that all 8 columns have not yet been displayed. Therefore, execution flow yet again descends to the innermost loop, where another complete column of information is written to the screen.

This process continues until all 8 columns of 16 items have been displayed. Simple arithmetic shows that there are 16 * 8 (or 128) passes through the loop body of the innermost loop, before execution flow ever percolates *above* line 20 again.

Finally, because the outermost loop executes in two passes (one display page per half the ASCII table), this whole process repeats a second time, so that the innermost loop body executes 256 times—the number of characters in the extended ASCII collating sequence on an IBM PC. Figure 7.4 illustrates the nested structure of the ASCII-chart generator program.

Fig. 7.4. Nested for*-loops generate a 2-page ASCII chart.*

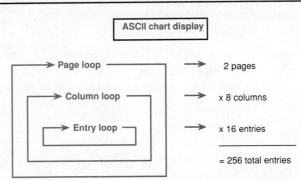

Finally, because all three expressions in a for statement are optional, you can write a never-ending loop like this:

```
for ( ; ; ) {
  /* do something here */
}
```

The problem is the same with a never-ending for-loop as with a while-loop. It is up to the logic—and that means you—to decide when the loop is done and to exit the loop. How do you do that? There are several ways, as you discover in the next section).

Altering Logic Flow in a Loop

Logic flow within a loop body is just like logic flow everywhere else. It proceeds in a sequential, linear flow (at least within the loop boundaries) unless you do something about it. Conditional logic (the C *selection statements*) can be used to tailor execution flow within a loop body (this is discussed shortly, in the "Programming Conditional Logic" section).

The special case (of altering logic flow in a loop) that we want to discuss here has to do with *changing the loop timing and sequencing*—that is, modifying the behavior of the loop itself. You can modify loop behavior by doing any of the following:

❏ *Enter the loop in a nonstandard way*. Normally, the while, do-while, or for statement initiates loop processing. It is possible, however, to use the goto statement to jump right into the middle of a loop body. The program might even work correctly. However, this is very dangerous, and is almost never done. You will see why in a moment.

❏ *Exit the loop in a nonstandard way.* The goto statement can be used also to jump directly out of a loop body. This is not as dangerous as jumping into the loop, but is still not a recommended practice.

❏ *Modify control variables to control the number of passes (iterations) through the loop body.* Consider the following example—a simple for loop controlled by an integer counter:

```
for ( i=0; i<10; i++ ) {
   --i;
}
```

From the definition of the for statement, you know that the postfix increment of i occurs as if it were at the back end of the block target statement. But the loop body also contains a prefix decrement of the control variable. What is the net effect on the loop? The value of i is *always the same at the top of the loop*. This is now a never-ending loop.

This code fragment illustrates the danger of using such a technique, but it is not always out of bounds. Suppose that the loop is processing the elements of an array (such that the control variable is also the array subscript). If one of the elements has an erroneous value *that can be corrected by the logic*, you might want to provide code that does the correction, sets the control variable back a notch, and allows the loop to reprocess that element. Be very careful, however, to limit sharply the conditions in which a control variable is modified.

❏ *Stop an iteration early, and immediately begin the next one.* You can use some of the nonstandard approaches already mentioned to do this, but by far the best way is to use the continue statement.

❏ *Exit the loop early, using a standard C verb to do so.* You can use two verbs here: return and break. The main difference is that return not only terminates the loop, but also exits the function. break just exits the innermost loop body in which it is found, and allows the remainder of the function to continue execution.

This list contains a mixture of standard and nonstandard approaches to changing the behavior of a loop. Clearly, you should know about the standard ways to do these things. But even the standard approaches, if not handled correctly, can get you in a bind. Because the nonstandard methods can be especially dangerous, we examine them to see why.

Quick-Reference: The C Jump Statements

Standard C provides four *jump*, or direct branching, statements to allow transferring control of execution to a statement other than the next sequential one. The jump is *unconditional*: if the statement is executed, the jump occurs. The general syntax and use of the four jump statements are

❑   `goto` *identifier* `;`

The `goto` statement causes an unconditional jump to the *label statement* (documented earlier in the book) named by *identifier*. The jumped-to location must be in the same function as the `goto` that references it. Remember that to jump outside the current function scope you must use the `longjmp()` facility.

❑   `continue ;`

The `continue` statement causes an unconditional jump to the *loop-continuation* part of the *smallest enclosing iteration statement* (loop body). That is, the jump is to the end of the loop body, skipping all intervening statements in the body. This allows the next iteration or pass of the loop to begin immediately. When `continue` appears in a loop body that is nested inside another loop, it does not "break out" to the next outer loop; it just causes the current one to skip to the next iteration.

❑   `break ;`

This statement terminates the execution of the smallest enclosing loop body—it "breaks out" to the next outer loop in a set of nested loops. `break` is used also to break out of a `switch` statement, as described in the section entitled "Programming Conditional Logic" later in this chapter.

❑   `return` *expression* `;`

The `return` statement terminates execution of a loop because it also terminates execution of the current function and returns control to the caller of the function. The related *expression* must have the same type as the function, unless the function has type `void`, in which case the *expression* should be omitted.

goto versus *break*

You have seen four ways to terminate loop-processing: allow the loop to complete normally, use the `return` statement, use the `goto` statement, and use the `break`. Of these, only the `goto` and the `break` statements both end the loop early and allow the function to continue execution.

Is there any reason you should choose the standard `break` statement, rather than the nonstandard `goto`, to terminate a loop early? Definitely. Look at the short program in listing 7.5.

LIsting 7.5. `goloop.c` *(Dangerous entry and exit from a loop).*

Zortech C 1.7

```
 1   #include <stdlib.h>
 2   #include <stdio.h>
 3
 4   main()
 5   {
 6     int i = 5;
 7
 8     goto target1;
 9
10     for ( i=0; i<10; i++ ) {
11   target1: ;
12       if ( i > 6 ) goto target2;
13       printf( "%d\n", i );
14     }                         ,
15   target2: ;
16   }
```

The first thing you should know about this program is that it does work correctly, in spite of the fact that the loop in lines 10–14 is both entered and exited "illegally."

The reason it works correctly is found in the object initializer in line 6, where i is set to 5. Thus, when the `goto` in line 8 transfers control into the middle of the loop, the control variable has a legitimate value. The loop body displays successive numbers beginning with 5.

What would have happened if there had been no initializer? To answer this question, you must resort again to scope, duration, and storage class. The control variable i is local to the function body and is by default an `auto` variable. Because it has no storage-class specifier overriding it (in other words, `static` is not specified), it has automatic duration.

By putting this information together with the fact that the ANSI standard specifies that an `auto` class variable with no initializer has an *undefined value* (anything at all could be in that storage location) until an assignment is made to it, you can conclude that the loop would have been completely unpredictable.

The obvious solution is to plan the program more carefully in the first place. There is no reason why you should not code the following:

```
for ( i=5; i<10; i++ ) { ... }
```

if you want the loop to begin with a value of 5.

Lines 12 and 15 of listing 7.5 demonstrate a nonstandard way to terminate the loop. All you have to do is `goto` some point outside the loop body that is still within the same function body. On the other hand, C provides a standard way of doing this that results in much safer, cleaner-looking code: the `break` statement. You could rewrite the loop in listing 7.5 as follows:

```
for ( i=5; i<10; i++ ) {
   if ( i > 6 ) break;
   printf( "%d\n", i );
}
```

Now the whole program is more controllable, not to mention more readable. The loop begins with the correct values, and terminates cleanly at the right time. The `break` statement causes the remainder of the loop body to be skipped. The next statement to be executed is the one just after the closing brace of the loop body (in general, the one after the loop's target statement).

If the `break` statement appears in a *nested loop*, *only the innermost* loop is terminated. A `break` in a nested loop allows, in effect, execution to percolate immediately up to the next outer loop.

The *automatic control* of the next statement selected to be executed is what makes the `break` statement the correct method for terminating a loop early. In listing 7.5, the closing brace of the loop body (line 14) is followed by a label statement (line 15) that is the target of the `goto`. What happens if you modify the code later, placing other statements between those two lines? They won't be executed when terminating the loop through `goto`.

If the new statements happen to be necessary for cleaning up after the loop, or are crucial to the program in any other way, you are in trouble. The program won't crash (not right there, anyway), but other parts of the program may not function correctly.

Using *continue* to Loop Early

The `continue` statement causes an unconditional jump to the loop-continuation part of the loop body, in effect skipping the statements from that point to the end of the loop body. The *loop-continuation* part of the loop body is just the point beyond the last statement in the loop body, prior to branching back or condition checking (depending on the loop type). This is shown graphically in figure 7.5.

Fig. 7.5. *The* `continue` *statement stops current iteration.*

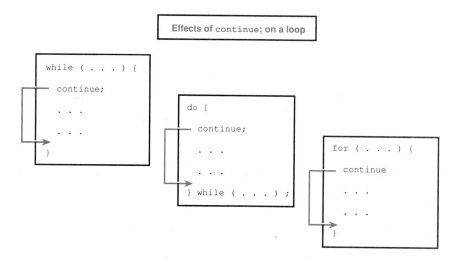

When should you use `continue`? Whenever you encounter during a pass a condition in which only some of the loop-body statements are required. For example, you might want to count both the total number of characters and the number of noncontrol characters in a text file. To get the total count, you always increment a counter; to get the noncontrol character count, you update only when the numeric value of the character is greater than or equal to that of a space character. The program in listing 7.6 performs such a character count.

Listing 7.6. `continue.c` *(Using* `continue` *to loop early).*   *Turbo C 2.0*

```
1    #include <stdlib.h>
2    #include <stdio.h>
3    #include <string.h>
4
5    main( int argc, char *argv[] )
6    {
7      FILE *infile;
8      char inname[41];
9      int ch;
10     int total = 0, notctl = 0;
11
12     if ( argc < 2 ) {
13       puts( "A file name is required." );
14       exit( 0 );
15     }
16     strcpy( inname, argv[1] );
17     if ( NULL == ( infile = fopen( inname, "r" ) ) ) {
18       puts( "File open error." );
19       exit( 0 );
20     }
21     while ( EOF != ( ch=fgetc( infile ) ) ) {
22       ++total;
23       if ( ch < ' ' ) continue;
24       ++notctl;
25     }
26     fclose( infile );
27     printf( "File name %s contained %d total characters, "
28             "of which %d were NOT control characters.\n",
29             inname, total, notctl );
30   }
```

Most of the code in listing 7.6 is support code. The loop that counts characters is in lines 21–25. This is a familiar `while` loop, and the process of checking for end-of-file while reading the file is also a familiar one by now.

Now look at the statement in line 22. This is the first statement in the loop body—it executes on every pass through the loop and counts the total number of characters in the file.

In line 23, however, the logic potentially prevents the bottom part of the loop body from executing. This happens whenever the numeric value of the character is less than that of a space character (notice that the statement tests for *less-than*, rather than *greater-than-or-equal-to*: this makes the logic both easier to handle and cleaner). The counter `notctl` is updated only if the value is *not* less than that of the space. Otherwise, the `continue` statement causes line 24 to be skipped.

Programming Conditional Logic

Conditional logic is the meat and potatoes of the programming trade. Conditional logic statements provide the only method of deviating from a strictly sequential execution flow. That is, conditional logic statements *make choices*, based on the value or values of data objects.

C provides all the conditional logic programming power you need in a surprisingly small set of statements. In fact, there are just two basic conditional or *selection* statements:

❏ *The* `if` *statement provides two-valued logic choices.* The general idea is that *if* the value of an object is one thing, do action *a*; *if it is not*, do action *b*. The `if` statement comes in two versions: the plain `if` and the `if-else` statement.

❏ *The switch statement provides multivalued logic choices.* When the value of an object may have more than two values (something other than just true and false values, say), each of which indicates some action to perform, a multivalued choice is necessary. The `switch` statement is useful in a number of situations.

The meanings of the terms *true* and *false* have been mentioned several times in this book, but this is the place to do it again. An expression (which may be just an object or something more complex) evaluates to a *true condition* when its *integral value is nonzero*. (The integral type may be arrived at by means of an implicit conversion. More on that in a moment.) Otherwise, an expression evaluates to a *false condition* when its integral value *is zero*.

Both the `if` and the `switch` statements have controlling-expressions. These statements are used in the same manner as in the iterations statements—a target statement either is or is not executed, depending on whether the controlling-expression is true or false.

> ## Quick Reference: The C Selection Statements
>
> C has surprisingly few conditional logic, or *selection*, statements.
> There are just two forms of the `if` statement, plus the extremely
> powerful `switch` statement. Their syntax is as follows:
>
> ```
> if ( expression ) statement
>
> if ( expression ) statement else statement
>
> switch ( expression ) statement
> ```
>
> This brief summary makes these powerful statements appear
> simpler than they are. For example, the syntax templates shown
> here fail reflect the complexity of punctuation possible. See the
> accompanying text for further details.

If-Then-Else Statements

If-then-else logic is the easiest form of conditional logic to grasp, because
it closely parallels the way people think and speak. *If* something is true, *then*
do a particular thing, *else* do something different.

C provides `if` logic both with and without `else` condition handling. The
syntax for the two forms of C `if` statement are

```
if ( expression ) statement

if ( expression ) statement else statement
```

The controlling-expression is the same as those used in forming program
loops. It is evaluated for a true or false condition and, if it was true, the target
statement is executed.

`if` logic differs from looping in that execution flow is linear, although
parts of the linear sequence of statements may not be executed. Figure 7.6
illustrates execution flow of the simple `if` statement.

Figure 7.6 shows logic flow as if the target statements were simple
statements. When that is the case, don't forget to punctuate the statements
with semicolons. The target statements also can be block statements, in
which case, *no* semicolon follows the closing brace (`}`).

Fig. 7.6. *Logic flow in a simple* `if` *statement.*

```
        if ( condition-expression ) /* if true */
            statement;                /* do this */
        statement;                /* then continue */
        . . .
```

```
        if ( condition-expression ) /* if false */
            statement;                /* skip this */
        statement;                /* then continue */
        . . .
```

`if-else` handling is similar to simple `if` handling, except that condition checking controls two target statements, not just one. Figure 7.7 shows program logic flow for the `if-else` construction.

Fig. 7.7. *Logic flow in an* `if-else` *statement.*

```
        if ( condition-expression )  /* if true */
            statement;                /* do this */
        else
            statement;                /* but not this */
        . . .
```

```
        if ( condition-expression )  /* if false */
            statement;                /* skip this */
        else
            statement;                /* and do this */
        . . .
```

Either or both of the target statements in an `if-else` may be a block statement. Figure 7.7 shows two simple statements, each of which has a terminating semicolon. Notice that a simple statement just before the `else` keyword *does* carry the semicolon.

The C-language specifications require that the controlling expression have a *scalar type*. A C scalar is either an arithmetic type or a pointer type. Thus, the controlling-expression can contain references to *floating-point* types, the *integral* types, and *pointers*.

There is nothing to prevent *nesting* `if` statements. A nested-`if` is handled in a hierarchical fashion, as in the following example:

```
int a = 6;
int b = 3;
...
if ( a > b )
  if ( b == 3 ) statement;
```

This code fragment causes *statement* to be executed. (But if the first `if` had not evaluated to true, the second `if` would never have been checked.)

Nested `if-else` constructions are possible also. When this is the case, each `else` keyword is associated with the *lexically immediately preceding* `if` keyword in the *same block*, but *not* if it is in an enclosed block. This just means that the curly brace characters (`{}`) enclosing a block statement work something like parentheses in forcing a certain grouping. For instance, the `else` in this code fragment is associated with the outermost `if`:

```
if ( a > b ) {    /* the if belonging to the else */
  if ( b == 3) { /* a completely independent if */
    a = 4;
    b = 2;
  }
}
else {              /* the else for the outermost if */
  a = 7;
  b = 8;
}
```

The classic nested-`if` construction looks like this:

```
if ( ... ) statement; ----------------+
  if ( ... ) statement; ----------+  |
    if ( ... ) statement; ----+  |  |
    else statement; ----------+  |  |
  else statement; ----------------+  |
else statement; -----------------------+
```

COBOL programmers can tell you two things about this kind of nested-if construction. First, think of grouping the if-else pairs like stacked bowls. The if-else pair in the "center" belong together, and then you work outward, associating pairs. The second thing an experienced COBOL programmer tells you is—don't do it. Because nested-if constructions of any length tend to become terribly confusing in practice, some other logic arrangement is preferred. Further, the statements in a nested-if are so interdependent that most attempts to change the interior code usually lead to disaster.

One approach to simplifying complex logic is to *modularize* it—use the higher levels of selection to call functions that handle the lower levels. Another approach to repackaging complex conditional logic is to "frame it in" with a switch statement. That is the topic of the following section.

More Complex Conditions: *switch( )*

You already have seen the switch statement in use several times in the sample programs in this and the earlier chapters. Most recently, the switch statement was used (listing 7.3) to determine what to do with the different kinds of input characters while detabbing a file.

The switch statement is useful whenever the logic path depends on the value of an object that can take *more than two* values. It is used frequently, for example, to "decode" menu-selection items entered from the keyboard.

The *switch( )* Statement

The ANSI documentation is about as unclear as it can be about writing a switch statement. The following is our own syntax template:

```
switch ( integral-expression ) {
  case constant-expression: statements
...
  case constant-expression: statements
  default: statements
}
```

The labeled statements within the braces constitute the switch *body*. There can be as many as 257 case labels, as well as a default label, in the switch body.

The controlling-expression of the switch statement must have an integral type: one of the integer or character types. The integral promotions are performed on the controlling-expression. When the controlling-expression has been evaluated, the `switch` statement causes a jump to one of three locations:

❏ *To the first statement associated with a* `case` *label with a matching constant expression value*. If the case value matches that of the controlling-expression, execution resumes at the associated statements for that `case` label.

❏ *To the first statement associated with the* `default` *label*. If none of the case values matches the controlling-expression value, and if there is a `default` label present, execution resumes at the first statement here.

❏ *To the first statement beyond the* `switch` *body*. If none of the case values matches the controlling-expression, and there is no `default` label, execution resumes completely beyond the `switch` body.

ANSI C Rationale: Controlling-expressions for *switch*

   The ANSI committee debated briefly on whether to allow floating-point types in the controlling-expression, but decided against it. They cited reasons such as the fact that it may not be possible to represent any particular value *exactly* as a floating-point, throwing the results of evaluation into some doubt.

---

case: Labels

   Clearly, the `case` labels and their associated statements are the core part of the `switch` construction. `case` labels are similar to the labeled statements you learned about earlier. The single exception is that the `case` keyword is followed by a constant expression, and then by the full colon of the label statement.

   The constant expression of a `case` label is just that—constant. This means that although the expression can indeed be complex, *it may not contain a reference to any variable*. Further, after all the `case` expressions have been evaluated, they *must all be unique*. This does *not* mean that they must be in any order, just that values must not be duplicated.

   The next important quality of `case` labels follows from the fact that *labeled statements are being written*, and have the same rules as any other labeled statements. The result is that the statements associated with a `case` label *do not necessarily* have to be written as a block statement. They already are part of the block statement that is the switch body. These statements can be function calls, expressions with side effects, or whatever you want them to be. Figure 7.8 shows the flow of execution through a switch body, as determined by the arrangement of case statements.

***Fig.** 7.8. Logic flow through a* switch *body.*

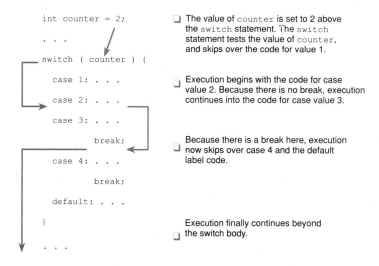

As you can see from figure 7.8, the controlling-expression of the switch evaluates to the value of the counter integer—just 2. The flow of execution jumps to the statements associated with case value 2, and continues from there. Some other interesting features shown here are covered in just a moment.

In the introduction to this section, we mentioned that switch statements frequently are used to control selection menus. Let's see how that is done. Listing 7.7 contains a program called select.c, which is driven by the switch statement in lines 37–47.

Listing 7.7. `select.c (switch` *statement in action).* *Turbo C 2.0*

```
1   #include <stdlib.h>
2   #include <stdio.h>
3   #include <bios.h>
4   #include <ctype.h>
5
6   /* +---------------------------------------------------+
7      + One of the following #defines should appear next,
8      + depending on which compiler you are using:
9      +    #define QUICKC
10     +    #define TURBOC
11     +    #define ZORTECH
12     +---------------------------------------------------+
13  */
14  #define TURBOC
15
16  int get_ch( void );
17
18  main()
19  {
20     int i;
21     char ch;
22
23     while ( 1 ) {
24        for ( i=0; i<25; i++ ) puts( "" ); /* clear the screen */
25        puts( "\t\t\tThe Menu Title Goes Here" );
26        puts( "" );
27        puts( "\t\t\t1 - First selection title" );
28        puts( "\t\t\t2 - Second selection title" );
29        puts( "\t\t\t3 - Third selection title" );
30        puts( "\t\t\t4 - Fourth selection title" );
31        puts( "" );
32        puts( "\t\t   Type a number key, the Enter, or type" );
33        puts( "\t\t\tX or x to exit the program." );
34        for ( i=0; i<6; i++ ) puts( "" );
35        ch = get_ch();      /* Input the character */
36        ch = toupper( ch ); /* Handle lowercase input */
37        switch ( ch ) {
38           case '1':
39           case '2':   /* You could call selected functions here */
40           case '3':
41           case '4': printf( "You selected item %c\n", ch );
42                     break;
43           case 'X': for ( i=0; i<25; i++ ) puts( "" );
44                     puts( "Terminating the program." );
45                     exit( 0 );
46           default: puts( "You struck an invalid key. Try again." );
47        }
48        puts( "Strike Enter to continue ..." );
```

Listing 7.7 *continues*

Listing 7.7. *continued*

```
49        ch = get_ch();
50    }
51  }
52
53  /* +---------------------------------------------------------+
54     + get_ch()
55     + Mimics the very common getch() function, for char.
56     + input from the console without echo, and without
57     + any interference or translation from the library
58     + functions. getc(), fgetc(), and getchar(), are
59     + unsuitable for most menu selection type functions.
60     +---------------------------------------------------------+
61  */
62  int get_ch( void )
63  {
64  /* +---------------------------------------------------------+
65     + The following #if defined uses the parenthesized
66     + form of the macro. Turbo C and QuickC don't care,
67     + but Zortech won't compile without it.
68     +---------------------------------------------------------+
69  */
70  #if defined( QUICKC )
71     return _bios_keybrd( _KEYBRD_READ );
72  #else
73     return bioskey( 0 );
74  #endif
75  }
```

Notice in lines 38–41 of listing 7.7 that using character constants for the case expression is perfectly legitimate. Using character constants is acceptable, because the characters are integral types, and the character constants are converted (at compile time) to their numeric equivalents.

Lines 43–45 illustrate the fact that code for a case label does not have to be a block statement. In this instance, the case's statements are "isolated" from the rest of the switch body by the call to exit(), which happens to terminate the program as well as the switch. A more normal way is to use the break statement (as seen in line 42 and discussed in the following section).

Examine listing 7.7 closely, and compare what you see with the following scenario of its execution:

... (program begins by painting the menu screen)

```
                    The Menu Title Goes Here

                    1 - First selection title
                    2 - Second selection title
                    3 - Third selection title
                    4 - Fourth selection title

          Type a number key, the Enter, or type
          X or x to exit the program.
```

... (user presses the 1 key here)

```
You selected item 1
Strike Enter to continue ...
```

... (user presses the Enter or Return key,
... and the program repaints the menu)

```
                    The Menu Title Goes Here

                    1 - First selection title
                    2 - Second selection title
                    3 - Third selection title
                    4 - Fourth selection title

          Type a number key, the Enter, or type
          X or x to exit the program.
```

... (user presses the x key here)

```
Terminating the program.
```

You should have noticed that no statements are associated with the first three `case` labels. To understand why, you have to understand how the `break` statement is used in a `switch` body—and that's next.

Using *break;* and *default:*

Both figure 7.8 and listing 7.7 show instances of execution resuming at a given `case` label and continuing straight down. In fact, the *entire remainder of the* `switch` *body* is executed, if you don't do something about it.

That something is the `break` statement. Look again at lines 38–42 in listing 7.7. If the `switch` expression evaluates to `'1'`, `'2'`, `'3'`, or `'4'` the jump to the `case` allows execution to "fall through" to case `'4'` statements. The `printf()` is sufficient to report any of these keystrokes.

At that point, however, we neither want to terminate the program nor to allow the `default` label code to tell us that the keystroke was invalid. The `break` statement in line 42 prevents that, by causing a jump to the first statement beyond the `switch` body. When you write real programs, be extremely careful where you place `break` statements in a `switch` body (and where you don't). Misplacement of `break` statements can be *very* difficult to find.

ANSI C Rationale: Why Not *case* Ranges?

The ANSI C committee seriously considered allowing the `case` statement constant expressions to include *ranges* of values, such as:

```
case 1..100: statements
```

which would mean that a `switch` controlling-expression whose value was anything from 1 to 100 would cause a jump to this `case` label. It was decided not to allow this for two reasons: it might cause the generation of a great deal of "jump table space"; and a programmer might inadvertently specify a range of not necessarily contiguous values (the range 'A'..'Z' may not be valid in the collating sequences of some machines).

The `default` label is provided in case (pardon the pun) none of the `case` values matches the controlling-expression. If that happens, and the `default` was provided, its code is executed. This label and its statements are completely optional, but having them is often a good idea. The logic of each individual situation dictates whether you need the label. You might use it as it is used in listing 7.7—this is a good place to inform the user that none of the expected values has appeared.

Terminating the Program Early

In line 45 of listing 7.7, the `break` statement is not used—rather, the `exit()` function is called. As mentioned earlier, this is a more extreme method of getting out of a `switch` body, because it also gets you out of the program. The `exit()` function can be called from *anywhere in the program*, and performs *normal program termination*. The function prototype for `exit()` is

```
void exit( int status );
```

`exit()` has a `void` function type because, by definition, it can never return to its caller—the program returns to the operating system.

This doesn't mean that nothing can be returned. The status argument is passed back to the operating system to indicate the success or failure of the program. This success or failure is a *logical* state—either way, the program didn't blow up. However, the program may have detected a condition that should not exist. In that case, you would call exit() with a status code that indicates "mission not accomplished."

Two predefined macros in stdlib.h can be used to set the status argument: EXIT_SUCCESS and EXIT_FAILURE, which have obvious meanings. The exact definition of these macros depends on the operating system. On MS-DOS systems, for example, calling exit(EXIT_SUCCESS) is equivalent to calling exit(0). Most compilers also permit more than just these two values.

When exit() is called, several important things happen and at least one important thing *may not* happen. These events are summarized in the following list:

1. *Any functions registered by the* atexit() *function are called.* Hold this thought; it is discussed next.

2. *The buffers for any open output streams are flushed (their contents written out and the buffers emptied).*

3. *All open streams are closed, and all files created by the* tmpfile() *are deleted (see Part II for a description of the* tmpfile() *function).*

4. *Control is returned to the host environment, passing back the* status *code.* However, any storage acquired dynamically is not necessarily freed. Whether or not dynamic storage is freed depends on several things (machine, operating system, particular compiler), but the only safe thing to assume is that if you acquired it (through malloc() or calloc(), both of which are covered later in the book), you should free it explicitly also.

The exit() function has a related function, atexit(), which can help you bulletproof your code. The atexit() function *registers* other functions that are to be called, in the reverse order of their registration, when the exit() function is invoked. The registered functions—at least 32 must be supported—can perform various clean-up tasks that might be otherwise overlooked. atexit() has the following prototype:

```
int atexit( void (*function)( void ) );
```

The call argument for atexit() is a *function pointer*. That is a pointer to the function to be called at exit time. You call atexit() as many times as there are functions to be registered. It returns zero if the registration is successful, nonzero if not.

Confused? Just remember how the signal() function used function pointers; this is similar. Listing 7.8 illustrates the use of atexit().

***Listing* 7.8.** atexit.c. *(Use of the* atexit() *function).*   *Turbo C 2.0*

```
 1   #include <stdlib.h>
 2   #include <stdio.h>
 3
 4   void work_exit( void );
 5   void mem_exit( void);
 6   void files_exit( void );
 7
 8   main()
 9   {
10     atexit( work_exit );
11     atexit( mem_exit );
12     atexit( files_exit );
13     exit( 0 );
14   }
15
16   void work_exit( void )
17   {
18     printf( "Task clean-up in progress.\n" );
19   }
20
21   void mem_exit( void)
22   {
23     printf( "Releasing dynamically acquired storage.\n" );
24   }
25
26   void files_exit( void )
27   {
28     printf( "Performing final file updates and closes.\n" );
29   }
```

The functions registered by atexit() are called in the *reverse order* of their registration. The last registered function is called first, and on down the list. You should exercise some caution here. What if performing the final file updates depended on using dynamically acquired buffers? If it did, you would have to retain the buffers until file-handling were finished.

Look carefully at the function prototypes for the registered functions in lines 4–6. They all have void type, and permit no parameters. This is how you must specify functions to be registered with atexit().

In listing 7.8, the exit() function is called explicitly, even though it is the last thing in main(). Explicitly calling exit() is not necessary when "falling through" the bottom of main()—an exit() is done implicitly then, and any registered functions are called. The explicit call is shown here for illustration, because exit() can be called from anywhere in the program.

There is one more way to terminate a program early. The abort() function causes *abnormal termination of the program*. Its prototype is

```
void abort( void );
```

The abort() function can be *extremely* dangerous to your files. Whether open files are flushed and closed is implementation-defined, but most compilers *do not do this*. Thus, potentially, calling abort() can cause the loss of data and even the corruption of files that happen to be open at the time.

The abort() function also can be called from anywhere in the program, but when you do it, be extremely careful to have control of files and dynamically allocated memory.

Invoking the System Command Processor

Perhaps no greater change in execution flow can be made than to invoke another program from within your program. ANSI C provides for this with the system() function, which has the following prototype:

```
int system( const char *string );
```

Calling system() is often termed "calling the shell," a term inherited from UNIX. The *shell* is just the system command processor—in DOS systems, it is command.com.

system() returns an integer that is similar to the status code passed to exit(), except that now the code is moving from the system to your program. This code has different meanings, depending on the arguments passed to system() as follows:

❑ *If the argument is a null pointer, a nonzero is returned if a command processor is available.* In ANSI C, this is how you can check for the presence of a command processor.

❑ *If the argument is a pointer to a string, the return value is implementation-defined.* Typically, it indicates the success or failure of the command processor's actions.

In practice, most implementations handle the returned value a little differently. Usually, calling `system()` with a null pointer invokes the command processor in such a way that its command prompt is displayed. You then type in the command you want processed. To get back to your program, you need to issue a special command (in DOS systems, that command is `exit`).

If the argument points to a string, the string should contain a legitimate command. For example, the following string

```
system( "dir *.*" );
```

scrolls a listing of the current directory on the screen (regardless of what your program is doing on the screen!) and returns to your program. In this slightly nonstandard world, the code returned may mean only that the command processor didn't blow up, not that any particular command processed was successful.

Common Extensions to the ANSI Standard

Most compilers, on most operating systems, provide other ways of invoking external programs. Some of these ways return to your program and some do not. Table 7.1 summarizes the function calls, the systems on which they are available, and whether your program gets control again.

Table 7.1. Summary of methods for invoking other programs.

Function call	Operating system	Returns to parent program
`system()`	UNIX, DOS	Yes
`exec...()`	UNIX, DOS	No
`fork()`	UNIX	Yes, synchronize with `wait()`
`spawn...()`	DOS	Yes
		Can be done in UNIX with a combination of `fork()`, `exec()`, and `wait()`

How the parent (invoking) and child (invoked) programs behave depends on the host system. UNIX, for example, is a true multitasking, multiuser system. Child "processes" can run simultaneously with the parent under UNIX. DOS cannot do this because it is strictly a single-task, single-user system (although some programs are able to cheat and fake multitasking). OS/2 is somewhere in between. It has some multitasking capabilities but is not meant to be a multiuser system.

Summary

Controlling logic flow is an extremely important part of building flexible, powerful programs. You have learned many of the techniques for controlling logic flow:

❏ *Program loops are probably the most useful, versatile means of molding your program into a powerful tool.* They are absolutely essential for performing repetitive work with any economy of effort.

❏ *Conditional logic increases the "intelligence" of your program by permitting flexible decision making.* A program without selection statements is similar to a car without a steering wheel. It may go fast, but only in one direction!

❏ *Controlled program termination also is important.* The `exit()`, `atexit()`, and `abort()` functions give you complete control over terminating program execution.

❏ *Invoking the system command processor is a good way to add impressive features easily to your program.* It is also a terrific convenience for the user—notice how many commercial packages provide just such a feature.

8

Programming with Pointers, Arrays, and Strings

Pointers, arrays, and strings may not be the most important topics in C programming, but they certainly rank near the top. It is a rare C program that does not use an array, a string, or a pointer. We have found it impossible, for example, to avoid references to, and uses of, these intriguing objects as we have developed sample code for this book. Their use so far has been on an intuitive basis, however, with a minimum of supporting theory.

In this chapter, you learn about pointers, arrays, and strings from the inside out. Specifically, you learn the following:

❑   *What pointers are, and how they are used in C to accomplish indirect addressing of objects.*

❑   *How to define, access, and manipulate arrays and strings. Using multidimensional arrays is covered also.*

❑   *That array subscript and pointer notation are different but equivalent ways of doing the same things, and how you can use this fact to pep up your programs.*

325

❑   *How to pass arrays and strings as arguments to functions, and how to refer to such arguments in the function body.*

Pointers and Composite Data Types

You can define a pointer to just about any object declarable in C syntax, including the basic object types. Objects with type *pointer to* int, for example, are perfectly legal, and are common in C programs. The same is true of the other basic types. You define a pointer to one of the basic types when you need the *address of the object*, rather than the object itself. This address may be used to access the object, or you can manipulate the pointer value directly.

The most common use of pointers, however, is to gain access to composite or *derived* object types. These objects may be too large to pass to a function by value, or there may be no way to refer to the individual elements in the object other than by pointer reference. This is the case with arrays and strings. Even using array subscripts is a "hidden" method of accessing array elements through a pointer, as you will see shortly.

In order to fully understand how C programs handle strings and arrays, then, you must understand how C handles pointers. To begin understanding pointers, you must get a firm grasp on *indirect addressing*.

Reviewing Indirect Addressing

Indirect addressing is a method of accessing variables that uses the contents of one object to find another object. In C, the first object is called a *pointer*, and its contents are just the *RAM address* of the second object. A pointer object contains the address of the pointed-to object. The pointed-to object is accessed indirectly through the pointer. Figure 8.1 illustrates this arrangement.

Every byte in the main memory of a computer has an address, beginning conceptually with an address of 0, and proceeding sequentially to the maximum address in the machine. (And 80x86 programmers are faced with a segmented memory scheme on top of this.) Clearly, every object stored in main memory has an address, which is just the "byte number" where its storage area starts.

Fig. 8.1. *Pointers and indirect addressing.*

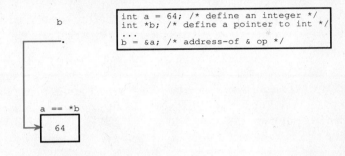

Now, remember the discussion of expressions and operators, particularly the *indirection operator* *. This is the operator that C uses both to declare a pointer, and to use that pointer to get to another object. The following are examples of pointer *declarations*:

```
int *a;        /* a is pointer to int */
char *s;       /* s is pointer to char or string */
double *dist;  /* dist is pointer to double */
```

Notice the comments for these sample declarations. a is *not* an integer; it is a *pointer* to type int. Neither is s a character, nor dist a double. These objects have a type of *pointer to type*, where *type* is the kind of object pointed to.

Referring to Pointers and Their Objects

After you have declared a pointer, you face two problems: how to initialize the pointer, and how to use it to get to other objects.

Initializing the pointer is critical. An uninitialized pointer is not the same thing as a null pointer. A null pointer contains binary zeros (a null value), which is the value used to signal the fact that the pointer *doesn't point to anything at all*. You can test for a null pointer in two ways:

```
char *s;
...
if ( s == 0 ) ... /* Test for 0 always permitted */
if ( s == NULL ) ... /* Most compilers #define NULL */
```

Compiler Dependency: Pointers and 80x86 Machines

The 80x86 CPU used for IBM and compatible PCs is peculiar in several ways. Not least in the list of oddities is the segmented memory scheme required by this processor to access all of its memory.

Memory addresses in the 80x86 CPU are composed of two parts: the *segment address* and the *offset address*. All pointers use the offset address, but pointers that also use the *segment address* are called *far* pointers. Those that do not are called *near* pointers. One or the other of these types of pointer is the default type used in compilation, depending on which *memory model* you pick for the program.

To declare a far pointer when near pointers are the default, you use an extra (nonstandard) type specifier in the declaration, as follows:

```
int far *counter;
```

Notice that the far qualifier appears after the type specifier, but before the * indirection operator. The actual implementation of memory models and pointer schemes may differ slightly from one compiler to the next. Be sure to check your product's manual before using this feature.

An uninitialized pointer, on the other hand, may contain garbage; it might or might not contain zero. Accidentally using an uninitialized pointer is a classic C programming error. It usually means the untimely demise of your program and, if it damages areas outside your program's boundaries, may even require a system reboot.

You initialize pointers as you would any other object. You can use an initializer in the declaration, or an assignment statement. You can also do address arithmetic on pointers to change their values (and hence the memory address pointed to).

In any case, it is an *address value* that is placed in a pointer, not the type of object that you mean to point to. Whether you write an initializer or an assignment statement, you can initialize a pointer in two ways.

❏ *Initialize the pointer by taking the address of the object pointed to*. The address-of operator & is used to do this, as follows:

```
int a = 64;
int *b = &a;  /* Using an initializer */
int *c;
...
c = &a;          /* Using an assignment statement */
```

❏ *Initialize the pointer with a copy of another pointer*. If a pointer to the appropriate object type already exists, its value can be assigned to another pointer referencing the same object type, like this:

```
int *a; /* Assume that this one is initialized */
int *b; /* Assume that this one is not */
...
b = a;  /* Don't use the & operator here */
```

Using a pointer to access a data object is called *dereferencing the pointer*. This is done also by using the indirection operator *, but in a statement rather than the declaration, as follows:

```
int a = 64;          /* Declare an int object */
int *b;              /* Declare the pointer */
...
b = &a;              /* Initialize it */
if ( *b == 64 )      /* Refer to the object */
  printf( "I found the object!\n" );
```

Again, the indirection operator is used both to *declare* the pointer, and to *dereference* it to access the object pointed to. This is a little confusing at first, but makes sense when you have some experience with C syntax.

There is a commonsense restriction to assigning values to pointers: You should be sure to mix apples only with apples. In other words, pointers to different object types usually don't mix. For example, the following code fragment:

```
long value = 37;
char *stuff;
.
stuff = &value;
```

should result at least in a compiler warning message that indirection to a different type is being attempted. And, of course, if you try to apply the indirection operator to something that isn't a pointer, you get an illegal-indirection error message from the compiler.

There are two exceptions to this rule: you can use the type cast operator to force conversion to a pointer to another object type; and the void pointer can point to anything.

Make it a rule of practice to use the type cast to avoid all error and warning messages—insist that a program compile completely clean when playing pointer conversion games. For example, if you want to access the individual bytes of a long int and dump them in hex, you could write the following code:

```
long value = 37;
char *stuff;
int i;
        /* The cast to pointer to char makes this work */
stuff = (char *)&value;
for ( i=0; i<4; i++ ) printf( "%.2x ", *stuff++ );
```

After taking the address of value, the resulting pointer is cast to a pointer to char, forestalling any warning messages. This code fragment worked without the cast, but insisting on a clean compile puts you in the position of *knowing* that something you did *not* intend is going on if a message appears.

The other way to mix different pointer types is to use the void pointer declaration. To declare a void pointer, write the following:

```
void *anyobject;
```

The void pointer can point to any object type, and can be assigned to a pointer to any object type without error. Many library functions use this kind of pointer, because it is impossible to predict what you want to use the pointer for. The dynamic allocation functions, for example, do not know what you will use the acquired memory for:

```
double *answer;
...
answer = malloc( sizeof( double ) );
```

Even though the malloc() function returns a void pointer, you can assign it with impunity to a pointer to double (or anything else).

The story is different, however, when you dereference a void pointer—doing so is illegal. A void pointer gives the compiler no information whatever about the kind of object to be dealt with. Rewriting the hex dump fragment using a void pointer gets you into immediate trouble:

```
long value = 37;
void *stuff;
int i;
                    /* The following statement gets by OK */
stuff = &value;
            /* But this results in "invalid indirection" */
for ( i=0; i<4; i++ ) printf( "%.2x ", *stuff++ );
```

The compiler flags the reference to *stuff in the printf() argument list as an error—illegal indirection, just as if you had applied the indirection operator to a nonpointer object—because it has no way of determining whether the dereferenced object can be applied to the %x conversion specification.

In this case, even a cast to another pointer type doesn't get you out of trouble. If you add the (char *) cast to the printf() argument, as in the following code:

```
long value = 37;
void *stuff;
int i;
                    /* The following statement gets by OK */
stuff = &value;
                /* Compiler doesn't know how to increment */
        /* the void pointer, even though there is a cast */
for ( i=0; i<4; i++ ) printf( "%.2x ", *(char *)stuff++ );
```

the compiler flags the postfix increment operator as an error. Because the compiler doesn't know how large the dereferenced object is, it cannot update the void pointer. (You see why in the next section, which discusses pointer arithmetic.)

Pointer Comparisons and Arithmetic

In the preceding section, you learned that you can always compare any pointer type to zero or the null macro value. You can also compare two pointers to each other, using the equality (== and ! =) or relational (<, >, <=, >=) operators, *under certain conditions*. First we'll look at how important pointer comparisons can be; then we'll talk about those conditions.

In the sample program cvtstr.c, in Chapter 5, there is a small function at the end of the program listing (listing 5.2). The purpose of this function—str_invert()—is to reverse the order of characters in a string. Here is a repeat of the code for that function:

```
void str_invert( char *s )
{
   static char *p;

   if ( !*s ) return;      /* Null string, no work */
   p = s;
   while ( *p ) p++; p--; /* Position to end of string */
   while ( s < p ) *s ^= *p, *p ^= *s, *s++ ^= *p-- ;
}
```

This function illustrates the importance of being able to freely compare (within limits) the values of pointers to each other (in other words, to *compare the address values*, not the values of the objects being pointed to). Without this capability, this function would be cumbersome and inefficient, though perhaps not impossible.

str_invert() is a compact, efficient function that is worth looking at closely. It reveals a great deal about how pointers are handled. The basic idea of the function is to define two pointers, one pointing to each end of the string, and "move" them toward each other, exchanging characters as they go. When the pointers "pass" each other, or become equal, the work is done. The algorithm is implemented in the following way:

❏ *Because a pointer to the beginning of the string is received as the function argument, only one temporary pointer needs to be defined to point to the end of the string.* This is char *p; it is given the static storage class so that it is not re-created at every call to the function (that is, it is a little faster this way).

❏ *A null (empty) string cannot be reversed, so this is checked for.* Dereferencing the pointer s—*s—yields the value of the first character pointed to. If it is a null string, its value is '\0', so that !*s then is *true*.

❏ *The temporary pointer p is initialized with the value of the argument pointer s.* It is incremented until the '\0' character is reached, and then backed-up one byte to point to the last character in the string.

❏ *The last line of the function contains all the power of the method.* It uses several techniques and concepts that you have learned from this book:

The whole process is controlled by the while condition s < p. This condition is no longer true when the pointers are equal or have passed each other; the loop stops.

The target statement (*one* statement) is composed of three assignment expressions separated by the *comma operator*.

These expressions are the three parts of exchanging the values of two objects with no temporary holding storage (through the exclusive-OR operation). (For a refresher on this concept, see listing 3.5.)

The first two of these expressions simply dereference the pointers to access the characters pointed to. The third adds the wrinkle of appending the postfix increment and decrement operators to the appropriate pointer. In order to understand this expression, you must remember the precedence of the operation. Because postfix increment and decrement have higher precedence, the pointers (not objects) are accessed for values to be updated at the next sequence point. However, because these are *postfix* operators, they do not interfere with the values fetched for use in dereferencing the pointers. The result is that the current value is used to access the characters indirectly, and only then are the pointers incremented or decremented.

Pointers clearly are powerful tools. But there *are* restrictions on how they can be compared.

❏ *When two pointers are compared, they both should point to the same kind of object.* The ANSI standard specifies that the objects pointed to must be of qualified or unqualified compatible types (or perhaps compatible incomplete types), as was discussed earlier in the book. If you compare a pointer to int to a pointer to double, for instance, your compiler should at least warn you that a suspicious pointer conversion occurred. When you need to get around this rule, use both type casts and extreme caution, as we mentioned earlier in this chapter.

❏ *If two pointers to a basic object type compare equal, then they point to the same object.* (See the "Compiler Dependency" C-Note later in this section for special cautions.)

❏ *Two pointers to elements of aggregate or derived objects (string, array, structure, or union) can be meaningfully compared only if the elements are members of the same aggregate object.* When this is the case, elements declared *later* in the aggregate compare *higher* than earlier elements. If the pointers refer to elements of *different* aggregate objects, the result is *undefined*—there is no guarantee what the result will be.

❑ *The preceding rule has one exception.* A pointer is allowed to point to *one position beyond the end of an array object* and still retain significance. If P and Q both point to the last element of an array, then P + 1 is guaranteed to compare higher than Q.

The ANSI standard specifies the results of comparisons of pointers that have been converted from one type to another (whether implicitly, during expression evaluation, or as a result of a cast operator you wrote).

❑ *A pointer to* void *may be converted to or from any object (or incomplete) pointer type.* Successive conversions ending with the original pointer type result in an address value identical to that of the original pointer (for example, a cast from (void *) to (int *) to (void *) produces no net change to the pointer value).

❑ *Conversion from an unqualified to a qualified pointer (or vice versa) does not change the address value of a pointer.* Thus the conversion from (int *) to (short *) produces an identical address value.

❑ *A null pointer (which has an address value of 0) is guaranteed to compare unequal to any pointer to an object or function.*

❑ *Any two null pointers are guaranteed to compare equal, regardless of the object type pointed to.*

Because addresses are integral things, pointers are related to integral values. In fact, the ANSI C document specifically permits the explicit (by cast) conversion of pointers to integers, and integers to pointers. In either case, the result is considered to be implementation-defined.

This can be quite useful, but requires detailed knowledge of machine and operating system internals. For example, an 80x86-based machine with CGA or compatible video modes has memory-mapped screen RAM located at segment address 0XB800. A Turbo C or Microsoft C program can access that RAM directly by declaring a pointer like this:

```
unsigned char far *screen;
...
screen = (unsigned char far *)0XB8000000L;
```

That's a little awkward to set up, but now your C program can place characters (and attributes) on the screen with a speed rivalled only by assembly language programs.

But do not forget that pointers are not integers! Remembering that fact is especially important when you write code that does address arithmetic. Arithmetic on pointers (meaning *addresses*) is carried out in a specific and special way in C. The difference between integers and pointers can be summed up as follows:

❏ *The address value contained in a pointer is the byte address of the object pointed to.*

❏ *Adding 1 to a pointer does not always increment the byte address by 1; the byte address may be increased by 1 but may also be more, depending on the object type pointed to.* Each increment (or decrement) of a pointer updates the byte address by an amount equal to the size of the object pointed to.

That is, updating a pointer always causes it to point to the "next" object of the type pointed to—the next character in a string, the integer in an array of integers, and so on, for the other basic types. How this affects the byte address stored in the pointer depends on the implementation of C. Remember that ANSI requires only that characters fit in one byte; all other types have an implementation-defined size, for which the only requirement is that the object type be able to store at least the minimum values defined for it.

This philosophy of pointers naturally and necessarily limits the kind of arithmetic operations that can be done on pointers. Exactly because pointers are not integers, the *only legal pointer arithmetic is additive*. There are further limitations on which additive operations are valid. Address arithmetic in C observes the following rules:

❏ *You can add or subtract an integral constant to or from a pointer.* Again, this causes the pointer to address the next object of the associated type, not the next byte address:

```
int a;      /* Set up a pointer to an integer */
int *b = &a; /* Take the address to get started */
...
b = b + 1; /* Point to next integer */
b += 1;     /* Same effect */
b++;        /* Still the same effect */
++b;        /* Still one more element */

int a[16]; /* An array of 16 integers (see below) */
int *b = a;  /* Notice the difference from just a pointer */
...
b = b - 1; /* Point to previous integer */
b -= 1;     /* OK for subtraction too */
b--;
--b;        /* Don't forget these */
```

Adding 1 to a pointer to int does not yield a pointer to the
second byte of the integer; it yields an address *beyond* the
integer, ready to access another integer following the first. This
is accomplished (by the compiler, not you) by first multiplying
the integral value by the size of the object pointed to, and then
performing the addition or subtraction.

❏ *You can subtract one pointer from another pointer.* When a
pointer subtraction is performed, the result is *not* another
pointer—it is a signed integral type. The ANSI document
requires that a conforming compiler provide a #define for this
type. It is ptrdiff_t and is defined in stddef.h.

When the subtraction is performed, the intermediate result
(which is the difference in byte address) is then *divided* by the
size of the object pointed to. The end result is a count of
elements between the two pointers:

```
ptrdiff_t distance;    /* Pointer difference object */
int a[16];             /* An array of integers */
int *c, *d             /* Two working pointers */
...
c = &a[0];             /* Address of first element */
d = &a[15];            /* Address of last element */
distance = d - c;      /* distance is now 15 */
```

Standard C provides a string-length function—strlen(). But
consider how pointer differences could help you develop an
efficient string-length algorithm.

```
#include <stdlib.h>
#include <stdio.h>
#include <stddef.h>
#include <string.h>

main()
{
   char text[41] = "Find the length of this string.";
   ptrdiff_t length;        /* Pointer difference object */
   char *s, *p;             /* Two working pointer */
   int count;
```

```
/* ---- Method 1: Count the bytes ---- */
count = 0;
s = p = text;                    /* Seems simple, but there is */
while ( *p++ ) count++;  /* hidden overhead in count++ */
printf( "%d %d\n", count, strlen( text ) );

/* ---- Method 2: Compute the length ---- */
s = p = text;
while ( *p++ ) ;
length = p - s - 1;              /* Only one calculation */
printf( "%d %d\n", length, strlen( text ) );
}
```

Both methods in this short example use the postfix increment operator to add 1 to a pointer and "step" down a string. In addition to the pointer arithmetic being done, the first method also updates a counter variable at *every iteration* of the `while` loop.

The second method uses the `while` loop only to find the end of the string. There is no other arithmetic in each iteration of the loop; all calculation is performed once after the loop is complete. You save a counter update for every pass through the loop.

For a quick and dirty program, either method is fine—the speed difference is not that great *for one use*. But if you are writing a production program that uses the string-length function frequently, every CPU cycle saved is a plus. Why not do it right in the beginning? (The standard `strlen()` function that comes with the compiler library is most likely much faster than either of these methods—it's probably written in assembler.)

❑ *You cannot add two pointers together*. The result would not make arithmetic (or pointer) sense. Generally, what you need is just a distance from one location to another, for which `ptrdiff_t()` is tailor-made.

❑ *You cannot perform multiplication, division, shift, or masking operations on pointers*. These operations make absolutely no sense for pointers. The restriction is not a heavy burden, however, as there is never a need for these operations on pointers.

Compiler Dependency:
Segmented Addresses and Pointer Arithmetic

Users of the 80x86 CPU have a special problem to deal with in handling pointers: the segmented address scheme of the processor. Because the memory of the 80x86 is linearly addressable only in 64K chunks, a pointer capable of pointing anywhere in memory must be composed of two parts: the *segment* and *offset* addresses. They are contained in two different integer (`unsigned int`) objects, from the machine's point of view.

C compilers for these machines are therefore compelled to implement several different nonANSI pointer types. The `near` pointer requires only 16 bits (an integer) and assumes a particular segment address (which is not directly available for manipulation). The `far` pointer has a behind-the-scenes structure: it is composed of 2 `unsigned ints`, 1 for the segment and 1 for the offset address.

`near` pointers conform to the ANSI standard in every respect. So do `far` pointers, but there are some vicious hidden pitfalls associated with them because the segment address can refer only to paragraph-size (16 byte) portions of memory. Thus a *single* location in the 80x86 address space can be represented by 65536 / 16 = 4096 separate and distinct `far` pointer values! None of this set of values compares equal, even though only one location is referenced. This can destroy pointer arithmetic; furthermore, only the offset portion of the address is affected by address arithmetic.

One way to ensure that `far` pointers behave properly is to load every pointer to a given object from the same base address, with no exceptions. Another way to do this is to provide a "normalized" `far` pointer type. Both the Borland (Turbo C) and Microsoft (QuickC and MS C) products do this—but Zortech does not. The type is called a `huge` pointer. Its offset part is never allowed to go over 16, the size of a paragraph. Maintaining normalized pointers involves considerable calculation overhead, but you can address arithmetic on the full 32-bit range.

QuickC 2.5 and Microsoft C 6.0 have a feature that offers a high-performance compromise: the `based` pointer. A `based` pointer resides in a single 16-bit (`near`-sized) pointer, but allows you to specify which memory segment the object resides in, without assuming that it is the current segment. `based` pointers offer the

(continues)

> *(continued)*
> best of all choices on 80x86 machines: addressability anywhere in
> the system's address space, ANSI conformity, and high
> performance—provided that you don't deal with an object over
> 65,536 bytes. This restriction may rule out the use of very large text
> buffers, for example.

When Do You Need a Pointer?

You can perform many tasks comfortably either with or without pointers.
For these tasks, the decision to use a pointer is a matter of personal taste.
There are other things for which a pointer is indispensable. How do you
know which is which? Here are some guidelines:

❑ *Passing function argument by reference.* Passing an object
value to a function makes only a *copy* of that value available to
the function. You cannot modify the value of the original
object. Passing parameters by *reference*—passing a pointer to
the object rather than its value—gets around this. You can
dereference the pointer and get to the original object.

❑ *Passing large structured objects as function arguments.*
Structures differ from arrays and strings in that, although they
are also derived objects, they normally are passed to functions
by value. A copy of the entire structure is passed to the
function. This may be too time-consuming for high-
performance programs and, on stack-driven machines, may
require too much stack space. Simply pass a pointer to the
structure, consisting of integral type data, in order to conserve
stack space as well as speed up call linkage considerably.

❑ *Dealing with arrays and strings.* Two instances here deserve
mention. In the first place, any reference to the identifier of an
array or string identifier *without subscripts* yields an address
value, not an object value. You already have seen this several
times:

```
char text[81] = "This is a text string!!";
char *s;  /* Define a pointer */
...
s = text; /* Refer to the string's address */
```

This does not mean, however, that the identifier t e x t in the preceding fragment is a pointer—t e x t = s ; would be an error—only a reference to it yields an address value, so that passing an array or string to a function necessarily means passing a pointer value.

In the second place, you frequently can use pointers *instead of* subscripts for greater performance. This is covered a little later in this chapter.

❑ *When you want to modify the value of a pointer passed as a function argument.* This can be a little tricky, until you remember that a pointer is also an object (a derived one, to be sure) that can be manipulated in its own right. When you pass a pointer to a function, only a *copy of the pointer's contents*—an address value—is passed to the function. This results in the same problem you faced in choosing between passing by value or by reference, it just deals with pointer values now. You can get around this by passing a *pointer to a pointer* to the function. Now the original pointer's contents (the address value in it) can be modified. This technique is explained in detail in Chapter 9.

Defining Arrays of Variables

Arrays of objects tend to be used extensively in C programs, which makes them an extremely important subject. Their implementation in this language is also tied intimately to pointers, which is why that subject was covered first.

What is an array? It is just a collection of related objects, much like a mathematical set. An array is composed of its *elements*, and in C every element must have the same type: there are arrays of i n t, of d o u b l e, of c h a r, and of all other basic types. You can even have arrays of derived types, such as structures. But there are *no* arrays that contain both i n t and d o u b l e objects, for example. (You can get around this by using arrays of structures.)

The elements of an array occupy *contiguous locations in memory*. If an integer requires 2 bytes of storage, then an array of integers places an integer element every 2 bytes, with no gaps in between. This concept is important because it affects not only the way elements are stored physically in memory, but also the means you can use to get to a particular element.

Defining One-dimensional Arrays

The simplest kind of array is the *one-dimensional* array. A one-dimensional array can be viewed as a list of items in memory, stored sequentially, one after the other. One-dimensional arrays can be used to represent simple vectors, lists, tables, the coefficients of an equation, or any number of other things.

Declaring the Array

All arrays require some means of locating a specific element. The means actually used makes sense, because it is just a number, called a *subscript*, that indicates which member element is the one to be used. One-dimensional arrays are characterized by the fact that they require only *one subscript* to access any element in the array. Other arrays, described a little later, may have more than one subscript.

You use subscript notation not only to declare the array but also to access member elements later in the program. Figure 8.2 shows the result of declaring (and initializing) a small array of integers. This array of integers, like all other arrays, occupies contiguous storage locations.

Fig. 8.2. *One-dimensional array in RAM.*

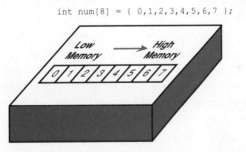

```
int num[8] = { 0,1,2,3,4,5,6,7 };
```

The array depicted in figure 8.2, num, has eight elements. Notice how the square brackets immediately follow the array identifier. Within the brackets, you write a number that tells the compiler how many elements to reserve space for—in this case it is 8. In the array *declaration*, this number is not an element locator, it is the *array size*.

The value used to declare the array size may be an expression, but the resulting value must be a constant—variables are not allowed here. One flexible way to do this, which allows for easy modification later, is to use a *manifest constant*. A manifest constant is defined with a #define directive, as follows:

```
#define SIZE 10
#define buildmsg(X) "Array size is: " ## #X

main()
{
    int num[SIZE];  /* Define array with SIZE elements */

    printf( "%s", buildmsg(SIZE) );       /* Report it */
}
```

In passing, notice how the buildmsg() function-like macro is arranged to use a manifest constant to build a string literal at preprocessing time. The string preprocessing operator # first creates the literal "10" (in this case), and the string concatenation preprocessing operator ## creates the token:

```
"Array size is: ""10"
```

The compiler performs (compile-time) string concatenation, so that the result is the equivalent of "Array size is: 10". This sort of flexibility was not available in preANSI C.

An initializer for an array differs from that of a basic object type, because more than one value must be specified. To initialize an array in the declaration, follow the identifier (and square brackets) with an assignment operator, just as you would for any object.

However, because you need a list of values for an array, you next write an opening (left) curly brace ({), then write the list of values separated by commas, and close with a closing (right) curly brace (}) *and a semicolon*. Because this is not a block statement, a semicolon *is* required. Note also that the ANSI standard allows you to leave a trailing comma at the end of the list; this makes it convenient to add values later and recompile without syntax errors:

```
int num[8] = { 0,1,2,3,4,5,6,7 };  /* This is the same */
int num[8] = { 0,1,2,3,4,5,6,7, }; /* as this! */
```

You do not *have* to write an initializer for an array. You can write code that initializes it at run-time (by reading values in a loop from a file, or the keyboard, and assigning the inputs to array elements, for example).

Referencing Array Elements

A reference to an array element involves the same [] operator as the declaration of the array. However, the element reference may now use an object identifier—a variable name—as the subscript, as follows:

```
#define SIZE 10
#define buildmsg(X) "Array size is: " ## #X

main()
{
  int num[SIZE];  /* Define array with SIZE elements */
  int i;          /* Define a subscript variable */

  printf( "%s", buildmsg(SIZE) );       /* Report it */
  for ( i=0; i<SIZE; i++ ) num[i] = 0; /* Initialize */
}
```

The last line of this fragment shows you something about the values that may be used in a subscript, and how to design loops that process the elements:

❑ *The first element of an array has subscript value 0, not 1.* The array declaration defines the size of an array with a value that is the *count* of the elements in it. Array subscripts are more like offsets, which specify a distance from the beginning of an object (whatever is being addressed). Thus the first subscript number is 0—no offset at all from the beginning of the array.

❑ *When processing an array in a loop, the maximum subscript value should therefore always be less than* SIZE, *where* SIZE is the number of elements in the array. This follows from the scheme of subscripting from 0; the maximum subscript possible is SIZE-1.

Of course, you can always use a constant value to subscript an array. You could write the initialization sequence for the array in the preceding code fragment like this, if you wanted to:

```
num[0] = 0;
num[1] = 0;
num[2] = 0;
...
num[SIZE-1] = 0;
```

Doing this is not generally profitable, for obvious reasons, but there will be times when you want to use constant values to subscript an array.

Defining Multidimensional Arrays

All that you have learned about one-dimensional arrays applies also to defining and using multidimensional arrays; you just have to add extra subscripts (or sizes) to define the extra dimensions.

Declaring the Array

Multidimensional arrays are useful for storing more complex groups of related items. You might want to describe a sequence of three-dimensional points, for example (you will see some code for this application shortly). Figure 8.3 depicts a conceptual layout of a multidimensional array.

Fig. 8.3. *Two- and three-dimensional arrays in RAM.*

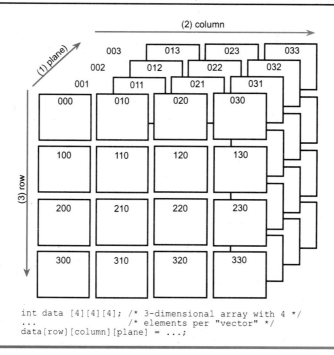

```
int data [4][4][4]; /* 3-dimensional array with 4 */
...                 /* elements per "vector" */
data[row][column][plane] = ...;
```

In Figure 8.3, the rightmost subscript describes elements in contiguous storage. All the [plane] elements are together. There are [column] groups of [plane] elements, and then there are [row] groups of [column][plane] elements. Element numbers shown in cells correspond to subscripts.

The most important thing to learn from figure 8.3 is that *arrays are stored in row-major order*—the *last* subscript varies the fastest. In figure 8.3, all the [plane] elements are stored in contiguous memory, and there are [row] times [column] elements in a "plane." Similarly, there are [row] elements that have the same [column] subscript number.

On a more intuitive level, think of a series of points in a graph. You might code the following:

```
int points[64][2];   /* Define 64 point-pairs */
```

This declaration would define 64 pairs of x-y points. For a given point i, for example, the x-value would be points[i][0], and the y-value points[i][1]. The C compiler doesn't care what the values signify. You could interpret the elements in this array to the number of eggs and apples, if you wanted to. The important thing to remember is that the last subscript varies fastest—x-y pairs are kept together (or egg and apple counts are kept together).

Referencing Array Elements

The same principles apply to referencing elements of multidimensional arrays as apply to any others. The following code fragment defines an array of five pairs of date and dollar numbers:

```
double revenue[5][2] = {
   90.001, 1000.00,
   90.002, 995.75,
   90.003, 1015.33,
   90.004, 877.44,
   90.005, 2000.01,
};
double total_income;
int i;

total_income = 0;
puts( "\t\t     Sales Revenue for the Week" );
puts( "\t\t    Date\t\t\t   Amount" );
for ( i=0; i<5; i++ ) {
   total_income += revenue[i][1];
   printf( "\t\t%8.3f\t\t%10.2f\n",
           revenue[i][0], revenue[i][1] );
}
printf( "\n\n\t\t\t Total Revenue: %10.2f\n",
        total_income );
```

Study carefully the initializer for the revenue array. The line breaks and spacing are written to emphasize the way the elements are stored in memory. The result in memory is a "stream" of double objects: 90.001, 1000.00, 90.002, 995.75, and so on, *in that order*. This reflects the fact the last subscript varies the fastest.

Notice that the first subscript is being referenced by means of a variable, whereas the second (last) subscript is referenced with a constant value. revenue[i]... locates the pair of figures for a date. revenue[i][0] locates the element containing a date in the pair, whereas revenue[i][1] refers to the corresponding income amount. When this code is run as part of a program, it produces the following output on-screen:

```
    Sales Revenue for the Week
   Date                  Amount
   90.001                1000.00
   90.002                 995.75
   90.003                1015.33
   90.004                 877.44
   90.005                2000.01

        Total Revenue:    5888.53
```

Pointer and Subscript Equivalence

The X3J11 ANSI committee very wisely brought forward the principle of *pointer and subscript equivalence*. This principle states that the *definition* of the [] postfix operator is that, for a pointer p and a subscript i, the expression p[i] is equivalent to (*(p+i)), which is, as you will recognize, a dereferenced pointer. As you might reasonably expect, i here can be an integral constant, identifier, or expression. If it is 0 (just *p) then the first element p[0] is the one accessed.

It is important to remember that even when using equivalent pointers to access arrays, the compiler regards the integral value added to (or subtracted from) a pointer as element-sized steps. This follows from the definition: *(p+2) is defined to be the same as p[2]—the *third* element of the array.

Using pointers rather than subscripts can *sometimes* result in better-performing code. But you must be careful of the hidden overhead that may be present. Consider, for example, the following three equivalent methods of stepping through an array on integers:

```
int numbers[64];
int *temp;
int i, sum = 0;
```

```
...
for ( i=0; i<64; i++ ) sum += numbers[i];
...
for ( i=0; i<64; i++ ) sum += *( numbers + i );
..
temp = numbers;
for ( i=0; i<64; i++ ) sum += *temp++;
```

Does any one of these methods increase performance? Probably not. The first two `for` loops are (by definition) exactly equivalent, and involve three arithmetic operations *per pass*:

❏ *The third expression in the* `for` *statement updates the variable* `i`.

❏ *The variable* `sum` *is updated.*

❏ *Address arithmetic is performed, adding the integral value* `i` *to the base address of the array* `numbers` *to locate a particular element.*

The third style of `for` loop looks as though it might save a few cycles, because the addition of `i` to `numbers` does not occur in the loop body. *However*, notice that the temporary pointer `temp` is postfix-incremented on every pass. This is equivalent to the expression `temp = temp + 1`, so that there are still three additions per pass.

On occasion, however, you can save cycles. What if you arrange the loop so that neither a subscript nor a count of the elements need be maintained? This would increase the speed of execution somewhat. You can achieve this by *fencing the array*, and allowing detection of the fence value to stop the loop, as in the following example:

```
int numbers[] = { 9, 3, 5, 2, 0 };
int *temp;
int sum;
...
temp = numbers;
while( temp ) sum += *temp++;
```

Now there are only two, not three, additions for each pass of the loop: the sum is updated, and the pointer is updated. The drawback is that this method requires that some value be set aside—in this case 0—the significance of which is *always* to act as a "fence" that terminates the array.

Usually, you might as well go ahead and use subscripts. This technique most often is as efficient as any other technique, and is more readable than complex pointer expressions. The one place that spending time rewriting with pointer notation is worthwhile is in string processing: a string is an array of characters that is always, by definition, terminated with a null (0) character.

Did you notice in the array declaration of the preceding code fragment that no array size was given? This is called an *incomplete type*—the compiler knows that it is an array and, in particular, that it is an array of integers. But it does *not* know how large the array is.

The size is unknown, that is, until the declaration is completed. In this case, the declaration is completed by writing an initializer. One other incomplete type, an incomplete structure type, is discussed later in the book.

Finally, you should understand that although pointers and subscripts can be used in equivalent ways, a pointer is still not an array *as such*:

```
int *numbers;    /* a pointer to int */
int numbers[4]; /* an array of int */
```

The pointer to int can be used to locate elements of an array, but before doing so, you must be careful to initialize it with the address of the array. Remember also that because an array identifier is not a pointer, it cannot appear on the left side of an assignment statement:

```
int *temp;
int number[];
int data[64];
...
number = data; /* ERROR */
temp = data;   /* Do it this way */
```

Using Arrays for Smoothing Geometric Curves

Now roll up your sleeves and get ready to put this knowledge to work. Two fairly major examples of using arrays are presented next. Both use most, if not all, of the array techniques discussed so far.

The two examples are moderately sophisticated. In fact, if you are not something of a mathematician, some of the theory behind the techniques may get by you. This is not important. What *is* important is that you pay attention to the way the arrays are handled (the basics of the theory are given, though). The first example involves alternative methods of geometric curve-smoothing.

Using Arrays To Represent Shapes

The simplest way to represent a curve is with a mathematical equation. You can use an equation to solve for points along the curve and plot each in turn. There is a very serious problem with this approach when implementing a computer graphics program: it's *slow*. The equation must be evaluated afresh at every plotted point on the curve. A compromise method is needed.

A common method of getting around the computational overhead of drawing a generalized curve is to store just a few points along the curve in an array, and "fit" a curve to them. Speed is achieved by simplifying the computations somewhat and "bunching" the calculations together. Then, drawing is rapid and uninterrupted.

The selected points—called *knots*, like knots in a curving string—can be stored in a relatively few elements; thus, the array required can be fairly small. In this example, the geometry is limited to two dimensions (in order to simplify the process). In particular, a curve is fitted to eight x-y points. The array for storing them is already familiar to you:

```
double knots[8][2] ...
```

This keeps the x-y pairs together, controlled by the rightmost (last) subscript.

Curve-smoothing Methods: *spline.c*

There are many methods for drawing a smooth curve through selected points. You can connect them with straight lines, or use a more-or-less sophisticated mathematical algorithm. The sample program `spline.c`, listing 8.1, illustrates the straight-line method, the fairly simple Bezier curve-smoothing algorithm, and the more sophisticated B-spline algorithm. Figure 8.4 shows the different results obtained with these methods.

Fig. 8.4. *Comparison of curve-smoothing methods.*

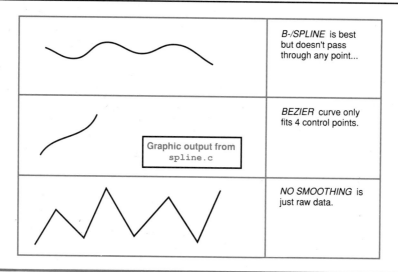

The Bezier method is not particularly discussed. If you like math, look at the derivation of the B-spline algorithm in Appendix E. Look over listing 8.1 now, and get the main features of the program in mind.

Listing 8.1. `spline.c` *(Using arrays to represent curves and shapes).*

ZortechC

```
 1   #include <stdlib.h>
 2   #include <stdio.h>
 3   #include <fg.h>
 4
 5   double knots[8][2] =     /* Define x/y point pairs */
 6      {
 7        10, 14,
 8        60, 101,
 9        110, 43,
10        160, 144,
11        210, 29,
12        260, 108,
13        310, 14,
14        360, 115
15      };
16                /*-------------------------------------*/
17                /* Define a pointer to an array of pairs */
18                /*-------------------------------------*/
19   double (*outpoly)[2];
```

```
20
21                 /*------------------------------------------*/
22                 /* General purpose draw for output pairs */
23                 /*------------------------------------------*/
24  void draw_polygon( double knots[][2], int N )
25  {
26    int i,j;
27    fg_line_t cline;
28
29    for ( i=0, j=1; j<N; i++, j++ ) {
30      cline[FG_X1] = (int)knots[i][0];
31      cline[FG_Y1] = (int)knots[i][1];
32      cline[FG_X2] = (int)knots[j][0];
33      cline[FG_Y2] = (int)knots[j][1];
34      fg_drawline( FG_RED,FG_MODE_SET,
35                   ~0,FG_LINE_SOLID,cline);
36    }
37  }
38
39                 /*------------------------------------------*/
40                 /* Bezier curve smoothing algorithm      */
41                 /*------------------------------------------*/
42  void bezier( double knots[][2], double poly[][2], int K )
43  {
44    static double t,tsq,tcu,a,b,c,d,omt,tmo,incr;
45    int cnt;
46
47    incr = 1 / (double)K;
48    for ( t=0.0,cnt=0; cnt<K; t+=incr,cnt++ ) {
49      omt =  1 - t; tmo = t - 1;
50      tsq = t * t; tcu = tsq * t;
51      a = omt * omt * omt;
52      b = 3.0 * t * tmo * tmo;
53      c = 3 * tsq * omt;
54      d = tcu;
55      poly[cnt][0] = a * knots[0][0] + b * knots[1][0]
56                   + c * knots[2][0] + d * knots[3][0];
57      poly[cnt][1] = a * knots[0][1] + b * knots[1][1]
58                   + c * knots[2][1] + d * knots[3][1];
59    }
60  }
61
62                 /*------------------------------------------*/
63                 /* B-spline curve smoothing algorithm    */
64                 /*------------------------------------------*/
65  void b_spline( double knots[][2], double poly[][2],
66                 int N, int K )
67  {
68    static double t,tsq,tcu,a,b,c,d,incr;
69    static int cnt,p;
70
```

Listing 8.1. continues

Listing 8.1. continued

```
71    incr = 1 / (double)K;
72    for ( p=1; p<N-2; p++ ) {
73      for ( t=0.0,cnt=0; cnt<K; t+=incr,cnt++ ) {
74        tsq = t * t; tcu = tsq * t;
75        a = ( -0.166*tcu + 0.500*tsq - 0.500*t + 0.166 );
76        b = ( 0.500*tcu - tsq + 0.666 );
77        c = ( -0.500*tcu + 0.500*tsq + 0.500*t + 0.166 );
78        d = 0.166*tcu;
79        poly[cnt][0] = a * knots[p-1][0] + b * knots[p][0]
80                     + c * knots[p+1][0] + d * knots[p+2][0];
81        poly[cnt][1] = a * knots[p-1][1] + b * knots[p][1]
82                     + c * knots[p+1][1] + d * knots[p+2][1];
83      }
84      draw_polygon( poly,K );
85    }
86  }
87
88  void part_screen( void )   /*---------------------------------*/
89  {                          /* Overhead routine for laying */
90    fg_line_t b;             /* out the graphics screen     */
91                             /*---------------------------------*/
92    b[FG_X1] = 0; b[FG_Y1] = 0; b[FG_X2] = 0; b[FG_Y2] = 479;
93    fg_drawthickline( FG_BLUE,FG_MODE_SET,~0,FG_LINE_SOLID,
94      b,fg_displaybox,4 );
95
96    b[FG_X1] = 0;
97    b[FG_Y1] = 479;
98    b[FG_X2] = 639;
99    b[FG_Y2] = 479;
100   fg_drawthickline( FG_BLUE,FG_MODE_SET,~0,FG_LINE_SOLID,
101     b,fg_displaybox,4 );
102
103   b[FG_X1] = 639;
104   b[FG_Y1] = 479;
105   b[FG_X2] = 639;
106   b[FG_Y2] = 0;
107   fg_drawthickline( FG_BLUE,FG_MODE_SET,~0,FG_LINE_SOLID,
108     b,fg_displaybox,4 );
109
110   b[FG_X1] = 639;
111   b[FG_Y1] = 0;
112   b[FG_X2] = 0;
113   b[FG_Y2] = 0;
114   fg_drawthickline( FG_BLUE,FG_MODE_SET,~0,FG_LINE_SOLID,
115     b,fg_displaybox,4 );
116
117   b[FG_X1] = 459;
118   b[FG_Y1] = 0;
119   b[FG_X2] = 459;
```

```
120     b[FG_Y2] = 479;
121     fg_drawthickline( FG_BLUE,FG_MODE_SET,~0,FG_LINE_SOLID,
122       b,fg_displaybox,4 );
123
124     b[FG_X1] = 0;
125     b[FG_Y1] = 161;
126     b[FG_X2] = 459;
127     b[FG_Y2] = 161;
128     fg_drawthickline( FG_BLUE,FG_MODE_SET,~0,FG_LINE_SOLID,
129       b,fg_displaybox,4 );
130
131     b[FG_X1] = 0;
132     b[FG_Y1] = 322;
133     b[FG_X2] = 459;
134     b[FG_Y2] = 322;
135     fg_drawthickline( FG_BLUE,FG_MODE_SET,~0,FG_LINE_SOLID,
136       b,fg_displaybox,4 );
137
138     fg_puts( FG_BLUE,FG_MODE_SET,~0,FG_ROT0,464,451,
139             "B-SPLINE is best,",fg_displaybox );
140     fg_puts( FG_BLUE,FG_MODE_SET,~0,FG_ROT0,464,439,
141             "but doesn't pass",fg_displaybox );
142     fg_puts( FG_BLUE,FG_MODE_SET,~0,FG_ROT0,464,427,
143             "thru any point.",fg_displaybox );
144
145     fg_puts( FG_BLUE,FG_MODE_SET,~0,FG_ROT0,464,293,
146       "BEZIER curve only",fg_displaybox );
147     fg_puts( FG_BLUE,FG_MODE_SET,~0,FG_ROT0,464,281,
148       "fits 4 control",fg_displaybox );
149     fg_puts( FG_BLUE,FG_MODE_SET,~0,FG_ROT0,464,269,
150       "points.",fg_displaybox );
151
152     fg_puts( FG_BLUE,FG_MODE_SET,~0,FG_ROT0,464,134,
153       "NO SMOOTHING is",fg_displaybox );
154     fg_puts( FG_BLUE,FG_MODE_SET,~0,FG_ROT0,464,122,
155       "just raw data.",fg_displaybox );
156   }
157
158   main()
159   {
160     char ch;
161     int i;
162
163     if ( fg_init_all() == FG_NULL ) exit(1);
164     fg_fillbox( FG_HIGHLIGHT,FG_MODE_SET,
165               ~0, fg_displaybox );
166
167     part_screen();
168
169     draw_polygon( knots,8 );
```

Listing 8.1. continues

Listing 8.1. continued

```
170            /*---------------------------------------------*/
171            /* Scale y values up to next screen partition */
172            /*---------------------------------------------*/
173     for ( i=0; i<8; i++ ) knots[i][1] += 158;
174
175     outpoly = calloc( 100,sizeof(double) );
176     bezier( knots,outpoly,50 );
177     draw_polygon( outpoly,50 );
178            /*---------------------------------------------*/
179            /* Scale y values up to next screen partition */
180            /*---------------------------------------------*/
181     for ( i=0; i<8; i++ ) knots[i][1] += 158;
182
183     b_spline( knots,outpoly,8,10 );
184            /*---------------------------------------------*/
185            /* Don't erase screen until user OKs it        */
186            /*---------------------------------------------*/
187     ch = getch(); if ( 0 == ch ) ch = getch();
188     fg_term();
189     free( outpoly );
190  }
191
```

The program in listing 8.1 is rather long, because we have included all the graphics overhead code (Zortech compiler-dependent). You can examine the overhead code at your leisure; most of the code from line 88 to the end has little to do with our example.(Readers who are just getting familiar with the Zortech Flash Graphics library should note that the graphics library must be specifically named when the linkage editor runs. If it is not, the graphics program will not link correctly.)

The data points along the sample curve are stored in the knots[][] array, lines 5–15 in listing 8.1. These are simple x-y pairs of points.

The number of points to plot calculated by the curve-smoothing algorithms needs to be larger to get the output points closer together—yielding a smooth-looking curve. Because 50 point-pairs should do the trick, 100 double sized chunks of storage are needed.

The acquired storage contains the *output polygon* array. Its name is outpoly, and it is declared in line 19. Be sure to notice the syntax: double (*outpoly)[2] declares *one* pointer to a one-dimensional array containing two elements. Clearly, we are going to play games—quite legal games—with pointer and subscript equivalence. The storage for this array is acquired through the `calloc()` function in line 175. (See Part II for an explanation of `calloc()`.)

The function `draw_polygon()`, lines 24–37, draws a curve by the simple expedient of connecting (with straight lines) all the data points passed to it. That is why we wanted points close together—if they are close enough, the curve looks smooth.

`draw_polygon()` has a couple of interesting features. First, notice that the formal parameter for the array is specified as an incomplete type, and that the number of points to connect is passed as a separate integer parameter. Even though `outpoly` is a pointer to `int`, you can pass it (legally) to the function as if it were an array reference; the base type is `int` in both cases. Inside `draw_polygon()`, the object *address* thus passed is treated as an ordinary two-dimensional array identifier (again, perfectly legally). You can treat `outpoly` this way anywhere, not merely within a function where its true nature is "hidden."

Both the `bezier()` (lines 39–60) and `b_spline()` (lines 62–86) functions also use an incomplete type to declare the array parameter (which, as you may recall, amounts to a pointer). Just how many subscript sizes can you leave out this way? Only *one*: the leftmost, or first, subscript size may be omitted.

Think about it for a moment, and you can see why. The last subscript varies fastest—all elements located by the last subscript are stored together. If any subscript to the right of the one being evaluated is incomplete, how does the compiler know how many objects to skip over to increment the left subscript by 1? For example, suppose that you specify a point-pair array as a function parameter, like this:

```
void show_stuff( int stuff[][] );
```

Now, *you* know that the right subscript indexes two integers (associated x-y values). To get to the next pair, the compiler needs to compute an address that skips over two integers. Simplicity itself, except that the compiler has no way of knowing this! This line of code causes a compile-time error message that says something to the effect that the size of the array is not known.

The rule of thumb, then, is that if there is a subscript to the right of one that is incomplete, the one to the right *cannot* be incomplete.

Using Arrays To Solve Systems of Equations

Algebra students reading this book are familiar with the techniques for using matrices to represent equations, and also with the manipulations necessary to solve equations using matrices.

Using arrays to represent such matrices is simple, and while solving equations may not be quite so simple, the method is extremely instructive on fancy subscripting for multidimensional arrays.

Using Arrays To Represent Equations

Suppose that you have three equations in three unknowns—x, y, and z. How can you represent these equations in arrays? The act of writing down some equations gives you a good idea how to start. Suppose that you want to solve the following equations:

```
 x +  3y -  4z =  8
 x +   y -  2z =  2
-x -  2y +  5z = -1
```

Notice the nice, neat pattern the coefficients of the variables make. This immediately suggests that the equations can be represented in a [3] x [4] array. This allows the coefficients and associated constant for one equation to be kept all together in memory; there are three groups of these items.

Solving the Equations: *gauss.c*

Matrices (arrays) can be used to solve (find the intersecting point for) any group of linear equations for which there are *n* variables and *n* equations to work with. The method is not limited the three-dimensional problems, provided that the coefficients form a square matrix *n* elements on a side.

The method is called *Gaussian elimination*. For a very good explanation of how the method works, refer to Sedgewick's *Algorithms*. The C implementation shown here, and indeed the specific equations, are converted from Sedgewick's Pascal-based example. Listing 8.2 contains the program gauss.c, which implements the method. Note that the Turbo C compiler will give you a warning message about line 59. The message is issued because the statement in line 59 is passing a two-dimensional array to gauss(), but the compiler expects a one-dimensional array. The program is deliberately designed this way; ignore the warning message.

Listing 8.2. `gauss.c` *(Gaussian elimination algorithm to solve equations with arrays).*   *Turbo C 2.0*

```
1   #include <stdlib.h>
2   #include <math.h>
3
4   void gauss( double eqs[], double sol[], int N )
5   {
6      double temp;
7      int i,j,k,max,r;
8
9      r = N + 1;        /* rowsize = N + 1 */
10
11     /* First do forward elimination (triangulation) */
12
13     for ( i=0; i<N; i++ ) {
14        max = i;
15        for ( j=i+1; j<N; j++ )
16           if ( fabs(eqs[j*r+i]) > fabs(eqs[max*r+i]) ) max = i;
17        for ( k=i; k<N+1; k++ ) {
18           temp = eqs[i*r+k];
19           eqs[i*r+k] = eqs[max*r+k];
20           eqs[max*r+k] = temp;
21        }
22        for ( j=i+1; j<N; j++ ) {
23           for ( k=N; k>=i; k-- ) {
24              eqs[j*r+k] =
25              eqs[j*r+k] - eqs[i*r+k] * eqs[j*r+i] / eqs[i*r+i];
26           }
27        }
28     }
29
30     /* Now do the back substitution */
31
32     for ( j=N-1; j>=0; j-- ) {
33        temp = 0;
34        for ( k=j+1; k<N; k++ ) temp += eqs[j*r+k] * sol[k];
35        sol[j] = (eqs[j*r+N] - temp) / eqs[j*r+j];
36     }
37   }
38
39   main()
40   {
41      double equations[3][4] =
42         {
```

Listing 8.2. *continues*

Listing 8.2. *continued*

```
43          1.0,   3.0,  -4.0,   8.0,
44          1.0,   1.0,  -2.0,   2.0,
45         -1.0,  -2.0,   5.0,  -1.0
46      };
47      double solution[3];
48      int i,j;
49
50      printf( "\n" );
51
52      for ( i=0; i<3; i++ ) {
53        for ( j=0; j<4; j++ ) {
54          printf( "%8.3f",equations[i][j] );
55        }
56        printf( "\n" );
57      }
58
59      gauss( equations,solution,3 );
60
61      for ( i=0; i<3; i++ ) printf( "%8.3f",solution[i] );
62      printf( "\n" );
63    }
```

---

gauss() works by first applying a method known as *forward elimination*. This method uses basic matrix operations to transform the matrix into an equivalent one that has all zeros below the diagonal of the matrix. This is sometimes known as *triangulation*. Next, a process called *back substitution* is used to solve for the variable. This involves beginning with the last row that has only one remaining nonzero coefficient, and solving immediately for that variable. Then it can be substituted in the preceding row to solve for the next, and so on.

The interesting thing about the gauss() function, lines 4–37 of listing 8.2, is that *it treats a two-dimensional array as a vector*—as a one-dimensional array. Here is yet another application of the equivalence of pointers and subscripts. (Note that this technique does not work with the Zortech C 1.7 compiler.)

As in listing 8.1, no prediction is made within the function about the ultimate size of the array. An incomplete type is used so that any array can be passed to the function (that is, its address can be passed). The number of rows and columns is determined here by the int type parameter N. (Only one such parameter is needed because a basically square matrix can be assumed.)

To handle the two-dimensional array as if it were a one-dimensional array, the function must compute how many objects to skip over to get from one row to the next. An `int` variable `r` is used for this purpose. Because all address and/or subscript arithmetic deals in numbers of elements—not byte addresses—rowsize in this example is $r = 3 + 1 = 4$.

Now suppose that you want to locate the kth element of the ith row. All you have to do is compute `i * r` to get to the first element of the ith row, and then add the k value to the result. The final result is the equivalent one-dimensional subscript for a two-dimensional array.

This program is not as complicated as it looks, but such machinations can be extremely confusing until you get used to them. We recommend that you study the addressing techniques here very carefully, and then write a few experimental programs until you get the hang of it.

Why are such techniques important? The answer is *size*. In real-world applications, you may need to work with extremely large arrays, in which mirror-image elements across the diagonal line through the matrix are identical. These are called *symmetric matrices*, and can be greatly reduced in size simply by not recording duplicate values. The result can be stored in a vector (as is done here in rudimentary form), and an algorithm can map array addresses to the correct values. Dr. Jack Purdum's book, *C Programmer's Toolkit*, also published by Que Corporation, has some very nice algorithms for dealing with symmetric matrices.

Strings Are Arrays of Characters

C strings are a very special case of array objects. A string is a *one-dimensional array of* `char`, or perhaps `unsigned char`. A string additionally has a *null fence*—the last character of a string is *always* a `'\0'`. Thus, although strings frequently are manipulated with subscripts, you often see them handled with pure pointers, as was discussed earlier.

The Internal Representation of Strings

A string is the one case of array structure in which incrementing the subscript by one also increases the byte address by exactly one. This is because the C standard requires a character to occupy just one byte (all other object types are constrained by minimum and maximum value ranges). A string object is a composite data type; specifically, it is an array of `char`, terminated by a null byte. Just as with any other array, referring to the string object name with no subscript results in a pointer reference. Figure 8.5 shows the internal memory arrangement of a string.

Fig. 8.5. *Memory layout of C strings.*

Declaring String Variables

Strings are declared like other array types. The postfix `[]` operator contains a maximum size for the object. The base type, of course, is `char` or `unsigned char`:

```
char text[81];       /* A line of text characters */
char command[41];    /* Use this string to receive a */
                     /*    keyboard command */
unsigned char data;  /* High-order bit might be on */
```

You might want to use the `unsigned char` type in cases in which special characters may be present that have the high-order bit on. This condition may not make much difference until you either explicitly (a cast) or implicitly (for example, assignment, stream I/O function call) convert one of the characters to an `int`. If the character is considered signed, the high-order bit is interpreted as a *sign bit*, and may be propagated to the high-order position of the new type.

If you look closely at figure 8.5, you will see that the array size given *includes* space for the `'\0'` fence character, even though it participates in the string value only to terminate the sequence. (It is not, for example, counted as part of the length of a string.)

You frequently will see a comment in code like this:

```
char *s;  /* String variable */
```

In this code line, is s really a string? No, it is not. This is a *pointer to a character*. However, because strings are composed of characters, this is also how you declare a *pointer to a string*. The comment really means that s is a pointer to a string (that is, a pointer to the first character in a string).

Initializing String Variables

All other array types require an initializer consisting of a list of comma-separated values, enclosed in curly braces (unless the array is initialized in a loop somewhere). Strings differ from other array types here also, in that they are initialized by a string literal, as follows:

```
char text1[81] = "Here is a string!";
char text2[255] = "This is a much longer string.";
char stuff[] = "How long can this string be?";
```

The strings text1 and text2 can contain 80 and 254 characters, respectively, *plus* the null character fence. The third string, stuff, is declared with an incomplete type specification (just as you have seen for other arrays), and is completed only by the initializer. Because there are 28 data characters in the literal, and the compiler supplies the '\0' character, a total of 29 characters are set aside for stuff.

Now, because a literal is used for initializer values, does this mean that you can assign a literal to a string identifier? For example, can you do this:

```
char holdit[41];
...
holdit = "A string literal";
```

No! A string identifier, like any other array identifier, is treated (when used without subscripts or a * operator) as an *address value*. Furthermore, also like other array types, this address value is not a true pointer and cannot be used on the left side of an assignment statement. How can you initialize a string, outside the declaration? You are about to find out.

Manipulating Strings

An ANSI-standard-conforming compiler provides several very useful string-manipulation library functions, all of which are declared in string.h. These functions are discussed in detail in Part II. Three of them deserve mention here:

❑   char *strcpy(char *s1, const char *s2) *copies the contents of one string (*s2*) into another (*s1*). It returns a pointer (*char **) to the receiving string (*s1*), although this is commonly ignored. You can use this function to initialize a string outside its declaration, as follows:*

```
char stuff[41];
...
strcpy( stuff, "Some characters for stuff." );
```

❏   char *strcat(char *s1, const char *s2)
concatenates string objects. Specifically, s2 is appended to
(tacked onto the end of) s1; the null characters are handled so
that there is only one at the end, as follows:

```
char stuff1[81] = "This is part 1, and ";
char stuff2[] = "this is part 2 !";
...
strcat( stuff1, stuff2 );
```

You must be careful to provide enough room in the receiving
string to hold it all. In this example, stuff1 must be at least
long enough to hold "This is part 1, and this is
part 2 !".

❏   size_t strlen(char *s) *reports the length of the string*
s *in a integral type* size_t, *as follows:*

```
size_t length;
char howlong[] = "How long is this string?";
...
length = strlen( howlong );
```

(You also can assign the results into an ordinary integer, if you
want.)

strlen() reports only the length of the *data* characters in the
string; the null terminator is not included in the byte count. If a
string contains *only* the null fence, it is said to be a null string
(literal value ""), and strlen() reports a length of zero.

You can use subscripts or dereference characters to manipulate strings
one character at a time. For example, you can initialize a string to a null string
by dereferencing the first character and assigning '\0', as follows:

```
char more_stuff[81];
...
*more_stuff = '\0'; /* Make it a null string */
```

As we mentioned earlier, you can gain some performance boost by using
pointer-only notation to process strings. For example, you could write your
own string copy function in-line by coding the following:

```
int i;
...
for ( i=0; s2[i] != '\0'; i++ ) s1[i] = s2[i];
```

This loop, short as it is, still involves data transfer, pointer arithmetic, and subscript update. It also fails to transfer the null terminator character. You could do it with just pointers and eliminate the subscript update:

```
while ( *s1++ = *s2++ ) ;
```

The problem is that this line, as short as it is, probably is a little slower than the `strcpy()` library function, which in all likelihood will be written in assembler. Still, this illustrates the kind of tricks you can use to cut down overhead and speed up your program. What it does not illustrate is that there is a time and place for both approaches. That is a matter for your judgement, in your situation.

Using Strings To Edit Text

One of the most important functions of your C program, from the user's point of view, is how he or she can get data into the program from the keyboard—and how easy (or difficult) doing so is. Most programs—somewhere—ask the user to enter a command, respond to a prompt, or input data. A program that does not allow *flexible* entry of commands and responses is one that will not be used often.

Normally, people don't type in hex or binary; data entry is in string format, and is converted internally to numeric formats. The C library functions `scanf()` and `gets()` and their variations can input string data—`scanf()` can even convert it to internal formats—but their editing capabilities are poor. In fact, about the only editing capability these functions have is the Backspace key. This allows you to correct typing mistakes, but becomes rather awkward when you discover that the second character in a 50-character input string is wrong.

What you need is a general-purpose string-editing (text-editing) function that, above all else, permits easy, flexible error correction. Developing such a function (and its support functions) is a good way for you to use what you have just learned about character strings. This function—we call it `edit_text()`—should have the following characteristics:

❑   *Flexible cursor movement and control.* The function should allow the user to use the keyboard arrow keys to move over existing text, one character at a time, in either direction—left or right. It should allow the use of the control-arrow keys to jump a whole word at a time, also either left or right. It should also permit the user to home the cursor (place it a the beginning of the line), or "end" the line (place the cursor at the rightmost position, just beyond the last character).

❏ *Easy correction or modification of string characters.* The function should allow text entry in either insert or overtype modes. It should also support uppercase-only input, deletion of characters anywhere in the string, erasing to end-of-line, or kill line (erase the whole line and continue), and destructive backspace.

Such a function is necessarily machine- and compiler-dependent. ANSI provides nothing for standardizing the tasks of screen control, cursor movement, or direct screen or console I/O.

In UNIX systems, this functionality is provided by the `curses` (cursor optimization) library functions, working with the `terminfo` database to acquire information about the terminal being used. These functions are found in the `curses.h` library header.

DOS systems handle screen I/O differently because the screen is connected directly to the system and its output is based on memory-mapped I/O. Different compilers access screen facilities in different ways; there is not as much uniformity as on UNIX systems. Typical library header files for DOS-based compilers are `conio.h` and `graph.h`. The `edit_text()` functions as developed here are written in Microsoft's QuickC Version 2.0. A later sample program using them requires the more recent QuickC 2.5. Notes for converting the routines to Turbo C appear a little later.

However screen-management is implemented, the first task in designing the routines is to decide which keys will be used for a given purpose. Table 8.1 shows the keyboard usage for `edit_text()`.

Table 8.1. `edit_text()` *keyboard map.*

Key name	Resulting action
F2 or Ctl-D	Erase to end-of-line
F3	Kill line (erase all)
Home	Cursor to start of string (left)
End	Cursor to end of string (right)
Left Arrow	1 position left, nondestructive
Right Arrow	1 position right, nondestructive
Ctl-Left Arrow	1 word left
Ctl-Right Arrow	1 word right
Backspace/Ctl-H	Erase character to left of current position, then 1 position left
Ins	Toggle insert/overtype modes; insert is starting default

Key name	Resulting action
Del	Delete 1 character at the cursor and close up
Enter/Return	Edit complete; accept string and return
Other keys	Text input

Inserting and Deleting Characters

The main purpose of edit_text() is to insert and delete characters in a string of text data. This not only requires enough logic of its own to warrant writing separate functions, but also is an intrinsically useful feature that can be used in other contexts. Accordingly, the source file cinsdel.c contains two functions—cinsert() and cdelete()—which are compiled separately to an object module. The code in cinsdel.c is shown in listing 8.3.

Listing 8.3. cinsdel.c (Inserting and deleting characters in a string).
Quick C 2.0 & 2.5

```
1    #include <string.h>
2    #include <ctype.h>
3
4    cinsert( char ccode,char *anystring,int spos )
5    {
6      int p;
7
8      p = strlen(anystring);
9      spos=( spos < 0 ) ? 0 : spos;
10     spos=( spos >= p ) ? p : spos;
11     for ( ; p>=spos; p--) anystring[p+1]=anystring[p];
12     anystring[spos]=ccode;
13   }
14
15   cdelete( char *anystring,int spos )
16   {
17     int p;
18
19     p=strlen(anystring);
20     if ( p>0 && spos>=0 && spos<=p) {
21       while ( spos < p ) {
22         anystring[spos]=anystring[spos+1]; spos++;
23       }
24     }
25   }
26
```

Both the insert and delete functions need arguments for the target string and the position within the string of the character to be affected. The insert function also requires the character to be inserted.

Whether you are inserting or deleting a character in a string, the rightmost end of the string (beyond the point of insertion or deletion) must be moved to accommodate the new number of characters. Therefore, the first step in either case is to determine the length of the argument string (lines 8 and 19 of listing 8.3, respectively).

Both routines require also that something be done with the right end of the string. Inserting a character requires that characters to the right of the insertion point be moved one space *to the right*, to make room for the new character. Deleting a character requires that characters to the right of the deletion point be moved *left*, in order to close the gap left by the character removed.

You can think of the insertion or deletion point as the "break" at which something has to be done to the string. The next task, accordingly, is to determine whether the break is within the boundaries of the string. Two different but equivalent methods are used to do this. cinsert() has a pair of statements that use the ternary operator (?:) to make the decision (lines 9–10), whereas cdelete() uses a single if statement (line 20) that does the same thing.

cinsert() moves the right fragment of the string to the right in line 11, and places the new character in position in line 12. cdelete() performs its move to the left in lines 21–22. Perhaps the most important thing to remember about these routines is that they do *not* allocate new space for the strings. The movement of characters occurs within the original string; you must be sure to define the string large enough to handle new characters.

Because cinsdel.c is to be compiled separately, you need a user header file for inclusion in other source files. The cinsdel.h header file is as follows:

```
#if !defined _CINSDEL
#define _CINSDEL
#include <string.h>
#include <ctype.h>

cinsert( char ccode,char *anystring,int spos );
cdelete( char *anystring,int spos );
#endif
```

To get ready for the next step, create the cinsdel.c source file and compile it, but do not link edit it (it has no main() function anyway, and can't be linked to an .EXE module). Then create the cinsdel.h header file and place it in the same directory with your other source code.

Screen I/O Considerations

In order for any string editor to be useful or pleasing to a user, you must be able to position the screen cursor *within the string*, to create the impression that the string is being manipulated directly, and to make that manipulation intuitive. To accomplish this, you must take direct control of the screen. Unfortunately, ANSI C makes no provision for this. Fortunately, most compilers do provide for it—but all in different ways.

For many terminals, screen control is not easy—but most are capable of it somehow. UNIX systems have a built-in package of functions called curses, together with a database of terminal information called terminfo that can be used to implement a full-screen edit. IBM PCs and compatibles have a memory-mapped screen I/O arrangement, plus some system BIOS calls that control the cursor.

The string editor as shown here is based on (and dependent on) cursor and screen functions peculiar to Microsoft QuickC. To convert the code to Turbo C, you must replace these functions with their Borland equivalents:

❑ _gettextpostion() *reports the current cursor position, placing the results in a structure object.* Turbo C has a pair of functions, wherex() and wherey(), that report the cursor position directly in integer objects.

❑ _settextposition() *sets the cursor position to a new location on the screen (moves the cursor).* The Turbo C equivalent is gotoxy().

❑ eraeol() *is not part of the QuickC library.* We wrote it. Its function is to erase characters from the current position to the end of the current edit line. In Turbo C, this function is built in. Alternatively, you could convert this function by replacing the _outtext() QuickC function call with a cprintf() call (both QC and Turbo C support this call, although it is not standard).

The library header files also differ between the two compiler products. Make the following changes to convert to Turbo C:

❑ *Change* memory.h *to* mem.h. The purpose of the two headers is the same, but the spelling differs.

❏   *Remove the* `#include` *for* `graph.h`. This is not needed in the Turbo C version (for this program).

Other compilers have other differences. You just have to know your own product well enough to determine for yourself what changes to make.

General-purpose String Edit: *stredit.c*

The source file `stredit.c`, listing 8.4, is of moderate length. As you read through it, notice the following features:

❏   *The integer variable* `inserton` *(line 8) is placed outside any block so that it can have external linkage.* It later is declared with the `extern` modifier in the `stredit.h` file, so that it can be accessed directly by calling functions instead of passing another argument. Notice that it is initialized to 1, or true, so that automatic insert mode is on by default.

❏   *The character insert and delete functions described earlier are used by the functions in this source file.* The `#include "cinsdel.h"` must be present.

❏   *The* `eraeol()` *function (lines 12–21) is not suitable for a windowed environment.* It assumes that a line is to be cleared all the way from the current position to the end of an 80-character line (see the way the overlaying string of blanks is built, in line 18). You may want to modify this so that it works in a windowed environment.

❏   *The* `getch()` *keyboard input function was borrowed by DOS implementations from the UNIX-based* `curses` *library functions.* It is used again here, with special emphasis on detecting extended ASCII keystrokes peculiar to IBM and compatible machines. If `getch()` returns a null character on first access, the extended code flag is set, and `getch()` is called again to get the scan code. Comments placed with the `case` statements beginning in line 51 show which keys the codes belong to.

❏   *The integer variables* x *and* X *are used initially to locate the starting position of the string on the screen, and the offset in the string to the first cursor location (see the use of the offset argument of* `edit_text()`*).* After initial placement, x (lowercase) locates the current cursor position, and X (uppercase) is made to track the offset of the cursor from the beginning of the string.

As written here, `edit_text()` is a void function. You may want to rewrite it to return an integer containing X, thus reporting where the cursor was when the edit finished. This would be useful when constructing a text-file editing program.

Listing 8.4. `stredit.c` *(General-purpose string editing functions).*

QuickC 2.0 & 2.5

```
1    #include <stdio.h>
2    #include <string.h>
3    #include <memory.h>
4    #include <conio.h>
5    #include <graph.h>
6    #include <ctype.h>
7
8    int inserton = 1;
9
10   #include "cinsdel.h"
11
12   void eraeol(void)
13   {
14     static struct rccoord scf;
15     static char empty[81];
16
17     scf = _gettextposition();
18     sprintf( empty,"%*c",81-scf.col,' ' );
19     _outtext( empty );
20     _settextposition( scf.row,scf.col );
21   }
22
23   void edit_text( char *anystring,
24                   int colno,  /* Display col - x */
25                   int lineno, /* Display row - y */
26                   int maxlen, /* Length allowed */
27                   int offset, /* Offset 0 = col 1 */
28                   int upcase  /* True = force upper */
29                 )
30   {
31     int X,x,y;
32     int x2,y2;
33     int oldlen, newlen;
34     char extcode,exitcode,ch;
35
36     extcode=0; exitcode=0;
37     X=0;
38     y=lineno; x=X+colno;
39     _settextposition(y,x);
```

Listing 8.4. continues

Listing 8.4. *continued*

```
40    cprintf("%s",anystring);    /* Position the cursor at the */
41    X=(offset > 0)?offset:0;    /* initial offset */
42    x=X+colno;
43    _settextposition(y,x);
44    do {              /* MAIN EDIT LOOP */
45      extcode=0;
46      ch=getch();
47      if (ch==0) { extcode=1; ch=getch(); }
48      if (!exitcode) {
49        if (extcode) {
50          switch ( ch ) {
51            case 60:     /* F2 = Erase EOL */
52                    eraeol();
53                    anystring[X] = '\0';
54                    break;
55            case 61:     /* F3 = Kill Line */
56                    X=0; x=X+colno;
57                    _settextposition(y,x);
58                    eraeol();
59                    *anystring='\0';
60                    break;
61            case 71:     /* HOME */
62                    X=0;
63                    x=colno;
64                    _settextposition(y,x);
65                    break;
66            case 75:     /* LEFT */
67                    if (X>0) {
68                      X--; x--; _settextposition(y,x);
69                    }
70                    break;
71            case 77:     /* RIGHT */
72                    if (X<strlen(anystring)) {
73                      X++; x++; _settextposition(y,x);
74                    }
75                    break;
76            case 79:     /* END */
77                    X=strlen(anystring);
78                    x=X+colno;
79                    _settextposition(y,x);
80                    break;
81            case 82:     /* INSERT */
82                    inserton = !inserton;
83                    break;
84            case 83:     /* DELETE */
85                    if (X<strlen(anystring) && X>=0) {
86                      cdelete(anystring,X);
```

```
 87                       eraeol();
 88                       cprintf("%s",anystring+X);
 89                       _settextposition(y,x);
 90                     }
 91                     break;
 92           case 115:   /* CTL LEFT = Prev. Word */
 93                     while (X>0 && anystring[X] != 32) {
 94                       X--; x--;
 95                     }
 96                     while (X>0 && anystring[X] == 32) {
 97                       X--; x--;
 98                     }
 99                     _settextposition(y,x);
100                     break;
101           case 116:   /* CTL RIGHT = Next Word */
102                     while (X<strlen(anystring)
103                           && anystring[X] != 32) {
104                       X++; x++;
105                     }
106                     while (X<strlen(anystring)
107                           && anystring[X] == 32) {
108                       X++; x++;
109                     }
110                     _settextposition(y,x);
111                     break;
112         }
113       }             /* end extcode */
114       else {
115         switch ( ch ) {
116           case 13: return; /* RETURN KEY TERMINATES */
117                     break;
118           case 4:                 /* CTL-D = Erase EOL */
119                     anystring[X] = '\0';
120                     eraeol();
121                     break;
122           case 8:                 /* CTL-H or BACKSPACE */
123                     if (X>0) {
124                       X--; x--; _settextposition(y,x);
125                     }
126                     if (X<strlen(anystring) && X>=0) {
127                       cdelete(anystring,X);
128                       eraeol();
129                       cprintf("%s",anystring+X);
130                       _settextposition(y,x);
131                     }
132                     break;
133           default:            /* FINALLY, PROCESS A TEXT KEY */
134 /* Check upcase */ if (strlen(anystring)<maxlen) {
135                       if ( upcase && islower(ch) )
136                         ch = toupper(ch);
```

Listing 8.4. continues

Listing 8.4. *continued*

```
137   /* If inserton /*      if (inserton) {
138                              cinsert(ch,anystring,X);
139                          }
140   /* If NOT insert */   else {
141                              if ( X >= strlen(anystring) )
142                                  cinsert(ch,anystring,X);
143                              else anystring[X] = ch;
144                          }
145                          cprintf("%s",anystring+X);
146                          X++; x++;
147                          _settextposition(y,x);
148                      }
149                      break;
150              }
151          }
152      }
153   } while (!exitcode);
154 }
```

After looking over listing 8.4 in some detail, you may realize that it does little with strings themselves. When `inserton` is false, lines 140–149 handle the overtype logic; other than that, all modifications to the string are done by the `cinsert()` and `cdelete()` functions! There is a lesson here. Many sophisticated tasks are basically fairly simple: the complications all arise in providing the support logic and features that make the core algorithm *useful*.

`stredit.c` should be compiled separately also. Developing the header file for use by other source files is mostly a matter of copying the declarations from the top of the program, and adding the `extern` modifier to `inserton`. The `stredit.h` header file is as follows:

```
#include <stdio.h>
#include <string.h>
#include <memory.h>
#include <conio.h>
#include <graph.h>
#include <ctype.h>

extern int inserton;

void eraeol(void);
void edit_text( char *anystring,
          int colno,
          int lineno,
          int maxlen,
          int offset,
          int upcase
      );
```

The edit_text() function can be useful in any number of ways. You may recall from Chapter 1, for example, that *environment variables*, or environment *strings*, need to be set up to run your compiler. Table 8.2 summarizes them.

Table 8.2. *Environment variables for compilation.*

String Name	Description of Use
PATH	Specifies the directory in which compiler programs and utilities can be found: PATH=C:\TC;C:\QC25\BIN;C:\ZORTECH\BIN
LIB	Specifies the directory in which vendor-supplied object files and libraries can be found: LIB=C:\TC\LIB;C:\QC25\LIB;C:\ZORTECH\LIB
INCLUDE	Specifies the directory in which vendor-supplied header files can be found: INCLUDE=C:\TC\INCLUDE; ...

Your program can use these environment strings to locate data files, programs, or anything else. The ANSI C standard requires that a function, char *getenv(const char *name), be provided and declared in stdlib.h. You can name your own environment strings and access them with getenv(), as follows:

```
#include <stdlib.h>
char *wheredat;
...
if ( NULL != ( wheredat = getenv( "DATA" ) ) ) {
 ... /* find the data */
}
else {
  puts( "Type the following system command and re-execute:" );
  puts( "SET DATA=[d:][\\path\\]filename[.ext]" );
  exit( 0 );
}
```

Some compilers provide also a nonstandard method of accessing environment strings, and more important, of updating them from within your program: the putenv() function. (This is something the standard should have included.) We took advantage of that to write sysenv.c, listing 8.5, to show off the string-editing functions just developed.

Listing 8.5. `sysenv.c` *(Editing DOS execution environment strings [PATH, LIB,* *INCLUDE, etc.]).*   *QuickC 2.5 Only*

```
 1   #include <stdlib.h>
 2   #include <stdio.h>
 3   #include <graph.h>
 4
 5   #include "cinsdel.h"
 6   #include "stredit.h"
 7
 8   #define LOWCASE 0
 9   #define UPCASE 1
10
11   void edit_environment( void );
12
13   main()
14   {
15     edit_environment();
16   }
17
18   void edit_environment( void )
19   {
20     int i,j;
21     int numstr;
22     char envstr[73];
23     char work[73];
24     char cmdstr[3] = "";
25     struct rccoord oldpos;            /* peculiar to QuickC */
26     struct videoconfig screen;        /* peculiar to QuickC */
27                        /* _MAXTEXTROWS is new in QC 2.5 */
28     _settextrows( _MAXTEXTROWS );     /* peculiar to QuickC */
29     _getvideoconfig( &screen );       /* peculiar to QuickC */
30     while ( *cmdstr != 'x' && *cmdstr !='X' ) {
31       _settextcolor( 0 );
32       _setbkcolor( 7L );
33       _clearscreen( _GCLEARSCREEN ); /* peculiar to QuickC */
34       oldpos = _settextposition( 0, 0 ); /* peculiar to QC */
35       /*-------------------------------------------------*/
36       /* char *environ[] not standard, may not be present*/
37       /*-------------------------------------------------*/
38     i = 0;
39     while ( environ[i] && i<screen.numtextrows-4 )
40       printf( "%.2d  %s\n", i, environ[i++] );
41     numstr = i;                       /* provide a backstop */
42     oldpos = _settextposition( screen.numtextrows-3, 2 );
43     printf( "Enter selection number, "
44             "S to recycle, A to add, or X to quit: " );
45     if ( NULL == gets( cmdstr ) ) break;
46     if ( *cmdstr == 'x' || *cmdstr == 'X' ) break;
47     if ( *cmdstr == 's' || *cmdstr == 'S' ) continue;
48     if ( *cmdstr == 'a' || *cmdstr == 'A' ) {
```

```
49          if ( numstr == screen.numtextrows-4 ) continue;
50          numstr++;
51          strcpy( envstr, "" );
52          edit_text( envstr, 2, screen.numtextrows-2,
53                     72, 0, UPCASE );
54          /* getenv() is std, but putenv() is not! */
55          putenv( envstr );
56          continue;
57       }
58       i = atoi( cmdstr ); /* get the item number user entered */
59       if ( i<0 || i>numstr ) continue;
60       else --i;                    /* adjust for subscript use */
61       strcpy( envstr, environ[i] );
62       strcpy( work, environ[i] );
63       for ( j=0; work[j] && work[j] != '='; j++ );
64       work[j] = '\0';      /* Clip string and delete first */
65       putenv( work );
66       edit_text( envstr, 2, screen.numtextrows-2,
67                  72, 0, UPCASE );
68                     /* getenv() is std, putenv() is not! */
69       putenv( envstr );
70    }
71    _clearscreen( _GCLEARSCREEN );
72 }
```

The edit_environment() function shown in listing 8.5 is yet another example of the fact that standard C functions are not enough—are *not designed to be enough*—to work in your actual environment. The standard only makes uniform those features that can be assumed to be present on every machine. Once more, screen handling is up to you and your compiler—and the code is not likely to be portable.

edit_environment() works by fetching a copy of an environment string, saving it, deleting it from the system environment, allowing the user to edit the copy, and replacing the result in the system.

Editing the environment string is done in the call to edit_text(), lines 66 and 67. Notice how the arguments are used to control the edit. The string is positioned at column 2, and 2 lines from the bottom of the screen (screen.numtextrows - 2). The edited string is limited to a maximum length of 72 characters, and is forced to uppercase.

Arrays and Strings as Function Parameters

A few words need to be said about passing arrays and strings to functions. You already have seen this done in this chapter, but some points need emphasis.

The most important thing to remember about arrays and strings as function arguments arises from the fact that a reference to an array or string identifier *without subscripts* is interpreted by the compiler as an *address reference*. Therefore, arrays and strings can be passed only by reference, *not by value*. Within the function, references to individual elements must be made by dereferencing the address of the object. There are several ways to do this.

Strings as Function Parameters

String arguments are sometimes confusing to beginning students because of the way you must refer to a string, as compared to the way you define it. That is, a reference to a string identifier is a pointer value, but pointers to strings are written as pointers to char, as in the following example:

```
char text[] = "One more line of text in a string.";
...
int count_chars( char *s )
{
   int i;

   for ( i=0; *s; i++, s++ ) ; /* Think about this loop! */
   return i
}

main()
{
   printf( "Character count: %d\n", count_chars( text ) );
}
```

Notice that count_chars() is called from within printf() with just the string identifier, text, as an argument, yet the function-declaration part describes the parameter as char *s. Within the function, references to the pointer and to the dereferenced object are handled just as they are for a string defined anywhere else.

Arrays as Function Parameters

Arrays are declared as parameters more consistently than strings:

```
double numbers[3][3]; /* A two-dimensional array */
...
void halve_elements( double data[3][3] )
{
  int i, j;

  for ( i=0; i<3; i++ ) {
    for ( j=0; j<3; j++ ) data[i][j] /= 2.0;
  }
}
```

As you saw earlier in the chapter, you can refer to array elements with pointers within a function, as follows:

```
int i, j, k;
int array2[3][3];       /* Two-dimensional */
int array3[3][3][3];    /* Three-dimensional */
...                     /* Initialize i,j,k in here */
printf( "%d", *( array2 + i * 3 + j ) );
printf( "%d", *( array3 + i * 9 + j * 3 + k ) );
```

The greatest problem with passing arrays as parameters to functions is that you cannot write a generalized array-handling routine without some trouble and planning. Ordinarily, you must specify the array size in the declaration, which limits your routine to handling arrays of exactly that size.

The simplest way around that dilemma is to use the incomplete type specification in the formal parameter declarations. This is exactly what was done in listing 8.2 because we wanted to write a function that could solve an array of equations of *any* size:

```
void gauss( double eqs[], double sol[], int N );
```

The trade-off, of course, is that you must provide another argument that specifies *at run-time* how many elements there are in the array. The gauss() further presumes that the array of equations is both two-dimensional and square as well.

Summary

At the end of every chapter, you are told, "This is important material—master it." That is no less true now than previously. Most robust C programs use at least a string somewhere, which brings with it the concept of pointers. Many programs also use arrays. These objects and ideas are almost impossible to do without. Review this chapter and make sure that you have picked up the following points:

❏   *What a C pointer is, how to manipulate address values, and how to dereference a pointer to its object.*

❏   *How to define one-dimensional and multidimensional arrays, and how to access individual elements within them.* You should understand also the equivalence of subscript and pointer notation. Perhaps more important than that is the knowledge that tells you when one or the other is appropriate.

❏   *How to define strings, and the peculiarities of using pointers to strings.* You should know how to access individual characters within strings, using both subscript and pointer notation.

❏   *What is required to declare an array or string as a parameter for a function, and how to reference the pointers and associated objects from within the function.*

❏   *How to declare and to use incomplete types.* You can do this with both arrays and strings. You should know how to complete the declaration (by initializing the object). You should know also how to use an incomplete declaration for an array type without ever completing it.

9

More about Using Pointers

Pointers are a critical resource for C programmers. They are the vehicle through which much of the flexibility—the *dynamic character*—of powerful programs is achieved.

Using pointers allows you to store and manipulate data at run time, without necessarily having to know beforehand how much data there will be, and without having to know how it will be arranged. In this chapter you will see how pointers help you write flexible, responsive programs, and do sophisticated things with a minimum of effort.

Using Pointers to Pointers

It stands to reason that, because a pointer contains the address of an object, and a pointer *is* an object, you can define a pointer that references another pointer. The trick, of course, is to realize when you are dealing with an address value, and when you are dealing with an object value.

Using Multiple Indirection

Using more than one pointer to access an object indirectly is called *multiple indirection*. The indirection operator is used for this purpose, as it is for simple pointers. The difference is the number of indirection operators used in the declaration of the pointer, as the following lines of code illustrate:

```
double a;       /* Declare a double object.*/
double *b;      /* Declare a pointer to a double */
double **c;     /* Object access is through two pointers */
double ***d;    /* Object access is through three pointers */
```

Simple pointers are quite common. Two levels of indirection, although not especially abundant, are still quite common. Three levels of indirection are almost never necessary, but the possibility of encountering it does exist.

Why would you ever want to define pointers to pointers? There are two major reasons:

❑ *To pass pointer values by reference, not value*. When you pass a pointer as an argument to a function, you are passing an address value *by value*. Stop and think about that for a second. Passing a pointer to a function really means that you are passing another object to the function *by reference*. Thus the object referenced can be modified by the function, but the original pointer to the object *cannot*. Only a copy of the pointer is available to the function. Therefore, if you want to pass a pointer to a function, and to modify the contents of the original pointer, you must use multiple indirection—you must pass another pointer to the one you want to modify.

❑ *To locate a list of pointers*. You should remember that an array identifier used without subscripts is interpreted as an address value. But what if the array (list) is an array of pointers? Again, an address pointing to a list of addresses is multiple indirection—access to a final object value is through two levels of address values. This is an especially powerful technique. We cover it in detail later in this chapter.

Referencing and Dereferencing Multiple Pointers

Recall what you already know about dereferencing pointers. If p is a pointer, then *p is a reference to the object pointed to. It works the same way with multiple indirection; there are just more indirection operators to keep up with. Figure 9.1 shows how multiple indirection governs references to addresses and underlying object values.

Fig. 9.1. *Dereferencing pointers to pointers.*

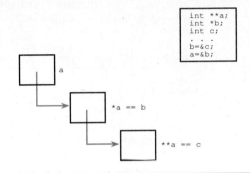

```
int **a;
int *b;
int c;
. . .
b=&c;
a=&b;
```

a

*a == b

**a == c

Using multiple indirection imposes some responsibilities on you, the programmer. A dereferenced pointer may now be another pointer, or it may be a reference to an object. You must keep track of which it is. Rewriting the code fragment shown in figure 9.1 illustrates this, as follows:

```
int **a;    /* Pointer to a pointer to an object */
int *b;     /* Pointer to an object */
int c;      /* An integer object *;
...
a = &b;     /* Initialize first pointer */
*a = &c;    /* Initialize second pointer */
**a = 64;   /* Initialize object */
```

The most interesting feature of this code fragment is the way a and b are initialized. a must be initialized with the address of b. Then b is initialized with the address of c, but it is done by dereferencing a. This is not necessary in the real world but is instructive here. Using this method, the precise order of statements seen here is required—a cannot be dereferenced to access b until a has been initialized.

Using Pointers To Scan and Parse Text

So far, you have seen only a few of the most primitive statements possible illustrating multiple indirection. A more realistic situation requiring multiple indirection arises in scanning and parsing text.

Roll up your sleeves, it's time to go to work! The programs and functions that follow can be confusing, simply because they must be a little lengthy to get the job done. We urge you to examine the code in detail and at length. The methods shown here for manipulating pointers are extremely important for building worthwhile programs. The routines themselves are also very useful—but only if you understand them thoroughly.

Creating a Lexical Scanner

Because you are reading a book on C programming, we can assume that you are a fairly experienced computer user. You almost certainly have used commercial software with a fairly complicated command set. Have you ever wondered how the software catches your keystroke and syntax errors, sometimes seeming very intelligent as it does it? For that matter, have you wondered just how the C compiler breaks down all that source code in an intelligible fashion?

Earlier in the book, you saw that one of the phases of compilation involves a lexical scanner, which examines the source code. Commercial software also uses scanners to process input commands (and perhaps data, as well). The scanner is the first step in handling text information in this seemingly intelligent fashion.

What a Scanner Does

The purpose of a scanner is to *process an input text stream and separate out tokens*. Tokens may be verbs, object identifiers, or whatever the application requires.

Scanners are sometimes referred to as *lexical scanners* (a *lexicon* is basically a word list) because the tokens retrieved from the input stream must conform to the syntax (language, command structure, and so forth). That is, unless tokens mean something to the application, an error exists. The scanner function presented shortly is designed to do several things. In particular, it is designed to do the following:

- ❏ *Recognize several fundamental object-type tokens, including alphanumeric symbols, string literals, integer, and real (floating point) constants.*

- ❏ *Recognize a suitable class of punctuation characters, including parentheses, colons and semicolons, commas, and periods.* Recognition of a period depends on the *context* in which it appears—a period embedded in a real literal is not counted as punctuation.

- ❏ *Recognize a group of operators that can be used to form regular expressions.* The operators recognized in this routine are a subset of C operators, plus one or two that don't exist in C. In particular, the caret (^) character is used as the *power operator*. That is, the expression x ^ y is interpreted to mean x raised to the y power.

Why *strtok( )* Won't Work Here

The function `char *strtok( char *s1, const char *s2)` is a standard library function (`string.h`) that performs scanning services. The string `s1` is searched for tokens, and a pointer to the found token is returned. This pointer indicates a location *within the original string pointed to*. No extra copy of the text is made.

The string `s2` determines *how* `strtok()` searches for tokens. String `s2` contains a set of characters that are to be considered *delimiters*, or separator characters that occur between tokens. A space, for example, is a commonsense choice of delimiters for scanning words out of an English sentence.

Because one call to `strtok()` returns a pointer to a single token, repeated calls must be made to scan a whole line. In support of this, `strtok()` is called in two different ways, as follows:

- ❏ *The first call passes a valid pointer in* `s1`. This locates the string to be scanned.

- ❏ *The second and following calls to* `strtok()` *pass a NULL pointer, not a pointer to* `s1`. This indicates to the function's logic that scanning is to continue for the same string. The delimiter characters contained in `s2` can be changed from one call to the next.

Because the same string is to be scanned over several calls, `strtok()` saves the location of the next character after the last found token between calls. There is an added wrinkle: `strtok()` also modifies the original string by placing a null character (`'\0'`) just after the last found token. It does this so that the caller does not have to search by another method to find the end of the token string just located. For example, suppose that you want to locate the second word in the following string:

```
char text[] = "Hello reader, this is a string!.";
```

To do so, you would use the following sequence of calls to `strtok()`:

```
char *t;
...
t = strtok( text, " " ); /* Blank delimiter */
t = strtok( NULL, "," ); /* Comma delimiter */
printf( "%s\n", t );     /* Display the token */
```

This sequence of code displays the word `reader` on the system console. This seems to work well. You can scan a large variety of input text with `strtok()`. Why not use it for our scanning purposes here? For the following reasons:

❏   *The original input string is modified.* This means that either the original text is corrupted, or a copy of the text must be made before scanning. This is not always desirable.

❏   *To some degree, the programmer must know which delimiter characters to expect in the input while writing the program.* This may be begging the question; not all users are so cooperative when entering text.

❏   *Detecting punctuation characters without treating them as delimiter characters—which* `strtok()` *overlays with '\0'—is difficult (but not impossible).* We want to be able to return punctuation characters as separate and legal tokens.

❏   *You want to be able to recognize a large number of punctuation and operator characters.* `strtok()` imposes an extra load on the programmer, in that successive calls frequently must specify different sets of delimiters.

   You should not get the idea that `strtok()` is not useful. It is extremely useful and can be used effectively in a variety of situations. You should pick and choose the situations in which you want to use it, however.

How the Scanner Uses Pointers

   The scanner function presented in this section avoids the problems raised by `strtok()`. The `scanner()` function (listing 9.1, source file `scanner.c`) scans a text string, copying the found tokens into an output string so that the original text is not modified. `scanner()` also identifies a variety of punctuators, operators, and named token types. The only delimiter characters are the space and end-of-line characters.

All arguments passed to `scanner()` are assumed to reside outside the function block. They do not have to have global scope; they just have to be available to the calling routine. It is the *manner* in which the arguments are used that gives the function its characteristics:

❏ `char **text;`

The caller must set up a pointer to the input text. It should be left undisturbed across all calls for scanning that line (string) of text. Multiple indirection is used so that the pointer can be updated by the function; thus it points in succeeding calls to the correct location in the input string. Ordinarily, the pointer used should be a temporary variable rather than the string identifier.

❏ `char *token;`

The second parameter is a pointer to a string that contains the output token. This avoids the necessity of modifying the input string to "mark" the end of the token. The caller need not initialize the token string. It is created and null-terminated by `scanner()` at each call (the same token string may be reused at each call, if you want).

❏ `int *ttype;`

The caller must also set up an integer-type object that is set to the token *type* by `scanner()`. The different token types are shown in the `#define` macros in lines 4–23 of listing 9.1. All of the token-type macro names are self-explanatory, except possibly for three: `LEXERR`, `EOL`, and `UNDEF`. The value of `LEXERR` is placed in `ttype` if the routine detects a nonblank string it cannot classify as any of the other token types. `EOL` is the one token-type value reported for which the output token string `token` does *not* contain a valid string; this is the end-of-line indicator. The `UNDEF` macro value is never reported—it is present only so that you may initialize `ttype` before the first call. You can see how `UNDEF` is used in lines 204–205 of listing 9.1.

Listing 9.1. `scanner.c` *(A lexical scanner routine).*   *All Compilers*

```
 1   #include <stdlib.h>
 2   #include <stdio.h>
 3
 4   #define LEXERR 0
 5   #define SYMBOL 1
 6   #define INTLIT 2
 7   #define REALLIT 3
 8   #define STRLIT 4
 9   #define LPAREN 5
10   #define RPAREN 6
11   #define SEMIC 7
12   #define COLON 8
13   #define COMMA 9
14   #define PERIOD 10
15   #define APOST 11
16   #define PLUSOP 12
17   #define MINUSOP 13
18   #define MUXOP 14
19   #define DIVOP 15
20   #define POWOP 16
21   #define ASSIGNOP 17
22   #define EOL 18
23   #define UNDEF 255
24
25   void scanner();
26   char *nmtoken();
27
28   char *nmtoken(ttype)
29     int ttype;
30   {
31     static char *tokennm[] = {
32                             "LEXERR",
33                             "SYMBOL",
34                             "INTLIT",
35                             "REALLIT",
36                             "STRLIT",
37                             "LPAREN",
38                             "RPAREN",
39                             "SEMIC",
40                             "COLON",
41                             "COMMA",
42                             "PERIOD",
43                             "APOST",
44                             "PLUSOP",
45                             "MINUSOP",
46                             "MUXOP",
47                             "DIVOP",
48                             "POWOP",
49                             "ASSIGNOP",
```

```
50                              "EOL",
51                              "UNDEF"
52                              };
53     return( tokennm[ttype] );
54  }
55
56  void scanner(text,token,ttype)
57     char **text;
58     char *token;
59     int *ttype;
60  {
61     for ( ; **text == ' ' || **text == '\t'
62          || **text == '\n' ; (*text)++ ) ;
63
64     if ( **text == '\0' ) {                    /* END OF LINE */
65       *ttype = EOL;
66       return;
67     }
68
69     if ( (**text >= 'A' && **text <= 'Z')        /* SYMBOLS */
70       || (**text >= 'a' && **text <= 'z') ) {
71         *ttype = SYMBOL;
72         while ( (**text >= 'A' && **text <= 'Z')
73              || (**text >= 'a' && **text <= 'z')
74              || (**text >= '0' && **text <= '9') ) {
75           *token++ = *(*text)++;
76         }
77         *token = '\0';
78         return;
79     }
80
81     if ( **text == '"' ) {                    /* STRING LITERALS */
82         *ttype = STRLIT;
83         (*text)++;              /* Skip first quote */
84         while ( **text != '"' && **text ) {
85           *token++ = *(*text)++;
86         }
87         (*text)++;              /* Skip last quote */
88         *token = '\0';
89         return;
90     }
91
92     if ( **text >= '0' && **text <= '9' ) {     /* NUMERICS */
93       *ttype =  INTLIT;
94       while ( **text >= '0' && **text <= '9' ) {
95         *token++ = *(*text)++;
96         if ( **text == '.' ) {
97           *ttype = REALLIT;
98           *token++ = *(*text)++;
99         }
```

Listing 9.1. continues

Listing 9.1. *continued*

```
100          if ( *ttype == REALLIT &&
101             ( **text == 'e' || **text == 'E' ) ) {
102            *token++ = *(*text)++;
103          }
104          if ( *ttype == REALLIT &&
105             ( **text == '+' || **text == '-' ) ) {
106            *token++ = *(*text)++;
107          }
108       }
109       *token = '\0';
110       return;
111    }
112
113    if ( **text == '(' ) {                    /* PUNCTUATION */
114       *ttype = LPAREN;
115       *token++ = *(*text)++;
116       *token = '\0';
117       return;
118    }
119    if ( **text == ')' ) {
120       *ttype = RPAREN;
121       *token++ = *(*text)++;
122       *token = '\0';
123       return;
124    }
125    if ( **text == ';' ) {
126       *ttype = SEMIC;
127       *token++ = *(*text)++;
128       *token = '\0';
129       return;
130    }
131    if ( **text == ':' ) {
132       *ttype = COLON;
133       *token++ = *(*text)++;
134       *token = '\0';
135       return;
136    }
137    if ( **text == ',' ) {
138       *ttype = COMMA;
139       *token++ = *(*text)++;
140       *token = '\0';
141       return;
142    }
143    if ( **text == '.' ) {
144       *ttype = PERIOD;
145       *token++ = *(*text)++;
146       *token = '\0';
147       return;
148    }
```

```
149     if ( **text == '\'' ) {
150         *ttype = APOST;
151         *token++ = *(*text)++;
152         *token = '\0';
153         return;
154     }
155
156     if ( **text == '+' ) {                    /* OPERATORS */
157         *ttype = PLUSOP;
158         *token++ = *(*text)++;
159         *token = '\0';
160         return;
161     }
162     if ( **text == '-' ) {
163         *ttype = MINUSOP;
164         *token++ = *(*text)++;
165         *token = '\0';
166         return;
167     }
168     if ( **text == '*' ) {
169         *ttype = MUXOP;
170         *token++ = *(*text)++;
171         *token = '\0';
172         return;
173     }
174     if ( **text == '/' ) {
175         *ttype = DIVOP;
176         *token++ = *(*text)++;
177         *token = '\0';
178         return;
179     }
180     if ( **text == '^' ) {
181         *ttype = POWOP;
182         *token++ = *(*text)++;
183         *token = '\0';
184         return;
185     }
186     if ( **text == '=' ) {
187         *ttype = ASSIGNOP;
188         *token++ = *(*text)++;
189         *token = '\0';
190         return;
191     }
192
193     *ttype=LEXERR;              /* IF NOTHING MATCHED, DO THIS */
194     return;
195 }
196
197 /* ---------- SAMPLE DRIVER FOR SCANNER ---------------
198 void parser(string)
199     char *string;
```

Listing 9.1. continues

Listing 9.1. continued

```
200   {
201      char *sp,*tp;
202      int ttype;
203.     char token[41];
204
205      sp = string;
206      ttype = UNDEF;
207      while ( ttype != EOL && ttype != LEXERR ) {
208         tp = token;
209         scanner(&sp,tp,&ttype);
210         if ( ttype != EOL )
211           printf( "Token type = %s, token = %s\n",
212                   nmtoken(ttype), token );
213      }
214   }
215   -------------------------------------------------------- */
```

Listing 9.1 shows `scanner.c` in a form suitable for separate compilation. If you want to compile it to an `.OBJ` file for inclusion in other programs, you could write the header file, `scanner.h`, like this:

```
#define LEXERR 0
#define SYMBOL 1
#define INTLIT 2
#define REALLIT 3
#define STRLIT 4
#define LPAREN 5
#define RPAREN 6
#define SEMIC 7
#define COLON 8
#define COMMA 9
#define PERIOD 10
#define APOST 11
#define PLUSOP 12
#define MINUSOP 13
#define MUXOP 14
#define DIVOP 15
#define POWOP 16
#define ASSIGNOP 17
#define EOL 18
#define UNDEF 255

extern void scanner();
extern char *nmtoken();
```

All the functions in listing 9.1 are written with *old-style declarations*. We thought about this at some length. Should we convert them to the new function-prototype syntax? After considering the question, plus the fact that this routine has been working just this way for a long time, *plus* the fact that the old-style declarations are perfectly legal, we decided to leave it alone. It serves as a reminder that C is a very flexible language, even with ANSI requirements laid on it.

Lines 61–62 perform the simple function of moving the "current position" to the right down the string until something other than whitespace is encountered—that is, until the first character of the next token is found. `scanner()` considers blanks, tabs, and newline characters to all be whitespace.

Notice the double dereference of `text` to access the character values in the string. This is simple enough, but updating the pointer is another matter when you use multiple indirection. Because the pointer actually resides in the caller's data area (this may be an `auto` variable, because the caller by definition has not yet returned and released that memory), the idea is to increment the pointer contents. This is done with the following expression:

```
(*text)++;
```

Consider carefully the grouping of operators in this expression: postfix ++ has higher precedence than indirection *. Thus, if the parentheses were *not* used, the equivalent grouping would be `*(text++)`. Now remember this: because `text` is the pointer passed to the function, `*text` is the original pointer, and `**text` refers to a character.

It is `*text`, the original pointer, that needs incrementing—hence the parentheses in `(*text)++` cause the original pointer to be updated. The other expression `*(text)++` would cause the *first*-level pointer (the one passed to the function) to be incremented, making it point not *to* the next pointer, but *in the middle* of the next pointer. In that case, `*text` would refer to garbage rather than a legitimate pointer.

Although `scanner()` seems complex, it only seems that way because of its length. *Every pointer update* is accomplished in the way just described.

The process of building the output tokens, once understood, is equally simple. They are built in blocks of `if` statements. First, `scanner()` identifies what token type has appeared, by comparing the character to a range of permissible characters for that type. It then continues scanning to the right, adding characters to the token as long as they belong to that subset of permissible characters.

Token building can be further simplified by using a standard library function: `strchr()`. Its prototype is

```
char *strchr( char *s, char c );
```

This function examines a string s, looking for the second argument character. If it is found, a pointer to the located character is returned; otherwise, a NULL pointer is returned.

The SYMBOL token is detected and built in lines 69–79. It might be rewritten as follows:

```
char sym_chars[] = "ABCDEFGHIJKLMNOPQRSTUVWXYZ"
                   "abcdefghijklmnopqrstuvwxyz"
                   "0123456789";   /* compiler concats these */
...
if ( strchr( sym_chars, **text ) ) {      /* SYMBOLS */
    *ttype = SYMBOL;
    while ( strchr( sym_chars, **text ) ) {
      *token++ = *(*text)++;
    }
    *token = '\0';
    return;
}
```

This code fragment takes about the same number of lines of code to accomplish nearly the same thing, because the sym_chars string takes up some space, but does it more legibly. Performance will still be good. The only difference is that scanner(), as originally coded, requires that a SYMBOL token begin with an alphabetic character, whereas this fragment accepts any alphanumeric character.

Such an improvement would be only a little more difficult for the INTLIT and REALLIT tokens, because numerics are assumed to be integers until a period is found, at which time the token type is converted to floating point. This search and possible type conversion is done in the same code fragment, lines 92–111. However, the improvement is possible and practical. Little is gained by converting the algorithm for the remaining token types, which mostly look for single characters.

The function nmtoken(), lines 28–54, is something you can use while experimenting with the scanner code. nmtoken() accepts an integer argument, the token type, and returns a pointer to a string containing the name of the token type. You already have seen the kind of static array declared in this function, but take a moment and study it again. How do you interpret the following declaration?

```
static char *tokennm[] = ...
```

Remember that [] has higher precedence than *. Therefore, tokennm is an array. An array of what? Of char *. Thus, this is an *array of pointers* to string. To reference one of the pointers for return, the `ttype` argument is used to subscript the array, as follows:

```
return( tokennm[ttype] );
```

where `tokennm[ttype]` is a pointer—and *not* a dereferenced pointer, either.

Lines 197–215 in listing 9.1 contain a sample scanner driver function, `parser()`, to show how the calls are engineered. This block of code is all in comments, because it is not meant to be actually compiled; it is only a suggestion. Suppose, for example, that you called `parser()` like this:

```
parser( "Scan this string!" );
```

The following output would be displayed on-screen

```
Token type = SYMBOL, token = Scan
Token type = SYMBOL, token = this
Token type = SYMBOL, token = string
Token type = LEXERR, token = string
```

In addition to three `SYMBOL` type tokens, a `LEXERR` is reported because the exclamation point is not a supported punctuator in `scanner()`. Notice that when a lexical error occurs, the token string is not modified; it still contains the string loaded in the last successful call.

Notice particularly how `scanner()` is called in line 209:

```
scanner(&sp,tp,&ttype);
```

The `sp` and `tp` objects are temporary pointers to the input string and the output token string, respectively. `ttype` is an integer variable that is loaded with the token type according to the `#define` macros at the top of listing 9.1.

The `sp` pointer itself is not passed to the function. Rather, its address is taken and passed. Because `sp` already is a pointer (to string), `scanner()` can modify the original pointer object—the `auto` variable `sp`.

Because the token pointer `tp` needs no multiple indirection, its address is not taken. In fact, because there is no multiple indirection, the original pointer object is not modified. You could use the `token` string identifier itself as the argument. Then you could eliminate the `tp` object declaration, as well as line 208 (which initializes it), in every pass through the loop. The tuning effect is small here, but serious applications may need every edge they can get.

Finally, the address of `ttype` *is* taken when passing it to `scanner()`. Thus scanner can load the riginal object with the token-type value. This is a good way to "cheat" the f tion-return mechanism and "return" several values, when it is otherwise restricted to returning just one value.

Creating a Parsing Routine

Many applications need no more than scanning services. Simply breaking out the parts of the input is enough, for example, when the input consists only of data items that will be used to update fields in a file record.

Other applications may need more than this, however. When you prompt a user for a command, for instance, the input may have a more or less complicated syntax. Then the input needs interpretation before any action can be taken. The act of interpreting scanned text is called *parsing*.

There is more than one way to create a parser. Commercial programs exist that can take tabularized summaries (grammars) and generate a parsing routine to match the specifications. Alternatively, you can "hard-code" a parser, using one of several different techniques.

We will now show you how to develop a hard-coded *recursive descent* parsing function. This special-purpose parser can evaluate regular expressions and return a result. It also provides limited support for variable names and value assignment. You can adapt it to any number of uses in your own programs.

What "Recursive Descent" Means

Before we discuss the development of the parser code, you need to know the meaning of *recursive descent*. The term is used in exactly the same sense used for the discussion of recursive function calls, as shown in figure 9.2.

As you can see from figure 9.2, recursive descent algorithms involve a hierarchy of functions. As functions call the next lower level (more detailed processing), program flow "descends" the hierarchy.

The recursive part enters the picture when the object being processed is complex, and can contain other—possibly also complex—objects of the same kind. In that case, it is possible for one of the lower-level functions to again call the first level routine.

This need not be as confusing as it sounds. Think of the algebraic expressions that we soon will parse. Such expressions may contain parenthesized subexpressions. When an opening parenthesis is encountered, you need only call the parsing routine from the top. When recursion has occurred, a return from the top-level routine returns control to the lower-level routine that reinvoked it. Clearly, you must forward-declare all the functions in the hierarchy (by prototyping them) so that the compiler knows what to do with the recursive references.

Fig. 9.2. *Control flow during recursive function calls.*

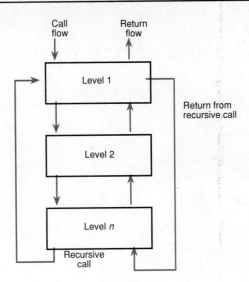

Building the Parser

The parsing routine that will be built here, `formula.c`, evaluates regular algebraic expressions and returns the result. For the sake of simplicity, only `double` values are allowed.

To save space, the operators allowed are simplified also. These operators, a subset of the C operators, determine precedence in a commonsense way. The expressions are considered to consist of the following parts, along with their associated operators, in descending order of precedence:

❑   Formula:

   (((... expression ...)))
   object name
   object name = expression
   object name = object name

❑   Expression:

   simpleexpr [+ simpleexpr] [- simpleexpr]

❑   Simple expression:

   term [* term] [/ term]

❏   Term:

signedfactor ^ *signedfactor [* ^ *signedfactor ...]*

❏   Signed factor:

[unary -] factor

❏   Factor:

integer literal
real literal
object name

Parentheses have the highest priority of all, and trigger a recursive call to evaluate a new subexpression. Thus they can force grouping and associativity.

The assignment operator, next in precedence, can also cause recursive processing; everything to the right of the = sign is considered a subexpression. The logic is arranged so that object-name (symbol-table) processing is reentrant; as a result, C-style expressions such as:

```
a = b = c = constant
```

can be used successfully.

Addition, subtraction, multiplication, and division follow the normal rules of algebra, with multiplication and division having the higher priority.

The ^ character is used as the *power operator*, so that there is no need for a function call to raise a number or variable to a power. Associativity for this operator is *right-to-left*, meaning that an expression such as:

```
a ^ b ^ c
```

first raises b to the c power, and then raises a to a power equal to the preceding result. This condition arises from the sequence of events during recursive descent.

This parsing routine does not support punctuation, except for space characters. Space characters can be embedded anywhere, as often as you like. Space characters are not required anywhere, except where omitting them would prevent recognizing a token. Note that the semicolon (;)—the C-style statement terminating character—is *not* supported.

Evaluating Formulas: *formula.c*

formula.c is shown in listing 9.2. The text to be parsed must be pointed to by the global variable char *sp (line 14). Lines 24–29 contain the prototype declarations for the hierarchy of functions that do the parsing. Lines 19–23 contain the prototypes for the support routines that provide user-variable and symbol-table support.

Listing 9.2. `formula.c`
(Parsing algebraic expressions with recursive descent logic).   *Turbo C 2.0*

```
 1   #include <stdlib.h>
 2   #include <stdio.h>
 3   #include <math.h>
 4   #include <string.h>
 5
 6   #include "scanner.h"
 7
 8   typedef struct var_struct
 9     {
10       char label[9];
11       double value;
12     } var_type;
13
14   char *sp,*tp;
15   char token[33];
16   int  ttype;
17   var_type (*vars)[16];
18
19   void   setup_vars( void );
20   void   free_vars( void );
21   void   list_vars( void );
22   var_type *find_var( char *vname);
23   int    add_var( char *vname, double vvalue );
24   double formula( void );
25   double expression( void );
26   double simpleexpr( void );
27   double term( void );
28   double signedfactor( void );
29   double factor( void );
30
31   main()
32   {
33     char request[40];
34
35     setup_vars();
36     strcpy( request, " NUM = 8.5" );
37     sp = request;
38     formula();
39     strcpy( request, " 1 + 3 * ( NUM / 0.2 ) ^ 2" );
40     sp = request;
41     printf( "The result is %.6f\n", formula() );
```

Listing 9.2. *continues*

Listing 9.2. continued

```
42    list_vars();
43    free_vars();
44  }
45
46  double formula( void )
47  {
48    if ( 0 != strpbrk( token,".+" ) ) ++sp;
49    scanner( &sp,token,&ttype );
50    return( expression() );
51  }
52
53  double expression( void )
54  {
55    double result = 0;
56
57    result = simpleexpr();
58    while ( ttype == PLUSOP || ttype == MINUSOP ) {
59      switch ( ttype ) {
60        case PLUSOP:  scanner( &sp,token,&ttype );
61                      result += simpleexpr(); break;
62        case MINUSOP: scanner( &sp,token,&ttype );
63                      result -= simpleexpr(); break;
64      }
65    }
66    return( result );
67  }
68
69  double simpleexpr( void )
70  {
71    double result = 0;
72
73    result = term();
74    while ( ttype == MUXOP || ttype == DIVOP ) {
75      switch ( ttype ) {
76        case MUXOP: scanner( &sp,token,&ttype );
77                    result *= term(); break;
78        case DIVOP: scanner( &sp,token,&ttype );
79                    result /= term(); break;
80      }
81    }
82    return( result );
83  }
84
85  double term( void )
86  {
87    double result = 0;
88
89    result = signedfactor();
```

```
90     while ( ttype == POWOP ) {
91       scanner( &sp,token,&ttype );
92       result = exp( log( result ) * signedfactor() );
93     }
94     return( result );
95  }
96
97  double signedfactor( void )
98  {
99    if ( *token == '-' ) return( 0-factor() );
100       else return( factor() );
101  }
102
103  double factor( void )
104  {
105    static double result = 0;
106    static var_type *temp;
107    char *holdvar;
108
109    switch ( ttype ) {
110      case REALLIT: result = atof( token ); break;
111      case INTLIT:  result = ( double )atol( token ); break;
112      case LPAREN:  scanner( &sp,token,&ttype );
113                    result = expression();
114                    break;
115  /* SYMBOL processing logic:
116        place current token in holdvar;
117        get the next token;
118        if ( variable DOES EXIST ) {
119          if ( new token is an = ) {        - reassign value -
120            get the next token;
121            evaluate the right side of the equation;
122            place result in variable bucket;
123            break out;
124          } ELSE {                          - fetch value -
125            return the variable's value;
126          }
127        } ELSE {                  - variable DOES NOT EXIST -
128          if ( current token is an = ) { - value provided -
129            get the next token;
130            evaluate the right side of the equation;
131            add variable to symbol table and set value;
132            if ( add failed ) exit( 8 );
133            break out in every case;
134          } ELSE {                        - value NOT provided -
135            set the value to 0;
136            add variable to symbol table and set value;
137            if ( add failed ) exit( 8 );
138            return 0;
139          }
```

Listing 9.2. continues

Listing 9.2. continued

```
140          }
141   */
142      case SYMBOL:
143                    holdvar = malloc( 9 );
144                    strcpy( holdvar, token );
145                    scanner( &sp,token,&ttype );
146                    temp = find_var( holdvar );
147                    if ( temp ) {
148                      if ( ttype == ASSIGNOP ) {
149                        scanner( &sp,token,&ttype );
150                        result = expression();
151                        temp->value = result;
152                        break;
153                      } else {
154                        result = temp->value;
155                        free( holdvar );
156                        return( result );
157                      }
158                    } else {
159                      if ( ttype == ASSIGNOP ) {
160                        scanner( &sp,token,&ttype );
161                        result = expression();
162                        if ( -1 == add_var( holdvar, result ) )
163                          exit( 8 );
164                        break;
165                      } else {
166                        result = 0.0;
167                        if ( -1 == add_var( holdvar, 0.0 ) )
168                          exit( 8 );
169                        free( holdvar );
170                        return( result );
171                      }
172                    }
173      }
174   if ( holdvar ) free( holdvar );
175   scanner( &sp,token,&ttype );
176   return( result );
177 }
178
179 void setup_vars( void )
180 {
181   int i;
182
183   vars = calloc( 16, sizeof( var_type ) );
184   for ( i=0; i<16; i++ ) {
185     strcpy( vars[i]->label, "" );
186     vars[i]->value = 0.0;
187   }
188 }
```

```
189
190   void free_vars( void )
191   {
192      free( vars );
193   }
194
195   void list_vars( void )
196   {
197      int i;
198
199      for ( i=0; i<16; i++ )
200        printf( "%s = %f\n", vars[i]->label, vars[i]->value );
201   }
202
203   var_type *find_var( char *vname )
204   {
205      static int i;
206
207      for ( i=0; i<16; i++ ) {
208        if ( 0 == strcmp( vname, vars[i]->label ) )
209          return( vars[i] );
210      }
211      return( NULL );
212   }
213
214   int add_var( char *vname, double vvalue )
215   {
216      int i;
217
218      if ( NULL != find_var( vname ) ) return( -1 );
219      for ( i=0; i<16; i++ ) if ( vars[i]->label[0] == '\0' ) break;
220      if ( i>15 ) return( -1 );
221      strcpy( vars[i]->label, vname );
222      vars[i]->value = vvalue;
223      return( 0 );
224   }
225
```

The basic plan of attack in parsing algebraic expressions is to loop at each level, calling the next-lower level, as long as the operators supporting the next-lower continue to be encountered. Each loop presumes that the scanner has been invoked beforehand and that the input token is ready in token.

Notice that the calls proceed from the lowest precedence to the highest as program flow moves *down* the hierarchy. This continues until factor() is entered; factor() deals with the "atomic" elements of the text. It is here also that parentheses and assignment operators are detected, and a recursive call is made to the top of the hierarchy [expression()].

In some instances, special cases are handled. Line 48, in `formula()`, advances the string pointer `sp` by 1 if the text to be parsed begins with a period or plus sign. Notice also the local variables in lines 105–107 in function `factor()`. The first two of these have the `static` specifier, for performance reasons (they do not have to be allocated again at every entry to the routine).

The variable `char *holdvar`, however, is not a `static` object. It is allowed to retain `auto` duration precisely because we *do* want it to be created afresh for every entry. This way there can be several copies of it during recursive entries to the function. Consider what happens when parsing the following expression, for example:

```
a = b = c = 6.28
```

At each entry to `factor()`, `holdvar` is created again (on the stack). In parsing this expression, one copy of `holdvar` saves the variable name `"a"`. Then the assignment operator causes recursion, and the function is entered again, only to encounter a reference to `"b"`, which also must be held in storage, and so on. If `holdvar` cannot be allocated dynamically (and uniquely) for every entry to `factor()`, only the rightmost variable name can be kept track of in parsing such expressions.

Lines 11–141 are of special interest. They contain (as comments) pseudocode that describes the flow of control during symbol processing.

Providing support for user variables and the symbol table requires that we look ahead a bit. The symbol table in `formula.c` holds as many as 16 variable names and associated values. Each variable in the symbol table is stored in a derived object called a *structure*, which can contain many atomic-type objects. In addition, the structure definition is given its own name, a `typedef`, so that it can be referred to easily. The structure type is defined like this:

```
 8   typedef struct var_struct
 9     {
10       char label[9];
11       double value;
12     } var_type;
...
17   var_type (*vars)[16];
```

The details of this syntax are covered in detail in Chapter 11. For now, pay attention especially to line 17. Presuming that you can legally write a type name of `var_type`, which was set up in lines 8–12, this line means that the symbol table consists of an *array of 16 pointers to the structure object*.

When dealing with structures, you normally refer to the individual elements within it by using the structure operator, which happens to be a period: a reference to `house.room` means that there is a structure called `house`, and that the reference is to the element `room` within it. There is, as you can see, some similarity to using the subscript operator `[ ]` to access an element of an array.

In `formula.c`, however, you go a little further. This program deals not merely with structures, but with *pointers to structures*. Now you must use the *structure pointer* operator (`->`), which consists of a minus sign followed by a greater-than sign. There must be no space between these two characters, although there can be space *around* them. Now `house->room` indicates that `house` is a pointer to a structure, and you are still accessing a particular `room`.

These considerations finally put you in a position to understand the references to symbol-table entries in `formula.c`. You need only take it one step further and introduce the notion that each structure is an element of an array. Lines 221 and 222, for example, initialize a user variable:

```
strcpy( vars[i]->label, vname ); /* init var name */
vars[i]->value = vvalue;         /* init var value */
```

Mixing Arrays and Pointers

In the preceding section, you encountered the interesting notion of an array of pointers. An array of pointers and a single pointer to an array are both possible in C. Each has its respective uses.

Defining Arrays of Pointer

Arrays of pointer are easy to define in C. Simply use both the indirection operator (`*`) and the subscript operator (`[ ]`) in the declaration. Figure 9.3 shows the syntax of the declaration and the memory configuration that this arrangement presumes.

An array of pointers is extremely useful for keeping track of a number of objects, not all of which may be in contiguous storage. You might be allocating storage dynamically for each object as they are created or read in, for example.

Fig. 9.3. Array of pointers in memory.

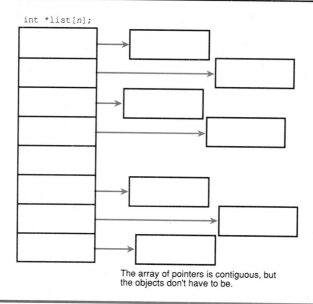

```
int *list[n];
```

The array of pointers is contiguous, but
the objects don't have to be.

The array itself, however, is in contiguous storage (refer to fig. 9.3). The array of pointers is easy to find, and makes finding the objects pointed to easy, as you can see in the following code fragment:

```
#include <stdlib.h>
#include <stdio.h>

main()
{
  int *list[16];
  int i;

  srand( 37 );    /* Seed the random number generator */
  for ( i=0; i<16; i++ ) {
    list[i] = malloc( sizeof(int) );   /* get storage */
    *list[i] = rand();             /* put something in it */
  }
  for ( i=0; i<16; i++ ) {
    printf( "%d\n", *list[i] );
  }
  for ( i=0; i<16; i++ ) {
    free( list[i] );               /* release the storage */
  }
}
```

In this code fragment, list is the array identifier; it is interpreted as an address value, as before. list[i] is also a pointer, whereas *list[i] is an integer.

Defining a Pointer to Array

You will sometimes encounter the companion case to the array of pointers: the *pointer to an array*. The syntax of this construction, which is determined by operator precedence, requires grouping parentheses to be interpreted correctly. Figure 9.4 shows this arrangement.

Fig. 9.4. *One pointer to an array of objects.*

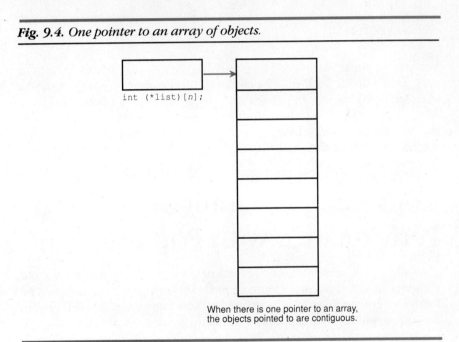

```
int (*list)[n];
```

When there is one pointer to an array,
the objects pointed to are contiguous.

The manner of manipulating the pointer and the array pointed to is similar to dealing with an array of pointers, but has some peculiarities. The following fragment shows how to define a pointer to an array and manipulate it:

```
#include <stdlib.h>
#include <stdio.h>

main()
{
  int (*list)[16];
  int i;

  srand( 37 );    /* Seed the random number generator */
  list = malloc( sizeof(int) * 16 );   /* get storage */
  for ( i=0; i<16; i++ ) {
    (*list)[i] = rand();         /* put something in it */
  }
  for ( i=0; i<16; i++ ) {
    printf( "%d\n", (*list)[i] );
  }
  free( list );                  /* release the storage */
}
```

You should notice in this code fragment that the malloc() function is used only once, outside the loop. The size of the entire array is calculated, and a corresponding amount of storage allocated. Further, the unqualified identifier list is a pointer to int, strictly speaking, and so is (*list). As you can see, the grouping parentheses plus the subscript operator are always required to dereference an array element.

Improving Program Performance with Pointers

In Chapter 8, we mentioned several times that using pointers to avoid subscripting does not always improve program performance—there may be hidden overhead in address calculations. You must examine each case to determine whether using pointers will help.

Program performance is not always a matter of mere speed, however. It may be a matter of functionality and flexibility, as well.

Using Pointers To Increase Flexibility

The previous sections illustrated a point that may not be obvious on the surface. Program performance (both speed and/or utility) can be affected drastically by the amount of data you can maintain in storage, rather than on disk (or other media).

Arrays of pointer and pointers to array can help you organize data in storage so that speed is much improved, and functionality is greatly increased, as well. A text-editing program, for example, would suffer greatly in both speed and functionality if only the line of text currently being edited were in RAM.

Examples of this kind are numerous and easy to find. You might go back through the sample programs in this book, for instance, and look for those that can be improved with these techniques.

Speeding Up Sorting with Pointers

ANSI standard C compilers provide a sorting function, `qsort()`, which is based on the Quicksort algorithm. It is fast and compact in most implementations. But there are times when you may want to save as much code space as possible, and thus write your own sort function. As you will see, you can write a snappy sort in about 20 lines of code. Furthermore, you can use arrays of pointer to achieve execution speeds that get fairly close to `qsort()` for file or table sizes under 5,000 entries.

Whether you use `qsort()` or roll your own, the first step is to design and code a set of functions that can compare two elements (called *sort keys* in this context). The idea is to keep the sort function itself small by passing to it a *function pointer* that designates the comparison method for a particular call. All the comparison routines, therefore, must have the same formal parameters so that multiple calls from the sort function are not necessary. Listing 9.3 shows `compares.c`, a separately compiled source file that contains a number of such comparison functions.

Listing 9.3. `compares.c` *(Comparison functions for use with the Shellsort function).* *Turbo C 2.0*

```
 1    #include <stdlib.h>
 2    #include <stdio.h>
 3
 4    #define INT     0
 5    #define CHAR    1
 6    #define DOUBLE  2
 7    #define LT     -1
 8    #define EQ      0
 9    #define GT      1
10    #if !defined( ASCENDING )
11    #define ASCENDING 0
12    #define DESCENDING 1
```

Listing 9.3. continues

Listing 9.3. continued

```
13   #endif
14
15   int comp_int( void *obj1, void *obj2, int order );
16   int comp_char( void *obj1, void *obj2, int order );
17   int comp_string( void *obj1, void *obj2, int order );
18   int comp_double( void *obj1, void *obj2, int order );
19
20   int comp_int( void *obj1, void *obj2, int order )
21   {
22     int result;
23
24     if ( order == ASCENDING )
25       result = *(int *)obj1 - *(int *)obj2;
26     else
27       result = *(int *)obj2 - *(int *)obj1;
28     if ( result ) result /= abs( result );
29     return result;
30   }
31
32   int comp_char( void *obj1, void *obj2, int order )
33   {
34     int result;
35
36     if ( order == ASCENDING )
37       result = *(char *)obj1 - *(char *)obj2;
38     else
39       result = *(char *)obj2 - *(char *)obj1;
40     if ( result ) result /= abs( result );
41     return result;
42   }
43
44   int comp_string( void *obj1, void *obj2, int order )
45   {
46     int result = 0;
47     char *s1 = obj1;  /* Do this because Turbo C doesn't */
48     char *s2 = obj2;  /* handle void pointers well */
49
50     while ( !result && *s1 && *s2 ) {
51       if ( order == ASCENDING )
52         result = *s1++ - *s2++;
53       else
54         result = *s2++ - *s1++;
55     }
56     if ( result ) result /= abs( result );
57     return result;
58   }
59
60   int comp_double( void *obj1, void *obj2, int order )
```

```
61  {
62    double result;
63
64    if ( order == ASCENDING )
65      result = *(double *)obj1 - *(double *)obj2;
66    else
67      result = *(double *)obj2 - *(double *)obj1;
68    if ( result < 0 ) return -1;
69      else if ( result == 0 ) return 0;
70        else if ( result > 0 ) return 1;
71  }
72
```

The comparison routines accept `void` pointers (not null pointers, remember) to the objects to be compared, plus another argument that specifies whether the sort is to be ascending or descending. If it is descending, the order of comparison is simply turned around to reverse the sense. All the sort function expects in return is an integer that is less than zero if `obj1` < `obj2`, zero if `obj1` == `obj2`, and > 0 if `obj1` > `obj2`.

The sort function neither knows nor cares if you swap the order internally to force a sort to descending order. In the case of `qsort()`, you would have to modify the comparison function in listing 9.3: eliminate the `order` argument, and make it a global variable that can be set before the program can call `qsort()`, because `qsort()` does not support a function parameter determining output order. The `shell_sort()` function we're about to show you supports the functions as written here.

The key to increasing sort speeds when using routines simpler than `qsort()`—such as `shell_sort()`, in listing 9.4—is to sort an array of *pointers* to objects, instead of sorting the objects themselves. This saves a great deal of time when large objects are sorted because only pointers, not the objects, physically exchange positions.

Listing 9.4. `shellsrt.c` (*Using the Shellsort algorithm with an array of pointers to the objects to be sorted*).   *Turbo C 2.0*

```
1   /* +-----------------------------------------------------+
2       +                    SHELL SORT                       
3       +    Input to shell_sort is an array of pointers to   
4       +    objects of your choice, plus a pointer to the    
5       +    appropriate comparison routine.                  
6       +-----------------------------------------------------+
7   */
8   #include <stdlib.h>
9   #include <stdio.h>
```

Listing 9.4. continues

Listing 9.4. continued

```
10                    /* Use defines with global var order */
11   #define ASCENDING 0
12   #define DESCENDING 1
13
14   #include "compares.h"
15   #include "timer.h"
16
17   /* +---------------------------------------------------+
18      + Shellsort test data.
19      + The SMALL MODEL used here assumes the near pointer
20      + type. To use in separate compiles, you might use
21      + the far override and always assume far pointers.
22      + Both shell_sort() and all comparison routines
23      + would then have to be modified to support this.
24      +---------------------------------------------------+
25   */
26   char *shell_list[] =
27     {
28          "Vermont                 ",
29          "Rhode Island            ",
30          "Oregon                  ",
31          "New York                ",
32          "New Hampshire           ",
33          "Mississippi             ",
34          "Montana                 ",
35          "Iowa                    ",
36          "Georgia                 ",
37          "California              ",
38          "Colorado                ",
39          "Alaska                  ",
40          "Alabama                 ",
41          "Arizona                 ",
42     };
43   /* +---------------------------------------------------+
44      + Quicksort test data.
45      +---------------------------------------------------+
46   */
47   char quick_list[][21] =
48     {
49          "Vermont                 ",
50          "Rhode Island            ",
51          "Oregon                  ",
52          "New York                ",
53          "New Hampshire           ",
54          "Mississippi             ",
55          "Montana                 ",
56          "Iowa                    ",
57          "Georgia                 ",
```

```
58          "California           ",
59          "Colorado             ",
60          "Alaska               ",
61          "Alabama              ",
62          "Arizona              ",
63     };
64
65     int q_comp_string( void *obj1, void *obj2 );
66
67     /* +----------------------------------------------------+
68        + Declare shell_sort().
69        +    All pointers at this level should be (void *).
70        +----------------------------------------------------+
71     */
72     void shell_sort( void *table[],
73                 int (*comp)( void *, void *, int ),
74                 int order,
75                 int sortsize );
76
77     main()
78     {
79        int i;
80
81        start_bench();
82        shell_sort( (void *)shell_list, comp_string,
83                    ASCENDING, 14 );
84        stop_bench();
85        for ( i=0; i<14; i++ ) printf( "%s", shell_list[i] );
86        puts( "\n" );
87        printf( "Shellsort required %.4f seconds.\n",
88            duration() );
89
90        start_bench();
91        qsort( quick_list, 14, 21, q_comp_string );
92        stop_bench();
93        printf( "Quicksort required %.4f seconds.\n",
94            duration() );
95
96        printf( "\nShellsort to descending order:\n" );
97        shell_sort( (void *)shell_list, comp_string,
98                    DESCENDING, 14 );
99        for ( i=0; i<14; i++ ) printf( "%s", shell_list[i] );
100       puts( "\n" );
101    }
102
103    /* +----------------------------------------------------+
104       + shell_sort().
105       +   INPUT: 1) A pointer to an array of pointers to
106       +              objects to be sorted.
107       +           2) A pointer to a function which will
```

Listing 9.4. continues

Listing 9.4. continued

```
108    +               perform the comparison between any
109    +               two elements in the array/list.
110    +            3) An integer whose value is either
111    +               ASCENDING or DESCENDING.
112    +            4) An integer whose value is the number
113    +               of elements to be sorted.
114    +  OUTPUT: NONE. The original array of pointers is
115    +          re-ordered in ascending or descending
116    +          sequence, depending on the global variable
117    +          order.
118    +  METHOD: h-partitioned insertion sort. The
119    +          sequence of values for h are:
120    +             1,4,13,40,121,364,1093,...
121    +          with the highest value depending on the
122    +          global variable sortsize. See the
123    +          appendices for more detail on method;
124    +          both Sedgewick and Knuth have much more
125    +          on sorting theory.
126    +----------------------------------------------------+
127 */
128 void shell_sort( void *table[],
129          int (*comp)( void *, void *, int ),
130          int order,
131          int sortsize )
132 {
133    int i, j, h;
134    void *v;
135
136    h = 1;
137    do h = 3 * h + 1; while (h <= sortsize - 1 );
138    do {
139      h /= 3;
140      for ( i=h; i<sortsize; i++ ) {
141        v = table[i];
142        j = i;
143        while ( 0 < (*comp)( table[j-h], v, order ) ) {
144          table[j] = table[j-h];
145          j -= h;
146          if ( j < h ) break;
147        }
148        table[j] = v;
149      }
150    } while ( h > 0 );
151 }
```

```
152
153   int q_comp_string( void *obj1, void *obj2 )
154   {
155     int result = 0;
156     char *s1 = obj1;   /* Do this since Turbo C doesn't */
157     char *s2 = obj2;   /* handle void pointers well */
158
159     while ( !result && *s1 && *s2 )
160       result = *s1++ - *s2++;
161     if ( result ) result /= abs( result );
162     return result;
163   }
```

Listing 9.4 shows how to set up and call `shell_sort()`. Notice particularly
lines 28–41 and 49–62. The test data for `shell_sort()` and `qsort()`, respectively, appears in these lines. Data for `shell_sort()` is set up as an
array of pointers to `char` so that only the pointers (not necessarily the strings
themselves) are presumed to be contiguous. In contrast, the `qsort()` test
data is arranged as a two-dimensional array of `char` so that the strings are
contiguous.

The Shellsort function itself is in lines 126–149. The array of pointers is
handled by using subscripts: it would be rather more difficult to use only
pointers, and that method would help little here. When the sample program
in listing 9.4 is run, output similar to the following is displayed on the system
console:

```
Alabama    Alaska   Arizona       California   Colorado
Georgia    Iowa     Mississippi   Montana      New Hampshire
New York   Oregon   Rhode Island  Vermont

Shellsort required 0.0025 seconds.
Quicksort required 0.0019 seconds.

Shellsort to descending order:
Vermont      Rhode Island   Oregon   New York   New Hampshire
Montana      Mississippi    Iowa     Georgia    Colorado
California  Arizona         Alaska   Alabama
```

Because this example sorts only 14 entries, the end-to-end run time is
small. The difference between `shell_sort()` and `qsort()` is also small,
about 0.6 milliseconds. (The difference in the length of time depends on
both the compiler and the machine you use.) For small numbers of records/
entries (less than 5,000), the simplicity of this implementation, plus the use
of pointers, nearly makes up for Quicksort's more efficient algorithm.

Summary

The techniques in this chapter, together with the more basic material in Chapter 8, provide just about everything you need to master the fine art of pointer programming in C. Before continuing, be sure you have mastered the following ideas:

❏ *Multiple indirection*. Pointers can point to other pointers in C. This is an extremely powerful and commonly used technique in C.

❏ *Arrays of pointer*. Arrays of pointers can help you organize a large number of discontiguous objects in memory. This technique adds power and flexibility to your C programs.

❏ *Pointers to array*. When you can load a number of objects simultaneously to memory, performance picks up. Using a pointer to an array allows you to allocate that memory dynamically so that it need not be a permanent part of your compiled program.

❏ *Text scanning and parsing*. With an understanding of scanning and parsing techniques, you can design and implement your own "intelligent" data- and command-input routines. Doing so provides not only an impressive interface for the user, but also more power and flexibility for your program.

10

File I/O Programming

File I/O programming is another of those C programming issues that can only be labeled as "crucial." The primary purpose of a computer program is to work with data, and most data is stored in files—usually on disk devices. The users of your programs would be perturbed, to say the least, if the information they laboriously typed in was not saved (written to a file).

The stream I/O functions discussed earlier in the book were those functions mostly related to the user-interface side of things. In this chapter, you are introduced to the process of bulk data storage and retrieval.

The subject of I/O programming is vast and often complicated. Although not a great deal of information is presented here about it, the fundamentals of disk file-handling, particularly as it applies to DOS- and UNIX-based systems (as opposed to mainframe environments), can be found here. In this chapter, you learn about the following:

❏ *File-management functions*. These are the functions that provide the facilities for what is usually termed *data-management* activities. This includes deleting and renaming files.

❏ *Buffer-management techniques*. Once into file I/O programming proper, you must give some consideration to moving data into and out of main memory (RAM). What kinds of files can be buffered? How? What is a good buffer size? These and other questions are answered.

❑   *File-access methods*. What methods are available for reading
and writing records? For that matter, what is a record? Can you
read or write a record in the middle of a file without having to
read (or write) all previous records to get to it? You can,
indeed, and you will discover some of the ways to do so.

Using C's File-Management Functions

Standard C provides an adequate, if not exhaustive, collection of file-
management functions. You can delete files, rename them, start over at the
beginning of a file that's already open, and create temporary files as well as
unique names (strings) for temporary files.

Deleting a File with *remove( )*

The `remove()` function can be used to delete a file. It is important to
understand that this function *physically removes the file from disk*. When
you execute this function, the file named by the argument for `remove()` is
gone. After you execute `remove()`, the file and its contents are forever
unavailable. Certain utilities on the market can "unerase" a deleted file, but
this is risky business at best.

The function prototype for `remove()` is as follows:

```
#include <stdio.h>
int remove( const char *filename );
```

When this function is called, the file named by `filename` should not be
open. If it is, the behavior is implementation-defined, meaning that it
depends on the compiler vendor (a given compiler may allow it, but it is
never guaranteed).

`remove()` returns a zero integer if the operation was successful, nonzero
if not. Here is an example of using `remove()`:

```
#include <stdio.h>
...
char fname[] = "\\usr\\junk.txt";
...
if ( !remove( fname ) )
  printf( "File: %s was erased.\n", fname );
else
  printf( "Could not erase %s\n", fname );
```

You can see from this example that ANSI does not care what string defines the file; it is just a string. Here, the file `junk.txt` is deleted from the `\usr` disk directory. Names like this are common in both DOS and UNIX systems (UNIX uses a forward slash). Because we coded the DOS version of the slash, a `\\` escape sequence was necessary.

Changing the File Name with *rename ( )*

The `rename()` function changes the name of a file on disk. That is, the directory entry (or volume table of contents, or whatever) is modified physically, so that the file can henceforth be accessed under its new name. The old name no longer exists. The function prototype for `rename()` is

```
#include <stdio.h>
int rename( const char *old, const char *new );
```

The `rename()` function returns zero if the operation was successful, nonzero if not. If `rename()` fails, the file is not damaged—it still exists under its old name.

You should make sure that the named file is not open when `rename()` is called. Some implementations (notably UNIX-based systems) must *copy* the file in order to rename it; there may be no operating system support for directly modifying the directory. Some systems (such as DOS) can directly modify a disk directory, but there is no guarantee that this capability will be available to you.

Why would you ever want to use this function? The obvious reason is so that you can maintain multiple copies, or versions, of a file. The program `versions.c`, listing 10.1, is extremely simplistic, but you could use it as a basis (as boilerplate code) to build a more complex archiving system.

Listing 10.1. `versions.c` *(Using the* `rename()` *function to change a file name).*   *Turbo C++*

```
1   #include <stdlib.h>
2   #include <stdio.h>
3   #include <string.h>
4   #include <conio.h>
5
6   main()
7   {
8     char newver[4];
```

Listing 10.1. continues

Listing 10.1. *continued*

```
 9      char oldver[] = "txt";
10      char fname[] = "junk.";
11      char oldname[13];
12      char newname[13];
13
14      clrscr();
15      printf( "Enter new archive version (3 digits): " );
16      gets( newver );
17      strcpy( oldname, fname);
18      strcpy( newname, fname);
19      strcat( oldname, oldver );
20      strcat( newname, newver );
21      if ( rename( oldname, newname ) )
22        printf( "Rename %s to %s failed.\n", oldname, newname );
23      else
24        printf( "Renamed %s to %s\n", oldname, newname );
25   }
```

Back to the Beginning with *rewind( )*

At times, you may want to process the same file more than once. You can
do this by using the `rewind()` function. `rewind()`, which is called while the
file is open, simply sets the current position (the point at which the next read
or write occurs) to the beginning of the file. The function prototype for
`rewind()` is

```
#include <stdio.h>
void rewind( FILE *stream );
```

Strictly speaking, `rewind()` is a file-positioning function. We include it
here because it performs only one function—although quite a useful one—
that amounts to setting up for I/O operations. Other functions detect and set
the current file position more flexibly (and hence are considered *processing*
functions, not management functions).

The `rewind()` function is probably most useful for processing a file
sequentially multiple times. *Sequential processing* is the processing of
reading (or writing) every record in the file, beginning with the first, and
(usually) going all the way to the end.

Suppose, for example, that you wanted to "send" multiple copies of a text
file to `stdout`. Because standard streams are used, you can incidentally use
redirection to put the output to another disk file. The program `copies.c`,
listing 10.2, performs this task.

Listing 10.2. `copies.c (Using rewind()).`   *Turbo C++*

```
 1   #include <stdlib.h>
 2   #include <stdio.h>
 3   #include <string.h>
 4
 5   main( int argc, char *argv[] )
 6   {
 7     int copies;
 8     char inname[41];
 9     FILE *infile;
10     char text[255];
11
12     if ( argc < 3 ) {
13       puts( "Command: copies infile n" );
14       puts( "To send to printer: copies infile n >prn" );
15       exit( 8 );
16     }
17
18     strcpy( inname, argv[1] );
19     copies = atoi( argv[2] );
20
21     if ( NULL == ( infile = fopen( inname, "r" ) ) ) {
22       printf( "Could not open %s\n", inname );
23       exit( 8 );
24     }
25
26     while ( copies ) {
27       while ( fgets( text, 255, infile ) ) fputs( text, stdout );
28       fputc( 12, stdout );   /* Formfeed for most printers */
29       --copies;
30       rewind( infile );
31     }
32
33     close ( infile );
34   }
```

One question about `rewind()` remains: Why use it, when you could just close and then reopen the file? The question is especially penetrating when you realize that there is a `reopen()` function (see Part II of this book) that can do the job with one function call. Because `reopen()` also allows you to specify a new processing mode, why use something as simple as `rewind()`?

The answer is *time*. The processing of closing and reopening a file is expensive, because it requires the handling of leftover buffers and updating the disk directory (which involves additional I/O, even if you, the programmer, do not see it). In contrast, `rewind()` just sets the current pointer back to the beginning. So if you are going to go back to the beginning a number of times, you can save time (translate that to the time the user sits there waiting) and wear and tear on the disk drive.

Creating and Using Temporary Files

Two other file-management functions—tmpfile() and tmpnam()—may prove very useful to you. Both are declared in stdio.h. The function prototype and a description of each of these functions are as follows:

❏   `FILE *tmpfile( void );`

tmpfile() creates *and opens* a temporary binary file (mode wb+ = create, binary, update read/write). If the create and open are successful, a standard stream pointer is returned; otherwise, a NULL pointer is returned. The name of the resulting file is generated automatically, as in the tmpnam() function (described next).

The temporary file created is deleted automatically when it is closed or when the program terminates normally. If the program terminates abnormally, ANSI leaves it to the implementation to determine whether the file is to be deleted.

❏   `char *tmpnam( char *s );`

tmpnam() does *not* create a file. It creates only a file *name*— that is, a string. Using tmpnam() creates a "temporary" name, only in the sense that the name generated is guaranteed not to collide with any existing file name. You still must use the file-name string to open, and later close, the temporary file. You might want to do this instead of calling tmpfile() if you do not want the file to be deleted automatically when closed, or if the file mode wb+ does not suit your purposes. You should (in every case) be sure to use the remove() function to erase the file after you finish with it.

You can invoke tmpnam() in two ways: the argument string pointer s can point to a valid string you have created, or it can be NULL. If it points to a string, it is presumed to be at least L_tmpnam (a predefined macro name) characters long, and the generated file-name string is placed in it. If it is NULL, the file-name string is stored in a static string internal to tmpnam(), and a pointer to it returned to the caller.

Temporary files can be very handy when you have intermediate results or data that is too massive to reside in memory. Most compilers use them, for example, as do some file-compression and archiving programs.

Buffered I/O Concepts

Earlier in the book, some aspects of the effect of buffering stream I/O were discussed. In standard C, "stream I/O" can encompass a variety of I/O programming techniques that usually are discussed separately.

In particular, stream I/O in C encompasses both character and block-device I/O programming. Console and communications port programming are examples of managing character devices, and disk file programming is an example of managing block devices.

Block devices, which can read and write many bytes at a time to and from the physical storage media, are the devices thought of as being "file-oriented" devices. These devices, therefore, are most susceptible to buffering techniques, and are the ones with which this chapter is concerned. (Although character devices can have buffering schemes imposed on them, this has little or no effect on their performance.)

An I/O buffer, as mentioned earlier, is an area of RAM reserved for receiving blocks of data; its main function is *speed matching*. The central processor of your computer is many times faster than any I/O device and, without some technique to "reduce" the speed differential, would spend (waste) a great deal of time just waiting for I/O to complete.

Buffering does nothing to change the physical speeds of the different kinds of electronics involved. It does work, however, because of a simple fact: programs "ask for data" only in spurts (most of the time). Between spurts, the program is busy processing the data just read (or getting ready to write more).

You can get an intuitive idea of why this concept works by thinking of your hot water heater. The water supply system is capable of providing a steady stream of water, but you can't heat it directly and send it straight to the faucet. Why? Because you can use hot water faster than you can heat it!

It's a different story if you introduce a tank large enough to hold sufficient hot water to satisfy a single fairly large demand. Now you can heat water and store it between demands. The supply, of course, corresponds to a disk or other device, the tank is the speed-matching buffer, and your shower is the program.

What Difference Does It Make?

Does buffering your files really make much of a difference? It surely does—the speed difference between even a *fast* disk and the central processor is enormous. The less you must cause something physical to happen at the drive, the better your program performs.

Up to this point, you have only been told that larger buffers (up to a point) make a big difference in program performance. Now it's time to see how to do that. A short program, speedbuf.c, listing 10.3, shows you how to use the setvbuf() standard library function to modify the buffer size used for a file.

This program uses some of the facilities of the DOS- and PC-based timer.c high-resolution timing routines, but high-resolution timing is not actually started. The reason is that high-resolution timing is too much of a CPU hog—the I/O interrupts don't work right, even on a fast machine. Therefore we must settle for a timer resolution of 18.2 ticks per second (which is sufficient for our purposes).

Listing 10.3. speedbuf.c *(Tuning I/O performance with buffer size).*

```
1   #include <stdlib.h>
2   #include <stdio.h>
3
4   #include "timer.h"
5
6   main()
7   {
8     FILE *infile;
9     char pline[255];
10
11    if ( NULL == ( infile = fopen( "finance.c", "r" ) ) )
12      abort();
13    if ( setvbuf( infile, NULL, _IOFBF, 512) ) abort();
14    begin_time = *clock;
15    while ( fgets( pline, 255, infile ) ) ;
16    end_time = *clock;
17    fclose( infile );
18    printf( "Time w/512 byte buffer: %.3f\n",
19            (double)( end_time - begin_time ) / 18.2 );
20
21    if ( NULL == ( infile = fopen( "finance.c", "r" ) ) )
22      abort();
23    if ( setvbuf( infile, NULL, _IOFBF, 4096) ) abort();
24    begin_time = *clock;
25    while ( fgets( pline, 255, infile ) ) ;
```

```
26      end_time = *clock;
27      fclose( infile );
28      printf( "Time w/4096 byte buffer: %.3f\n",
29              (double)( end_time - begin_time ) / 18.2 );
30  }
```

When the `speedbuf.c` program runs, the output it produces on the system console is something like this:

```
Time w/512 byte buffer: 0.604
Time w/4096 byte buffer: 0.220
```

The figures may not be the same on your machine, because you may be running something either faster or slower than the 80386-20Mhz machine on which this sample was run. The relative differences should be reflected, however.

`speedbuf.c` reads the same text file twice, with two different buffer sizes. Note that if you are going to use the `setvbuf()` function, you must call it *after opening* the file and *before any I/O* calls are made. Once you start reading and writing, it is too late. (The details on `setvbuf()` are given later in this chapter in the section "Writing High Performance File Routines.")

This program is dependent on PC- or compatible-based architecture. It begins timing by the simple expedient of recording the current system clock tick count (lines 14 and 24), and concludes by recording it again (lines 16 and 26). Then the tick rate is used to compute the elapsed time for reading with each buffer size (lines 19 and 29).

Even in this trivial example, the results are encouraging. Just increasing the buffer size from 512 bytes to 4K bytes speeded up the file-read (about three times faster). Even more satisfying results can be achieved in more sophisticated applications.

Buffering and *stdin*, *stdout*, and *stderr*

Buffering is a coin with two sides. It may actually impede your attempts to control the console, for instance. The `stdin` stream normally is line-buffered, which means that you must type characters and press Enter to have them input to the program, even if you are using character-input functions such as `getchar()`. `getchar()` and its companion functions also echo keyboard characters to the screen whether you want them to or not.

For character devices, therefore, you occasionally may want to turn off buffering completely. This is the case, for example, with the common DOS implementation of getch(), which originated in the UNIX-based curses library functions. In DOS systems, getch() ordinarily is used to get keystrokes, one at a time, with no echo to the screen (hopefully without having to press Enter).

For direct console I/O using a function like getch(), you need to turn buffering off so that the keystroke is reported to your program immediately. You can use the setbuf() function to do this. The sample program keyio.c, shown in listing 10.4, illustrates how to go about it.

Listing 10.4. keyio.c *(Controlling keyboard I/O buffering).*   *Turbo C 2.0*

```
1    #define BORLAND
2
3    #include <stdlib.h>
4    #include <stdio.h>
5    #if defined( BORLAND )
6    #include <conio.h>
7    #elif defined( MS )
8    #include <graph.h>
9    #endif
10
11   int get_ch( void )
12   {
13      static int is_open = 0;
14      static FILE *istream = NULL;
15
16      if ( !is_open ) {
17         if ( NULL == ( istream = fopen( "CON","rb" ) ) ) exit( 1 );
18         setbuf( istream, NULL );
19         is_open = 1;
20      }
21      return( fgetc( istream ) );
22   }
23
24   main()
25   {
26      char ch;
27
28   #if defined( BORLAND )
29      clrscr();
30   #elif defined( MS )
```

```
31      _clearscreen( _GCLEARSCREEN );
32  #endif
33    ch = 32;
34    while ( ch != '.' ) {    /* Type a period to quit */
35        ch = get_ch(); if ( ch == 0 ) ch = get_ch();
36  #if !defined( MS )
37        fputc( ch,stdout );
38  #endif
39    }
40  }
```

In listing 10.4, the setbuf() function is not used to alter the behavior of the stdin stream; another stream is provided instead (see line 14). Nor is the curses-like function name duplicated. The underscore character is used to form a similar but unique name for the function: get_ch() (lines 11–22). Static local variables are used (lines 13–14) so that the status of the stream (open or closed) can be retained across multiple calls to the function.

Line 1 of listing 10.4 contains a macro definition that structures the code for Turbo C 2.0 and Turbo C++ compilers. You can change this macro to #define MS if you want to compile it with Microsoft QuickC 2.0 , 2.5, or Microsoft C 6.0. In either case, type a period to terminate the program.

You should be aware that the behavior of the program is different when it is run with different compilers. Using the Borland (Turbo) products, the get_ch() behaves just like the common getch() function; DOS input calls are completely bypassed and you get every keystroke. The Microsoft products, however, do not bypass DOS input functions. You can use the DOS editing keys, and you must press Enter before the period character terminates the program. The vendor-provided getch() function works the same in either product line.

Selecting an I/O Mode for File Streams

Standard C provides I/O modes with which you can read, write, update, and append data to files, and you can do it in either text or binary modes. It is important that you understand what the various modes mean, and what you can do with them.

Selecting the Access Mode

The mode parameter of the fopen() function determines the *file access mode* (or just *file mode*) that is associated with the file *while it is open this time*. You can select different modes at other times. The mode parameter is a string, which can be a string literal. The following code fragment shows how to place the mode string in fopen() call arguments:

```
#include <stdio.h>
...
FILE *stream;
...
if ( NULL == ( stream = fopen( "anyfile.dat", "mode" ) ) )
    abort();
```

The values that the mode string may take on are discussed in the following sections. In general, the mode string can contain up to three characters, which must be selected from the set of five characters shown in table 10.1.

Table 10.1. *Characters used in the mode string.*

Mode Character	Meaning
r	Read from file
w	Write to file
a	Append to end of file
b	I/O is in binary mode (no text transformations)
+	Updates are permitted

The difference between text and binary mode access is discussed again later in this chapter in the section "Using Text and Binary File Modes."

Open Options for Input Mode

When you want to access the file in a read-only mode, you use an input mode—either text input or binary input. Examples of each method follow:

❏   fopen(*filenamestring,* "r")

Opens, for reading in text mode, the file named by *filenamestring*. Some transformations of the data (discussed later in the chapter) are performed on the input data.

❏ fopen(*filenamestring*, "rb")

Opens, for reading in binary mode, the file named by *filenamestring*. Input operations do not cause any transformations of data.

Open Options for Output Mode

You use an output mode when you want to access the file in write-only mode (an obvious example—creating the file in the first place). Generalized examples of using the output modes follow:

❏ fopen(*filenamestring*, "w")

Opens the file for writing, in text mode. If the file already exists, it is truncated to zero length, effectively overlaying the original data. If it does not exist, it is created.

❏ fopen(*filenamestring*, "wb")

Opens the file for writing, in binary mode. This mode also destroys (overlays) an existing file. If you open an existing file accidentally, there is no way back—closing it immediately still leaves it with a zero length. A word of caution: earlier we mentioned the existence of commercial "unerase" programs that can undo the effect of a call to remove(). These programs *cannot help you here*. Removing and truncating a file are two entirely different things.

❏ fopen(*filenamestring*, "a")

Opens the file for appended writing, in text mode, with the current position at end-of-file. That is, the next write occurs just beyond the last line of text previously written. Opening an existing file does not destroy it. Opening a nonexistent file creates it.

❏ fopen(*filenamestring*, "ab")

Opens the file for appended writing, in binary mode, with the current position at end-of-file. This mode also creates. if needed.

Open Options for Update Mode

You use an update mode when you want to access the file for both reading and writing. Briefly, you should append the + character to the end of any of the preceding six modes to get one of the update modes.

❏   fopen(*filenamestring*, "r+")

Opens the text file for update—both reading and writing. It is assumed that the initial I/O request will be for reading. This mode does not destroy existing files, but the current position is placed at the beginning of the file at file open time. On the other hand, this mode does not create a file. (You cannot open a nonexistent file with this mode.)

❏   fopen(*filenamestring*, "w+")

Opens the text file for update. This mode is similar to the "r+" mode, but it is assumed that the initial I/O request will be for writing. If the file does not exist, it is created; if it does, it is truncated to zero length and overlayed. Opening a file in this mode generally will not fail, unless there is a directory error or no space left on the disk or directory for the new file.

❏   fopen(*filenamestring*, "a+")

Opens, or perhaps creates, the text file for update. In any case, the current position is placed at end-of-file. This means that a write request tacks the data on the end of the file, but a read request fails (with EOF). To read immediately after opening the file with this mode, you must move the current position elsewhere. How to do this is discussed later in the chapter, in the section "Direct Access File Programming."

Note that all writes to a file opened with append mode are forced to the then current end-of-file position. It makes no difference whether there has been a call to one of the file-positioning functions. For all practical purposes, append mode is for writing to end-of-file locations only. In addition, some implementations may have padded the last block with null characters, so that the next appended record is *beyond* the previous end-of-file position.

If you want to append records *and* update elsewhere in the file, open it with the "r+" or "rb+" mode strings and manually position to end-of-file.

❏   fopen(*filenamestring,* "rb+")

Opens the binary file for update. Opening a nonexistent file will fail.

❏   fopen(filenamestring, "wb+")

Opens or creates the binary file for update processing.

❏   fopen(filenamestring, "ab+")

Opens or creates the binary file for update processing, writing at end-of-file. The same warning about where writes occur applies for this mode string: they *always* are at end-of-file.

When the mode string contains three characters, the update character + may be either the second or the third character in the string: "r+b", "w+b", and "a+b" are all valid mode strings.

Summary of Modes

Table 10.2 summarizes all the combinations of mode-string characters, with a brief explanation of their meaning.

Table 10.2. *A Summary of all ANSI C file modes.*

Mode String	Meaning
"r"	Open text file for reading
"w"	Truncate to zero length or create text file for writing
"a"	Append; open or create text file for writing at end-of-file
"rb"	Open binary file for reading
"wb"	Open binary file for writing
"ab"	Append; open or create binary file for writing at end-of-file
"r+"	Open text file for update (both reading and writing)
"w+"	Truncate to zero length or create text file for update
"a+"	Append; open or create text file for update, positioned at end-of-file

Table 10.2 continues

Table 10.2 *continued*

Mode String	Meaning
"rb+"	Open a binary file for update
"wb+"	Truncate to zero length or create a binary file for update
"ab+"	Append; open or create binary file for update, positioned at end-of-file
"r+b"	Same as "rb+"
"w+b"	Same as "wb+"
"a+b"	Same as "ab+"

Mixing Reads and Writes in Update Modes

Update-mode file access is distinguished by the fact that, once a file is open in the correct mode, you can both read data from and write data to the file. This is the characteristic of disk files that makes them so useful. They can be updated without your having to rewrite the whole file.

In combining both reading and writing to a single file, you frequently have to switch from reading to writing, or from writing to reading. Some attention must be paid to what happens to the file buffers when you do this. If file buffers are not handled correctly, you probably will lose some data. Almost invariably so, in fact.

The process of switching from writing to reading in update mode is particularly vulnerable to data loss. The reason is that the write-type library functions don't actually cause disk I/O—*they just send data to the buffer*. The data is not physically written to disk until the buffer is full. Thus, switching to read functions may simply overlay the data already in the buffer. Consider the following code fragment, for example:

```
#include <stdlib.h>
#include <stdio.h>
....
main()
{
   FILE *data;
   int i;
   unsigned char record[100];   /* The data record */

   if ( NULL == ( data = fopen( ..., "rb+" ) ) ) ...
   setvbuf( data, NULL, _IOFBF, 1000 ); /* 10 recs/buf */
```

```
...
    for ( i=0; i<5; i++ ) fwrite( record, 100, 1, data );
    fread( record, 100, 1, data );
...
    fclose( data );
}
```

The for loop in this fragment writes five records (only half a bufferful). Then, without further ado, a read is performed. What happens to the five output records? They are lost. Some means of forcing the remaining data in a buffer to be written to the disk when switching access types is needed. This method exists—it is called *flushing* the buffer. Incidentally, you should flush the buffer no matter which type of switch is involved—whether read to write or write to read. The ANSI standard says that the contents of a buffer area are indeterminate *at all times* (from the point of view of the program).

There are two ways, not just one, to flush a buffer. They are as follows:

❑   *Call the* fflush() *library function*. You can flush a buffer manually by calling fflush(*ptr), where *ptr is a FILE * pointer. To flush *all* buffers, call fflush(NULL).

❑   *Call one of the file-positioning functions*. These functions, which include fseek(), fsetpos(), and rewind(), all change the location in the file of the current position, making it safe for these functions to "assume" that you intend to switch access types. Even if you do not switch access types, thc data in the buffer will no longer match data on disk at the new position.

Knowing the rules for buffer handling, you can rewrite the last few lines of the preceding code fragment, as follows, so that it is guaranteed to work correctly:

```
    for ( i=0; i<5; i++ ) fwrite( record, 100, 1, data );
    fread( record, 100, 1, data );
    fclose( data );
    fflush( data );   /* Resynchronize the buffer */
}
```

Using Text and Binary File Modes

Before leaving the topic of file modes, you should know something about using text and binary modes to access your files. Many files can be processed either way, but the distinction is important.

Two things need to be clarified: what is and isn't a text stream and which read/write functions apply to the text and binary modes.

A *text stream* is a sequence of lines, each composed of zero or more characters (an implementation is required to support *at least* 255 characters per line), terminated by an end-of-line character or characters that are converted internally to the '\n' character. On disk, a line is not necessarily a string: the null character '\0' is not recorded. The string-oriented character stream functions add the '\0' when reading a line, and remove it when writing a line. Briefly, a text line is meant to be readable by a human being.

A *binary stream* is anything else; all characters are unprocessed—they are read or written as is, with no transformation. A '\0' character appearing in a binary stream has no significance for string termination or anything else. It is just data.

These two concepts must now be combined with the families of I/O library functions, matching the function purpose to file mode. There are five classes of I/O functions, the first of which (the file-management group of functions) does not apply to this discussion. The other four classes of functions are the *formatted*, *character*, *direct*, and *file-positioning* I/O groups of functions. Table 10.3 summarizes these function classes and which I/O modes can be used with them.

Table 10.3. *I/O function families and permitted I/O modes.*

Function Class	Modes Available
Formatted I/O	Text only
Character I/O	Text and binary, with caution
Direct I/O	Binary only
File positioning	All modes, use caution with text mode

The formatted I/O functions include the printf() and scanf() families of functions. They clearly are intended for text-mode use and should not be used for anything else.

The character I/O functions include the fgetc(), fputc(), fgets(), and fputs() families of functions. Of these, the string-oriented functions also are clearly text-mode-dependent. The single-character functions, however, can be used (under certain circumstances) with binary-mode operations. This was done deliberately in the keyio.c program, listing 10.4, for instance. Understand, however, that this is not the normal use of the function, and should be done with caution—and only when you must approach the extreme limits of what C can do (in that case, in fact, an assembler subroutine may be called for).

The direct I/O class of functions includes the `fread()` and `fwrite()` functions, which are used with binary-mode files. However, a file created in text mode can be opened in binary mode and read or written to in binary mode.

In fact, this is commonly done in order to load text files to memory at very high speeds. The catch is that now you must deal with the end-of-line characters, and any other characters transformed in some way by text-mode functions.

The file-positioning functions are examined in detail a little later in the chapter, but a special caveat is needed right now. Table 10.3 indicates that the file-positioning functions can be used with either text- or binary-mode file processing. This is perfectly true—but using the file-positioning functions in *text mode* can be tricky. If you fail to account for this, you may destroy the validity of a file.

Specifically, the transformation of characters during text-mode processing may "fool" the positioning functions—they may not know the current position as an exact byte count. Consider the DOS-based task of writing a string to a text-mode file, as shown in this short program:

```
1   #include <stdlib.h>
2   #include <stdio.h>
3
4   main()
5   {
6      FILE *text;
7      long numbytes;
8      char testline[20] = "test data\n";
9
10     text = fopen( "junk.txt", "w+" );
11     printf( "testline contains 11 bytes internally\n" );
12     fputs( testline, text );
13     numbytes = ftell( text );
14     printf( "current position is %d\n", numbytes );
15     fseek( text, numbytes, SEEK_SET );
16     fputs( testline, text );
17     fclose( text );
18  }
```

Count the bytes in the string in line 8 of this code sample. There are 9 characters, the `'\n'` newline escape sequence, and the (invisible) null string terminator `'\0'`, for a total of 11 bytes.

The physical characters placed on disk by the `fputs()` call in line 12 depend on the implementation. This usually means that special characters are transformed according to the requirements of the host system. On DOS systems, the newline character is transformed to the carriage return-line feed pair of characters, `"\x0D\x0A"`. This is confirmed when you run the hex dump utility `sdump.c` (Chapter 3) against the output file:

```
======== SDUMP Output for: junk.txt ========
74657374 20646174 610D0A ... "test.data..        "
                      ^
```

We have added the caret character to the third line of the dump output to show what the `ftell()` function thinks is the current position in the file (see line 13 of the sample code). Clearly, `ftell()` has not taken into account the fact that the newline character has been transformed to *two* characters.

You can prove this by using `fseek()` to set the current position to the location reported by `ftell()`, and writing the line again (lines 15–16). Another dump of the file at that point would show the following byte sequence:

```
======== SDUMP Output for: junk.txt ========
74657374 20646174 610D7465 73742064 6174610D
0A                 ^  ^
```

Now the first caret on the third line indicates the last surviving byte from the first line, and the second caret points to the first byte of the next line. Notice that the line-feed character `'\x0A'` has been overlayed in error.

This does not mean that DOS has lost track of the output location. Had the `fseek()` *not* been called, DOS would have continued to place output at the correct locations in the file. And you can use `fseek()` and `fsetpos()` with text files, but you must seek to a position that has been reported by `ftell()` or `fgetpos()` and that contains display text (in contrast to this example).

You can implement I/O tasks in many ways, some more and some less complex. To be generally safe, however, consider the character and formatted I/O functions as part of your text-processing tool kit, and the direct and file-positioning functions as belonging to binary-mode processing.

Direct-Access File Programming

Direct-access file programming is a greater challenge than the concepts and techniques presented earlier in this book. But the price of power and flexibility always seems to be increased complexity, and greater demands on the programmer's skills.

Fortunately, the demands on a programmer's skill need not be overwhelming. You can get respectable service and I/O performance with some fairly basic concepts and techniques. The next few sections introduce you to I/O programming techniques whose sophistication lies in their simplicity and adaptability.

We have chosen to concentrate on direct-access methods in the following sections for two reasons:

❏ *First, direct-access method (DAM) files require either no support files or only simple ones, and are well suited to applications running on PC-sized machines simply because the data sizes are smaller.*

❏ *Second, the reduced overhead of DAM files permits speed and performance that frequently rival more complex indexed sequential and B-tree methods, and in some situations can out-perform them.* Naturally, this is true only if you go about it correctly.

Direct-Access Concepts

Direct-access files are a subset of the larger class of random-access files. The purpose of any *random-access file* is to provide the means of reading or writing *any* record immediately, without having to read or write from the beginning of the file to get to the desired record. To accomplish this, the access routines must either record each record's disk address, or be able to compute it on demand.

Indexed files use the former method, and require a physically distinct file for recording the index. The index must be consulted for every read or write. Direct file-access routines compute each record's address (or close to it, as you will see) for each access. In either case, a given record must contain some item or value unique to that record. This is called the record *key*.

Direct file access requires not only that you supply some method of converting the record key value into a disk address, but also that the method produce addresses which distribute the records evenly over the space allocated to the file. If an inefficient algorithm is chosen, the records may cluster together in groups. This can cause exaggerated search times, and may make the file appear full when it is not.

The most widely used method of computing addresses from keys is called *hashing*. Hashing can be used to address disk files or memory-resident tables, but this discussion focuses only on disk usage. The hashing function not only must produce a good spread of values as nearly random as possible, but it also must be *quick*. Algorithms that go beyond simple arithmetic are unacceptable.

First of all, some provision must be made for alphanumeric keys, such as a name string. Is there any convenient method for converting a string to a fairly unique number? In Chapter 3, you saw a sample program (crc16.c, in listing 3.4) that returns a value. The function embedded in this program returns a 16-bit checking code developed from a string of characters. The algorithm is designed (for error-checking purposes) to produce a code as nonrepetitive as possible. Such a function is made to order for this application. The following discussion assumes that such a method has been applied to alpha keys, and that a resulting numeric value is available.

After the key has been reduced to a numeric value, it must be hashed—its disk (or table) address must be calculated. One very popular method (it works well in most cases) is the *modulus (remainder) method*. This method divides the numeric key value by another number and preserves the remainder as the *hashkey*. How to select the number for the divisor is explained in the following paragraphs.

Suppose that you want to add a record directly to a file that has space for *N* records, where *N* must be a *prime number* for the algorithm to work well. To compute the record's address, divide the key value by *N* and take the remainder, as follows:

```
address = key % N
```

Now you can fseek() to this position (which is discussed after the next section), and write the record. Or can you? The problem with this and all other similar methods is that they are not *truly* random so that *different* keys may hash to the *same* address—the keys may *collide*.

To recover from collision, you must be able to detect a record location—a *slot*—where you *can* write the record. The most common method is to have preinitialized the file so that unused slots have a null (zero) key field. Then you can read records sequentially from the computed address until an empty slot is found, and then write the record. To retrieve the record, the same logic is followed.

Collision recovery introduces a new wrinkle. Searching forward from the computed address for the desired record or empty slot is called *open addressing*. It implies that you may well have to search to end-of-file before you can determine when the search is a hit or a miss (the desired record was found or not found). Search times can become drastically longer as the file is more fully populated.

One solution is to divide (conceptually) the available record slots into groups of slots called *buckets*. The key is hashed to the disk address of the corresponding bucket, and searching is confined to the slots in that bucket only. In order to approach a random (uniform) distribution of records, the divisor still needs to be prime. And you must provide a total number of slots somewhat greater than the number of records to be stored—some clustering of records occurs despite everything you do. Figure 10.1 illustrates these ideas.

Fig. 10.1. *The remainder dividing a numeric key by a prime number divisor is the bucket number. The bucket number times the number of bytes in a whole bucket equals the bucket's disk address.*

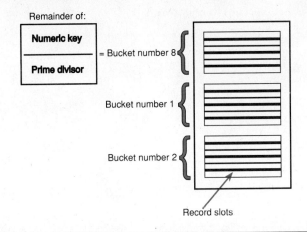

Suppose, for example, that you want to store 100 records in about 10 buckets of 10 slots each. Because 11 is the next prime number higher than 10, assume that there are 11 buckets and 110 total slots. This provides about 10 percent free space to alleviate clustering problems. The bucket number is computed as follows:

```
bucket = keyvalue % 11
```

and this value, in turn, can be used to compute the correct disk address of the first record in the bucket. Of course, having a function that computes the required prime number would be nice. Listing 10.5 shows a new version of prime.c, which was presented in a different form earlier in the book. You pass it a long int parameter that indicates the minimum number of buckets, and it computes the next higher or equal prime number.

Listing 10.5. `prime.c` *(Calculating the next higher prime number for "bucket" divisor).*   *Microsoft C 6.0*

```
1   #include <stdlib.h>
2   #include <stdio.h>
3
4   long next_prime( long );
5
6   /* +------------------------------------------------------+
7      +  Calculate the next prime after the seed number.
8      +------------------------------------------------------+
9   */
10  long next_prime( long seed )
11  {
12     long n;
13     int j, k;
14     ldiv_t ans;
15     long *primes;
16
17     if ( NULL == ( primes = calloc( 350, sizeof(long) ) ) )
18        return 3L;
19     primes[0] = 2;
20     n = 3;
21     for ( j=1; j<350 && seed>primes[j-1]; j++ ) {
22        primes[j] = n;                /* Store the prime */
23  nextprime: n += 2;
24        k = 1;
25  checkprime: ans = ldiv( n, primes[k] );
26        if ( ans.rem == 0 ) goto nextprime;
27        if ( ans.quot <= primes[k] ) continue;
28        k++;
29        goto checkprime;
30     }
31     free( primes );
32     return( primes[j-1] );
33  }
```

The first few lines of the `prime.c` program can be used to create the header file for it, as follows:

```
#include <stdlib.h>
#include <stdio.h>

long next_prime( long );     /* <prime.h> */
```

The material so far provides the conceptual framework you need for computing direct disk addresses. Now you need the technology to control the file's current position.

Using *ftell( )* and *fgetpos( )*

The ftell() and fgetpos() functions report the current position in the file. Although these functions are quite similar in operation, the wording of the ANSI standard implies the possibility that a given compiler could implement them differently. The function prototype for ftell() is

```
#include <stdlio.h>
long int ftell( FILE *stream );
```

Call ftell() after opening the file; there is no "current position" for a closed file. ftell() returns a long int that reports the current position in the file as an *offset from the beginning of the file, in bytes*. That is, the offset of the first byte is 0, of the second byte, 1, and so on. If 10 bytes have been read, the current position is 10 (bytes 0 through 9 were read). File position is always reported as a byte offset, no matter what size record you may be reading or writing. As you already have seen, ftell() does not necessarily provide a meaningful measure of bytes written for a *text file*. But it reports exact byte offsets for binary files. The following code fragment shows how to use ftell():

```
#include <stdio.h>
...
long position;
FILE *input;
unsigned char *data;
unsigned request_size = 32768U;
... /* No error checking in this sample, for brevity */
data = malloc( request_size );       /* get a buffer */
input = fopen( "junk.dat", "rb" );    /* open binary */
                /* read all the records in the file */
while( fread( data, request_size, 1, input ) );
position = ftell( input );        /* current position */
printf( "junk.dat contains %ld bytes\n", position );
fclose( input );
```

fgetpos() differs in that the position reported is not necessarily just a long int. The function modifies a derived object that has a (derived) type of fpos_t and is declared in stdio.h. The object with type fpos_t contains "unspecified information," as allowed by the standard, and can be implemented in any way the implementation sees fit. The prototype for fgetpos() is

```
#include <stdio.h>
int fgetpos( FILE *stream, fpos_t *pos );
```

The arguments for `fgetpos()` are a pointer to the stream, and a pointer to the object with type `fpos_t`. The value returned is a success or failure flag—zero when successful, and nonzero when the call fails. (Upon failure also, an error code is stored in `errno`.) Because the `fpos_t`-type object contains unspecified information, we cannot duplicate the preceding code fragment; there is no way to know what to report in the `printf()` call. We can, however, show the function call in context, as follows:

```
#include <stdio.h>
...
fpos_t position;
FILE *input;
unsigned char *data;
unsigned request_size = 32768U;
... /* No error checking in this sample, for brevity */
data = malloc( request_size );        /* get a buffer */
input = fopen( "junk.dat", "rb" );    /* open binary */
                    /* read all the records in the file */
while( fread( data, request_size, 1, input ) );
if ( fgetpos( input, &position ) ) {
  printf( "Position report failed.\n" );
}
fclose( input );
```

Notice in this code fragment that the address-of operator & was used to get the address of the object `position`.

Using *fseek( )* and *fsetpos ( )*

`fseek()` and `fsetpos()` are the companion functions, respectively, to `ftell()` and `fgetpos()`. Both `fseek()` and `fsetpos()`, with their different calling sequences, set a new current position in the file (if successful).

The function prototype for the `fseek()` function is

```
#include <stdio.h>
int fseek( FILE *stream, long int offset, int whence );
```

The first parameter, `FILE *stream`, is the same stream pointer you already have seen. The second is the offset value discussed earlier—you never need *absolute* disk addresses in C because all the functions work with offset values. The third parameter is something new. The `int` type variable `whence` contains a value that identifies the relative starting point in the file *from which* the offset will be measured in the file. The three possible values all have macros defined for them in `stdio.h`. These macros are `SEEK_SET`, `SEEK_CUR`, and `SEEK_END`.

❏ SEEK_SET *indicates that the seek (positioning) operation is to be performed relative to the beginning of the file.* For example, the following lines of code:

```
rewind( stream );
fseek( stream, 0, SEEK_SET );
```

are equivalent. Both place the current position at the beginning of the file.

❏ SEEK_CUR *indicates that the seek operation is to be performed relative to the current file position.* For example, if ftell() reports that the current position is 100, then the following function call:

```
fseek( stream, 100, SEEK_CUR );
```

causes the current position to be changed to 200. This is one that you probably will not use much until you begin to write extremely sophisticated file-access functions. Then it becomes very useful.

❏ SEEK_END *indicates that the seek operation is to be performed relative to the end of the file.* Suppose, for example, that 100 bytes are already in a file. The following call:

```
fseek( stream, 0, SEEK_END );
```

sets the current position to end-of-file, plus an offset of zero— or just end-of-file. This is how you could avoid the problems (mentioned earlier in the chapter) associated with opening a file with append mode.

Some implementations (DOS, for example) support a call with SEEK_END and an offset greater than zero; others do not. The ANSI standard states that an implementation is not required to do so. Figure 10.2 depicts the positions of the three seek origins.

Direct Access with Hashed Keys

Now let's bring it all together. damfile.c, listing 10.6, contains samples of all the techniques presented. It provides the capability for creating/ initializing a DAM file, and for adding, deleting, and randomly retrieving records.

Fig. 10.2. `fseek()` *sets the new current position relative to* `SEEK_SET`, `SEEK_CUR`, *and* `SEEK_END`.

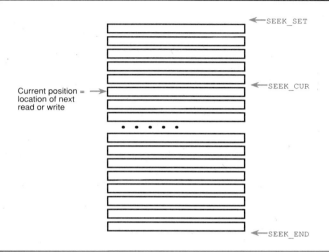

For purposes of illustration, we simply used a random-number generator to create 25 key values, corresponding to 25 records. Because the record key values are already numeric, the code is somewhat simplified.

The records in this example have only the key field (presumed to be the first thing in the record area), and a couple of bytes of padding. The file itself is designed to have exactly 25 record slots, one for each input record, arranged in five buckets. This arrangment has consequences that become apparent shortly.

Listing 10.6. `damfile.c` *(Direct file-access create, read, add, and delete functions).*   *Microsoft C 6.0*

```
1    #include <stdlib.h>
2    #include <stdio.h>
3
4    #include "prime.h"
5
6    FILE *d_create( char *dname, int numrecs, int reclength );
7    int d_addrec( FILE *dfile, int hashkey, int recs_bucket,
8                  void *rec, int lng );
9    int d_delrec( FILE *dfile, int hashkey, int recs_bucket,
10                 void *rec, int lng );
11   int d_getrec( FILE *dfile, int hashkey, int recs_bucket,
12                 void *rec, int lng );
```

```
13
14   struct rtype {    /* Test record format */
15     int keyfield;
16     char data[8];
17   };
18
19   struct rtype record;
20   int num_bucket;
21   int recs_bucket = 5;
22   int total_recs;
23   int reclength = 10;
24   int testkeys[] = {
25      159,   12194, 26852, 8043,  30046,
26      26014, 25222, 22280, 31555, 32510,
27      381,   29730, 1081,  22671, 22447,
28      2070,  18170, 19890, 5197,  356,
29      17366, 14862, 20148, 23302,  712,
30   };
31
32   main()
33   {
34     FILE *damfile;
35     int i;
36
37                              /* Create the direct access file */
38                        /* Write binary zeros in every slot */
39     num_bucket = (int)next_prime( 5L );        /* 5 buckets */
40     total_recs = recs_bucket * num_bucket;
41     if ( NULL ==
42        ( damfile = d_create( "test.dam", total_recs, 10 ) ) ) {
43        printf( "Could not create the direct file.\n" );
44        exit( 8 );
45     }
46
47     for ( i=0; i<25; i++ ) {         /* Load all the records */
48        record.keyfield = testkeys[i]; /* Build dummy record */
49        memset( record.data, ' ', 8 );
50        if ( EOF == d_addrec( damfile, testkeys[i] % num_bucket,
51                          recs_bucket, &record, 10 ) ) {
52           printf( "Could not add record key %d\n", testkeys[i] );
53        }
54     }
55
56     record.keyfield = 22280; /* Delete a couple of records */
57     if ( EOF != d_delrec( damfile, 22280 % num_bucket, recs_bucket,
58                 &record, 10 ) )
59        printf( "Deleted record key %d\n", record.keyfield );
60     else
61        printf( "Could not delete %d\n", record.keyfield );
62
```

Listing 10.6. continues

Listing 10.6. continued

```
63     record.keyfield = 381;
64     if ( EOF != d_delrec( damfile, 381 % num_bucket, recs_bucket,
65               &record, 10 ) )
66       printf( "Deleted record key %d\n", record.keyfield );
67     else
68       printf( "Could not delete %d\n", record.keyfield );
69
70     record.keyfield = 26852;   /* Direct read some records */
71     if ( EOF != d_getrec( damfile, 26852 % num_bucket, recs_bucket,
72               &record, 10 ) )
73       printf( "Read record key %d\n", record.keyfield );
74     else
75       printf( "Could not locate %d\n", record.keyfield );
76
77     record.keyfield = 22671;
78     if ( EOF != d_getrec( damfile, 22671 % num_bucket, recs_bucket,
79               &record, 10 ) )
80       printf( "Read record key %d\n", record.keyfield );
81     else
82       printf( "Could not locate %d\n", record.keyfield );
83
84     close( damfile );
85   }
86
87   FILE *d_create( char *dname, int numrecs, int reclength )
88   {
89     FILE *dfile;
90     int i;
91     unsigned char *recd; /* Dummy record */
92
93     if ( NULL == ( dfile = fopen( dname, "w+b" ) ) ) return NULL;
94     if ( NULL == ( recd = malloc( reclength ) ) ) return NULL;
95     memset( recd, '\0', reclength );  /* Init dummy record */
96     for ( i=0; i<numrecs; i++ )
97       fwrite( recd, reclength, 1, dfile );
98     rewind( dfile );
99     return( dfile );
100  }
101
102  int d_addrec( FILE *dfile, int hashkey, int recs_bucket,
103               void *rec, int lng )
104  {
105    int i;
106    long address;
107    static unsigned char hold[10];  /* For performance */
108
109    /* Compute bucket adrs */
110    address = (long)( hashkey * recs_bucket * lng );
```

```
111    if ( fseek( dfile, address, SEEK_SET ) ) return -1;
112    for ( i=0; i<recs_bucket; i++ ) {
113      address = ftell( dfile );        /* Note where you are */
114      fread( hold, lng, 1, dfile );
115      if ( *(int *)hold && *(int *)hold != 0xFFFF ) continue;
116      fseek( dfile, address, SEEK_SET ); /* Also flushes */
117      fwrite( rec, lng, 1, dfile );
118      return 0;
119    }
120    return -1;
121  }
122
123  int d_delrec( FILE *dfile, int hashkey, int recs_bucket,
124                void * rec, int lng )
125  {
126    int i;
127    unsigned delkey = 0xFFFF;
128    long address;
129    static unsigned char hold[10];
130
131    /* Compute bucket adrs */
132    address = (long)( hashkey * recs_bucket * lng );
133    if ( fseek( dfile, address, SEEK_SET ) ) return -1;
134    for ( i=0; i<recs_bucket; i++ ) {
135      address = ftell( dfile );        /* Note where you are */
136      fread( hold, lng, 1, dfile );
137      if (*(int *)hold != *(int *)rec) continue; /*No match*/
138      fseek( dfile, address, SEEK_SET ); /* Also flushes */
139      fwrite( &delkey, sizeof(int), 1, dfile );
140      return 0;
141    }
142    return -1;
143  }
144
145  int d_getrec( FILE *dfile, int hashkey, int recs_bucket,
146                void *rec, int lng )
147  {
148    int i;
149    long address;
150    static unsigned char hold[10];
151
152    /* Compute bucket adrs */
153    address = (long)( hashkey * recs_bucket * lng );
154    if ( fseek( dfile, address, SEEK_SET ) ) return -1;
155    for ( i=0; i<recs_bucket; i++ ) {
156      address = ftell( dfile );        /* Note where you are */
157      fread( hold, lng, 1, dfile );
158      if ( *(int *)hold != *(int *)rec ) continue;
159      memmove( rec, hold, lng );
```

Listing 10.6. continues

Listing 10.6. *continued*

```
160        return 0;
161     }
162     return -1;
163 }
164
```

As you can see from lines 14–19 of listing 10.6, we have anticipated structured objects a bit in order to provide a convenient record-holding area. The `main()` function, lines 32–85, serves only to drive the functions to be demonstrated.

Lines 87–100 contain the `d_create()` function, which creates and initializes the DAM file. It writes the 25 empty records, and returns a pointer to the stream opened.

Alert readers will have noticed that the `FILE *` object is declared as a local (`auto`) variable in `d_create()`. Don't `auto` variables go away when the function returns to its caller? Yes, they do. We can get away with it *in this case*, however, because the stream control information is actually external to the function and has static duration. Only the *pointer* object is lost, but not before a copy of it has been returned.

The purpose of the `d_addrec()` function (lines 102–121) is to add randomly received records to the file. Notice how the *offset address* of the first record in the required bucket is developed in line 110:

```
110     address = (long)( hashkey * recs_bucket * lng );
```

The hashkey is nothing more than the bucket number (starting with bucket 0) computed from taking the remainder, as discussed earlier. The hashkey is multiplied by the number of records in the bucket and the length of each record to get the *byte* offset of the beginning of the bucket.

After seeking to the right address, the function loops a number of times no greater than the number of records in the bucket (lines 112–119). Because the file was initialized with null records, the first slot whose key is all zero can receive the new record. Notice that the routine also permits a slot whose first bytes are `'\xFFFF'` to receive a new record. This is explained shortly.

The `d_delrec()` and `d_getrec()` functions follow a similar line of logic. Both of these functions expect you to place the desired key value in a dummy record that is passed to the function and used to compare key values.

Selection criteria differs a little between the two functions, however. Line 137 in d_delrec() has the if statement with the test criteria; the record keys must match exactly before the record can be deleted. Line 158 shows that this is true also for record retrieval.

Records are deleted in a special way. They are not simply reset to zero. Rather, the key value is set to all 'OxFF' values (two bytes in this case). There are two reasons for doing this. First, it allows other functions to examine the file and determine how many records have been deleted; a valuable statistic for full-blown database systems. Second, deleting records this way is necessary for a modification we suggest (shortly) for these two functions.

Now let's see how the program works. When it is run, the following output is produced on the console:

```
Could not add record key 18170
Could not add record key 19890
Could not add record key 17366
Could not add record key 23302
Could not add record key 1712
Deleted record key 22280
Deleted record key 381
Read record key 26852
Read record key 22671
```

There are 25 records, and a total of 25 slots are available. Why were there 5 records that could not be added? Because of the phenomenon of clustering, mentioned earlier. The 5 victimized records all hashed to buckets that already were full. Hex-dumping the file shows that slots are still available—they just are not in the correct bucket. Here is the file dump:

```
======== SDUMP Output for: test.dam ========
·FFFF2020 20202020 2020437B 20202020 20202020
FE7E2020 20202020 20202274 20202020 20202020
16082020 20202020 20205E75 20202020 20202020
FFFF2020 20202020 20203904 20202020 20202020
8F582020 20202020 20206401 20202020 20202020
E4682020 20202020 20208662 20202020 20202020
AF572020 20202020 20204D14 20202020 20202020
0E3A2020 20202020 20206B1F 20202020 20202020
B44E2020 20202020 20200000 00000000 00000000
00000000 00000000 00000000 00000000 00000000
9F002020 20202020 2020A22F 20202020 20202020
9E652020 20202020 20200000 00000000 00000000
00000000 00000000 0000
```

Having slots available in buckets that aren't hashed to for a given key highlights the fact that, for efficient implementation of a DAM file, *the number of buckets must be much greater than the number of records per bucket*. As much greater, in fact, as the space available combined with the number of records to store will allow. For these methods to work well, direct files must contain some free space. After modifying this program so that there were 30 buckets with 5 records per slot and then rerunning the program, all the records could be added with no problem. Furthermore, another file dump showed that the distribution of the records was more even, reducing the amount of clustering. Thus, the new file could be loaded much nearer full capacity before encountering problems.

A few paragraphs ago, we mentioned a modification for the delete and retrieve functions. This modification increases the performance (speed) of the functions by reducing the number of unsuccessful comparisons—*probes*—when searching for a key in the bucket.

To make the modification, insert the following line of code after lines 137 and 158 of listing 10.6:

```
if ( ! *(int *)hold ) break;
```

The effect of this statement causes the loop probing successive slots to terminate when a null slot is encountered. Now you can see why it was undesirable to simply reset a deleted slot back to nulls—the slot might be in the middle of a group of valid records.

With this modification, all the null slots are toward the bottom of the bucket. Thus you can terminate a scan when a null slot is encountered during either delete or get processing; you know that there are no more valid records after that point.

This modification greatly improves the performance of the access functions in many cases, especially if the file is only sparsely populated. Always checking all the slots in a bucket is no longer necessary.

Finally, you have to cope in some way with *overflow records*—records that cannot be added to the file. This always is true, no matter how efficiently you design the direct-access structures. (It is true also of indexed files.) Several options are open to you. Of these, two are particularly interesting because they are easy to implement and effective. Both of them involve providing another file, used strictly to hold overflow.

First, you might simply use a *flat* (sequential) file to hold the overflow records. To add an overflow record, just append it to the end of the overflow file. Append mode might seem suitable in this case, but it is not. You may well have to update records in the middle of the overflow file and, as you may recall, append mode forces *all* writes to go to end-of-file. The advantage of this method is its simplicity; the disadvantage is that the process of locating a record that resides in overflow may be very slow. Such a search necessarily requires that the file be read from the beginning whenever a record located here is requested.

The second solution is to provide another direct file. The overflow file could conceivably have fewer slots with more records per slot, but the best bet would be to use the same slot-bucket arrangement, with only the overall file size being smaller (fewer buckets, but more than in the first case).

Either way, eventually a time will come when the only remaining alternative is to move the data to a file with more space, provided that the file continues to grow. If you initially design the file sizes correctly, this should happen infrequently.

When should direct files be used? The following recommendations are derived from Sedgewick's *Algorithms*:

❏ *When you want very fast access with relatively constant search times*. The trade-off is that if the file must support an extremely unpredictable number of insertions (additions), designing the size efficiently may be impossible, thus costing performance.

❏ *When code space is at a premium*. That is, when the amount of code must be small, and the program as compact as possible. The code needed to support index or B-tree structures is not all that expensive, but is more than that required for direct-access methods.

❏ *When ordered, sequential access is not necessary*. If you think about it for a moment, you will realize that the continual addition and deletion of records to and from the file may leave the records in a particular bucket in no particular order at all. All that can be guaranteed is that any null slots are toward the bottom of the bucket. Of course, you could use a file-sort utility, after extracting only used slots. You must still account for the records in overflow, however, and that may be a different matter. This would also require a good deal of disk space. If ordered access is required, you have to resort to an indexed structure, or perhaps a linked-list approach.

Writing High-Performance File Routines

Everyone naturally wants the programs he or she writes (or uses!) to be as fast as possible. Speed is all the user sees, but the programmer is faced with additional considerations.

What is *performance*? It is *the best speed possible while still providing all the function required*. Invariably, you (the programmer) have to make space-time trade-off decisions. This issue is especially acute with I/O programming.

Choosing the File Mode

The file mode you choose for processing a file depends more on the functionality required than the speed of execution you want to achieve. In *most* cases, you will want to process text files with text mode because it performs character conversions and detects line-ends. In *all* cases, binary files that contain data in internal formats must be processed in binary mode.

On the flip side, binary mode can achieve execution speeds greater (sometimes much greater) than text-mode access, because no character conversion or variable-line detection is necessary. If you are willing to write the code required, you can process text files in binary mode and get really impressive speeds. This would be important, for example, in a word- or text-processing system that handles large documents.

In general, however, the file mode is dictated by the file type. Tuning efforts must be restricted to selecting proper buffer sizes and writing the surrounding code as efficiently as possible.

Minimizing I/O Overhead

In several places in this book, we have pointed out the potential sources of overhead—indeed, of bottlenecks—in I/O programming, particularly disk I/O. One of these, especially, bears repeating yet again. *The physical set-up time required by the disk is several orders of magnitude slower than all other phases of I/O.*

In order to read or write data on a disk, the disk must rotate into position to bring the required sector under the read/write head (rotational delay or *latency*), the read/write head must be moved physically across the surface to the correct track (seek time), and, for disks with multiple recording surfaces, the proper head must be activated. (Head switching is mostly electronic, however, and usually ignored in performance studies.)

On many of the disk drives available today, the time required for these operations has been reduced to a handful of milliseconds. But this still is a couple of orders of magnitude slower than the CPU. Essentially, the only way to tune I/O is to *eliminate as many I/O events as possible* while still providing the necessary I/O flow. Beyond that, you can "spread out" the overhead so that it is less noticeable. The following sections deal with ways to do this.

Using *setbuf( )* and *setvbuf( )*

Standard C provides just two library functions with which you can tune I/O performance: setvbuf() and setbuf(). This may not seem like much, but generally is all you need to get really good results.

setvbuf() is used to control buffering for a stream—both the kind of buffering (full, line, or none), and the buffer size. It should be called *after* opening the file, and *before* any reading or writing. The prototype for setvbuf() is

```
#include <stdio.h>
int setvbuf(FILE *stream,char *buf,int mode,size_t size);
```

The pointer to stream, of course, identifies the stream for which buffering is to be modified. The pointer to char has two uses. If it is NULL, it indicates that setvbuf() is to allocate a buffer on behalf of the caller; otherwise, it indicates a buffer you have allocated to be used.

The mode parameter indicates what kind of buffering is to be used: full buffering, line buffering, or no buffering. The stdio.h header declares the following three macros for this purpose:

❏ _IOFBF, *which indicates that full buffering should be used during this open of the file, ordinarily is used with block devices and direct files.*

❏ _IOLBF *means that line buffering is to be used.* This buffering mode is used with text streams and nonblock devices. stdin usually is line-buffered, for example.

❏ _IONBF *indicates that the stream is associated with a character device that cannot tolerate buffering.* Note that some current compilers do not actually turn off buffering for console devices when this parameter is used, because the operating system may be buffering behind the scenes. Sometimes you can use `setbuf()` to get around this, but it doesn't always work. These failures are points of nonconformity to the ANSI standard in such compilers. Only experimentation will tell what does and what does not do the job.

If taking full control of a character device is absolutely necessary, you can resort to programming the I/O ports directly, although that will take a bit of research. In Chapter 2, for example, we pointed to the program in Appendix D (a communications program) as an example of programming I/O ports. Keep in mind, however, that this approach is *highly* nonstandard, and almost certainly is not portable to other compilers and systems.

The `size` parameter of `setvbuf()` has a derived (integral) type of `size_t`, which is also declared as a macro in `stdio.h`. It states the size of the buffer that `setvbuf()` is to allocate, or that you have allocated already. The choice of this parameter, particularly, is critical to adequate I/O performance.

`setvbuf()` returns an integer to the caller. This integer is zero if the operation was successful, nonzero if not. You can test for successful completion with an `if`, as follows:

```
if ( setvbuf( stream, NULL, _IOFBF, 16384 ) ) {
   printf( "Could not acquire a buffer for the stream.\n" );
   fclose( stream );
   abort();
}
```

In this fragment, the `if` is satisfied only if `setvbuf()` *fails*. Notice that, for extra safety, the stream is closed—even though, presumably, there has not yet been a read or write.

`setbuf()` is used also to control buffering for a stream, but in a slightly different (less flexible) fashion. The prototype for `setbuf()` is

```
#include <stdio.h>
void setbuf( FILE *stream, char *buf );
```

`setbuf()` returns no value, does not support a buffer type parameter, and assumes the default buffer size (BUFSIZE macro declared in `stdio.h`, frequently 512 bytes).

If `setbuf()` is invoked with `buf == NULL`, it is equivalent to `setvbuf( stream, NULL, _IONBF, 0 )`. If `buf != NULL`, the function call is equivalent to `setvbuf( stream, mybuf, _IOFBF, BUFSIZE )`, where `mybuf` is a pointer to a buffer you have allocated.

Reducing I/O Events

The whole point of manipulating the buffers associated with a stream, of course, is to reduce the number of physical I/O events. This section includes some tips on how buffers can help do this.

❑ *In general, a larger buffer is better than a smaller one, but don't get carried away.* A trade-off is involved here. While it is certainly true that larger buffers give your program better performance, there is a point of diminishing returns. Several things can prevent increases in buffer size from increasing performance. Over time, for example, disks tend to become fragmented (that is, the sectors belonging to a particular file may be scattered all over the disk). In this case, even if you specify a buffer larger than the entire file, multiple I/O's are required to get all the sectors. It makes no difference that you do not "see" these events, they are there (performed by the operating system) anyway.

Furthermore, allocating more memory to buffer space by definition reduces the amount of memory available to your program for data, work areas, and so forth. There is a point of diminishing returns here, also.

❑ *For fixed-length records, use* setvbuf() *to set the buffer size to a multiple of the record size.* Suppose that you are reading 1024-byte records from a disk file, and suppose further that you have allowed the default buffer size (controlled by the macro BUFSIZ, and usually 512 bytes) to remain in place. How many physical reads do you suppose are now required to get that one record? You are correct if you answered "Two." In such a case, you should have set the buffer size—your friend setvbuf() again—to some multiple of 1024.

❑ *For text files and other kinds of variable-length records, use as large a buffer as is practical in your environment.* This decreases the number of instances in which only part of a line or record is in the buffer, which would require more I/O to read or write the rest. Secondly, text-mode processing is already expensive, because of the examination and possible transformation of each byte read or written. Thus, reducing I/O overhead is even more important for text files than for binary files.

❑ *For direct files, in which record slots are arranged in buckets, consider making the buffer size equal to or—even better—a multiple of the bucket size in bytes.* In this way, the entire bucket is read into the buffer. When you then read the records in the bucket sequentially, probing for a match, `fread()` will more often find the record available in the buffer instead of starting a new I/O operation.

❑ *If your operating system has some disk caching software with it, use it.* A caching routine can read many tracks at a time into the cache. Because a cache is nothing more than a high-performance buffer, the savings associated with buffering can be increased in proportion to the amount of storage you can spare for the cache. Even a small cache can help, however, if it is large enough to hold a few tracks of data. You can get as much as 30 to 40 percent increases in disk I/O speed with caching software, because it helps to eliminate more rotational delays and seek times.

Releasing the Buffers at Close

The performance of your program as a whole must be considered also. The performance of any one part of the program depends on the amount of resources (both CPU time and memory) consumed by the other parts of the program. If you spend too much RAM in file buffers, other parts of the program may suffer.

You should use the buffers you need, then. But when you have finished with them, free them. If you allocate the buffer yourself with `calloc()` or `malloc()`, don't forget to call `free()` to release that memory. If you allow `setvbuf()` to allocate the buffer, don't forget to close the file when you have finished with it—`setvbuf()` has no other way to know that the buffers no longer are necessary.

Loading Directly to RAM

It may be possible to load smaller files directly to RAM and keep them there while processing them. Examples of files suited to this include small note or text files and sometimes even large text files.

This procedure has the advantage of completely eliminating I/O while processing the file. The disadvantage is that, somewhere in the program, you must provide the logic to get to the records in memory. Whether you decide to do this depends on how much memory your machine has, and just how fast you require the program to be. A useful trade-off is to load large chunks of the file at one time (but this is little different from beefing up the buffer sizes).

Common Extensions to the ANSI Standard

Some aspects of I/O programming are impossible to include in any language standard, because they depend entirely on the platform on which the compiler is implemented (that is, the hardware and host system).

For example, no standard whatsoever yet exists for screen I/O programming, because it differs greatly from one machine to the next. Still, there may be some progress in that direction eventually. The UNIX-based `curses` package is beginning to appear on some DOS-based platforms and may someday provide a certain basis for a standard interface. And a few graphical user interfaces (GUIs) for workstation-type machines (which include the PC and UNIX machines) are being implemented on different hardware types.

Low-Level I/O Practices

At one time, the stream I/O library of various C compilers could only be characterized as poor. Because older library functions just didn't perform well, many compiler vendors included (nonstandard) low-level functions that corresponded to the basic operating system I/O calls.

Recently, however, this is not true. The stream I/O libraries of all the leading C compiler vendors are quite capable of providing acceptable (and sometimes outstanding) performance. The message here is that if you want to write portable code, don't use nonstandard functions unless it is *absolutely necessary*.

Files in a Networking Environment

Finally, something must be said about I/O practices in a networking environment. PC communications and LANs are proliferating. You may find yourself writing programs in that environment, in which files are shared by many users.

DOS versions 3.x and 4.x provide for shared file access (this includes multitasking environments, as well as networks) mainly through DOS interrupt 0x21, function 0x3D, the open-file (handle) function. Many DOS-based C compilers support this function through variations on `fopen()`, such as `sopen()`. Some networking and file-management packages hook into this interrupt, supporting the basic DOS functionality as well as their own extensions. If you want to delve more deeply into this subject, you can read *Network Programming in C* by Barry Nance (Que Corporation).

UNIX-V systems also support file sharing, through the `fcntl()` system calls as well as through the `/usr/group` standards-compatible `lockf()` calls. Record-level locking is built into the libraries, whereas it may or may not be present on DOS systems, depending on the third-party software being used.

File I/O programming necessitates some research for each system on which you implement your programs. In any event—for our purposes, shared file access, however common it may become, must be viewed in the same light as low-level I/O practices. Both are distinctly nonstandard, and nonportable.

Summary

The following five areas of importance to file I/O programming have been covered in this chapter:

❏   *File-management functions.* ANSI C provides some basic but useful file-management functions, including the means to delete, rename, and "restart" files. By adding the functions to your program, you can add a nice, finished touch to the final product.

❏   *Buffer-management functions.* Buffer management is the most important consideration in file I/O programming. Controlling the kind of buffering and the size of the buffers to be used is an important skill.

❏   *Direct file I/O programming.* This is but one example of how you can use the stream direct I/O functions to implement sophisticated database structures and methods.

❏   *High-performance file-programming considerations.* The combination of intelligent design and clever buffer control are the keys to high-performance I/O routines.

❏   *Areas where the standards don't reach.* Two important environments—multiuser systems and networked systems—are becoming increasingly prevalent. The ANSI standard says nothing about these areas, but they are topics to which you should pay attention. They become increasingly important.

CHAPTER 11

Deriving New Complex Data Types

I n the last few chapters you have seen increasingly frequent references to a "derived type declared in this or that header file." In each instances, we actually were referring to complex objects known as *structures*.

Structures are in fact only one of five kinds of object considered to have *derived types*, constructed from the basic types with which you already are familiar. ANSI recognizes the following derived types:

- ❑ *Array type*. A contiguously allocated set of objects, all of which have the same basic type, the element type. An array is said to be derived from its element type, so that an array of integers is said to have type "array of int." The construction of an array from its element type is called *array type derivation*.

- ❑ *Function type*. All functions return an object with a specified type. The function is said to have type "function returning *type*." Even a void function has type "function returning void." The construction of a function type from the returned type is called *function type derivation*.

- ❑ *Pointer type*. Pointers reference some other object that has a type. A pointer has type "pointer to *type*." The construction of a pointer type from the referenced type is called *pointer type derivation*.

The three preceding derived types are already familiar to you. You have been using them for several chapters now. The next two have been hinted at, but are new. They (and a couple of other things) are the subject of this chapter.

❑   *Structure type*. Structures contain a set of contiguously allocated *member objects*, which may have diverse basic types, and may also include other structures.

❑   *Union type*. A union is best described as "overlapping structures." One way to think of unions is that they contain *different views of the same structure*. Each "view" has a name and is a structure definition. You could write a union declaration, for example, that describes an integer as an integer under one name, and a collection of unsigned characters under another (many compilers describe the system registers this way).

In programs with any vitality, getting away from structures is difficult. In Chapter 10, for example, we used a structure to define the record layout for a direct file. This is only one example of an almost infinite set of uses.

Defining Structures of Items

Before you can define unions, you must be able to define a structure. Structures give you a way to regard a diverse collection of objects as a single entity.

Basic Structure Declarations

Structured objects can be declared in several ways. Each method is discussed in this chapter, beginning with the simplest. The most sophisticated—structures with tags used as part of a user type definition—are discussed later in this chapter, in the section "Deriving Types with typedef."

Defining Structured Data Objects

The first way to declare a structure is the simplest, and the least useful. The syntax is best seen in an example. Suppose that you want to use a structure to define a record in a property list file. You would write something like this:

```
struct {
  int serialno;
  char brand[21];
  char model[21];
  char description[41];
  char location[21];
} prop_rec;
```

The `struct { ... }` declaration defines the type for the object `prop_rec`. `prop_rec` has type `struct`. In general, begin the declaration with the `struct` keyword, followed by the *structure declaration list* (the list of objects contained within the structure). Notice that each declaration within the structure declaration list—each *member*—is coded and terminated with a semicolon, just as if the object were being declared outside the structure. Notice also that the object identifier, `prop_rec`, is terminated with a semicolon.

This is a simple, straightforward way to declare a structure, but it has a serious shortcoming, one that prevents this particular construction from seeing widespread use. It provides no convenient shorthand type name for declaring other objects; indeed, this syntax can be used only to declare objects, not types, immediately. You can declare several objects at once, however, aas in the following example:

```
struct {
  int serialno;
  char brand[21];
  char model[21];
  char description[41];
  char location[21];
} prop_rec, new_rec, hold_rec;
```

In this fragment, three objects are defined. But it is still an object definition, not a type declaration. As such, this last definition reserves memory space for all three objects. Figure 11.1 demonstrates how a block of memory is used to hold a structure.

The following four rules govern what kinds of objects and declarations a structure can contain:

❑ *A structure cannot contain a member with in*complete *or* function *type*. An example of an incomplete type is an array declaration with no size specified:

```
int stuff[];
```

An incomplete type does not provide the compiler with enough information to determine the size of the structure.

Fig. 11.1. *A single block of memory holds all the member variables of a structure.*

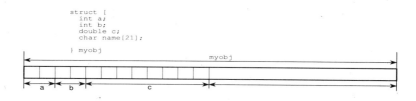

```
struct [
    int a;
    int b;
    double c;
    char name[21];

] myobj
```

The restriction that a structure cannot contain a function type does not mean that it cannot contain a function *pointer*— pointer types are not excluded. You simply cannot write a function inside a structure.

❏ *A structure cannot contain an instance of itself.* A structure is considered incomplete until the closing curly brace (}) is encountered, and a structure cannot contain an incomplete type. It can, however, contain a *pointer* to an instance of itself. This is called a *self-referential* structure. We show you how to write a self-referential structure a little later.

❏ *A structure can contain derived objects, including other structures and unions.* You can make structures as complex as you like, provided that you can keep up with the naming conventions (see the "Accessing Structure Members" section later in this chapter).

❏ *The compiler may introduce unnamed padding bytes within the structure, if any of the members required a particular byte alignment.* There may also be unnamed padding after the members, to achieve a whole-byte object size if there are any bit-fields (discussed a little later) in the structure. Make no assumptions about the size of a structure, unless you are extremely familiar with your machine's requirements, the compiler's characteristics, and the nature of the members. The safest route is to use the `sizeof` operator, instead of trying to compute the object's size yourself.

You can pack a great deal of complexity into a structure definition. Like bowls stacked within one another, structures can contain other structures, in just about any fashion you choose. Listing 11.1 shows how to declare nested structures, and how to initialize them.

Listing 11.1. `struct.c` *(Declaring and initializing structures without tags).* *Microsoft C 6.0*

```
1   #include <stdlib.h>
2   #include <stdio.h>
3
4   main()
5   {
6     struct {
7       int header;
8       struct {
9         int part1;
10        int part2;
11      } parts;
12    } assem = { 1,
13              { 37, 64 }
14            };
15    struct {
16      int trailer;
17      struct {
18        int sub1;
19        int sub2;
20      } subs;
21    } subassem = { 2, 16, 32 };
22
23    printf( "Header %d has parts %d and %d\n",
24            assem.header, assem.parts.part1,
25            assem.parts.part2 );
26
27    printf( "Trailer %d has subassemblies %d and %d\n",
28            subassem.trailer, subassem.subs.sub1,
29            subassem.subs.sub2 );
30  }
```

Listing 11.1 shows how to initialize a structure in the declaration. The initializer list must be enclosed in curly braces (`{}`) in the same manner as the declaration part, and also terminated with a semicolon.

If the structure declaration is a nested one, you can use *interior* curly braces on the initializer parts for the contained structures to help you stay organized (refer to listing 11.1, lines 12–14).

Nested curly braces in the initializer list are considered optional, however. Line 21 shows the initializer list for the `subassem` object as a straightforward list. Neither method of using curly braces in the initializer list is required nor preferred. Suit yourself on this one.

Using Structure Tags

The method of defining structures (outlined so far) has an extremely serious shortcoming: it is impossible to use it like a type definition in the general sense. Declare the structure; declare the object or objects, and that's it.

The ability to reuse a structure declaration to define objects elsewhere in the program that have the same structure would be nice. You can use structure tags to do this. A *structure tag* is just a name for the structure that is not the name of any object that may be defined with it later. The general syntax of a structure declaration with a tag is as follows:

```
struct tagname { declarator-list };
```

The tag name follows the same rules for naming as every other name in C. In concrete terms, a structure declaration and corresponding object definition now look like this:

```
struct locator {
  char subject[21];
  char keywords[81];
  char booktitle[81];
  int room;
  int aisle;
  int shelf;
};
...
struct locator index;
```

Here there is an *index* object that has type `struct locator`. This syntax greatly simplifies the definition of various objects in the source file, whereas the structure *declarations* are packed away neatly in their own group of lines. Program readability is much increased this way.

Initializers for structures with tags are the same as before. Listing 11.2 shows the use of structure tags and associated objects with initializers. Compare this program with listing 11.1, particularly from line 36 on. The initializers and manner of reference are basically the same.

Listing 11.2. `struct2.c` *(Declaring and initializing structures with tags).*
Microsoft C 6.0

```
 1   #include <stdlib.h>
 2   #include <stdio.h>
 3
 4   main()
 5   {
 6   /* +-----------------------------------------------------+
 7       + Declares structure types first, not objects
 8       + Use structure tags to clarify and simplify code
 9       +-----------------------------------------------------+
10   */
11      struct part_t {
12        int part1;
13        int part2;
14      };
15
16      struct assem_t {
17        int header;
18        struct part_t parts;
19      };
20
21      struct sub_t {
22        int sub1;
23        int sub2;
24      } subs;
25
26      struct suba_t {
27        int trailer;
28        struct sub_t subs;
29      };
30
31   /* +-----------------------------------------------------+
32       + Now declare the structure objects
33       + No difference in initializers or references
34       +-----------------------------------------------------+
35   */
36      struct assem_t assem = {
37        1,
38        { 37, 64 }
39      };
40
41      struct suba_t subassem = { 2, 16, 32 };
42
43      printf( "Header %d has parts %d and %d\n",
44               assem.header, assem.parts.part1,
45               assem.parts.part2 );
46
```

Listing 11.2. continues

Listing 11.2. continued

```
47      printf( "Trailer %d has subassemblies %d and %d\n",
48              subassem.trailer, subassem.subs.sub1,
49              subassem.subs.sub2 );
50   }
```

Accessing Structure Members

Because structures share the same environment with all other objects in C, it is reasonable to expect that many of the same things can be done with them. You can declare them, assign the "value" of one structure to another with the same type, access structure members in a manner analogous to accessing the elements of an array, and form pointers to them. You can use pointer techniques also to build self-referential structures. The importance of this last technique becomes apparent later in this chapter.

First, consider how to reference the individual members of a structure without involving pointers (for the time being). Just as an array reference requires the postfix subscript operator ([ ]), reference to a structure member requires the postfix *structure dot operator* (.). This not a typo; the dot operator is a period. The general form of its use is as follows:

```
object.member
```

where `object` has a type of `struct`, and `member` has whatever type belongs to that member object. Early in the chapter, for example, we defined a structure for describing a property record, `prop_rec`. To refer to the integer `serialno` and the string `brand` members of that structure, you might write the following code:

```
prop_rec.serialno = 12345;   /* integer member type */
strcpy( prop_rec.brand, "Acme" ); /* string member type */
```

Structures differ from arrays in that references to the unqualified structure object identifier *are not* interpreted as address values. To illustrate what this means, rewrite the `prop_rec` structure with a tag so that it can be referenced conveniently, as follows:

```
struct prop_type {
   int serialno;
   char brand[21];
   char model[21];
   char description[41];
   char location[21];
};
```

```
struct prop_type prop_rec;
struct prop_type hold_rec;
```

Now if you write the following assignment statement:

```
hold_rec = prop_rec;
```

the whole structure contents are transferred to the other structure. Naturally, in order to do this, the exact types must be compatible. The point is that neither `prop_rec` nor `hold_rec` are pointers. To get the address of a structure, you must take its address explicitly with the address-of operator, as follows:

```
struct prop_type *hold_rec;
...
hold_rec = &prop_rec;
```

Observe also how the pointer to the structure was declared in the first line of this fragment. The indirection operator is required, just as for any basic type object, and the address-of operator (&) is required to take the address.

Once you have a pointer to a structure, how do you reference the members? Accessing structure members through a pointer to the structure changes things a bit; the structure dot operator no longer applies. Now you need the *structure pointer operator* (->), a two-character operator designed to look like an arrow pointing to the right. To write this character, use the minus sign followed *immediately* by the greater-than sign, as follows:

```
hold->serialno = 12345;
```

You can put whitespace *around* the structure pointer operator, but *not between* the - and the >.

While you are dealing with structures and pointers, you may want to take the *offset address* (the number of bytes from the beginning) of a structure member. The `offsetof` macro does this for you, as in the following example:

```
#include <stdlib.h>
#include <stdio.h>
#include <stddef.h>

struct anytype {
  int a;
  double b;
  char text[40];
  int c;
};
```

```
main()
{
  printf( "The offset of \"c\" is %d\n",
          offsetof( struct anytype, c ) );
}
```

Support for the offsetof macro is fairly new on DOS-based systems. It is supported by Turbo C++, and by QuickC 2.0 and 2.5, but not by Turbo C 2.0.

Now let's get really fancy. You know that a structure can contain a pointer, and now you know how to form a pointer to a structure. With these two pieces of knowledge, you can construct a self-referential structure. A *self-referential structure* points to *an instance* of itself—of that particular structure *type*. It is not an object that points directly to itself (which would serve little purpose). This kind of construction is most often used to create *linked lists*. For example, suppose that the property record examined earlier is just one of a list of items of property. We rewrite it again, as follows:

```
struct prop_type {
  struct prop_type *next;
  int serialno;
  char brand[21];
  char model[21];
  char description[41];
  char location[21];
};
...
struct prop_type *anchor;
struct prop_type *current;
```

Do you recognize the structure pointer declarations in the first member, and in the separate pointer declarations? This is called a *singly linked list*. The first "free standing" pointer is said to *anchor the list*. It is not a structure; it is just a pointer that contains the address of the first structure in the list, and can always be accessed. (Initializing the anchor and member pointers is covered later in this chapter, in the "Managing Data in Dynamic Memory" section.) To get the link list started, the current pointer can be set from anchor, as follows:

```
current = anchor; /* These ARE pointers */
```

At this point, you can access any member in the first structure in the list by using the structure pointer operator:

```
current->serialno = 12345;   /* OBJECT has type int */
```

Now think about the *member* pointer for a moment. You access it like any other member in this pointed-to structure, and the referenced object has a pointer type. The following statement shows how this is done:

```
current = current->next; /* Go to the next list entry */
```

Look carefully at this last statement. This is much like the snake that ate its own tail. *First*, the right side is evaluated, so that `current->next` is dereferenced, the result being *another pointer to structure*. That address value is then assigned back into `current`. You have just begun the process of *running the chain*—continually updating the current object pointer with another pointer that leads to the next list entry. Presumably, the last structure in the list has `next` set to NULL, so that you can determine when to stop. The following code is an example of how you could run the entire chain:

```
current = anchor;
while ( current ) {
   printf ( "Serial number: %d\n", current->serialno );
   current = current->next; /* Go to the next list entry */
}
```

When the loop is complete, `current` points to the last structure in the list. If you use `current` alone, there is no way to get back to the beginning of the list. That is why a separate pointer is used to anchor the list. A little later in this chapter, you will see how to construct *doubly linked lists*, which can be run both forward and backward.

Using Bit-fields in Structures

A bit-field can occur only as a member of a structure. Because you cannot use the address-of operator with a bit-field, there can be no such thing as a pointer to a bit-field. A bit-field member may have only the `int`, `signed int`, and `unsigned int` types assigned to it. For optimum portability, use the `signed` or `unsigned` qualifiers explicitly.

What does a bit-field *do*? It is a mechanism for *saving space*. Throughout the book you have seen, again and again, instances of a whole integer being used as a true-false flag. Because most integers are 16 bits (2 bytes) long, and the only values that such a flag needs are 0 and 1, for false and true conditions, you might well argue that 15 of those bits are being wasted. In other cases, you might want to define a variable, for example, that has values only from 0 to 3, and never more than that. This actually requires only 2 bits: the decimal number 3 can be expressed as the binary number 11.

Bit-fields provide a way to define an integer type variable that has a limited number of bits. You certainly would want to do this when memory is at an absolute premium, but it may be wise to use the facility to prevent using up too much of that precious but limited commodity—RAM.

The declaration of a bit-field structure member requires the addition of a *field-width specifier*. Declare the integer type and name, as mentioned earlier, followed by a colon and the number of bits in the field. Listing 11.3 shows how to declare, initialize, and reference bit-fields.

Listing 11.3. `struct3.c` *(Declaring bit-field structure members).*

Microsoft C 6.0

```
 1   #include <stdlib.h>
 2   #include <stdio.h>
 3
 4   struct anytag {
 5     unsigned int flag1       : 1;   /* Boolean true-false */
 6     unsigned int group       : 2;   /* values 0 - 3 */
 7     unsigned int foldernum   : 4;   /* values 0 - 15 */
 8                              : 1;   /* 1 bit padding */
 9     unsigned int casenum     : 6;   /* values 0 - 63 */
10                              : 0;   /* force word alignment */
11     int total_cases;              /* normal integer */
12   };
13
14   struct anytag myobj = {
15     0, 3, 15, 63, 324
16   };
17
18   main()
19   {
20     if ( myobj.flag1 )
21       printf( "Case number %d is currently open.\n",
22         myobj.casenum );
23     else
24       printf( "Case number %d is currently closed.\n",
25         myobj.casenum );
26
27     printf( "This case belongs to group %d, folder %d.\n",
28             myobj.group, myobj.foldernum );
29     printf( "There are %d total cases.\n",
30             myobj.total_cases );
31   }
```

Bit-field objects can be treated just as if they were "miniature" integers. Refer to them by member name, as you would any other member.

Notice the *unnamed bit-fields* in lines 8 and 10. In line 8, the field width is greater than zero. This unnamed field is used only for padding. The unnamed field in line 10 has length 0, and causes *padding up to the next word boundary*; if the bit counts are such that a word boundary coincides with this field, there is no padding. Finally, the initializer list in line 15 has values only for named fields. Unnamed fields cannot be initialized. (How would you refer to them?)

ANSI leaves several bit-field characteristics dependent upon the implementation. A bit-field may or may not overlap a word boundary. A given bit-field may be stored in memory from left to right, or from right to left (the sequence of fields as a whole moves from left to right; that is, from low to high memory). Finally, bit-fields are not, and should not be thought of as, arrays.

Combining Structures and Arrays

Considering the flexibility of C syntax as you have seen it so far, you probably will not be surprised to learn that you can combine structure and array declarations to achieve some pretty sophisticated objects. You can combine arrays and structures in several powerful ways.

First, you can write a structure declaration that contains a member that is an array. Listing 11.4 illustrates the syntax required for this.

Listing 11.4. `struct4.c` *(A structure with a member having array type).*

Microsoft C 6.0

```
1   /* +----------------------------------------------------+
2       + EXAMPLE OF A STRUCTURE WITH AN ARRAY MEMBER
3       +----------------------------------------------------+
4   */
5   #include <stdlib.h>
6   #include <stdio.h>
7
8   struct p_type {
9      int pair[2][10];
10  };
11
12  struct p_type points;
13
14  main()
15  {
16     int i;
17
18     srand( 37 );   /* Seed the random number generator */
```

Listing 11.4. continues

Listing 11.4. *continued*

```
19      for ( i=0; i<10; ++i ) {
20        points.pair[0][i] = rand() % 100;
21        points.pair[1][i] = rand() % 100;
22      }
23      for ( i=0; i<10; ++i ) {
24        printf( " %d, %d\n",
25          points.pair[0][i], points.pair[1][i] );
26      }
27    }
```

There is nothing surprising about the declaration itself; common sense tells you how to declare the array member. Furthermore, because the *member* is an array, the subscript postfix operator clearly belongs with the member name, not with the structure name. This is seen in line 20–21, and line 25 of listing 11.4.

The step from the concept of a structure having an array type member, to constructing an *array of structures*, is a small one. Listing 11.5 shows you how to do this.

Listing 11.5. struct5.c *(An array of structures).*   *Microsoft C 6.0*

```
1    /* +----------------------------------------------------+
2        + EXAMPLE OF A ARRAY OF STRUCTURES
3        +----------------------------------------------------+
4    */
5    #include <stdlib.h>
6    #include <stdio.h>
7
8    struct p_type {
9      int x;
10     int y;
11   };
12
13   struct p_type points[10];
14
15   main()
16   {
17     int i;
18
19     srand( 37 );  /* Seed the random number generator */
20     for ( i=0; i<10; ++i ) {
21       points[i].x = rand() % 100;
```

```
22       points[i].y = rand() % 100;
23   }
24   for ( i=0; i<10; ++i ) {
25     printf( " %d, %d\n",
26       points[i].x, points[i].y );
27   }
28 }
```

The structure definition in line 13 has the added feature of the array dimensions appended to the structure object name. As you might expect, the subscript postfix operator now belongs to the *structure identifier*, not to any member name. Lines 21–22 and line 26 illustrate how to refer to structure array elements, and the members that belong to each (structure) element. When you build the concept a layer at a time, it's still not particularly complicated. Figure 11.2 shows the memory arrangement for an array of struct.

Fig. 11.2. *A structure can be an array element.*

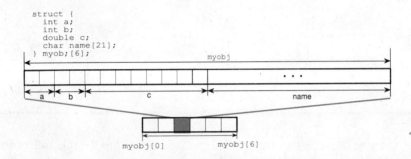

Take it one more step, and you can build an *array of pointers to structure*. Listing 11.6 shows how to implement this process.

Listing 11.6. struct6.c *(An array of pointers to structure).*

Microsoft C 6.0

```
1  /* +----------------------------------------------------------+
2     + EXAMPLE OF A ARRAY OF POINTERS TO STRUCTURE
3     +----------------------------------------------------------+
4  */
5  #include <stdlib.h>
```

Listing 11.6. *continues*

Listing 11.6. continued

```
 6   #include <stdio.h>
 7
 8   struct p_type {
 9      int x;
10      int y;
11   };
12
13   struct p_type *points[10];
14
15   main()
16   {
17      int i;
18
19      srand( 37 );   /* Seed the random number generator */
20      for ( i=0; i<10; ++i ) {
21        points[i] =
22            (struct p_type *)malloc( sizeof( struct p_type ) );
23        points[i]->x = rand() % 100;
24        points[i]->y = rand() % 100;
25      }
26      for ( i=0; i<10; ++i ) {
27        printf( " %d, %d\n",
28        points[i]->x, points[i]->y );
29      }
30      for ( i=0; i<10; ++i ) {
31        free( points[i] );
32      }
33   }
```

The first difference in listing 11.6 can be seen in line 13: the indirection operator has been added to the declaration. The result is an array of pointers; as yet, no memory is reserved for the structures themselves. Keep in mind that when you subscript this array, each element is a *pointer*.

The next step is found in lines 21–22. Here the malloc() function is used to allocate memory dynamically for each structure. When the memory for the structure has been obtained, each array element (pointer) is initialized to point to it.

The final step is to replace the dot operator with the structure pointer operator (see lines 23–24 and 28). In this part of the program, this is the only difference from listing 11.5. Notice the relative placement of the subscript and structure pointer operators when referring to a member object.

Defining Unions of Structures

Now that you have mastered the basics of handling structures, you are ready to approach *unions*. Structures are at the heart of unions, whereas unions can be thought of as providing different "views" of structures.

The Overlay Concept of Unions

A *union* can be thought of as a set of structures, every one of which *begins at the same storage address*. This is what is meant by the *overlay concept* of unions. There is only one object in the union at any time, no matter how many views of it exist.

A union, like a structure, has member objects that can be of just about any type. *But every member of the union begins at offset 0 of the union.* Unions really are useful only as containers of structures providing "alternate views" of structures. Unions also are similar to structures in that their declaration syntax is the same, and the address-of operator & works the same way with both. Figure 11.3 illustrates the concept of unions as overlays.

Fig. 11.3. Members of a union "redefine" the same area of memory in different ways.

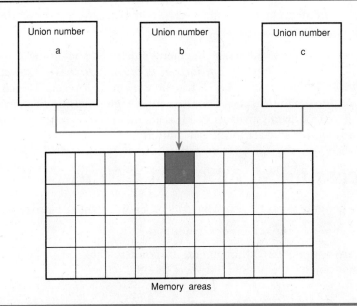

Declaring a Union

You can define the structures that make up a union directly within the union, without using structure tags, but the resulting code looks unnecessarily complex. In the following sample code, we use tags to simplify the appearance:

```
struct INTEGERS {     /* The caps are not required */
  int ai, bi, ci;
};
struct BYTES {
  unsigned char al, ah, bl, bh, cl, ch;
};
...
union {
  struct INTEGERS i;
  struct BYTES b;
} codes = { 37, 16, 24 };
```

Did you notice that the union was declared without a tag? The principles for tags that apply to structures are the same as those that apply to unions—this union is a discrete object, and cannot be used as a type specification anywhere else. The union object in this case is codes.

This union is meant to give two different views of integer codes. When member objects are accessed by means of the INTEGER structure declaration, the whole integer value is obtained. When member objects are accessed by means of the BYTES structure declaration, you can manipulate the component bytes of the integers.

The initializer in this code fragment illustrates something important about initializing unions: *the initializers apply only to the first structure in the union.* struct INTEGERS i has three member integers. Hence, there are three integer initializers. Of course, you can reference the elements of the second and following structures with assignment statements, but that is not as handy as an initializer in the declaration.

Accessing Members of a Union

The general syntax for referring to member objects in a union is as follows:

```
unionname.structname.memname
```

Thus, in the previous code fragment, you could refer legitimately to the same member object several different ways, like this:

```
codes.i.bi = 3;         /* an integer view */
codes.b.bl = '\x00';    /* first byte of bi */
codes.b.bh = '\x03';    /* second byte of bi */
```

In this particular case, the two member structures are designed to be the same size. This does not always have to be so. Suppose that you want to define an object, for example, that could contain different data types—with different lengths—depending on a "switch" variable. Here's an example of such a field:

```
struct vtype {
   int type;
};
struct ctype {
   int type;
   char cvar;
};
struct itype {
   int type;
   int ivar;
};
struct dtype {
   int type;
   double dvar;
};
...
union var_type {
   struct vtype v;
   struct ctype c;
   struct itype i;
   struct dtype d;
};
```

Now the union can contain several different kinds of variables, depending on the variable type v.type. All the member structures have the type member object in common in the same relative position, so that the object type can be determined. The following code puts this complicated object to use; the task is easier because it is declared with a tag this time:

```
#define CHAR 0
#define INT 1
#define DOUBLE 2
...
union var_type vars;   /* declare the union */
...
switch ( vars.v.type ) {
   case CHAR:   vars.c.cvar = '$';
```

```
                        break;
    case INT :          vars.i.ivar = 16;
                        break;
    case DOUBLE:        vars.d.dvar = 2.14;
                        break;
    default:            printf( "Don't know what kind of object"
                                " this is.\n" );
    }
```

How large, incidentally, is the union `vars`? It is large enough to contain the *largest object within it*. In this case, because the largest object is a `double`, the union's size is the same as a `double`.

Deriving Types with *typedef*

Earlier in this book, we mentioned that one of the goals of the ANSI standards advisory committee was to strengthen the typing mechanism of C. The original K & R was a deliberately weakly typed language. Evidently, the committee felt that weak typing was a defect, even though it was a powerful tool, rightly used.

Whether an implementation supports strong or weak object typing, the type of an object is a matter of some detailed concern and importance to the programmer. Data typing is so important, in fact, that ANSI C has carried forward the facility for *declaring user-defined types*, as embodied in the `typedef` specifier. We begin by immediately showing you an example, and then discuss its implications. Here is a simple `typedef` declaration:

```
typedef int STUFF;
...
STUFF height = 32;      /* same as int height = 32 */
STUFF *width;           /* a pointer to an integer */
```

These lines define a new type name: `STUFF`. Clearly, the underlying objects have type `int`. The `typedef` does nothing to change that. In fact, the type of `STUFF` *is* `int`.

At this level, you have achieved little more than the convenience of calling basic types by some other name should they happen to irritate you. Type definitions become more useful when applied to structures and unions. You can assign a new type name to an imaginary database-control structure type, for example, by writing the following:

```
typedef struct {
  int isopen;
  long offset;
  unsigned reclength;
  int recordingmode;
  long juldatemod;
} db_control;   /* This is a type name, not object name */
```

If you had written a collection of independently compiled database functions, you could place this typedef in the header file for the source file. Then, you just would need to include that header in any "main program" source modules, and declare database-control structures by writing:

```
db_control inventory_db;
```

db_control is an object with type db_control. All the inner complexity is hidden within the typedef. Thus typedef names can go a long way to enhance the readability of complicated code.

In this last code fragment, you may have noticed that the structure declaration had no tag. Does this make any difference? No, not in any practical sense *for this construction*. The new type name is db_control whether a tag is present or not. On the other hand, you may prefer to write the declarations in the following equivalent manner:

```
struct dbctl_t {
  int isopen;
  long offset;
  unsigned reclength;
  int recordingmode;
  long juldatemod;
};

typedef struct dbctl_t db_control;
```

The new type name is still db_control. The only difference is that this way of building the type *does* require the structure tag. However you write the declarations, remember that no intrinsically new data type has been introduced, only a synonym for existing constructions.

Managing Data in Dynamic Memory

When you run your program, the host operating system loads the executable file into memory, from whence the program executes. From your program's point of view, there are now two general areas of memory—one "inside" and one "outside" the program. The part of main memory "outside" your program is what we mean by *dynamic memory*. Your program doesn't own dynamic memory, and has no business trying to use it unannounced.

This does not mean that dynamic memory is inaccessible, however. Standard C provides four *memory-management functions* that allow your program to acquire (allocate) and control portions of dynamic memory. These are the `calloc()`, `malloc()`, `realloc()`, and `free()` functions. The use of these functions is covered in the next two sections.

Before jumping directly into that discussion, however, we need to mention one more technical term. Those of you who have had some prior exposure to C probably already know that most C implementations frequently mention the *heap*, meaning precisely dynamic memory.

Standard C knows nothing of a heap, which doesn't mean that compilers that support one are nonconforming. The manner of implementing dynamic memory support is implementation-dependent, however common heap space may be. In any event, the following discussion proceeds as if there were no such thing as a heap, but you should be aware that *your* compiler may make distinctions based on the presence of a heap.

Allocating Memory at Run-time

Of the four memory-management functions, three acquire new (dynamic) memory, or resize it, and one releases it. The first implication of this situation is that when your program begins execution, it is not known where such memory resides, because it *doesn't exist yet*.

The functions acquiring memory return a pointer to the memory acquired, if successful, and you are responsible for noting it. If the function call is unsuccessful, a null pointer is returned, and you are still responsible for doing something about it. This is quite different from just writing an object definition and assuming that it is there: you have to write code to handle instances in which memory allocation may fail. Figure 11.4 illustrates dynamic memory allocation in a DOS system.

Fig. 11.4. *C compilers on DOS systems can allocate memory on either the near or far heap.*

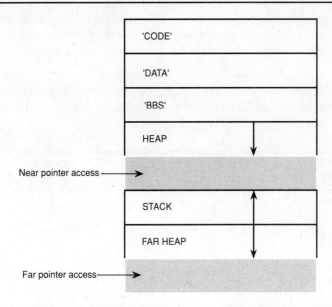

You can allocate dynamic memory in two ways: in groups of objects, or in groups of bytes. The first method, acquiring groups of objects, is handled by the calloc() function. Its prototype is

```
#include <stdlib.h>
void *calloc( size_t nmemb, size_t size );
```

Note carefully that calloc() is *not* a void function—it returns a void *pointer*, or NULL if it fails. Remember—the void type pointer can be assigned to any other pointer type. For example, if you wanted to allocate memory for a large array of integers—say for 4096 integers—instead of taking up code space in your program, you could write the following:

```
int i;
int *data; /* define a pointer to int */
...
if ( NULL == ( data = calloc( 4096, sizeof(int) ) ) ) {
  puts( "Can't get the memory for the data array." );
  abort();
}
for ( i=0; i<4086; ++i )
  data[i] = 0; /* initialize the array */
```

This code fragment illustrates the fact that the arguments to `calloc()` are the *number of objects*, and the *size of each object*, respectively. The returned pointer is placed in a pointer to `int`. An incomplete array type (such as `int data[]`) was not used, because the compiler would try to reserve space in the program's data areas (not dynamic memory) for the array. Because type would have been left incomplete, this would have resulted in a compile-time error.

You can do the same thing in allocating dynamic memory for a large array of structures. In fact, we'll use `typedef` just for fun and see how it helps (see listing 11.7).

Listing 11.7. `struct7.c` *(Implementing a pointer to array of* `struct` *in dynamic memory).* *Microsoft C 6.0*

```
1   #include <stdlib.h>
2   #include <stdio.h>
3
4   main()
5   {
6     int i;
7     typedef struct { int x, y; } p_type;
8     p_type *points;   /* pointer to array of struct */
9
10    if ( NULL == ( points = calloc( 4096, sizeof(p_type) ) ) ) {
11      puts( "Can't get the memory for the points array." );
12      abort();
13    }
14
15    srand( 37 );
16    for ( i=0; i<4086; ++i ) { /* init the array */
17      points[i].x = rand() % 100;
18      points[i].y = rand() % 100;
19    }
20    for ( i=0; i<4086; ++i ) { /* print the array */
21      printf( " %d   %d\n",
22        points[i].x, points[i].y );
23    }
24    free( points );
25  }
```

The use of `typedef` simplifies the declaration (lines 7, 8 listing 11.7), as well as the `sizeof()` operator in the `calloc()` argument list (line 10). It makes for much neater code, which can be extremely important in complicated code.

There is another interesting feature in this code fragment. The way the declarations are written, we have defined a *pointer to an array of* struct. This is quite different from the array of struct, or the array of pointers to struct that you saw earlier in this chapter. It is *one* pointer to a whole array of struct. *However*, it *does not* require different treatment when referring to member elements. See lines 17, 18, and 22: you subscript the array identifier, and use the structure dot operator to access members.

Line 24 of listing 11.7 is important also. A given implementation of C may clean up (release dynamically acquired memory) automatically after such an allocation, but *don't count on it*. Always take the time and effort to release the allocated memory with the free() function.

The malloc() and realloc() functions can be covered rather quickly. Their prototypes are as follows

```
#include <stdlib.h>
void *malloc( size_t size );
void *realloc( void *ptr, size_t newsize );
```

Pointer returns (or NULL) from these functions are the same as for calloc(). You should use malloc() when you want to allocate an amorphous chunk of dynamic memory with size_t size number of *bytes*. Object sizes do not enter into it.

realloc() is a little more interesting. Its first argument is a pointer to the area of memory allocated originally, and the size is the *new* size you want the area to have. realloc() returns a pointer because it may allocate a completely new area with the requested new size. The contents of the (possibly new) area, however, are guaranteed to be the same as the old area, *up to the lesser of the old and new sizes*. If the new area is smaller, the data is "truncated"; if larger, the added area has indeterminate contents, and may contain garbage.

realloc() has one other important feature. If the first argument pointer is NULL, realloc() acquires a brand new area and returns its address to the caller, just as if malloc() had been the function called. You can take advantage of this characteristic when coding a loop that contains reallocation calls. If the area doesn't exist yet, realloc() works anyway.

Keeping Track of Allocations

Now take a moment and reflect on what keeping track of dynamically allocated memory costs you, in terms of writing code. Throughout the chapter, the following methods have cropped up:

❑ *A simple pointer suffices to keep track of a single area.* This is the easiest method to implement, because it requires only one declaration.

❑ *An array of pointers can be used to keep track of a number of separately allocated areas that are not contiguous.* Slightly more complex, this still requires only a single array declaration.

❑ *An anchor pointer locates the first structure in a linked list of structures.* This is the most complicated method, because another pointer within each element structure must be maintained also. When we introduce doubly linked lists (shortly), you will see how complicated it can be.

In addition to the simple consideration that you don't want to lose allocated areas while you are still working with them, keeping track of dynamically allocated areas is important so that you can release them with the `free()` function when they no longer are needed.

Structures and Unions as Function Parameters

We delayed discussing structures and unions as function parameters until after the discussion of dynamically allocated memory so that dynamic objects as parameters could be included. This point is more subtle than you might at first think—frequently, structures and unions are large objects, and thus may equally frequently be dynamically allocated.

How you choose to pass structures (unions) to a function is affected most by the fact that *reference to a structure or union identifier does not result in an address value*. Just the opposite is true with arrays, so that passing an array to a function always means passing a pointer.

Simply naming a structure in the argument list, however, results in that structure's contents being passed *by value*, not reference. That is, a copy of the whole structure, however large, is passed to the function. On stack-oriented machines, that could present quite a problem—you conceivably could cause the stack to overflow. The problem only gets worse when you think of passing arrays of structures.

The solution is to take the address of the structure explicitly and pass it to the function. This requires the following modification of the function prototype:

```
typedef struct anytag { ... } typename;
typename myobject;
void myfunc( typename *anyobject ); /* prototype */
...
myfunc( &myobject );                /* function call */
```

The indirection operator must be added to the function-prototype parameter-declaration list, and the address-of operator must be used to take the address when the function is called.

Now, what about dynamically allocated structures or arrays of structures? Look back at line 8 of listing 11.7. You could pass the array of dynamically allocated structures defined in that program to a function, as follows:

```
void myfunc( p_type * ); /* unnamed formal parameter */
...
myfunc( points );
```

That is, the object points is already a pointer; there is no need to take its address. Each case merits a little thought. Just stop and consider how you defined the object or objects in the first place.

Building Linked Lists with Structures

As always, theory is one thing, and performance another. In this section we develop (for the PC in the DOS environment) a directory-listing program that uses just about every trick you have learned in this chapter. This is *not* a simple demo program—mastering it takes some effort.

A description of what we want the directory program (xdir.c) to do is deceptively simple, however. It produces an alphabetized directory listing based on the command-line argument received. The argument can contain DOS wildcard characters (but cannot consist of just a path name; *some* file specification is required). The command-line sequence is as follows:

```
xdir [path]filespec
```

After the directory has been read, it is stored in a doubly linked list, so that it can be scrolled with the paging and arrow keys (nothing is as irritating as a directory list that scrolls off the screen).

The ordered directory list is scrolled within a window on the screen. Another window at the top of the screen displays both the number of bytes occupied by files in the directory being listed, and the remaining free space on that disk.

Scrolling is controlled both by the up- and down-arrow keys and the page-up and page-down keys. In addition to being able to scroll the screen, the arrow keys control the selection of a "current file" by moving a highlighted cursor over the file name. If the file is a standard ASCII text file, you can press the V (for View) key to scroll the text file.

The entire file is read into memory for scrolling, so that viewing is as fast as scrolling the directory. The scrolling keys are the same as those for scrolling the directory. The program refuses to select a directory entry or volume label as if it were a text file. To stop scrolling a text file, press F3. Press F3 also to stop scrolling a directory (leave the program).

Finally, all scrolling and screen displays must be *fast*. Those of you who have the old CGA display adapters can expect snow on the screen when scrolling.

Keep in mind that, despite its length and complexity, xdir.c is not a commercial product. It is in fact just a sample program developed for this book, and has relatively few features. This may give you some idea of the amount of code and effort that goes into a good commercial package. xdir.c is shown in listing 11.8.

Listing 11.8. xdir.c *(Using doubly linked lists to implement a directory listing program).*   *Turbo C 2.0*

```
 1    /* +----------------------------------------------------+
 2        + XDIR.C Extended Directory List
 3        + Compile with LARGE MODEL   so that the FAR HEAP is
 4        + used — needed by long linked lists
 5        + for View, etc.
 6        +----------------------------------------------------+
 7    */
 8    #include <stdlib.h>
 9    #include <stdio.h>
10    #include <conio.h>
11    #include <dos.h>
12    #include <dir.h>
13    #include <string.h>
14
15    union REGS reg;
16    char dirmask[81];
17    long totsize;
18    long totfree;
19    struct text_info screen;
20    unsigned char far *vram;
21    int x, y;
22
23    typedef struct l_type {
24       struct l_type *prev;
```

```
25    struct l_type *next;
26    char flag;                /* Reserved future use */
27    char line[255];
28  } text;
29
30  text *dir_ent = NULL;  /* anchor directory list */
31  text *flist = NULL;    /* anchor text file list */
32
33  void get_entries( char *dirmask, text **list );
34  void free_entries( text *list );
35  void scroll_entries( text *list, int height );
36  text *paint_dir( text *list, int height );
37  void get_flist( char *dirmask, text **list, text *select );
38  void scroll_flist( text *list, int height );
39  text *paint_flist( text *list, int height );
40  void scroll_up( void );
41  void scroll_down( void );
42  void ch_out( unsigned char data );
43  void string_out( char * );
44  void overlay( char * );
45  void draw_boxes( void );
46  void highlight_on( void );
47  void highlight_off( void );
48
49  /* +-------------------------------------------------------+
50     + main()
51     +    Initialize screen mode and kick it off
52     +-------------------------------------------------------+
53  */
54  main( int argc, char *argv[] )
55  {
56    if ( argc < 2 ) strcpy( dirmask, "*.*" );
57    else strcpy( dirmask, argv[1] );
58    strupr( dirmask );
59    textmode( 3 );
60    textbackground( BLUE );
61    textcolor( LIGHTGRAY );
62    clrscr();
63    gettextinfo( &screen );
64    switch ( screen.currmode ) {
65      case 1:
66      case 2:
67      case 3:
68      case 4:
69      case 5:
70      case 6: vram = MK_FP( 0xB800, 0 ); break;
71      case 7: vram = MK_FP( 0xB000, 0 ); break;
72      default: vram = MK_FP( 0xA000, 0 ); break;
73    }
74    draw_boxes();
```

Listing 11.8. continues

Listing 11.8. continued

```
75    window( 2, 2, 79, 3 );
76    get_entries( dirmask, &dir_ent );
77    window( 2, 5, 79, 21 );
78    gettextinfo( &screen );
79    scroll_entries( dir_ent,
80      screen.winbottom - screen.wintop + 1 );
81    free_entries( dir_ent );
82    window( 1, 1, 80, 25 );
83    clrscr();
84  }
85
86  /* +--------------------------------------------------------+
87     + Get Directory Entries in a Linked List
88     +--------------------------------------------------------+
89  */
90  void get_entries( char *dirmask, text **list )
91  {
92    struct ffblk entry;    /* DOS disk information is not */
93    struct dfree diskfree;   /* portable across systems */
94    unsigned char drive;
95    char work[81];
96    char work2[41];
97    text *hold, *base, *temp;
98    int finito;
99
100   if ( dirmask[1] != ':' ) {  /* drive id if missing */
101     drive = getdisk();
102     sprintf( work, "%c%c%s", drive+65, ':', dirmask );
103     strcpy( dirmask, work );
104   }
105   if ( !strchr( dirmask, '\\' ) ) { /* If no entered */
106     strncpy( work, dirmask, 2 );   /* preserve drive */
107     work[2] = '\0';  /* strncpy() doesn't carry null */
108     strcat( work, "\\" );              /* first slash */
109     getcurdir( work[0]-64, work+3 );   /* path spec */
110     strcat( work, "\\" );              /* last slash */
111     if ( work[3] == '\\' )   /* two slashes together */
112       work[3] = '\0';               /* mean root dir */
113     strcat( work, dirmask+2 );  /* copy rest of mask */
114     strcpy( dirmask, work );
115   }
116   drive = dirmask[0] - 64;
117   getdfree( drive, &diskfree );
118   if ( diskfree.df_sclus == 0xFF ) abort();
119   totfree = (long)diskfree.df_sclus *
120             (long)diskfree.df_bsec  *
121             (long)diskfree.df_avail;
122   gotoxy( 2, 1 );
```

```
123    cprintf( "Directory( %s ) Free Space( %ld )",
124            dirmask, totfree );
125    totsize = 0;
126    finito = findfirst( dirmask, &entry, 0xFF );
127    while ( !finito ) { /* Format & link the dir entry */
128       sprintf( work, "%-13s%8ld ", entry.ff_name,
129               entry.ff_fsize );
130       sprintf( work2, "%02d:%02d:%02d ",
131               entry.ff_ftime >> 11,
132               ( entry.ff_ftime << 5 ) >> 10,
133               ( entry.ff_ftime << 11 ) >> 11
134           );
135       strcat( work, work2 );
136       sprintf( work2, "%02d/%02d/%02d ",
137               ( entry.ff_fdate << 7 ) >> 12,
138               ( entry.ff_fdate << 11 ) >> 11,
139               ( entry.ff_fdate >> 9 ) + 80
140           );
141       strcat( work,work2 );
142       if ( entry.ff_attrib & FA_RDONLY ) strcat( work, "R " );
143       if ( entry.ff_attrib & FA_HIDDEN ) strcat( work, "H " );
144       if ( entry.ff_attrib & FA_SYSTEM ) strcat( work, "S " );
145       if ( entry.ff_attrib & FA_LABEL ) strcat( work, "V " );
146       if ( entry.ff_attrib & FA_DIREC ) strcat( work, "D " );
147       if ( entry.ff_attrib & FA_ARCH ) strcat( work, "A" );
148       base = *list;                      /* Point to first entry */
149       if ( !base ) {         /* If there isn't one create it */
150          base = (text *)malloc( 2 * sizeof(text *)
151             + strlen( work ) + 2 );
152          base->next = base->prev = NULL;
153          *list = base;                    /* Update the anchor */
154       }
155       else {               /* Otherwise, link-in the new entry */
156
157    /* First, position to entry BEFORE WHICH this one goes */
158       /* Might as well insert them in order to begin with */
159
160          while ( base->next
161                  && strncmp( work, base->line, 12 ) > 0 )
162              base = base->next;
163          hold = (text *)malloc( 2 * sizeof(text *)
164             + strlen( work ) + 2 );
165          if ( !hold ) goto nomore; /* Stop short, no memory */
166          if ( !base->next
167                  && strncmp( work, base->line, 12 ) > 0 ) {
168             base->next = hold;              /* Append the entry */
169             hold->prev = base; hold->next = NULL;
170             base = hold;
171          }
172          else {                             /* Insert the entry */
```

Listing 11.8. continues

Listing 11.8. continued

```
173            temp = base->prev;
174            hold->prev = temp;
175            hold->next = base;
176            base->prev = hold;
177                                    /* Fix anchor when prepending*/
178            if ( !temp ) *list = hold;
179            else temp->next = hold;
180            base = hold;
181        }
182      }
183      strcpy( base->line, work );
184      base->flag = ' ';
185      totsize += entry.ff_fsize;
186      finito = findnext( &entry );
187    }
188  nomore: ;
189    gotoxy( 2, 2 );
190    cprintf( "Total Allocated in Directory( %ld )", totsize );
191  }
192
193  /* +----------------------------------------------------+
194     + Free Far Memory Used for Linked List
195     +----------------------------------------------------+
196  */
197  void free_entries( text *list )
198  {
199    text *hold;
200
201    while ( list->prev ) list = list->prev;
202    while ( list ) {
203      hold = list->next;
204      free( list );
205      list = hold;
206    }
207  }
208
209  /* +----------------------------------------------------+
210     + Scroll Directory Entries in a Linked List
211     +----------------------------------------------------+
212  */
213  void scroll_entries( text *list, int height )
214  {
215    char ch = ' ';
216    int i, numpage, savey;
217    text *page_top = NULL;
218    text *page_bot = NULL;
219    text *current = NULL;
```

```
220
221    clrscr();
222    page_top = list;  /* Display a page and note bounds */
223    page_bot = paint_dir( list, height );
224    current = page_top;
225    for ( numpage=1; current != page_bot; numpage++ )
226      current = current->next;
227    current = page_top;
228    gotoxy( 3, 1 );
229    highlight_on();
230
231    while ( ch != 61 ) {              /* position screen */
232      ch = getch(); if ( !ch ) ch = getch();
233      switch ( ch ) {
234        case 72:  if ( current == page_top ){
235                    if ( current->prev ) {
236                      current = current->prev;
237                      page_top = page_top->prev;
238                      if ( numpage == height )
239                        page_bot = page_bot->prev;
240                      else numpage++;
241                      highlight_off();
242                      scroll_down();
243                      highlight_on();
244                      x = 3; gotoxy( x, y );
245                      string_out( current->line );
246                    }
247                  }
248                  else {
249                    current = current->prev;
250                    highlight_off();
251                    y--; gotoxy( x, y );
252                    highlight_on();
253                  }
254                  break;
255        case 80:  if ( current == page_bot ){
256                    if ( current->next ) {
257                      current = current->next;
258                      page_top = page_top->next;
259                      page_bot = page_bot->next;
260                      highlight_off();
261                      scroll_up();
262                      highlight_on();
263                      x = 3; gotoxy( x, y );
264                      string_out( current->line );
265                      x = 3; gotoxy( x, y );
266                    }
267                  }
268                  else {
```

Listing 11.8. continues

Listing 11.8. continued

```
269                         current = current->next;
270                         highlight_off();
271                         y++; gotoxy( x, y );
272                         highlight_on();
273                     }
274                     break;
275         case 73:    highlight_off();          /* page up */
276                     for ( i=0; i<height && page_top->prev; i++ )
277                         page_top = page_top->prev;
278                     page_bot = paint_dir( page_top, height );
279                     current = page_top;
280             for ( numpage=1; current!=page_bot; numpage++ )
281                         current = current->next;
282                     current = page_top;
283                     x = 3; y = 1; gotoxy( x, y );
284                     highlight_on();
285                     break;
286         case 81:    if ( !page_bot->next ) break;
287                     highlight_off();          /* page down */
288                     page_top = page_bot->next;
289                     page_bot = paint_dir( page_top, height );
290                     current = page_top;
291             for ( numpage=1; current!=page_bot; numpage++ )
292                         current = current->next;
293                     current = page_top;
294                     x = 3; y = 1; gotoxy( x, y );
295                     highlight_on();
296                     break;
297         case 'V':
298         case 'v':   highlight_off();
299                     savey=y;
300                     get_flist( dirmask, &flist, current );
301                     if ( flist ) {
302                       scroll_flist( flist, height );
303                       free_entries( flist );
304                     }
305                     flist = NULL;
306                     window( 2, 23, 79, 23 );
307                     clrscr();
308                     window( 2, 5, 79, 21 );
309                     gotoxy( x, y );
310                     paint_dir( page_top, height );
311                     x = 3; y = savey; gotoxy( x, y );
312                     highlight_on();
313                     break;
314     }
315   }
316 }
317
```

```
318  /* +-----------------------------------------------------+
319     + Paint a Whole Screen of Directory Entries
320     +-----------------------------------------------------+
321  */
322  text *paint_dir( text *list, int height )
323  {
324    int i;
325
326    clrscr();
327    for ( i=1; i<=height; i++ ) {
328      if ( !list ) break;
329      gotoxy( 3,i );
330      string_out( list->line );
331      if ( !list->next ) break;
332      else list = list->next;
333    }
334    if ( i > height ) return( list->prev );
335    else return( list );
336  }
337
338  /* +----------------------------------------------------+
339     + Get Text File Lines in a Linked List
340     +----------------------------------------------------+
341  */
342  void get_flist( char *dirmask, text **list, text *select )
343  {
344    FILE *infile;
345    int i;
346    char *ch;
347    char work[255];
348    text *hold;
349
350    strcpy( work, dirmask);
351    i = strlen( work ) - 1; /* index last char */
352
353    /* trim off search mask and tack on selected name */
354
355    for ( ; i>0 && work[i]!='\\' && work[i] != ':'; --i ) ;
356    if ( !i ) strncpy( work, select->line, 12 );
357    else {
358      ++i; work[i] = '\0';
359      strncat( work, select->line, 12 );
360    }
361
362    if ( NULL == ( infile = fopen( work, "r" ) ) ) {
363      *list = NULL;
364      return;
365    }
366    x = wherex();
367    y = wherey();
368    window( 2, 23, 79, 23 );
```

Listing 11.8. continues

Listing 11.8. continued

```
369      gotoxy( 1, 1 );
370      printf( "Scrolling file: %s", work );
371      window( 2, 5, 79, 21 );
372      gotoxy( x, y );
373
374      while ( fgets( work, 255, infile ) ) {
375        if ( ch = strchr( work, '\n' ) ) *ch = '\0';
376        if ( !*list ) {
377          *list = (text *)malloc( 2 * sizeof(text *)
378            + strlen( work ) + 2 );
379          (*list)->next = (*list)->prev = NULL;
380        }
381        else {
382          hold = (text *)malloc( 2 * sizeof(text *)
383            + strlen( work ) + 2 );
384          if ( !hold ) goto notext;
385          (*list)->next = hold;
386          hold->prev = *list; hold->next = NULL;
387          *list = hold;
388        }
389        strcpy( (*list)->line, work );
390        (*list)-> flag = ' ';
391      }
392  notext: ;
393      fclose( infile );
394      while ( (*list)->prev ) *list = (*list)->prev;
395  }
396
397  /* +---------------------------------------------------------+
398     + Scroll Text Lines in a Linked List
399     +---------------------------------------------------------+
400  */
401  void scroll_flist( text *list, int height )
402  {
403      char ch = ' ';
404      int i,numpage;
405      text *page_top = NULL;
406      text *page_bot = NULL;
407      text *current = NULL;
408
409      clrscr();
410      page_top = list;   /* Display a page and note bounds */
411      page_bot = paint_flist( list, height );
412      current = page_top;
413      for ( numpage=1; current != page_bot; numpage++ )
414        current = current->next;
415      current = page_top;
416      x = y = 1;
417      gotoxy( x, y );
```

```
418
419     while ( ch != 61 ) {            /* position screen */
420       ch = getch(); if ( !ch ) ch = getch();
421       switch ( ch ) {
422         case 72:  if ( current == page_top ){
423                     if ( current->prev ) {
424                       current = current->prev;
425                       page_top = page_top->prev;
426                       if ( numpage == height )
427                         page_bot = page_bot->prev;
428                       else numpage++;
429                       scroll_down();
430                       x = 1; gotoxy( x, y );
431                       string_out( current->line );
432                     }
433                   }
434                   else {
435                     current = current->prev;
436                     y--; gotoxy( x, y );
437                   }
438                   break;
439         case 80:  if ( current == page_bot ){
440                     if ( current->next ) {
441                       current = current->next;
442                       page_top = page_top->next;
443                       page_bot = page_bot->next;
444                       scroll_up();
445                       x = 1; gotoxy( x, y );
446                       string_out( current->line );
447                       x = 1; gotoxy( x, y );
448                     }
449                   }
450                   else {
451                     current = current->next;
452                     y++; gotoxy( x, y );
453                   }
454                   break;
455         case 73:                          /* page up */
456                   for ( i=0; i<height && page_top->prev; i++ )
457                     page_top = page_top->prev;
458                   page_bot = paint_flist( page_top, height );
459                   current = page_top;
460               for ( numpage=1; current!=page_bot; numpage++ )
461                     current = current->next;
462                   current = page_top;
463                   x = 1; y = 1; gotoxy( x, y );
464                   break;
465         case 81:  if ( !page_bot->next ) break;
466                   page_top = page_bot->next;
467                   page_bot = paint_flist( page_top, height );
468                   current = page_top;
```

Listing 11.8. continues

Listing 11.8. *continued*

```
469                      for ( numpage=1; current!=page_bot; numpage++ )
470                          current = current->next;
471                      current = page_top;
472                      x = 1; y = 1; gotoxy( x, y );
473                      break;
474          }
475      }
476  }
477
478  /* +---------------------------------------------------------+
479        + Paint a Whole Screen of Text Lines
480        +---------------------------------------------------------+
481  */
482  text *paint_flist( text *list, int height )
483  {
484    int i;
485
486    clrscr();
487    for ( i=1; i<=height; i++ ) {
488      if ( !list ) break;
489      gotoxy( 1,i );
490      string_out( list->line );
491      if ( !list->next ) break;
492      else list = list->next;
493    }
494    if ( i > height ) return( list->prev );
495    else return( list );
496  }
497
498  /* +---------------------------------------------------------+
499        + Scroll the Display Screen One Line Up
500        +---------------------------------------------------------+
501  */
502  void scroll_up( void )
503  {
504    reg.x.ax = 0x0601;                    /* Scroll up 1 line */
505    reg.h.bh = screen.attribute;       /* Use attribute */
506    reg.h.ch = screen.wintop - 1;       /* Area to use */
507    reg.h.cl = screen.winleft - 1;
508    reg.h.dh = screen.winbottom - 1;
509    reg.h.dl = screen.winright - 1;
510    int86( 0x10, &reg, &reg );
511  }
512
513  /* +---------------------------------------------------------+
514        + Scroll the Display Screen One Line down
515        +---------------------------------------------------------+
516  */
517  void scroll_down( void )
```

```
518  {
519    reg.x.ax = 0x0701;              /* Scroll down 1 line */
520    reg.h.bh = screen.attribute;       /* Use attribute */
521    reg.h.ch = screen.wintop - 1;       /* Area to use */
522    reg.h.cl = screen.winleft - 1;
523    reg.h.dh = screen.winbottom - 1;
524    reg.h.dl = screen.winright - 1;
525    int86( 0x10, &reg, &reg );
526  }
527
528  /* +---------------------------------------------------+
529     + Display a Character on the Screen
530     +---------------------------------------------------+
531  */
532  void ch_out( unsigned char data )
533  {
534    /* Do it all within current window boundaries */
535
536    *(vram + ( screen.winleft + x++ - 2 ) * 2
537      + ( screen.wintop + y - 2 ) * 160 ) = data;
538    if ( x > screen.winright ) { x = screen.winleft; ++y; }
539    if ( y > screen.winbottom ) {
540      scroll_up();
541      y = screen.winbottom;
542    }
543  }
544
545  /* +---------------------------------------------------+
546     + Write a String to the Screen
547     +---------------------------------------------------+
548  */
549  void string_out( char *string )
550  {
551    x = wherex();
552    y = wherey();
553    while ( *string ) {
554      if ( *string == '\t' ) {
555        do ; while ( ++x % 8 != 1 );
556        string++;
557        continue;
558      }
559      *(vram + ( screen.winleft + x++ - 2 ) * 2
560        + ( screen.wintop + y - 2 ) * 160 ) = *string++;
561      if ( x > screen.winright - screen.winleft + 1 ) break;
562    }
563    gotoxy( x, y );
564  }
565
566  /* +---------------------------------------------------+
567     + Overlay One String With Another
568     +---------------------------------------------------+
```

Listing 11.8. continues

Listing 11.8. continued

```
569    */
570    void overlay( char *string )
571    {
572      x = wherex();
573      y = wherey();
574      while ( *string ) {
575        if ( *string != ' ' ) *(vram + ( screen.winleft + x - 2 )
576           * 2 + ( screen.wintop + y - 2 ) * 160 ) = *string;
577        if ( *string != ' ' ) *(vram + ( screen.winleft + x - 2 )
578           * 2 + ( screen.wintop + y - 2 ) * 160  + 1 )
579           = screen.attribute;
580        x++; string++;
581        if ( x > screen.winright - screen.winleft + 1 ) break;
582      }
583      gotoxy( x, y );
584    }
585
586    /* +---------------------------------------------------------+
587       + Draw Box Outlines on the Screen
588       +---------------------------------------------------------+
589    */
590    void draw_boxes( void )
591    {
592      int i, j;
593
594      x = y = 1; ch_out( 213 );                /* Top line */
595      for ( i=2; i<80; i++ ) ch_out( 205 );
596      ch_out( 184 );
597
598      for ( j=2; j<24; j++ ) {               /* Lines 2 - 23 */
599        x = 1; y = j; ch_out( 179 );
600        x = 80; y = j; ch_out( 179 );
601      }
602
603      x = 1; y = 4; ch_out( 195 );     /* First crossbar */
604      for ( i=2; i<80; i++ ) ch_out( 196 );
605      ch_out( 180 );
606
607      x = 1; y = 22; ch_out( 195 );   /* Second crossbar */
608      for ( i=2; i<80; i++ ) ch_out( 196 );
609      ch_out( 180 );
610
611      x = 1; y = 24; ch_out( 192 );   /* Bottom crossbar */
612      for ( i=2; i<80; i++ ) ch_out( 196 );
613      ch_out( 217 );
614
615      window( 1, 25, 80, 25 );
```

```
616    textbackground( LIGHTGRAY );
617    textcolor( BLACK );
618    clrscr();
619    gotoxy( 2, 1 );
620    gettextinfo( &screen );
621    string_out( "\x18\x19 PgUp PgDn    Quit    View" );
622
623    textbackground( LIGHTGRAY );
624    textcolor( RED );
625    gotoxy( 2, 1 );
626    gettextinfo( &screen );
627    overlay( "                F3-      V-      " );
628
629    window( 1, 1, 80, 25 );
630    textbackground( BLUE );
631    textcolor( LIGHTGRAY );
632    gettextinfo( &screen );
633  }
634
635  /* +---------------------------------------------------+
636     + Turn on Highlight for Current Line
637     +---------------------------------------------------+
638  */
639  void highlight_on( void )
640  {
641    int p;
642
643    y = wherey();
644    for ( p=3; p<16; p++ ) {
645    *(vram + ( screen.winleft + p - 2 ) * 2
646      + ( screen.wintop + y - 2 ) * 160  + 1 )
647        = ( LIGHTGRAY << 4 ) + BLACK;
648    }
649  }
650
651  /* +---------------------------------------------------+
652     + Turn Off Highlight for Current Line
653     +---------------------------------------------------+
654  */
655  void highlight_off( void )
656  {
657    int p;
658
659    y = wherey();
660    for ( p=3; p<16; p++ ) {
661    *(vram + ( screen.winleft + p - 2 ) * 2
662      + ( screen.wintop + y - 2 ) * 160  + 1 )
663        = screen.attribute;
664    }
665  }
```

Macros defined through #define take up symbol-table space at compile time, whereas enumerated variables take up symbol-table space at compile time *and* reserve an integer object in the object code. The notational convenience is well worth the extra couple of bytes, however.

The basic structure for holding both the directory-entry information and lines from a text file is declared in lines 23–29 of listing 11.8. This typedef for the text structure describes the layout for an entry in a *doubly-linked list*.

The items in a linked list are allocated separately. Each item—typically a structure—contains a pointer (or pointers) that connect it to other items in the list. A *singly-linked list* item has only one pointer connecting it to the following item in the list. This is called *forward chaining* and is illustrated in Figure 11.5.

Fig. 11.5. *Forward chaining in a single-linked list.*

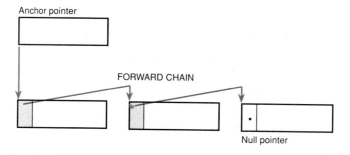

Doubly-linked list items have two pointers. One pointer forward chains the items, and the other *backward chains* them. Backward chaining connects an item to the previous item in the list. This is illustrated in Figure 11.6.

Note that, for forward chaining, the *last* forward chaining pointer in the list is null—there are no more items to point to. The *first* backward chaining pointer is null—there are no items before the beginning of the list.

There are two self-referential pointers within the structure declaration for the linked list in program listing 11.8: prev and next. The meaning of these pointers is obvious, because they are used in the same way as the pointer in a singly linked list. The difference is that prev contains NULL in the first entry in the list, whereas next contains NULL in the last entry in the list.

Fig. 11.6. *Forward and backward chaining in a doubly-linked list.*

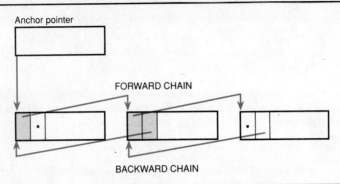

The anchor pointers for the directory-list entries and the text-file list entries appear in lines 30 and 31, respectively. They are initialized to NULL. This is important, because there is no other way to determine whether there actually is a list yet.

The get_entries() function reads the disk directory and formats the entries into suitable form for the linked list. Because this function contains all the linked-list technology we want to demonstrate, only this function is explained in detail. The function prototype for get_entries() appears in line 33; the function definition, in lines 90–191.

First, look at the formal parameter list in line 90. The first argument to get_entries() is a string that contains the *directory mask*. This string is just a file specification with optional path information and wildcard characters. There is nothing surprising about this argument.

The second argument is a little different. The formal parameter text **list is a *pointer to the anchor pointer*. The pointer to a pointer is used so that the original anchor can be updated when the linked list is built.

Most of the lines of code down to line 147 deal with accessing the DOS disk directory and formatting the contents of a directory entry into a displayable string that can be loaded into the linked list. Because this is not a DOS tutorial, we leave those details alone. Suffice it to say that the results are placed in the line member of the structure.

But how is the anchor pointer used to access member objects? This can be seen most clearly in lines 148–153, where the first entry in the list is built.

In `get_entries()` the solution is to assign the pointer value to a simple pointer to `struct`, so that double-dereferencing is not necessary, and then assigning it back again to initialize the anchor, as follows:

```
base = *list;
...
*list = base; /* this initializes the anchor pointer */
```

A different solution is used in `get_flist()`, which reads the selected text file and builds a linked list for it. In this function, the multiple indirection must be considered explicitly. In line 379, for example you see the following:

```
(*list)->next = (*list)->prev = NULL;
```

In this case, the parentheses are required to enclose the dereferenced pointer `list`, because the structure pointer operator `->` has higher precedence than the indirection operator `*`.

Returning to `get_entries()`, dereferencing the pointers is taken care of, but chaining the entries can get a little tricky. The compilation appears because we chose to insert the entries in the list in *alpha order*, rather than just tacking them onto the end of the list. This is one of the powerful features of doubly linked lists. It costs a lot less code to insert the entries in order in the first place, than to sort them in an array, for example.

The first step in inserting an entry in an ordered list is to run the list to the point at which the entry is inserted. In lines 160–162, the list is "run" until either the current pointer (`base`, in this function) is pointing to the entry *before which* the new entry is inserted, or until it points to the last entry in the list. Space for the new entry is allocated dynamically in lines 163–165; the `goto` jumps out of the loop if the allocation fails. `hold`, another temporary pointer to `struct`, is used to point to the newly allocated entry's memory until it can be inserted in the list.

Three distinct possibilities exist for inserting the new entry. It may have to be prepended to the beginning of the list, or inserted between two existing entries, or appended to the end of the list, depending on the way the new `line` string compares to the one in `base->line`.

If the new string (held in the temporary string `work`) is greater than the member string in the current entry pointed to by `base` (detected by the `if` statement in lines 166–167), the new entry must be appended to the list. This is the simplest operation, because it requires the least pointer manipulation. Just three lines of code are required (lines 168–170), as follows:

```
base->next = hold;              /* Append the entry */
hold->prev = base; hold->next = NULL;
base = hold;
```

Because `base` was pointing to the end of the list, its `next` pointer is made to point to the new entry (located by `hold`). Then the new entry's `prev` pointer is made to point to the old end-of-list entry, and its `next` pointer is assigned a value of `NULL` (no more entries).

Next, part of the logic for inserting a new entry between two existing entries is the same as that for prepending it to the beginning of the list. The first part of the common code is seen in lines 173–176. Because three pointers to `struct` are involved in this process, another temporary pointer, `temp`, is introduced. It holds the address of the current entry (`base->`) while all the pointers are chained together.

Line 178 detects the condition in which the new entry is actually to be the new first entry (prepending is required). Notice that if the new entry is to become the first entry, the original anchor pointer, located by `*list`, must be updated to reflect this. This is the only difference between prepending and true insertion.

Line 179 goes back to the instance in which the entry is inserted, and finishes the chaining process by making the original preceding entry point to the new one. Finally, the current pointer `base` is made to point to the new entry (line 180), and the new entry members are initialized (lines 183–184).

Clearly, setting up doubly linked lists takes some time and trouble. There is one outstanding reason you should accept this price: a doubly linked list is an extremely powerful and flexible data structure.

Using Enumeration Constants

Earlier in the chapter, you saw the `#define` directive being used to set up manifest constants for deciding variable type, as follows:

```
#define CHAR 0
#define INT 1
#define DOUBLE 2
```

This is perfectly acceptable, but a cleaner way to do this is *enumeration*. An enumeration is just a list of *named* integer values. Enumerations provide a handy way to associate many constants to names, as an alternative to `#define`. You could write the following line, for example:

```
enum { CHAR, INT, DOUBLE };
```

Now the names `CHAR`, `INT`, and `DOUBLE` are *enumeration constants*, not manifest constants. They *are* constants, however, not variables, and can be used anywhere constants can be used. Enumeration constants are integral constant values; when specified as in the preceding line of code, they assign values, beginning with 0 and proceeding sequentially.

The fact that the names are constants would have made no difference to the `switch` statement that used them, however. You can still write the following:

```
switch (...) {
  case CHAR: ...; break;
}
```

Enumerations support tags as structures do. The tag goes in the same relative position, as in the following example:

```
enum list { CHAR, INT, DOUBLE };
```

where list is the tag name. Why would you want to use tags with enumerated lists? Because you can define enumerated variables, as in this example:

```
enum list { CHAR, INT, DOUBLE };
enum list which;
```

It is important that you understand that `CHAR`, `INT`, and `DOUBLE` *are still constants*—the variable is `which`, and it has type `int`. The purpose of writing an enumerated variable definition is to define a *discrete set of values that the variable can take on*. The variable `which`, for example, can have values of 0, 1, and 2.

This doesn't buy you a whole lot, as is. But you can control the value of the constant names, as follows:

```
enum list { room1 = 233, room2, room3 = 277 };
enum list where;
```

Now the `where` variable can take on the values corresponding to `room1`, `room2`, and `room3`, which are 233, 234, and 277. Notice that if the value of one name is assigned in the declaration, and the next is not, the value of the next follows sequentially.

Enumerations take a little effort to set up, but can yield unexpected utility. If you are writing a school class-assignment program, for example, you can use enumerations to limit the number of places you must make changes when the room numbers change, as in the following example:

```
enum list { room1 = 233, room2, room3 = 277 };
enum list where;
...
if ( where == room1 ) { ... }
```

Now the only place you have to change the code is in the first enumerated list. The remainder of the logic can be left safely alone, without fear of missing something.

Summary

This chapter has taught you some important new techniques for controlling and defining data objects. You have learned the following:

❏ *Structures and unions provide a way to declare complex objects composed of more than one basic type, or even combinations of other complex types.* Structures and unions, together with arrays, are also called *aggregates*.

❏ *Type definitions allow you to define synonyms for other types.* This is especially useful for writing compact code when you deal with complex types.

❏ *Memory-management functions let you determine where and how memory-resident data is handled.* They also provide a way to keep relatively large amounts of data in memory.

❏ *Linked lists are a particularly powerful technology with great flexibility for organizing large numbers of objects.* You will continue to find many applications for linked lists.

❏ *Enumerations give you a handy way to control a number of constant values, and to constrain the values that an enumerated variable may take on.* They also help you minimize the amount of change to your source code when values change.

At this point, you have mastered all the basic syntax and techniques of standard C. The final chapter in Part I deals with portability and conversion issues, without introducing any new techniques or rules. That should give you a breather before you tackle Part III, and C++ object-oriented programming! (Part II is strictly reference material for the library functions. You don't need to read that straight through.)

CHAPTER 12

Portability and Conversion Issues

C is a very popular language, one that is used on a wide variety of computer hardware. Most recently, the latest and greatest in RISC (Reduced Instruction Set Computer) machines has seen rapid and widespread growth because the UNIX operating system platform provides easy implementation and fast times to production. And UNIX is written mostly in C.

The very reason for any language standard—whether the ANSI C standard or another—is precisely to support the process of "porting" software to the different hardware and operating system platforms on which it runs. There lies the rub, however. A standard can incorporate only those aspects of the software—C compilers, in this case—that are fairly certain to be *common to all machines and environments*. A great deal about any *particular* machine and system is unique to them. Most notable are the I/O systems, including display technology.

This is why we have usually refused to limit sample code in this book only to ANSI standard features. Such code would be largely useless. This is true even though there are many places in which the ANSI committee required only that a certain functionality be present, leaving the exact implementation to the various vendors.

Thus the portability of C programs, and the conversion of those aspects that can never be portable, is a topic of considerable interest to C programmers. Even if you are not a professional programmer, you probably will be faced sooner or later with the prospect of upgrading your personal system—perhaps by changing brands. What will happen to your established base of C source code? Will you still be able to use it?

It must be said that the ANSI C committee has made every effort to be fair about this issue. Its members recognized, and spoke out about, these very issues. This chapter, in fact, is largely a summary of material published in the proposed standard and in the rationale document.

Keeping the Spirit of C

By the time the ANSI C advisory committee convened, C was already an established language, with *de facto* standards governing C programming practices. Most compiler vendors adhered to those standards; there was a remarkable continuity and portability among different products in an otherwise ungoverned industry.

The ANSI C rationale document recognized that those *de facto* standards already existed. The ANSI committee went further and set for themselves the task of never violating these *de facto* standards unless absolutely necessary. They termed the body of standards and practice the *spirit of C*.

The Programmer Is King

The foremost principle of the spirit of C is that *the programmer is king*. This is only right: a compiler is not an end unto itself; it is a working tool in the hands of programmers. If programmers cannot get the job done using a particular tool, they will lay it down and get another, more appropriate, tool. Certainly, the ANSI committee's purpose was not to cause a mass abandonment of the C language.

The basic attitude is to "trust the programmer." If the programmer is using sophisticated extensions to the language, it is to be presumed that he knows what he is doing. It is further to be presumed that he has enough sense to isolate instances of nonstandard code so that porting to another platform requires a minimum of conversion of environment-dependent code.

Keep It Simple

The rule here is "keep the language small and simple." This is in keeping with the original philosophy expressed by Kernighan and Ritchie. A language that is small and simple is likely to perform well under a variety of conditions, as well as being easier to port to other systems.

Make It Unique

"Make it unique" is another way of saying "provide only one way to do an operation." Endless proliferation of variant techniques is a good way to destroy compatibility, because variations tend to "run away," out of control. Obviously, a language that fails to control methods for accomplishing a task is neither predictable nor portable.

Performance Is the Rule

One of the most important aspects of the spirit of C is summed up as "make it fast, even if it is not guaranteed to be portable." Speed of execution is important, but the emphasis here is not to throw portability to the winds.

What the ANSI C committee had in mind was that requiring a particular capability is not at all the same as requiring a specific method of implementation. There are many places in the standard where the manner of accomplishing a task is considered *implementation-defined*.

This leaves the vendor free to implement functionality in a way that takes advantage of the strengths of the machine and system hosting the compiler, while (hopefully) avoiding their weaknesses.

A Treaty between Vendor and Programmer

The ANSI committee sees any standard as being a treaty between the implementor and the programmer. A standard gives both parties an understanding of what must be provided by an implementation, and what can be expected and depended upon to exist.

A Meeting of the Minds

The use of *minimum maxima* in setting numerical limitations is a case in point. These limitations are lower boundaries placed on the maximum values supported by the different object types. That is, the limitations express the fact that a given type must be able to support *at least* a stated maximum value; an implementor is free to provide support for greater limits.

When It Backfires

The understanding cuts both ways, however. Whenever a programmer takes advantage of the more generous limits, it must be understood that that the program is not guaranteed to work properly with another compiler.

The same can be said for the use of extensions to the language. An implementation is free to go beyond the minimum requirements for the language, adding extra functionality, and still be considered conforming. The catch is that no other implementation is required to support any particular extensions. You may have to recode such features from the ground up when running with another compiler. A summary of common extensions appears at the end of this chapter.

Unspecified Behavior

Aside from well-defined behavior, the ANSI standard speaks of three kinds of compiler behavior that can have a serious impact on portability. These are *unspecified*, *undefined*, and *implementation-defined behavior*. Unspecified behavior is discussed first.

What It Means

Unspecified behavior means that the ANSI standard requires nothing of an implementation, one way or another. The only defense you have against these potential trouble spots is to be thoroughly familiar with *your* compiler.

What to Look for

The ANSI standard does not specify the following:

The manner and timing of static initialization

Output display or printer behavior when a printable character is written in the final position of a line. That is, no specification is made as to whether automatic line-wrap occurs.

Output display or printer behavior when a backspace character is written in the first character of a line

Output display or printer behavior when a horizontal tab character is written past the last defined tab position

Output display or printer behavior when a vertical tab character is written past the last defined vertical tab position

The internal format of floating-point objects

The order of expression evaluation. Evaluation always occurs *as if* algebraic associative rules are followed, but this does not necessarily mean that internal events exactly follow that order.

The order in which side effects take place. The only guarantee is that side effects will be complete at the next sequence point.

The order in which the function designator and the arguments in a function call are evaluated. Remember that a sequence point occurs only when all evaluation is complete and the function actually entered.

The alignment of the addressable storage unit used to contain a bit-field. Bit-fields may or may not overlap word boundaries, depending on the machine and particular compiler.

The layout of storage for function parameters. The reason for this is that some machines are physically stack-oriented, and some are not. There is no guarantee as to what the parameter-passing internal mechanism will be.

The order in which the preprocessing "stringizing" operator # and the "token pasting" operator ## are evaluated

Whether `errno` is a macro or an external identifier

Whether `setjmp()` is a function-like macro or an external identifier

Whether `va_end` is a macro or an external identifier

What the value of the file position indicator is after a successful call to the `ungetc()` function for a text file, until such time as all pushed-back characters are either read or discarded

The details of the value stored by a call to `fgetpos()`. This may be an aggregate structure, or it might simply be a `long`.

The details and accuracy of the value stored by a call to the `ftell()` function, when used in *text mode*

The order and contiguity of storage allocated by the `calloc()`, `malloc()`, and `realloc()` functions. This can be critical if you must have contiguous storage for an application.

Which of two elements that compare equally will be returned by a call to `bsearch()`

The relative order of two elements that compare equally when `qsort()` is used to sort an array. Be careful here—this can be the deathblow to *many* business-oriented applications that require the preservation of the original order of appearance of otherwise equal elements. Consider this a *severe* shortcoming of the standard implementation of `qsort()`.

The internal structure of the calendar time returned by the `time()` function

Undefined Behavior

If your program encounters a situation in which the behavior of the program will be undefined, you almost always have a serious problem. Debugging is in order.

What It Means

Basically, *undefined behavior* gives an implementation the elbowroom to *not catch an error condition*. If your program (meaning you, the programmer) allows such a condition to develop, anything at all may happen next—all the way from nothing at all to a severe system crash.

What to Look for

Program behavior in the following circumstances is undefined:

When a nonempty program source file does *not* end in a newline character, when it *does* end in a newline character immediately preceded by a backslash (continuation) character, or when it ends with a *partial* preprocessing token or comment

When a character not in the source character set is encountered during compilation, *except* when it appears in a preprocessing token that is never converted to a token, character constant, string literal, or comment

When a comment, string literal, character constant, or header name contains an invalid multibyte character, or does not begin and end in the "initial shift state"

When an unmatched ' or " is encountered on a logical source line during tokenization (preprocessing)

When the same identifier name is used more than once as a label (for `goto`s) in the same function

When an identifier is used that is not visible in the current scope

When identifiers that are supposed to denote the same object differ beyond the minimal number of significant characters (that is, when there is a difference in the name in, say, the 33rd position)

When an identifier has both internal and external linkage in the same translation unit (source file)

When an identifier with external linkage is used, but there is more than one declaration for the object with the `extern` specifier

When a pointer is used that was made to point to an object with `auto` duration, and the function owning the object is now out of scope (has returned). Usually this means a crash.

When a redeclaration of an object or function fails to specify compatible types (for the object, returned value, or parameters)

When an unspecified escape sequence appears in a character constant or string literal. An unspecified escape sequence is one that is not explicitly supported by the standard

When an attempt is made to modify a string literal in any form

When a character string literal is adjacent to a wide string literal. Adjacent literals are of the form:

```
L"This is a""" string"
```

where the *L* preceding the first string literal denotes a wide character string literal. Normally, the compiler concatenates adjacent strings, building one result string, but normal and wide character strings don't mix.

When unneeded punctuation is encountered within the `<name>` or `"name"` specification for a header file

When an arithmetic conversion produces a result that cannot be contained in the space provided

When an lvalue with an incomplete type is used in a context that requires the value of the designated object

When the value of a `void` expression is used, or when an implicit conversion (except to `void`) is applied to a void expression

When an object is modified more than once between two sequence points. It is valid to *access* an object more than once between sequence points, but only once to modify it; other access must be "read-only."

When an arithmetic operation is either invalid (for example, divide by zero), or the results cannot be stored in the space provided (for example, when there is an under- or overflow condition)

When an object has its stored value accessed by an lvalue with an incompatible type

When an argument to a function is a void expression

When a function without a full function prototype (that is, an old-style declaration) is called with the wrong number of arguments

When a function having a prototype is called with incompatible parameters—that is, when the function is not defined with a compatible type

When a function accepting a variable number of parameters is called without a prototype that ends with an ellipsis (the . . . characters)

When an invalid array reference occurs, a null pointer is dereferenced, or reference is made to a local variable with `auto` duration that resides in a block that has gone out of scope

When a pointer to a function returning a type is cast to a pointer to a function returning another (incompatible) type, and is used to call the function

When a pointer to an object is converted to a pointer to function, or vice versa

When a pointer is cast to something other than an integral type or another pointer

When addition or subtraction is performed on a pointer that does *not* point to an array element

When two pointers that do not reference the same array aggregate are subtracted

When a bit-wise shift count is negative or greater than or equal to the number of bits in the object (or expression type). This tactic frequently is used to clear bits from an object, even though it is "nonstandard."

When pointers that do not point to the same aggregate are compared

When an object is assigned to an overlapping object. For example, you could use pointer casts to access individual bytes in an integer, but modifying the bytes may not have the expected effect.

When an identifier is declared for an object with no linkage and an incomplete type. Declarations with incomplete types generally are used to refer to objects that are defined completely elsewhere; an object with no linkage cannot be defined elsewhere.

When a function is declared within a block without the `extern` storage-class specifier

When a bit-field is declared with a type that is not `int`, `signed int`, or `unsigned int`. (See the common extensions at the end of this chapter.)

When an attempt is made to modify a `const` object with an lvalue that is *not* qualified as `const`

When an attempt is made to modify a `volatile` object with an lvalue that is *not* qualified as `volatile`

When an uninitialized object with `auto` duration is used

When an aggregate `auto` object has an initializer that is not brace-enclosed, or an aggregate `static` object is initialized with something other than another aggregate of the same type or a brace-enclosed initializer

When an attempt is made to use the return value of a `void` function

When a function accepting a variable number of arguments has a formal parameter list that does not end with the . . . ellipsis

When an identifier for an object with internal linkage and incomplete type is declared with a tentative definition

When the preprocessing token `defined` is generated during the expansion of an `#if` or `#elif` directive

When an `#include` directive is generated by macro expansion, and its form is incorrect

When a macro argument consists of no preprocessing tokens

When the list of macro arguments contains preprocessing tokens that ordinarily would be directives themselves

When the result of the token paste preprocessing operator `##` is not a valid preprocessing token

When a macro expansion results in a `#line` directive that does not match one of the two well-defined forms

When you attempt to `#define` or `#undef` one of the following predefined directives:

```
defined
    __LINE__
    __FILE__
    __DATE__
    __TIME__
    __STDC__
```

When an attempt is made to copy an object to an overlapping object by some means other than the `memmove()` library function (which is designed to handle overlapped argument objects)

When a program redefines a reserved external identifier

When a standard header is included within an external definition, or when it is included for the first time *after* reference is made to anything it declares, or when it is included while a current macro definition has the same name as a keyword

When a macro definition of `errno` is suppressed to obtain access to an actual object

When the `offsetof` macro refers to a structure member that is a bit-field. (Bit-fields cannot be addressed separately by either pointer or offset, because they may not be on a byte boundary.)

When an argument to a library function has an invalid value, except in those cases where the behavior is explicitly stated

When a library function that accepts a variable number of arguments is not declared

When the macro definition of `assert` is suppressed to obtain access to an actual object

When the argument to one of the character-handling functions is outside the domain of characters it can handle

When a macro definition of `setjmp()` is suppressed to gain access to an actual function

When you invoke `setjmp()` and then fail to test the returned value by a selection, iteration, or comparison statement

When, between calls to `setjmp()` and `longjmp()`, an `auto` object that has *not* been declared as `volatile` is modified, and then is accessed to fetch its value

When the `longjmp()` function is invoked from a *nested* signal-handling function

When a truly asynchronous signal occurs—that is, it is not the result of calling `abort()` or `raise()`—and

> the signal handler calls any library function *other than* `signal()`

> the signal handler refers to any object that is *not* of static duration and declared to have type `volatile sig_atomic_t`

When a truly asynchronous signal occurs, and the signal handler calls `signal()`, only to receive the return value `SIG_ERR`, and then `errno` is referred to

When the `va_arg` macro is invoked with the same `ap` pointer that was passed to and used by a lower-level function. That is, the lower-level function has altered `ap` so that the current function must call `va_end` to resynchronize the pointer and variable argument list. (See Chapter 15 for a list of this and other caveats on variable argument processing.)

When a macro definition of `va_start`, `va_arg`, `va_end`, or any combination of them is suppressed to gain access to an actual function. (There may *be no* such function.)

When the `parmN` parameter of the `va_start` is declared with `register` storage class, array or function type, or any type that is not compatible with the default argument promotions

When all variable arguments have been exhausted and you invoke `va_arg` again

When the type of the next actual variable argument disagrees with that requested by `va_arg`

When the `va_end` macro is invoked *before* `va_start`

When a function that accepts variable arguments and has initialized the argument list with `va_start` returns without invoking `va_end`. In many implementations this would have no effect at all, *but it could*.

When you call `fflush()` against an input stream, or against an update stream whose last operation was input. The latter is a little contradictory, because other parts of the literature (both the ANSI document and others) indicate that you should flush an update stream whenever you switch from write to read, *or* from read to write. In any event, when the last operation on an update stream was a read operation, you most likely will call a seek or positioning function before writing again, which also flushes the buffer.

When you switch read/write access on an update stream without properly flushing the buffer. Most likely, you will lose data somehow.

When the format string of `fprintf()` or `fscanf()` type functions does not match the actual argument list

When an invalid conversion specification is encountered in the format string of `fprintf()` or `fscanf()` functions

When the `%%` conversion occurs in the format string of `fprintf()` or `fscanf()` and there are characters between the two percent signs. This is a real syntax error, but presumably, some compiler has permitted it in the past.

When the format string for `fprintf()` contains a conversion specification with an `h` or `l` (ell) character that is not part of the following conversions: `d, i, n, o, u, x, X`. Also, the `L` character must be a part of the following conversions: `e, E, f, g, G`. The same is true for `fscanf()`, except that `fscanf()` does not have any of the uppercase conversion characters.

When the format string for `fprintf()` contains a `#` flag for a conversion other than `o, x, X, e, E, g, G`

When the format string for `fprintf()` contains the 0 (zero-fill) flag for a conversion other than: `d, i, o, u, x, X, e, E, f, g, G`

When an aggregate object, or a pointer to one, is an argument to `fprintf()`, unless the conversion specifies `%s` (string) or `%p` (pointer to `void`)

When a single conversion performed by `fprintf()` results in more than 509 characters of output

When a pointer value produced by the `fprintf()` function's `%p` conversion *in a previous program execution* is used as input to the `fscanf()` function's `%p` conversion. Note that this works in the *same* program execution, because both program and data are still in the same locations.

When the receiving internal object of an `fscanf()` conversion has the wrong type, or cannot hold the resulting value

When the results of converting a string to internal format by `atoi()`, `atol()`, or `atof()` cannot be properly represented (for example, if the value is too large)

When you refer via pointer to dynamically allocated memory that already has been freed by `free()`

When you try to `free()` dynamically allocated memory with the wrong address, or when the memory has been freed already

When a program executes more than one `exit()` function. You might trip over this one if you have defined several `atexit()` routines.

When the result of `abs()`, `div()`, `labs()`, or `ldiv()` cannot be represented properly

When the shift states for the `mblen()`, `mbtowc()`, and `wctomb()` functions are not reset explicitly to the initial shift state when the `LC_CTYPE` category of the current locale is changed

When the output array targeted by a copying or concatenation function is too small

When the `strftime()` contains an invalid conversion specification

Implementation-defined Behavior

In keeping with the spirit of C—where performance is important even if portability suffers—there are several areas where the standard indicates that behavior is implementation-defined.

What It Means

Implementation-defined behavior gives the implementor elbowroom—room to implement a given task in such a way that the full native powers of the hardware and software platform can be brought to bear. However, the standard requires that the *choice of implementation be explained to the user*.

What to Look for

Compiler implementors are required to document their product's behavior in several specific areas. These statements are taken nearly verbatim from the ANSI-proposed standard for C, because of their importance to you, the programmer. An implementor must state the following items.

Environment

The semantics of the arguments to `main()`

What constitutes an interactive device

Identifiers

The number of initial significant characters beyond 31 for an identifier with internal linkage

The number of initial significant characters beyond 6 for an identifier with external linkage

Whether case distinctions are significant for an identifier with external linkage

Characters

The members of the source and execution character sets, except as explicitly specified in the standard

The shift states used for encoding multibyte characters

The number of bits in a character in the execution character set

The mapping of source-set characters to execution-set characters (in string literals and character constants)

The value of an integer character constant that contains a character or escape sequence not represented in the basic execution character set for a wide character constant

The value of an integer character constant that contains more than one character, or a wide character constant that contains more than one multibyte character

The current locale used to convert multibyte characters into corresponding wide characters (codes) for a wide character constant

Whether a "plain" `char` has the same range of values as `signed char` or `unsigned char`

Integers

The representations and sets of values of the various types of integers

The results of converting an integer to a shorter signed integer, or the result of converting an unsigned integer to a signed integer of equal length, if the value cannot be represented

The results of bit-wise operations on signed integers

The sign of the remainder after integer division

The result of a right shift of a negative-valued signed integer

Floating Point

The representations and sets of values of the different types of floating-point numbers

The direction of truncation when an integral number is converted to a floating-point number that cannot *exactly* represent the original value

The direction of truncation or rounding when a floating-point number is converted to a narrower floating-point number

Arrays and Pointers

The type of integer required to hold the maximum size of an array—that is, the type of the `sizeof` operator, `size_t`

The result of casting a pointer to an integer, and vice versa

The type of integer required to hold the difference between two pointers to members of the same array, `ptrdiff_t`

Registers

The extent to which objects can actually be placed in registers by use of the `register` storage-class specifier

Structures, Unions, Enumerations, and Bit-fields

A member of a union object is accessed using a member of a different type

The padding and alignment of members of structures. This should present no problem unless binary data is written by one implementation to be read by another.

Whether a "plain" `int` bit-field is treated as a `signed int` bit-field or as an `unsigned int` bit-field

The order of allocation of bit-fields within an `int`

Whether a bit-field can straddle a storage-unit boundary

The integer type chosen to represent the values of an enumerated type

Qualifiers

What constitutes an access to an object that has `volatile`-qualified type

Declarators

The maximum number of declarators that may modify an arithmetic, structure, or union type

Statements

The maximum number of `case` values in a `switch` statement

Preprocessing Directives

Whether the value of a single-character character constant in a constant expression that controls conditional inclusion matches the value of the same character constant in the execution character set, and whether such a character constant may have a negative value

The method for locating includable source files

The support of quoted names for source-file inclusion

The mapping of source-file character sequences

The behavior for each recognized `#pragma` directive

The definitions for `__DATE__` and `__TIME__`, respectively, when the date and time of translation are not available

Library Functions

The null-pointer constant to which the macro `NULL` expands

The diagnostic printed by and the termination behavior of the `assert()` function

The sets of characters tested for by the `isalnum()`, `isalpha()`, `iscntrl()`, `islower()`, `isprint()`, and `isupper()` functions

The values returned by the mathematics functions on domain errors

Whether the mathematics functions set the integer expression `errno` to the value of the macro `ERANGE` on underflow range errors

Whether a domain error occurs or zero is returned when the `fmod()` function has a second argument of zero

The set of signals for the `signal()` function

The semantics for each signal recognized by the `signal()` function

The default handling and the handling at program startup for each signal recognized by the `signal()` function

If the equivalent of `signal( sig, SIG_DFL );` is not executed prior to the call of a signal handler, then state the blocking of the signal that *is* performed

Whether the default handling is reset if the `SIGILL` signal is received by a handler specified to the `signal()` function

Whether the last line of a text stream requires a terminating newline character

Whether space characters that are written out to a text stream immediately before a newline character appear when read in

The number of null characters that may be appended to the data written to a binary stream

Whether the file-position indicator of an append-mode stream is positioned initially at the beginning or end of a file

Whether a write on a text stream causes the associate file to be truncated beyond that point

The characteristics of file buffering

Whether a zero-length file actually exists

The rules for composing valid file names

Whether the same file can be open multiple times (concurrently)

The effect of the `remove()` function on an open file

The result of trying to `rename()` a file when the new name already exists

The output for the `%p` conversion of `fprintf()`. (80x86 addresses must account for the segment and offset parts, for example.)

The input for the `%p` conversion of `fscanf()`

The interpretation of the [-] character when it is neither the first nor the last character in the scanlist for the `%{` conversion of `fscanf()`

The value assigned to `errno` when `fgetpos()` or `ftell()` is unsuccessful

The messages generated by the `perror()` function

The behavior of `calloc()`, `malloc()`, and `realloc()` when the requested allocation size is zero

The behavior of the `abort()` function with respect to open and temporary files. Many implementations make no attempt to clean these up, which can cause problems later.

The status returned by the `exit()` function if the value of the argument is not zero, `EXIT_SUCCESS`, or `EXIT_FAILURE`

The set of environment names and the method for altering the environment list used by the `getenv()` function

The contents of the error message strings returned by the `strerror()` function

The local time zone and daylight saving time

The era for the `clock()` function

Locale-specific Behavior

The following characteristics of a hosted environment are locale-specific (that is, dependent):

The content of the execution character set, in addition to the required members

The direction of printing

The decimal point character

The implementation-defined aspects of character-testing and case-mapping functions

The collating sequence of the execution character set

The formats for time and date information

The subject of common extensions to the language also fits in the category of implementation-defined behavior. We have deferred that discussion until the end of this chapter.

Quiet Changes to K & R C

An area of portability and compatibility that would be dangerous to overlook concerns the vast amount of preexisting C code. There is a vast body of commercial code "out there" that must be supported somehow—presumably with the newer ANSI-conforming compilers.

By now it should be quite clear to you that the original K & R C and ANSI C are substantially compatible, but that the operative word is *substantially*. There are differences between the two standards (K & R compatibility *is* a standard, and a very good one).

How can you cope with the changes from one C platform to the next? What, in particular, may catch you unaware? The ANSI rationale document identifies a number of danger areas, called *quiet changes*, of which you should be aware.

What Is a Quiet Change?

Understanding quiet changes means knowing the difference between syntax and semantics. *Syntax* defines how you write code: the reserved words, punctuation, operators, their grouping, and so forth. *Semantics*, on the other hand, defines what a given syntax *means*.

What does this mean to you? It means that it is entirely possible for the same syntax (manner of writing code) *to be interpreted in two different ways*. This is the danger you face when compiling old code with new compilers. What if a line of code is still syntactically valid, but now means (and hence *does*) something different?

This is the crux of the quiet changes introduced into the C language by the new ANSI standard. They are points of difference between the old and new standards that invisibly cause code to behave differently. This is an insidious problem, and ANSI was aware of its danger. Moreover, the committee acknowledged the problem and made efforts to minimize the number of instances in which this can happen.

There are instances of quiet changes in C semantics, though, however few they may be. You should be aware of them, and be prepared to correct for them when recompiling old code.

Converting K & R C Programs

This section details the quiet changes in C semantics introduced by the ANSI standard for C. Keep in mind that these changes do not comprise *all* the changes. This section deals only with those changes that may be "invisible"—code that still compiles without error but now works differently.

The exact text of the ANSI rationale's documentation of quiet changes is given in italics in each case, followed by explanations in normal text.

Programs with character sequences such as ??! in string constants, character constants, or header names now produce different results. This happens because such sequences duplicate the new *ternary escape sequences* that formerly did not exist.

A program that depends upon internal identifiers matching only in the first (say) eight characters may change to one with distinct objects for each variant spelling of the identifier. ANSI C allows identifiers to have up to 31 case-sensitive characters, as opposed to the older 8-character limit. A name may now vary in the 20th digit for example, and be considered different, where formerly spelling differences this far down the sequence were ignored.

A program relying on file scope rules may be valid under block scope rules but behave differently. This is a particularly subtle change. Many older compilers assigned file scope to identifiers with external linkage, *even if they were declared within a block*. Under the ANSI standard, an object declared within a block is governed within by block scope rules. *However*, if the object had external linkage, but is now gone out of scope (for example, the function has returned), an implementation is not required to diagnose a failure to redeclare the external identifier. In other words, there may be some confusion as to the type of such an object, but there may still be no compiler error message.

Unsuffixed integer constants may have different types. In K&R, unsuffixed decimal constants greater than INT_MAX, and unsuffixed octal or hexadecimal constants greater than UINT_MAX are of type long. That is, previously, an integer constant with value 43777 (greater than INT_MAX) was understood to be type long. Now, it may be interpreted as a normal int, with the accompanying danger that it is truncated before use. If you mean for a constant to be long, or unsigned, use the L or U constant suffix, as in 43777L.

A constant of the form '\078' (an octal escape sequence) is valid, but now has different meaning. It now denotes a character constant whose value is the (implementation-defined) combination of the values '\07' and '8'. In some implementations the old meaning is the character whose code is 078 (70 *octal* + 87) = 100 *(octal)* = 64 *(decimal)*. This is in contrast to hex escape sequences (\x . . .), which extend until the first nonhex character is encountered.

A constant of the form '\a' or '\x' may now have different meaning. The old meaning, if any, was implementation dependent. The alert special character '\a', and hex escape '\x' did not exist in K & R C; thus, a compiler may have used these sequences for other purposes.

It is neither required nor forbidden that identical string literals be represented by a single copy of the string in memory; a program depending on either scheme may behave differently. That is, do not count on the address of a string literal.

Expressions of the form x=-3 change meaning with the loss of the old-style assignment operators. Operators such as =-, =+, and so on were used by very old compilers. Now only the forms -=, +=, and so on are permitted. Thus, the preceding expression would be interpreted to mean that "x is equal to minus three."

A program that depends upon unsigned preserving arithmetic conversions behaves differently, probably without complaint (from the compiler). This is considered to be the most serious semantic change made by the committee to a widespread current practice. This has to do with the new *integral promotion rules*. Formerly, when any shorter unsigned value was widened, the result was always unsigned. This is the *unsigned preserving rule*. Now, when an unsigned char or unsigned short is widened (say in being assigned to a signed int), the ANSI standard requires that the value preserving rules be used. This means that *if the unsigned value permits it*, the result will be signed; otherwise (if the value was too large) the result will be unsigned. This was deemed to be safer for novice programmers, but introduces the possibility that an expression no longer evaluates to the same result (because of the unexpected participation of a signed value).

Expressions with float operands may now be computed at lower precision. The Base Document (K & R) *specified that all floating point operations be done in* double. This change was well-meant (it increases computational speed), but may backfire on you. You may begin a computation with float types, and the result may also fit in a float. However, *intermediate results frequently may require greater precision*, causing loss of precision, and possibly a significant error. If you need to be sure, use double in the first place.

Shifting by a long *count no longer coerces the shifted operand to* long. The second operand of the bitwise shift operators << and >> is a count of the number of bits to be shifted in the indicated direction. Formerly, if this count operand had type long, this implied that the object being shifted should be promoted to long also.

A program that uses #if expressions to determine properties of the execution environment may now get different answers. Some C compilers, called *cross-compilers*, are used in one environment to produce code for another. The ANSI committee felt that requiring that equal precision of floating-point numbers, minimum maxima, and other environment characteristics be provided in both the translation and execution environments imposed too great a burden on some cross-compilers.

The empty declaration `struct x;` *is no longer innocuous*. Such a declaration hides an outer declaration of x, and "opens" an new instance of the object in the current block. That is, the declaration is no longer empty.

Code that relies on a bottom-up parse of aggregate initializers with partially elided braces does not yield the expected initialized object. In Chapter 11, you saw that the initializer for a `struct` that contained other complex objects could specify only the outer curly braces in the initializer. In some instances of older code, only part of the internally contained curly braces would be omitted, because of the way the initializer was parsed. Because the ANSI document has reaffirmed the top-down parse originally described by K & R, such constructions may not work correctly now. Either use all internal braces, or omit them all.

`long` expressions and constants in switch statements are no longer truncated to `int`. The ANSI standard allows the `case` variables to have any integral type; original C required a type of `int`. This may produce some unexpected results when recompiling older code that relied on this truncation.

Functions that depend on `char` *or* `short` *parameter types being widened to* `int`, *or* `float` *to* `double`, *may behave differently*. Formerly, such function arguments were subject to a different set of automatic integral promotions that widened the mentioned types. The result was that you could pass a `char` to a function that actually specified a formal parameter of type `int`. The ANSI standard requires that the received argument be converted *as if* by assignment, but such type rewriting is no longer permitted.

A macro that relies on formal parameter substitution within a string literal produces different results. This process is called *stringizing*, and is important to many programs. The ANSI standard introduced another preprocessing operator to solve this and other token handling problems. This is the `##` or *token paste* operator. In Chapter 8 you saw how to use it to implement the pasting of manifest constants in a string, as in the following example:

```
#define SIZE 10
#define buildmsg(X) "Array size is: " ## #X
```

```
main()
{
    int num[SIZE];   /* Define array with SIZE elements */
    printf( "%s", buildmsg(SIZE) );        /* Report it */
}
```

In this fragment, both the stringizing and token pasting operators are used to form the string. The paste operator not only gets around the limitation, but provides added flexibility.

A program that relies on size-0 allocation requests returning a non-null pointer behaves differently. This is the last of the quiet changes, and the only one that affects a standard library function. Some older compilers would allow a zero-size `calloc()` or `malloc()` request, and return a valid pointer to the "object." An ANSI-conforming compiler does not allow this.

Environmental Considerations

C compilers do their work in many environments, and sometimes even produce object code for environments other than the translation environment. This imposes some limitations on how a compiler can be implemented.

Some limitations, such as numerical (value) limits, were discussed in earlier chapters. Two aspects that have not yet been discussed are translation limits and common but nonstandard functions. The next two sections deal with these.

Translation Limitations

An ANSI-conforming implementation of C must be able to compile a program that contains at least one instance of every one of the following limits:

15 nesting levels of compound statements, iteration control structures, and selection control structures

8 nesting levels of conditional inclusion

12 pointer, array, and function declarators (in any combinations) modifying an arithmetic, structure, union, or incomplete type in a declaration

31 declarators nested by parentheses within a full declarator

32 expressions nested by parentheses within a full expression

31 significant initial characters in an internal identifier or macro name

6 significant initial characters in an external identifier

511 external identifiers in one translation unit (source file)

127 identifiers with block scope that are declared in one block

1,024 macro identifiers simultaneously defined in one translation unit

31 parameters in one function definition

31 arguments in one function call

31 parameters in one macro definition

31 arguments in one macro invocation

509 characters in one logical source line

509 characters in one character-string literal or wide-string literal (after concatenation)

32,767 bytes in an object (only in hosted, not freestanding, environments)

8 nesting levels for #included files

257 case labels for a switch statement (excluding those for any nested switch statements)

127 members in a single structure or union

127 enumeration constants in a single enumeration

15 levels of nested structure or union definitions in a single *struct-declaration-list*

Common Extensions to ANSI Standard C

We have pointed out several times in this book that any *particular* machine or system on which a C compiler runs has its own peculiarities that cannot be accounted for in any standard. These peculiarities are often handled by a vendor's extensions to the language, and it is often impossible to write high-performance code without using them. This is *not contrary* to the intent of the ANSI committee; extensions do not replace requirements— they go beyond them.

Some of the more common extensions are discussed in the proposed standards document, and are covered here. Their inclusion here does *not* mean that your compiler must support them. Nor are they necessarily portable to other implementations.

Environment Arguments

In addition to the `int argc` and `char *argv[]` arguments that `main()` receives from the environment, in a hosted environment `main()` may receive a third argument of the form `char *envp[]`. This is handled much like `argv` pointers, but points to a null-terminated array of pointers to string. Each string provides information about the environment during this execution of the program (or process).

Some compilers set up a similar environment variable using this information. The sample program `sysenv.c` in this book used such a variable.

Specialized Identifiers

Letters, digits, and the underscore character are required for the formation of identifiers in the source character set. Other characters, such as the so-called national characters $, @, and #, may be allowed by some compilers in the formation of names.

Length and Case of Identifiers

Some compilers go beyond the 31 characters required for internal, and 6 characters required for external identifiers, and consider all characters significant, whatever the linkage, including case distinctions.

Scope of Identifiers

A function identifier, or an object declaration containing the `extern` keyword, may have file scope wherever it is written. Minimal conformity to the ANSI standard would permit some such declarations (not definitions, remember) to have only block scope.

Writable String Literals

Some compilers allow modification of string literals. In such a case multiple appearances of otherwise identical literals are distinct objects.

Other Arithmetic Types

An implementation may define additional object types, such as `long long int`, or BCD (binary coded decimal—packed decimal) objects.

Function Pointer Casts

Ordinarily, function and data objects are kept severely separated. Some implementations, however, may allow a cast of an object pointer to a pointer to function. This would have the effect of allowing a program to invoke data as if it were code.

Non-*int Bit*-field Types

Types other than `int`, `signed int`, or `unsigned int` may be declared as bit-fields, with the appropriate widths.

The *fortran* Keyword

The `fortran` specifier may be written in a function declaration to indicate that the function was written in that language.

The *asm* Keyword

Some compilers permit the use of the `asm` keyword for the direct insertion of inline assembler code in a C program. Depending on the compiler, an external assembler program may or may not have to be present.

Multiple External Definitions

A given object may be declared, with or without the explicit use of the `extern` keyword, more than once. This is dangerous in any case: if the declarations disagree, or more than one is initialized, the behavior is "undefined."

Empty Macro Arguments

In several places in this book, we have used macros such as the following:

```
#define COMPILER
...
#if defined( COMPILER )
...
#endif
```

Such a macro definition has an *empty argument list*. Strictly speaking, this is nonstandard, because the whole point of macros is string substitution. This use is so widespread, however, that we do not know of a compiler that fails to support the usage. If a macro *has* arguments, then the macro invocation must supply the correct number of arguments.

Predefined Macro Names

An implementation may provide macros, which describe the translation and execution environments, that do not begin with the underscore character.

Extra Arguments for Signal Handlers

Handlers for a specific type of signal may be called with arguments (in addition to the signal type argument) for handling special conditions.

Additional Stream Types and File Modes

Special applications may require special mappings from file to stream, and extended processing modes.

Defined File-position Indicator

When this extension is implemented, the file-position indicator is decremented by each successful call to the `ungetc()` function for a text stream, unless the position was already zero.

Summary

In this chapter you learned about portability and conversion of C programs from one platform to another. The following topics were covered:

❏ *The spirit of C controls the shape of the ANSI standard for C.* This means several specific things to you, not the least of which is that *performance is important*, and using extensions to the language is both necessary and expected.

❏ *Undefined, unspecified, and implementation-dependent behavior are important aspects of your compiler.* Particularly with regard to implementation-defined behavior, you should take the time and trouble to become intimately familiar with your own compiler.

❏ *Extensions to the language give your program added power and flexibility.* The language standard provides a solid, predictable base for your C programming efforts. The extensions allow you to tailor the application to the machine and operating system on which it runs, and to extract their full power and efficiency—but there is a corresponding decrease in portability.

This is the final chapter in Part I of *Using C*. Nearly every important aspect of using the C programming language has been covered in this part of the book. Part II is a reference section. It contains all the library functions specified in the ANSI C standard, with short examples for most. Part III introduces you to the more timely and advanced, but less standard, subject of object-oriented programming with C++.

Part II

Using the Standard C
Function Library

13

Debugging, Error Handling, and Character Handling

Debugging, error handling, and character handling may be some of the less glamorous aspects of C programming, but they are necessary for a full range of programming tools. The three header files covered in this chapter—assert.h, errno.h, and ctype.h— contain macros and functions not usually given much consideration. Yet one of these, ctype.h, is used in almost every program. The others—assert.h and errno.h—are not used as often, but when necessary are indispensable.

In this, and all the chapters in Part II, each header file is signalled by simply using the #include for that file as the major head for the section. Under each major head, the functions are presented by writing the prototype for the function, or the *call syntax* for the macro. Any parameters, returned values, or defined values are presented with the entry, as appropriate.

#include <assert.h>

```
void assert(int expression);
```

Type: Function-type macro

Returns: None

The assert() macro is a diagnostic tool that evaluates an expression you specify. This expression can contain a variable you want to test, or some combination of variables, constants, and operators. If the expression is *false* (evaluates to 0), `assert()` gives an error message and aborts program execution, as in the following example:

```
int blow_up;
...
blow_up = 0; /* Error condition detected */
assert( blow_up );
```

`assert()` is implemented as a macro, not as a function, although it is invoked like a function. `assert()` tests for the existence of another macro name, `NDEBUG` (meaning *no debug*), which is *not defined* in `assert.h`. You define it, when you want to turn off debugging and thereby nullify the effect of `assert()`. For example,

```
#define NDEBUG
int blow_up = 0;
...
assert( blow_up );
```

causes nothing to happen.

Because `assert()`, if successful, terminates the program (by calling `abort()`), it does not need to return a value. It is therefore of type `void`. Being of type `void` also means that the *assert* macro can be placed anywhere in the program without producing unwanted *side effects*. *Side effects* are simply changes that modify the execution environment (change the value of an object). (Refer to Chapters 3 and 5 for discussions of side effects.)

If the expression in the following line:

```
assert( expression );
```

evaluates to zero, an error message is sent to `stderr` and program execution is halted. The error message includes the expression, the name of the file, and the line number where the assert macro failed. The file name and line number come from the predefined macros __`FILE`__ and __`LINE`__ (refer to Chapter 4).

#*include* <*errno.h*>

`errno.h` contains the declarations for a series of macros that define and document run-time errors.

```
int errno;
```

Type: Macro

Returns: N/A

Some of the library functions post an error code in `errno` when unable to complete processing correctly. `errno` is usually an object of type `int`, but it may also be a function that returns a pointer to an object of type `int`. In either case, the ANSI standard requires that `errno` be accessible, modifiable, and have a base type of `int`. It can be used with most compilers to index into an array of pointers to characters (strings) that contain text messages describing the error condition.

`errno` is set to zero when the program begins execution, but it *is not* set back to zero by any library function. Therefore, when you want to make use of `errno`, it is wise to set it to zero before calling the function that may place error codes in it, so that you can distinguish between genuine errors and leftover values.

EDOM

Type: Macro

Returns: N/A

`EDOM` is an object-like macro that defines a value that can be placed in `errno` when an *input argument* to a math function is outside the domain of possible values for that function.

For example, the library function `pow( double x, double y )` computes x^y. `pow()` sets `EDOM` in `errno` if x is less than or equal to zero when y is not a whole number.

ERANGE

Type: Macro

Returns: N/A

`ERANGE` is an object-like macro that defines a value that can be placed in `errno` when the *result* returned from a math function is too large for the defined data type.

For example, you might call `exp( double x )` with a value of x that causes e^x to be larger than a `double` type can hold, causing `ERANGE` to be placed in `errno`. The ANSI standard does not specify what value should be returned from the function after such an error, but many compilers return some predetermined value, such as `DBL_MAX` (refer to `math.h`, in Chapter 14).

Exxxxxxx

Type: Macro

Returns: N/A

The ANSI standard does not require, but does allow, a compiler to implement any number of macros to define error conditions for that particular environment. These macro names must begin with an uppercase *E* plus a digit character, or *E* and another uppercase letter. Although these macros are not required, they are usually present, and show a remarkable uniformity in the names chosen for them.

#include <ctype.h>

`ctype.h` declares two groups of character-related functions. The first group of functions includes the `is...()` family of functions. These functions determine whether a character belongs to a certain class of related characters. Examples of these classes of characters are the alphabetic characters, the numeric characters, and the control characters.

The second group of functions contains only two members, the `to...()` functions. These two functions convert uppercase letters to lowercase, and lowercase letters to uppercase.

All the parameters to these functions are type `int`, so that the (integer) returns from the character I/O functions can be used as arguments for these functions. Additionally, some of the I/O functions return the `EOF` value (–1, which cannot be represented in one byte). The `is...()` and `to..()` functions accept `EOF`, but leave it unchanged. The ANSI document specifies, however, that arguments to these functions be representable as `unsigned char`, except for `EOF`, or else the behavior of the functions is undefined.

`int isalnum( int c );`

Type: Function; may be implemented as a macro

Returns: >0 if alphanumeric
0 if not alphanumeric

The `isalnum()` function returns nonzero if `c` is an alphanumeric character, or 0 if `c` is not alphanumeric. An alphanumeric character can be an uppercase `A-Z`, a lowercase `a-z`, a decimal digit `0-9`, or any other locale-specific alphabetic character.

`int isalpha( int c );`

Type: Function; may be implemented as a macro

Returns: >0 if alphabetic
0 if not alphabetic

The `isalpha()` function returns nonzero if c is an alphabetic character, or 0 if c is not alphabetic. The alphabetic characters are the uppercase letters `A–Z`, the lowercase letters `a–z`, and any other locale-specific alphabetic characters.

`int iscntrl( int c );`

Type: Function; may be implemented as a macro

Returns: >0 if control character
             0 if not control character

The `iscntrl()` function returns nonzero if c is a control character, or 0 if c is not a control character. The control characters include the horizontal and vertical tab, form-feed, newline, carriage return, backspace and bell characters.

`int isdigit( int c );`

Type: Function; may be implemented as a macro

Returns: >0 if digit
             0 if not digit

The `isdigit()` function returns nonzero if c is a decimal digit, or 0 if c is not a decimal digit. A decimal digit is a character in the range of `0–9`. If c is not a decimal digit, 0 is returned.

`int isgraph( int c );`

Type: Function; may be implemented as a macro

Returns: >0 if graphic character
             0 if not graphic character

The `isgraph()` function returns nonzero if c is a printable character, or 0 if c is not a printable character. In this particular instance, the space, " ", is not included with the printable characters.

`int islower( int c );`

Type: Function; may be implemented as a macro

Returns: >0 if lowercase
             0 if not lowercase

The `islower()` function returns nonzero if c is a lowercase alphabetic character, or 0 if c is not a lowercase alphabetic character. This includes the letters `a–z`, and any other locale-specific lowercase letters.

```
int isprint( int c );
```

Type: Function; may be implemented as a macro

Returns: >0 if printable
                0 if not printable

The isprint() function returns nonzero if c is any printable character, or 0 if c is not a printable character. Unlike the isgraph() function, this function includes the space character with the other printable characters.

```
int ispunct( int c );
```

Type: Function; may be implemented as a macro

Returns: >0 if punctuation character
                0 if not punctuation character

The ispunct() function returns nonzero if c is a printing character but *not* an alphanumeric or space character. In other words, a value of nonzero is returned if c isprint(), but not isalnum() and isspace(). 0 is returned if c is not a punctuation character.

```
int isspace( int c );
```

Type: Function; may be implemented as a macro

Returns: >0 if space
                0 if not space

The isspace() function returns nonzero if c is a space character, or 0 if c is not a space character. The space characters include the space, form feed, newline, carriage return, and horizontal and vertical tabs.

```
int isupper( int c );
```

Type: Function; may be implemented as a macro

Returns: >0 if uppercase
                0 if not uppercase

The isupper() function returns nonzero if c is an uppercase letter, or 0 if c is not an uppercase letter. The uppercase letters include A–Z and any other locale-specific uppercase letter.

```
int isxdigit( int c );
```

Type: Function; may be implemented as a macro

Returns: >0 if hexadecimal digit
                0 if not hexadecimal digit

The isxdigit() function returns nonzero if c is a hexadecimal digit, or 0 if c is not a hexadecimal digit. The hexadecimal digits include the decimal digits 0–9, and the hexadecimal digits A–F and a–f.

```
int tolower( int c );
```

Type: Function; may be implemented as a macro

Returns: Lowercase of c if isupper(c)
               c if !isupper(c)

If isupper(c) and there is a corresponding lowercase letter, tolower() returns the lowercase letter. Otherwise c is returned.

```
int toupper( int c );
```

Type: Function; may be implemented as a macro

Returns: Uppercase of c if islower(c)
               c if !islower(c)

If islower(c) and there is a corresponding uppercase letter, toupper() returns the uppercase letter. Otherwise c is returned.

Listing 13.1 shows you how all of the ctype.h functions work in the context of a whole program. isfunct.c prompts you to enter a character from the keyboard (press Enter after it), and then tells several interesting things about that character.

Listing 13.1. isfunct.c *Show is...() and to...().*   *Microsoft C 6.0*

```
 1   #include <stdio.h>
 2   #include <ctype.h>   /* header for the is functions */
 3
 4   main()
 5   {
 6     char c;
 7
 8     printf("Enter a character and learn more about it => ");
 9     scanf("%c",&c);
10     if (isalnum(c))
11       printf("%c is an alphanumeric character.\n",c);
12     if (isalpha(c))
13       printf("%c is an alphabetic character.\n",c);
14     if (iscntrl(c))
15       printf("Your character is a control character.\n");
16     if (isdigit(c))
17       printf("%c is a decimal digit.\n",c);
18     if (isgraph(c))
19       printf("%c is a printing character and not a space.\n",c);
20     if (islower(c))
21       printf("%c is a lowercase letter.\n",c);
22     if (isprint(c))
```

Listing 13.1. continues

Listing 13.1. continued

```
23        printf("%c is a printing character.\n",c);
24    if (ispunct(c))
25        printf("%c is a punctuation character.\n",c);
26    if (isspace(c))
27        printf("Your character produces a space.\n",c);
28    if (isupper(c))
29        printf("%c is an uppercase letter.\n",c);
30    if (isxdigit(c))
31        printf("%c is a hexadecimal digit.\n",c);
32    if (islower(c))
33        printf("%c is the uppercase version of your letter.\n",
34                         (toupper(c)));
35    if (isupper(c))
36        printf("%c is the lowercase version of your letter.\n",
37                         (tolower(c)));
38  }
```

Summary

The macros and functions presented in this chapter are simple and easily overlooked. However, they contribute a great deal to completeness and reliability and add that finishing touch to your programs.

❏ *The assert macro is a diagnostic tool that lets you specify an expression and abort program execution, if necessary.* It also gives you an error message on the stderr device that lets you know why your program stopped.

❏ *The errno header contains declarations for macros used to define and document run-time errors.* The macro errno has a base type of int and is accessible by the library functions when they post error codes. These error codes can be used to index into an array of error messages.

❏ EDOM *and* ERANGE *are macros, declared in the* errno *header, that post error codes to* errno *when certain math errors occur.* The ANSI standard allows other error-type macros to be included in the errno header file, but these other macros are not required.

❏   *The ctype header contains useful character-testing and
    conversion function definitions.* The `is...()` functions are
    related, in that each function tests a character to determine
    whether it belongs in a certain class of characters. An example is
    the `isalpha()` function, which tests the character passed to it
    to determine whether it is an alphabetic character.

❏   *The `to...()` functions are also defined in* `ctype.h`. These
    two functions convert the character passed to them to the
    opposite case, if there is one. For example, the `toupper()`
    function converts the character passed to it to an uppercase
    letter, if it can.

❏   *All the functions defined in the* `ctype.h` *header require that
    an integer that is within the range of unsigned* `char` *be passed
    to them.*

❏   *The return value of the* `is` *functions is nonzero if the function
    is true, and 0 if it is false.* The `to` functions don't return a true
    or false; rather, they return the appropriate upper- or lowercase
    letter. If the `to` functions cannot return a converted character,
    they pass the argument back unchanged.

14

Math, Numbers, and Conversions

The ANSI standard for C specifies for floating-point numbers a particular *model*, or format, that guarantees certain arithmetic properties. The mathematical formulation of floating-point theory can be quite complex and is not covered here. Two characteristics of floating-point numbers, however, have a significant bearing on C programming. They are as follows:

❑ *The floating-point model specified by ANSI is formulated such that only sign-and-magnitude values are possible.* Every floating-point number can (possibly) be negative—there is no such thing as an "unsigned float" representation.

❑ *The floating-point model also requires that any floating-point number be capable of being normalized. Normalization* is the process in which the exponent and fraction parts of the number are manipulated so that the *maximum possible number of significant digits* is preserved in the number. If this is not done, accumulating errors in intermediate results during lengthy calculations can completely destroy the validity of the results.

#include <float.h>

The float.h header file contains macros that define the properties of the floating-point data types. The ANSI standard requires that only the macro FLT_RADIX be a constant expression that can be used in #if preprocessing directives. Other macro values do not have to be constant expressions.

There are three different versions of almost every macro in the following list, one for each of the floating-point data types: float, double and long double. In the following discussion, macros that are the same except for the floating-point type are listed together. The exceptions to this are the FLT_ROUNDS and the FLT_RADIX macros, which have only one version each.

FLT_ROUNDS

Type: Macro

Returns: N/A

The macro FLT_ROUNDS determines how the floating-point numbers are rounded during addition. The following values of FLT_ROUNDS and their meanings are standard:

n	Rounding behavior
-1	Indeterminable
0	Toward zero
1	Toward nearest representable value
2	Toward positive infinity
3	Toward negative infinity

Other values for FLT_ROUNDS are allowed. Their meaning is implementation-defined.

FLT_RADIX   2

Type: Macro

Returns: N/A

The FLT_RADIX macro defines the radix (base number system) for exponent representation. FLT_RADIX must be greater than or equal to 2.

FLT_MANT_DIG

DBL_MANT_DIG

LDBL_MANT_DIG

Type: Macro

Returns: N/A

The `..._MANT_DIG` macros define the number of base-`FLT_RADIX` digits in the floating-point mantissa (fraction part).

`FLT_DIG`	6
`DBL_DIG`	10
`LDBL_DIG`	10

Type: Macro

Returns: N/A

The `..._DIG` macros define the number of *decimal digits of precision* for the floating-point values. A conforming compiler must provide *at least* the number of decimal digits of precision shown here.

`FLT_MIN_EXP`

`DBL_MIN_EXP`

`LDBL_MIN_EXP`

Type: Macro

Returns: N/A

The `..._MIN_EXP` macros define a minimum negative integer such that `FLT_RADIX` raised to that power minus 1 yields a normalized floating-point number, e_{min}.

`FLT_MIN_10_EXP`	-37
`DBL_MIN_10_EXP`	-37
`LDBL_MIN_10_EXP`	-37

Type: Macro

Returns: N/A

The `..._MIN_10_EXP` macros define a minimum negative integer such that 10 raised to that power yields a result that falls within the range of normalized floating-point numbers. The value -37 is the smallest negative value allowed (that is, -36 would be nonconforming).

`FLT_MAX_EXP`

`DBL_MAX_EXP`

`LDBL_MAX_EXP`

Type: Macro

Returns: N/A

The `..._MAX_EXP` macros define a maximum integer such that `FLT_RADIX` raised to that power minus 1 yields a representable finite floating-point number, e_{max}.

`FLT_MAX_10_EXP`	+37
`DBL_MAX_10_EXP`	+37
`LDBL_MAX_10_EXP`	+37

Type: Macro

Returns: N/A

The `..._MAX_10_EXP` macros define the maximum integer power to which 10 can be raised, yielding a result that is the range of representable finite floating-point numbers.

`FLT_MAX`	1E+37
`DBL_MAX`	1E+37
`LDBL_MAX`	1E+37

Type: Macro

Returns: N/A

The `..._MAX` macros define the maximum representable finite floating-point numbers. The implementation-defined values should be equal to or greater than the values in the preceding list.

`FLT_MIN`	1E-37
`DBL_MIN`	1E-37
`LDBL_MIN`	1E-37

Type: Macro

Returns: N/A

The `..._MIN` macros define the minimum positive floating-point numbers. The implementation-defined values should be equal to or smaller than the listed values.

`FLT_EPSILON`	1E-5
`DBL_EPSILON`	1E-9
`LDBL_EPSILON`	1E-9

Type: Macro

Returns: N/A

The `..._EPSILON` macros define the minimum floating-point numbers that, when added to 1, yield a result that is not equal to 1. In other words, these are the smallest values that cause a floating-point number to change when it's used in a calculation.

#include <limits.b>

`limits.h` contains constant expressions that define the maximum and minimum values of the integral types. The ANSI standard requires that a conforming implementation define the following constants with equal or greater (absolute) values.

`CHAR_BIT`	8

Type: Macro

Returns: N/A

`CHAR_BIT` defines the maximum number of bits that can be used to represent an object of type `char`.

`SCHAR_MIN`	−127

Type: Macro

Returns: N/A

`SCHAR_MIN` defines the minimum value for an object of type `signed char`.

`SCHAR_MAX`	+127

Type: Macro

Returns: N/A

`SCHAR_MIN` defines the maximum value for an object of type `signed char`.

`UCHAR_MAX`	255

Type: Macro

Returns: N/A

`UCHAR_MAX` defines the maximum value for an object of type `unsigned char`.

CHAR_MIN   0 (or see SCHAR_MIN)

Type: Macro

Returns: N/A

CHAR_MIN defines the minimum value for an object of type char. If the object of type char sign-extends, or becomes negative, the value of CHAR_MIN equals the value of SCHAR_MIN. If the object keeps a positive value (doesn't sign-extend), the value of CHAR_MIN is 0.

CHAR_MAX   (see SCHAR_MAX or UCHAR_MAX)

Type: Macro

Returns: N/A

CHAR_MAX defines the maximum value for an object of type char. If the object of type char sign-extends, or becomes negative, the value of CHAR_MAX equals the value of SCHAR_MAX. If the object keeps a positive value (doesn't sign-extend), then the value of CHAR_MAX equals the value of UCHAR_MAX.

MB_LEN_MAX   1

Type: Macro

Returns: N/A

MB_LEN_MAX defines, for any supported locale, the number of bytes in a multibyte character. Notice that the minimum allowed value implies that single-byte characters are a special subset of multibyte characters.

SHRT_MIN   32767

Type: Macro

Returns: N/A

SHRT_MIN defines the minimum value for an object of type short int.

SHRT_MAX   +32767

Type: Macro

Returns: N/A

SHRT MAX defines the maximum value for an object of type short int.

USHRT_MAX 65535

Type: Macro

Returns: N/A

`USHRT_MAX` defines the maximum value for an object of type `unsigned short int`.

`INT_MIN`   −32767

Type: Macro

Returns: N/A

`INT_MIN` defines the minimum value for an object of type `int`.

`INT_MAX`   +32767

Type: Macro

Returns: N/A

`INT_MAX` defines the maximum value for an object of type `int`.

`UINT_MAX`   65535

Type: Macro

Returns: N/A

`UINT_MAX` defines the maximum value for an object of type `unsigned int`.

`LONG_MIN`   −2147483647

Type: Macro

Returns: N/A

`LONG_MIN` defines the minimum value for an object of type `long int`.

`LONG_MAX`   +2147483647

Type: Macro

Returns: N/A

`LONG_MAX` defines the maximum value for an object of type `long int`.

`ULONG_MAX`   4294967295

Type: Macro

Returns: N/A

`ULONG_MAX` defines the maximum value for an object of type `unsigned long int`.

#include <locale.h>

The header file `locale.h` contains several macros, two functions, and one type that are used in the formatting of numeric values.

The type defined in `locale.h` is `struct lconv`. To conform to the ANSI standard, the `lconv` structure must contain the members shown in the following structure definition. The members of the structure do not have to be in any particular order, and other implementation-defined members can be placed in the structure.

A member of the structure with the type *pointer to char* points to a string. The string can be null (""), which means that a value is either not available in the current locale or has zero length. A member of type `char` must be a nonnegative number. If a member of type `char` has the value `CHAR_MAX`, that value is not available in the current locale.

In the following structure definition, the comments indicate the value of the members in the "C" locale. A description of each member is given in the discussion of the `localeconv()` function.

```
struct lconv {
     char *decimal_point;        /* "." */
     char *thousands_sep;        /* "" */
     char *grouping;             /* "" */
     char *int_curr_symbol;      /* "" */
     char *currency_symbol;      /* "" */
     char *mon_decimal_point;    /* "" */
     char *mon_thousands_sep;    /* "" */
     char *mon_grouping;         /* "" */
     char *positive_sign;        /* "" */
     char *negative_sign;        /* "" */
     char int_frac_digits;       /* CHAR_MAX */
     char frac_digits;           /* CHAR_MAX */
     char p_cs_precedes;         /* CHAR_MAX */
     char p_sep_by_space;        /* CHAR_MAX */
     char n_cs_precedes;         /* CHAR_MAX */
     char n_sep_by_space;        /* CHAR_MAX */
     char p_sign_posn;           /* CHAR_MAX */
     char n_sign_posn;           /* CHAR_MAX */
};
```

LC_ALL

Type: Macro

Returns: N/A

The `LC_ALL` macro is used as a `category` argument for the function `setlocale()`. `LC_ALL` specifies the entire program's locale. The other locale macros specify the locale for only part of the program's locale.

LC_COLLATE

Type: Macro

Returns: N/A

The `LC_COLLATE` macro is used as a `category` argument for the function `setlocale()`. `LC_COLLATE` affects only the behavior of the functions `strcoll()` and `strxfrm()`.

LC_CTYPE

Type: Macro

Returns: N/A

The `LC_CTYPE` macro is used as a `category` argument for the function `setlocale()`. `LC_CTYPE` affects the character-handling functions and the multibyte functions.

LC_MONETARY

Type: Macro

Returns: N/A

The `LC_MONETARY` macro is used as a `category` argument for the function `setlocale()`. `LC_MONETARY` affects the information returned from the `localeconv()` function about monetary formats.

LC_NUMERIC

Type: Macro

Returns: N/A

The `LC_NUMERIC` macro is used as a `category` argument for the function `setlocale()`. `LC_NUMERIC` affects the nonmonetary format information returned from `localeconv()`, and the decimal-point character used in the formatted I/O functions and the string-conversion functions.

LC_TIME

Type: Macro

Returns: N/A

The LC_TIME macro is used as a category argument for the function setlocale(). LC_TIME affects the behavior of the strftime() function.

```
char *setlocale( int category, const char *locale );
```

Type: Function

Returns: Character pointer or null

The setlocale() function is used to modify or query the program's current locale. By using the proper arguments in the function call, you can change all or part of the program's locale.

For the category argument of setlocale(), any of the LC_... macros can be used. The macro LC_ALL is used to select the entire program's locale. The other LC_... macros select only part of the program's locale. The implementation can define other macros to be used as category arguments to setlocale(). The only requirement is that the new macro name start with the characters LC_ and an uppercase letter.

ANSI lists only two values that can be used as the second argument, locale. A value of "C" for locale specifies that the minimal environment for C translation is used. A value of "" specifies that the implementation-defined *native environment* is used. Any other values for locale are implementation-defined.

The pointer to string *returned* by setlocale() depends on the value of the locale pointer passed as the second argument, as follows:

❑ *When locale points to a valid category string, the function returns a pointer to the old string.* You should not modify this string; it can be used later as a locale argument to restore that part of the program's locale. If the argument string was not valid, the locale is not changed and the function returns a null pointer.

❑ *When locale is a null pointer, the function returns only a pointer to that category string.* That is, this is the query-mode function call.

ANSI specifies that an implementation must behave as if no library functions call setlocale(). However, when a program begins execution, a command equivalent to

```
setlocale( LC_ALL, "C" );
```

is executed.

```
struct lconv *localeconv( void );
```

Type: Function

Returns: Pointer to structure

The `localeconv()` function is used in the formatting of numeric values, including monetary values, in accordance with the formatting rules of the current locale. This numeric formatting information is found in the structure `lconv`.

The members of `lconv` have two types. The first is type `char *`, pointers to strings, and the second is type `char`, which must be nonnegative numbers.

Most of the members of `lconv` that are `char *` can point to a null string, `""`. This indicates that a value is not available in the current locale or that it has zero length. The exception to this rule is the member `decimal_point`: it should not be null string.

A value of `CHAR_MAX` for the members of `lconv` that are of type `char` means that a value is not available in the current locale.

Brief descriptions of the members of the `lconv` structure follow.

```
char *decimal_point
```

The decimal-point character used to format the nonmonetary values.

```
char *thousands_sep
```

The character to the left of the decimal point, used to separate groups of digits. Used for nonmonetary values.

```
char *grouping
```

This is a string whose elements give the size of each group of digits in a formatted numeric value. Used for nonmonetary values.

```
char *int_curr_symbol
```

The international currency symbol used in the current locale. The first three characters indicate which international currency sumbol will be used. The fourth character indicates the character used to separate the international currency symbol and the monetary value.

```
char *currency_symbol
```

The local currency symbol used in the current locale.

```
char *mon_decimal_point
```

The decimal-point character used to format monetary values.

`char *mon_thousands_sep`

The character to the left of the decimal-point, used to separate groups of digits. This is used for monetary values.

`char *mon_grouping`

A string whose elements give the size of each group of digits in a formatted monetary numeric value.

`char *positive_sign`

The string used to indicate a positive, or nonnegative, formatted monetary value.

`char *negative_sign`

The string used to indicate a negative formatted monetary value.

`char int_frac_digits`

Contains a number that indicates the number of fractional digits, digits to the right of the decimal point, to be displayed in a monetary value. This member is used for the internationally formatted monetary values.

`char frac_digits`

Contains a number that indicates the number of fractional digits, digits to the right of the decimal point, to be displayed in a monetary value.

`char p_cs_precedes`

Determines whether a currency symbol precedes or succeeds a nonnegative formatted monetary value. If set to 1, the currency symbol precedes the value. If set to 0, the currency symbol succeeds the value.

`char p_sep_by_space`

Determines whether a currency symbol is separated from a nonnegative formatted monetary value by a space. If set to 1, the currency symbol is separated by a space. If set to 0, the currency symbol is not separated by a space.

`char n_cs_precedes`

Determines whether a currency symbol precedes or succeeds a negative formatted monetary value. If set to 1, the currency symbol precedes the value. If set to 0, the currency symbol succeeds the value.

`char n_sep_by_space`

Determines whether a currency symbol is separated from a negative formatted monetary value by a space. If set to 1, the currency symbol is separated by a space. If set to 0, the currency symbol is not separated by a space.

char p_sign_posn

Contains a number that determines how a positive sign is placed in a nonnegative formatted monetary value. For a list of acceptable values, see the description of `char n sign posn`, which follows.

char n_sign_posn

Contains a number that determines how a negative sign is placed in a negative formatted monetary value.

The following list contains the acceptable values that can be placed in `char p sign posn` and `char n sign posn`:

Value	Effect
0	The quantity and the `currency symbol` are enclosed in parentheses.
1	The quantity and the `currency symbol` are preceded by the sign string.
2	The quantity and the `currency symbol` are succeeded by the sign string.
3	The `currency symbol` is preceded immediately by the sign string.
4	The `currency symbol` is succeeded immediately by the sign string.

#include <math.h>

The `math.h` header file contains the function prototypes and the one macro that are used for floating-point library functions. All the floating-point functions require that double-precision values be passed to them. After a function performs its calculations, it returns a double-precision value.

Although the name of the header file is `math.h`, not all of the math functions are contained here. Only the floating-point functions are declared in this header. The functions dealing with integer mathematics are contained in the `stdlib.h` header file. If you want to use both floating point and integer libraries, you must include both the `stdlib.h` and the `math.h` header files.

The macro defined in `math.h` is `HUGE_VAL`. This macro expands to a positive `double` expression. This value does not have to be representable as a `float`.

Error Conditions

Many math functions are defined to work within specified value limits. The set of allowed values is called the function's *domain*. When an argument is passed to a function, the function checks to see whether it is within the defined domain. If not, a *domain error* occurs.

The following descriptions list any domain errors for a function. These, of course, are the domain errors specified by ANSI C. An implementation can define other domain errors if they are consistent with the mathematical definition for the function.

When a domain error occurs, two things happen. One is that the macro EDOM is stored in errno (refer to Chapter 13). The other is that the function returns an implementation-defined value.

Even if a function is given arguments that are within the proper domain, another error can occur. It may be that the result of the function's calculations cannot be represented by an object of the function's return type. When this happens, a *range error* has occurred.

The result of a function's computation could either *overflow* or *underflow* the object type required to hold it. An overflow occurs when the result is too large to fit in the specified type. An underflow occurs when the result is too small to be represented by the specified type.

If a function results in an overflow condition, the function returns the value of the macro HUGE_VAL, and the macro ERANGE is stored in errno. The return value of HUGE_VAL has the same sign as the correct value of the function.

If a function results in an underflow condition, the function returns zero. Whether the macro ERANGE is stored in errno is implementation-defined.

Trigonometric Functions

```
double acos( double x );
```

Type: Function

Returns: The arc cosine in the range [0, PI] radians

The acos() returns the principal arc cosine value for x in the range [0, PI] radians. The argument, x, passed to acos() must be in the range [−1, +1]; otherwise, a domain error occurs.

```
double asin(double x );
```

Type: Function

Returns: The arc sine in the range [–PI/2, +PI/2] radians

The asin() function returns the principal arc sine value for x in the range [–PI/2, +PI/2] radians. The argument, x, passed to asin() must be in the range [–1, +1]; otherwise, a domain error occurs.

```
double atan( double x );
```

Type: Function

Returns: The arc tangent in the range [–PI/2, +PI/2] radians

The atan() function returns the principal arc tangent value for x in the range [–PI/2, +PI/2] radians.

```
double atan2( double y, double x );
```

Type: Function

Returns: The tangent of y/x in the range of [–PI, +PI] radians

The atan2() function returns the principal arc tangent value for y / x in the range [–PI, +PI] radians. The arguments passed to atan2() can be signed. The signs of the arguments are used to determine the quadrant of the return value. If both arguments, y and x, are zero, a return value cannot be calculated and a domain error occurs.

The code fragment in listing 14.1 shows the usage of the inverse trigonometric functions.

```
double cos( double x );
```

Type: Function

Returns: The cosine value

The cos() function returns the cosine value of x in radians. If the magnitude of x is large, the return value may have little or no significance.

```
double sin( double x );
```

Type: Function

Returns: The sine value

The sin() function returns the sine value of x in radians. If the magnitude of x is large, the return value may have little or no significance.

Listing 14.1. *The inverse trig functions.*

```
1     double x, y;
2
3     x = 0.87;
4     y = acos( x );
5       printf( "y = the angle, in radians, whose cosine = x.\n");
6       printf( "The given cosine x = %f.\n", x);
7       printf( "y = %f radians.\n\n", y);
8
9     x = 0.50;
10    y = asin( x );
11      printf( "y = the angle, in radians, whose sine = x.\n");
12      printf( "The given sine x = %f.\n", x);
13      printf( "y = %f radians.\n\n", y);
14
15    x = 0.58;
16    y = atan( x );
17      printf( "y = the angle, in radians, whose tangent = x.\n");
18      printf( "The given tangent x = %f.\n", x);
19      printf( "y = %f radians.\n\n", y);
20
```

```
double tan( double x );
```

Type: Function

Returns: The tangent value

The `tan()` function returns the tangent value of x in radians. If the magnitude of x is large, the return value may have little or no significance.

The code fragment in listing 14.2 shows examples of the trigonometric functions in action.

Listing 14.2. *The regular trig functions.*

```
1     double x, y;
2
3     x = 0.52;
4     printf( " x = %f radians.\n\n", x );
5
6     y = cos( x );
7     printf( "The cosine of x = %f.\n\n", y );
8
9     y = sin( x );
10    printf( "The sine of x = %f.\n\n", y );
11
12    y = tan( x );
13    printf( "The tangent of x = %f.\n\n", y );
```

Hyperbolic Functions

```
double cosh( double x );
```

Type: Function

Returns: The hyperbolic cosine value

The cosh() function returns the hyperbolic cosine of x. If the argument passed to cosh() is too large, a range error occurs.

```
double sinh( double x );
```

Type: Function

Returns: The hyperbolic sine value

The sinh() function returns the hyperbolic sine of x. If the argument passed to sinh() is too large, a range error occurs.

```
double tanh( double x );
```

Type: Function

Returns: The hyperbolic tangent value

The tanh() function returns the hyperbolic tangent of x.

The use of the hyperbolic trig functions is shown in listing 14.3.

Listing 14.3. The hyperbolic trig functions.

```
1     double x, y;
2
3     x = 1.00;
4     printf( "x = %f.\n\n", x );
5
6     y = cosh( x );
7     printf( "The hyperbolic cosine of x = %f.\n\n", y );
8
9     y = sinh( x );
10    printf( "The hyperbolic sine of x = %f.\n\n", y );
11
12    y = tanh( x );
13    printf( "The hyperbolic tangent of x = %f.\n\n", y );
```

Exponential and Logarithmic Functions

```
double exp( double x );
```

Type: Function

Returns: The exponential value

The `exp()` function returns the value of e^x, where e is the natural logarithm base (this is not the natural log function). If the argument passed to `exp()` is too large, a range error occurs.

```
double frexp( double arg_val, int *exp );
```

Type: Function

Returns: A `double` normalized fraction in the range [1/2, 1] or 0

The `frexp()` function takes a floating-point argument and divides it into a normalized fraction and an integral power of 2. The normalized fraction is returned and the integral power of 2 is pointed to by the integer pointer `*exp`.

Therefore, if you take the return from `frexp()` and multiply it by 2 raised to the `*exp` power, the result equals `arg_val`. If a value of 0 is passed to the function in `arg_val`, both parts of the result equal zero.

```
double ldexp( double x, int exp );
```

Type: Function

Returns: The value of x times 2 raised to the `exp` power

The `ldexp()` function requires two arguments: the first is a `double` floating-point number; the second, an integer. The `ldexp()` function computes and returns $x * 2^{exp}$. When you use this function, a range error may occur.

The exponential class of functions can be seen in context in the code fragment in listing 14.4.

Listing 14.4. The exponentiation functions.

```
1     double x, y, z;
2     int i;
3
4     x = 100.00;
5     y = exp( x );
6     printf( "The exponential of x = %f.\n\n", y );
7
8     x = 100;
9     y = frexp( x, &i );
10    printf( "x = y * ( 2 to the i power )\n\n" );
11    printf( "y = %f.\n", y );
12    printf( "i = %d.\n", i );
13    z = pow( 2.0, ( double ) i );
14    printf( "z = 2 to the i power = %f.\n", z);
15    printf( "y * z = %f.\n\n", y * z );
16
17    x = 3.00;
18    i = 4;
19    y = ldexp( x, i );
20    printf( "y = x * ( 2 to the i power ).\n");
21    printf( "x = %f, i = %d, y = %f.\n\n", x, i, y);
```

```
double log( double x );
```

Type: Function

Returns: The natural logarithm

The log() function returns the natural logarithm of x. When you use this function, encountering either a domain error or a range error is possible. A domain error occurs if the argument, x, is negative. A range error occurs if the argument, x, is 0 and the logarithm of 0 cannot be represented.

```
double log10( double x );
```

Type: Function

Returns: The base-ten logarithm

The log10() function is similar to the log() function, except that the base-10 logarithm is returned instead of the natural logarithm. A domain error occurs if the argument, x, is negative. A range error occurs if the argument, x, is 0 and the logarithm of 0 cannot be represented.

The log() and log10() functions are extremely easy to use. The fragment in listing 14.5 shows what they look like in code.

Listing 14.5. *The* `log()` *and* `log10()` *library functions.*

```
1    double x, y;
2
3    x = 10;
4
5    y = log( x );
6    printf( "The base 2 log of x = %f.\n\n", y );
7
8    y = log10( x );
9    printf( "The base 10 log of x = %f.\n\n", y );
```

`double modf( double x, double *ptr );`

Type: Function

Returns: The signed fractional part of x

The `modf()` function separates a floating-point number x into two parts, the fractional and the integer parts of the number. The integral part of the floating-point number, x, is stored in the double object pointed to by `*ptr`. The fractional part of the floating-point number is returned by the function. Each separated part has the same sign as x.

The `modf()` function name seems similar to the `fmod()` function discussed later in this chapter. However, their purposes differ: `modf()` separates a floating-point number into its component parts; `fmod()` results in the *remainder* of a floating-point division (reminiscent of the % *modulus* operator for integers). Listing 14.6 shows the `modf()` function in action.

Listing 14.6. *The* `modf()` *function.*

```
1    double x, integral, frac;
2
3    x = 3.1416;
4    frac = modf( x, &integral);
5    printf( "x is broken into integral and fractional "
6             " parts.\n" );
7    printf( "The integral part = %f.\n", integral );
8    printf( "The fractional part = %f.\n\n", frac );
```

Power Functions

```
double pow( double x, double y );
```

Type: Function

Returns: The value of x raised to the y power

The `pow()` function returns the result of x raised to the power y. Domain and range errors may occur. A domain error occurs if x is a negative number and y is not an integral value. A domain error occurs also when the result cannot be represented and x is equal to 0 and y is less than or equal to 0.

```
double sqrt( double x );
```

Type: Function

Returns: The square root of x

The `sqrt()` function returns only nonnegative square roots. A domain error occurs if the argument passed to the function is negative.

In a real sense, the `sqrt()` is a power-manipulating function, because taking the square root of x is exactly equivalent to computing $x^{0.5}$. The use of the power functions is shown in listing 14.7.

Listing 14.7. The `pow()` and `sqrt()` functions.

```
1    double x, y, z;
2
3    x = 2.05;
4    y = 5.34;
5    z = pow( x, y );
6    printf( "x to the y power = %f.\n\n", z );
7
8    x = 25.78;
9    y = sqrt( x );
10   printf( "x = %f, the square root of x = %f.\n\n", x, y );
```

Closest Integer, Absolute Value, and Remainder Functions

`double ceil( double x );`

Type:　　Function

Returns:　　The lowest integral value that is not less than x

Although the `ceil()` function calculates a whole-number value, notice that the type of the return value is `double`.

`double fabs( double x );`

Type:　　Function

Returns:　　The absolute value

The `fabs()` function returns the absolute value of the floating-point number passed to it. (Remember that floating-point numbers always have a sign, possibly negative. This function in effect reverses the sign only if the argument is negative.)

`double floor( double x );`

Type:　　Function

Returns:　　The highest integral value that is not greater than x

Although the `floor()` function calculates an integral value, notice that the type of the return value is `double`.

`double fmod( double x, double y );`

Type:　　Function

Returns:　　The floating-point remainder of x / y

The function `fmod()` takes the arguments passed to it, x and y, divides them, and then returns the floating-point remainder from the division operation. This remainder is computed in much the same way as a remainder from integer division. Consider this algebraic expression:

$$x / y = i + r$$

In this example, i is an integer (whole number), and r is the remainder, which in this case *may have a fractional part*. Hence, the returned type is `double`. If the argument y is zero, the implementation can choose whether to simply return zero, or trigger a domain error.

The use in code of these "miscellaneous" floating-point functions is shown in the code fragment in listing 14.8.

Listing 14.8. *Closest integer, absolute value, and remainder functions.*

```
1    double x, y, z;
2
3    x = 6.5;
4
5    y = ceil( x );
6    printf( "The smallest integer not less than x = %f.\n\n",
7            y );
8
9    y = floor( x );
10   printf( "The largest integer not greater than x = "
11           "%f.\n\n", y );
12
13   x = -6.5;
14   y = fabs( x );
15   printf( "The absolute value of x = %f.\n\n", y );
16
17   x = 13.00;
18   y = 4.00;
19   z = fmod( x, y );
20   printf( "The remainder of x / y = %f.\n\n", z );
```

Summary

This chapter contains reference material pertaining to the following four standard header files:

- ❏ float.h Macros defining important floating-point values and properties.

- ❏ limits.h Minimum and maximum values for the integral types.

- ❏ locale.h Macros and functions for locale control. The most important impact of these resources is their effect on formatting monetary numeric values.

- ❏ math.h The floating-point math function library. C may perhaps not possess the richness of function found in FORTRAN, but it certainly has more than most languages.

15

Alternate Transfers of Control and Variable Argument Lists

The setjmp.h, signal.h, and stdarg.h header files declare function prototypes for some of the most sophisticated functions in standard C.

The functions declared in setjmp.h can jump directly from one function to another, without the normal call sequence. Some implementations require the target function to be a direct "parent" of the function invoking the jump; others do not. Because ANSI is silent on the issue, either implementation is acceptable.

Frequently, conditions confronting your program can be unpredictable. The functions declared in signal.h provide a flexible means of coping with unexpected events. In addition, one of the functions can *cause* a signal event. The ability to cope with the unexpected gives users of your program a sense of solidity and of flexibility.

Other conditions, in which predicting the exact number of parameters that will be passed to a function is impossible, may arise. The capability of handling this condition is a particularly powerful tool, and is provided by the functions declared in stdarg.h.

#include <setjmp.h>

setjmp.h declares functions that can bypass the normal function-call-and-return protocol, together with a supporting type declaration. Typically, setjmp.h functions are required in only two situations. First, they are used when unusual conditions are encountered during program execution. Second, `setjmp.h` functions permit a quick return from a set of deeply nested functions.

`jmp_buf env;`

Type: Type declaration

Returns: N/A

`jmp_buf` is the declaration for an array type used to store information about the program environment.

```
1    #include <stdlib.h>
2    #include <stdio.h>
3    #include <setjmp.h>
4
5    jmp_buf env;
6
7    main()
8    { ... }
```

Line 3 of the preceding code fragment shows the declaration of a jump buffer.

In the preceding code fragment, the jump buffer, `env`, is declared with global scope. Because `env` was declared with global scope, it can be used in any function in the program.

`int setjmp( jmp_buf env );`

Type: Function-like macro

Returns: If `setjmp()` is invoked directly, it returns a value of zero. If `longjmp()` causes `setjmp()` to return a value, the value is nonzero.

`setjmp()` stores information about the program environment in the jump buffer `env`. The environment information is used by `longjmp()` to restore the program environment.

`void longjmp( jmp_buf env, int val );`

Type: Function

Returns: `longjmp()` is a void function; it does not return a value. It does, however, cause `setjmp()` to return the value `val`.

`longjmp()` is used to bypass the normal function call and return mechanisms. When `longjmp()` is called, it performs the following basic functions:

1. longjmp() restores the program environment in env.

2. longjmp() causes setjmp() to return the value val.

3. longjmp() continues program execution immediately following the corresponding setjmp() macro.

The env argument is used to hold information about the program environment. When longjmp() is invoked, this environment information is restored.

The val argument is the integer value that longjmp() causes setjmp() to return. val should not be a negative number or zero. If val is zero, longjmp() causes setjmp() to return a value equal to 1.

Listing 15.1 shows how to set up and use the longjmp() function and the setjmp() macro.

Listing 15.1. jump.c (Demonstration of setjmp.h).   Microsoft C 6.0

```
1   #include <stdio.h>
2   #include <stdlib.h>
3   #include <setjmp.h>
4
5   void func1( void );
6   void func2( void );
7
8   jmp_buf env;
9
10  main()
11  {
12    int i;
13
14    i = setjmp( env );
15    printf( "If setjmp() is used more than once,\n" );
16    printf( "longjmp() can only return to the last one.\n" );
17
18    i = setjmp( env );
19    if( i == 0 ) {
20      printf( "Initial invocation of setjmp().\n" );
21      printf( "setjmp() returned a value of: %d\n", i );
22      func1();
23    }
24    else {
25      printf( "setjmp() invoked by longjmp().\n" );
26      printf( "setjmp() returned a value of: %d\n", i );
27    }
28
```

Listing 15.1. continues

Listing 15.1. *continued*

```
29    printf( "main() completed, program ending.\n" );
30  }
31
32  void func1()
33  {
34    printf( "In func1(), 1 level below main().\n " );
35    func2();
36  }
37
38  void func2()
39  {
40    printf( "In func2(), 2 levels below main().\n" );
41    printf( "Preparing to longjmp() to main().\n" );
42
43    longjmp( env, 3 );
44  }
```

On line 8 of listing 15.1, the jump buffer env is declared as a global variable. (As a global variable, env can be used anywhere in the program.) Lines 18 through 27 show how setjmp() is used to distinguish between when it initially is invoked and when longjmp() has been called. When setjmp() initially is invoked, it returns 0; the first part of the if is therefore executed. When longjmp() causes setjmp() to return a nonzero value, the else part of the if condition is executed.

func1() and func2() are designed to show how longjmp() can be used to return from nested functions. main() calls func1(), which in turn calls func2(). Normally, program flow would travel back up this chain of functions. This program bypasses normal return procedures by calling the longjmp() function in line 43. The longjmp() function causes program flow to return immediately to the last setjmp() in main(). In this example, longjmp() causes setjmp() to return a value of 3 (the value detected in the if statement).

When using the setjmp() and longjmp() functions, you should remember the following precautions:

❑ longjmp() *restores the environment saved by the most recent invocation of* setjmp()*.* However, if the function containing the setjmp() macro has terminated, longjmp() cannot be counted upon to work.

❑ *Some implementations require that the function containing the* longjmp() *call be a direct descendent of the function containing the initial* `setjmp()` *call.* Others require that you observe the first precaution, but do not require the second.

❏ *The values of some objects can be indeterminate if their value is changed between* `setjmp()` *and* `longjmp()`. These objects have automatic duration and do not have a `volatile` type.

#include <signal.h>

The declarations in `signal.h` are for code that associates a signal-handling routine with a signal. A signal is a condition that can arise at *any time* during program execution. Because a signal can occur at any time, without reference to the execution flow of the program, it is called an *asynchronous event*.

sig_atomic_t

Type: Type definition

Returns: N/A

`sig_atomic_t` declares an integral object that can be accessed as an *atomic entity*. The assignment of a value to an atomic entity cannot be interrupted, not even by an asynchronous event. Thus, an assignment operation to an object of `sig_atomic_t` cannot be suspended when a signal is raised.

SIG_DFL

Type: Macro

Returns: N/A

`SIG_DFL`, a macro that can be used as the second argument to the `signal()` function, indicates that a signal is to be handled in the default manner. This macro expands to a constant expression with a type compatible with the `*func` argument in `signal()`.

SIG_IGN

Type: Macro

Returns: N/A

`SIG_IGN`, a macro that can be used as the second argument to the `signal()` function, indicates that a signal is to be ignored. This macro expands to a constant expression that has a type compatible with the `*func` argument in `signal()`.

SIG_ERR

Type: Macro

Returns: N/A

  SIG_ERR, a macro used as a return value for the signal() function, indicates that an error occurred when signal() was called.

SIGABRT

Type: Macro

Returns: N/A

  The SIGABRT macro, used as a sig argument in the signal() function, indicates an abnormal termination. The termination can be initiated by the abort() function.

SIGFPE

Type: Macro

Returns: N/A

  SIGFPE, a macro used as a sig argument for signal(), signals that an erroneous arithmetic operation has occurred. (An example of such an operation is trying to divide by zero.)

SIGILL

Type: Macro

Returns: N/A

  SIGILL, the macro used to signal that an invalid function image has been detected, is used as a sig argument for the signal() function.

SIGINT

Type: Macro

Returns: N/A

  SIGINT, the macro that tells the program there has been an interactive attention signal, is used as a sig argument for the signal() function.

SIGSEGV

Type: Macro

Returns: N/A

This macro indicates that there has been an invalid storage access. `SIGSEGV` is used as a `sig` argument for `signal()`.

SIGTERM

Type: Macro

Returns: N/A

`SIGTERM`, the macro that indicates that an asynchronous termination signal has been sent to the program, is used as a `sig` argument for `signal()`.

`void ( *signal( int sig, void ( *func )( int ) ) ) ( int );`

Type: Function

Returns: A pointer to function *func, if signal( ) is successful.
             If signal( ) is not successful, a value of SIG_ERR is
             returned.

`signal()` is the function that associates a signal-handling routine with a signal. The signal is indicated by the first argument, `sig`. The signal-handling function is indicated by the second argument, `*func`. `signal()` returns a pointer to the signal-handling function. The function pointed to by `*func` is called whenever the corresponding signal occurs.

In ANSI C, a macro is used for the `sig` argument. The standard ANSI macros are included in the preceding list. An implementation is allowed to include other signal macros in its compiler. ANSI requires only that the implementation-defined macros start with `SIG`.

`( *func )( int )` is the second argument for the `signal()` function. The purpose of this argument is simply to point to a function that is to be used when its corresponding signal is raised. The `*func` parameter can use the predefined macros, `SIG_DFL` and `SIG_IGN`, or a user-defined function. If `signal()` is successful, it returns the function pointer `func`.

The `int` argument to `*func` passes the value of the `sig` argument to the signal handler. Thus, the signal-handling function knows which signal it is handling. This is useful when one signal handler deals with more than one signal. You do not have to specify this integer value; it is done automatically.

`int raise( int sig );`

Type: Macro

Returns: Zero if successful, nonzero if unsuccessful.

The `raise()` function sends the signal, `sig`, to the program. Any signal used in the `signal()` function can be used in `raise()`.

Calling the `signal()` function with the following parameters:

```
signal( SIGTERM, SIG_DFL );
```

tells the program to handle an interactive attention signal in the default manner.

In the following:

```
signal( SIGTERM, myfunc );
```

the `signal()` function associates a user-supplied function with the interactive termination signal. Now, when the termination signal occurs, `myfunc()` is called.

At program start up, the equivalent of this function:

```
signal( sig, SIG_IGN );
```

can be executed for some implementation-specified signals. For all other signals, default signal handling is specified.

Listing 15.2 demonstrates some of the ways that `signal()` and `raise()` can be used.

___

Listing 15.2. `sigdemo.c` *(A demonstration of signal handling).*   *QuickC 2.5*

```
 1   #include <stdio.h>
 2   #include <stdlib.h>
 3   #include <signal.h>
 4
 5   void my_func( int sig );
 6
 7   main()
 8   {
 9     int i;
10
11     signal( SIGINT, my_func );
12     signal( SIGABRT, my_func );
13
14     printf( "Enter a CNTRL-BREAK during the loop.\n" );
15     for( i = 1; i <= 250; i++ )
16       printf( "Iteration # %d.\n", i );
17
18     printf( "\n\nNow, the abort signal is raised.\n" );
19     raise( SIGABRT );
20   }
21
22   void my_func( int sig )
23   {
```

```
24      char ch;
25
26      printf( "In the signal-handler.\n" );
27
28      if( sig == SIGINT )
29        printf( "Handling a user interruption.\n\n" );
30      else
31        printf( "Handling an abort signal.\n\n" );
32
33      printf( "Press Return to continue.\n\n" );
34      ch = getchar();
35
36      signal( SIGINT, my_func );
37      signal( SIGABRT, my_func );
38
39      return;
40    }
```

In this listing, the heart of the `main()` function is a loop that provides the opportunity for a user interrupt to be entered. The interactive attention signal is handled in the user-supplied function, `myfunc()`. After the loop is completed, the `raise()` function sends the abort signal to the program. `myfunc()` also handles the abort signal.

`myfunc()` is a signal-handling routine capable of processing more than one signal. This is accomplished by passing a copy of the signal to `myfunc()` in its `sig` parameter. `myfunc()` can use `sig` to select which signal-handling routine to use (see line 28). The `signal()` function handles passing of the `sig`; the programmer does not have to pass this value explicitly.

#include <stdarg.h>

`stdarg.h` provides the capability for processing a variable argument list passed to a function (also called a *variadic* argument list). In a variable argument list, the number of arguments and the type of each argument can change from one invocation of a function to the next.

`va_list`

Type: Type definition

Returns: N/A

`va_list` declares an object used to point to the arguments in a variable argument list. All the macros in `stdarg.h` make use of the `va_list` type argument pointer. A function with a variable argument list must declare an object of `va_list` type, as follows:

```
1  void func1( int i, ... )
2  {
3    va_list ap;
4    ...
5  }
```

This code fragment shows a function definition for a function with a variable argument list. On line 3, a variable of type `va_list` is declared. This argument pointer object, `ap`, is used later to retrieve arguments from the variable argument list.

void va_start(va_list ap, parmN);

Type: Macro

Returns: N/A

`va_start` initializes `ap` so that it can be used by the `va_arg` and `va_end` macros. The `va_start` macro must be invoked before any reference is made to the variable argument list. The argument, `parmN`, is the rightmost parameter in the function definition. In the following code fragment, `parmN` is the argument just before the `, ... )`:

```
1  void func1( int i, ... )
2  {
3    va_list ap;
4    va_start( ap, i );
5    ...
6  }
```

This code fragment declares the argument list `ap` and initializes the argument pointer. `i` is the rightmost parameter in the fixed part of the argument list. That is, `i` is the last parameter before the variable arguments start.

type va_arg(va_list ap, type);

Type: Macro

Returns: After the invocation of the `va_start` macro, the first invocation of `va_arg` returns the value of the argument following `parmN`. Subsequent calls to `va_arg` return the values of the remaining arguments in order.

`va_arg` is used to extract the next argument value from the variable argument list. This macro expands to an expression that has the same type *and* value as the next argument in the list. The `ap` argument given to `va_arg` is the same argument pointer that was initialized in `va_start`. Each time `va_arg` is called, `ap` is modified so that it points to the next argument in the list.

Listing 15.3 shows how to set up and use a function with a variable argument list.

Listing 15.3. `bar.c` *(Using a variable argument list).*   *QuickC 2.5*

```
 1   #include <stdio.h>
 2   #include <stdlib.h>
 3   #include <stdarg.h>
 4
 5   void plot_bar( int scale, ... );
 6
 7   main()
 8   {
 9      printf( "This program creates a simple bar graph.\n\n" );
10      plot_bar( 2, 2, 3, 0, 8, 11, -1 );
11   }
12
13   void plot_bar( int scale, ... )
14   {
15      /* The first argument to this function is a scaling
16         factor. The scaling factor adjusts the size of the
17         bars in the graph. The other arguments should be
18         positive integers. These integers are the values
19         that will be graphed. -1 signals the end of the list.
20      */
21
22      va_list ap;
23      int i;
24      int number;
25
26      va_start( ap, scale );
27
28      number = va_arg( ap, int );
29      while( number != -1 ) {
30         if( number != 0 ) {
31         for( i = 1; i <= ( number / scale ); i++ )
32            printf( "*" );
33         }
34         printf( "\n" );
35
36         number = va_arg( ap,int );
37      }
38
39      va_end( ap );
40   }
```

In this listing, `plot_bar()` plots a number of stars for each argument in its variable argument list. The `plot_bar()` argument, `scale`, adjusts the number of stars printed for each value. If `scale` equals 1, 10 stars are printed for the number 10. If `scale` equals 2, 5 stars are printed for a value of 10.

In both the function declaration and definition, the *ellipsis* characters (`...`) signify a variable argument list. The argument pointer is declared on line 22 and initialized on line 26. The value of the first argument is placed in `number` on line 28. After `number` is set up, the `while` statement loops through the argument list until –1 is encountered. `va_arg()` retrieves the next argument at the bottom of the `while` loop, on line 36. When all values are graphed, `va_end()` cleans up on line 39.

```
void va_end( va_list ap );
```

Type: Macro

Returns: N/A

`va_end` performs the clean-up necessary for a normal return from a function using a variable argument list. `va_end` may modify the value of `ap` so that it cannot be used until it is reinitialized.

When using a variable argument list, you should keep in mind the following guidelines:

❑ *The argument pointer,* `ap`, *can be passed as an argument to another function.* A problem may arise if both functions attempt to process the variable argument list. In the *new* function, if `va_arg()` is invoked with an argument of `ap`, `ap`'s value in the *calling* function is indeterminate. Before any further reference to `ap` can be made in the calling function, `ap` must be passed to the `va_end` macro. This is necessary because using `ap` in more than one function can leave `ap` with an indeterminate value.

❑ *If there is not an invocation of* `va_start` *for each* `va_end` *macro, the behavior is undefined.*

❑ *If* `va_end` *is not called before the function return, the behavior is undefined.*

Summary

The `setjmp.h` header is included when the capability of bypassing the normal function call-and-return process is needed. This capability is useful for dealing with severe errors, or for increasing return speed from deeply nested functions.

`signal.h` provides utilities that allow easy handling of asynchronous, or nonpredictable, events. `signal.h` gives you three choices for handling signals. The default action can be taken, the signal can be ignored, or you can provide your own signal-handling routines.

The `stdarg.h` macros are used for handling the variable argument list of a function header. A variable argument list can have a variable number of arguments as well as different types of arguments.

16

Common Macros and I/O Functions

This chapter covers the stddef.h and stdio.h header files. The former contains definitions and declarations of some of the standard types and macros; the latter, declarations for a large number of input/output functions.

#include <stddef.h>

The stddef.h header file contains definitions of several types, and declarations of two macros. Some of these definitions occur also in other header files. (Compiler vendors usually provide enough #ifdef macros in their headers to prevent a collision of definitions.)

Types

ptrdiff_t

Type: Type definition

Returns: N/A

ptrdiff_t, which means *pointer difference type*, is the type of the result from the subtraction of one pointer from another. Remember that pointers can be meaningfully subtracted only if they are based on the same basic or aggregate object.

`size_t`

Type: Type definition

Returns: N/A

   `size_t` is the *unsigned integral type*. It is used for the result from the `sizeof` operator.

Macros

`wchar_t`

Type: Macro

Returns: N/A

   `wchar_t` is an integral type, large enough to represent all the characters in the largest extended character set specified by the supported locales. In these character sets, the value of the null character should equal zero. There is a restriction also on the values of the characters in the basic character set specified by ANSI. The `wchar_t` type value for a given character should equal its integer character constant value.

`NULL`

Type: Macro

Returns: N/A

   `NULL` is a macro that expands to an implementation-defined null pointer constant.

`offsetof( type, member-designator )`

Type: Function-like macro

Returns: N/A

   `offsetof()` is a macro that expands to an expression with a type of `size_t`. The result of this macro is an offset in bytes from the beginning of a structure to a structure member. The structure is specified by the *type* argument; the structure member, by the *member_designator*.

#include <stdio.h>

   The `stdio.h` header file declares the types, macros, and functions that handle the basic input/output chores in a C program.

Types

stdio.h contains two type declarations: FILE and fpos_t.

FILE

Type: Type definition

Returns: N/A

FILE is the type definition for a pointer to an object that stores information about a stream. This object contains a file-position indicator, a pointer to the buffer associated with the stream, an error indicator, and an end-of-file indicator. The error indicator is used to note whether a read/write error has occurred.

fpos_t

Type: Type definition

Returns: N/A

fpos_t is the type definition for an object that can hold enough information to identify uniquely every position in a file.

Macros

stdio.h contains several predefined macros describing the I/O environment, processing limits, and manifest constants.

_IOFBF
_IOLBF
_IONBF

Type: Macro

Returns: N/A

These three macros expand to integer constant expressions. Used as third argument to the setvbuf() function, specifying the type of buffering to use on a stream, they indicate *full*, *line*, and *no* buffering, repectively.

BUFSIZ

Type: Macro

Returns: N/A

BUFSIZ expands to an integral constant expression. It is both the size of the buffer used by default for I/O operations, and the size assumed by setbuf(). You can change this value (redefine the macro) to affect all subsequent file opens, or you can use setvbuf() to control buffer size on an individual basis.

EOF

Type: Macro

Returns: N/A

EOF is the end-of-file marker. This macro, which expands to a negative integer constant, is used by several functions to indicate that there is no more input from a stream.

FOPEN_MAX

Type: Macro

Returns: N/A

This integer constant expression specifies the maximum number of files the implementation can have open at one time.

FILENAME_MAX

Type: Macro

Returns: N/A

This macro expands to an integer constant expression equal to the maximum length of a file-name string.

L_tmpnam

Type: Macro

Returns: N/A

L_tmpnam is a macro that expands to an integer constant expression. This expression specifies the size of a character array that holds a temporary file name created by the tmpnam() function.

SEEK_CUR
SEEK_END
SEEK_SET

Type: Macro

Returns: N/A

These three macros are integer constant expressions used as the third argument to the `fseek()` function. They indicate that a seek is to be done relative to the currect position, end-of-file, or beginning-of-file, respectively.

TMP_MAX

Type: Macro

Returns: N/A

`TMP_MAX` is an integer constant expression that represents the minimum number of unique file names that can be generated by the `tmpnam()` function.

stderr

Type: Macro

Returns: N/A

`stderr` is a pointer to an object of type `FILE`. `stderr` points to the object associated with the standard error stream.

stdin

Type: Macro

Returns: N/A

`stdin` is a pointer to an object of type `FILE`. `stdin` points to the object associated with the standard input stream.

stdout

Type: Macro

Returns: N/A

`stdout` is a pointer to an object of type `FILE`. `stdout` points to the object associated with the standard output stream.

File Utilities

```
int remove( const char *filename );
```

Type: Function

Returns: Zero if the function is successful; otherwise, nonzero.

`remove()` is used to make a file inaccessible by the file name pointed to by `*filename` (typically, by erasing it from disk). Until the file is recreated, any attempt to reopen it fails. If the file is open when the remove() function is executed, the behavior is implementation-defined.

In the following code fragment, the remove() function removes the file test.txt:

```
i = remove( "test.txt" );
if( i == 0 )
  printf( "remove() worked correctly.\n" );
else
  printf( "remove() did not work.\n" );
```

The value returned by remove() is used to indicate whether the function executed correctly.

`int rename( const char *old, const char *new );`

Type: Function

Returns: Zero, if the function is successful; nonzero, if unsuccessful. If unsuccessful, the file (if it existed) is known by its previous name.

The rename() function is used to rename files. The string pointed to by *old is the file's old name; that pointed to by *new is its new name. If the string pointed to by *new is the name of a file already in existence, the behavior is implementation-defined.

In the following code fragment, the rename() function is invoked to change the name of the file old.txt to new.txt:

```
i = rename( "c:old.txt", "c:new.txt" );
if( i == 0 )
  printf( "rename() worked correctly.\n" );
else
  printf( "rename() did not work.\n" );
```

The value returned by rename() is used to indicate whether the function worked correctly.

`FILE *tmpfile( void );`

Type: Function

Returns: If tmpfile() can create a temporary file, it returns a pointer to the stream of the temporary file. If the file cannot be created, tmpfile() returns a null pointer.

tmpfile() creates a temporary binary file, which is removed either when it is closed or when the program terminates. The implementation defines whether the temporary file is removed when the program terminates abnormally. When the file is created, it is opened in wb+ mode, which means that the temporary file is ready to be updated.

Listing 16.1 shows how the tmpfile() function can be used to create temporary files.

Listing 16.1. temp.c *(Using the* tmpfile() *function).*   *Turbo C++*

```
 1   #include <stdio.h>
 2   #include <stdlib.h>
 3
 4   main()
 5   {
 6     FILE *file_ptr;
 7     int i;
 8
 9     file_ptr = tmpfile();
10
11     if( file_ptr != NULL ) {
12       printf( "The tmpfile() function successfully "
13                  "created a temporary binary file.\n" );
14
15       for( i = 1; i <= 20; i++ )
16         fputc( i, file_ptr );
17       printf( "Binary file updated.\n" );
18
19       rewind( file_ptr );
20       while( ( i = fgetc( file_ptr ) ) != EOF )
21         printf( "i = %d.\n", i );
22       }
23     else
24       printf( "tmpfile() couldn't open a file.\n" );
25   }
```

In line 9 of listing 16.1, tmpfile() creates a temporary binary file and opens it in append mode. The pointer to the stream is stored in the variable file_ptr. Line 11 checks to see whether the file was created. If the file exists, the numbers 1 through 20 are stored in it (see lines 15 and 16). Line 19 resets the file-position pointer. Lines 20 and 21 print the contents of the file.

---

char *tmpnam(char *s);

Type: Function

Returns: The string pointer argument determines the return value of *tmpnam().

If the argument is a null pointer, `*tmpnam()` places the file name in an internal static object. The return value is a pointer to this static object. Subsequent calls to `*tmpnam()` can change the value of the static object. If the argument is not a null pointer, it is assumed to be a pointer to an array of characters that can hold at least `L_tmpnam` chars. In this case, the file name is written to the character array and a pointer to the array is returned by `*tmpnam()`.

`*tmpnam()` creates a new, unique, file name. A different file name is created whenever `*tmpnam()` is called. `*tmpnam()` can create a maximum of `TMP_MAX` new file names. The result of calling `*tmpnam()` more than `TMP_MAX` times is implementation-defined.

In the following code fragment, the `tmpnam()` function is used with a string argument:

```
int i;
char s[80];
.
for( i = 1; i <= 10; i++ ) {
  tmpnam( s );
  printf( "The temporary name is: %s.\n", s );
}
```

On line 5, `tmpnam()` creates a file name and stores it in the string s. On line 6, the temporary file name is printed.

The following line of code:

```
printf( "The file name is: %s.\n", tmpnam( NULL ) );
```

calls the `tmpnam()` function with a null pointer instead of a pointer to a string. In this case, `tmpnam()` stores the temporary file name in an internal static object. A pointer to that object is returned.

Accessing Files

```
int fclose(FILE *stream );
```

Type: Function

Returns: A value of zero, if the `fclose()` is successful; returns
              a value of EOF if `fclose()` encounters problems.

`fclose()` is the function that closes files. `fclose()` flushes the stream pointed to by `*stream` and closes the file associated with that stream. When the file is closed it is disassociated from the stream. Any buffered data that has not been written is sent to the host environment to be written to the file. Any buffered data that has not been read is simply discarded. Automatically allocated buffers are deallocated automatically when `fclose()` is called.

The following code fragment shows how `myfile.dat` is opened for writing and associated with the stream pointed to by `file_ptr`:

```
FILE *file_ptr;
.
file_ptr = fopen( "myfile.dat", "w" );
.
fclose ( file_ptr );
```

When the program is finished with the file, the function `fclose()` is called. The only argument needed for `fclose()` is the pointer to the stream. `fclose()` writes any buffered data to the file, closes the file, and disassociates the stream from the file.

`int fflush(FILE *stream );`

Type: Function

Returns: A value of zero, if the `fflush()` function is successful; a value of EOF, if `fflush()` encounters problems.

`fflush()` flushes the stream pointed to by `*stream`. The behavior of `fflush()` is defined only for output and update streams where the most recent action was output. The `*stream` argument can be a null pointer also. When `*stream` is a null pointer, `fflush()` flushes all files for which its behavior is defined.

Listing 16.2 is a simple program that reads integer numbers and stores them in a binary file.

On lines 19 and 20, the `fflush()` function is used to make sure that all the buffered data has been written to the file.

`FILE *fopen( const char *filename, const char *mode );`

Type: Function

Returns: If `*fopen()` is successful, returns a pointer to the object controlling the stream. If `*fopen()` is unsuccessful, a null pointer is returned.

`fopen()` opens a file and prepares for reading, writing, or appending operations. `fopen()` works with either binary or text files.

Listing 16.2. `flush.c` *(Using the* `fflush()` *function).*   *Turbo C++*

```
 1   #include <stdio.h>
 2   #include <stdlib.h>
 3
 4   main()
 5   {
 6     FILE *file_ptr;
 7     int n = 0;
 8
 9     file_ptr = fopen( "data.fil", "wb" );
10
11     printf( "Enter numbers to store in the data file.\n" );
12     printf( "When complete enter -1.\n" );
13
14     while( n != -1 ) {
15        scanf( "%d", &n );
16        fprintf( file_ptr, "%d ", n );
17     }
18
19     if( fflush( file_ptr ) != EOF )
20        printf( "File flushed successfully.\n" );
21   }
```

The first argument to `fopen()`, `*filename`, points to a string that is the name of the file to be opened. `*fopen()` opens the file and associates a stream with it.

The second argument to `fopen()`, `*mode`, specifies what kind of file to open and what type of operation is to be performed on the file. The following values can be assigned to the `*mode` argument:

Value	Result
`"r"`	Opens a text file for reading
`"w"`	Opens a text file for writing. If file does not exist, it is created; otherwise, file is truncated.
`"a"`	Opens a text file for appending to end of the file. If file does not exist, it is created.
`"rb"`	Opens a binary file for reading
`"wb"`	Opens a binary file for writing. If file does not exist, it is created; otherwise, file is truncated.

"ab"	Opens a binary file for appending to end of the file. If file does not exist, it is created.
"r+"	Opens a text file for updating. Both read and write operations are allowed.
"w+"	Truncates an existing text file to zero length, or creates a new file for updating. Both read and write operations are allowed.
"a+"	Opens or creates a text file for updating at end of the file. Both read and write operations are allowed.
"r+b" or "rb+"	Opens a binary file for updating. Both read and write operations are allowed.
"w+b" or "wb+"	Truncates an existing binary file to zero length or creates a new file for updating. Both read and write operations are allowed.
"a+b" or "ab+"	Opens or creates a binary file for updating at the end of the file. Both read and write operations are allowed.

When the *mode argument specifies a read operation, and the file specified by *filename cannot be opened, the *fopen() function fails.

In append mode, all subsequent writes to the file are made at the end of the file. This is true even if fseek() is called between write operations. When append mode is specified for a binary file, the file-position indicator may be placed beyond the actual end of file because of null-character padding at the end of the file.

In update mode, both read and write operations may be performed. However, read and write operations may not be able to follow each other immediately. A write operation cannot be followed by a read operation until fflush() or a file-positioning function has been called. After a read operation, a file-positioning function must be called before a write operation can take place. (The exception is when the read operation encounters the end of the file.)

When a stream is opened, the indicators for end-of-file and errors are cleared.

Only noninteractive devices can be fully buffered.

In the following code fragment:

```
FILE *file_ptr;
.
if( ( file_ptr = fopen( "my.txt", "a" ) ) != NULL )
   printf( "File opened successfully.\n" );
else
   printf( "Could not open file.\n" );
```

the fopen() function is used to open the text file my.txt in append-update mode. If the value returned by fopen() is equal to NULL, my.txt cannot be opened successfully.

```
FILE *freopen( const char *filename, const char
      *mode,FILE *stream );
```

Type: Function

Returns: If *freopen() can open the file successfully, the value of *stream is returned. If the file cannot be opened successfully, a null pointer is returned.

*freopen() tries to close any file associated with the specified stream. Any errors that occur when closing the file are ignored. After the file associated with the stream has been closed, *freopen() opens the file specified by *filename, and associates it with the stream. *freopen() is used primarily to change the file associated with the standard text streams. The arguments for 1 freopen() follow:

*filename points to a string that contains the name of the file to be reopened.

*mode specifies the mode in which to open the file. (See the discussion of *fopen for a list of the values that can be used for the *mode argument.)

*stream points to the stream object with which the file is associated when it is reopened.

Listing 16.3 uses the freopen() function to redirect the stdout stream to the file temp.txt.

On line 10, the freopen() function is called and the stdout stream is redirected. Thus (on line 15) the putchar() sends output to temp.txt instead of to the screen.

Listing 16.3. `reopen.c` *(Redirecting standard output to a file).*

Turbo C++

```
1    #include <stdio.h>
2    #include <stdlib.h>
3
4    main()
5    {
6      FILE *file_ptr;
7      char c;
8
9      file_ptr = fopen( "test.txt", "r" );
10     if( freopen( "temp.txt", "w", stdout ) == NULL )
11       printf( "Could not redirect.\n" );
12
13     while( !feof( file_ptr ) ){
14       c = fgetc( file_ptr );
15       putchar( c );
16     }
17
18     fclose( file_ptr );
19     fclose( stdout );
20   }
```

void setbuf(FILE *stream, char *buf);

Type: Function

Returns: N/A

`setbuf()` sets up the buffer for the stream pointed to by `*stream`. Normally, `setbuf()` is equivalent to the `setvbuf()` function with the `mode` argument of `IOFBF` and a `size` argument of `BUFSIZE`. If `*buf` is `NULL`, however, `setbuf()` works like `setvbuf()` with a mode argument of `IONBF`. The arguments to `setbuf()` follow:

`*stream` points to a stream object.

`*buf` points to a character array that is used as a buffer for the stream pointed to by `*stream`.

In the following example, `setbuf()` uses the character array `in_buf` to buffer the stream pointed to by `file_ptr`.

```
FILE *file_ptr;
char in_buf[BUFSIZE];
...
file_ptr = fopen( "test.txt", "r" );
setbuf( file_ptr, in_buf )
```

```
int setvbuf( FILE *stream, char *buf, int mode,
    size_t size );
```

Type: Function

Returns: A value of zero, if successful. A nonzero value is
               returned if unsuccessful, or if an invalid value is
               given for mode.

setvbuf() determines how a stream is buffered. It is used after a stream is associated with a file (by open), *but before any operations are performed on the stream*. The arguments for setvbuf() follow:

*stream points to the stream to be buffered.

*buf points to a character array that is used as a buffer for the stream. If *buf is a null pointer, setvbuf() allocates a buffer to be used with the stream. When the file associated with the stream is closed, the buffer is deallocated automatically.

mode specifies the type of buffering for the stream. The values that can be used for the mode argument are as follows:

_IOFBF   I/O is fully buffered.

_IOLBF   I/O is line buffered.

_IONBF   No buffering

size   Specifies the size of the buffer.

Listing 16.4 reads a text file and prints it on the screen.

On line 13, setvbuf() is used to control buffering for the stream. In this example, the stream pointed to by file_ptr is to be line-buffered in the in_buf character array. setvbuf() specifies that the buffer uses only 20 characters of space.

If line 13 in the preceding example were replaced by the following line of code:

```
setvbuf( file_ptr, NULL, _IONBF, 0 );
```

there would be no buffering of the stream pointed to by file_ptr.

Listing 16.4. `buffer.c` *(File buffer setup).*   *Turbo C++*

```
1   #include <stdio.h>
2   #include <stdlib.h>
3
4   main()
5   {
6     FILE *file_ptr;
7     char in_buf[81];
8     char chars[81];
9
10    if( ( file_ptr = fopen( "test.txt", "r" ) ) == NULL )
11      printf( "Could not open file.\n" );
12    else{
13      setvbuf( file_ptr, in_buf, _IOLBF, 20 );
14      while( !feof( file_ptr ) ) {
15        fscanf( file_ptr, "%s", chars );
16        printf( "chars => %s\n", chars );
17      }
18    }
19  }
```

Formatted I/O

```
int fprintf( FILE *stream, const char *format,
    ... );
```

Type: Function

Returns: The number of characters transmitted, if successful. If an output error occurs and `fprintf()` is unsuccessful, a negative number is returned.

`fprintf()` performs formatted output to the stream pointed to by `*stream`. The format of the output is controlled by the string pointed to by `*format`. The format string determines how all the following arguments are to be converted. When the end of the format string is reached, the `fprintf()` function returns.

The conversion specifications in the format string should match the arguments following the format string. The behavior is undefined when there are not enough arguments to match the conversion specifications. If there are more arguments than conversion specifications, the excess arguments are evaluated in the normal manner, but otherwise ignored. The arguments for `fprintf()` are as follows:

`*stream` points to the stream to which the output of the `fprintf()` function is sent.

*format points to the format string. The *format string* is simply a string composed of multibyte characters and conversion specifications. Multibyte characters usually are normal characters and are sent directly to the output stream. These characters appear the same in the format string and in the output stream.

A conversion specification gets zero or more arguments from the variable argument list of the fprintf() function and determines how the argument appears in the output stream. A conversion specification always starts with the % character.

You can list a variable number of arguments that you want converted and sent to the output stream. The number of arguments given must match the number of conversion specifiers in the format string.

Immediately after the % start-conversion character, you can write optional modifier character(s), followed by the required conversion type characters. The following list shows the modifiers in the order in which they should appear:

1. *Flags*. Zero or more flags can be used. A flag changes the meaning of the conversion specification. The optional flags are as follows:

   –   The left adjustment flag. When used, the converted number is left-justified in the display field.

   +   The sign flag, which specifies that a signed number starts with either a plus or minus sign.

   space   When the first character in a signed conversion is not a sign, or when a signed conversion does not produce any character, a space is added before the result. If both the *space* and sign flags appear, the *space* flag is ignored.

   #   Specifies a certain display form for several of the conversion specifications. When used with the o conversion specification, the result is forced to a precision large enough to display a leading zero character. When used with the x or X specification, the result has the leading characters 0x. With the e, E, f, g, and G conversion specifications, a decimal point always is displayed. With the g and G specifications, trailing zeros always are displayed.

2. *Field width*. The field-width specification is entered as a decimal integer. It determines the minimum width of the field in which a converted value is placed. If the converted value is smaller than the field width, the excess space is padded with blanks. The use of the left adjustment flag determines whether padding is to the left or right of the value. Field width is an optional argument.

3. *Precision*. Precision determines how many digits are displayed. The precision argument has slightly different meanings for integer type and floating-point type numbers. For integer type numbers (d, i, o, u, x, and X) the precision argument specifies the minimum number of digits to display. For floating-point type numbers (e, E, f, g, and G) the precision argument specifies the number of digits to follow the decimal point. The precision argument can also specify the number of characters to be written when the conversion type is s. The precision argument is entered as a decimal point followed by an integer. If the integer value is not given, it is assumed to be zero. The precision argument is optional.

4. h, l, L. The h can be used in the following two ways:

   When used with the d, i, o, u, x, and X conversion specifications, h specifies that the conversion specification is for a short int or an unsigned short int. When either type of short int is included in the argument list, it undergoes automatic type conversion. h forces the integer to be converted to a short int or an unsigned short int before it is printed.

   When used with the n conversion specification, h specifies that the pointer points to a short int.

   The l argument works like the h argument except that the l is used for long int. l can be used with the d, i, o, u, x, X, and n conversion specifiers.

   L is used with the e, E, f, g, and G conversion specifiers to indicate that the argument in fprintf()'s variable argument list is a long double.

   The h, l, L arguments are optional. The behavior of h, l, and L is undefined if they are used with conversion specifiers other than the ones listed.

5. *Conversion specifier.* The conversion specifier is a character that indicates the type of the argument to be converted. The following discussion includes a list of the conversion specifiers and their meanings.

An asterisk (*) can be used to specify the field width or precision. When an asterisk is used, the fprintf() variable argument list must contain an int argument to supply the value for the field width, precision, or both. In the argument list, the int argument for the field width should be first, followed by the argument for precision (if needed), and then by the argument to be converted (if there is one). If the field-width argument is a negative number, it is assumed to be a – flag followed by a positive field-width argument. If the precision argument is negative, it is treated as if it were missing.

The many conversion specifier characters for fprintf() apply to the whole family of ...printf() functions. They are as follows:

❑ *The* d, i, o, u, x, *and* X *conversion specifications are used with integer arguments.* Each conversion specification results in a specific display format. d and i result in a signed decimal format. o results in an unsigned octal format. u results in an unsigned decimal format. x or X result in an unsigned hexadecimal format. x denotes that the hexadecimal characters, a, b, c, d, e, and f are used. X denotes that the hexadecimal characters A, B, C, D, E, and F, are used. The precision argument specifies the minimum number of digits to be displayed (the default value is 1). If a value cannot fill the field, the value is converted with leading zeros.

❑ *The* e *and* E *conversion specifications are used with a floating-point number of type* double. The number is converted to the format *[-]d.ddde+-dd*. There is one digit before the decimal point. If the number is nonzero, the first displayed digit is nonzero. The number of digits following the decimal point is specified by the precision. The default value for precision is 6 digits after the decimal point. No decimal point is displayed when the precision is zero. The number is rounded to the nearest digit. When the conversion specification is E, an E is used before the exponent. If the conversion specification is e, an e is used before the exponent. The exponent is always two digits long. When the exponent is equal to zero, a zero is displayed.

❑ *The* f *conversion specification is used with a* double *floating-point number.* The number is displayed in the format *[-] ddd.ddd*. At least one digit appears before the decimal point (when a decimal point is used). The number of digits following the decimal point is determined by the precision argument. The default value for the precision argument is 6. If the precision is equal to 0, the decimal point is not displayed. The value of the number is rounded to the appropriate number of digits.

❏ *The g and G conversion specifications are used with double floating-point numbers.* The value is converted to either the e or f format if g is used; to the E format if G is used. When used with the g and G arguments, the precision argument specifies the number of significant digits. The precision argument is forced to the value of 1 when a value of zero is specified. The output style depends on the value of the number to be converted. The e format is used only when the exponent of the converted number is less than –4 or greater than or equal to the specified precision. A decimal point is used only when it is followed by a digit. Any trailing zeros are eliminated.

❏ *c is used with an integer argument.* The integer is converted to an unsigned char and printed.

❏ *For a conversion specification of s, the argument should be a pointer to a string.* The contents of the string are printed up to, but not including, the terminating null character. A precision value can be specified for the s conversion. The precision value indicates how many characters from the string (character array) should be printed. If the precision is greater than the size of the character array, or if the precision is not given, the character array should have a terminating null character.

❏ *The p conversion specification is used with a pointer to type* void. A sequence of printable characters is generated from the value of the pointer. This operation is carried out in an implementation-defined manner (the usual action is to hex-dump the pointer).

❏ *The n specification has no argument.* It indicates a pointer to an integer that receives the number of characters fprintf() has written during its current call. The argument must be a pointer to int.

❏ *When the % character is used as a conversion specification, no argument is converted.* The only effect is that the % character is written to the output stream.

Listing 16.5. `get_name.c` *(A simple example of using* `fprintf()`*).*

Turbo C++

```
 1   #include <stdio.h>
 2   #include <stdlib.h>
 3
 4   main()
 5   {
 6     FILE *file_ptr;
 7     char first[10];
 8     char last[10];
 9     int age;
10
11     file_ptr = fopen( "data.fil", "w" );
12
13     printf( "Enter a first name, last name and age.\n" );
14     printf( "When finished, enter a ^Z.\n " );
15
16     while( scanf( "%s %s %d", first, last, &age ) != EOF )
17       fprintf( file_ptr, "%s %s .%d ", first, last, age );
18
19     fclose( file_ptr );
20   }
```

Listing 16.5 contains a simple example of using `fprintf()`. (Listing 16.6 is a more complicated example.)

The program in this listing uses `fprintf()` to write formatted data to a text file. The `...printf()` always produces display-text type information. Lines 1 through 11 perform the program's setup. On line 16, the `scanf()` function is used to get a person's first and last names and his or her age. When a `^Z` is entered, `scanf()` returns a value of `EOF`. The routine then closes the text file and returns. On line 17, the `fprintf()` sends formatted data to the file `data.fil`. The formatted data sent to the file includes two strings and an integer.

The example in listing 16.6 illustrates a wider range of conversion specifiers.

Listing 16.6 demonstrates some of the many ways the `fprintf()` function can output data. Lines 16 through 20 print integers. Line 16 left-justifies a decimal integer in a field 10 characters wide. Line 17 right-justifies an integer in a field 10 characters wide. On lines 18 and 19, octal and hexadecimal numbers are preceded with `0` and `0x`, respectively. On line 20, the conversion specification `%hd` signifies that a short integer was printed.

In the `print_it()` function, lines 23 through 26 print floating-point numbers. On line 23, the minimum field width is 11 characters (including

Listing 16.6. `print_it.c` *(Second example of* `fprintf()`*).*   *Turbo C++*

```
 1  #include <stdio.h>
 2  #include <stdlib.h>
 3
 4  main()
 5  {
 6     int i = 10;
 7     short int j = 128;
 8     double c = 186282.3976;
 9     long double d = 15000000.00;
10     char ch = 'A';
11     char *str = "Hello";
12     FILE *fp;
13
14     fp = fopen( "print.out", "wb" );
15
16     fprintf( fp, "i as a decimal integer     : %-10d\n", i
);
17     fprintf( fp, "i as unsigned integer      : %10u\n", i );
18     fprintf( fp, "i as an octal integer      : %#o\n", i );
19     fprintf( fp, "i as a hexadecimal integer: %#x\n", i );
20     fprintf( fp, "j is a short integer       : %hd\n", j );
21     fprintf( fp, "\n" );
22
23     fprintf( fp, "c in normal format      : %6.4f\n", c );
24     fprintf( fp, "c in exponential format: %e\n", c);
25     fprintf( fp, "c in optimal format     : %g\n", c);
26     fprintf( fp, "d is as long double     : %10.0Lf\n", d );
27     fprintf( fp, "\n" );
28
29     fprintf( fp, "str is the string: %s\n", str );
30     fprintf( fp, "ch is the character: %c\n", ch );
31  }
```

the decimal point and the following digits). Line 26 prints a `long double` floating-point number.

Lines 29 and 30 in the `print_it()` function print characters and strings. On line 29, the `%s` specification is used to print a string. On line 30, the `%c` specification is used to print a single character.

```
int fscanf( FILE *stream, const char *format,
        ... );
```

Type: Function

Returns: The number of elements input and converted. This can be fewer than called for, or even zero because of matching errors. `EOF` is returned if an error occurs before any conversions.

`fscanf()` retrieves data from a stream, according to a specified format. The format determines what data can be read and how that data is converted for storage. Following the input specification is a list of objects where the input data is stored. The arguments for `fscanf()` apply to the whole `...scanf()` family of functions. They are as follows:

`*stream` designates the stream the input comes from.

`*format` points to a format string. The format string specifies what data is read and how that data is converted for storage. The format string is a multibyte character sequence that forms zero or more directives. A directive can be one or more whitespace characters, a regular multibyte character, or a conversion specification. Each conversion specification is preceded by the % character.

. . . The variable argument list contains arguments *that must be pointers to objects* in which the input data is stored.

The following parameters can precede and modify the conversion specification:

❏ *The assignment-suppression character (*).*

❏ *Field width.* A decimal integer can be used to specify the maximum field width.

❏ *The* h, l, *or* L *characters indicate the size of the object in which the data is stored.* The conversion specifiers d, i, and n can be preceded by h and l. h indicates that the object in the variable argument list is a pointer to a `short int` instead of an `int`. l indicates that the object pointed to is a `long int`. The conversion specifiers o, u, and x can be used with h and l. h indicates that object pointed to is an `unsigned short int`. l indicates that the object is an `unsigned long int`. e, f, and g can be used with the modifiers l and L. l specifies that the object pointed to is of type `double` instead of type `float`. L specifies that the object should be of type `long double`. When using h, l, or L with any other conversion specifiers, the behavior is undefined.

The format string is composed of a series of directives. A directive does not have to be a conversion specification. The directives and their effects are as follows:

❏ *Whitespace.* A whitespace character in the format string causes the input data to be read up to, but not including, the first nonwhitespace character (or until no more input data can be read).

❏ *Multibyte character*. A multibyte (or normal) character causes characters in the stream to be read. It is expected that the characters read *exactly match* the characters in the directive. When the characters in the stream do not match the multibyte directive, the directive fails. The unmatched character causing the failure is not read.

❏ *Conversion specification*. A conversion specification retrieves enough data from the stream to match the specification. The conversion specifier characters are

d   Inputs a decimal integer. The format of this input should be the same as the argument for the `strtol()` function when used with 10 for the `base` argument. Optionally, the input can be signed. The matching argument in the variable argument list should point to an integer.

i   Inputs an integer. The format of this input should be the same as the argument for the `strtol()` function when used with 0 for the `base` argument. Optionally, the input can be signed. The matching argument in the variable argument list should point to an integer.

o   Inputs an octal integer. The format of this input should be the same as the argument for the `strtol()` function when used with 8 as the `base` argument. Optionally, the input can be signed. The matching argument in the variable argument list should point to an unsigned integer.

u   Inputs a decimal integer. The format of this input should be the same as the argument for the `strtol()` function when used with 10 as the `base` argument. Optionally, the input can be signed. The matching argument in the variable argument list should point to an unsigned integer.

X and x
    Input a hexadecimal integer. The format of this input should be the same as the argument for the `strtoul()` function when used with 16 as the `base` argument. Optionally, the input can be signed. The matching argument in the variable argument list should point to an unsigned integer.

e, E, f, G, and g

> Input a floating-point number. The format of this input should be the same as the argument for the `strtod()` function. Optionally, the input can be signed. The matching argument in the variable argument list should point to a floating-point type.

s

> Inputs a sequence of nonwhitespace characters. The matching argument in the variable argument list should point to a character array large enough to hold all the input characters plus a terminating null character. The null character is added automatically after the last input character.

[

> This character starts a set of characters against which input characters are checked. All input characters found in the set are read. The matching argument in the variable argument list should point to a character array large enough to hold all the input characters plus a terminating null character. The null character is added automatically following the last input character. The characters between the [and] characters form a *scanlist*. All the characters found in the scanlist are read. If the ^ character is the first character in the scanlist, all characters *except* those in the scanlist are read. The [character can be used in the scanlist if it is the first character following the [character or if it follows the ^ character. When the – character is not the first character in the scanlist, or the second, with ^ being first, the behavior of the conversion specification is implementation-defined.

c

> Inputs a number of characters specified by the field width. The argument in the variable argument list points to an array large enough to hold all the characters. A terminating null character is not added to this array. The default field width for the c conversion specification is 1.

p

> This conversion specification works with an implementation-defined sequence of characters that matches the `fprintf()` %p conversion specification. The argument in the variable argument list should be a pointer to type `void`.

This specification does not input any data. It is used to record the number of characters read from the stream, up to that point, by the `fscanf()` function. The matching argument in the variable argument list should be a pointer to an integer. The `n` specification does not add to the assignment count returned by the `fscanf()` function.

%   Inputs a single % character. No assignment or conversion is performed. The specification is used simply to read the % character.

There are three steps to processing a conversion specification. In the first step, the whitespace characters in the input stream normally are skipped. When the `[`, `c`, or `n` conversion specifiers are used, whitespace is not skipped.

In the second step, an input item is read. An *input item* is a group of characters that matches the type of the conversion specification. As many characters as possible, up to the maximum field width, are used for an input item. The character immediately following the input item is left unread. An input or a matching failure can occur at this point. An input failure occurs if the data cannot be read, and a matching failure occurs if the length of the input item is zero.

Finally, in the third step, the input item is converted to the type indicated by the conversion specification. If the input item does not match, a matching failure occurs. After the input item has been converted, it is stored in the appropriate object from the variable argument list. If the `*` conversion specification is used, the input item is not stored. When an `n` conversion specifier is encountered, the number of characters read is placed in the storage object. If the input item's type does not match the type of the storage object, the behavior of the conversion specification is undefined.

`fscanf()` is a sophisticated function that uses a format string, a variable argument list, and input data. Unpredictable behavior or errors result when these parts do not match. There are two general types of mismatches.

The first type of mismatch occurs between the format string and the variable argument list. If the variable argument list does not contain enough arguments to match the format string, the behavior is undefined. Each implementation may handle this situation differently. If the variable argument list contains more arguments than conversion specifications, the extra arguments are evaluated and ignored.

The second type of mismatch can occur between the format string and input data. When the format string and the input data do not match, a failure occurs that causes fscanf() to return. An input failure occurs when there is not enough data for the format string. An end-of-file encountered during the input process generally causes an input failure. A matching failure occurs when the input data does not match the format string.

Listing 16.7 shows how fscanf() is used to read records from a data file.

Listing 16.7. get_data.c *(Using fscanf() to read information from a file).*
Microsoft C 6.0

```
 1   #include <stdio.h>
 2   #include <stdlib.h>
 3
 4   main()
 5   {
 6      FILE *file_ptr;
 7      int emp_num;
 8      char first[15];
 9      char last[15];
10      char class;
11      double hours;
12      double rate;
13
14      file_ptr = fopen( "scan.dat", "r" );
15
16      while(  fscanf( file_ptr, "%d %s %s %[1-9] %lf %lf ",
17                     &emp_num, first, last, &class, &hours,
18                     &rate ) != EOF ) {
19         printf( "Employee number :%d\n", emp_num );
20         printf( "Name : %s %s\n", first, last );
21         printf( "Employee classification : %c\n", class );
22         printf( "Hours worked : %4.1f\n", hours );
23         printf( "Hourly rate : $%5.2f\n", rate );
24      }
25
26      fclose( file_ptr );
27   }
```

Listing 16.7 shows how fscanf() can retrieve information from a file. In this example, employee information is read from the scan.dat file. On lines 16 through 18, fscanf() is used inside a while loop to step through the data file. Because fscanf() advances the file pointer automatically, a scpa- rate statement is not needed. Notice that fscanf() can be compared to the value EOF, a capability that permits checking for the end-of-file condition.

fscanf() scans a stream and stores the data it retrieves at the *address* specified in the variable argument list. That is why variables such as emp_num, class, hours, and rate are preceded by the address-of character (&). Because the variables first and last are strings, preceding them with the address-of character is not necessary. The name of the string yields the address of the first character of the string. The conversion specification %[1-9] stores any character between 1 and 9 in the variable class. The %lf conversions match input to variables of type double.

The next code fragment shows how fsconf() can retrieve a hexadecimal value.

```
int i;
...
fscanf( stdin, " %x ", i );
```

When fscanf() is used with the %x conversion specifier, it scans in a hexadecimal number. In the last line of this code fragment, a hexadecimal number is scanned and stored in the integer variable i. The hexadecimal number can be signed.

In the following example:

```
char char_in[10];
FILE *my_file;
...
fscanf( my_file, " %10c ", char_in );
```

fscanf() scans in ten characters from the file pointed to by my_file. The characters are stored in the character array char_in. When the %c conversion specification is used, the array in which the characters are stored must be large enough to hold all the input characters. A null character is not added to the end of the string.

The next code fragment shows how fsconf() can count the number of characters it has read.

```
char my_str[256]
int scan_in;
...
fscanf( std_in, " %s %n ", my_str, &scan_in );
```

The %n conversion specification stores the number of characters read by fscanf(). The %n does not read data from the stream, but does store the number of characters read in a variable. In this example, scan_in is used to hold the number of characters read by this invocation of fscanf().

```
fscanf( std_in, " %% " );
```

%% specifies that the % character should be matched in the input stream. However, no conversion takes place and the % character is not stored in a variable.

```
int printf( const char *format, ... );
```

Type: Function

Returns: The number of characters printed, if successful. If an
               output error occurred, a negative value is returned.

The `printf()` function is the same as `fprintf()` with `stdout` used as
the output stream.

```
int scanf( const char *format, ... );
```

Type: Function

Returns: The number of elements input and converted. (This can
               be fewer than called for, or even zero because of
               matching errors. EOF is returned if an error occurs
               before any conversions.

The `scanf()` function is the same as `fscanf()` with `stdin` used as the
input stream.

```
int sprintf( char *s, const char *format, ... );
```

Type: Function

Returns: The number of characters output to the array. The
               terminating null character is not included in the
               character count.

The `sprintf()` function works much the same as `fprintf()`. The only
difference is that `sprintf()` sends its output to an array instead of a stream.
At the end of the characters written to the array, `sprintf()` appends a
terminating null character. The arguments for `sprintf()` are as follows:

`*s` is a pointer to the character array where the output is to be sent.

`*format` is a pointer to a format string. The format string controls which
data is printed and how it appears.

`...` indicates the variable argument list. In the variable argument list are
all the variables that are printed under control of the format string.

```
int sscanf( const char *s, const char *format,
      ... );
```

Type: Function

Returns: The number of elements input and converted. This can be
               fewer than called for, or even zero because of matching
               errors. EOF is returned if an error occurs before any
               conversions.

The `sscanf()` function works much the same as the `fscanf()` function. `sscanf()` gets its input from a string, however, whereas `fscanf()` gets its input from a file. When `sscanf()` reaches the end of the string, it behaves as `fscanf()` does when it reaches the end of the file.

`*s` is a pointer to the string `sscanf()` scans. The format string and the variable argument list work the same as in `fscanf()`.

```
int vfprintf( FILE *stream, const char *format,
    va_list arg );
```

Type: Function

Returns: The number of characters printed, if successful. If an
               output error occurred, a negative value is returned.

The `vfprintf()` function works much the same as the `fprintf()` function, but `vfprintf()` accesses the variable argument list in a different way. The variable argument list in `fprintf()` is replaced by the single argument `arg` in `vfprintf()` (see the discussion of `vprintf()`). The arguments for `vfprintf()` follow:

`*stream` points to the stream to which data is printed.

`*format` is a pointer to a format string. The format string controls which data is printed and how it appears.

`arg` is a pointer to a variadic argument list. In `vfprintf()`, the variable argument list is not in the function call; only a pointer to a variable argument list is in the function call. `arg` should be initialized by the `va_start` macro before `vfprintf()` is called. `vfprintf()` does not call the `va_end` macro automatically. The programmer should call `va_end` for `arg` when `vfprintf()` is finished.

```
int vprintf( const char *format, va_list arg );
```

Type: Function

Returns: If successful, returns the number of characters printed.
               If an output error occurred, a negative value is returned.

The `vprintf()` function works much the same as the `printf()` function, except that the variable argument list is handled differently in `vprintf()`. In `vprintf()` the variable argument list is replaced by a pointer to a variable argument list. The arguments for `vprintf()` are as follows:

`*format` is a pointer to a format string. The format string controls which data is printed and how it appears.

arg points to a variable argument list. The va_start() macro should be called for arg before the vprintf() function is invoked. After vprintf(), the va_end() macro should be called for arg.

Listing 16.8 shows how vprintf() is used.

Listing 16.8. vprint.c *(A demonstration of* vprintf()).   *Turbo C++*

```
1    #include <stdio.h>
2    #include <stdlib.h>
3    #include <stdarg.h>
4
5    void diags( char *f_name, char *format, ... );
6
7    main()
8    {
9      int i;
10     char c;
11     double x;
12
13     printf( "Enter an integer, character and float.\n" );
14     printf( "==>   " );
15     scanf( "%d %c %ld", &i, &c, &x );
16
17     diags( "main", "i = %d, c = %c, x = %ld\n", i, c, x );
18   }
19
20   void diags( char *f_name, char *format, ... )
21   {
22     va_list arg_ptr;
23
24     va_start( arg_ptr, format );
25
26     printf( "*****************************\n" );
27     printf( "Diagnostic report\n\n" );
28     printf( "Executing function %s\n\n", f_name );
29
30     vprintf( format, arg_ptr );
31
32     printf( "*****************************\n" );
33
34     va_end( arg_ptr );
35   }
```

This listing shows a simple example of the use of vprintf(). In the function diags(), vprintf() prints part of a diagnostic report. vprintf() uses the format string and variable argument list that was passed to diags().

A pointer to the variable argument list must be set up before the list can be used. (This is done with the variable argument macros on lines 22 and 24.) vprintf() is then called on line 30. In vprintf(), format points to the format string passed to diags(). arg_ptr is the pointer to the variable argument list. When finished with the variable argument list, the va_end() macro must be called.

```
int  vsprintf(  char  *s,  const  char  *format,
         va_list arg );
```

Type: Function

Returns: The number of characters output to the array. The terminating null character is not included in the character count.

The vsprintf() function works much the same as the sprintf() function, except that the variable argument list is handled differently in vsprintf(). In vsprintf(), the variable argument list is replaced by a pointer to a variable argument list (see the discussion in vprintf()). The arguments for vsprintf() follow:

*s is a pointer to the character array where the output is sent.

*format is a pointer to a format string. The format string controls which data is printed and how it appears.

arg points to a variable argument list. The va_start() macro should be called for arg before the vsprintf() function is invoked. After vsprintf(), the va_end() should be called for arg.

Character I/O

```
int fgetc( FILE *stream );
```

Type: Function

Returns: If successful, fgetc() returns the next character from the stream pointed to by *stream. If the stream is at the end of the file, EOF is returned and the EOF marker for the stream is set. If fgetc() is unsuccessful, a value of EOF is returned and the error marker for the stream is set.

fgetc() inputs the next character from the stream pointed to by *stream. The character is read as an unsigned char and returned from the fgetc() function as an int. After fgetc() reads a character, it advances the stream's file-position indicator, if it exists.

*stream points to an input stream. The following simple example:

```
char in;
...
while( ( in = fgetc( stdin ) ) != EOF )
  printf( "%c" in );
```

uses the fgetc() function to get characters from the standard input stream until an end-of-file condition is signaled. The input characters are echoed by the printf() statement.

```
char *fgets( char *s, int n, FILE *stream );
```

Type: Function

Returns: If successful, fgets() returns s. If no characters have been read and an end-of-file has been encountered, a null pointer is returned. The array is left unchanged. If fgets() is unsuccessful because of a read error, a null pointer is returned. The contents of the array are indeterminate.

The fgets() function reads a string from the stream pointed to by *stream and stores it in the array pointed to by *s. fgets() reads up to (n–1) characters. fgets() stops before (n–1) characters are read if a newline or end-of-file character is encountered. The newline character is stored in the array. fgets() appends a null character to the end of the string it stores in the array. The arguments for fgets() are as follows:

*s points to the array in which fgets() stores characters.

n specifies the maximum number of characters to be read. A maximum of (n–1) characters are read.

*stream specifies the input stream. This is the stream from which fgets() reads characters.

Listing 16.9 shows how fgets() can be used to read a string from a text file.

Listing 16.9. fget_str.c *(Reading a file with* fgets()*).*   *Turbo C++*

```
1   #include <stdio.h>
2   #include <stdlib.h>
3
4   main()
5   {
6     #define MAX_IN 256
7
```

```
8     FILE *file_ptr;
9     char str[MAX_IN];
10
11    file_ptr = fopen( "test.txt", "r" );
12
13    while( !feof( file_ptr ) ) {
14       fgets( str, MAX_IN, file_ptr );
15       printf( "%s", str );
16    }
17
18    fclose( file_ptr );
19  }
```

On line 14, `fgets()` reads a string from the file pointed to by `file_ptr`. Line 15 prints the string on-screen.

```
int fputc( int c, FILE *stream );
```

Type: Function

Returns: If `fputc()` is successful, it returns the character `c`.
If `fputc()` encounters a write error, it returns a
value of `EOF`. When a write error is encountered,
`fputc()` sets the error indicator for the stream.

`fputc()` writes one character to the output stream pointed to by `*stream`. The integer `c` is converted to an `unsigned char` before it is written to the output stream. `fputc()` writes the character at the position specified by the file-position indicator and then advances the indicator. In streams that do not support a position indicator or that were opened in append mode, the character is appended to the stream. The arguments for `fputc()` are as follows:

The integer `c` is the character that is output.

`*stream` is a pointer to the output stream where the character is written.

Listing 16.10, a file-copying program built around two lines of code, illustrates the use of `fputc()`.

Listing 16.10. `f_copy.c` *(Copying files using `fputc()`).*   *Turbo C++*

```
1   #include <stdio.h>
2   #include <stdlib.h>
3
4   main()
5   {
```

Listing 16.10. continues

Listing 16.10. continued

```
 6     FILE *file_ptr1;
 7     FILE *file_ptr2;
 8     int c;
 9
10     file_ptr1 = fopen( "test.txt", "r" );
11     file_ptr2 = fopen( "new.fil", "w" );
12
13     while( ( c = fgetc( file_ptr1 ) ) != EOF )
14       fputc( c, file_ptr2 );
15
16     fclose( file_ptr1 );
17     fclose( file_ptr2 );
18  }
```

In listing 16.10, `fgetc()` repetitively reads characters from a file until the end of the file is reached. `fputc()` is used to copy the input characters to another file. The `while()` that does the file copy is on line 13 and 14. The rest of the program is set up for variables and the opening and closing of files.

```
int fputs( const char *s, FILE *stream );
```

Type: Function
Returns: A nonnegative value, if successful. A value of `EOF` is
               returned if a write error occurs.

The `fputs()` function writes the string pointed to by `*s` to the stream pointed to by `*stream`. The arguments for `fputs()` follow:

`*s` points to the string to be output.

`*stream` points to the output stream.

Listing 16.11 demonstrates how `fputs()` can be used to write strings to a file.

Listing 16.11. `fput_str.c` *(A demonstration of* `fputs()`*).*   *Turbo C++*

```
1  #include <stdio.h>
2  #include <stdlib.h>
3
4  main()
5  {
6     FILE *file_ptr;
7     char str[256];
8
```

```
 9      file_ptr = fopen( "myfile.txt", "w" );
10
11      printf( "Type text for 'myfile.txt'.\n" );
12      printf( "Enter ^Z on a blank line when finished.\n\n" );
13
14      while( gets( str ) != NULL ) {
15         fputs( str, file_ptr );
16         fputs( "\n", file_ptr );
17      }
18
19      fclose( file_ptr );
20   }
```

The `while()` loop on lines 14 through 17 reads strings from `stdin`. The only thing to notice about this `while()` loop is how the end of the file is detected. A `^Z` (end-of-file marker) is entered on a line by itself. When `gets()` reads the end-of-file indicator, `gets()` returns a null pointer. `fputs()` takes the string stored in `str` and puts it in the file pointed to by `file_ptr`. `fputs()` is called again to put a newline character at the end of the string, because `gets()` discards the newline character it read.

`int getc( FILE *stream );`

Type: Macro implementation of a function

Returns: If successful, `getc()` returns the next character from
              the stream. If the end-of-file is encountered, the
              value `EOF` is returned and the end-of-file indicator for
              the stream is set. If unsuccessful because of a read
              error, a value of `EOF` is returned and the error
              indicator for the stream is set.

Normally `getc()` is equivalent to the `fgetc()` function. In some implementations, `getc()` is a macro that may be able to evaluate the stream more than once. `*stream` points to an input stream.

`int getchar( void );`

Type: Function

Returns: If successful, `getchar()` returns the next character
              from the stream. If the end-of-file is encountered, the
              value `EOF` is returned and the end-of-file indicator for
              the stream is set. If unsuccessful because of a read
              error, a value of `EOF` is returned and the error
              indicator for the stream is set.

`getchar()` is exactly the same as `getc()` with the `*stream` argument specified as `stdin`.

`char *gets( char *s );`

Type: Function

Returns: If successful, `gets()` returns s. If no characters have been read and an end-of-file has been encountered, a null pointer is returned. The array is left unchanged. If `gets()` is unsuccessful because of a read error, a null pointer is returned. The contents of the array are indeterminate.

`gets()` reads a string from the stream `stdin` and stores it in the array pointed to by `*s`. `gets()` works like the `fgets()` function with the stream specified as `stdin`. `gets()` reads characters until it encounters the end-of-file or a newline character. The newline character is discarded and a null character is added to the end of the string stored in the array.

`int putc( int c, FILE *stream );`

Type: Macro implementation of a function

Returns: If successful, `putc()` returns c, the character it has written. If a write error occurs, `putc()` returns a value of `EOF` and sets the error indicator for the stream.

Normally, `putc()` is equivalent to the `fputc()` function. In some implementations, however, `putc()` can be a macro that can evaluate the stream more than once. Its arguments are as follows:

The integer value c is the character that is to be written.

`*stream` is a pointer to the output stream.

`int putchar( int c );`

Type: Function

Returns: If successful, `putchar()` returns c, the character it has written. If a write error occurs, `putchar()` returns a value of `EOF` and sets the error indicator for the stream.

`putchar()` is the same as `putc()` with a `*stream` argument of `stdout`. c is the character to be written.

This line of code writes the character *a* to the screen:

`putchar( 'a' );`

And this call to `putchar()`:

```
char a;
putchar( a );
```

writes the character stored in the variable a to the screen:

`int puts( const char *s );`

Type: Function

Returns: A nonnegative value, if `puts()` is successful. If a write error occurs and `puts()` is unsuccessful, a value of `EOF` is returned.

`puts()` writes the string pointed to by `*s` to the stream `stdout`. The terminating null character for the string is not written, but a newline character is appended to the string and output.

The following two lines of code write the string "C is great!" and a newline character to the standard output device:

```
char str[20] = "C is great!";
...
puts( str );
```

`int ungetc( int c, FILE *stream );`

Type: Function

Returns: If successful, `ungetc()` returns the `unsigned char` that was pushed back to the input stream. If unsuccessful, a value of `EOF` is returned.

`ungetc()` returns, or *pushes back*, a character to the input stream. Although a character is pushed back onto the stream, the external device associated with that stream is not changed.

`ungetc()` cannot push back a character with a value equal to `EOF`. If this is done, the operation fails and the input stream is left unchanged.

It is guaranteed that one character can be pushed back. Additional characters may be able to be pushed back. However, if too many calls are made to `ungetc()` without any read or file-positioning operations, `ungetc()` may fail.

A character pushed back on the stream can be retrieved by a read operation. If more than one character was pushed back, the characters are retrieved in *LIFO* (Last In, First Out) order. Any pushed-back characters is discarded if a file-positioning function is called.

On a successful call to ungetc(), the end-of-file indicator is cleared if it was already set.

After all the pushed-back characters have been read or discarded, the value of the file-position indicator should be the same as it was before ungetc() was called. On text streams, the value of the file-position indicator is indeterminate until all pushed-back characters are cleared by either a read operation or a file-positioning operation. On binary streams, the value of the file-position indicator is decremented for each successful call to ungetc(). However, if the initial value of the file-position indicator was zero, its value is indeterminate after a call to ungetc().

The arguments for ungetc() are as follows:

c is the character to be pushed back onto the input stream.

*stream is a pointer to the input stream onto which a character is pushed back by ungetc().

Listing 16.12 shows how ungetc() pushes characters back on the stream.

Listing 16.12. un_read.c *(Using the* ungetc() *function).*   *Turbo C++*

```
 1   #include <stdio.h>
 2   #include <stdlib.h>
 3
 4   main()
 5   {
 6      FILE *file_ptr;
 7      int c;
 8      int pass;
 9      int uc = 32;
10
11      file_ptr = fopen( "test.txt", "r" );
12      pass = 0;
13
14      while( !feof( file_ptr ) ) {
15         if( pass == 0 ) {
16            ungetc( uc, file_ptr );
17            pass = 1;
18         }
19         else {
20            c = fgetc( file_ptr );
21            putchar( c );
22            c = fgetc( file_ptr );
23            putchar( c );
24            pass = 0;
```

```
25        }
26     }
27
28     fclose( file_ptr );
29  }
```

In this program, a `while()` loop is used move through the file. On every other pass through the `while()` loop, the `ungetc()` function pushes back a blank character on the stream. On the other passes through the loop, the `fgetc()` functions read characters from the stream. On the first call to `fgetc()`, the character that was pushed back is read (see line 20). The second call to `fgetc()` retrieves an original character from the file (see line 22). On output, every other character printed is a blank.

Direct I/O

```
size_t fread( void *ptr, size_t size, size_t
    nmemb,FILE *stream );
```

Type: Function

Returns: If successful, `fread()` returns the number of characters read. The number of characters read can be less than specified by `nmemb`, if read errors occur or the end of the file is encountered. If size or `nmemb` is zero, a value of zero is returned. In this case, nothing is read into the array and the stream is left unchanged.

`fread()` reads data from the file specified by `*stream` and places it in the array pointed to by `*ptr`. The size of each object in the file is specified by `size`. The number of objects to be read from the file is specified by `nmemb`. The file-position indicator is advanced by the number of characters successfully read. If a partial member is read, or a file error occurs, the value of the file-position indicator is indeterminate. The arguments for `fread()` are as follows:

`*ptr` points to an array in which data from the file is to be stored.

`size` specifies the size of each member in the file.

`nmemb` specifies the number of members to read from the data file.

`*stream` points to the stream associated with the file from which data is being read.

In listing 16.13, `fread()` reads a group of characters from the file pointed to by `file_ptr`.

Listing 16.13. `dir_io.c` *(A demonstration of* `fread()`*).*   *Turbo C++*

```
1   #include <stdio.h>
2   #include <stdlib.h>
3
4   main()
5   {
6     FILE *file_ptr;
7     size_t size = 1;
8     size_t n_memb = 5;
9     size_t loop;
10    size_t i;
11    char store[255];
12
13    file_ptr = fopen( "test.fil", "r" );
14
15    do {
16      loop = fread( store, size, n_memb, file_ptr );
17        for( i = 0; i <= loop - 1; i++ ) putchar( store[i] );
18    } while( loop == n_memb );
19
20    fclose( file_ptr );
21  }
```

The characters read in this program are stored in the array `store[]`. The number of characters to be read is determined by the value of the variable `n_memb`. If the value of `n_memb` is changed, the number of characters read is changed. The size of each member is determined by the value of the variable size. Because characters are being read, the value of size was set to 1. `fread()` returns a value equal to the number of characters it was able to read. Normally, this value equals `n_memb`. At the end of the file, however, the return of `fread()` and the value of `n_memb` is not equal. (This permits checking for the end of the file.) The `for` loop on line 17 is used to display the data read into the array `store[[` by the `fread()` function.

```
size_t fwrite( const void *ptr, size_t size,
        size_t nmemb, FILE *stream );
```

Type: Function

Returns: The number of characters successfully written. This value is less than `nmemb` only if a write error occurs.

fwrite() writes data from the array pointed to by *ptr to the file associated with the stream pointed to by *stream. The size of each data item written to the file is specified by the size argument. The number of members to write to the file is specified by the nmemb argument. The value of the file-position indicator is incremented by the number of successfully written characters. If a write error occurs, the value of the file-position indicator is indeterminate. The arguments for fwrite() are as follows:

*ptr points to an array from which data id written.

size specifies the size of each member written to the file.

nmemb specifies the number of members to write to the file.

*stream points to the stream where data is written.

In listing 16.14, the fwrite() function writes, with one statement, an entire array to a file.

Listing 16.14. dir_wrt.c *(Directly writing data with* fwrite()*).*

Turbo C++

```
1   #include <stdio.h>
2   #include <stdlib.h>
3
4   main()
5   {
6      FILE *file_ptr;
7      double temp_num;
8      double d[10];
9      int i;
10
11     for( i = 0; i <=9; i++ ) d[i] = 0.0;
12     i = 0;
13
14     printf( "Enter up to 10 floating point numbers.\n" );
15     printf( "Enter a -1 when finished.\n\n" );
16
17     do {
18        scanf( "%lf", &temp_num );
19        d[i++] = temp_num;
20     } while( temp_num != -1.0 );
21
22     file_ptr = fopen( "float.dat", "wb" );
23     if( fwrite( d, sizeof( d ), 1, file_ptr ) == 1 )
24        printf( "fwrite() was successful.\n" );
25     else
26        printf( "fwrite() was not successful.\n" );
27  }
```

In this listing, lines 11 and 12 initialize the array elements to zero. Lines 14 through 20 get up to 10 floating-point numbers from the user and store them in the array. Line 23 opens a file for fwrite() to use. On line 24, the fwrite() function is executed.

The first argument in fwrite() points to the data to be written. (In this example, the data to be written is the array d.) The second argument specifies the size of the data item. Here, the sizeof() function returned the size of the whole array. The third argument specifies how many data items to write. Because the whole array is written, only one item needs to be transferred. The last argument points to the stream to which the data is written. If the value returned by fwrite() equals the number of items to write, then fwrite() executed successfully.

```
int fgetpos( FILE *stream, fpos_t *pos );
```

Type: Function

Returns: If successful, fgetpos() returns a value of zero. If unsuccessful, a nonzero value is returned and a positive implementation-defined value is placed in errno.

fgetpos() gets the current position of the file-position indicator for the stream pointed to by *stream. The value of the file-position indicator is stored in the object pointed to by *pos. Other (unspecified) information also is stored in the object pointed to by *pos; this information is used by fsetpos() to restore the file-position indicator to its position when fgetpos() was called. The arguments for fgetpos() follow:

*stream points to the stream on which fgetpos() get the value of the file-position indicator.

*pos points to an object in which the value of the file-position indicator is stored.

In the following code fragment, the fgetpos() function stores the current value of the file-position indicator for the stream pointed to by file_ptr:

```
FILE *file_ptr;
fpos_t position;
...
if( fgetpos( file_ptr, position ) == 0 )
  printf( "fgetpos() executed correctly.\n" );
```

The value of the file-position indicator is stored in the variable position. fgetpos() returns a value that indicates whether the function was successful. If the value returned by fgetpos() equals zero, fgetpos() was successful.

```
int fseek( FILE *stream, long int offset, int
    whence );
```

Type: Function

Returns: A value of nonzero is returned only if `fseek()` was
                  unable to process the seek request.

`fseek()` sets the file-position indicator to a value specified by `offset` and `whence` for the stream specified by `*stream`. The arguments `offset` and `whence` are set up differently for binary and text files.

In a binary file, `whence` can have three different values: `SEEK_SET` sets `whence` to the beginning of the file; `SEEK_CUR` sets `whence` to the current value of the file-position indicator; `SEEK_END` sets `whence` to the end of the file (this argument does not have to be meaningfully supported). `offset` is added to the value of `whence` to obtain the total offset, measured in characters, from the beginning of the file.

In a text stream, `whence` is set to the value `SEEK_SET`. `offset` can either be zero or the value returned by the `ftell()` function.

If `fseek()` is successful, the end-of-file indicator is cleared and any characters pushed back by `ungetc()` are discarded. After a successful call to `fseek()`, a read or write operation can be performed on a stream opened in update mode.

The arguments for `fseek()` are as follows:

`*stream` points to the stream that has the value of its file-position indicator changed by `fseek()`.

`offset` specifies the number of characters of offset to add to the value of `whence`.

`whence` specifies an offset from the beginning of the file. The arguments for `whence` are the macros listed in the preceding discussion.

Listing 16.15 uses the `fseek()` function to pull every fifth character from the file pointed to by `file_ptr`.

In line 14, `fseek()` locates the position of the end of the file. The `while()` statement on line 21 uses this information to loop through the file without going past the end of the file. The `fseek()` function on line 24 moves the current file position 5 characters forward on every pass through the loop. At the end of the loop, `fgetpos()` gets the current file position so that it can be compared to the position of the end of the file.

Listing 16.15. `seek.c` *(A demonstration of* `fseek()`*).*   *Turbo C++*

```
 1   #include <stdio.h>
 2   #include <stdlib.h>
 3
 4   main()
 5   {
 6     FILE *file_ptr;
 7     fpos_t curr_p;
 8     fpos_t end_p;
 9     long int offset = 5;
10     char c;
11
12     file_ptr = fopen( "test.txt", "rb" );
13
14     fseek( file_ptr, 0, SEEK_END );
15     fgetpos( file_ptr, &end_p );
16
17     rewind( file_ptr );
18     fgetpos( file_ptr, &curr_p );
19
20
21     while( curr_p < end_p ) {
22       c = getc( file_ptr );
23       putchar( c );
24       fseek( file_ptr, offset, SEEK_CUR );
25       fgetpos( file_ptr, &curr_p );
26     }
27
28     fclose( file_ptr );
29   }
```

```
int fsetpos( FILE *stream, const fpos_t *pos );
```

Type: Function

Returns   If successful, `fsetpos()` returns the value zero. If
              unsuccessful, `fsetpos()` returns a nonzero value and
              stores a positive implementation-defined value in `errno`.

Like the `fseek()` function, `fsetpos()` is used to set the value of the file-position indicator. However, the position specified by `fsetpos()` is the file-position value stored by an earlier call to the `fgetpos()` function.

If `fsetpos()` is successful, the end-of-file indicator is cleared and any characters pushed back by `ungetc()` are discarded. After a successful call to `fsetpos()`, a read or write operation can be performed on a stream that was opened in update mode. The arguments for `fsetpos()` are as follows:

`*stream` points to the stream that has its file-position indicator reset.

*pos points to the object in which fgetpos() stored the file-position indicator information.

Listing 16.16 uses fsetpos() to restore the file-position indicator after a random change.

Listing 16.16. set_pos.c *(Using the* fsetpos() *function).*　　　　*Turbo C++*

```
 1   #include <stdio.h>
 2   #include <stdlib.h>
 3
 4   main()
 5   {
 6      FILE *file_ptr;
 7      long int offset;
 8      fpos_t position;
 9      char store[256];
10
11      file_ptr = fopen( "test.txt", "rb" );
12
13      fseek( file_ptr, 0L, SEEK_END );
14      offset = ftell( file_ptr);
15
16      rewind( file_ptr );
17      fgetpos( file_ptr, &position );
18
19      printf( "Enter a value between 0 and %d.\n", offset );
20      printf( "This value indicates the new file offset.\n" );
21      printf( "==> " );
22      scanf( "%ld", &offset );
23
24      fseek( file_ptr, offset, SEEK_SET );
25      printf( "%d characters from the beginning of file.\n",
26              offset );
27
28      fsetpos( file_ptr, &position );
29      printf( "Returning to offset specified by fgetpos.\n" );
30
31      printf( "The next string in the file is:\n" );
32      fgets( store, 256, file_ptr );
33      puts( store );
34   }
```

Lines 13 and 14 determine the length of the file. Lines 16 and 17 store the value of the file-position indicator when it is at the beginning of the file. Lines 19 through 25 randomly change the file-position indicator, using input from the user. On line 28, the `fsetpos()` function uses the value stored in `position` to restore the file-position indicator.

`long int ftell( FILE *stream );`

Type: Function

Returns: If successful, `ftell()` returns the value of the file-position indicator. If unsuccessful, a value of –1L is returned and a positive implementation-defined value is stored in `errno`.

`ftell()` gets the current value of the file-position indicator. This return value is different for binary and text streams. For a binary stream, the value of the file-position indicator is expressed as the number of characters from the beginning of the file. For a text stream, the value of the file-position indicator includes unspecified information usable by the `fseek()` function on the same stream. `*stream` points to the stream on which `ftell()` gets the value of the file-position indicator.

If this code fragment were used with a binary file, as follows:

```
FILE file_ptr;
long int offset;
...
offset = ftell( file_ptr );
```

the value of `offset` would indicate the current offset of the file-position indicator. For a binary file, the offset from the beginning of the file is specified in characters.

The following code fragment could be used in a text file:

```
FILE file_ptr;
long int position;
...
position = ftell( file_ptr );
...
fseek( file_ptr, position, SEEK_SET );
```

In this fragment, `ftell()` stores the value of the file-position indicator in `position`. After some other intermediate operations, the `fseek()` function uses `position` to restore the file-position indicator. Using `ftell()` and `fseek()` in this manner is similar to using `fgetpos()` and `fsetpos()`.

`void rewind( FILE *stream );`

Type: Function

Returns: N/A

The `rewind()` function sets the value of the file-position indicator to the beginning of the file and clears the error indicator for the stream. `*stream` points to the stream that has its file-position indicator reset to the beginning of the file.

Listing 16.17 opens a text file, reads to the end of the file, invokes `rewind()` to return to the beginning of the file, and then prints the first string in the file.

Listing 16.17. `rewind.c` *(Using* `rewind()` *to reset the file-position indicator).* *Turbo C++*

```
1   #include <stdio.h>
2   #include <stdlib.h>
3
4   main()
5   {
6     #define MAX_LEN 256
7     FILE *file_ptr;
8     char c;
9     char store[MAX_LEN];
10
11    file_ptr = fopen( "test.txt", "r" );
12
13    while( !feof( file_ptr ) ) {
14      c = fgetc( file_ptr );
15      putchar( c );
16    }
17
18    rewind( file_ptr );
19
20    fgets( store, MAX_LEN, file_ptr );
21    puts( store );
22  }
```

On lines 13 through 16, each character in the file is read. On line 18, `rewind()` resets the file-position indicator to the beginning of the file. Lines 20 and 21 print the first string in the file to prove that the file-position indicator was reset.

Error-handling Functions

```
void clearerr( FILE *stream );
```

Type: Function

Returns: N/A

`clearerr()` clears the error *and* the end-of-file indicators on the stream pointed to by *stream.

Listing 16.18 reads characters from the keyboard until an end-of-file character (^Z) is entered. The end-of-file indicator is then cleared.

Listing 16.18. `clear.c` *(Clearing the end-of-file and error indicators).*

Turbo C++

```
 1   #include <stdio.h>
 2   #include <stdlib.h>
 3
 4   main()
 5   {
 6      #define MAX_LEN 256
 7
 8      char c;
 9      char store[MAX_LEN];
10      int i = 0;
11
12      printf( "Enter up to 255 characters of text.\n" );
13      printf( "When finished, hit ^Z to indicate the \n" );
14      printf( "end of your input.\n\n" );
15
16      while( ( c = getchar() ) != EOF )
17        store[i++] = c;
18
19      clearerr( stdin );
20
21      i = 0;
22      while( putchar( store[i++] ) != NULL );
23   }
```

In this program, `clearerr()` is invoked to clear the end-of-file indicator for the `stdin` stream. The data is then output for display. Lines 16 and 17 store data until the end-of-file character is entered. On line 19, `clearerr()` clears the end-of-file indicator. Lines 21 and 22 simply print the data that was entered.

`int feof( FILE *stream );`

Type: Function

Returns: Nonzero, if the end-of-file indicator for the stream pointed to by *stream is set.

`feof()` tests the value of the end-of-file indicator for the stream pointed to by *stream. If the end-of-file indicator is set, a nonzero value is returned.

The following code fragment reads characters from the file pointed to by file_ptr until the end-of-file marker is encountered:

```
FILE *file_ptr;
char c;
.
while( !feof( file_ptr ) ) {
  c = fgetc( file_ptr );
  putchar( c );
}
```

The expression !feof(file_ptr) remains true as long as the end-of-file indicator is not set. However, when fgetc() reaches the end of the file, it sets the end-of-file indicator. This causes !feof() to return a value of FALSE. The FALSE value ends the while() loop.

```
int ferror( FILE *stream );
```

Type: Function

Returns: Nonzero, if the error indicator for the stream pointed
              to by *stream is set.

ferror() tests the value of the error indicator for the stream pointed to by *stream. If the error indicator is set, a nonzero value is returned.

The following code fragment reads characters from the stream pointed to by file_ptr until either the end-of-file or file error indicators are set:

```
FILE *file_ptr;
char c;
.
while( !ferror( file_ptr ) && !feof( file_ptr ) ) {
  c = fgetc( file_ptr );
  putchar( c );
}
```

The expression !ferror(file_ptr) returns TRUE as long the file error indicator is not set.

```
void perror( const char *s );
```

Type: Function

Returns: N/A

perrno() is used to print error messages for the error codes stored in errno. These error messages are output to the stderr stream. perror() maps the value of the error code in errno to an error message. After this, perror() is ready to print an error message. First, the string pointed to by *s is printed, followed by a colon and a space. Next, the error message corresponding to errno is printed, followed by a newline character. The string pointed to by *s is printed only if *s is not a null pointer and the character pointed to is not a null character. The error messages printed are the same as those returned by the strerror() function when an argument of errno is used.

The following code fragment uses perror() to give a more detailed error message when there is a problem opening myfile.dat:

```
FILE *file_ptr;
 .
if( ( file_ptr = fopen( "myfile.dat", "r" ) ) == NULL )
    perror( "myfile.dat " );
```

If fopen() cannot open the file, it returns a null pointer, and an error code is placed in errno. The return of a null pointer causes the perror() function to be called. perror() prints the string pointed to in its argument list, along with the standard error message.

Summary

The stddef.h header file declares and defines some of the most common type definitions and macros. Some of these declarations and definitions occur also in other header files.

The stdio.h header file declares the basic I/O functions. The functions declared in stdio.h range from basic character I/O functions to the powerful printf() and scanf() functions. stdio.h declares functions for almost every I/O and file chore.

String, Time, and Miscellaneous Functions

The stdlib.h header file declares a general assortment of utility functions. Along with stdio.h, stdlib.h is included in most C programs. The string.h header file declares functions that are useful for manipulating character strings. The time.h header file has declarations for functions that work with time and date values.

#include <stdlib.h>

The stdlib.h header file declares two new types and several functions and macros. Included in the stdlib.h are declarations for functions that do everything from memory management to string conversion. Most programs use some of the functions declared in stdlib.h.

Type Declarations

div_t

Type: Type declaration

Returns: N/A

div_t is a type declaration for the structure that holds the value returned by the div() function.

ldiv_t

Type: Type declaration

Returns: N/A

ldiv_t is a type declaration for the structure that holds the value returned by the ldiv() function.

Macro Definitions

EXIT_FAILURE

Type: Macro definition

Returns: N/A

EXIT_FAILURE is a macro that can be used as the argument to the exit() function. It indicates an unsuccessful status at program termination. EXIT_FAILURE expands to an integral expression.

EXIT_SUCCESS

Type: Macro definition

Returns: N/A

EXIT_SUCCESS is a macro that can be used as the argument to the exit() function. It indicates a successful status at program termination. EXIT_SUCCESS expands to an integral expression.

RAND_MAX

Type: Macro definition

Returns: N/A

RAND_MAX is a macro definition for an integral expression equal to the maximum value that can be returned by the rand() function.

MB_CUR_MAX

Type: Macro definition

Returns: N/A

`MB_CUR_MAX` is the macro definition for the integral expression that is equal to the maximum number of bytes that can be used for a multibyte character in the extended character set. The value of `MB_CUR_MAX` is never greater than the value of `MB_LEN_MAX`.

Converting Strings to Numbers

```
double atof( const char *nptr );
```

Type: Function

Returns: A double floating-point number

`atof()` converts the first part of the string pointed to by `*nptr` to a floating-point number of type `double`. Other than error handling, `atof()` works like this:

```
strtod( nptr, ( char ** )NULL );
```

The difference is that when `atof()` encounters a conversion error, an error code is not necessarily stored in `errno`.

In the following code fragment:

```
double x;
char *str_dbl = "100.75";
...
x = atof( str_dbl );
```

the `atof()` function converts the string `"100.75"` to a floating-point `double`. The `double` returned by `atof()` is stored in the variable `x`.

```
int atoi( const char *nptr );
```

Type: Function

Returns: An integer

`atoi()` converts the first part of the string pointed to by `*nptr` to an integer. Other than error handling, `atoi()` works like this:

```
strtol( nptr, ( char ** )NULL, 10 );
```

The difference is that when `atoi()` encounters a conversion error, an error code is not necessarily stored in `errno`.

In the following code fragment:

```
int i;
char *str_int = "123";
...
i = atoi( str_int );
```

the `atoi()` function converts the string `"123"` to an integer. The return value from `atoi()` is stored in the variable `i`.

`long int atol( const char *nptr );`

Type: Function

Returns: A long integer

`atol()` converts the first part of the string pointed to by `*nptr` to a long integer. Other than error handling, `atol()` works like this:

```
strtol( nptr, ( char ** )NULL, 10 );
```

The difference is that when `atol()` encounters a conversion error, an error code is not necessarily stored in `errno`.

In the following code fragment:

```
long int i;
char str_int = "5430798";
...
i = atol( str_int );
```

the `atol()` function converts the string `"5430798"` to a long integer. The long integer that is returned is stored in the variable `i`.

`double strtod( const char *nptr, char **endptr );`

Type: Function

Returns: If possible, `strtod()` returns the converted value. Zero is returned if no conversion could be made. If the converted value would cause an overflow, the macro `ERANGE` is placed in `errno`, and plus or minus `HUGE_VAL` is returned. If the converted value would cause an underflow, the macro `ERANGE` is placed in `errno` and zero is returned.

`strtod()` converts the initial part of the string pointed to by `*nptr` to a floating-point `double`. `strtod()` breaks the string into three pieces: beginning whitespace, the subject sequence, and subsequent characters up to and including the terminating null character. The subject sequence is the longest string of characters that can compose a floating-point number.

The subject sequence can consist of the following: an optional plus or minus sign, a sequence of digits with an optional decimal point, and an optional exponent notation. No floating suffix is allowed.

If the subject sequence can be converted correctly, a pointer to the final string is placed in the object pointed to by `endptr`. The subject sequence can fail to be converted because it does not match correctly or because it is empty. If the subject string is not converted, the value of `nptr` is stored in the object pointed to by `endptr`. These values are stored only if `endptr` is not a null pointer.

The arguments for `strtod()` are as follows:

`*nptr` is a pointer to the string from which a `double` is to be converted.

`**endptr` is a pointer to the final string.

In listing 17.1, the `strtod()` function converts the string `"732899.576"` to a floating-point `double`. The converted number is stored in the variable x.

Listing 17.1. `fltcnvrt.c` *(Converting a string to a floating-point double).*
Turbo C++

```
1    #include <stdio.h>
2    #include <stdlib.h>
3
4    main()
5    {
6       double x;
7       char *flt_num = "732899.576";
8       char *endptr;
9
10      x = strtod( flt_num, &endptr );
11
12      printf( "x = %f\n", x );
13   }
```

```
long int strtol( const char *nptr, char **endptr,
        int base );
```

Type: Function

Returns: If a conversion was possible, the converted number is returned. If a conversion was not possible, a value of zero is returned. If the converted value would cause an overflow, the value of the macro `ERANGE` is placed in `errno` and the value `LONG_MAX` or `LONG_MIN` (the sign of the converted number determines which) is returned.

`strtol()` converts the first piece of the string pointed to by `nptr` to a long integer. `strtol()` breaks the string pointed to by `nptr` into three pieces: a beginning section composed of whitespace; the subject sequence; and the remaining characters up to and including the terminating null character.

If `base` is equal to zero, the subject sequence should be composed of an optional plus or minus sign and integer digits. An integer suffix is not allowed. If `base` equals a number between 2 and 36, the subject sequence should be composed of an optional plus or minus sign and a sequence of letters or digits. The letters and digits comprising the subject sequence should form an integer that represents a number with the radix equal to `base`. The letters `a` through `z` represent the numbers 10 through 35. Uppercase letters can be used also. If `base` equals 16, the subject sequence can be preceded by an optional `0x` or `0X`.

The subject sequence is the longest string of characters that can represent an integer value.

If the subject sequence can be converted correctly, a pointer to the final string is placed in the object pointed to by `endptr`. The subject sequence can fail to be converted because it does not match correctly or because it is empty. If the subject string is not converted, the value of `nptr` is stored in the object pointed to by `endptr`. These values are stored only if `endptr` is not a null pointer.

The arguments for `strtol()` are as follows:

`*nptr` is a pointer to the string from which an integer value is converted.

`**endptr` is a pointer to the final string.

`base` specifies the radix of the integer to which the subject string is converted.

In listing 17.2, the `strtol()` function is used to convert the string `"9876"` to an integer value. On line 11, strtol() is called. It converts the string pointed to by `int_str` to a long integer that is stored in i.

```
unsigned long int strtoul( const char *nptr,
          char **endptr, int base );
```

Type: Function

Returns: If a conversion was possible, the converted value is returned. If no conversion was possible, a value of zero is returned. If the converted value would cause an overflow, the value of the macro `ERANGE` is stored in `errno`, and `ULONG_MAX` is returned.

Listing 17.2. `lcnvrt.c` *(Converting a string to a long integer).*

TurboC++

```
 1   #include <stdio.h>
 2   #include <stdlib.h>
 3
 4   main()
 5   {
 6      int base = 10;
 7      long int i;
 8      char *int_str = "9876";
 9      char *endptr;
10
11      i = strtol( int_str, &endptr, base );
12
13      printf( "i = %ld\n", i );
14   }
```

`strtoul()` converts the first piece of the string pointed to by `nptr` to a long integer. `strtoul()` breaks the string pointed to by `nptr` into three pieces: a beginning section composed of whitespace, the subject sequence, and the remaining characters up to and including the terminating null character.

If `base` is equal to zero, the subject sequence should be composed of an optional plus or minus sign and integer digits. An integer suffix is not allowed. If `base` equals a number between 2 and 36, the subject sequence should be composed of an optional plus or minus sign and a sequence of letters or digits. The letters and digits comprising the subject sequence should form an integer that represents a number with the radix equal to `base`. The letters a through z represent the numbers 10 through 35. Uppercase letters can be used also. If `base` equals 16, the subject sequence can be preceded by an optional `0x` or `0X`.

The subject sequence is the longest string of characters that can represent an integer value.

If the subject sequence can be converted correctly, a pointer to the final string is placed in the object pointed to by `endptr`. The subject sequence can fail to be converted because it does not match correctly or because it is empty. If the subject string is not converted, the value of `nptr` is stored in the object pointed to by `endptr`. These values are stored only if `endptr` is not a null pointer.

The arguments for strtoul() are as follows:

*nptr is a pointer to the string from which an integer value is converted.

**endptr is a pointer to final string.

base specifies the radix of the integer to which the subject string is converted.

In listing 17.3, the strtoul() function is used to convert a string to an unsigned long integer. On line 11, strtoul() is called to convert the string pointed to by int_str to an integer that is stored in the variable i.

Listing 17.3. ulcnvrt.c *(Converting a string to an unsigned long integer).*   *Turbo C++*

```
1   #include <stdio.h>
2   #include <stdlib.h>
3
4   main()
5   {
6      int base = 10;
7      unsigned long int i;
8      char *int_str = "235478";
9      char *endptr;
10
11     i = strtoul( int_str, &endptr, base );
12
13     printf( "i = %lu\n", i );
14  }
```

Generating Pseudorandom Numbers

```
int rand( void );
```

Type: Function

Returns: A pseudorandom integer

rand() generates a *sequence* of pseudorandom numbers. If rand() is called enough times, the sequence of pseudorandom numbers is repeated. The numbers generated by rand() are in the range 0 RAND_MAX.

The following code fragment assigns the pseudorandom integer generated by rand() to the variable i.

```
int i;
...
i = rand();
```

void srand(unsigned int seed);

Type: Function

Returns: N/A

srand() *seeds* the pseudorandom number generator, rand(). If srand() is called more than once with the same seed argument, rand() generates the same *sequence* of numbers each time. If srand() is called more than once with different seed arguments, rand() generates different *sequences* of numbers each time.

rand() can be called before the srand() function is called. In this situation, rand() acts as if srand() has been called with a seed argument equal to 1.

seed is an integer argument used to initialize the pseudorandom number generator.

In the following code fragment, scanf() retrieves a new value for the variable i:

```
int i;
...
scanf( "%d", &i );
...
srand( i );
```

srand() then uses i to reseed the pseudorandom number generator.

Managing Memory

void *calloc(size_t nmemb, size_t size);

Type: Function

Returns: If successful, returns a pointer to the allocated memory; otherwise, a null pointer is returned.

calloc() allocates a section of memory to hold an array of objects. Enough space is allocated to hold nmemb number of objects. The size of each object is equal to the argument size. Every bit in the allocated space is initialized to a value of zero. The arguments for calloc() are as follows:

nmemb specifies the number of objects for which space is allocated.

size specifies the size of each object for which space is allocated.

Listing 17.4 demonstrates the calloc() function by allocating memory for a list of integers.

Listing 17.4. cmem.c *(Using* calloc() *to allocate memory).*   *Turbo C++*

```
1   #include <stdio.h>
2   #include <stdlib.h>
3
4   main()
5   {
6      size_t nmemb;
7      size_t loop;
8      int *int_array;
9
10     printf( "Enter the size of the integer array. == > " );
11     scanf( "%d", &nmemb );
12
13     int_array = calloc( nmemb, sizeof( int ) );
14
15     for( loop = 0; loop <= nmemb; loop++ )
16        int_array[loop] = loop;
17
18     for( loop = 0; loop <= nmemb; loop++ )
19        printf( "%d\n", int_array[loop] );
20
21     free( int_array );
22  }
```

On line 11, the user enters the size of the array. This value is used as the nmemb argument for calloc(). On line 13, the calloc() function is called. The sizeof() function has been used to determine the size of each integer element. The pointer array stores the value returned by calloc(). The for() on lines 15 and 16 store values in the new array. The for() loop on lines 18 and 19 prints the values in the array. Notice that on line 21 the allocated space is released by the free() function.

```
void free( void *ptr );
```

Type: Function

Returns: N/A

The free() function deallocates a section of memory. After the memory has been deallocated, it is available for further use.

*ptr is a pointer to the block of memory to be deallocated. *ptr should point exactly to a block of memory allocated by the calloc(), malloc() or realloc() functions. If it does not, the behavior is undefined. If *ptr is NULL, no action is taken.

In the following code fragment:

```
char *my_space;
my_space = malloc( 1000 );
...
free( my_space );
```

malloc() allocates a section of memory. The pointer to the beginning of this section of memory is stored in the pointer my_space. free() deallocates the memory pointed to by my_space.

```
void *malloc( size_t size );
```

Type: Function

Returns: If successful, malloc() returns a pointer to the allocated space. If unsuccessful, a null pointer is returned.

malloc() allocates a section of memory. The size of the allocated area is equal to the size argument. malloc() differs from calloc() in that it does *not* initialize the allocated storage to any particular value—that is up to you.

Listing 17.5 uses malloc() to allocate a section of memory for a list of integers to be summed. The declaration on line 8 creates an array of MAX integer pointers. The scanf() function on line 15 inputs the number of integers the user wants to sum. The for() on lines 18 through 21 allocates memory and stores the input. Notice on line 19 that malloc() allocates memory for every integer and stores the address for each integer in the num_ptr pointer array. The loop on lines 24 through 27 retrieves the integers and sums them. On each pass through this loop, the memory for the integer pointed to by num_ptr[loop] is deallocated.

```
void *realloc( void *ptr, size_t size );
```

Type: Function

Returns: If successful, realloc() returns a pointer to the reallocated space. This space does not necessarily begin where the original allocation did. If realloc() is not successful, a null pointer is returned.

Listing 17.5. mmem.c *(Allocating memory with* malloc()*).*   *Turbo C++*

```
 1  #include <stdio.h>
 2  #include <stdlib.h>
 3  #include <string.h>
 4  #define MAX 100
 5
 6  main()
 7  {
 8    int *num_ptr[MAX];
 9    int num, count, loop;
10    int sum = 0;
11    size_t size;
12
13    printf( "How many integers do you want to sum?\n" );
14    printf( "==> " );
15    scanf( "%d", &count );
16    printf( "\n" );
17
18    for( loop = 0; loop < count; loop++ ) {
19      num_ptr[loop] = malloc( sizeof( int ) );
20      printf( "\nInteger ==> " );
21      scanf( "%d", num_ptr[loop] );
22    }
23
24    for( loop = 0; loop < count; loop++ ) [
25      sum += *num_ptr[loop];
26      free( num_ptr[loop] );
27    }
28
29    printf( "\nSum = %d\n", sum );
30  }
```

The realloc() function changes the amount of space allocated for the pointer ptr. The size of the reallocated section of memory is specified by the size argument. The data being pointed to is still there, but if the new size is smaller than the old size, data is lost. If the new size is larger, the old data is there, but extra, uninitialized memory is appended to it.

The arguments for realloc() are as follows:

*ptr is a pointer to the object that is to have its space reallocated. If ptr is null, realloc() acts like malloc() with the same size argument. If the pointer value in ptr did not come from a call to calloc(), malloc(), or realloc(), the behavior of realloc() is undefined. If the pointer value in ptr has been deallocated, the behavior of realloc() is undefined.

size specifies how much memory is used for the new memory allocation. If the value of size is zero, and ptr is a valid pointer, realloc() deallocates the memory for that object.

Listing 17.6 illustrates how to use realloc().

Listing 17.6. rmem.c *(Reallocating memory).*   *Turbo C++*

```
1   #include <stdio.h>
2   #include <stdlib.h>
3
4   main()
5   {
6       int *reg_int;
7       long int *long_int;
8
9       reg_int = malloc( sizeof( int ) );
10      *reg_int = 32767;
11      printf( "reg_int = %d\n", *reg_int );
12
13      long_int = realloc( reg_int, sizeof( long int ) );
14      *long_int = 2147438647;
15      printf( "long_int = %ld\n", *long_int );
16  }
```

In this listing, two pointers are used. The first, reg_int, points to a normal integer; the second, long_int, points to a long integer. On line 9, memory for a regular integer is allocated and the address is stored in reg_int. On line 13, realloc() is called to reallocate the memory for the object pointed to by reg_int. Because realloc() is allocating memory for a long integer, its return value is stored in a pointer to a long integer, long_int.

Communicating with the Environment

void abort(void);

Type: Function

Returns: N/A

Calling the abort() function raises the SIGABRT signal and causes abnormal program termination. The flushing and closing of streams and the removal of temporary files is implementation-defined. The `SIGABRT` signal causes an *unsuccessful termination* message to be sent to the host environment. The format of this message is determined by the implementation. The programmer can supply his or her own routines to trap the `SIGABRT` signal and pass control to a signal-handling routine. The signal-handling routine then determines how processing will continue.

In the following code fragment:

```
int catastrophic_error = 0;
...
if( catastrophic_error ) abort();
```

a variable called `catastrophic_error` is declared. If the value of this variable is changed to a positive value, it is evaluated as `TRUE` by the `if()` statement. When this happens, program execution is terminated.

int atexit(void (*func)(void));

Type: Function

Returns: If registration of the function succeeds, a value of zero is returned. If registration fails, nonzero is returned.

`atexit()` *registers* functions to be called at normal program termination. In other words, `atexit()` creates a list of programs that is called when the program terminates. The implementation should be able to register at least 32 functions. The functions are called in LIFO order, which means that the last function to be registered by `atexit()` is the first function called at termination. The registered functions do not accept arguments and do not return values. There is only one argument for `atexit()`. This argument, `*func`, is a pointer to a function. It points to a function you want to register to be called at normal program termination.

Listing 17.7 demonstrates how to use the `atexit()` function. On lines 4 and 5, two functions are declared. Both are of type `void`, and neither takes an argument. On lines 15 through 25, the functions are defined. In the function `main()` on lines 9 and 10, the `atexit()` is called. It registers `exit_func2()` and then `exit_func1()`. Because the functions are invoked in LIFO order, `exit_func1()` is called first. Notice that `atexit()` does not call the functions, it *registers* them. The functions are called at normal program termination.

void exit(int status);

Type: Function

Returns: N/A

Listing 17.7. `atexit.c` *(How to register a function).*   *Turbo C++*

```
1   #include <stdio.h>
2   #include <stdlib.h>
3
4   void exit_func1( void );
5   void exit_func2( void );
6
7   main()
8   {
9     atexit( exit_func2 );
10    atexit( exit_func1 );
11
12    printf( "Processing main() function.\n\n" );
13  }
14
15  void exit_func1( void )
16  {
17    printf( "In exit_func1().\n" );
18    printf( "Preparing to exit.\n\n" );
19  }
20
21  void exit_func2( void )
22  {
23    printf( "In exit_func2().\n" );
24    printf( "Exiting program ...NOW!\n" );
25  }
```

The `exit()` function causes the program to terminate normally. If any functions have been registered by the `atexit()` function, they are executed in LIFO order. Next, output streams are flushed, all streams are closed, and temporary files are removed. After this, control can return to the host environment. If the value of the argument `status` is zero or `EXIT_SUCCESS`, a successful termination message is sent to the host environment. If the value of `status` is equal to `EXIT_FAILURE`, an unsuccessful termination message is sent.

In the following code fragment:

```
FILE file_ptr;
...
if( ( file_ptr = fopen( "myfile.txt", "r" ) ) == NULL )
  exit( EXIT_FAILURE );
```

the `exit()` function is called when the file `myfile.txt` cannot be opened. In this example, the `status` argument is equal to `EXIT_FAILURE`. So, `exit()`

returns an unsuccessful termination message to the host environment. The program is shut down normally, however—all streams are flushed and closed, and temporary files are removed.

```
char *getenv( const char *name );
```

Type: Function

Returns: If successful, a pointer to the appropriate host environment string is returned. If a matching string cannot be found, a null pointer is returned.

getenv() searches the host's environment list to find a string that matches the argument name. If a match is found, a pointer to the appropriate string in the host's environment list is returned.

The following line of code:

```
printf( "%s\n", getenv( "PATH" ) );
```

prints the current path stored in the environment list.

```
int system( const char *string );
```

Type: Function

Returns: If the string argument is a null pointer, a nonzero value is returned if a command processor is available. If the string argument is not a null pointer, the return value is implementation-defined.

The system() function invokes the command processor, which then executes the command pointed to by the string argument.

On the first line of the following code fragment:

```
if( system( NULL ) != 0 )
   system( "DIR" );
```

the system() function determines whether a command processor is available. If the processor is available, the second system() function is executed. The second system() function performs a directory of the current disk drive.

Searching and Sorting

```
void *bsearch( const void *key, const void *base,
      size_t nmemb, size_t size,
        int ( *compar )( const void *, const void * ) );
```

Type: Function

Returns: If successful, `bsearch()` returns a pointer to the matching member in the array. If two members of the array compare equal, it is left to the implementation to decide which is returned. If unsuccessful, a null pointer is returned.

The `bsearch()` function is used to search an array of objects. The objects in the array should already be sorted in an ascending order suitable for use by the function pointed to by `compar`. The function pointed to by `compar` is called with two arguments, which point to the `key` object and to an array member. The value returned by the comparison function depends on how the `key` object compares to the array member. The return values and the conditions possible are listed here:

Return value	Condition
Less than zero	`key` less than member
Zero	`key` equals member
Greater than zero	`key` greater than member

The arguments for `bsearch()` and their significance are as follows:

`*key` points to the object that is being searched for.

`*base` points to the first object in the array.

`nmemb` denotes how many objects are in the array.

`size` specifies the size of each member in the array.

`*compar` points to a comparison function.

Listing 17.8 uses the `bsearch()` function to search an array of structures. Lines 5 through 8 are the type definition for the `PHONE_LIST` structure. On lines 10 through 12, an array of `PHONE_LIST` structures is initialized. Lines 23 through 26 set up the arguments for the `bsearch()` function. `key` is the string to search for. `base` identifies the beginning of the array. Line 24 calculates the number of members in the array and then places the result in `nmemb`. `size` is the size of a single `PHONE_LIST` structure. `bsearch()` returns a pointer to the `PHONE_LIST` object. (This pointer is stored in the `search` pointer.) On line 31, the value of the `search` pointer is checked to determine whether the search was successful. Then the result of the search is printed.

Listing 17.8. `search.c (Binary search).`   *Turbo C++*

```
1   #include <stdio.h>
2   #include <stdlib.h>
3   #include <string.h>
4
5   typedef struct {
6     char name[20];
7     char number[9];
8   }  PHONE_LIST;
9
10  PHONE_LIST friends[] = {"Abe Adams", "555-1234",
11                          "Bob Barns", "555-2345",
12                          "Chuck Clay", "555-3456" };
13
14  main()
15  {
16    PHONE_LIST *search;
17    PHONE_LIST *base;
18    size_t nmemb;
19    size_t size;
20    char *key;
21    int strcmp();
22
23    base = friends;
24    nmemb = sizeof( friends ) / sizeof( friends[0] );
25    size = sizeof( PHONE_LIST );
26    key = "Chuck Clay";
27
28    search = bsearch( key, base, nmemb, size, strcmp );
29
30    if( search == NULL )
31      printf( "Search not successful.\n" );
32    else
33      printf( "%s  %s\n", search->name, search->number );
34  }
```

```
void qsort( void *base, size_t nmemb, size_t size,
    int ( *compar ) ( const void *, const void * ) );
```

Type: Function

Returns: N/A

The `qsort()` function sorts an array of objects. The array is sorted into ascending order as determined by the comparison function, which is pointed to by the argument `compar`. The value returned by the comparison function depends on the relationship between the two arguments passed to it. The following return values and relationships between arguments are possible:

Return value	Relationship between arguments
Less than zero	First less than second
Zero	First and second
Greater than zero	First greater than second

The arguments for qsort() and their significance are as follows:

*base points to the beginning element in the array.

nmemb specifies the number of elements in the array.

size specifies the size of each object in the array.

*compar points to the comparison function.

Listing 17.9 sorts a short array of character strings with the qsort() function.

Listing 17.9. sort.c *(Using the* qsort() *function).*   *Turbo C++*

```
1    #include <stdio.h>
2    #include <stdlib.h>
3    #include <string.h>
4
5    main()
6    {
7       char list[4][10] = {"David", "Bill", "Charles", "Art"};
8
9       int strcmp();
10      int i;
11
12      qsort( list, 4, sizeof( list[0] ), strcmp );
13
14      for( i = 0; i < 4; i++ )
15         printf( "%s\n", list[i] );
16   }
```

On line 7, the array of strings is initialized. On line 12, qsort() is called to sort the array. The list argument points to the beginning of the array, 4 indicates the number of elements in the array, and the sizeof() function calculates the size of each member in the array. strcmp is the function called to compare pairs of strings. Lines 14 and 15 print the sorted array.

Arithmetic for Integers

```
int abs( int j );
```

Type: Function

Returns: An integer that is the absolute value of the j argument.

abs() computes the absolute value of the j argument. The behavior is undefined when the result cannot be represented.

j is the integer from which the absolute value is calculated. For example:

```
i = abs( -32000 );
```

calculates the absolute value of -32000 and stores the result in i.

```
div_t div( int numer, int denom );
```

Type: Function

Returns: Returns a structure of type div_t. The members of the struc-
                  ture (quot and rem) are both of type int. These integers
                  represent the quotient and remainder from integer division.

div() performs integer division. The argument numer is divided by denom. The result is placed in a structure of type div_t. The behavior is undefined when the result cannot be represented. The arguments for div() are as follows:

numer   The numerator

denom   The denominator

Here is a short demonstration of div():

```
div_t result;
result = div( 10, 3 );
printf( "Quotient = %d, Remainder = %d",
        result.quot, result.rem );
```

In this code fragment, result is declared with type div_t. The div() function divides 10 by 3 and places the answer in result. The printf() statement prints each part of the result structure.

```
long int labs( long int j );
```

Type: Function

Returns: A long integer that is the absolute value of the argument j.

labs() calculates the absolute value of j. In the following code fragment, for example:

```
long int i;
i = labs( -2147483647 );
```

the absolute value for the long integer, –2147483647, is calculated, and the result is placed in i.

```
ldiv_t ldiv(long int numer, long int denom );
```

Type: Function

Returns: A structure of type ldiv_t. Both members of the structure (quot and rem) are long integers. These integers are the quotient and remainder from the integer division.

The ldiv() function performs integer division on long integers. The result of the division is placed in a structure of type ldiv_t. The behavior is undefined if the result cannot be represented. The arguments for ldiv() are as follows:

numer   The numerator

denom   The denominator

The following fragment of code demonstrates the ldiv() function:

```
ldiv_t result;
result = ldiv( 100, 30 );
printf( "Quotient = %ld, Remainder = %ld",
        result.quot, result.rem );
```

result is declared as an ldiv_t type structure. ldiv() divides two integers and places the long integer results in result. The printf() statement is used to print the values of the members of the structure.

Handling Multibyte Characters

```
int mblen( const char *s, size_t n );
```

Type: Function

Returns: The meaning of the return values is determined by whether s is a null pointer. If s is a null pointer, the return value indicates whether multibyte character encodings have state-dependent encodings. A nonzero return indicates that they do have state-dependent encodings. A zero return indicates that the multibyte characters do not have state-dependent encodings. If s is not a null pointer, the return value indicates whether a multibyte character is pointed to, and how long it is. If the return equals zero, s pointed to a null *character* (not a null pointer). If s is less than 1, the next n or fewer bytes did not compose a valid multibyte character.

If s is not a null pointer, `mblen()` calculates how many bytes make up the multibyte character pointed to by s. The arguments for `mblen()` are as follows:

`*s` points to a multibyte character or is a null pointer.

`n` specifies the maximum number of bytes to check to determine whether a multibyte character exists.

Because the compilers available to us did not support this function, no sample code is provided.

```
int mbtowc( wchart *pwr, const char *s, size_t n );
```

Type: Function

Returns: The meaning of the return values is determined by whether s is a null pointer. If s is a null pointer, the return value indicates whether multibyte character encodings have state-dependent encodings. A nonzero return indicates that they do have state-dependent encodings. A zero return indicates that the multibyte characters do not have state-dependent encodings. If s is not a null pointer, the return value indicates the number of converted multibyte characters. If the return equals 0, s pointed to a null character. If the return is –1, the characters pointed to did not form a valid multibyte character.

If s is not a null pointer, `mbtowc()` first calculates how many characters comprise the multibyte character pointed to by s. Next, the `wchart` type code value that matches the multibyte character is determined. If the multibyte character is valid and `pwc` is not a null pointer, the code value is stored in the object pointed to by `pwc`. The arguments for `mbtowc()` are as follows:

`*pwc` points to an object in which the code value that matches the multibyte object is stored.

`*s` points to the character where the multibyte character is to begin.

`n` specifies how many characters to check to determine whether a valid multibyte character exists.

Because the compilers available to us did not support this function, no sample code is provided.

```
int wctomb( char *s, wchar_t wchar );
```

Type: Function

Returns: The meaning of the return values is determined by whether s is a null pointer. If s is a null pointer the return value indicates whether multibyte character encodings have state-dependent encodings. A nonzero return indicates that they do have state-dependent encodings. A zero return indicates that the multibyte characters do not have state-dependent encodings. If s is not a null pointer, the return value equals the number of bytes of the multibyte character that corresponds to the code in wchar. If the return value is –1, the code in wchar does not correspond to a multibyte character.

wctomb() determines how many bytes are needed to generate a multibyte character that corresponds to the code in wchar. The number of bytes needed includes any bytes needed to indicate a change in shift state. The multibyte character generated is stored in the array pointed to by *s. The maximum number of characters that can be stored is determined by the macro MB_CUR_MAX. If the value of wchar is equal to zero, wctomb() is left in its initial shift state.

Because the compilers available to us did not support this function, no sample code is provided.

Handling Multibyte Strings

```
size_t mbstowcs( wchar_t *pwcs, const char *s,
size_t n );
```

Type: Function

Returns: The number of array elements modified. Terminating zero codes are not included in the return value. If an invalid multibyte character is encountered, a value of –1 is returned.

mbstowcs() converts multibyte characters from the array pointed to by *s to the corresponding codes, and stores the codes in the array pointed to by pwcs. The multibyte characters pointed to by s begin in the initial shift state. No multibyte characters are converted after a null character is encountered. The multibyte string is converted as if repetitive calls were made to the mbtowc() function. The only difference is that the shift state is not affected. At most, n codes are stored in the array pointed to by pwcs.

The arguments for mbstows() are as follows:

*pwcs points to the array where the codes corresponding to the converted multibyte characters are placed.

*s points to the string that contains the multibyte codes to be converted.

n specifies the maximum number of codes that can be placed in the array pointed to by pwcs.

Because the compilers available to us did not support this function, no sample code is provided.

```
size_t wcstombs( char *s, const wchar_t *pwcs,
size_t n );
```

Type: Function

Returns: The number of bytes modified. The terminating null character is not included in the count. If a code that does not correspond to a valid multibyte character is encountered, a value of –1 is returned.

wcstombs() converts the codes in the array pointed to by pwcs to multibyte characters that are stored in the array pointed to by s. The multibyte characters begin in the initial shift state. The codes are converted as if repetitive calls were made to the wctomb() function. The difference would be that the shift state of wctomb() would not be affected.

No more than n number of bytes are modified in the array pointed to by s. The conversion stops if a null character is stored.

Because the compilers available to us did not support this function, no sample code is provided.

#include string.h

Include string.h when you want to work with strings. A string is simply an array of characters. string.h also can work with other objects that can be treated as an array of characters. For all character arrays, there should be either a character pointer or a void pointer to the first character in the array. Several methods are used for determining the size of the array. The behavior of going beyond the end of the array is undefined.

Copying

```
void *memcpy( void *s1, const void *s2, size_t n );
```

Type: Function

Returns: The pointer value stored in s1

memcpy() copies n number of characters from the string pointed to by s2 to the string pointed to by s1. The behavior of the function is *undefined for objects that overlap*. The arguments for memcpy() are as follows:

s1 is the string into which data is copied (the *receiving* string).

s2 is the string from which data is copied (the *sending* string).

n specifies how many characters are copied from s2 to s1.

In the following code fragment, the first 4 characters of s2 are copied into the first 4 positions of s1:

```
char s1[81] = "First string.";
char s2[81] = "Next string.";
memcpy( s1, s2, 4 );
```

In this example, the return value from memcpy() is placed in ptr. This return value is the same as the value of s1. s1 is a pointer to the first string:

```
char *ptr;
...
ptr = memcpy( s1, s2, 4 )
```

```
void *memmove( void *s1, const void *s2, size_t n );
```

Type: Function

Returns: The pointer value stored in s1

memmove() copies n number of characters from the string pointed to by s1 to the string pointed to by s2. Copying takes place as if a temporary storage area were used. First, the characters from s2 are copied to the temporary storage area. Then the characters in the storage area are copied into s1. The arguments for memmove() are as follows:

s1 points to the string to which data is moved.

s2 points to the string from which data is copied.

n specifies the number of characters to copy from the string s2.

The principal difference between `memcpy()` and `memmove()` is that `memmove()` *can* handle overlapping operands correctly.

In the following code fragment, the first 4 characters of s2 are moved into the first 4 positions of s1:

```
char s1[81] = "First string.";
char s2[81] = "Next string.";
memmove( s1, s2, 4 );
```

```
char *strcpy( char *s1, const char *s2 );
```

Type: Function

Returns: The pointer value stored in s1

`strcpy()` copies the string pointed to by s2 into the string pointed to by s1. All characters from s2 are copied, including the terminating null character. The behavior of the function is undefined for objects that overlap. The arguments for `strcpy()` are as follows:

s1 is a pointer to the string into which s2 is copied.

s2 is a pointer to the string to be copied.

n specifies the number of characters to copy.

The next code fragment shows how the `strcpy()` function works. The string s2 is copied into the string s1.

```
char s1[81] = "Initial string";
char s2[81] = "String to be copied";
...
strcpy( s1, s2 );
```

```
char *strncpy( char *s1, const char *s2, size_t n );
```

Type: Function

Returns: The pointer value stored in s1

`strncpy()` copies n number of characters from the string pointed to by s2 to the character array pointed to by s1. If the string pointed to by s2 is shorter than n characters, only characters up to and including the null character are copied from s2. If the string pointed to by s2 is shorter than n characters, `strncpy()` still copies n characters to s1, but the extra characters are nulls. The arguments for `strncpy()` are as follows:

s1 points to a character array to which data is copied.

s2 points to a character array from which n characters is copied.

n specifies the number of characters to copy.

In the following example, strncpy() copies 6 characters from the string pointed to by s2 to the string pointed to by s1:

```
char s1[81] = "Initial string.";
char s2[81] = "String to copy to s1.";
strncpy( s1, s2, 6 );
```

Concatenation

```
char *strcat( char *s1, const char *s2 );
```

Type: Function

Returns: The pointer value stored in s1

strcat() concatenates the string pointed to by s2 to the string pointed to by s1. The terminating null character in s1 is overwritten by the first character from s2. However, the terminating null character from s2 is retained when the concatenation is performed. The behavior of the function is undefined when the two strings overlap. The arguments for strcat() are as follows:

s1 points to the string onto which another string is concatenated.

s2 points to the string to be added to s1.

The following code fragment uses strcat() twice to concatenate three strings:

```
char name[81] = "Bob";
char space[2] = " ";
char last[81] = "Barns";
...
strcat( name, space );
strcat( name, last );
```

First, space is concatenated to name. Second, last is concatenated to name. The final string pointed to by name would be "Bob Barns".

```
char *strncat( char *s1, const char *s2, size_t n);
```

Type: Function

Returns: The pointer value stored in s1

strncat() concatenates up to n number of characters from s2 to s1. If n is greater than the length of s2, the terminating null and following characters are not concatenated to s1. When the two strings are concatenated, the first character of s2 overlays the terminating null character in s1. The terminating null from s2 is not copied to s1. However, the concatenation operation always adds a terminating null character to the final string. The behavior of the function is undefined when the two strings overlap.

The arguments for strncat() are as follows:

s1 points to the string onto which another string is concatenated.

s2 points to the string that is concatenated to s1.

n specifies the maximum number of characters from s2 to add to s1.

In the following code fragment, 5 characters from last are appended to name:

```
char name[81] = "Bob";
char last[81] = "Barns";
strncat( name, last, 5 );
```

Comparing Strings

```
int memcmp( const void *s1, const void *s2,
size_t n );
```

Type: Function

Returns: An integer that indicates how s1 and s2 compare. If s1 < s2, a value less than zero is returned. If s1 == s2, a value of zero is returned. If s1 > s2, a value greater than zero is returned.

memcmp() compares the first n number of characters from the string pointed to by s1 to the first n number of characters from the string pointed to by s2. The arguments for memcmp() are as follows:

s1 points to the first string to be compared.

s2 points to the second string to be compared.

n indicates how many characters from each string are compared.

Listing 17.10 shows how to set up the memcmp() function and test the value returned by it. On line 11, memcmp() compares the first 6 characters of s1 and s2. The return value is stored in the variable i. The value of i is tested on lines 13 through 19. The appropriate message indicating whether s1 was less than, equal to, or greater than s2 is printed.

Listing 17.10. `compare.c` *(Comparing strings with* `memcmp()`*).*
                                                                    TurboC++

```
1   #include <stdio.h>
2   #include <stdlib.h>
3   #include <string.h>
4
5   main()
6   {
7     char s1[81] = "String 1";
8     char s2[82] = "String 2";
9     int i;
10
11    i = memcmp( s1, s2, 6 );
12
13    if( i < 0 )
14      printf( "s1 < s2\n" );
15    else
16      if( i == 0 )
17        printf( "s1 = s2\n" );
18      else
19        printf( "s1 > s2\n" );
20  }
```

```
int strcmp( const char *s1, const char *s2 );
```

Type: Function

Returns: An integer indicating how s1 and s2 compare. If s1 < s2, a
               value less than zero is returned. If s1 == s2, a value of zero
               is returned. If s1 > s2, a value greater than zero is returned.

The `strcmp()` function compares two complete strings. Its arguments
are as follows:

s1 points to the first string to be compared.

s2 points to the second string to be compared.

The following code fragment compares the string pointed to by s1 to
the string pointed to by s2; the returned integer value is stored in the
variable i:

```
char s1[81] = "May";
char s2[81] = "June";
int i;
i = strcmp( s1, s2 );
```

```
int strcoll( const char *s1, const char *s2 );
```

Type: Function

Returns: An integer that indicates how s1 and s2 compare. If s1 < s2, a value less than zero is returned. If s1 == s2, a value of zero is returned. If s1 > s2, a value greater than zero is returned.

Like strcmp(), strcoll() compares two strings. The difference between the two functions is that strcoll() depends on the current locale. Specifically, strcoll() depends on the setting of LC_COLLATE for the current locale.

The following code fragment compares the string pointed to by s1 to the string pointed to by s2; the returned integer value is stored in the variable i:

```
char s1[81] = "May";
char s2[81] = "June";
int i;
i = strcoll( s1, s2 );
```

```
int strncmp( const char *s1, const char *s2,
size_t n );
```

Type: Function

Returns: An integer indicating how s1 and s2 compare. If s1 < s2, a value less than zero is returned. If s1 == s2, a value of zero is returned. If s1 > s2, a value greater than zero is returned.

strcmp() compares up to n number of characters in the string pointed to by s1 to the string pointed to by s2. If n is greater than the size of s1, the characters following the terminating null character are not used in the comparisons. A terminating null character may not be necessary in either s1 or s2. The arguments for strncmp() are as follows:

s1 points to the first string to be compared.

s2 points to the second string to be compared.

n specifies how many characters from s1 are to be compared to s2.

In the following code fragment, the first 11 characters from the string pointed to by s1 are compared to the string s2, and the integer result is stored in the variable i:

```
char s1[81] = "Test string no. 1";
char s2[81] = "Test string no. 2";
int i;
...
i = strncmp( s1, s2, 11 );
```

Because the strings differ only after the 11th character, in this instance they compare equal.

`size_t strxfrm( char *s1, const char *s2, size_t n );`

Type: Function

Returns: The length of the string pointed to by `s1`. The length of the string does not include space for the terminating null character. If the value returned by `strxfrm()` is greater than n, the contents of the string pointed to by `s1` are indeterminate.

`strxfrm()` is a *string transformation* function. `strxfrm()` transforms up to n number of characters from the string pointed to by `s2`. The transformation made depends on the current locale. The transformation is such that the value returned by `strcmp()` for the *transformed* strings equals the value returned by `strcoll()` for the *original* strings.

Up to n number of characters are transformed from the string pointed to by `s2`. The transformed sting is placed in the array pointed to by `s1`, and the terminating null character from `s2` is copied to `s1`. However, the value returned, which indicates the length of `s1`, does not include the terminating null character.

In plain language, `strxfrm()` is equivalent to a call to `strncpy()`, except that the sending string characters are "transformed" in a way controlled by the current locale.

The arguments for `strxfrm()` are as follows:

`s1` points to the string where the transformed string is copied. `s1` can be a null pointer if n is zero. In this case, the value returned equals the amount of space needed to store the string pointed to by `s2`. This return value does not include the space needed for the terminating null character.

`s2` points to the string from which a transformed string is generated.

n specifies the number of characters to be transformed from the string pointed to by `s2`.

In listing 17.11, the `strxfrm()` function is used to transform 4 characters from the string pointed to by `s2`.

Listing 17.11. xfrm.c *(Transforming strings with* strxfrm()*).*

TurboC++

```
1   #include <stdio.h>
2   #include <stdlib.h>
3   #include <string.h>
4
5   main()
6   {
7     char s1[81] = "String 1";
8     char s2[81] = "My stuff";
9     size_t i;
10
11    i = strxfrm( s1, s2, 4 );
12
13    printf( "i = %d\n", i );
14    printf( "s1 = %s\n", s1 );
15    printf( "s2 = %s\n", s2 );
16  }
```

The strxfrm() function is on line 11. Because the return value is greater than n in this example, the contents of the string pointed to by s1 is indeterminate. If n were equal to 9, the entire contents of the string pointed to by s2 would be transformed. The transformed string would then be stored at the address specified by s1.

String Searching

```
void *memchr( const void *s, int c, size_t n );
```

Type: Function

Returns: A pointer to the located character, if successful. If unsuccessful, a null pointer is returned.

memchr() searches the first n number of characters in the string pointed to by s for the character c. Only the first occurrence of c is reported. The arguments for memchr() are as follows:

*s points to the string to be searched.

c is the character to be located. c is converted to an unsigned char for the search.

n specifies the portion of the string to search. Only the first n characters are searched.

The following code fragment searches the string pointed to by s for the first occurrence of the character *'a'*:

```
char *s[81] = "This is a test string.";
char *ptr;
ptr = memchr( s, 'a', 12 );
```

Only the first 12 characters of the string are searched. The return value, which is stored in ptr, is a pointer to the first occurrence of *'a'*.

```
char *strchr( const char *s, int c );
```

Type: Function

Returns: A pointer to the located character, if successful. If unsuccessful, a null pointer is returned.

strchr() searches the string pointed to by s for the first occurrence of the character c. The terminating null character is part of the string that is searched. The arguments for strchr() are as follows:

s points to the string to be searched.

c is the character to be located in the target string.

The following code fragment searches the string pointed to by s for the first occurrence of the character *'a'*.

```
char *s[81] = "This is a test string.";
char *ptr;
ptr = strchr( s, 'a' );
```

The return value, which is stored in ptr, is a pointer to the first occurrence of *'a'*.

```
size_t strcspn( const char *s1, const char *s2 );
```

Type: Function

Returns: The length of the segment

strcspn() returns the length of the longest initial segment of s1 composed of characters not found in s2. Its arguments are as follows:

s1 points to the string to be searched.

s2 points to a string of characters. These are the characters *not* to be found in s1.

In the following code fragment, strcspn() checks the string pointed to by s1 for the characters found in the string pointed to by s2:

```
char s1[81] = "This is a test string.";
char s2[81] = "a";
size_t = len;
len = strcspn( s1, s2 );
```

The return value is the length of the longest sequence of characters not composed with the characters found in s2.

```
char *strpbrk( const char *s1, const char *s2 );
```

Type: Function

Returns: A pointer to the located character, if successful. If unsuccessful, a null pointer is returned.

strpbrk() locates in the string pointed to by s1 the first occurrence of *any one* of the characters in the string pointed to by s2. The arguments for strpbrk() are as follows:

s1 points to the string to be searched.

s2 points to a string of characters. The string pointed to by s1 is to be searched for the initial occurrence of any of these characters.

In the following code fragment, strpbrk() locates the first occurrence of "a" in the string pointed to by s1; the character pointer returned is stored in ptr:

```
char s1[81] = "This is a test string.";
char s2[81] = "a";
char *ptr;
ptr = strpbrk( s1, s2 );
```

```
char *strrchr( const *s, int c );
```

Type: Function

Returns: A pointer to the located character, if successful. If unsuccessful, a null pointer is returned.

strrchr() searches the string pointed to by s for the last occurrence of the character c—that is, the target string is searched *in reverse*. The terminating null character is part of the string to be searched. The arguments for strrchr() are as follows:

*s points to the string to be searched.

c is the character to be located in the string pointed to by s.

In the following code fragment, strrchr() searches the string pointed to by s for the last occurrence of 's'; a pointer to the last occurrence of 's' is returned and stored in the variable ptr:

```
char s[81] = "This is a test string.";
char *ptr;
ptr = strrchr( s, 's' );
```

size_t strspn(const char *s1, const char *s2);

Type: Function

Returns: The length of the segment

strspn() returns the length of the longest *initial* segment of the string pointed to by s1. (The segment must be composed entirely of characters found in the string pointed to by s2.) This is not a strict comparison function, because the order of characters found has nothing to do with it. The arguments for strspn() are as follows:

*s1 points to the string to be searched.

*s2 points to a string of characters. strspn() searches the string pointed to by s1 for the longest section composed entirely of these characters.

In the following code fragment, for example:

```
char str1[22] = "This is a test string";
char str2[6]  = " sihT";

printf( "Found a segment %d bytes long\n",
        strspn( str1, str2 ) );
```

strspn() searches the string pointed to by str1 for the longest segment composed entirely of the characters, " sihT". The length of the longest initial segment of str1 is reported as 8, including the substring "This is ".

char *strstr(const char *s1, const char *s2);

Type: Function

Returns: A pointer to the located substring, if successful. If unsuccessful, a null pointer is returned. s1 is returned if s2 points to a string of zero length.

The strstr() function searches the string pointed to by s1 for the first occurrence of the string pointed to by s2. The arguments for strstr() are as follows:

s1 points to the string to be searched.

s2 points to a string to be located in the string pointed to by s1.

In the following code fragment:

```
char s1[81] = "This is a test string.";
char *ptr;
...
ptr = strstr( s1, "test" );
```

strstr() searches the string pointed to by s1 for the first occurrence of the string "test". A pointer to the first occurrence of "test" is returned. This pointer is stored in the character pointer variable ptr.

```
char *strtok( char *s1, const char *s2 );
```

Type: Function

Returns: A pointer to the first character of the token. If there are no tokens, a null pointer is returned.

strtok() searches for tokens in the string pointed to by s1. If there are tokens in this string, they must be delimited by some character. The string pointed to by s2 specifies the delimiting character to search for.

The strtok() function is called for each token to be retrieved. On the first call to strtok(), the s1 argument points to a string that is searched. On subsequent calls, the s1 argument is a null pointer. The delimiter pointed to by s2 can change from call to call.

When strtok() is first called, it searches for the first character that is not a delimiter found in the string pointed to by s2. This point begins the token string. The string is then searched for the first character that is a delimiter; this is the end of the token string. It is marked by overlaying the token character with a null character. If a delimiter is not found, the token string extends to the normal end of the string.

A pointer to the token string is returned by strtok(). The strtok() function also stores a pointer to the character that followed the preceding delimiter. If such a character did not exist, a null pointer is stored.

Subsequent calls to strtok() use a null pointer as the s1 argument. strtok() retrieves the pointer it stored earlier (the pointer to the character following the last delimiter). strtok() then searches the string for other tokens, as it did before. The arguments for strtok() are as follows:

*s1 points to the string to search for tokens.

*s2 points to the string that specifies the delimiter characters.

Listing 17.12 uses the strtok() function to pull two tokens from the string pointed to by s1.

Listing 17.12. `token.c` *(Pulling tokens from a string).*   *Turbo C++*

```
1   #include <stdio.h>
2   #include <stdlib.h>
3   #include <string.h>
4
5   main()
6   {
7     char s1[81] = "!First token!Second token!";
8     char *ptr;
9
10    ptr = strtok( s1, "!" );
11    printf( "%s\n", ptr );
12
13    ptr = strtok( NULL, "!" );
14    printf( "%s\n", ptr );
15  }
```

On the first call to `strtok()`, the address of the string to search is given as the `s1` argument. The delimiter is defined as the `"!"` character. `strtok()` returns a pointer to the first token, and `printf()` prints the first token. On the second call to `strtok()`, a null pointer is given as the `s1` argument. `strtok()` has already stored a pointer to the rest of the string. The programmer does not need to supply a second pointer. `strtok()` returns a pointer to the second token, and `printf()` prints the second token.

Other String Functions

```
void *memset( void *s, int c, size_t n );
```

Type: Function

Returns: A pointer to the string pointed to by the `s` argument.

`memset()` initializes, with the character `c`, the first `n` number of characters in the string pointed to by `s`. `c` is converted from an integer to an `unsigned char` before it is written to the string.

The following two lines of code declare, initialize, and print a character string:

```
char s[10];
printf( "%s", memset( s, 'a', 5 ) );
```

memset() initializes, with the letter 'a', the first 5 characters of the string pointed to by s. Because memset() returns the value of the pointer s, it can be used as the argument in a printf() statement.

`char *strerror( int errnum );`

Type: Function

Returns: A pointer to the string associated with the number specified by errnum.

The strerror() function takes the error-number argument and returns a pointer to the string associated with that argument. errnum is the error number for which an error message is needed.

The following line of code prints the error message associated with the current value of errno:

```
printf( "%s", strerror( errno ) );
```

Because strerror() returns a pointer to a string, it can be used as an argument in printf().

`size_t strlen( const char *s );`

Type: Function

Returns: The length of the string pointed to by s. The terminating null character is not included in the string length.

strlen() calculates the length of the string pointed to by s. The returned value indicates the length of the string without the terminating null character.

In the following code fragment, strlen() calculates the length of the string pointed to by s, and the returned value is printed by printf():

```
char s[81] = "My string";
printf( "The length of s is : %d", strlen( s ) );
```

#include time.h

The time.h header file declares several functions for working with time values. time.h has declarations for functions that work with local, calendar, and daylight saving time.

Macros

CLK_TCK

Type: MACRO

Returns: N/A

CLK_TCK is an implementation-defined macro that indicates how many clock ticks per second the clock() function can count.

Type Definitions

clock_t

Type: Type definition

Returns: N/A

clock_t is a type definition used to declare variables capable of holding an object that represents a time value.

time_t

Type: Type definition

Returns: N/A

time_t is a type definition used to declare variables capable of holding an object that represents a time value. The contents of the underlying structure for that object are as follows:

struct tm {

Type: Structure definition

Returns: N/A

The tm structure holds the values for date and time information. The date and time information in this structure is called *broken-down time*. The structure should contain at least all the members listed in the following code. The order of the members is not important. The comment to the side of each member describes it and lists its acceptable values.

```
     int  tm_sec;          Seconds  after  the  minute  [0,  60]
     int  tm_min;          Minutes  after  the  hour  [0,  59]
     int  tm_hour;         Hours  after  midnight  [0,  23]
     int  tm_wday;         Days  since  Sunday  [1,  6]
     int  tm_mday;         Day  of  the  month  [1,  31]
     int  tm_yday;         Days  since  January  1  [0,  365]
     int  tm_mon;          Months  is  January  [0,  11]
     int  tm_year;         Years  since  1900
     int  tm_isdst;        Flag  for  daylight  saving  time
}
```

Notice that the value of `tm_sec` can range from 0 to 60—a total of *61* seconds. The extra second is to allow for an occasional leap second. The value of the `tm_isdst` flag is zero if daylight saving time is not in effect. The value of the flag is 1 if daylight saving time is in effect. The value is negative if information about daylight saving time is not available.

Manipulating Time

```
clock_t  clock( void );
```

Type: Function

Returns: The number of clock ticks since the program began. The value
              (`clock_t`)–1 is returned if the time is not available or cannot
              be represented.

`clock()` computes how long the program has been running. The implementation determines how precise the value returned by `clock()` can be. The value returned by `clock()` is in clock ticks, not seconds. To determine the number of seconds of program execution, the value returned by `clock()` must be divided by the macro `CLK_TCK`.

Listing 17.13 uses the `clock()` function twice to determine the time needed for a loop to complete. On line 10, the time is stored in the variable `time0`. Then the loop on line 11 is executed. Next, the `clock()` function is called again and the time is stored in `time1`. The difference between `time1` and `time0` gives a close approximation of the time needed for the loop. (This difference is calculated on line 14.)

```
double  difftime( time_t  time1,  time_t  time0 );
```

Type: Function

Returns: The number of seconds between `time1` and `time0`. The value
              returned is of type `double`.

The `difftime()` function computes the difference in time between `time1` and `time0`. Its arguments are as follows:

time1 is   the *ending* time.

time0 is   the *beginning* time.

Listing 17.13. `clock.c` *(Timing a loop using* `clock()`*).*   *Turbo C++*

```
 1   #include <stdio.h>
 2   #include <stdlib.h>
 3   #include <time.h>
 4
 5   main()
 6   {
 7     clock_t time0, time1;
 8     long int i;
 9
10     time0 = clock();
11     for( i = 0; i < 500000; i++ );
12     time1 = clock();
13
14     time1 = ( ( time1 - time0 ) / CLK_TCK );
15     printf( "loop time = %d\n", time1 );
16   }
```

Listing 17.14 uses the `difftime()` function to calculate the length of time needed for the `for()` loop.

Listing 17.14. `difft.c` *(Timing a loop using* `difftime()`*).*

TurboC++

```
 1   #include <stdio.h>
 2   #include <stdlib.h>
 3   #include <time.h>
 4
 5   main()
 6   {
 7     time_t time0, time1;
 8     long int i;
 9
10     time( &time0 );
11     for( i = 0; i < 500000; i++ );
12     time( &time1 );
13
14     printf( "loop time = %f\n", difftime( time1, time0 ) );
15   }
```

On line 10, the first time value is stored in `time0`. On line 11, the loop is executed. On line 12, the ending time is stored in `time1`. On line 14, `difftime()` computes the difference between `time1` and `time0`. The returned value is used as an argument of the `printf()` statement.

```
time_t mktime( struct tm *timeptr );
```

Type: Function

Returns: The value of the specified calendar time, modified so that it can be represented as type `time_t`. If the specified calendar time cannot be represented, a value of –1 is returned.

`mktime()` converts the values in the structure pointed to by `timeptr`. Before `mktime()` is called, the values in the structure are expressed in *local time*. For local time, the value of some of the components in the array do not have to be within their normal values. `mktime()` forces the values of the components to their normal values. After `mktime()` adjusts the values of these components, the values for `tm_wday` and `tm_yday` are calculated and stored. The return value is encoded so that it can be represented by a variable of type `time_t`.

`timeptr` points to a structure of type `tm`. The values in this structure are adjusted and converted.

Listing 17.15 uses the `mktime()` function to calculate the day of the week for a given date. The `scanf()` function on line 16 scans in month, day, and year values. These values are stored in the `calctm` structure (see lines 18 through 24). `mktime()` normalizes the structure values and calculates values for `tm_wday` and `tm_yday`. The value of `tm_wday` is output in the `printf()` statement found on line 27. The return value from `mktime()` is checked on line 26. If the return value equals –1, `mktime()` was not successful. In this case, because the day of the week was not calculated, no output is performed. The return value when `mktime()` is successful was not needed in this example.

```
time_t time( time_t *timer );
```

Type: Function

Returns: If successful, the return value is the closest approximation of the current calendar time. If unsuccessful, a value of –1 is returned. If `*timer` is not a null pointer, the return value is stored in the object pointed to.

`time()` gets the current calendar date. The return value is as close to the exact date as is possible for the implementation. The implementation specifies the encoding of the return value.

Listing 17.15. `mktime.c` *(Using* `mktime()` *to calculate the day of the week for a given date).*   *Turbo C++*

```
1   #include <stdio.h>
2   #include <stdlib.h>
3   #include <time.h>
4
5   char *wkday[] = {"Sunday", "Monday", "Tuesday",
6                    "Wednesday", "Thursday", "Friday",
7                    "Saturday"};
8   main()
9   {
10    int mm, dd, yy;
11    struct tm calc_tm;
12
13    printf( "Enter your next pay date.\n" );
14    printf( "Enter the date as: MM DD YYYY\n" );
15    printf( "==> " );
16    scanf( "%d %d %d", &mm, &dd, &yy );
17
18    calc_tm.tm_year  = yy - 1900;
19    calc_tm.tm_mon   = mm - 1;
20    calc_tm.tm_mday  = dd;
21    calc_tm.tm-hour  = 0;
22    calct_m.tm_min   = 0;
23    calc_tm.tm_sec   = 0;
24    calc_tm.tm_isdst = -1;
25
26    if( mktime( &calc_tm ) != -1 )
27      printf( "Your next payday is on: %s\n",
28               wkday[calc_tm.tm_wday] );
29    else
30      printf( "The day could not be calculated.\n" );
31  }
```

`*timer` can be either a null pointer or a pointer to an object. If `timer` points to an object, the current calendar date is stored in that object. If `timer` is a null pointer, `time()` returns the current time but does not store the time in an object.

The following two lines of code declare a `time_t` object and store the current calendar date in the object:

```
time_t time_obj;
time( &time_obj );
```

The next two lines of code are equivalent to the two preceding lines:

```
time_t time_obj;
time_object = time( NULL );
```

In this example, the value returned by time() is *assigned* to time_obj. (In the first example, the return value was not used.) The current calendar date was stored directly in the object specified by the address &time_obj.

Converting Time

```
char *asctime( const struct tm *timeptr );
```

Type: Function

Returns: A pointer to a string that contains the converted form of the broken-down time.

asctime() converts the broken-down time in the tm type structure to a character string. *timeptr points to a tm type structure that contains a broken-down time.

The following lines of code are used to print a string representation of the current time:

```
time_t timer;
struct tm *my_time;
time( &timer );
my_time = localtime( &timer );
printf( "my_time  = %s", asctime( my_time ) );
```

The time() function determines the current calendar time. The result is stored in timer. localtime() converts the calendar time to the local, broken-down, time. my_time points to the structure where the broken-down time is stored. Finally, asctime() converts the broken-down time to a string representation, and the string is printed by the printf() function.

```
char *ctime( const time_t *timer );
```

Type: Function

Returns: A pointer to a string that contains the converted form of the broken-down time.

ctime() converts the calendar time pointed to by timer to a string representation of the broken-down time. *timer points to a time_t type object that contains the current calendar time.

The following code fragment gets the current calendar time and converts it to string representation of the broken-down time:

```
time_t timer;
time( timer );
printf( "The current time is: %s", ctime( &timer ) );
```

This code fragment is equal to the code fragment in the discussion of `asctime()`, earlier in this section.

```
struct tm *gmtime( const time_t *timer );
```

Type: Function

Returns: A pointer to the `tm` type structure that contains the broken-down time. A null pointer is returned if UTC time is not available.

gmtime() converts the current calendar time into local, broken-down, time. The time is converted also to indicate the equivalent Coordinated Universal Time (UTC), previously known as Greenwich mean time (GMT). (Pilots still refer to "Zulu" time when talking by radio with Flight Service.)

The following code fragment prints the UTC time as a string:

```
time_t timer;
struct tm *my_time;
time( &timer );
my_time = gmtime( &timer );
printf( "The UTC time is: %s", asctime( my_time ) );
```

The `time()` function gets the current calendar time. This time is stored in `timer`. `gmtime()` takes the value of `timer` and converts it to UTC time. The converted time is in the local, broken-down form. `my_time` points to the structure where the broken-down time is stored. The `asctime` function converts the broken-down time to a string representation, and `printf()` displays the string representation of the UTC time.

```
struct tm *localtime( const time_t *timer );
```

Type: Function

Returns: A pointer to the structure where the converted, broken-down time is stored.

localtime() converts the current calendar time pointed to by `timer` into the local, or broken-down, representation. `*timer` points to the calendar-time value.

In the following code fragment, the current calendar time is retrieved by the `time()` function:

```
time_t timer;
struct tm *my_time;
time( &timer );
my_time = localtime( &timer );
```

The calendar time is stored in the `timer` variable. `localtime()` takes the calendar time from `timer` and converts it to local time. The local time is stored in the structure pointed to by `my_time`.

```
size_t strftime( char *s, size_t maxsize,
    const char *format, const struct tm *timeptr );
```

Type: Function

Returns: If the number of characters written, including the terminating null character, is less than `maxsize`, the return value equals the number of characters written. The return value does not include the terminating null character. In any other case, the return value is zero. The contents of the array written to are indeterminate.

`strftime()` generates a formatted string that contains date and time information. The formatted string is pointed to by the s argument. No more than `maxsize` number of characters are placed in the string. The `format` string consists of a number of characters and conversion specifications.

Each conversion specification begins with %. The regular characters in the format string are copied unchanged to the destination string. The date and time information to be used comes from the structure pointed to by `timeptr`. The arguments for `strftime()` are as follows:

*s points to the string where the formatted output is sent.

`maxsize` specifies the maximum size of the formatted string.

*`format` points to the string that contains the formatting information.

*`timeptr` points to a structure of type `tm` that contains date and time information.

Table 17.1 lists the conversion-specification characters for the `strftime()` function. Each specification is followed by a brief description of what replaces the specification in the put string. The exact representation of many of the output values is determined by the implementation.

Table 17.1. Conversion specifiers for strftime().

Specifier	Description
%a	Abbreviated weekday name
%A	Full weekday name
%b	Abbreviated month name
%B	Full month name
%c	The locale's appropriate date and time representation.
%d	Decimal value for day of the month (01–31)
%H	Decimal value for 24-hour time (00–23)
%I	Decimal value for 12-hour time (01–12)
%j	Decimal value for the day of the year (001–366)
%m	Decimal value for the month (01–12)
%M	Decimal value for the minute (00–59)
%p	The locale's equivalent of AM or PM
%S	Decimal value for the second (00–60)
%U	Decimal value for the week number, with Sunday as the first day of the week (00–53)
%w	Decimal value for the weekday; Sun. = 0. (0–6)
%W	Decimal value for the week number, with Monday as the first day of the week (00–53)
%x	The locale's appropriate date representation
%X	The locale's appropriate time representation
%y	Decimal value of the year, w/o century (00–99)
%Y	Decimal value of the year, with century
%z	Time-zone name, if available. No characters, if unavailable.
%%	The % character

Listing 17.16 uses the `strftime()` function to generate a formatted string containing date information.

Listing 17.16. `frmtime.c` *(Formatted time strings).*   *Turbo C++*

```
1   #include <stdio.h>
2   #include <stdlib.h>
3   #include <time.h>
4
5   main()
6   {
7     time_t timer;
8     struct tm *my_time;
9     char hold[81];
10
11    time( &timer );
12    my_time = localtime( &timer );
13
14    strftime( hold, 81, "Today is %A %b %d %Y", my_time );
15    printf( "%s\n", hold );
16  }
```

On line 11, the current calendar time is obtained from the system. Line 12 converts the calendar time to local time. The local time is stored in the structure pointed to by `my_time`. On line 14, `strftime()` generates a formatted string. The formatted string is pointed to by `hold`. The value 81 indicates that no more than 81 characters are to be sent to `hold`. The format string is next, followed by the pointer to the `tm` type structure. `printf()` prints the formatted string pointed to by `hold`.

Summary

When you need a function that does not seem to fit in the normal categories, look in the `stdlib.h` header. `stdlib.h` has a useful assortment of utility functions. When you are working with strings (character arrays), include the `string.h` header file. When calculating time values, you need the `time.h` header file.

Part III

C++ Programming Basics

18

Objects and Object-Oriented Programming

Object-oriented programming (OOP) and object-oriented programming systems (OOPS) are the current cutting edge of software technology. An object-oriented language—such as C++—can be used for anything from sprucing up existing programs written in procedural languages, to providing an architectural platform for implementing that latest wonder of artificial intelligence: neural networks.

If you have no prior experience with C programming, we urge you to stop reading right now, go back to the beginning of this book, work your way through it, write lots of practice code, and master that material thoroughly. If you do not, you will be quickly and utterly lost.

If, on the other hand, you have a moderate amount of experience with C— enough so that you feel comfortable writing C programs—C++ and object-oriented programming will present no particular difficulty. C++ implements "objects" by using the structured object technology you already know about, adding some new syntax for notational convenience, and some new rules to cope with the expanded capabilities of this new environment.

Objects Are Working Models

What is an object? This is the first and crucial question that must be answered before C++ can be understood. There is much discussion about this and related issues; to begin with, we like Bruce Eckel's generalized definition of an object : *an object is anything with boundaries*.

Comparing an object-oriented program to a more conventional procedural program shows why this definition is appropriate. In a procedural program, the program is built around the idea of functionality—a program does something. Data is what you "do something to." Thus a procedural program is conceived of as a collection of procedures or functions, and data flows openly through the program (see fig. 18.1).

Fig. 18.1. Data flow in a procedural language.

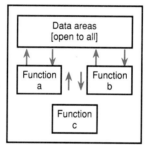

An object-oriented program, in contrast, is conceived of as a collection of objects—which includes both data and the methods to use it—that communicate with each other through messages, to get the job done (see fig. 18.2). The central question is why you should want to write programs this way. Two features of object-oriented architecture make it desirable, especially for complex projects. These features are *data abstraction* and the association of methods for handling objects *with the objects themselves*.

Data Abstraction Is Data Hiding

The first feature that makes object-oriented design desirable is *data abstraction*, also known as *encapsulation*. Data abstraction is nothing more than data hiding—concealing some parts of the program's data structures

Fig. 18.2. Message flow in an object-oriented program.

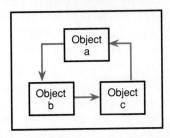

from ordinary view to avoid inadvertent or erroneous modification. Only the parts of the program the data "belongs to" can either access or modify it. Note that this is not the same thing as abstract data typing, which we get to shortly.

The need for such a mechanism in procedural languages is more acute than you might think. The larger a program grows, the easier it is for the programmer to become disorganized, and the more difficult to keep in mind all the details. Fighter pilots call the ability to mentally retain and juggle many factors simultaneously *situational awareness*, or SA. You could say that large procedural programs make it impossible to maintain adequate SA.

Structured programming techniques were the first real attempt to untangle the complex web of logic and interdependent data areas (and increase SA). These techniques dictated how logic should be designed, how procedures could be accessed (logic flow), and a host of other things all aimed at forcing a programmer to stay organized.

Put bluntly—it didn't work. The most difficult program in the world to debug is the poorly written structured program. There were two main reasons for this failure. First, the programmer generally is not at fault (there are bad programmers, but there are many more good ones). The programmer's problem was not mental laziness, nor stupidity, nor any such thing. His real problem was (and often is) *overload*. Large programs simply can exceed normal human capacity to cope with them effectively.

Second, structured coding techniques required, *but provided no real tools to accomplish*, better organization. Admonishing programmers to "Get organized: write structured code" is like telling a hungry man to be filled, but giving him no food. Whatever else structured techniques did, *they failed to prevent the open flow of data in and through a program*. The result is that the programmer continues to be confronted by all the complexity of a large program, which in turn snowballs. More data and logic is required to control previous data and logic, and so on.

In the down-to-earth world of the real data-processing shop, structured programming has proven inadequate for coping with ever-larger and more complex programs. Object-oriented languages can do better, but are not the final answer either.

And you must recognize yet another consideration before you decide to take on a new object-oriented coding project. For exactly the reasons just discussed, you don't need OOPS (including C++) unless the project is going to be large and complex. The very purpose of techniques like data abstraction is to conceal and manage complexity. If there is no real complexity, all you accomplish by using these tools is, ironically, a needlessly complex program!

In fact, data hiding can be accomplished to some degree in conventional procedural languages. C is more capable than most languages of data hiding; to accomplish it, C uses structures, type definitions, header files, and pointers to functions.

C Functions as Object Methods

One of the most significant advances incorporated into C++ is the *binding of method to the object to which it belongs*. C++ supports functions (as C does) but goes farther, requiring that functions which manipulate the object belong to the object—they must be *member functions*.

This is the crux of *abstract typing*, or defining your own object types (not data abstraction or encapsulation). The compiler already knows how to deal with its built-in types, but you must "teach" it how to handle types you define. Hence a need for member functions that goes beyond the simple goal of protecting the object's contents from accidental or illegal access.

You may wonder why a whole new syntax is necessary to provide object-oriented behavior. The answer is simply *convenience and power*. Writing an object-oriented program with ordinary C is entirely possible. To get started, all you need is a mastery of C structures and function pointers to provide object boundaries and member functions.

Using ordinary C to write a (somewhat) object-oriented program will help you appreciate just what we mean by "convenience"—but it's not worth doing more than once. Listing 18.1 contains the source code for `cminus.c`, which implements some crude screen functions in a somewhat "object-oriented" fashion.

Listing 18.1. `cminus.c` *(Implementing abstract types with ordinary C structures).* *Zortech C*

```
1   #include <stdlib.h>
2   #include <stdio.h>
3   #include <disp.h>
4   #include <conio.h>
5
6   typedef struct {     /* DEFINE SCREEN "CLASS" */
7      int border[4];
8      int curpos[2];
9      int cur_attr;
10
11     void (*clr)( void * );                /* Methods */
12     void (*loc)( void *, int, int );
13     void (*put)( void *, char * );
14     int* (*query_scr)( void * );
15  } screen;
16
17  void clr( screen * );
18  void loc( screen *, int, int );
19  void put( screen *, char * );
20  void init_scr( screen *, int, int, int, int);
21  int*  query_scr( screen *);
22
23  #define CLR(a)  (*a.clr)( &a )
24  #define LOC(a,b,c) (*a.loc)( &a,b,c )
25  #define PUT(a,b)   (*a.put)( &a,b )
26  #define INIT(a,b,c,d,e) (*init_scr)( &a,b,c,d,e )
27  #define QUERY(a) (*a.query_scr)( &a )
28
29  void init_scr( screen *this, int topx, int topy,
30                 int botx, int boty )
31  {
32     this->query_scr = query_scr;
33     this->clr       = clr;
34     this->loc       = loc;
35     this->put       = put;
36     this->border[0] = topx-1;
37     this->border[1] = topy-1;
38     this->border[2] = botx-1;
39     this->border[3] = boty-1;
40     this->cur_attr = 0x1E;
41     if ( !disp_inited ) {
42       disp_open();
43       disp_scroll( 0,0,0,disp_numrows-1,
44                    disp_numcols-1,0x40 );
```

Listing 18.1. *continues*

Listing 18.1. continued

```
45        disp_setattr( this->cur_attr );
46      }
47      disp_scroll( 0,this->border[1],this->border[0],
48                   this->border[3],this->border[2],
49                   this->cur_attr );
50      disp_box( 0,this->cur_attr,this->border[1],
51                this->border[0],this->border[3],
52                this->border[2] );
53  }
54
55  int*  query_scr( screen *this )
56  {
57     return( this->curpos );
58  }
59
60  void clr( screen *this )
61  {
62      disp_scroll( 0,this->border[1]+1,this->border[0]+1,
63                   this->border[3]-1,this->border[2]-1,
64                   this->cur_attr );
65  }
66
67  void loc( screen *this, int x, int y )
68  {
69     disp_move( this->border[1] + y, this->border[0] + x );
70     this->curpos[0] = disp_cursorcol - this->border[0];
71     this->curpos[1] = disp_cursorrow - this->border[1];
72  }
73
74  void put( screen *this, char *msg )
75  {
76     int *p;
77
78     p = QUERY( (*this) );
79     LOC( (*this),*p,*(p+1) );
80     disp_printf( "%s",msg );
81     this->curpos[0] = disp_cursorcol - this->border[0];
82     this->curpos[1] = disp_cursorrow - this->border[1];
83  }
84
85  main()
86  {
87     screen screen1, screen2;
88     char ch;
89
90
91     INIT( screen1,1,1,39,12 );
92     INIT( screen2,40,13,80,25 );
```

```
93
94      LOC( screen1,17,6 );
95      LOC( screen2,17,6 );
96
97      PUT( screen1,"Hello" );
98      PUT( screen2,"Hello" );
99
100     while ( !(ch = getch()) ) ;
101 }
```

Listing 18.1 shows what is probably the most complicated "hello" program you will ever see. This program defines and uses multiple "virtual screens" that may all appear simultaneously on the physical screen. (A real object-oriented virtual screen manager, complete with pulldown menus is presented in the next chapter.)

Each virtual screen is an object, and must have a type (known as a *class* in true C++). This program implements the screen type in an ordinary structure, however, which can be seen in lines 6–15. Both the data items belonging to the object (lines 7–9) and the pointers to "member" functions (lines 11–14) are contained within the boundaries of the object type.

Before the object can be used, it must be initialized. This is done in lines 29–53, function init_scr(). This activity corresponds to the C++ *constructor*. The major difference is that true C++ objects do not require you to take addresses and initialize pointers in this way, although you have to initialize member variables.

Lines 23–27 contain several macros intended to mimic the C++ way of accessing an object. Although the syntax cannot be matched exactly, using macros to mask the syntax does allow you to pass objects by "reference," much as C++ does, without having to use the address-of operator for every reference. What "passing by reference" means becomes clear later when the C++ reference operator is discussed. Meanwhile, notice how complicated the macro structure must be to permit this simplified method of access.

Without belaboring the point, you can see that implementing objects in ordinary C costs something in effort, and possibly in confusion, as you deal with the awkward syntax. Implementing objects in C++ also costs some effort—just not as much—and can be done much more powerfully than in C. Without further delay, then, you can see how all this is done with C++.

Classes Are Abstract Data Types

Objects, like structures in general, are relatively complex. And as with structures, the compiler has no advance "knowledge" of what an object contains or how it is handled. That is, the compiler knows nothing about the object's type.

Typing objects in C++ is entirely your problem: you must decide what goes in the object, and how that data is to be handled. In C++, such user-defined types are called *classes*. A class is the method used by C++ to implement *abstract data types*, which in turn means only that the compiler knows nothing about them beforehand (as it does its built-in types).

Now, let's pull together some terminology. C++ provides for *data abstraction* (encapsulation of related complex data) as well as for *abstract data typing* (user-defined types or classes). And the *structure*, a feature you already know about from C, should be knocking at the door of your mind.

If all this reminds you of structures, you are entirely correct. Underneath all the new terminology and syntax of C++, the basic vehicle for implementing objects is the C struct. But it is a structure with a twist, with new and improved powers! If you keep this one fact in mind as you approach learning C++, it all is much easier to retain.

The new kind of structure in C++ is the class. Its declaration syntax is similar to your old friend the struct. Details on declaring classes and defining objects are given in the next chapter, but comparing some real C++ code to the program in listing 18.1 is enlightening. Therefore, in the next three program listings, we show briefly the source files required for defining and using a keyboard object. As you read over the listings, watch for the way the code treats the keyboard object as something that can *act*, rather than simply being acted upon—objects have more "intelligence" than simple data because they contain their own method functions.

The keyboard object appears in the next three source file listings, which correspond to the header file, the member (method) functions source file, and the main program file. We definitely mean to convey to you that the best way to write C++ code is in separately-compiled modules, but you should know also that it can all be done in one file.

The first source file, shown in listing 18.2, contains the header file for the keyboard object. In addition to the more mundane matters of manifest constants, the object header contains the object's type, or *class*, declaration. This header is included in *both* the source file that contains the actual member functions, *and* the main program that uses it all.

Listing 18.2. `keyboard.hpp` (Header file for the keyboard object). Turbo C++

```
1   #define NORM 0
2   #define EXT  1
3
4   #define F1 59
5   #define F2 60
6   #define F3 61
7   #define F4 62
8   #define F5 63
9   #define F6 64
10  #define F7 65
11  #define F8 66
12  #define F9 67
13  #define F10 68
14  #define INS 82
15  #define DEL 83
16  #define HOME 71
17  #define END 79
18  #define UPA 72
19  #define DNA 80
20  #define LFA 75
21  #define RTA 77
22  #define PGU 73
23  #define PGD 81
24
25  class keyboard {          // Declare the class (type)
26     int state;
27     int ch;
28     int lastpush;
29     int pushbuf[80][2];      //LIFO push buffer
30  public:
31     keyboard( void );
32     void next( void );       // get next state and character
33     void nexte( void );      // get next state, character, echo
34     void push( int, int ); // push specified state, character
35     friend int keystate( keyboard & );
36     friend int keyval( keyboard & );
37  };
38
```

Notice how much the class keyboard declaration (lines 25–37 of listing 18.2) resembles a struct declaration with a tag. It has member elements, just like a struct.

Differences appear immediately, however. The members elements in lines 26–29 are encapsulated—*they are visible only to the member func-*

tions. That, in fact, is the purpose of the `public` keyword in line 30: it signals that the member elements (all functions, in this case) can be seen and accessed by calls from outside the object (when one is later defined—this is just the declaration, remember). The one exception to this rule is the `friend` function (see lines 35–36). These are nonmember functions that nevertheless can access private member elements. They are covered in detail in Chapter 21.

So much for the `keyboard` header file and prototype declarations. What about the member functions themselves? They are found in the source file `keyboard.cpp`, listing 18.3. One very good reason for defining the member functions in a separate file is that doing so enhances the effect of encapsulating the object.

Listing 18.3. `keyboard.cpp` *(Source file containing member functions for keyboard object).* *Turbo C++*

```
 1   #include <stdlib.h>
 2   #include <stdio.h>
 3   #include <conio.h>
 4
 5   #include "keyboard.hpp"
 6
 7   keyboard::keyboard( void )
 8   {
 9     if ( !this ) {  // assigning to this is now obsolete
10       if ( NULL == ( this =
11         (keyboard *)malloc( sizeof( keyboard ) ) ) ) {
12         printf( "Could not allocate %d bytes\n",
13           sizeof( keyboard ) );
14         abort();
15       }
16     }
17     else this = this; // assign for every possible path
18     state = NORM;
19     ch = '\0';
20     lastpush = 80;
21   }
22
23   void keyboard::next( void )
24   {
25     if ( lastpush < 80 ) {    // get it from push buffer
26       state = pushbuf[lastpush][0];
27       ch = pushbuf[lastpush][1];
28       ++lastpush;
29     }
30     else {
31       state = NORM;
```

```
32        ch = getch();
33        if ( !ch ) {
34          state = EXT;
35          ch = getch();
36        }
37      }
38   }
39
40   void keyboard::nexte( void )
41   {
42     if ( lastpush < 80 ) {    // get it from push buffer
43       state = pushbuf[lastpush][0];
44       ch = pushbuf[lastpush][1];
45       ++lastpush;
46     }
47     else {
48       state = NORM;
49       ch = getch();
50       if ( !ch ) {
51         state = EXT;
52         ch = getch();
53       }
54     }
55     if ( !state ) putchar( ch ); // if not ext ASCII
56   }
57
58   void keyboard::push( int kstate, int kval )
59   {
60     if ( lastpush > 0 ) {
61       --lastpush;
62       pushbuf[lastpush][0] = kstate;
63       pushbuf[lastpush][1] = kval;
64     }
65   }
66
67   int keystate( keyboard &kybd )
68   {
69     return kybd.state;
70   }
71
72   int keyval( keyboard &kybd )
73   {
74     return kybd.ch;
75   }
```

Writing the member function definitions in a separate source file does require one particular extra bit of effort. Notice in the declaration part of every function declaration (except the two that were declared as friend functions) that every function name is preceded by the tokens keyboard::.

This is done so that the compiler knows *which class declaration these member functions belong to*. The `::` operator, which is new in C++, is the *scope resolution operator*. This is an important concept—if the header and source file were combined, the scope resolution operator might not be necessary (if only one class were being defined).

Lines 7–21 of listing 18.3 show something interesting: a function with the same name as the class. This is the *constructor* member function; it has the special purpose of initializing the object when it is defined (created). Remember that we said you must teach the compiler everything it knows about how to handle the new object.

The constructor function also contains a peculiar reference to something named `this`. The identifier `this` is a very special pointer identifier in C++. It is always assumed to be present (notice that it was not declared), and can always be referenced by member functions to access a particular object—*this* object, with the obvious meaning. The use of `this` is explained in great detail in the next chapter. For now, we keep moving along with the introduction to C++.

All that remains to be done is to create an object by defining it, and use it. This is done in the main program `testkey.cpp`, listing 18.4. This program illustrates the use of the `keyboard` class object to retrieve characters from the keyboard, with echo to the screen automatically included, to receive special-purpose keystrokes (the extended-ASCII function keys and other keys on the IBM PC), and to show briefly how keyboard macros might be implemented. That's quite a lot from this little bit of code, but it is a perfect illustration of what the power of C++ buys for you.

Listing 18.4. *testkey.cpp (Test driver for keyboard object).*   *Turbo C++*

```
1   #include <stdlib.h>
2   #include <stdio.h>
3   #include <string.h>
4
5   #include "keyboard.hpp"
6
7   main()
8   {
9       int i;              // declare an ordinary object ...
10      keyboard kybd;      // Create the keyboard object ...
```

```
11                         // No constructor parms were needed,
12                         // so parens weren't needed either
13
14    char *p;
15    char msg[80] = "Create keyboard macros easily!\r";
16                         // string simulates console input ...
17
18    printf( "\nType some normal text:\n" );
19    do { kybd.nexte(); } while ( keyval( kybd ) != 13 );\
20
21    printf( "\nStrike a function or other extended key:\n" );
22    kybd.nexte();
23    if ( keystate( kybd ) == NORM ) {
24      printf( "That wasn't an extended ASCII key\n" );
25      exit( 0 );
26    }
27
28    switch( keyval( kybd ) ) {
29      case F1 :
30                    printf( "You struck F1\n" ); break;
31      case F2 :
32                    printf( "You struck F2\n" ); break;
33      case F3 :
34                    printf( "You struck F3\n" ); break;
35      case F4 :
36                    printf( "You struck F4\n" ); break;
37      case F5 :
38                    printf( "You struck F5\n" ); break;
39      case F6 :
40                    printf( "You struck F6\n" ); break;
41      case F7 :
42                    printf( "You struck F7\n" ); break;
43      case F8 :
44                    printf( "You struck F8\n" ); break;
45      case F9 :
46                    printf( "You struck F9\n" ); break;
47      case F10 :
48                    printf( "You struck F10\n" ); break;
49      case INS :
50                    printf( "You struck Ins\n" ); break;
51      case DEL :
52                    printf( "You struck Del\n" ); break;
53      case HOME :
54                    printf( "You struck Home\n" ); break;
55      case END :
56                    printf( "You struck End\n" ); break;
57      case UPA :
58                    printf( "You struck UpArrow\n" ); break;
59      case DNA :
```

Listing 8.4. continues

Listing 2.2. continued

```
60                       printf( "You struck DownArrow\n" ); break;
61      case LFA :
62                       printf( "You struck LeftArrow\n" ); break;
63      case RTA :
64                       printf( "You struck RightArrow\n" ); break;
65      case PGU :
66                       printf( "You struck PageUp\n" ); break;
67      case PGD :
68                       printf( "You struck PageDown\n" ); break;
69      }
70
71      p = msg + strlen( msg ) - 1; // push down kybd macro
72      for( i=strlen(msg); i>0; --i ) kybd.push( 0, *p-- );
73
74      printf( "\nYou don't have to do anything here:\n" );
75      do { kybd.nexte(); } while ( keyval( kybd ) != 13 );
76  }
```

The program in listing 18.4 is shown to be dependent on Turbo C++. Only one line—line 15—prevents this particular program from being compiled directly by the Zortech C++ 1.07 compiler. The Zortech compiler complains that you cannot write an initializer with an `auto` array object. This is in keeping with the original K&R C on which Zortech C++ 1.07 is based. Turbo C++ permits this line to compile correctly because it conforms to the ANSI C practice of allowing initializers for aggregate objects anywhere.

The point of overwhelming interest in listing 18.4 is line 10. With the one short statement `keyboard kybd;` the object is created, initialized, and ready for use! All you had to do was declare it like any other "variable." There is a moral here: *after you have conceived and defined a class properly, you can write extremely powerful code very quickly*. That is what C++ is all about.

Going Beyond *typedef*

Clearly, the `class` declaration goes considerably beyond even `typedef` in its descriptive and syntactical power. Further, it puts that power in *your* hands.

We mentioned earlier that one of the glaring failures of structured programming was that it required good organization without supplying the proper tools. Well, C++ doesn't so much require organization as it does supply the tools—the organization happens pretty much automatically.

That is perhaps the greatest beauty of C++ (and other OOPS vehicles). It definitely makes large and complex projects possible. After you have gotten over the learning curve, writing badly disorganized code is nearly impossible. And, in the long run, C++ simplifies complex projects, not so much by being complex (although it can be) as by *not* requiring you to continue dealing with complexity after you have solved a particular problem. You can fix it, file it, and forget it.

Is C++ the answer to every programming dilemma? It most certainly is not. You still can stumble into several dark corners, but the language is young and growing. Pitfalls are bound to exist. With a little work and experimentation, you will find it worthwhile (we hope!).

What Encapsulation Means

Admittedly, the `keyboard` class object developed in this chapter was somewhat contrived. The `friend` functions were included even though they were not strictly necessary in this object class.

Why would we do that? Simply to illustrate something about what encapsulation means in the context of C++. Encapsulation, or data hiding, is meant to be an ally, not an enemy. It should be a tool to work with, not something that defeats you at every turn.

Thus the `friend` nonmember functions were included in this example to show you that C++ has the flexibility to do what you need it to do—it even provides a legitimate way to get around data hiding. The spirit of C is at work also in C++, and it can be a `friend`ly language when approached with a little patience!

Class Inheritance Is Type Derivation

In ordinary C, you can derive new objects from old. For example, defining an array of `int` is a type derivation, but you don't have to redefine `int` to the compiler to do it. Of course, plain C provides only a synonym facility in deriving arrays, `struct`s, and `typedef`s.

C++ also provides for type derivation, but it is more than just a synonym facility. You can derive a class from another similar class and *easily change part of its definition*. That is somewhat like being able to define a brand-new basic type to C, but better.

This feature of C++ is called *inheritance*. The derived class can inherit most of its logic from the old class, but you can redefine parts of the new class to suit slightly (or greatly) different purposes.

Inheritance is perhaps one of the most powerful features of C++, and indeed of any OOPS language. There are, however, differences of opinion as to what inheritance does, or should, mean. In fact there are differences of opinion on exactly what "object-oriented" should mean. A review of some of these opinions may help you form your own mental filing system in which you can arrange your understanding of C++.

Definitions of Object-Oriented Systems

There are multitudes of definitions of "object-oriented." We have already given you a first working definition of an object as something that has boundaries. This helps to get started in forming a conceptual framework for the subject, but does little to help you understand just how objects might be represented in a concrete programming language.

Accordingly, three different views on the subject are presented for your inspection. You might keep in mind that while these three views don't agree everywhere, they don't necessarily disagree everywhere, either. We briefly discuss the statements of Peter Wegner of Brown University; of Zortech Ltd., the company that produced the first true C++ compiler for the IBM PC environment (Bruce Eckel contributed to the tutorial parts of the Zortech manual); and finally, of Bjarne Stroustrup (who originally conceived and developed C++—we can hardly miss his comments).

It might be added that C++ is object-oriented by any of the views about to be examined. Certain OOPS purists, however, would claim that no *compiled* language can ever be object-oriented. These devotees would limit such rarified achievement only to implementations that can resolve the type and validity of objects and their "messages" completely dynamically at run-time: that is, only to interpretive languages. Understandably, most of us differ with this extreme view.

Wegner's Definition

Peter Wegner, who earned a Ph.D in Computer Science from London University, is currently a professor of that subject at Brown University in

Providence, Rhode Island. He is deeply involved in OOPS and has written about it in a variety of learned and popular publications. His views, as briefly summarized here, appeared in an article, "Learning the Language," in the March, 1989, issue of *Byte Magazine* (Vol. 14, No. 3).

Of the three views presented here, Wegner has the most well-considered and technically oriented perspective. The essentials of his definition are not overly complex, however. Figure 18.3 shows the progressively restrictive requirements for languages imposed by Wegner's definition.

Fig. 18.3. *Wegner's definition begins with object-based languages, adds classes to yield class-based languages, and finally adds class-inheritance to arrive at object-oriented languages.*

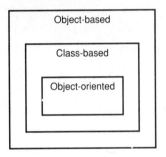

The most permissive class of languages in this view are the object-based languages. They provide for data abstraction and access to an object's "state" through its own operators, and not much else. Data abstraction provides the data-hiding qualities of objects, but doesn't include the qualities of abstract typing. Strong data typing—when the type characteristics of all objects are completely determined at compile time—may appear in these languages, as it does in C++, but is not an indispensable ingredient.

Adding abstract data types, or classes, to object-based languages yields the more restrictive set of languages known as class-based. In these languages, objects do not stand alone against the world, but belong to classes—their abstract types. All previous qualities of objects are brought forward.

A class is to be thought of more as a *template* for an object than as a strict type. This has important consequences for the way the language behaves. Typed languages have type-checking semantics that do little more than prevent errors and nail down the identification of an object. Classes, on the other hand, are oriented toward instance-creation semantics, which allows the class's template to be copied, and perhaps modified in being copied. This is why you have seen comments to the effect that type derivation in standard C is a synonym mechanism, whereas class derivation is a true abstract type derivation—much more than a simple synonym.

Class derivation leads directly to the third requirement for a fully object-oriented language: inheritance. Class derivation is more properly called *class inheritance*. Inheritance is the mechanism by which one class (a subclass) acquires many of its properties or methods from its "parent" (a superclass, or base class).

Class inheritance is a key concept in C++. When one class is derived from another, it is assumed that it inherits from its base class all the methods belonging to the base class, *except those specifically overridden by new definitions*. In this way, member functions from the base class can be reused without having to be redefined or recoded. Such a feature is called *code reusability* (you can also reuse code without inheritance, by including objects from one class in a new class).

The capability of a class to act as a template for its subclasses while allowing for *incremental modification* is an important part of what classes are and do. This aspect of classes is called *polymorphism*. Polymorphism is just the flip-side of code reusability. It refers to the process of only partially changing class methods, so that there is still much in common with the superclass. A shape superclass, for example, might be used to derive square and circle subclasses. Each subclass might have draw() methods, but they would necessarily differ in internal detail. You will see how to perform class derivations, and all the rest, in the next two chapters.

In fairness to all those who have labored long over OOPS theory, it must be said that Wegner did not invent all of these terms. His discussions of them, however, are illuminating in a sea of often confusing literature. C++ users need not fear the confusion of the OOPS debate—C++ characteristics are quite clear-cut.

Zortech's Definition

The Zortech C and C++ programs in this book are all based on the version 1.07 compiler. Zortech has released version 2.1, but the introductory remarks in the 1.07 manual, on what constitutes an object-oriented language, still apply.

The Zortech version 1.07 C++ manual manages to coherently and understandably introduce and define object-oriented programming in one page. On that page, the following brief definition of "object-oriented" is given:

Object-Oriented = Abstract Data Typing

+ Type Derivation

+ Commonality

You already are familiar with the first of these ingredients. *Abstract data typing* still means the ability to define your own classes. *Type derivation* is also familiar; it is used by Zortech (and everyone else) as a synonym for class inheritance. *Commonality* is another word meaning polymorphism, as discussed earlier.

This manual does make an interesting comment about polymorphism. It is defined here as the ability of a C++ object to determine, at run-time, the meaning of a message sent to it. In terms of C++, because "messages" are sent to objects by means of calling member functions, this means the ability to determine at run-time which of several identically named functions to invoke. The example of the `draw()` function mentioned in the previous section is a case in point.

Commonality, or polymorphism, is another very important issue in C++. A method (which can involve a member function or a redefined operator) can take several forms, all with the same name, in a C++ program. The use of a common function name for a superclass and its subclasses is only one instance. You can also *overload* both functions and operators. You will learn how to do this shortly.

What the Zortech manual doesn't mention is that object-oriented languages are also object-based. This aspect is assumed.

Stroustrup's Comments

Not very surprisingly, C++ was conceived and developed in the Bell Telephone Laboratories in Murray Hill, New Jersey. Although both Kernighan and Ritchie have been involved in the project, the principal architect of C++ is Bjarne Stroustrup.

Stroustrup has also written a book, patterned after the famous "base document," entitled *The C++ Programming Language*. One would think that this document would include some pointed comments about which aspects of OOPS theory have been incorporated into the new language. But it isn't so, and that *is* surprising.

Much of what has just been discussed here is simply assumed by Stroustrup. His own characterization of C++ is that it is "C with classes," and he spends most of his time discussing C++ as actually implemented. This important book can be considered the C++ base document, but understandably cannot mention many important developments in C++ since it was published.

Other Issues in Object-Oriented Systems

As we have intimated, there has been much discussion in computer trade publications as to what exactly is meant by object-oriented. Other parts of that continuing discussion deal more with the varieties of implementations of OOPS, and what that means for specific products. We touch on two of these issues before leaving this chapter.

Multiple Inheritance

When C++ was very new, there were many claims that C++ was not truly object-oriented. One of the reasons cited was that it did not (in the earliest compilers) support multiple inheritance.

What is multiple inheritance? An intuitive guess might lead you to the conclusion that multiple inheritance is the condition in which a subclass of a class is itself a superclass. That is, when there are successive generations of derived classes. But this has always been possible (within limits) from the first implementations of C++.

Multiple inheritance is rather that facility by which a *subclass inherits from more than one superclass simultaneously*. This is something like saying that a child has two parents, not just one.

The first implementation of C++, AT&T C++ 1.0, did not support multiple inheritance. As a consequence, some OOPS theorists claimed that C++ was not object-oriented. C++ adherents, naturally, claimed that it was, and that multiple inheritance was merely an unnecessary luxury.

More recently, the concensus is that multiple inheritance is very useful. It is present in AT&T C++ 2.0, which sets the standard, and in all other products seeking conformity to it.

Conformity to a standard C++ is also a growing issue. ANSI has very recently formed the X3J16 committee to begin work on a proposed C++

standard. Well, given the new ANSI C standard, it was bound to happen. We can only wait and hope that X3J16 does as well with C++ as X3J11 did with C.

Object Implementations: Functional, Server, Autonomous, and Slot-based

The manner in which an object is implemented influences directly and drastically the actions of which the object is capable. It is by no means a universal law of nature that an object must be implemented exactly as in C++. What are some of these implementations, and where does C++ fit in?

In the same article cited earlier, Wegner defines four fundamental kinds of objects: functional, server, autonomous, and slot-based.

Functional objects fulfill the requirement of data abstraction, but do not have an identity that persists between two operations on an object. Any operation that changes the object's state (you can think of this as the "internal, hidden variables") causes the creation of a new object—a physically distinct entity—that has the same programming interface as the old object, with a new state arising from the operation. Wegner cites OBJ2 and Vulcan as languages that have this characteristic.

Server objects are passive objects: they are active only when a message (such as a member-function call) is received that triggers the object's internal operations. C++ objects fall into this category, as do those of Smalltalk, Ada, Modula-2, Simula, and CLU.

Autonomous objects are active objects. Their methods (member functions) can execute even in the absence of a triggering message. Such objects might appear in multitasking systems, or perhaps in parallel processors. One of the sample programs used frequently in this book, the `timer.c` program, might well be implemented as an autonomous object, because it runs "in the background" all the time. C++, however, does not provide native support for autonomous object definitions.

Slot-based objects focus strongly on instance-variables, called slots, rather than on classes. The distinguishing characteristic of these languages is the capability to add methods to an object. Thus, you might characterize these languages as having methods that belong to objects, rather than objects that belong to classes. Two languages predicated on this philosophy are Flavors and CLOS (meaning Common Lisp Object System).

Summary

From the perspective of C++, an object is something that has definite boundaries, hides information (its state or internal variables), has methods implemented as member functions, receives messages in the form of member function calls, and belongs to a class. That is certainly quite a bit more complex than even the derived objects of standard C!

The controlling notion of C++ is really *class*. A class is a user-defined type that goes far beyond the synonym-assigning capability of standard C. Classes are what give C++ its power and flexibility, especially because of their capability for inheriting characteristics from predecessor classes (subclasses inherit superclass characteristics), and for efficiently reusing code.

C++ is still a young language, but is growing even faster than C did (perhaps because C had already opened the floodgates). Stroustrup published his landmark base document for C++ in 1986, and developed the first C++ compiler (AT&T 1.0).

Now, the AT&T compiler is in version 2.0, Borland has released Turbo C++ on May 14, 1990, and Zortech (which produced the first true compiler version of C++ for the IBM PC) also has a version 2.0 compiler. We had for a while hoped that Microsoft C 6.0 would feature C++ support, but it didn't happen. MS-C 6.0 was recently (as of this writing) released without it, but Microsoft is in the meantime recommending that its clientele acquire the Glockenspiel C++ 2.0 preprocessor.

C++ compilers have come a long way in the short time since their introduction. Current compilers support such fancy items as multiple inheritance, virtual base classes, and type-safe linkages.

C++ is a complex language—one that is probably impossible for the non-C programmer to master. There is little doubt that its syntax and many of its features are quite advanced, even arcane, at least in its current form.

Still, the basic concepts are really quite simple; like good engineering, simple modular pieces come together into a complex whole. Mastering those first concepts and modular tools is not particularly difficult, it is just *different*. They are simple enough, in fact, that you will have a firm grasp of the foundations when you finish the next two chapters. So let's get started . . . .

CHAPTER 19

Defining Classes and Objects

The greatest obstacle facing the proficient C programmer who wants to learn C++ *is* his or her proficiency. There is a correct way of thinking about C — and another way of thinking about C++. You must realize that, in many respects, *C++ is a different language*. Frequently, the similarities between the two languages are more deceptive than they are helpful. Fortunately, not *all* the time.

C++ is a different language, but not in the sense that it arises from a completely alien ancestry. C++ is C, plus a lot more—plus classes, in particular. What is a class? It is a structure, with some features added, as indicated in the following two partial declarations:

```
struct tag {
  ... member elements
};

class name {
  ... member elements
};
```

Structures *can* have tags; classes *must* have names. C++ structures can do everything that C structures can do — plus allowing you to define member functions in the C++ style.

C++ classes hide data and functions (that is the default, in fact) and *can* declare some elements or member functions as publicly available. C++ structures do not hide data or functions; everything in a structure has the public attribute. But you can build objects from either structures or classes.

The predominance of the class concept in C++ is the clue to its fundamental difference from C: The main idea in C is *executing functions*, whereas the main idea in C++ is *referencing objects*. The big difference is that the member function is *part of* the object. Failure to grasp this difference can make writing C++ programs quite difficult. Once you have changed mental gears, however, you will find that C++ programming is not terribly difficult, in spite of its esoteric appearance. Figure 19.1 illustrates the idea of referencing a C++ (class) object.

Fig. 19.1. *Reference a C++ object by calling a member function.*

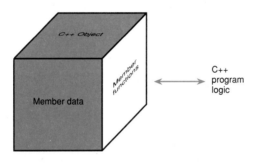

Defining Classes to C++

Before you can define or use an object, you must declare a class for it. The class declaration contains encapsulated data and member-function prototypes, public data and member-function prototypes, and perhaps inline member-function definitions. Not every permutation of class-declaration syntax is illustrated in this chapter and the next, but many of them are.

We strongly recommended in Chapter 18 that you write separate files for the object header and member-function definitions. When you do this, make the header and member-function source-file names the same, except for the extension. For example, suppose that you are writing a definition for a gadget object. The header file will be gadget.hpp, and the member-function source file will be gadget.cpp (or whatever extensions your compiler requires). And don't forget to #include the header name in the member-function source file, as in the following example (notice how you can write C++ commands):

```
#include <stdlib.h>    // gadget.cpp source file
#include <stdio.h>
... // any other includes
#include "gadget.hpp"
... // continue with member function definitions
```

The advantages of building the program this way are greatest in the development phase of writing your program, rather than at the time you run the program. The member-function source file can be compiled separately (after adequate debugging) and easily included in programs that use the functions by writing an #include for the appropriate header. This is the way the keyboard object was handled in Chapter 18.

It is possible to write all the declarations and member-function definitions directly in the program that will use the objects defined (we do this in listing 19.1). There are two good times to do this.

1. *When the program is very short.* A short program probably will use simple objects and be simple overall. If this is not the case, you should go to the trouble of writing separate files for the header and member functions. Writing class declarations and member-function definitions in C++ is easy once you get the hang of it, but these declarations quickly tend to get long and complex for objects that have many capabilities. You will find, however, that this is actually one of the benefits of C++ — it naturally encourages you to write object definitions that are robust, full-functioned, and more bug-free than standard C. The trade-off is code space, and overall complexity, but that has always been the price of powerful programs. At least C++ helps you manage and conceal that complexity.

2. *When you have no need to reuse the objects defined.* Writing the class declarations directly into the main program that is supposed to use them carries the cost of loss of availability. Clearly, they can be used only in that program. This is fine for practice coding and for illustrations, but real-world projects should produce classes that can be used again and again.

Setting Up the Class Definition

How do you define your own object types with a class declaration? The best way to learn is "hands on," so we begin by presenting a class. It is packaged together with a `main()` function to drive it, because it is fairly short.

The program in listing 19.1 contains an `array` class. It is informative because it is short enough to remember while you are getting acquainted with classes, and because it resembles the vector class built into your C++ compiler. The array class contains declarations for an array-based object that can initialize itself, display itself, reverse itself, and sum itself. This class also has facilities for accessing individual elements just like a standard array. In short, it demonstrates quite handily that C++ objects tend to be more "intelligent" than derived objects in standard C—in several ways.

Listing 19.1. `array.cpp` (A class for an array object, C++ style). Turbo C++

```
1    #include <stdlib.h>
2    #include <stdio.h>
3    #include <stdarg.h>
4    #include <string.h>
5
6    class array {
7       int value;
8       int numelem;
9       int *elem;
10      char *name;
11   public:                      // two constructors first
12      array( char *, ... ); // with name and init list
13      array( array & );       // copied from another object
14      ~array( void );          // now a destructor
15      void *operator new( unsigned );
16      void operator delete( void * );
17      int &operator[](int);
18      void reverse( void );
19      void display( void );
20      void newname( char * );
21   };
22
23   array::array( char *sname, ... ) // variadic declaration
24   {
25      va_list ap;
26      int work;
27      value = 0;                   // sum starts at zero
28      numelem = 0;
29      name = new char[strlen(name)+1];
30      strcpy( name, sname );   // init name string
```

```
31     va_start( ap, sname );   // just count them this time
32     while ( 0 <= (work = va_arg( ap, int ) ) ) ++numelem;
33     va_end( ap );
34     if ( numelem > 0 )        // if there were any elements
35     elem = new int[numelem];
36     va_start( ap, sname);    // now load the array
37     for ( work=0; work<numelem; ++work )
38       elem[work] = va_arg( ap, int );
39     va_end( ap );
40   }
41
42   array::array( array &copy )     // copy constructor
43   {
44     int i;
45
46     value = copy.value;    // ref op makes -> op unnecessary
47     numelem = copy.numelem;
48     name = new char[strlen(copy.name)+1];
49     strcpy( name, copy.name );    // init name string
50     elem = new int[copy.numelem];
51     for ( i=0; i<copy.numelem; ++i )
52       elem[i] = copy.elem[i];
53   }
54
55   array::~array( void )
56   {
57     delete elem;
58     delete name;
59   }
60
61   void *array::operator new( size_t size )
62   {
63     return ::new unsigned char[size];
64   }
65
66   void array::operator delete( void *objptr )
67   {
68     ::delete objptr;
69   }
70
71   int &array::operator[]( int n )
72   {
73                                  // returning a reference ensures
74                                  // that the [] op can be used on
75                                  // either side of the = operator
76     if ( n<0 || n >= numelem ) return elem[0];
77     return elem[n];
78   }
79
80   void array::reverse( void )
81   {
```

Listing 19.1. continues

Listing 19.1. *continued*

```
82     int a, b;
83     a = 0;
84     b = numelem - 1;
85     while ( b > a ) {
86       elem[a]^=elem[b];
87       elem[b]^=elem[a];
88       elem[a]^=elem[b];
89       ++a; --b;
90     }
91   }
92
93   void array::display( void )
94   {
95     int i;
96      for ( i=0; i<numelem; ++i ) {
97        printf( "%s[%d]=%d ", name, i, elem[i] );
98      }
99      printf( "\n" );
100  }
101
102  void array::newname( char *n )
103  {
104    delete name;                   // deallocate old name
105    name = new char[strlen(n)+1];  // allocate new name
106    strcpy( name, n );             // copy it in
107  }
108
109  main() {
110                   // define an object on the stack
111    array x( "X", 1,2,3,4,5,6,7,8,9,0,-1 );
112
113    x.display(); // send various messages to object
114    x.reverse();
115    x.display();
116    x[0] = 99;    // use the overloaded [] operator
117    x[1] = 101;   // you couldn't do this if op[]()
118    x[2] = x[1];  // returned other than int&
119    x.display();
120
121    array y = x; // use the copy constructor
122    y.newname( "Y" );
123    y.display();
124  }
```

If you were writing separate modules, lines 1–21 are the part of listing 19.1 you would place in the .HPP file. These lines include the standard C #includes, and the class declaration proper. Lines 23–107 contain the member-function prototype declarations. To package them separately, you need to add an `#include "array.hpp"` at the beginning of that `.CPP` source file. In this case, an `#include "array.hpp"` and the `main()` function would occupy a third `.CPP` file.

Now turn your attention to lines 6–21 of listing 19.1, which contain the class declaration. You form the class declaration by writing the `class` keyword, the class name (which is formed like every other identifier), and then the declarations for the member objects, surrounded by curly braces and terminated with a semicolon. When we speak of member objects, we may mean a standard C object, or we may mean another C++ object, as you will see later.

This class is arranged like many you will see and write yourself. It is divided neatly into two parts: some *data objects* precede the `public:` keyword, and *member-function prototype declarations* follow it. This is often, but *not always,* the case. Figure 19.2 shows a schematic arrangement of the `array` class declaration.

Fig. 19.2. *Typical arrangement of member elements in the array class.*

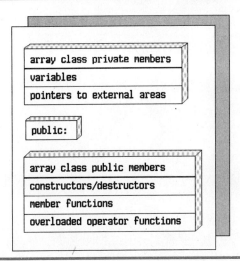

When you declare a class by using the `class` keyword, member elements are considered `private:` by default. You must code a `public:` keyword before those elements or function declarations you want to be able to access from outside the object having that class name (see line 11).

You can declare a class also by using the struct keyword. A struct in C++ is something more than it is in standard C. It is in fact a class, with all the members public: by default. You can reference, from outside the object, any member element of an object having a class declared with struct.

All this raises an interesting issue having to do with scope. What is "inside" an object, and what is "outside"? The very phrasing of the question implies that "inside" an object there is a local scope, something like a block statement in standard C.

This is so. All data objects declared within the class, together with all the member functions belonging to the class, comprise a scope local to the object. This is why, for example, you see the *scope resolution operator* :: used in the member-function *definitions*. Because the member functions appear outside the braces delimiting the class or struct, how else can the compiler know which class a given function belongs to — if any? This may seem a trivial question until you realize that different classes may have member functions with the same name. In the following code fragment, for example:

```
class c1 {  // declare a class
...
public:
   void printobj( void );
...
};

class c2 {  // declare another class
...
public:
   void printobj( void );
...
};

void c1::printobj( void )  // this belongs to class c1
{
   puts( "..." );
}

void c2::printobj( void )  // this belongs to class c2
{
   printf( "%8.3f\n", ... );
}

void printobj( char *s )  // this belongs to no class
{
   ...
}
```

total confusion would result if you tried to declare all these functions without the scope resolution operator.

Member-function prototypes, therefore, are declared in a normal fashion within the class declaration. Member-function definitions generally are written outside and after the class declaration, using the scope resolution operator.

Arguments are allowed in member-function declarations, just as in standard C. C++ gives you a little more help, however, by allowing you to define *default argument values* for member functions, as in the following example:

```
class c3 {
   int a, b;
public:
   c3() { ... }              // constructor function decl
   ~c3() { ... }             // destructor function decl
                // default args must be last in list
   int transform( int delta, int cval = 0 );
};

int c3::transform( int delta, int cval )
{
   return a + b + delta + cval;
}
```

Default arguments for C++ functions are written in the function prototype declaration, not the function definition. You can also write prototypes that mix parameters , those with and without default arguments. If you do, however, the parameters with default arguments must be written last in the argument list, as shown in the preceding example.

Member Elements: *private:*, *public:*, and *protected* :

A more precise definition is in order now. There are three kinds of member elements: `private:`, `public:`, and `protected:`. In listing 19.1, only one of these, `public:`, was used. How can you know which to pick, and where to code it? The `public:` and `private:` keywords can be thought of as complementary in their meanings, whereas `protected:` may be thought of as a mixture of the first two. The following points may help make the differences clear:

> `public:` indicates that all member objects or functions following this keyword are available for general access. Member functions, as well as any other functions not associated with the class declaration, may access (or call) the member object (or function). Member objects and functions are publicly available

from this point to the end of the class declaration, or until another of these three keywords is encountered. You normally use this keyword in `class` declarations, because its members are `private:` by default.

`private:` indicates that all member objects or functions following this keyword are available for access *only by member or friend functions of this class*. Because this is the default for class declarations, you normally use this keyword to hide member objects or functions in a class declared by a struct.

`protected:` indicates that all members or functions following this keyword are available for access by member functions, friend functions, or *member functions of subclasses derived from this one*. They are not, however, at any time available to other functions generally. This subject comes up again later in the discussion of class inheritance.

The nature of the keywords determines where you code them in the class declaration. Simply decide what must be hidden from public access, and make it private, or perhaps protected. Keep in mind that the spirit of C++ implies that you should make public only the absolute minimum number of objects necessary—the goal is to create objects that perform "intelligently" and need no outside help to get the job done. Such assistance is often an inadvertent return to standard C-style thinking and will prove to be a hindrance, not a help.

What Is *this*

Look closely at listing 19.1, and see whether you can find the C++ keyword `this`. It is conspicuous for its absence, isn't it? Then why, you might ask, do I need to know anything about it? Because you sometimes need to use it explicitly, even though that need may not arise often.

`this` is a *pointer-to-self*. It points to the object currently being dealt with. `this` is the means by which a *member function* can know which particular instance of the object it is handling. It is a pointer to the object: `classname* this;` is *declared implicitly in every member function* of a class. You do not need to declare it yourself, but you can refer to it explicitly as `this`.

It is the keyword `this` that makes such a high level of syntactic convenience possible in C++. In line 27 of listing 19.1, for example, the constructor member function of the `array` class initializes a private member element like this:

```
value = 0;  // refer to a class member simply using this
```

To do this in standard C, you would have to declare a pointer as a function parameter, take the address of the particular object, and pass it to the function. Furthermore, you would have to refer to the member object using the structure pointer operator (presuming that you explicitly declared this to be the pointer) in the following fashion:

```
this->value = 0;  /* looks familiar, doesn't it? */
```

Because C++ provides the self-reference pointer `this`, and also knows beforehand how it should be used, all that syntactic complexity can be hidden. Remember that it is *always* a *hidden parameter* for every member function (but clearly not for ordinary functions). It is the presence of `this` that permits you to write references to members of the class directly, without structure pointer operators.

Another important use of `this` is to provide a means for returning the address of the current object, or the object itself, from a member function. This maneuver permits such expressions as `a = b;` for example, where both sides of the assignment refer to C++ objects. Just as in standard C, with ordinary objects, you can do this by value or by reference. Listing 19.2 shows how to return an object by value, for instance.

Listing 19.2. `this1.cpp` *(Return an object by value).*　　　　*Turbo C++*

```
1   #include <stdlib.h>
2   #include <stdio.h>
3
4   class c1 {
5     int value;
6   public:
7     c1( int init ) { value = init; } // constructors inline
8     c1( void ) { value = 0; }
9     c1( c1& otherc1 ) { value = otherc1.value; }
10    c1 operator=( c1& rval )      // assign op, return value
11       { value = rval.value; return *this; }
12    void printv( void ) { printf( "%d\n", value ); }
13  };
14
15  main()
16  {
```

Listing 19.2. continues

Listing 19.2. continued

```
17     c1 obj1( 37 ); // declare one with initializer
18     c1 obj2, obj3; // and two without
19
20     obj3 = obj2 = obj1;
21     obj1.printv();
22     obj2.printv();
23     obj3.printv();
24   }
```

The program in listing 19.2 declares a class c1. Before you go any further, notice that in this program, the member functions are *defined*, not just declared, in the class declaration. You can do this when function bodies are *very* short and don't contain complex constructions such as while loops. Member functions defined in this manner are called *inline functions*.

Now look at line 10. This line contains a function-declaration part that looks strange to standard C programmers:

```
c1 operator=( c1& rval )      // assign op, return value
```

This member function declares the method for handling the assignment operator = for objects with class c1. The declaration part indicates that = is a binary operator—the function parameter declares what kind of right hand operand is required. The function also returns an object with type (class) c1.

Later, you are shown how to overload operators, in detail. For now, just observe how the object is returned (return *this, line 11). Because this is a pointer, it must be dereferenced before it can be returned by value.

Do you remember reading earlier in this book that passing and returning pointers to structures, not the objects themselves, usually is wise? The reason was *size*. Values are passed and returned on the system stack, which is relatively small, and pushing large objects on the stack may cause an overflow. (It also can degrade *performance*.)

Classes and structures differ in many ways, but they are similar in that a reference to an object's identifier does *not* result in an address value (as it does with arrays). Classes and structures are similar also in that they tend to be large. Thus, for exactly the same reasons, passing and returning C++ objects by reference usually is wise. Listing 19.3 shows how to rewrite the previous short program to return the current object by reference, still using this to do it.

Listing 19.3. `this2.cpp` *(Return an object by reference).* *Turbo C++*

```
1   #include <stdlib.h>
2   #include <stdio.h>
3
4   class c1 {
5     int value;
6   public:
7     c1( int init ) { value = init; } // constructors inline
8     c1( void ) { value = 0; }
9     c1( c1& otherc1 ) { value = otherc1.value; }
10    c1& operator=( c1& rval )      // assign op, return ref.
11        { value = rval.value; return *this; }
12    void printv( void ) { printf( "%d\n", value ); }
13  };
14
15  main()
16  {
17    c1 obj1( 37 ); // declare one with initializer
18    c1 obj2, obj3; // and two without
19
20    obj3 = obj2 = obj1;
21    obj1.printv();
22    obj2.printv();
23    obj3.printv();
24  }
```

There is exactly *one* difference between listings 19.2 and 19.3. It is in line 10 again. Look at the following comparison of line 10 from each program:

```
c1 operator=( c1& rval )      // assign op, return value
c1& operator=( c1& rval )      // assign op, return ref.
```

The *only difference* is in the *return-type specification* of the declaration part. The first returns an object with type `c1`, and the second returns a *reference to* an object with type `c1`. This is the meaning of the return-type specifier `c1&`. In C++, the `&` operator is the *reference* operator when used in a context like this one, and the *address-of* operator when used in more normal contexts.

The interesting thing about listing 19.3 is that, even when returning by reference rather than value, you still write `return *this`. This is because the C++ compiler is once again giving special assistance; the return-type specifier `c1&` (which you can also write as `c1 &...`) completely determines how the `return` is to be handled. In either case, you write the statement just as though you were dealing with an object (rather than an address). You will read much more about pointers and references in C++ in the next chapter.

Now, which of the two programs is more efficient? The more efficient is this2.cpp, listing 19.3, for precisely the same reasons pointers are more efficient in standard C — less physical data has to be hauled around when passing and returning parameters with address values. C++ references are the same, but you get more help with the syntax.

Initializing and Destroying Class Objects

The next step in writing a C++ object-oriented program is to initialize objects with particular values. And when you are done with them, you must have some way to get rid of them. Initializing class objects is accomplished by *constructor* functions, and destroying (freeing) an object is accomplished by the class's *destructor* function.

Constructors and Destructors

Think back to the lowly integer for a moment. How are integers created and initialized in standard C? The answer depends on the storage class of the particular instance of integer.

Integers that have static storage class are created by the compiler as a result of a declaration you wrote. If you also wrote an initializer, the variable is set to that value; if you did not write an initializer, it is set to zero. All this takes place at *compile time*.

Integers declared within a block (local variables) have auto storage class, unless you override it. These variables are created at *run-time*, typically on the system stack, by compiler-provided routines. If you provide an initializer, it will be used; otherwise, the contents of the object remain indeterminate until you do something about it.

Now make the mental switch back to C++ objects. How much does the C++ compiler do for you in creating and initializing user-defined objects? Ironically, it does relatively less than the standard C compiler does for basic objects. The key to user-defined objects in C++ is that they are user-defined. It's up to you to define what is to be done with them — the C++ compiler makes almost no assumptions about how objects declared for a class are to be handled. Also, C++ objects are *always* created at run-time, never at compile time, even though you write the object definitions into the source code.

When you write your own classes, you are defining what must be included in such objects, what class members are to be visible to functions outside the object, how member variables should be initialized, what operators are associated with the class, and how they are to work — you define everything.

There is one exception. If you do not write any code that tells the compiler how to initialize the object, it automatically generates a *constructor* function for the object. Such a constructor does nothing but allocate memory sufficient to contain the object. Likewise, if you don't tell the compiler what to do about destroying the object when it goes out of scope, it generates a *destructor* function that performs the reverse task.

You must write your own constructor and destructor member functions for each class, if you want more than simple allocation done — as you almost always will. Constructors and destructors are the means of controlling the *creation*, *initialization*, *copying*, and *destruction* of objects. All of the sample programs in this chapter have constructors and destructors. Look at them as you read the following text, to see them in action.

First, constructors and destructors have the *same name as the class to which they belong*. The following code fragment, for example:

```
class tool {
  int kind;
  char *descrip;
public:
  tool( int type, char *use ); // a constructor
  ~tool( void );  // destructor name has a tilde
};
                // constructor function definition
tool::tool( int type, char *use )
{
  kind = type;
  descrip = new unsigned char[strlen(use)+1] ;
  strcpy( descrip, use );
}
                // destructor function definition
tool::~tool( void )  // use void or leave empty
{
  delete descrip;
}
main()
{
  tool wrench( 1, "Turn nuts and bolts" );
  tool hammer( 2, "Drive nails" );
...
}
```

defines only the constructor and destructor member functions for the class tool. The constructor and destructor names are the same as the class name. Additionally, the destructor function has a tilde (˜) character prepended to the function name, identifying it as the destructor.

What you *don't see* is also important—*there must be no return-type specifier, not even* void. C++ has its own internal return type for these special functions, and you may not declare one.

You can also declare more than one constructor for a class (but not for a destructor). In listing 19.3, there are two constructors for the c1 class (lines 7, 8). One of them accepts an integer argument, and one accepts no argument at all. Lines 16–17 show how to declare objects of this class, corresponding to each of these constructor methods. Specifying more than one constructor (or other member functions, for that matter) is called *overloading* the function. When you make a call to an overloaded function, constructor or otherwise, the C++ compiler determines which one you mean by examining the arguments to be passed to it.

The constructors you have seen so far initialize the object by the simple expedient of assigning values to the hidden members of the class. This probably is the most frequently used way of doing it, but several other ways are provided by the more recent compilers. Two specific forms of initializer list can be used, implemented in radically different ways.

The first form of initializer list provides variable substitution support; it is not used for plugging in constant values. The list is specified with the constructor function *definition*, after the declaration part and a full colon, and before the function body. The following short program, for example, supplies a variable initializer list for both of the hidden variables for an object of class A:

```
#include <stdlib.h>
#include <stdio.h>

class A {
   int a, b;
public:
   A(int, int);
   void display();
   void operator()();   // overload function call () op
};

         // define initializer list for constructor
A::A( int i = 0, int j = 0 ) : a(i), b(j) {}
```

```
void A::display()
{
  printf( "a = %d, b = %d\n", a, b );
}
void A::operator()() // define function call operator
{
  display();
}
main()
{
  A obj1;                // take advantage of default args
  A obj2( 16, 64 );        //use init list for this one

  obj1();      // use overloaded function call operator
  obj2();                  // to display object values
}
```

The constructor declaration is written in the normal way. The constructor definition contains the initializer list. Note the following about the initializer list:

❑ *A full colon appears immediately after the declaration part of the function definition.* The list follows the colon.

❑ *The variable initializer list is composed of comma-separated entries.* The list as a whole is not terminated by any punctuation; the function body begins immediately.

❑ *Each entry in the initializer list is composed of the member variable name it is to initialize, followed by the initial value it is to take on.*

❑ *The parenthesized value of an entry in the list is most often one of the arguments to the constructor.* This need not be the case, however. It can be an expression, or even a constant (which, as you recall, is an expression).

❑ *The number of entries in the initializer list does not necessarily have to correspond either to the number of constructor arguments or to the number of class members to be initialized.* You can mix and match methods in any way you want — some members can be initialized from the initializer list, and some by assignment within the constructor function body. It is up to you to get the object properly initialized.

This form of initializer list is often convenient, and can help you write concise, compact code in the old tradition of C. It also is important later for passing initial value to base class constructors when you are designing derived classes (implementing class inheritance), but more on that later.

The second form of initializer list is one with which you already are familiar. It is the initializer list, enclosed in curly braces, written as though for an aggregate object in standard C, as in the following example:

```
#include <stdlib.h>
#include <stdio.h>

struct A {               // struct means all members public
    int a, b;            // there is no constructor, either
    void display();
    void operator()();   // overload function call () op
};


void A::display()
{
    printf( "a = %d, b = %d\n", a, b );
}

void A::operator()() // define function call operator
{
    display();
}

main()
{
    A obj1 = { 16, 64 };                // initializer list

    obj1();    // use overloaded function call operator
}
```

To use this kind of initializer, the class must satisfy three requirements: there may be no private members, there may not be any constructor, and there may not be any base class (that is, it cannot be a subclass that inherits a superclass). Such classes typically are declared through struct rather than class. Note the following about aggregate initializers for classes:

❑ *This is a true aggregate initializer; treat it just as you do when writing standard C code.* This form can initialize an array, or a class, struct, or union. (In C++, the last three are referred to collectively as a *class*.)

❑ *If you don't provide enough initial values, the remainder of the members are set to zero or null.*

❑ *For complex aggregates, the initializer list can omit or retain interior curly braces.* ANSI standard C borrowed this convention from C++. For multidimensional arrays of objects or class objects, however, you can use interior curly braces to force the way initial values are assigned (for example, when subgroups don't provide all values).

❑ *Arrays of class objects can be initialized by this method, as long as other requirements are fulfilled, as in the following example:*

```
class X { public: int a, b, c }; // define a class
X objs[2] = { 1, 2, 3, 4, 5, 6 }; // array of class objs
```

With these methods of initializing objects or objects of class, you can write code that's as flexible as you like. You can do anything—from nothing at all, to taking complete control of initializing even the most complex objects.

Finally, declarations for an object of a class—which cause the constructor to be invoked—don't have to be at the top of a block, as standard C requires. Object declarations can be scattered throughout a block. Each causes the constructor function for the class to be invoked. There is no other way to call a constructor, in fact. Calling a constructor directly is illegal.

Destructors are a little different from constructors. There can be only one destructor function, and it may not have any parameters. Note that in C++, using the `void` specifier for the argument list is not strictly necessary. Writing an *empty* list in C++ means that no arguments are permitted as shown in this line of code:

```
tool::~tool(); // don't need ANSI void arg spec
```

Destructors are like constructors, however, in that you can leave them out. In such a case, the compiler generates code that releases the memory used by the object when it goes out of scope. The only problem with this is that the constructor function may have specifically and dynamically allocated storage, which is outside the object, for its use. If so, allowing the destructor to default leaves that dynamic storage still allocated, with no way now to locate and release it.

Although you cannot call a constructor directly, you may call a destructor, if you use the *fully qualified name* of the destructor function, as in the following example:

```
main()
{
  tool wrench( 1, "Turn nuts and bolts" );
  ...
  wrench::~tool(); // legal destructor call
  tool::tool();    // illegal constructor call
}
```

When is a destructor called automatically? Ordinarily, for dynamic (`auto` class) class objects, whenever the object goes out of scope — when the current scope no longer exists. This happens, for instance, when a function that declares a local object returns.

Global objects have file scope, however. When are their destructors called? If you have declared any `atexit()` functions, the destructor call would necessarily follow their execution. But matters may get complicated if you explicitly invoke `exit()` or `abort()`.

When you explicitly invoke `exit()` from within a function (ordinary or member function), the destructors for *static objects* are called. This means that objects with file scope, or which were created with the `new` operator, are taken care of. Dynamic object destructors are not called (but this hardly matters, because they ordinarily exist on the stack).

Calling `exit()` from within the destructor function itself could be especially dangerous, however — it might cause infinite recursion. This could happen if the object were global or just static, because `exit()` causes the destructor to be called, which calls exit(), which .... Well, you get the idea.

Destructors are not called at all if you explicitly call `abort()`, because `abort()` is not required to perform any particular cleanup. This may or may not be dangerous, depending on what an object was doing. If its constructor had opened an output file, for example, this might cause the last bufferful of data to be lost. Note that this also could happen to dynamic objects when `exit()` is called.

Copy Initializers

Listing 19.1 shows the use of a special kind of constructor function: the *copy constructor*, or copy initializer. The copy constructor is invoked automatically when an object is declared — created *with reference to an existing object*. Here is the copy-constructor function for the `array` class of listing 19.1:

```
array::array( array &copy )      // copy constructor
{
  int i;

  value = copy.value;    // ref op makes -> op unnecessary
  numelem = copy.numelem;
  name = new char[strlen(copy.name)+1];
  strcpy( name, copy.name );   // init name string
  elem = new int[copy.numelem];
  for ( i=0; i<copy.numelem; ++i )
    elem[i] = copy.elem[i];
}
```

The copy constructor always takes one argument: a *reference* (careful— not a pointer!) to an object of the same class (see the next chapter for details).

For a class X, declare the copy constructor as `X::X( X& );` (here, `&` is the reference operator).

Two ways of declaring an object can cause the copy constructor to be invoked: declaration with an assignment initializer, and declaration with an argument that is an object. (Note that using a reference means you do *not* have to take the address; it's done for you.) Examples of these two ways of declaring an object follow:

```
array y = x; // use the copy constructor
array y(x);  // also invokes copy const.
```

If you don't declare a copy constructor, the C++ compiler generates one for you. The automatically generated copy constructor is built assuming that you want a one-to-one copy of every member in the object. This is fine in many cases, but not all. A closer look at the copy constructor for the `array` class reveals why you would want to write your own.

The `new` operator (discussed later in this chapter) is used twice in this constructor function. In each case, a pointer is returned and stored in a member object. That is, each `array` object has its own dynamically allocated memory, *which exists outside the bounds of the object*, for storing array elements and the string array name. If another `array` object is created from the first one in either of the two ways just mentioned, thus *using the default copy constructor*, the member pointers are copied as is. This results in two `array` class objects pointing to the same dynamic memory — the storage fails to be unique for each object. In such a case, writing your own copy constructor ensures that separate dynamic storage is allocated for each unique object.

Using Class Objects

At this point, you can declare a class and write some pretty sophisticated code to initialize objects of that class. Now you need to know how to "send messages to the object," and to see an extended example of class implementation.

Calling Member Functions

Calling member functions is much the same as calling ordinary functions, except that you must indicate the object on behalf of which you are making the call. This is the C++ way of sending a "message" to the object. The syntax is

```
objectname.memberfunction( arg list );
```

where *objectname* is the identifier of an already declared object (in other words, an object whose constructor has been called), the period is the familiar structure operator, and the remainder is just like a normal function call. For example, the following code fragment shows how to call the reduce() member function of object X, which has class c1:

```
class c1 {
   int i;
public:
   c1() { i=37; } // inline constructor
   int reduce();
};
...
int c1::reduce() // same as void arg list
{
   return --i;
}
...
main()
{
c1 X; // declare an object (and invoke constructor)
...
printf( "Value minus 1 is %d\n", X.reduce() );
}
```

Notice that you can return basic (C-style) objects from calls to member functions, as well as objects or references to objects.

An exception to this syntax arises when you have defined a constructor member function with an empty argument list (meaning that that particular constructor may not have arguments). With such a constructor, do not code argument parentheses — even if they are empty — when declaring an object that invokes that constructor. For example, the following short program does not compile correctly with Turbo C++:

```
#include <stdlib.h>
#include <stdio.h>

class c1 {
   int i;
public:
   c1() { i = 37; }  // empty arg list means no args!
   int reduce() { return --i; }
};
```

```
main()
{
   c1 X;    // this is the correct way
   c1 Y();  // makes compiler expect reference to object

   printf( "%d\n", Y.reduce() );
}
```

The compiler flags the last line of this program — which contains a call to
Y.reduce()—as being in error. The error message informs you that a
reference to an object is expected to be returned. If you simply rewrite the
object declaration as c1 Y; the program compiles and runs correctly.

You will learn how to simplify the member-function call syntax a little
later, when we discuss how to overload the function call operator (). Right
now, it's time to apply what you have learned so far.

Building a Virtual Screen Class

Because the extended example of a class implementation might as well be
a useful one, we present a class, screen, that is capable of virtual-screen
management functions. A virtual screen is something like a window, but not
exactly.

The example is based on an older copy of the Zortech C++ compiler
(version 1.07) for the IBM and compatible PCs. Because it is a slightly older
compiler, some of the features already discussed were not available when we
wrote the class (this was one of our very first C++ projects—which gives you
some idea of how easy it is to write complex code quickly with C++). It gives
us the opportunity to illustrate an interesting and important constructor
technique involving this, however.

What is a virtual screen? As implemented here, a "virtual screen" resembles a panel that overlays part of the system display screen more than it
resembles a true window. This doesn't make much difference in practice, but
the subtle difference did influence the way virtual screens can be moved
around the display. Briefly, a virtual screen is a movable panel.

What does a virtual screen do? Several requirements must be met if the
class is to be truly useful. A virtual screen must be able to appear and
disappear. When it disappears, it must restore the underlying display area to
its original state. That is, it must be able to save itself and the underlying
screen area. Allocating dynamic memory for these save areas is done in the
constructor.

Although only text mode is supported, color must be supported in a virtual screen. The constructor function's arguments include color values for background and text.

Multiple boundaries for the panel area allow for attractive presentation formats on virtual screens. Three boundary types are supported: none (plain border), box (double lines), and a drop-shadow box. The drop-shadow box border is particularly attractive, because it gives the virtual screen the appearance of "floating" above the underlying display. The color attributes of text falling in the shadow are changed to gray-on-black, greatly enhancing this effect.

A virtual screen must be able to appear anywhere on the real display. Providing this support [screen::move()] makes a trivial exercise of writing a driving program that allows the user to slide the virtual screens around the display by using the arrow keys. (We show such a program, demo.cpp, a little later.)

In a virtual screen, "normalized" cursor control is required. This means that a driving program should be able to make cursor-positioning requests that specify values relative only to the border of the virtual screen, not the real display. A companion function, screen::query(), reports current cursor position relative to the border.

Corresponding to normalized cursor control, virtual screens need clipped and bounded message-display support. A message string that would go beyond the virtual screen boundary is clipped to fit. Because it would be nice if the message display function (screen::put()) also allowed variable arguments, like printf(), we include the trivial amount of code necessary for va_arg() processing. Tab and newline characters are supported (and accounted for in clipping), and all is done so that the user sees RAM-poke write speeds. The routines work on all display types, from old monochrome to VGA. In addition to display message support, a virtual-screen clear function (screen::clr()) is included.

A special member function in virtual screens adds sauce to the goose. This is screen::pulldown(), which turns a virtual screen into a pull-down menu, complete with highlighted selection bar.

Whew! The preceding paragraphs about virtual screens sum up a lot of functions! The fact is, however, that this really is a fairly trivial exercise in C++ — OOPS technology makes this kind of project easily feasible (although the display technology is confusing if you are not accustomed to it). All this can be implemented with a 53-line .HPP header, and only 365 lines of code for the member-function source file. That isn't much of a dime to pay for so much candy, if you think about it.

Separate compilation was used for this project; it is a bit much for one source file. Besides, we hope that class s c r e e n is useful enough to be used in many projects. The header for s c r e e n is shown in listing 19.4.

Listing 19.4. `screen.hpp` *(Class for a virtual-screen manager supporting multiple border types, colors, screen movement, clipped/detabbed messages, and pull-down menus).* *Zortech C++*

```
1   #ifndef NULL            /*----------------------------*/
2   #define NULL 0          /*-------- SCREEN.HPP --------*/
3   #endif                  /* Begin header file for      */
4                           /* screen.cpp module          */
5   #ifndef PLAIN           /*----------------------------*/
6   #define PLAIN   0
7   #define BOX     1
8   #define SHADOW 2
9   #endif
10
11  #ifndef COLORS
12  #define COLORS
13  #define BLACK 0
14  #define BLUE 1
15  #define GREEN 2
16  #define CYAN 3
17  #define RED 4
18  #define MAGENIA 5
19  #define BROWN 6
20  #define LIGHTGRAY 7
21  #define DARKGRAY 8
22  #define LIGHTBLUE 9
23  #define LIGHTGREEN 10
24  #define LIGHTCYAN 11
25  #define LIGHTRED 12
26  #define LIGHTMAGENTA 13
27  #define YELLOW 14
28  #define WHITE 15
29  #endif
30
31  class screen {
32    int border[4];
33    int border_t;
34    int curpos[2];
35    int cur_attr;
36  public:
37    void *save;        // pointer to copy of self
38    void *olds;        // pointer to copy of underlying screen
39    screen( int back, int fore, int bor,
40            int topx, int topy, int botx, int boty );
41    ~screen() { delete save; delete olds; }
```

Listing 19.4. continues

Listing 19.4. *continued*

```
42    void clr( void );
43    void loc( int x, int y );
44    void put( char *format, ... );
45    void pushold( void );
46    void popold( void );
47    void push( void );
48    void pop( void );
49    void move( int x, int y );
50    int pulldown( int elements, char *list[] );
51    int *query( void );
52  };
53
```

The screen.hpp header contains #define directives for NULL, the screen border types, and the colors available. To further protect the header against redefinition (multiple inclusion), you could surround the entire file with the following:

```
#if !defined( VSCREEN )
#define VSCREEN
... header contents
#endif
```

There is a prototype declaration for only one constructor function, and it contains no default arguments. You might want to write default arguments for this one, and perhaps some overloaded constructor declarations that require no arguments or fewer arguments.

The screen class member functions depend on the Zortech compiler's disp family of functions for manipulation of the system display. These functions are extensions to the language and are unique to Zortech. The greatest difference between these functions and the Borland and Microsoft screen-handling functions is that Zortech does not translate cursor coordinates from the (0,0) origin address as do other vendors. Because the member functions here presume a (1,1) screen-origin cursor address, some internal translation is necessary. This makes for some added complexity in the Zortech version of the class, but simplifies the code somewhat when converting to the other compilers. The member functions for screen are presented in listing 19.5.

Listing 19.5. `screen.cpp` *(Member functions for the* `screen` *class).*

Zortech C++ 1.07

```
1   #include <stdlib.h>
2   #include <stdarg.h>
3   #include <disp.h>
4   #include <dos.h>
5   #include <ctype.h>
6
7   #include "screen.hpp"
8
9   /* ----------------------------------------------------------*/
10  /*------------------- SCREEN.CPP -----------------------*/
11  /* Begin screen.cpp source for use in separate     */
12  /* compilation.                                     */
13  /* ----------------------------------------------------------*/
14
15  /* ----------------------------------------------------------*/
16  /*           Screen-class object constructor        */
17  /* Input parameters:                                */
18  /*              int back         Background attribute */
19  /*              int fore         Foreground attribute */
20  /*              int bor          Border; PLAIN, BOX,  */
21  /*                                    or SHADOW       */
22  /*              int topx,topy    1-origin coordinates */
23  /*                               top left corner      */
24  /*              int botx,boty    1-origin coordinates */
25  /*                               bottom left corner   */
26  /* ----------------------------------------------------------*/
27  screen::screen( int back, int fore, int bor,
28                  int topx, int topy, int botx, int boty )
29  {
30    if ( !this ) {
31      if ( NULL ==( this = malloc( sizeof( screen ) ) ) ) {
32        printf( "Could not allocate %d bytes\n",
33          sizeof( screen ) );
34        abort();
35      }
36    }
37    else this = this;        // assign for every possible path
38    border_t = bor;
39    cur_attr = (back << 4) + fore; // Build display attribute
40    if ( !disp_inited ) disp_open();
41    disp_setattr( cur_attr );
42    if ( botx == 0 ) {
43      border_t = PLAIN; // Force border type for whole screen
44      border[0] = 0;
45      border[1] = 0;
46      border[2] = disp_numcols-1;
47      border[3] = disp_numrows-1;
48    } else {
```

Listing 19.5. continues

Listing 19.5. *continued*

```
49        if ( border_t == SHADOW ) {  // Check size/positioning
50          if ( botx >= disp_numcols-1 )
51            botx = disp_numcols-2;
52          if ( boty >= disp_numrows-1 )
53            boty = disp_numrows-2;
54        }
55        border[0] = topx-1;
56        border[1] = topy-1;
57        border[2] = botx-1;
58        border[3] = boty-1;
59      }
60          // Allocate this screen and old screen save buffers
61      if ( border_t == SHADOW ) {
62        save = new char[ (border[lb]2]-border[lb]0]+2)
63          * (border[3]-border[1]+2) * 2 ];
64        olds = new char[ (border[lb]2]-border[0]+2)
65          * (border[3]-border[1]+2) * 2 ];
66      }
67      else {
68        save = new char[ (border[2]-border[0]+1)
69          * (border[3]-border[1]+1) * 2 ];
70        olds = new char[ (border[2]-border[0]+1)
71          * (border[3]-border[1]+1) * 2 ];
72      }
73      pushold();  // and save old screen area
74
75      if ( border_t == SHADOW ) {
76        int ofs,cnt;
77        unsigned char *p;
78        unsigned char a = (BLACK << 4) + DARKGRAY;
79        ofs = 160*(border[1]+1) + 2*(border[2]+1);
80 /* ------------------------------------------------------------*/
81 /*   Locate and draw vertical stripe for shadow box     */
82 /* ------------------------------------------------------------*/
83        p = MK_FP( disp_base,ofs+1 );
84        for ( cnt=border[1]; cnt<=border[3]; ++cnt ) {
85          *p = a; p += 160;
86        }
87 /* ------------------------------------------------------------*/
88 /*   Locate and draw horizontal stripe for shadow box   */
89 /* ------------------------------------------------------------*/
90        ofs = 160*(border[3]+1) + 2*(border[0]+1);
91        p = MK_FP( disp_base,ofs+1 );
92        for ( cnt=border[0]; cnt<=border[2]; ++cnt ) {
93          *p = a; p += 2;
94        }
95      }
96
```

```
 97    disp_scroll( 0,border[1],border[0],
 98      border[3],border[2],cur_attr );
 99
100    if ( border_t == BOX )
101      disp_box( 0,cur_attr,border[1],border[0],
102        border[3],border[2] );
103
104    push(); // save a copy of self
105  }
106
107  void screen::clr()
108  {
109    if ( border_t == BOX )
110      disp_scroll( 0,border[1]+1,border[0]+1,
111        border[3]-1,border[2]-1,cur_attr );
112    else
113      disp_scroll( 0,border[1],border[0],
114        border[3],border[2],cur_attr );
115  }
116
117  // This member function converts x,y notation to internal
118  // y,x and converts 1-origin to internal 0-origin
119
120  void screen::loc( int x,int y )
121  {
122    if ( border_t == BOX ) {
123      disp_move( border[1] + y, border[0] + x );
124      curpos[0] = disp_cursorcol - border[0];
125      curpos[1] = disp_cursorrow - border[1];
126    }
127    else {
128      disp_move( border[1]+y-1, border[0]+x-1 );
129      curpos[0] = disp_cursorcol - border[0] + 1;
130      curpos[1] = disp_cursorrow - border[1] + 1;
131    }
132  }
133
134  int*  screen::query()
135  {
136    return( curpos );
137  }
138
139  void screen::put( char *format, ... )
140  {
141    int i;
142    int *p;
143    va_list arg_ptr;
144    static char ibuf[256], obuf[256];
145    char *a, *b;
146
147    p = query();
```

Listing 19.5. continues

Listing 19.5. continued

```
148    loc( *p,*(p+1) );
149    va_start( arg_ptr,format );
150    vsprintf( ibuf,format,arg_ptr );
151    a = ibuf; b = obuf;
152    i = 0;
153    while ( *a ) {  // detab the line
154      switch( *a ) {
155        case '\t': do *b++ = ' '; while ( ++i % 8 != 1 );
156                   a++; break;
157        default:   *b++ = *a++; ++i; break;
158      }
159    }
160    *b = '\0';  // terminate the output line
161    i = strlen( obuf );
162    i = ( i > border[2] - disp_cursorcol ) ?
163        border[2] - disp_cursorcol : i;
164    disp_printf( "%.*s",i,obuf ); // clip it, too
165    va_end( arg_ptr );
166    if ( border_t == BOX ) {
167      curpos[0] = disp_cursorcol - border[0];
168      curpos[1] = disp_cursorrow - border[1];
169    }
170    else {
171      curpos[0] = disp_cursorcol - border[0] + 1;
172      curpos[1] = disp_cursorrow - border[1] + 1;
173    }
174    if ( curpos[0] < 1 ) curpos[0] = 1;
175  }
176
177  void screen::pushold( void )
178  {
179    static void *p;
180    static void *q;
181    static int i,size;
182    static unsigned ofs;
183
184    q = olds;
185    ofs = 160*border[1] + 2*border[0];
186    p = MK_FP( disp_base,ofs );
187    if ( border_t == SHADOW )
188      size = (border[2]-border[0]+2)*2;
189    else
190      size = (border[2]-border[0]+1)*2;
191    for( i=border[1]; i<=border[3]; i++ ) {
192      memcpy( q,p,size );
193      p += 160; q += size;
194    }
195    if ( border_t == SHADOW ) memcpy( q,p,size );
196  }
```

```
197
198   void screen::popold( void )
199   {
200     static unsigned char *p;
201     static unsigned char *q;
202     static int i,size;
203     static unsigned ofs,cnt;
204
205     q = olds;
206     ofs = 160*border[1] + 2*border[0];
207     p = MK_FP( disp_base,ofs );
208     if ( border_t == SHADOW )
209       size = (border[2]-border[0]+2)*2;
210     else
211       size = (border[2]-border[0]+1)*2;
212     for( i=border[1]; i<=border[3]; i++ ) {
213       memcpy( p,q,size );
214       p += 160; q += size;
215     }
216     if ( border_t == SHADOW ) memcpy( p,q,size );
217     disp_setattr( cur_attr );
218   }
219
220   void screen::push( void )
221   {
222     static void *p;
223     static void *q;
224     static int i,size;
225     static unsigned ofs;
226
227     q = save;
228     ofs = 160*border[1] + 2*border[0];
229     p = MK_FP( disp_base,ofs );
230     size = (border[2]-border[0]+1)*2;
231     for( i=border[1]; i<=border[3]; i++ ) {
232       memcpy( q,p,size );
233       p += 160; q += size;
234     }
235   }
236
237   void screen::pop( void )
238   {
239     static unsigned char *p;
240     static unsigned char *q;
241     static int i,size;
242     static unsigned ofs;
243
244     q = save;
245     ofs = 160*border[1] + 2*border[0];
246     p = MK_FP( disp_base,ofs );
247     size = (border[2]-border[0]+1)*2;
```

Listing 19.5. continues

Listing 19.5. continued

```
248    for( i=border[1]; i<=border[3]; i++ ) {
249      memcpy( p,q,size );
250      p += 160; q += size;
251    }
252    if ( border_t == SHADOW ) {  // repaint the shadow
253      unsigned char a = (BLACK << 4) + DARKGRAY;
254      ofs = 160*(border[1]+1) + 2*(border[2]+1);
255      p = MK_FP( disp_base,ofs+1 );
256      for ( i=border[1]; i<=border[3]; ++i) {
257        *p = a; p += 160;
258      }
259      ofs = 160*(border[3]+1) + 2*(border[0]+1);
260      p = MK_FP( disp_base,ofs+1 );
261      for ( i=border[0]; i<=border[2]; ++i ) {
262        *p = a; p += 2;
263      }
264    }
265    disp_setattr( cur_attr );
266  }
267
268  void screen::move( int x,int y )
269  {
270    push();
271    popold();
272    if ( border_t == SHADOW ) {
273      if ( 0<=border[0]+x && border[2]+x+1<disp_numcols ) {
274        border[0] += x; border[2] += x;
275      }
276      if ( 0<=border[1]+y && border[3]+y+1<disp_numrows ) {
277        border[1] += y; border[3] += y;
278      }
279    }
280    else {
281      if ( 0<=border[0]+x && border[2]+x<disp_numcols ) {
282        border[0] += x; border[2] += x;
283      }
284      if ( 0<=border[1]+y && border[3]+y<disp_numrows ) {
285        border[1] += y; border[3] += y;
286      }
287    }
288    pushold();
289    pop();
290  }
291
292  int screen::pulldown( int elements, char *list[] )
293  {
294    int selected,mline,numline,ofs,cnt;
295    unsigned char a;
296    char ch;
```

```
297      char *p,**q;
298
299      selected = numline = 0;
300      mline = 1;
301      clr();
302      q = list;
303      for ( ;; ) {
304        loc( 2,mline++ ); numline++; put( "%s", *q++ );
305        if ( numline >= border[3]-border[1]+1
306            || numline >= elements ) break;
307      }
308      if ( numline == 0 ) {
309        popold();
310        return( 0 );
311      }
312      selected = 1;
313      loc( 2,selected );
314      ofs = 160*(border[1] + selected - 1) + 2*(border[0] + 1);
315      p = MK_FP( disp_base,ofs+1 );
316      for ( cnt=border[0]+1; cnt<border[2]; ++cnt ) {
317        if ( cnt == border[0] + 1 )
318          a = ( LIGHTGRAY << 4 ) + RED;
319        else
320          a = ( LIGHTGRAY << 4 )  + BLACK;
321        *p = a; p += 2;
322      }
323      for ( ;; ) {                              // roll selection bar
324        ch = '\0'; while( !ch ) ch = getch();
325
326 // Turn selection bar back off
327        ofs = 160*(border[1] + selected - 1) +
328          2*(border[0] + 1);
329        p = MK_FP( disp_base,ofs+1 );
330        for ( cnt=border[0]+1; cnt<border[2]; ++cnt ) {
331          *p = cur_attr; p += 2;
332        }
333        switch( ch ) {
334
335          case 13: popold();
336                   return( selected );
337          case 72: if ( --selected < 1 ) selected = 1; break;
338          case 80: if ( ++selected > numline )
339                     selected = numline;
340                   break;
341          default: selected = 0;
342                   q = list;
343                   for ( ;; ) {
344                     if ( ++selected > elements ) break;
345                     q++;
346                     if ( toupper( **q ) == toupper( ch ) ) {
347                       popold();
```

Listing 19.5. continues

Listing 19.5. continued

```
348                          return( selected );
349                     }
350                 };
351                 selected = 1;  // nothing matched
352     }
353
354  // Turn selection bar on in new position
355      ofs = 160*(border[1]+selected-1) + 2*(border[0]+1);
356      p = MK_FP( disp_base,ofs+1 );
357      for ( cnt=border[0]+1; cnt<border[2]; ++cnt ) {
358        if ( cnt == border[0] + 1 )
359          a = ( LIGHTGRAY << 4 ) + RED;
360        else
361          a = ( LIGHTGRAY << 4 )  + BLACK;
362        *p = a; p += 2;
363      }
364    }
365  }
```

When you compile `screen.cpp`, be sure to use the large memory model and to compile to object code without linking. You can use the following command to do this:

```
ztc -ml -c screen
```

A brief introduction to the Zortech `disp` functions may help you follow the code. The Zortech display-management facilities consist of several globally defined variables, and the group of functions whose names all begin with `disp_`.

Before any of the functions can be used, you must check the value of the variable `disp_inited` to determine whether display processing has been started. This is a true-false variable. If it is false, you must call `disp_open()` to begin display processing.

Several other global variables are maintained automatically by the display package. The variable `disp_base` contains a `void far *` pointer to the beginning of screen RAM in the current video mode. This is how `screen` functions can be made to work on all video display types.

Other variables include `disp_numrows` and `disp_numcols` for determining screen size, and `disp_cursorrow` and `disp_cursorcol` for reporting the current display cursor position. The function `disp_move()` is used to control this position. One serious drawback to this package is the fact that the `disp_` package cursor position does not necessarily correspond to the physical cursor, so the cursor may be left somewhere visible on the screen. This is, however, the only shortcoming of the package.

The `disp_scroll()` function invokes system services directly to scroll the display either up or down. We take advantage of this to scroll only the portion of the physical display involved in the current virtual screen. `disp_box()` is also very handy, because we can draw the `BOX` type border with a single function call.

Finally, `disp_printf()` is used to provide `printf()` service at RAM-poke speeds. To fully implement the service, variadic arguments (variable argument list) are used to format the output line into a buffer string, where it is detabbed. The output of this operation is then passed to `disp_printf()`.

The constructor for class `screen` appears in lines 27–105 of listing 19.5. In some ways, the constructor is the most difficult technology to implement; the various box-types must be distinguished, storage for the screen-save buffers acquired, and everything else set up.

The most interesting feature of the `screen()` constructor, from the point of view of C++ programming, is the use of `this`. The constructor function assigns the address of the object being created to `this`.

Let us say at the outset that this *ordinarily* is an obsolete technique with most current C++ compilers — including AT&T 2.0. There are new and better ways to accomplish the same effect using `::operator new()`. That operator is described fully in the next chapter, in the discussion of the C++ *free store*.

But why would you want to assign a value to `this` even with an older compiler, and perhaps most important, would you ever want to do this with a current-level compiler? The answer to the first question is that, with previous C++ compilers, the value of `this` was not valid in the constructor until an assignment to it *had been made*. The resultant effect is that, although you could initialize member data objects, you could not call other member functions from within the constructor unless you initialized `this` yourself.

This problem may not sound serious, but often can be. In `screen` objects, for example, we have a requirement: to save a copy not only of the virtual screen's contents, but also of the underlying screen area itself. This necessitates a call to `screen::pushold()` *from within the constructor*, so that the area's contents are not be lost when the new panel is painted.

If you are going to assign a value to `this`, you must realize that the compiler detects what you are doing and *no longer generates the hidden code* to perform that function for you. Therefore, you must perform the assignment to `this` along *every possible entry path to the constructor*, as follows:

```
30     if ( !this ) {   // from listing 19.5
31       if ( NULL ==( this = malloc( sizeof( screen ) ) ) ) {
32         printf( "Could not allocate %d bytes\n",
33           sizeof( screen ) );
34         abort();
35       }
36     }
37     else this = this; // assign for every possible path
```

The arrangement of the if statement implies that this already may be a valid pointer, or it may be NULL on entry to the constructor function. Basically, there are three ways you can cause the creation of an object (and hence a constructor call).

For the first two of these ways, the value of this is already valid when the constructor is entered. You can declare an object at file scope, thus creating a global static object. The relative position of this kind of object is known even at compile time, and is resolved completely when the system loader brings the program into memory for execution. You can also declare an object local to a function or interior block. Again, because such an object (C++ or otherwise) is allocated on the stack, the address of the object is known when the constructor is entered.

The third way of creating an object is to create it dynamically, using the new operator. Such an object has static duration and must be destroyed by using the operator delete. However, if you have assigned a value to this, you must now detect the fact that new was used to create the object and take over the destruction of the object. This also implies the answer to the question "Why should you ever assign a value to this?" You assign values to this when you want total control over the creation and destruction of an object. For example, the following code fragment shows how to set up the destructor function for an object created with new:

```
#include <stdlib.h>
#include <stdio.h>

class stuff{
  int dynalloc; // true-false: allocated via new?
public:
  stuff();
  ~stuff();
};
```

```
stuff::stuff()
{
  if ( !this ) {
    this = (stuff *)malloc( sizeof(stuff) );
    dynalloc = 1; // set dynamic flag to true
  }
  else {
    this = this;
    dynalloc = 0; // set dynamic flag to false
  }
}
stuff::~stuff()
{
  if ( dynalloc ) {
    free( this ); // release storage first
    this = 0;     // prevent normal deallocation
    printf( "Took over destruction of object.\n" );
  }
}
main()
{
  stuff* thing = new stuff;

  delete thing;  // implicitly invoke destructor
// -------------------------------------------------
//  Or, you can explicitly call the destructor,
//  with a statement like this:
//            thing->stuff::~stuff();
// -------------------------------------------------
}
```

With all that under your belt, now notice line 73 of listing 19.5. This line is within the constructor, and is executed as soon as control over t h i s has been established. The sole purpose of the call to s c r e e n : : p u s h o l d ( ) is to save a copy of the underlying screen area. Notice that, because the member function is called from within another member function, you call it just like any other C function — there is no need to prepend an object name and structure operator (.). Indeed, doing so would be an error.

All the work done in the s c r e e n constructor paves the way for extremely straightforward implementation of some other fairly sophisticated features. The s c r e e n : : m o v e ( ) function, for example, shifts the position of the virtual screen from one position on the display to another (lines 268 – 290). Because everything has already been taken care of, the logic consists simply of the following sequence of events:

1. push() saves a copy of the current virtual screen.

2. popold() restores the underlying screen area.

   The cursor coordinates are modified by the requested amount, checking to be sure that the virtual screen is not shifted off the display.

3. pushold() saves a copy of the underlying screen at the new coordinates.

4. pop() restores the contents of the virtual screen, now in its new location.

Such a simple implementation of moving virtual screens around can result in quite pleasing visual effects. The program demo.cpp, shown in listing 19.6, demonstrates virtual-screen movement under the user's control, displays all three kinds of screen borders, and uses the screen::put() message-display function. Figure 19.3 shows the appearance of the demo.cpp screen.

Fig. 19.3. The demo.cpp *program shows off all three border types, plus movable virtual screens.*

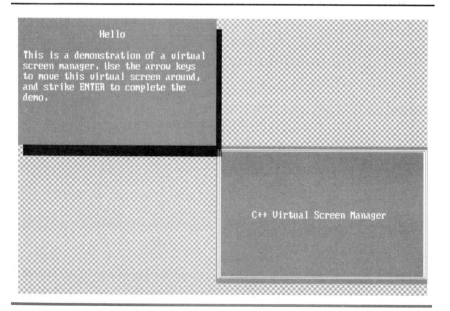

Listing 19.6. `demo.cpp` *(Demonstrates the basic* `screen` *class capabilities).*
Zortech C++

```
1    #include <stdlib.h>
2    #include <stdio.h>
3    #include <stdarg.h>
4    #include <disp.h>
5    #include <dos.h>
6
7    #include "screen.hpp"
8
9    main()
10   {
11      char ch = ' ';
12      int i;
13      screen screen0( RED,WHITE,PLAIN,0,0,0,0 );
14      screen screen2( BLUE,WHITE,BOX,40,13,80,25 );
15      screen2.loc( 7,6 );
16      screen2.put( "%s","C++ Virtual Screen Manager" );
17      screen0.push();
18      screen screen1( BLUE,WHITE,SHADOW,1,1,39,12 );
19
20      screen1.loc( 17,2 );
21      screen1.put( "%s","Hello" );
22      screen1.loc( 1,4 );
23      screen1.put( "%s\n",
24               " This is a demonstration of a virtual" );
25      screen1.put( "%s\n",
26               " screen manager. Use the arrow keys" );
27      screen1.put( "%s\n",
28               " to move this virtual screen around," );
29      screen1.put( "%s\n",
30               " and strike ENTER to complete the" );
31      screen1.put( "%s\n"," demo." );
32
33      while ( ch != 13 ) {
34        ch = getch(); if ( ch == 0 ) ch = getch();
35        switch ( ch ) {
36          case 72: screen1.move( 0,-1 ); break;
37          case 75: screen1.move( -1,0 ); break;
38          case 77: screen1.move( 1,0 );  break;
39          case 80: screen1.move( 0,1 );  break;
40        }
41      }
42   }
43
```

The program in listing 19.6 assumes that `screen.cpp` has already been compiled separately and will be linked in only here. Therefore, you should use the MAKE utility to control the compilation and linking of all the source files. Here is the MAKE file we used (`demo.mak`) to build the complete sample program:

```
demo.exe: demo.obj screen.obj
               ztc demo.obj screen.obj -odemo.exe
demo.obj: demo.cpp
               ztc -c demo.cpp -odemo.obj -mL

screen.obj: screen.cpp screen.hpp
               ztc -c screen.cpp -oscreen.obj -mL
```

The amazing thing is the ease with which virtual screens can be implemented and used, once the class has been written and member functions compiled. Even more amazing is the simplicity of implementing the reasonably sophisticated feature of pull-down menus, which is demonstrated in listing 19.7, `menus.cpp`.

Listing 19.7. `menus.cpp` (Demonstrate the `screen` class pull-down menus).   Zortech C++

```
 1   #include <stdlib.h>
 2   #include <stdio.h>
 3   #include <disp.h>
 4   #include <string.h>
 5   #include "screen.hpp"
 6
 7   FILE *menu;
 8   char menuname[41];
 9   char work[81];
10   char in_line[81];
11   char *mentry[16];
12   char *mcommand[16];
13   char *s, *r;
14   int longest = 0, numentries = 0;
15
16   main( int argc, char *argv[] )
17   {
18     char ch = ' ';
19     int i,j;
20
21     if ( argc > 1 ) strcpy( menuname, argv[1] );
22     else {
23       puts( "Supply a menu file name: "
24             "C:>menus [\\path\\]name[.ext]" );
25       exit( 8 );
```

```
26      }
27      for ( i=0; i<16; ++i ) {   // Init labels & commands array
28        mentry[i] = NULL;
29        mcommand[i] = NULL;
30      }
31      if ( NULL == ( menu = fopen( menuname, "r" ) ) ) {
32        printf( "Menu file %s was not found\n", menuname );
33        exit( 8 );
34      }
35      i = 0;
36      while ( fgets( in_line, 81, menu ) ) {
37        if ( ++numentries == 16 ) break;
38        if ( *in_line == ' ' || *in_line == '\n' ) {
39          numentries--;
40          continue;
41        }
42        s = in_line; r = work;
43        while ( *s && *s != '@' && *s != '\n' )
44          *r++ = *s++;                  // Copy menu label part
45        *r = '\0';
46        j = strlen( work );
47        mentry[i] = malloc( j+1 );
48        strcpy( mentry[i], work );
49        if ( j > longest ) longest = j;
50
51        // No command part if null or tab
52        if ( !*s || *s == '\n' ) break;
53        s++;                            // Get past @
54        r = work;                       // And restart work
55        while ( *s && *s != '\n' )
56          *r++ = *s++;                  // Copy command part
57        *r = '\0';
58        j = strlen( work );
59        mcommand[i] = malloc( j+1 );
60        strcpy( mcommand[i], work );
61        i++;                            // Now you can update it
62      }
63      fclose( menu );
64      screen screen0( LIGHTGRAY,BLACK,PLAIN,0,0,0,0 );
65      screen0.loc( 10, 12 );
66      screen0.put( "Strike Return to pop up the menu" );
67      ch = getch();
68      screen screen1( BLUE,WHITE,SHADOW,1,1,
69                      longest+2,numentries );
70      //
71      // Screen object now makes actual use of menu simplicity
72      //
73      i = screen1.pulldown( numentries, mentry );
74      screen0.pop();
75      screen0.clr();
76      screen0.loc( 10, 12 );
```

Listing 19.7. continues

Listing 19,7. continued

```
77    screen0.put( "You selected item: %s", mentry[i-1] );
78    screen0.loc( 10, 13 );
79    screen0.put( "Strike any key to return to the system" );
80    ch = getch();
81    for ( i=0; i<16; i++ ) {
82       free( mentry[i] ); free( mcommand[i] );
83    }
84    screen0.popold();
85 }
```

The `menus.cpp` program in listing 19.7 assumes that `screen.cpp` will be compiled separately. The MAKE file used to build the complete program is `menus.mak`. It has the following control statements:

```
menus.exe: menus.obj screen.obj
            ztc menus.obj screen.obj -omenus.exe
menus.obj: menus.cpp
            ztc -c menus.cpp -omenus.obj -mL
screen.obj: screen.cpp screen.hpp
            ztc -c screen.cpp -oscreen.obj -mL
```

Creating, displaying, and processing pull-down menus is easy when you use the `screen` class. Lines 68–73 of listing 19.7 show the proper way to do this. For your convenience, the necessary statements are extracted here:

```
char *mentry[nn]; // substitute num of items
int numentries;   // num items here, too
int selected;     // to return item selected
...
screen screen1( BLUE,WHITE,SHADOW,1,1,
                longest+2,numentries );
selected = screen1.pulldown( numentries, mentry );
```

This is just an example. The name of the `screen` object does not have to be `screen1`, nor do the colors and position of the screen have to be as shown here. Notice, however, that when you declare the object, the screen width is specified as `longest+2`, and the screen height is specified as `numentries`, the number of lines in the selection list. The integer `longest` is the length of the longest string in the list of selection items. It is kept updated (line 49) as the selection item strings are read in from the file.

C++ object control is not the hardest part of this program. Building the list of strings containing the selection items is. All that `screen::pulldown()` requires is an array of pointer to string for the selection items; we have chosen to build a second array of pointer to string, `char *mcommand[]`, which contains actions to perform that correspond to each possible selection. Figure 19.4 shows the appearance of the sample pull-down menu screen.

Fig. 19.4. *Tell a screen object to display itself as a pull-down and provide the label strings.*

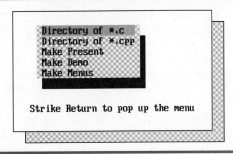

Thus, the text file (or, if you want, it could be an internal `array static char *name[] = {};`) supporting this approach is composed of lines, each of which has the selector display string and the command part, like this:

```
Directory of *.c@dir *.c
Directory of *.cpp@dir *.cpp
Make Present@make -fpresent.mak
Make Demo@make -fdemo.mak
Make Menus@make -fmenus.mak
```

Lines 36 – 62 contain the logic for reading the file, splitting out the string parts, and loading the corresponding array elements. This approach assumes that you have used the @ character in the line to indicate the end of the selector part and the beginning of the command string part.

If you eliminated the logic for menu text-file handling, and perhaps hard-coded the selector string array, you could implement a function supporting color pull-down menus in 20 to 30 lines of code. Such is the power of C++ objects.

Summary

This chapter described concepts and facilities basic to the use of C++ object-oriented programming tools. Before you go on to the next chapter (which assumes that you *read* this one!), be sure that you understand the following:

❑   *What a class is, and how to declare one to C++.* This involves more than just syntax, as important as that is. Class design and declaration is where you find out whether you have understood correctly the differences in perspective between C and C++. If you have not, your class designs will be awkward, and you will find it necessary to redesign and change them frequently (the voice of experience speaks!). When you have begun to understand the "object-oriented mind-set," such things as what to make `private:` and what to make `public:` begin to fall into place.

❑ *Constructors are the way you teach C++ how to initialize your objects.* You can't call a constructor explicitly; this happens when you declare the object. Do you understand what `this` is? If not, review a little and let it soak in. It will be important later when you want to take complete control over object creation and initialization. Don't forget the copy initializer — it is often overlooked and is very important. You should understand also what the *destructor function* does, and when you can call a destructor explicitly.

❑ *Calling a member function of an object is the C++ way of sending a "message" to an object.* If you declare a static object, use the structure member operator to qualify the function name; if a pointer to an object is being used, use the structure pointer operator as follows:

```
class A { ... };
...
A obj1;
A *obj2 = new A;
...
A.function(); // call the member function
A->function(); // also call the member function
```

20

Controlling Classes and Objects

This chapter goes into more detail about controlling the creation and initialization of class objects. Specifically, you will learn more about the C++ free store, controlling object duration, and reusing class code already written:

❑ *In Chapter 19, we mentioned two operators,* `new` *and* `delete`, *without explaining much about them.* They *are* operators, like `sizeof`, and are used to create and delete objects dynamically. The pool of memory used to hold is called the *free store.* You can use `new` and `delete` for other things besides creating and deleting class objects. And you can *overload* (redefine) `new` and `delete` on a class-by-class basis with recent versions of the C++ compiler.

❑ *Understanding object duration is important, if for no other reason than that you don't want to refer to an object that has gone out of scope.* The `new` and `delete` operators can be used to get around all duration issues.

❑ *Code reusability and polymorphism are extremely important topics in object-oriented systems.* C++ allows you to reuse existing code by two means: *object composition*, in which objects of an existing class can be declared in a new class, or pointers to existing objects can be recorded; and *class inheritance*, in which classes are derived from old ones. Polymorphism can be thought of as inheritance with slight modifications to the methods. C++ implements polymorphism through *virtual functions*.

Understanding C++'s Free Store

You are already familiar with the standard C functions `malloc()`, `calloc()`, `realloc()`, and `free()`. These library functions allocate and deallocate memory on the C heap—which is exactly what the C++ *operators* `new` and `delete` do. The C heap is called the *free store* in C++.

With all the power of the library functions available, why would you want to use the `new` and `delete` operators? There are two reasons.

First, when you dynamically create objects, it is the use of the `new` operator that triggers the constructor function. Simply declaring a pointer to a class, and using `malloc()`, as in the following example:

```
class S { ... };
...
S *obj; // a pointer to class object;
obj = (S *)malloc( sizeof(s) ); // no constructor call
```

does not do this. These lines of code certainly allocate space for the pointer, the `malloc()` call allocates the correct amount of space to hold an object of class S, and the returned pointer is correctly assigned. But you still don't have an *object*, because the constructor was never called.

Second, and somewhat more philosophically, storage allocation in C++ was felt to be important enough to make it an integral part of the language, rather than a library function. There are advantages to using `new` and `delete`. Doing so automatically calculates the size of the object (you don't have to use that operator) and also returns a pointer of the correct type, so that no cast is necessary. These operators also give better performance at run-time.

Nevertheless, because `new` and `delete` are reported to *compile* more slowly than the library function calls, you might want to substitute `malloc()` or `calloc()` in certain circumstances during program development.

Using the Global *new* and *delete* Operators

You write the `new` operator to allocate storage for both class objects and other objects in C++. You write the `delete` operator to release storage acquired through `new`. The general syntax for these operators is as follows:

```
pointer-to-type = new typename(optional initializer);

delete pointer-to-type;
```

The `new` operator returns either a pointer of the correct type (actually a `void *` pointer) or a null pointer. You should check the returned value just as you do when using the `malloc()` or `calloc()` library functions.

The `typename` used as the operand (not argument!) for `new` can be a basic type, an ordinary derived type, or a class name. `new` implicitly computes the size of the object so that you never need write the `sizeof` operator. For example,

```
int *i = new int;  // operand is int, not i
int *array = new int[3][3]; // size computed for you
class X { ... };
...
X *obj1 = new X;
```

Getting fancy with `new` is not particularly difficult, once you get it firmly in mind that its operand is a *type*. For example, listing 20.1 shows how to declare an array of pointers to class objects and create the class objects to go with them.

The array of pointers is mundane, being formed just like anything you have already done in standard C. The only difference is that the type is now a class. Simply defining an array of pointers to class objects creates no objects, however. The loop in line 38 creates four objects of class `multiple`, including the implied call to the constructor function. Because this is not an array of objects, the constructor can have arguments, if you want (the default constructor with no arguments is not required).

Listing 20.1 also illustrates another interesting feature of class declarations: the initialization of `static` member data objects. Line 7 declares the `static` variable `instances`, placing it in the `public:` part of the declaration. Line 37 then initializes this data member object before the constructor is ever called, and before memory for the object is allocated.

Think for a minute about what that implies. Such initialization is not possible unless the variable physically resides outside the object (which does

Listing 20.1. `arraycla.cpp` *(Using* `new` *and* `delete` *to create and destroy multiple objects).*   *Turbo C++*

```
1   #include <stdlib.h>
2   #include <stdio.h>
3
4   class multiple {
5      int which;
6   public:
7      static int instances;
8      multiple();
9      ~multiple();
10     void display();
11  };
12
13  multiple::multiple()
14  {
15     which = instances;
16     ++instances; // update number of object created;
17  }
18
19  multiple::~multiple()
20  {
21     printf( "Help! Object %d is dying!\n", which );
22     --instances;
23  }
24
25  void multiple::display()
26  {
27     printf( "I am object number %d of %d\n",
28             which, instances );
29  }
30
31
32  main()
33  {
34     int i;
35     multiple *x[4]; // array of pointers to object
36
37     multiple::instances = 0; // pre-init static data member;
38     for ( i=0; i<4; i++ ) x[i] = new multiple;
39     for ( i=0; i<4; i++ ) x[i]->display();
40     for ( i=0; i<4; i++ ) delete x[i];
41  }
```

not exist at this point, remember). That is why `instances` also gets updated correctly as multiple instances of the object are created. Look at the output from the program:

```
I am object number 0 of 4
I am object number 1 of 4
I am object number 2 of 4
I am object number 3 of 4
Help! Object 0 is dying!
Help! Object 1 is dying!
Help! Object 2 is dying!
Help! Object 3 is dying!
```

If instances physically resided within the object, then a new version of it would come into being each time a new object was created—the first four lines of the output report would not report correctly the total number of instances of the object.

To initialize a static member data object, you must code the fully qualified name of the item, but *do not attempt to include an object identifier.* Use only the classname, scope resolution operator, and data member name, as in the following example:

```
multiple::instances = 0;  // or whatever value you want
```

Finally, notice in the output from the program in listing 20.1 that the destructor is called for every instance of the object pointed to by the array, because separate applications of new created the instance objects.

You don't have to do it this way to create multiple objects at one time. You can use new to create an array of objects at one lick, and still do it on the free store so that program space is not used. Listing 20.2 shows how to do this.

Listing 20.2. arraycl2.cpp *(Using a single call to* new *and* delete *to allocate and destroy a whole array of objects)*   *Turbo C++*

```
1    #include <stdlib.h>
2    #include <stdio.h>
3
4    int instances = 0; // make this global just for fun
5
6    class multiple {
7      int which;
8    public:
9      multiple();
10     ~multiple();
11     void display();
12   };
13
14   multiple::multiple()
15   {
```

Listing 20.2. continues

Listing 20.2. continued

```
16      ++instances; // update number of object created;
17      which = instances;
18   }
19
20   multiple::~multiple()
21   {
22      printf( "Help! Object %d is dying!\n", which );
23      --instances;
24   }
25
26   void multiple::display()
27   {
28      printf( "I am object number %d of %d\n",
29              which, instances );
30   }
31
32
33   main()
34   {
35      int i;
36                  // pointer to array of objects
37      multiple *x = new multiple[4];
38
39      for ( i=0; i<4; i++ ) x[i].display();
40      delete x;   // kill one pointer only
41   }
```

Before anything else is said about listing 20.2, note this: When you define (create) an array of objects (on the free store or otherwise), *the default constructor is used to initialize the objects.* If you have defined one or more constructors, be sure to include one with no arguments or one that has defaults for *all* the arguments. Here is a skeleton of a class whose constructor has arguments with defaults:

```
class ZZ {
...
public:
ZZ( int = 0, int = 0 ); // qualifies as default
...                     // when called with no args
};
```

This makes sense if you think about it. When you declare an array of class objects, where would you place any initializers? Hence the default constructor is used (yours or the one generated by the compiler).

Now, back to listing 20.2. When you look at the output from this version of the program:

```
I am object number 1 of 4
I am object number 2 of 4
I am object number 3 of 4
I am object number 4 of 4
Help! Object 1 is dying!
```

you can see that the constructor for each instance of the object is indeed called when a whole array of class objects is created with a single application of new.

The delete operator takes as an operand a pointer to the object to be deallocated (and destroyed, if a class object). Stroustrup says that applying delete to a pointer that was not obtained from new is undefined (meaning an error that your compiler is free to handle in its own way). Deleting a pointer that is already zero is said to be harmless, but is at least a logical error indicating that you have lost control of your program.

The delete operator is not as smart as the new operator, either. Looking once more at the output from listing 20.2, it is apparent that because only one pointer is being processed, only one destructor is called.

What about using new in a constructor function? This is perfectly fine, provided that you *do not refer to the class to which the constructor belongs*. For example, in the following code:

```
class odd {
...
public:
  odd();
};

odd::odd()   // BIG mistake here!
{
  odd *obj = new odd;
}
...
main ()
{
  odd job; // declare the object
}
```

everything is fine when the object is declared in main(). When execution reaches the code in the constructor, however, matters are different. It is the *constructor* that is executing, but the new odd object creation invokes the constructor—the *same* constructor—that invokes the constructor, and on to infinity (or until memory is exhausted). Using new to allocate memory for nonclass objects is acceptable and common, however.

Defining Your Own *new* and *delete*

The new and delete operators discussed so far are also called the *global* new and delete operators. They are predefined by your compiler and are available everywhere, in every scope.

It is possible to *overload* them—redefine them by providing your own functions, if you want to provide very special handling of allocation requests. You may need to do this when normal new does not work—when, for example, allocation may involve virtual storage manipulation. Another example is garbage collection in a memory-constrained or fragmented environment—when allocation is likely to fail frequently. But first, let's look at the facilities C++ provides for recovering a failed new request *without* overloading the function.

We said that new returns a pointer, or null if it fails. This is true only if you do not take over handling allocation failures for new. You can take over this function by writing a function that either recovers enough memory to allow the allocation to succeed or terminates the program. C++ provides a pointer to function object, _new_handler, and a function, set__new_handler(), with which you can reset the function that new_handler points to. The following code fragment shows how to hook into this function:

```
#include <stdlib.h>
#include <stdio.h>

void handle_new_failure()
{
   printf( "Tough cookies!\n" );
   // if you take over handling new failures, you must
   // either free up some storage, or terminate the
   // program
   exit( 8 );
}

// see Stroustrup p. 93
// for this typedef & declaration:

typedef void (*PF)();
extern PF set_new_handler( PF );

main()
{
   set_new_handler( handle_new_failure );
   while( new int ) ;
}
```

This is just the skeletal framework of the facilities necessary to do adequate garbage collection. If you choose to use this vehicle to enhance `new` processing, note carefully the `typedef` and `extern` declaration for `set_new_handler()`. Note also that if you define a `_new_handler` routine, the function must either free sufficient storage for the request to be satisfied, or terminate the program. If the `exit(8)` call is removed from this fragmentary program, for example, the program loops infinitely when storage has been exhausted.

How can you use this method to control storage fragmentation? In his book, *Using C++*, Eckel presents a satisfying though short program. The outlines of the method are as follows:

1.   Define an array class. This class is used to hold pointers to all objects created during the life of the program.

2.   Define all classes to include private data member objects that indicate whether the object is in use or is finished processing. Add also a method common to every class, which can be called to query the in-use flag. All class objects must be created with `new` only. That is, a class object's space, and any space acquired on its behalf, must be acquired through `new` (you can't `delete` objects from the stack or those that are `static`).

3.   Write your `_new_handler` function, including logic to traverse the array class object. As each pointer to an object is fetched, call the object's query function and determine whether it is in use or not. If not, use `delete` to free the space.

You can provide most of the recovery function you will ever need by using this method. One limitation, however, is the fact that the `_new_handler` is a `void` function, unable to return a go or no-go indication—it cannot report complete failure to recover.

If that is a problem, or you have other special memory-allocation needs, you can replace `new`, `delete`, *and* the failed allocation handler. Just override (replace completely) global `new` and `delete`, designing them to do what you want them to, and provide your own handler protocol from the ground up. Listing 20.3 shows how to do this.

Listing 20.3. `glblnew.cpp` (*Overloading the global operator* `new()` *and operator* `delete()`). *TurboC++*

```
 1   #include <stdlib.h>
 2   #include <stdio.h>
 3   #include <stream.h>
 4
 5                    // override global new and delete functions
 6   int (*_my_handler)();  // pointer to handler function
 7
 8   int garbage_collector()  // return true if try again is OK
 9   {
10     printf( "Garbage collector is on duty!\n" );
11     return 0;  // force a no-recovery return for test
12   }
13
14   void *operator new( size_t size )
15   {
16     void *thing;
17
18   oncemore: ;
19     if ( size % 2 != 0 ) {
20       printf( "operand for new must be an even"
21               " number of bytes.\n" );
22       return 0;
23     }
24     else {
25       if ( 0 == ( thing = calloc( size/2, sizeof(int) ) ) ) {
26         if ( (*_my_handler)() ) goto oncemore;
27       }
28       return thing;
29     }
30   }
31
32   void operator delete( void *obj )
33   {
34     free( obj );
35   }
36
37   main()
38   {
39     _my_handler = garbage_collector; // set up handler;
40
41     while ( new int ) ; // guaranteed to exhaust storage!
42   }
```

You override global `new` and `delete` by writing functions for them outside any class, as shown in listing 20.3. Code the declaration part as shown here, but handle memory allocation any way you see fit. This does not mean that you begin calling these functions like any other functions—you still use the new and delete syntax (as in line 41).

There is a difference between the AT&T 2.0 C++ implementation and Turbo C++. The AT&T compiler expects a long argument to the new function, whereas Turbo C++ expects a type of size_t (which is just an unsigned int—see line 14).

The program in listing 20.3 completely redesigns the _new_handler facility, replacing it with its own. The handler routine (lines 6–12) now returns a fail-success integer value so that the override new function can determine whether to retry. It is not necessary to exit() or abort() during garbage collection, because failure can be easily caught and handled.

In older versions of the C++ compiler, new and delete could only be overridden globally. Either you did it this way, for the whole program, or you left it alone. But compilers compatible with the AT&T 2.0 compiler allow you to overload new and delete on a class-by-class basis—you can tune them up for a class without affecting any other classes. This feature has also made the need to assign pointers to this obsolete, as you will see in a moment. Listing 20.4 shows how to overload the new and delete operators for a single class.

The overloaded new operator must return a void pointer. In the Turbo C++ implementation, the method function must also accept an unsigned argument. Other compilers may require a long. The delete method function accepts a void pointer, as always.

The syntax for the class overloaded operators is the same as for the global versions. Further, the global versions can still be accessed. How do you sort out which is used and when?

The rule is that when new has been overloaded for the class, and you write a reference to the *class for which it is defined*, classname::operator new() is called. Otherwise, global operator new() is called, as in the following example:

```
class redefined {
...
public:
void *operator new( unsigned );
...
};
void *redefined::operator new( unsigned size )
{
```

```
    return new unsigned char[size]; // global new
}
...
main()
{
  redefined A;                    // overloaded new
  char *s = new char[81];              // global new
...
}
```

Listing 20.4. `newcp.cpp`, *overloading* `::operator new()` *and*
`:operator delete()`.   *Turbo C++*

```
 1   #include <stdlib.h>
 2   #include <stdio.h>
 3
 4   class A {
 5     int holdit;
 6   public:
 7     void *operator new( unsigned );
 8     void operator delete( void *obj );
 9   };
10
11   void * A::operator new( unsigned size )
12   {
13     return ::new unsigned char[size];
14   }
15
16   void A::operator delete( void *obj )
17   {
18     ::delete obj;
19   }
20
21   main()
22   {
23     A *myobj = new A;
24     delete myobj;   // calls A::operator delete();
25   }
```

Notice that the `new` method function in listing 20.4 is slightly different
from the one in this code fragment. It uses the global `new`, but with a strange
looking syntax (line 13), as follows:

```
13       return ::new unsigned char[size];
```

The double colon with no prepended class name is, of course, the scope
resolution operator. But because no class name is attached, the scope is
global. All this accomplishes is to guarantee that the `new` method function
used is in fact the global one.

You can force the selection of the overloaded `new` or `delete` method function from within a member function by using the scope resolution operator with the class name attached, as in the following example:

```
#include <stdlib.h>
#include <stdio.h>

class big {
  char *bigdata;
public:
  big()
      { bigdata = (char *)big::operator new( 32768U ); }
  ~big() { big::operator delete( (void *)bigdata ); }
  void *operator new( unsigned size )
      { return (void *)malloc( size ); }
  void operator delete ( void *obj )
      { free( obj ); }
};

main()
{
  big deal; // declare object
  // and let it go out of scope
}
```

You can do this if you want, but the question remains—why would you want to? Look at the disadvantages suddenly accruing to the technique: the syntax is complicated by scope resolution; you may have to do your own size calculations; the pointer type must be coerced by a cast, because it is no longer automatic; and instead of writing a simple operand, you must resort to a function call. In summary, overloading the `new` and `delete` operators is handy for acquiring space for a *class object*, and that is what you should use it for.

What about *this* and *::operator new()?*

For historical reasons, we introduced you earlier to the notion of acquiring your own storage and assigning a pointer to `this` in the constructor. We did this for two reasons: first, `this` was not valid in the constructor until *you* assigned a value to it (limiting access to other member functions from within the constructor); and second, you occasionally might want to be explicitly aware when an object had been created with `new`. Let's reexamine those ideas in light of the ability to overload `new` and `delete` on a class basis.

When you have overloaded `new`, `this` is not valid at only one point in the process of creating the object—in the `class::operator new()` method function itself. To illustrate this, listing 20.5 shows a program that does *not* compile correctly.

Listing 20.5. `newcp2.cpp` (*When is* `this` *valid, using* `::operator new()`?). *Turbo C++*

```
 1   #include <stdlib.h>
 2   #include <stdio.h>
 3
 4   class A {
 5      int flag1;
 6      static int flag2;
 7   public:
 8      void *operator new( unsigned );
 9      void operator delete( void *obj );
10   };
11
12   void * A::operator new( unsigned size )
13   {
14      flag1 = 0;   // ERROR--flag1 does not exist yet!
15      flag2 = 1;
16      return ::new unsigned char[size];
17   }
18
19   void A::operator delete( void *obj )
20   {
21      ::delete obj;
22   }
23
24   main()
25   {
26      A *myobj = new A; // calls A::operator new()
27      delete A;   // calls A::operator delete();
28   }
```

Because `flag1` is a normal private data member, meaning particularly that it is *not* static, it does not exist until object creation is complete. Line 14 shows code in the `new` method function attempting to access that data member. This produces a compile-time error, because the compiler knows very well that the data member doesn't exist. `flag2`, on the other hand, *is* defined as `static`. As you learned earlier, this data member does exist, and can even be initialized by code outside the member functions for the class.

After the `new` method function has executed, however, a valid `this` pointer for the new dynamic object does exist. Because it is only at this point that the constructor function is invoked, there is no further need to assign to `this` to gain access to any data or function member within the class.

The second reason for assigning to `this` was to enable you to write code that could detect when the object was dynamically created (for example, with `new`). Knowing this was necessary when it was mandatory to substitute your own code for releasing storage in the destructor function. In other words, you did this when you wanted to override what `delete` does, without redefining global `delete` as shown earlier. This is even more easily disposed of. The overloaded class `delete` takes care of all that—if your class `delete` is entered at all, it is because the object was dynamically created. *Voila*, you don't need other code to detect that fact.

The only other reasons for knowing about `this` (at all) with the newer compilers are that a knowledge of internals is always beneficial, and you may often want to return a reference to `this` (to *self*) from a member function. You will see that done frequently later.

Defining Objects to C++

In C++, scoping issues are as important as they are in standard C—perhaps even more so. When and where you declare or create a class object makes all the difference in the world to how you can get to it. By now, you have enough experience with C programming so that this is hardly surprising.

The way objects appear to the programmer in C++ has a different, more complex behavior, however. This is largely because class objects contain member functions within their boundaries, and the way they are accessed and behave is necessarily more complex.

You can declare class objects that have static, dynamic, or purely arbitrary duration. And, because C++ is what it is, some of the categories overlap slightly. The following sections detail which declarations create which kind of object.

What Are Static and Dynamic Objects?

The terms *static* and *dynamic* have approximately the same significance in C++ that they have in standard C. The terms still refer primarily to the duration of the object, although the terms do have connotations for its visibility.

Because static objects (class or otherwise) are those objects for which space can be set aside at compile time, their duration is permanent—static— for the duration of program execution.

Dynamic objects, in contrast, are objects for which no space is set aside at compile time; rather, it is set aside at run-time. The compiler does know something about the kind and expected size of the object, but nothing whatever about where it exists—when it gets around to being created. Now, how does all this shake out for class objects in C++?

Dynamic Objects on the Stack

You can declare class objects locally within ordinary C functions. When you do, the object is allocated on the stack, and the constructor is called, as follows:

```
class workhorse { ... };
...
void myfunction( void )
{
   workhorse bigdata;
   ...
}
...
```

This is essentially what we have been doing all along in the sample code. It was the `main()` function that declared the objects, but that is still a function. When the function containing the declaration returns, the dynamically created object goes out of scope, and the destructor is called automatically. Local class objects have `auto` duration, just like any other local object. Figure 20.1 graphically depicts dynamic objects created on the stack.

Fig. 20.1. Class objects declared local to a function or block are given space on the stack.

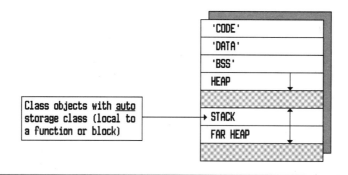

When a declaration local to a block creates a dynamic object, it does *not* involve `::operator new()`. That is not the function of the `new` operator. As a result, you need not, and should not, use the `delete` operator or call the destructor explicitly.

Dynamic objects on the stack can be declared also within class member functions. The only restriction is that they may not be declared within a constructor or destructor function.

Strictly speaking, a constructor function may not contain a declaration for an object that has the *same class as the constructor*. Declaring such an object would cause endless recursion of the constructor function, leading finally to an exhaustion of memory and a program crash.

You could, however, declare an object with a *different* class, if that were needed in the process of setting up *this* class object. Remember that the local object is destroyed when the constructor goes out of scope (returns). Declaring a static class object within a constructor would be pointless, because you could never get to it again after the constructor returned. Here is a short program sporting a constructor declaring another local object:

```
#include <stdlib.h>
#include <stdio.h>

struct junk1 {
junk1() {}
~junk1() { puts( "Bye, bye! Junk1 is dead." ); }
};

struct junk2 {
junk2();
~junk2() { puts( "Bye, bye! Junk2 is dead." ); }
};

junk2::junk2()
{           // local object has *different* class
  junk1 stuffa; // this goes out of scope FIRST,
}               // when this constructor returns

main()
{
  junk2 stuffb; // NEXT, the junk2 destructor
}               // produce its cute message
```

The comments in this short piece of code indicate which destructor's message appears first on the display. Needless to say, you are going to be hard pressed to find a meaningful application for this technique. But if you do, enjoy!

The behavior of the destructor function is analogous to that of the constructor function. The only difference is that if you declare an object of the same class in a destructor, it is the destructor that recurs forever.

In the next chapter, you will see sample code with *many* examples of member functions creating objects on the stack. None of them involve the constructor or destructor, however.

Global Static Objects

Class objects can have file scope also. Nothing whatever prevents you from writing object declarations outside any function or block. These objects, like ordinary objects, have global visibility and s t a t i c duration. These are the objects whose space is set aside at compile time. Using global static objects makes them available to all functions in the file. They can be declared e x t e r n as well. Figure 20.2 illustrates the placement of global static class objects.

Fig. 20.2. *Turbo C++ places global class objects in the DATA or BSS segments, depending on whether or not they are initialized.*

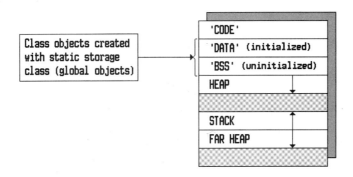

You can do this, but should you? If you think about it, one of the key components of C++ is compartmentalization, an important aspect of encapsulation. Writing all your object declarations with file scope violates no hard rule, but it does contradict the spirit of C++ (to a lesser degree, this is true even of standard C).

In addition to making your program very large, the danger of making everything global and static is *confusion*. If everything is global, nothing gets cleaned out. In the interests of having as few objects as possible to keep track of at any one time, you need to allow all objects that can reasonably be released to be destroyed. Only terminating the program destroys a global static object.

You can declare *objects that are static, but not globally visible*. You do this the same way you did it in standard C: use the `static` specifier keyword in the object's declaration within a function block.

Now such an object does have `static` duration, and it resides neither on the stack nor on the heap. But what parts of the program can "see" it and how many copies there are depend on what kind of function created it. The visibility and number of copies of an object are independent of the kind of *object*, as such (class or ordinary).

Think first of objects declared with ordinary functions. Static objects declared in ordinary functions have a *truly local scope*, and *declarations in multiple functions result in multiple copies of an object*. In the following code fragment, for example:

```
void func1( void )
{
  static object a;
  ...
}
void func1( void )
{
  static object a;
  ...
}
```

the *identifier* a is local to the function in which it appears. Thus there is an a of `func1`, and an a of `func2`, they exist in different *name spaces*. That is, there really are two different objects, with no confusion between them.

When `static` objects are declared within class member functions, the whole story changes. For instance, in the following code:

```
class anything {
...
public:
...
void do_something( void );
};
...
void anything::do_something( void )
{
  static int a;
  ...
}
```

```
...
main()
{
   anything X;
   anything Y;
   ...
}
```

how many copies of the static integer a are there? Just one, in spite of the
fact that there are two objects of class anything.

The reason is not really mysterious. Because the member function exists
because of its declaration as part of the *class* definition, there is only one copy
of it, regardless of the number of *objects* declared having that class. Thus,
static objects declared within a class member function are unique and
available to all objects of that class, but not to objects of other classes. You
might think of such objects as "semiglobal."

The moral of this story is that if you want a local object within a member
function to be unique to an *object*, and not merely to the *class*, don't make
it static. Let it default to an auto variable (you might also dynamically
acquire space for it in the constructor and use a pointer to get to it).

Static Objects on the Free Store

Objects created through new share some of the characteristics of both
dynamic and static objects. You create objects on the free store like this:

```
class modata { ... };
...
main()
{
   modata *motown = new modata;
}
```

Remember that because new returns a pointer, objects on the free store
are referenced by pointer. To call a member function of the motown object,
for example, you would write the following:

```
motown->memberobject();
```

using the structure pointer operator (->).

In this particular code fragment, the motown object is created within the
boundaries of the main() function. Thus, the *pointer* motown is local to
main() and not known outside the function.

You can write object declarations (class and ordinary) at file scope,
however—including objects created with new. The syntax is just like that for

any object declared at file scope with an initializer. The only difference is that now `motown` is a global static *pointer*, and the class object it points to can also be considered as global static.

Objects created with `new` are like dynamic objects created on the stack, in that they are not created and no space is allocated for them until run time. The space allocated is in the heap (free store), rather than the stack.

They are also somewhat similar to global static objects in that they don't ever go out of scope—whether declared in block scope or file scope. But true global objects are destroyed only at program termination. Static objects on the free store can be destroyed by using the `delete` operator or by explicitly calling the class destructor. It is more accurate, therefore, to speak of the duration of objects created with `new` as having *arbitrary* duration. Figure 20.3 shows the placement of class objects on the free store.

Fig. 20.3. *Turbo C++ uses either the near or far heap for free store memory, depending on the active memory model.*

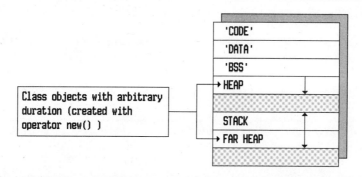

Derived Classes and Inheritance

Deriving classes corresponds to deriving types from basic C types. A derived class, or type, is generally more complex and has more functionality than its base class or type.

Because C++ objects have not only *attributes* (represented by data members) but also behavior (represented by the member functions), inheritance in C++ goes beyond the carrying-over of attributes when deriving objects from basic C types. C++ inheritance provides for the transmission of both attributes and behavior in derived classes. Inheritance provides a programming context in which you can easily *reuse code that has already been written*—and extend its capability in the process, if you want.

Understanding Code Reusability

The idea of reusing code that already has been written is intuitively clear. If you have written certain functions in class A, and they apply to the behavior of class B, why not just use them in place, rather than writing them into multiple class declarations? That is, why can't B inherit the functions of A, without the functions having to be rewritten?

C++ certainly provides the means for doing that. Even better, it provides two ways of doing it. The two methods have similarities and—even more important—differences. You can reuse code by either *composition* or *inheritance*.

These methods represent two different perspectives on what objects are. Reusing code by composition views objects as simply *collections of other objects*. Reusing code by inheritance views an object as a (perhaps slightly different) *kind* of its parent object.

Reusing Code by Composition

First, let's examine the consequences of viewing objects as collections of other objects. When this perspective is assumed, you naturally think of reusing the member functions of another class by *declaring objects of that other class in the current one*. Figure 20.4 illustrates this concept.

Fig. 20.4. *Reusing code by composition means defining class objects within a class declaration.*

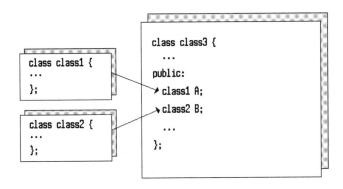

Suppose, for example, that you create a report class whose objects are capable of printing themselves. This report class describes reports in connection with a billing-record class. Billing-record objects also should be able to print themselves, but the report class object is used to do the printing. But you don't want to have to write classes for each kind of report—you want to reuse the code for a report class object.

A report object is necessarily general; it presumes that the billing record using it can be either a new invoice or a credit memo reporting a credit balance update. The kind of report is determined solely by the billing record itself, which then "informs" its included report object of the record type. Listing 20.6 shows a possible implementation of such a system, using the composition of classes by including other class objects.

Listing 20.6. `compose.cpp` *(Reusing member functions by composing collections of objects).*   *Turbo C++*

```
1   #include <stdlib.h>
2   #include <stdio.h>
3   #include <string.h>
4   #include <iostream.h>              // introduce streams
5
6   #define INVOICE    0
7   #define CREDITMEMO 1
8           //
9           // Define a general billing record format
10          //
11  typedef struct { // typedef for billing rec. data
12    int acctno;
13    char name[41];
14    double amt;
15  } billdata;
16          //
17          // Define a billing report object class
18          //
19  class report {    // class for included object
20    int rpttype;
21    char title[12];
22  public:
23    report( int );
24    void display( billdata &);
25  };
26
27  report::report( int btype )
28  {
29    switch( btype ) {
30      case INVOICE:    rpttype = btype;
```

Listing 20.6. continues

Listing 20.6. continued

```
31                         strcpy( title, "Invoice" );
32                         break;
33      case CREDITMEMO: rpttype= btype;
34                         strcpy( title, "Credit Memo" );
35                         break;
36    }
37  }
38
39  void report::display( billdata &billrec )
40  {
41    if ( rpttype == CREDITMEMO )
42      billrec.amt *= -1; // neg for credit balances
43    cout << title << " -----\n\n";
44    cout << "Account number: " << billrec.acctno
45        << "\n";
46    cout << "Customer Name: " << billrec.name
47        << "\n";
48    if ( rpttype == INVOICE )
49      cout << "Amount Due: ";
50    else
51      cout << "Credited to your account: ";
52    cout << billrec.amt << "\n";
53  }
54            //
55            // Define a billing record object class
56            //
57  class billrecord {        // billing record class
58    billdata brec;
59  public:
60    billrecord( int = 0, int = 0, char * = "",
61                double = 0 );
62    report billrep;          // be sure no args here
63    void printrep();
64  };
65                  // notice how the include object's
66                  // constructor is called here
67  billrecord::billrecord( int btype, int bacct,
68    char *bname, double bamt ) : billrep( btype )
69  {
70    brec.acctno = bacct;
71    strcpy( brec.name, bname );
72    brec.amt = bamt;
73  }
74
75  void billrecord::printrep()
76  {
77            // reference used, don't take address
78    billrep.display( brec );
```

```
79  }
80
81  main()
82  {
83     char nm[41] = "Smith, J.D.";
84     billrecord cust1( CREDITMEMO, 9939, nm, 125.55 );
85
86     cust1.printrep();
87  }
```

The output from the program looks like this:

```
Credit Memo -----

Account number: 9939
Customer Name: Smith, J.D.
Credited to your account: -125.55
```

In listing 20.6, we have begun purposely to introduce C++ streams to do the display I/O. Streams, which are discussed in the last sections of this chapter, are included in this program so that you can begin to get accustomed to their appearance.

Two classes are declared in listing 20.6. The report class (lines 19–53 contain the class declaration and member functions) describes report objects. The conceptual framework is that a report is a "thing" that can display itself when requested to do so. How it is stored (or the parts collected) internally is irrelevant to the end user.

The end user of reports, however, is the billing-record class object. The billrecord class is shown in lines 57–79 of listing 20.6. Notice that line 63 declares a member function printrep(). The billing-record object also is expected to be able to print itself. The vehicle for doing so is to "send a message" to the included report class object, billrep (declared in line 62). Now, how do the classes work?

Learning how to compose collections of objects requires that you understand two things: how constructors are called in this context, and how (and from where) the various member functions can be called.

First things first. How do you write an *object* declaration within a class declaration, and how can you get any arguments to the constructor?

Declaring an object within a class declaration is easy: do it just as you would anywhere else, with only one exception. In listing 20.6, the general framework for this declaration looks like this (with other material removed for clarity):

```
class billrecord {
...
public:
   report billrep;
   ...
};
```

That's simple enough so far. The exception mentioned above complicates things a little, however. When declaring an object within a class, never write constructor arguments for the included object. Now that doesn't mean that the default constructor is the only one used in this situation. You can pass arguments to the included object's constructor, you just can't do it *here*.

Where can you do it? You can specify the member object in the containing class's constructor function *definition*, as shown in lines 67–68:

```
billrecord::billrecord( int btype, int bacct,
   char *bname, double bamt ) : billrep( btype )
{
   ... constructor function body
}
```

The syntax is exactly the same as the constructor initialization list you have already seen, which follows:

```
class X {
   int a, b, c;
public:
   X( int = 0, int = 0, int = 0 );
...
};
X::X( int arg1,arg2,arg3 ) : a(arg1),
                             b(arg2),
                             c(arg3)
{
   ...
}
```

Now you know why the arguments in the initializer list have their peculiar-looking syntax—to allow for having a *class* object, with its constructor function arguments, in the list.

The syntax can be a little more complicated when one of the initializers is a class object. The initialization arguments for a class object can contain a list of its own constructor arguments (or none if you want—you can use a default constructor for the included object), as follows:

```
class X {
   int a, b, c;
public:
```

```
   X( int = 0, int = 0, int = 0 );
...
};
X::X( int arg1,arg2,arg3 ) : a(arg1),
                             b(arg2),
                             c(arg3)
{
...
}

class Y {
   int a, b, c;
public:
   Y( int = 0 , int = 0, int = 0 );
   X xobj; // no args here
...
};
Y::Y( int arg1,arg2,arg3 ) :
     xobj( arg1, arg2+3, arg3*2 )
{
...
}
```

In summary, you can do all the constructor argument jockeying you want. You just have to do it in the declaration part of the *containing class's constructor definition*.

The second thing you need to understand is how you can get to the various member functions. In the current example, the `billrecord` class contains a member function `printrep()`, and the contained object's class, `report`, contains a member function `display()`. That is, the `cust1` billing record object contains the `billrep` report object.

In line 86, the `main()` function calls the `cust1.printrep()` member function. This in turn calls the `billrep.display()` member function. Can you take a shortcut and go straight to the contained object's member function, bypassing the container class function? To do so, you would have to rewrite line 86, something like this:

```
   cust1.printrep.display( brec ); // INVALID !!!
```

An attempt to do this generates not one, but *two* compiler error messages. In the first place, there is no correct syntax to support such a shortcut: the compiler expects to see `printrep()` with its function-call arguments immediately following the function identifier. Writing `printrep.display...` implies that `printrep` is a structure—and the compiler has no idea what to make of that.

In the second place, the `report` class's `display()` member function expects a reference to the billing-record structure as its argument. The only available billing-record data is in the *private member declarations* of the `cust1` object. The structure cannot be accessed from `main()`—it is *private*. Hence the second compiler error.

What you should get from all this is a simple rule of thumb: When a class contains an object of another class, *the containing class is the sole manager of that object*. Outside functions communicate directly only with the containing class. This is perfectly in line with the philosophy of hiding complexity and encapsulation in C++.

Reusing Code by Inheritance

The other way of viewing objects is to consider them to be slightly different kinds of their parent objects. This perspective leads to the notion of *class inheritance*.

In C++, class inheritance is implemented in the syntax for declaring a *derived class* (subclass), in such a way that it inherits (almost) all the data and functions of its parent class: the *base class* (superclass). Figure 20.5 illustrates the concept of class inheritance.

Fig. 20.5. *Class inheritance means deriving a new class from an old one. The new class also has unique characteristics of its own.*

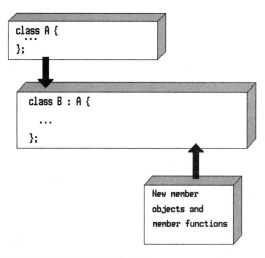

The idea is to provide a syntax such that the derived class *automatically* uses the functions (and the private data members, if you ask for them) of the base class, *unless you do something to change that*. This reuses the maximum amount of code with the least effort. The general syntax for writing base and derived classes is as follows:

```
class A { ... };        // the BASE class
...
class B : A { ... };   // the DERIVED class
```

The subclass B *inherits* the base class A. Does it inherit everything? No, there are exceptions. When a derived class is declared as in this sample syntax, it inherits the base class's member functions, *except* the constructor, destructor, and any defined operator=() (overloaded or redefined assign operator). These three things are assumed to be unique to each class, derived or not.

Furthermore, the sample syntax *does not allow inheritance of the private data members of the base class*. This makes sense—because the derived class applies to objects outside the base class, they are not automatically permitted access to encapsulated data. But there is a way around this. You can declare the base class to be public, in the derived class's declaration, and to inherit private data as well, as in the following example:

```
class A { ... };                    // the BASE class
...
class B : public A { ... };  // the DERIVED class
                // now inherits private data, too
```

This second form is the one you usually see and use.

What goes into the class declarations for the base and derived classes? At this level, *declare the base class just as you would if it were going to stand alone*. That includes private data members, constructors, destructors—the whole works.

When you do this, however, keep in mind that the *base class should define the most general case of object*. Derived classes inherit all the base class capability, and can add their own functionality to handle more specific cases. The conceptual result is a hierarchy of classes, with the most basic at the top of the tree and the most specific and detailed at the bottom.

What happens if the derived class contains a member having the same name as one in the base class? Running the following short program is instructive:

```
#include <stdlib.h>
#include <stdio.h>
#include <iostream.h>

class A {
  int a;
public:
  A() { a = 0; }
  void print() { cout << a << "\n"; }
};

class B : public A {
  int a;
public:
  B() { a = 255; }
  void print() { cout << a << "\n"; }
};

main()
{
  B myobj;

  myobj.print();      // displays 255
  myobj.A::print(); // displays 0
}
```

In this example, both the base class A and the derived class B feature a member function named `print()`. As you can see from the code in `main()`, you get access to the derived class's member function, unless you use the scope resolution operator `::` to override the specification.

Now it's time to see inheritance in context. Listing 20.7 shows the billing-record program, rewritten to use inheritance.

Listing 20.7. `inherit.cpp` *(Reusing code by inheritance (deriving new classes)).*   *Turbo C++*

```
 1   #include <stdlib.h>
 2   #include <stdio.h>
 3   #include <string.h>
 4   #include <iostream.h>              // introduce streams
 5
 6   #define INVOICE    0
 7   #define CREDITMEMO 1
 8             //
 9             // Define a general billing record format
10             //
11   typedef struct { // typedef for billing rec. data
12      int acctno;
13      char name[41];
14      double amt;
```

```
15  } billdata;
16              //
17              // Define a billing record BASE class
18              //
19  class billrecord {          // billing record class
20    billdata brec;
21  public:
22    billrecord( int = 0, char * = "",
23                double = 0 );
24    void print();
25  };
26
27  billrecord::billrecord( int bacct,
28                          char *bname,
29                          double bamt )
30  {
31    brec.acctno = bacct;
32    strcpy( brec.name, bname );
33    brec.amt = bamt;
34  }
35                  // base class report writer function
36  void billrecord::print()
37  {
38    cout << "Account number: " << brec.acctno
39         << "\n";
40    cout << "Customer Name: " << brec.name
41         << "\n";
42    cout << "Posted to your account: "
43         << brec.amt << "\n";
44  }
45          //
46          // define an invoice record DERIVED class
47          //
48  class invrecord : public billrecord {
49    char title[12];
50  public:
51    invrecord( int = 0, char * = "", double = 0 );
52    void report();
53  };
54
55  invrecord::invrecord( int bacct,
56                        char *bname, double bamt ) :
57                  billrecord( bacct, bname, bamt )
58  {
59    strcpy( title, "Invoice" );
60  }
61
62  void invrecord::report()
63  {
64    cout << title << "-----\n\n";
65    print();                          // it's easy, now!
```

Listing 20.7. continues

Listing 20.7. continued

```
66   }
67          //
68          // define a credit memo record DERIVED class
69          //
70   class credrecord : public billrecord {
71     char title[12];
72   public:
73     credrecord( int = 0, char * = "", double = 0 );
74     void report();
75   };
76
77   credrecord::credrecord( int bacct,
78                           char *bname, double bamt ) :
79            billrecord( bacct, bname, bamt *= -1 )
80   {
81     strcpy( title, "Credit Memo" );
82   }
83
84   void credrecord::report()
85   {
86     cout << title << "-----\n\n";
87     print();                        // it's easy, now!
88   }
89
90   main()
91   {
92     char nm[41] = "Smith, J.D.";
93     credrecord cust1( 9939, nm, 125.55 );
94
95     cust1.report();
96   }
```

In listing 20.7, things are arranged much as before, except that billrecord is now a base class, and there are two derived classes, invrecord and credrecord. The base class has a member function print() with which the generic billing record can display all its data except the title. Each of the derived classes has a report() member function, which provides the title for the unique cases. The *derivedclass*:report() functions then call the *baseclass*:print() member functions for detailed reporting.

Notice that the derived classes declare the bare minimum necessary to differentiate them from the base class. Otherwise, the base class is permitted to handle as much of the required function as possible. One advantage of this is that writing the derived class declarations is often very quick and fairly easy.

The base class billrecord constructor has arguments, just as before. The base class also declares all the private data members; the derived classes do not. Given that information, notice how the constructor function declaration part for the derived classes is written in the following code:

```
credrecord::credrecord( int bacct,
                    char *bname, double bamt ) :
        billrecord( bacct, bname, bamt *= -1 )
{
...
}
```

The arguments for the derived class are once more followed by a colon and a constructor initialization list. This time, however, the constructor call in the initialization list is preceded, not by an object name, but by the *base class name*.

In older versions of C++, it was not necessary to use the base class name in the constructor call. Current compilers still support such a declaration without the base class name, when only single inheritance is being implemented (there is only *one* base class). You should get in the habit of writing the base class name, though, because it is required when implementing *multiple inheritance* (the derived class inherits from more than one base class).

Extending Class Capability with Virtual Functions

C++ *virtual functions* provide the facility of *polymorphism*, literally "different forms" of the same function when inherited by a derived class. Such functions are *virtual* because the selection of the correct copy of the function is transparent to the outside caller of the function.

This is not the same as overloading functions in the same class, although there are similarities. Overloaded and virtual functions are alike in that each allows several different declarations of a single function name, and each function may have different arguments.

Virtual functions go beyond overloading, however. First, you can have a function of exactly the same name, arguments, and return type in a derived class as in the base class. With virtual functions, you can use the scope resolution operator to get to the base class copy, as you saw in the last section, whereas this is illegal (and pointless) for overloaded functions. Second, you can change the arguments, or both the arguments and the return type, but not just the return type of the function in the derived class. Calls to that member-function name are sorted out by the compiler, based on the combination of arguments and return type, and the correct one selected.

The point of having virtual functions is to provide a way to write a function name that can be used in the base class *and* its derived classes, but to keep the user from having to decide which one to select. The classic example of a virtual function is a `draw()` function for geometric shapes (base class `shape`), where the logistics of `draw()` varies for each kind of shape (classes `point`, `circle`, `square`, etc.). All the user needs to know is that he or she has a shape and wants to `draw()` it.

You declare a function as virtual by using the `virtual` specifier keyword in front of the function declaration, as follows:

```
class A {
   int idata;
public:  // declare a virtual function
   virtual int getdata( int );
};
...
int A::getdata( int delta) { return data+delta; }
...
class B : public A {
   double ddata
public:  // the virtual function in the derived class
   double getdata( double );
};
...
double B::getdata( double delta )
    { return ddata+delta; }
...
main()
{              // demonstrate detection of correct function
   int change1;
   double change2;
   B obj1;        // declare derived class object
                        // call derived class getdata()
   cout << "Integer change is " << obj1.getdata( change1 );
                        // now call base class getdata()
   cout << "Double change is " << obj1.getdata( change2 );
}
```

In this code fragment, the declaration of `getdata()` in the derived class does not have the `virtual` keyword; this is optional. The function is presumed to be virtual anyway, because it was inherited from a declared virtual function. That means that you can use a subclass as a superclass, and derive other subclasses from it.

We rewrote the billing-record class program once more, implementing the reporting function with a single function name, `print()`. Listing 20.8 shows the result.

Listing 20.8. `vinherit.cpp` *(Reusing code by inheritance, and extending class capability with virtual functions).*   Turbo C++

```
1   #include <stdlib.h>
2   #include <stdio.h>
3   #include <string.h>
4   #include <iostream.h>              // introduce streams
5
6   #define INVOICE     0
7   #define CREDITMEMO 1
8           //
9           // Define a general billing record format
10          //
11  typedef struct { // typedef for billing rec. data
12    int acctno;
13    char name[41];
14    double amt;
15  } billdata;
16          //
17          // Define a billing record BASE class
18          //
19  class billrecord {          // billing record class
20    billdata brec;
21  public:
22    billrecord( int = 0, char * = "",
23                double = 0 );
24    virtual void print(); // VIRTUAL FUNCTION
25  };
26
27  billrecord::billrecord( int bacct,
28                          char *bname,
29                          double bamt )
30  {
31    brec.acctno = bacct;
32    strcpy( brec.name, bname );
33    brec.amt = bamt;
34  }
35              // base class report writer function
36  void billrecord::print()
37  {
38    cout << "Account number: " << brec.acctno
39         << "\n";
40    cout << "Customer Name: " << brec.name
41         << "\n";
42    cout << "Posted to your account: "
43         << brec.amt << "\n";
44  }
45          //
46          // define an invoice record DERIVED class
47          //
```

Listing 20.8. *continues*

Listing 20.8. *continued*

```
48   class invrecord : public billrecord {
49     char title[12];
50   public:
51     invrecord( int = 0, char * = "", double = 0 );
52     void print();
53   };
54
55   invrecord::invrecord( int bacct,
56                         char *bname, double bamt ) :
57                    billrecord( bacct, bname, bamt )
58   {
59     strcpy( title, "Invoice" );
60   }
61
62   void invrecord::print()
63   {
64     cout << title << "-----\n\n";
65     billrecord::print();
66   }
67       //
68       // define a credit memo record DERIVED class
69       //
70   class credrecord : public billrecord {
71     char title[12];
72   public:
73     credrecord( int = 0, char * = "", double = 0 );
74     virtual void print();
75   };
76
77   credrecord::credrecord( int bacct,
78                           char *bname, double bamt ) :
79              billrecord( bacct, bname, bamt *= -1 )
80   {
81     strcpy( title, "Credit Memo" );
82   }
83
84   void credrecord::print()
85   {
86     cout << title << "-----\n\n";
87     billrecord::print();
88   }
89
90   main()
91   {
92     char nm[41] = "Smith, J.D.";
93     credrecord cust1( 9939, nm, 125.55 );
94
95     cust1.print();
96   }
```

In this case, `print()` has exactly the same arguments and return type in both the base and derived classes. Yet both functions are used to generate the billing report. How is that done? You can see the answer in lines 65 and 87. After each derive class `print()` has printed the correct title for its report, the base class `print()` function is invoked by using the scope resolution operator: `billrecord::print()`. This variation on using virtual functions to select the correct operation is not common, but is quite handy when you need it.

C++ Stream I/O

You are already familiar, from standard C, with the notion of *streams*. C++ streams include all that C streams imply, and more—C++ streams are class objects. To use C++ streams, you `#include` the header for them. The precise name of the header may vary from one compiler to the next. Zortech's header is `stream.hpp`, and Turbo C++'s is `iostream.h`.

C++ stream I/O can be simple or complex, depending on what you do with it. How C++ streams behave also depends greatly on whether you are using an older C++ compiler (compatible with AT&T 1.2 or earlier) or a newer one such as Turbo C++ (which is AT&T 2.0 compatible).

C++ streams have changed a good deal since early releases of C++ compilers, particularly in their internals. This is not terribly surprising. The original streams were weak and awkward, and needed considerable tweaking. Current implementations are no longer weak. Each C++ user must decide for him- or herself whether they are still awkward.

Because there are considerable differences in implementations of old and new streams, and those differences are sometimes quite technical, we avoid them in this brief introduction to C++. The usage of C++ streams seen here is basic and should work with any C++ compiler compatible with version 2.0.

Reading and Writing with *cin* and *cout*

In C++, as in standard C, no provision for input and output is built into the compiler. Also like standard C, standard libraries (though not yet *ANSI* standard) provide for such things.

The C++ standard stream library provides for many kinds of operations, but we discuss only two: the `cin` and `cout` predefined stream objects.

`cin` and `cout` are connected to `stdin` and `stdout`, respectively. They perform I/O functions done in standard C with `puts()`, `gets()`, `printf()`, `scanf()`, and their related functions. The basic mechanisms for using `cin` and `cout` are the overloaded operators `<<` (for `cout`) and `>>` (for `cin`). The `<<` operator for `cout` is called an *inserter*, because it inserts data into the output stream. The `>>` operator for `cin` is called an *extractor*, because it extracts data from the input stream. They look like this in context:

```
int a:
...
cin >> a;  // data flows INTO the variable
cout << a; // data flows OUT OF the variable
```

Of course, integers are not the only thing that can be processed by `cin` and `cout`. `cout` can handle signed and unsigned characters, signed and unsigned short integers, signed and unsigned integers, signed and unsigned longs, `char *` pointers to string (for outputting a whole string), floats, doubles, long doubles, and `void *` for dumping pointers in hex. `cout` generates *no* automatic padding or whitespace to separate output items—you must handle that yourself.

`cin`, as described so far, *does* automatically skip whitespace in the input stream. `cin` recognizes (in the input stream) *display* formats of the integer, float, and character constants as described for `cout` (that is, constants as you would write them in your source code). Because `cin` skips whitespace, you cannot input a text stream character-by-character, unless you do something else about it (you learn what you must do in the next section).

The inserter and extractor operators are defined so that they return a reference to the `iostream`. This means that you can "string things together," much like the expression a = b = c. This syntactical arrangement is called *cascading*. Listing 20.9 shows what we mean by that.

It is important for you to understand that inserters and extractors, when cascaded, don't behave like the assignment operator. That is, line 13 in listing 20.9 doesn't mean that a value is read from the input stream and then successively assigned to a, b, c, and d. What it *does* mean is that whitespace is skipped, a is extracted from the stream, whitespace is skipped, b is extracted from the stream, and so on.

Listing 20.9. `cinout.cpp` *(Input and output using the predefined* `cin` *and* `cout` *streams).*   *Turbo C++*

```
1   #include <stdlib.h>
2   #include <iostream.h>  // Turbo C++ stream header
3
4   main()
5   {
6      int a, b, c, d;
7
8      cout << "Enter an integer number: ";
9      cin >> a;
10     cout << a << '\n';
11
12     cout << "Enter 4 integers, separated by whitespace: ";
13     cin >> a >> b >> c >> d;
14
15     cout << "Dumping all the variables:\n";
16     cout << a << ' ' << b << ' '
17          << c << ' ' << d << '\n';
18
19     cout << "Hex dumping all the variables:\n";
20     cout << hex << a << ' ' << hex << b << ' '
21          << hex << c << ' ' << hex << d << '\n';
22  }
```

You should notice a couple of other things in listing 20.9. First, note that blank characters are inserted in the `cout` stream to provide separation of the output items. Remember—that is a manual operation. You must do it. You can take advantage of that fact to insert newline characters and other formatting characters.

Second, note the token `hex` in lines 20 and 21. This is called a *manipulator*. The manipulator's job is to perform a format conversion on the data being inserted in the output stream. The expression `cout << hex << a`, for example, means that `a` is first converted to a hex display format (like the `%x` conversion of `printf()`), and the resulting character string is inserted in the output stream. Version 2.0 compilers sport a number of useful manipulators. The manipulators supported by Turbo C++ are shown in Table 20.1.

Table 20.1. *Turbo C++ stream manipulators*

Manipulator (arg)	Use	Description
dec	ostr<<dec istr>>dec	Set decimal conversion base
hex	ostr<<hex istr>>hex	Set hex conversion base
oct	ostr<<oct istr>>oct	Set octal conversion base
ws	istr>>ws	Extract white space
endl	ostr<<endl	Insert newline and flush
ends	ostr<<ends	Insert '\0'
flush	ostr<<flush	Flush stream
setbase(int)	ostr<<setbase(n)	Set conversion base to 0,8,10,16
resetiosflags(long)	istr>>resetiosflags(n) ostr<<resetiosflags(n)	Reset ios flags given in n
setiosflags(long)	istr>>setiosflags(n) ostr<<setiosflags(n)	Set ios flags given in n
setfill(int)	istr>>setfill(n) ostr<<setfill(n)	Set fill char to n
setprecision(int)	istr>>setprecision(n) ostr<<setprecision(n)	Set floating-point precision to n digits
setw(int)	istr>>setw(n) ostr<<setw(n)	Set field width to n

Mixing Input and Output Streams

You can mix `cin` and `cout` in the same statement, if you you go about it carefully. You could copy an input stream directly to an output stream, for example. Stroustrup shows a copy loop that looks like this:

```
while (cin >> z) cout << z << "\n";
```

The problem with this loop is that it can't handle whitespace. If z is a `char`, then it is impossible to read blanks, and the loop produces just one character per physical line. If z is a pointer, `char *`, it results in one token (a "word", if you like) per line. To get a true character-image copy, you must do something like the program shown in listing 20.10.

Listing 20.10. `mixstr.cpp` *(Combining input and output in the same statement, with character I/O).*   *Turbo C++*

```
1   #include <stdlib.h>
2   #include <stdio.h>
3   #include <iostream.h>
4
5   main()      // Character-based copy program
6               // Note that cin uses stdin which is
7               // normally line buffered with this
8               // compiler. If I/O is not redirected,
9               // you get multiple echoes on screen.
10  {
11    unsigned char k = ' ';
12    cout << "Type something until you are tired of it,\n"
13         << "then strike Ctl-Z or F6 to emulate EOF.\n";
14    while( cin.get(k) ) cout << k;
15  }
```

Clearly, `get()` is a member function of `cin`. This member function reads a stream one character at a time, *including* whitespace.

I/O Redirection and Streams

We said that `cin` and `cout` are connected to `stdin` and `stdout`. The implication, of course, is that `cin` and `cout` can be redirected. That is correct. For example, you can run the program `mixstr` in listing 20.10 with no command-line parameters; input is gotten from the keyboard, and placed on the screen. Or you can redirect input from a text file, with the result being a `type` command-replacement utility. Finally, you can redirect both input and output, and have a text-file copy utility.

Summary

This chapter covered four topics of some importance to C++ programming. You learned about the free store, static and dynamic objects, class derivation and inheritance, and were introduced to C++ streams:

❑ *The C++ free store is the way that C++ handles the C heap.* This is where space for dynamic objects (class and otherwise) is allocated. One of the most important things you should have learned from this discussion is how to redefine `operator new()` and `operator delete()`, what that means for writing your constructor and destructor functions, and how it makes assigning values to `this` an obsolete practice.

❑ *Scoping for static and dynamic class objects is also a matter of some critical importance.* You need to know when and how both constructors and destructors are invoked, and when you need to invoke the destructor manually. You also need to understand the implications for object duration and accessibility from other objects.

❑ *Class derivation and inheritance are the C++ way of reusing code, which means that you don't have to rewrite it.* Inheritance plus virtual functions is an especially powerful technique for managing extremely complex objects. And don't forget that you can reuse code also by composing objects from other objects.

❑ *Finally, C++ streams provide an easy way to send messages to the console and get simple input from the keyboard.* Although C++ streams have evolved to the point that a complete mastery of them may take a little time, their major use is still console display and keyboard input.

Frankly, this chapter has bombarded you with a great deal of new material. If it hasn't settled to the bottom yet, you may want to let it simmer a while, and perhaps review some, before going on to the next chapter. Remember —we warned you! The price of power is at least some complexity. And C++ is extremely powerful—the wonder is that it is no more complex than it is.

21

More on C++
Methods and Objects

C ++ is a tremendously *flexible* language. What makes C++ so powerful and flexible? There are many contributing factors, among them the
two things we discuss in this chapter: C++ *references* and *overloading*.

References, like pointers, deal with address values — but they do it with
a difference. Declaring a reference to an object (class or ordinary) simplifies
life quite a bit when you're writing expressions involving that object.
References, in short, provide a syntax that simplifies dereferencing the object pointed to.

Overloading is the process of defining something more than once. You
can overload functions and most operators, but not data or class objects.
What does overloading do for you? It allows you to write functions and
operators, the meaning of which is dependent on *context*. Based on arguments and operands actually used, the compiler takes over the job of
deciding *which* function, or *which* operator, you mean to use. This is a *very*
powerful concept — as you will see later in this chapter.

Pointers and References in C++

Both pointers and references deal with the addresses of objects. Both are necessary. In fact, the existence of references implies that a pointer is at work behind the scenes (which is the case).

What is the great difference between pointers and references? Just that, to access the object located by the address value, you must *dereference a pointer* but *not a reference*. Now, we'll see how that concept is implemented in C++.

The Reference Operator

Because the reference operator deals with addresses of objects, it makes sense that the reference operator is an overload of the address-of operator &. The compiler can tell the difference between the two operators by noting the context in which an operator is used.

To develop an understanding of references, we begin with a review of pointer syntax and see how reference syntax grows out of it. Here, for example, is the way you declare a pointer as a function argument:

```
void myfunc( char *s )
{
  if ( *s == 'A' || *s == 'a' ) {
    puts( "I got an 'A'!" );
  }
  ...
}
```

That is simple enough. The dereference operator, when used in the declaration part or prototype of a function (or in its original declaration, for that matter), means "you have to dereference to get to the actual object." When used in a function body, it means "don't treat this identifier as an lvalue; go get what it points to."

Simple, indeed. But what if the object pointed to is a structure? (Remember, C++ classes are basically structures at heart, and structure reference syntax applies to them just as it does to ordinary structures in standard C.) Structures make it just a little more difficult to access member variables, because now you need the structure pointer operator like this:

```
typedef struct {
  int a, b, c;
} sometype;
...
main()
{
  sometype *mystruct;
  ...
  mystruct = malloc( sizeof( sometype ) );
  mystruct->a = 0;
  mystruct->b = 1;
  mystruct->c = 2;
  ...
}
```

That's still not so bad. It is nice and clean, and is familiar to you — it may even make intuitive sense to you by now.

But now we must start moving toward the technology required to implement C++ class objects. Class objects don't contain nice simple integers only. Remember the `cminus.c` program in Chapter 18 (listing 18.1)? Look back and refresh your memory on how function pointers are stored — and then used — within the ordinary structure mimicking a class. It's not so easy any more, is it?

When you deal with complex C++ programs, you may face having to cope with arrays of class objects, a pointer to an array of class objects, an array of pointers to class objects, and so on. And each of these class objects contains (implicitly) pointers to the member functions, as well as containing other member objects that may be just as complicated. Some assistance is needed in controlling the explosion of dereferencing operators, grouping parentheses, structure pointer operators, and all the rest.

The answer to simplifying all this complexity is the *reference operator* &. When Bjarne Stroustrup made the design decision to make the address-of operator do double-duty, it was one of those decisions whose very simplicity has the mark of genius. For the following example, we rewrote the preceding code fragment again, adding a function that must access the structure and using a reference to do so:

```
//
// C++ version of structure handling
//
typedef struct {
  int a, b, c;
} sometype;
```

```
...
int getsum( sometype &s )    // arg is a reference
{
  return s.a + s.b + s.c;    // no -> op !
}
...
main()
{
  sometype *mystruct;   // still a pointer here
  ...
  mystruct = new sometype;
  mystruct->a = 0;
  mystruct->b = 1;
  mystruct->c = 2;
          // the function calls for a reference,
          // and references always BIND TO OBJECTS,
          // NOT addresses, so ...
  printf( "The sum is: %d\n", getsum( *mystruct ) );
  ...
}
```

This short piece of code shows all the basic techniques you need to implement references in your C++ programs. First of all, note that mystruct is still a pointer. That is your first rule of thumb: *the original declaration of a pointer* is *a pointer*, not a reference. At this point in the code, it would be illegal to write the following:

```
sometype &mystruct;   // WRONG!
```

The reason for this is also your second rule of thumb: *references always bind (refer to) objects, never pointers or addresses*. This is in keeping with the desire for a syntax where you, the programmer, are largely freed from the task of dereferencing addresses to objects. The first and immediate benefit is a relief from a tedious chore — keeping up with and writing dereference operators for pointers and address-of operators for objects. The second benefit is more subtle, but correspondingly more important. It reduces the possibility of making a nearly invisible, hard-to-find error.

This second rule of thumb reveals why the previous statement is in error. Because references always bind to objects, this statement says that there already exists an object mystruct, and there emphatically does *not* exist any such object, yet. Alternatively, you could view this as saying, "Take the address of mystruct." The very fact that there are multiple ways of interpreting this statement is the first and best clue that it is in error.

The third rule of thumb derives directly from the second, and involves knowing where you can code the reference operator. You write the reference operator to describe a *formal function parameter*, or to describe a *return type* (not object). For example, the function prototype:

```
mystruct &myfunc( mystruct &astruct );
```

means that `myfunc()` receives an argument that is the address of a structure and *is to be treated like an object, not a pointer*; and returns the address of a structure (the same or another) *which is also to be treated like an object, not a pointer*. Now, did you notice how many times the term "address of" was just used? If so, you are beginning to understand why the address-of operator was overloaded to perform this task.

Finally, the last rule of thumb is this: if you use the `&` operator anywhere else (if it is not an error), it is treated as the original address-of operator, and used to take the address of something, resulting in a pointer.

Now you have the background to understand the remainder of the code fragment. Notice, in the following line, how the argument to `getsum()` is formed:

```
printf( "The sum is: %d\n", getsum( *mystruct ) );
```

References always bind to *objects*; because `mystruct` is a *pointer*, you must dereference it this one time to get things rolling. After that, you may refer to the structure (or class) members as if no pointer were involved, while within the called function. Of course there is a pointer involved, behind the scenes, but the compiler is handling all those details for you now. Using a referenced *object* as a function argument would also have permitted you simply to write the following:

```
printf( "The sum is: %d\n", getsum( mystruct ) );
```

Defining Pointers to Objects

Now we apply to class objects what you have learned about references. Anticipating an example later in this chapter, here is part of the class declaration, and one of the member functions, for a class `vli` (meaning *very large integer*):

```
class vli {    // Very Large Integer class
   unsigned int *vdata;
   int vlioflow; // overflow indicator
   int vliuflow; // underflow indicator
public:
...
   vli &operator+( vli & );    // define addition
...
};
...
vli &vli::operator+( vli &addend )    // addition
{
```

```
unsigned long x, y;
unsigned carry = 0;
int i;
static vli SUM;

SUM = 0;
for ( i=0; i<8; ++i ) {
  x = vdata[i]; y=addend.vdata[i];
  x += y + carry; // add with carry
  SUM.vdata[i] = x & 0x0000FFFF;      // partial
  carry = (unsigned)( x >> 16 );   // save carry
}
if ( carry ) SUM.vlioflow = 1;
else SUM.vlioflow = 0;
return SUM;
}
```

Because vli is supposed to be a (new) class of numbers, what we are doing here is overloading the + operator. That means that we are defining addition for objects of this class.

Now here is a very short program that uses this class and this member function to sum two vli numbers. The only catch is that one of the vli "variables" is an object, and the other is a *pointer*, initialized by new:

```
#include "vli.hpp"

main()
{
  vli X;                    // static object
  vli *Y = new vli;         // dynamic object

  X = "4294967295";         // give'em values
  *Y = "4294967295";
  X = X + *Y;               // add'em up
  printf( "Big number is %s\n", (char *)X );
}
```

When this program is run, it produces the following output:

```
Big number is 8589934590
```

which is, of course, the correct answer to the addition problem.

But notice the statement X = X + *Y;. Why is it written like this? Naturally, the design of vli::operator+() is meant to allow you to write what appear to be normal expressions combining vli objects. If you look at the function-declaration part of the vli::operator+() member function, you see that it expects to both receive as a parameter, and return as a value, a *reference* to a vli class object — vli &. Thus the operands of + must always be objects, never pointers.

But how does that affect the code within the `vli::operator+()` member function? It allows this member function to be *coded only one way*, and still manipulate objects directly, as well as manipulate objects that are only pointed to. That is, specifying `vli&` as the type of argument expected, the member function is always passed the address of an object (behind the scenes), and the C++ compiler allows the function to always refer to arguments as if directly — with *no* structure qualifier for private data within `*this`, and only the structure operator (`.`) for private data within `addend`. To be consistent (and for other reasons) the function also returns a reference to a `vli` object.

When calling a member function of a class located by a pointer, you use the structure pointer operator, just as you would for any other structure, as follows:

```
class SP {
  ...
public:
  int sfunc() { return 37; }
  ...
};

main()
{
  SP *s = new SP;
  int x;

  x = s->sfunc();
}
```

Passing Objects as Parameters

Writing C++ programs means that you frequently will pass objects as arguments to functions (member functions and ordinary functions). When you do, you should remember that a class is a structure, and that using the identifier of a structure does *not* result in an address value, as it does with an array identifier.

This is just another reason to be sure that you always pass a *reference* to a class object, and not the object itself. The following short program makes that mistake, with predictable results:

```
#include <stdlib.h>
#include <stdio.h>
#include <iostream.h>
```

```
class OP {
  int DataValue;
public:
  OP() { DataValue = 37; }
  void listit();
  friend void ChangeIt( OP ); // declare friend function
};

void OP::listit()
{
  cout << "The value of DataValue is " << DataValue;
}
              // Here is the friend function definition

void ChangeIt( OP SomeOP ) // Notice, not a reference
{
  SomeOP.DataValue = 64;
}

main()
{
  OP a; // default constructor sets DataValue to 37

  ChangeIt( a ); // now call friend function
  a.listit();    // show the result
}
```

When you run this program as is, you receive the following message on `stdout`:

```
The value of DataValue is 37
```

Nothing whatever changed in the `OP` class object a, because nothing but a *copy* of the object was passed to the friend function.

A *friend function* is usually an ordinary function, that is specifically granted access to the private data and function members of objects for that class. The following is an example of the correct way to declare a friend function:

```
class OP {   // DEFINE A FRIEND FUNCTION CORRECTLY
  int DataValue;
public:
  OP() { DataValue = 37; }
  void listit();
  friend void ChangeIt( OP & ); // declare friend function
};
...
void ChangeIt( OP &SomeOP ) // Notice, not a reference
{
  SomeOP.DataValue = 64;
}
```

A friend function must have a reference to an object of the target class, if it is to gain access to a particular object. That is, even though there is a `friend` declaration in the class granting access, the friend function is not a *member* function. It therefore has no `this` pointer, and needs to be told *which* object to work on.

You can declare a friend function by writing the declaration *anywhere* within the class granting access. Even if the `friend` declaration is listed among the private data and function members of a class, the friend function itself is *not* private — it is not a member *per se* and therefore cannot be made private.

Referencing Other Objects

Can the member functions of one class access objects of other classes? Of other objects of the same class? Yes, they can, but you must observe not only ordinary scoping rules, but also class scoping rules, as follows:

❏ *If a class has not yet been declared, you cannot refer to objects of that class.* This is just like the scoping rules for ordinary objects in standard C. However, as shown in the following example, you can forward declare classes, much as you can write function prototypes:

```
class one; // forward declare class one
class two{
  ...
public:
  ...
  void do_something( two &, one & );
  ...
};

class one { // now finish the class declaration
  ...
public:
  ...
};
```

Now the member function `two::do_something()` can access the *public* data and function members of class `one` objects. Because this function is not a friend, however, private data and functions of class `one` objects are still invisible to class `two` member functions.

❑ *Because member functions of a class are called on behalf of specific objects of that class, a member function can declare an object of that same class, as follows:*

```
class one {
   int priv_data;
public:
   ...
   int sum_it();
   ...
};

int one::sum_it()
{
   one otherobj; // declare obj of same class locally
   ...             // manipulate otherobj somehow
   return priv_data + otherobj.privdata;
}
```

In this code fragment, the member function declares an object of the same class. That object has local scope (is destroyed when the member function returns). In the meantime, the member function has access to both private and public members of otherobj, because it is of the same class.

❑ *A member function may also either be passed a reference to, or locally declare, an object of another class (provided that the other class has been fully or forward declared).* In either case, the member function has access only to the public members of objects of the other class.

❑ *Member functions may serve as friend functions of another class.* Indeed, you may declare *all* the member functions as friends of another class.

To declare a member function as a friend of another class, you grant it access in the other class's declaration, as follows:

```
class two ;

class one {
   ...
public:
   ...
   void function_one( two & );
   ...
};

class two {
   ...
```

```
        public:
    ...
    friend void one::function_one();
    ...
};
```

Notice how the class name and scope resolution operator are used in the *granting* class's declaration to identify which member function in the other class is the friend.

To declare *all* the member functions of another class as friends, you write the `friend` keyword followed by the class name of the other class, as in the following example:

```
class one { ... };

class two {
...
    friend one;
};
```

❏ *Class friendship is not transitive, but can be inherited.* Thus if A is a friend of B, and B is a friend of C, this does *not* mean that A is a friend of C.

Class friendship is inherited, however. If B is a friend of A, and C is derived from A, then B *is* a friend of C.

❏ *If B is derived from A, then all members of A by default become private members of B.* If the `public` keyword is used in the base list, as follows:

```
class A { ... };
class B : public A { ... };
```

Then the public members of A are public members of B and protected members of A become protected members of B. However, in all circumstances, private members of A remain private to A (not B).

❏ *If members of a class are declared* `protected` *in a base class, those members are accessible to member functions and friends of derived classes, but only in objects of the derived type.* Note that even when you use the `public` keyword in a base list, the private members of the base class remain private to it, unless you explicitly declare `friend` functions in the base class granting access.

Overloading Functions

C++ allows you to write multiple definitions of both functions and operators. This is called *overloading* and, as you know, is something we have already mentioned several times.

Because you are responsible for "teaching the compiler" how to deal with user-defined types (classes), being able to overload functions and operators is important. Not only does this capability permit you to define what should happen to your objects, it permits you to define what should happen in multiple circumstances and contexts. We mentioned the concept of overloading earlier, but only briefly. Now, you get the details. We look first at how you go about overloading functions.

For historical reasons and for background on the subject, you should know that older versions of C++ required you to declare function names that were to be overloaded. Listing 21.1 shows a program that overloads an ordinary function definition, using an older copy of the Zortech C++ compiler.

Listing 21.1. `ovloadf.cpp` *(Function overloading using older compiler version).*
Zortech C++ 1.07

```
1    #include <stdlib.h>
2    #include <stream.hpp>
3
4    overload show_var;
5    void show_var( int );
6    void show_var( double );
7
8    void show_var( int arg )
9    {
10       cout << "This is an integer argument: " << arg << "\n";
11   }
12
13   void show_var( double arg )
14   {
15       cout << "This is a double float argument: " << arg << "\n";
16   }
17
18   main()
19   {
20       int i = 2;
21       double x = 3.1415926;
22
```

```
23    show_var( i );
24    show_var( x );
25  }
26
```

Line 4 declares that the function show_var() is to be overloaded, using the (now obsolete) overload keyword. Lines 5 and 6 give the function prototypes (plural) for the function (singular).

How does the compiler know which version of the function to invoke? For example, lines 23 and 24 both call show_var(), with the obvious intent of invoking a different version each time. The C++ compiler detects the difference by *examining the arguments for the function call*. Then these arguments are matched (once more, at compile time) against the formal parameter declarations to determine which copy of show_var() to invoke.

This leads directly to the next rule of function overloading: you can *vary the arguments*, and you can vary *both the arguments and the return type*, but you *cannot vary only the return type* of an overloaded function. If the compiler checks arguments as the primary means of detecting the difference between two versions of an overloaded function, and the argument lists are the same, the compiler cannot determine which version to use. Hence, you must alter the argument list if you want to change the return type.

It was a very short step from providing overloaded function support at all to automating the process. The overload keyword is now obsolete, and should not be used. Your current compiler may still allow it (only to ignore it), but you should expect that at some future time, the overload keyword is flagged as an error. Listing 21.2 shows how to overload an ordinary function with version 2.0 compatible compilers.

Listing 21.2. multif.cpp *(Function overloading using newer versions of the C++ compiler. The* overload *keyword is now obsolete.)*

Turbo C++

```
1   #include <stdlib.h>
2   #include <stdio.h>
3
4   void f1( int arg )
5   {
6      printf( "Integer value %d\n", arg );
7   }
8
9   void f1( double arg )
10  {
```

Listing 21.2. continues

```
11      printf( "Floating point value %lf\n", arg );
12    }
13
14    main()
15    {
16      f1( 3 );
17      f1( 3.1415926 );
18    }
19
```

Overloading Member Functions

Member functions of a class can be overloaded. Indeed, this is the primary purpose of the facility. You just need to observe the rules for changing argument lists and return types, as you would for ordinary functions, as shown in the following code fragment:

```
class A {
  int a_value:
public:
  ... // functions are very short, use inline
  int getit() { return a_value; }
  long getit() { return (long)a_value; }
  double getit() { return (double)a_value; }
};
```

Overloading Friend Functions

Although friend functions are not members of a class, they can be overloaded. The same rules still apply, except that it isn't possible to declare a friend function in-line. Here is an example of overloading friend functions:

```
class A {
  int a_value:
public:
  ... // functions are very short, use inline
friend int getit();
friend long getit();
friend double getit();
};

int getit() { return a_value; }
long getit() { return (long)a_value; }
double getit() { return (double)a_value; }
```

Overloading Operators

When you declare a class, establishing a true user-defined type (not just the synonym facility of standard C), the compiler assumes nothing whatever about the operations that can be performed on objects of that class. If you don't define those operations, they aren't available.

To define the operations that can be performed on your class objects, you must *overload the operators that you want to have apply to the class*. We say "overload," even though it seems that you are defining them for the class for the first time, because they already exist at the global level.

What Can Be Overloaded?

You heard it correctly: most of the standard C operator set can be overloaded (defined for class objects). *You cannot invent your own operators*; you can only apply existing ones to your class.

That is not a terrible restriction, however, when you think of the power inherent in the C operator set. The following list shows the C operators that can be overloaded.

```
[]   ()        ->    ++    --    &     *     +     -     ~

!    sizeof          /     %     <<    >>    <     >     <=

>=   ==        !=    ^     |     &&    ||    =     *=    /=

%=   +=        -=    <<=   >>=   &=    ^=    |=    ,
```

The ternary operator (?:) and the structure operator (.) cannot be overloaded. Additionally, the following three operators, which are specific to C++, cannot be overloaded: :: (scope resolution), .* (member dereference, structure container), and ->* (member dereference, pointer to structure container). Finally, the # stringizing operator, and the ## token pasting "operators" are used only by the preprocessor.

To overload an operator, you use the `operator` keyword when declaring a member function to provide that service. The general syntax for doing this is as follows:

```
class classname {
...
public:
...
returntype operator op ( [type [,type]] );
...
};
...
returntype classname::operator op ( [arg [,arg]] ) {
   ... // handle the operation
}
```

Replace the *op* placeholder with the actual operator you want to overload. The whitespace around it is optional. The number of arguments specified depends on two things: whether the operator is a unary or binary operator; and whether the operator function is a nonstatic member function or a nonmember (friend) function.

Consider first the case in which the operator function is a nonstatic member function (the nonstatic attribute is required here). If the operator is *unary*, there must be no arguments. Use of a unary operator is interpreted as a call to

```
obj.operator op ();
```

and the operator function works directly on `*this`. If the operator is *binary*, there must be *one* argument. Use of the binary operator is interpreted as a call to

```
obj.operator op ( otherobj );
```

and the operator works on a combination of `*this` and `*otherobj`. Incidentally, if you define a unary operator function (member of friend) it is impossible in the operator function body to determine whether the operator was prefix or postfix. In general, `*this` refers to the left operand, and `*otherobj` to the right, but this depends on the grouping and associativity of the operator.

To help you understand what all this means, look at the declarations for a hypothetical class of numeric object A. In the following code fragment, two operators are overloaded: addition + and unary increment ++. Nonstatic member functions are used. You would write the declarations something like this:

```
class A {
  long value; // holds the value of the object
  ...          // other private members
public:
  ...
  A& operator++();
  A& operator+( A& );
  ...
};
...
A& A::operator++()
{
  ++value;        // works only on *this
  return *this; // return reference to self
}
A A::operator+( A& otherA )
{
  A SUM; // you will understand this shortly
         // also assumes that = has been overloaded
  SUM = value + otherA.value;
  return SUM;
}
```

Before we explain why we coded the statement `A SUM;` in the `operator+()` function, we are going to talk for a moment about references, arguments, and return types.

First, when the operator function should modify the contents of `*this`, return a reference; when it should not, return an *object* (by value). Thus, in the preceding example, the ++ operator returns a reference, and the + operator returns an object by value. That is, because a reference serves as an *object locator*, the result of an operation can serve as an lvalue in subsequent evaluation of an expression involving your classes.

But if an operator associates operands right to left, it doesn't matter whether you return a reference or an object value (if you aren't considering performance). For example, consider the process of simple assignment for the hypothetical class A, as follows:

```
A x, y, z;   // declare objects of class A
...
x = y = z = 10;
```

This last expression assumes that assignment has been overloaded a couple of different ways — assignment from an integer, as well as from another object of class A. The point, however, is that if the `operator=()` functions don't return a reference, the expression still is evaluated correctly. In this case, z is first set to 10, and then y gets a copy of z with which to update itself, and x does likewise. That is, arguments requiring references and arguments requiring objects both bind to objects; thus, either works in this situation.

Returning by value has the disadvantage of possible poor performance, but it can keep you out of trouble when you evaluate complex expressions involving your objects. Overloading the [] subscript operator, on the other hand, requires that you return a reference if you want to be able to subscript on either side of an assignment operator. In Chapter 19, we presented an array class that does just this. Here is an extract of the code showing the []

operator overload:

```
class array {
  int value;
  int numelem;
  int *elem;
  char *name;
public:
  array( char *, ... );
  array( array & );
  ~array( void );
  void *operator new( unsigned );
  void operator delete( void * );
  int &operator[](int);
  void reverse( void );
  void display( void );
  void newname( char * );
};
...
int &array::operator[]( int n )
{
                         // returning a reference ensures
                         // that the [] op can be used on
                         // either side of the = operator
    if ( n<0 || n >= numelem ) return elem[0];

    return elem[n];
}
```

In the array class, the subscript operator function returns a reference to an individual element of the array. To say that another way: *it returns an object locator* so that a subscripted class object *can stand on the left side of an assignment*. Suppose that it returned a simple integer *value* instead, as one might be tempted to do. Then the following expression:

```
array X( "My array", 1, 2, 3, 4 );
...
X[3] = 5;
```

actually evaluates to 4 = 5, which naturally is going to fail in compilation. Because the subscript operator in fact returns a reference to the third array element, the expression is interpreted to mean:

```
address-of-X[3] = 5;
```

which allows X[3] to stand as an lvalue (an object locator); consequently, the value 4 is changed to 5 in the array — as intended.

Generallly then, return a reference from operator functions that should update and return *this, and return by value from just about everything else. This prevents much grief in attempting to set up operator overloads that allow general expressions to be evaluated correctly.

A word of warning is in order, however. If the class objects contain pointers to dynamically allocated data, this rule can cave in on you. If you declare temporary objects to hold intermediate results, a copy of the object is indeed placed on the stack for return. *But* the dynamic data pointed to by that copy no longer exists after the temporary object has gone out of scope (and the destructor has released it). Usually, objects that point to data outside themselves should be either s t a t i c or arbitrary (allocated through new) in duration.

Now we can explain why we wrote the A SUM; declaration into the operator+() function for the hypothetical class A. Suppose that we had blithely written the operator+(); function like this:

```
A& A::operator+( A& otherA )
{                    // this code kills *this
   value = value + otherA.value;
   return *this
}
```

There doesn't appear to be anything wrong with this function. In fact, it works — as far as it goes. But if you stop and consider what gets modified, you realize that it is a disaster waiting to happen. Consider the expression in the following code fragment:

```
A x, y, z;
...
x = 3; y = 4;
z = x + y;        // what happens here?
```

The intent is clearly to sum x and y, *without changing either of them*, and place the result in z. With the operator+() written as it is here, however, the value in x is replaced with the sum before the assignment operator is ever encountered. That is, in evaluating x + y, *this refers to x, and *otherA refers to y.

That is why the SUM object was declared, and used as the return value. It serves as an accumulator to hold an intermediate result, without accidentally altering the contents of *this. Even though it is a local (auto) object, and goes out of scope when the function returns, a copy of it is placed on the stack before this happens, because the function returns by value.

As we have mentioned, you can use friend functions also to perform the task of overloading an operator. If you do, remember that a friend function is *not* a member function, and has to be told where everything is. That is why friend operator functions require one more argument than member operator functions do. For binary operators, the first argument locates the first operand (for example, the left side of an assignment), and the second locates the other operand object. For unary operators, the argument locates *this.

There is one operator you do not have to overload: the assignment operator (=). If you do not overload = for a class, the compiler generates an operator=(const class&); function for you. The generated function works by copying one object to the target object on a member-by-member basis. This may be sufficient, but if some of the data members are pointers to unique data, it may get you in trouble.

You should understand also that nothing you do can change the *precedence of operators*. This is fixed by the compiler just as it was in standard C. Therefore, the C++ compiler generates code to evaluate expressions involving your class objects just as it would for basic data objects. The only difference is that, if you have overloaded an operator, the generated code implicitly invokes your operator member function at the right moment during evaluation. If you failed to overload the operator, you receive a compile-time message informing you that the compiler cannot locate a function to support the operation.

An extended example illustrates the potential power of operator overloading. For this purpose, we declare a class vli (meaning *very large integer*) that has the following properties:

> A vli object has data-content capability of 16 bytes, with a temporary capability of 32 bytes (particularly for the division algorithm). This gives a vli number a range of $2^{128}-1$ to -2^{128}, or about 3.4E+38. Thus vli numbers can compete with long double floating point for sheer magnitude, and have many

digits greater precision. Don't expect them to compete in performance, however. Repetitive multiplication and division, in particular, are very slow. You would need to rewrite for high performance, and do it in assembler, to get `vli` objects to run quickly. You could do this with in-line assembler, but that is beyond the scope of this book.

Because `vli` objects can have a much greater value than any native form of number, it is desirable to be able to "assign a string" to a `vli` number, and to cast a `vli` number to a string. That is, we want to permit statements such as these:

```
vli X; // declare a vli object
...
X = "999999999999" // 999 trillion
printf( "%s\n", (char *)X);
```

For more ordinary number values, assignment from, and casting to, `long` and `int` are also supported.

`vli` numbers are subject to *signed arithmetic*. This is implemented by recording negative numbers in 2's complement form. Addition, subtraction, and multiplication produce results with the correct algebraic sign. The quotient of `vli` division also records the correct algebraic sign, but the remainder of such division (accessed through the modulus % operator) is always positive.

Only the assignment operators and the internal member functions affect the value of `*this`. That is, in an expression such as `X = X + 1`; the value of `X` is not changed physically until evaluation encounters the assignment operator. Internal temporary "accumulators" are used to guarantee that object values are not modified inadvertently, and do not become confused during expression evaluation.

The header file for the `vli` class is shown in listing 21.3. As you look over it, pay particular attention to those member-function declarations that return references, and those that return objects. Because the addition, subtraction, multiplication, and division operator functions return *values*, not references, the evaluation of complex algebraic expressions is possible with `vli` objects. Notice also which operators are *not* overloaded. You can supply those as an exercise, if you want.

Listing 21.3. `vli.hpp` *(Header file for Very Large Integer class declaration).*
Turbo C++, Zortech C++

```
 1   #include <stdlib.h>
 2   #include <stdio.h>
 3   #include <string.h>
 4
 5   class vli {    // Very Large Integer class
 6     unsigned int vdata[16];
 7     int vlioflow; // overflow indicator
 8     int vliuflow; // underflow indicator
 9   public:
10     vli();         // default constructor
11     vli( vli & ); // copy constructor
12     vli( long );  // constructor with long
13     vli( int );   // constructor with int
14     void dump();
15     vli &operator=( vli & );        // assign op overload
16     vli &operator=( long );         // assign op overload
17     vli &operator=( int );          // assign op overload
18     vli &operator=( char * );       // assign op overload
19     operator long();                // cast to long
20     operator int();                 // cast to int
21     operator char*();               // cast to string
22     vli operator+( vli & );      // define addition
23     vli operator+( long );       // define addition
24     vli operator+( int );        // define addition
25     vli &operator+=( vli & );      // compound addition
26     vli &operator+=( long );       // compound addition
27     vli &operator+=( int );        // compound addition
28     vli operator-( vli & );      // define subtraction
29     vli operator-( long );       // define subtraction
30     vli operator-( int );        // define subtraction
31     vli &operator-=( vli & );      // compound subtraction
32     vli &operator-=( long );       // compound subtraction
33     vli &operator-=( int );        // compound subtraction
34     void shiftleft();
35     void shiftright();
36     vli operator<<( int );       // define left shift
37     vli operator>>( int );       // define right shift
38     vli operator*( vli & );      // multiplication
39     vli operator*( long );       // multiplication
40     vli operator*( int );        // multiplication
41     vli operator/( vli & );      // define division
42     vli operator/( long );       // define division
43     vli operator/( int );        // define division
44     vli operator%( int );        // define modulus
45   };
```

The member functions definitions for the `vli` class are shown in listing 21.4. Look them over, and then we will explain how some of the more sophisticated algorithms work.

Listing 21.4. `vli.cpp` *(Member functions for Very Large Integer class declaration)* .   *Turbo C++, Zortech C++*

```
 1   #include "vli.hpp"
 2
 3   static char outstr[81];
 4
 5   vli::vli()                      // default constructor
 6   {
 7     int i;
 8
 9     for ( i=0; i<16; ++i ) vdata[i] = 0;
10     vlioflow = 0;
11     vliuflow = 0;
12   }
13
14   vli::vli( vli &old )            // copy constructor
15   {
16     int i;
17
18     for ( i=0; i<16; ++i ) vdata[i] = old.vdata[i];
19     vlioflow = old.vlioflow;
20     vliuflow = old.vlioflow;
21   }
22
23   vli::vli( long value )          // constructor with long
24   {
25     int i;
26
27     memset( (void *)vdata, 0, 32 );
28     memmove( (void *)&vdata[0], (void *)&value, 4 );
29     if ( vdata[1] & 0x8000 )     // 2's comp neg, so
30       for ( i=2; i<8; ++i ) vdata[i]=0xFFFF;
31     vlioflow = 0;
32     vliuflow = 0;
33   }
34
35   vli::vli( int value )           // constructor with int
36   {
37     int i;
38
39     memset( (void *)vdata, 0, 32 );
40     memmove( (void *)&vdata[0], (void *)&value, 2 );
41     if ( vdata[0] & 0x8000 )     // 2's comp neg, so
42       for ( i=1; i<8; ++i ) vdata[i]=0xFFFF;
```

Listing 21.4. continues

Listing 21.4. continued

```
43      vlioflow = 0;
44      vliuflow = 0;
45   }
46
47   void vli::dump()                 // debugging dump
48   {
49      int i;
50      unsigned char *v;
51
52      v = (unsigned char *)vdata;
53      for (i=0; i<16; ++i ) printf( "%.2X ", v[i] );
54      printf( "\n" );
55   }
56
57   vli &vli::operator=( vli &other ) // assign op
58   {
59      int i;
60
61      memmove( (void *)vdata, (void *)other.vdata, 32 );
62      vlioflow = other.vlioflow;
63      vliuflow = other.vliuflow;
64      return *this; // return reference
65   }
66
67   vli &vli::operator=( long value ) // assign op
68   {
69      int i;
70
71      memset( (void *)vdata, 0, 32 );
72      memmove( (void *)&vdata[0], (void *)&value, 4 );
73      if ( vdata[1] & 0x8000 )
74        for ( i=2; i<8; ++i ) vdata[i]=0xFFFF;
75      vlioflow = 0;
76      vliuflow = 0;
77      return *this; // return reference
78   }
79
80   vli &vli::operator=( int value ) // assign op
81   {
82      int i;
83
84      memset( (void *)vdata, 0, 32 );
85      memmove( (void *)&vdata[0], (void *)&value, 2 );
86      if ( vdata[0] & 0x8000 )
87        for ( i=1; i<8; ++i ) vdata[i]=0xFFFF;
88      vlioflow = 0;
89      vliuflow = 0;
90      return *this; // return reference
91   }
```

```
92
93   vli &vli::operator=( char *s ) //assign ASCII->VLI
94   {
95      int neg, i;
96      if ( *s == '-' ) {
97        neg = 1; s++;
98      }
99      else neg = 0;
100     *this = 0;
101     while ( *s ) {
102       *this = *this * 10; // shift running total
103       *this += (int)( *s++ - '0' );
104     }
105     if ( neg ) {
106       for ( i=0; i<8; ++i )
107         vdata[i] = ~vdata[i];
108       *this += 1;
109     }
110     return *this;
111  }
112
113  vli::operator long()          // cast to long
114  {
115     return *(long *)vdata;
116  }
117
118  vli::operator int()           // cast to int
119  {
120     return *(int *)vdata;
121  }
122
123  vli::operator char*()                 // cast VLI -> ASCII
124  {
125     int neg, i;
126     char *s, *p;
127     vli VA = *this;
128
129     s = outstr;
130     if ( VA.vdata[7] & 0x8000 ) {
131       neg = 1;
132       for ( i=0; i<8; ++i )
133         VA.vdata[i] = ~VA.vdata[i];
134       VA += 1;
135     }
136     else neg = 0;
137     while( 1 ) {
138       VA -= 10;
139       if ( VA.vdata[7] & 0x8000 ) break; // done
140       VA += 10;
141       *s++ = '0' + (int)( VA % 10 );
142       VA = VA / 10;
```

Listing 21.4. continues

Listing 21.4. continued

```
143     }
144     VA += 10;                    // fixup from loop
145     if ( (int)VA > 0 ) *s++ = (int)VA + '0';
146     if ( neg ) *s++ = '-';
147     *s = '\0'; // terminate the string
148     s = outstr;
149     p = s + strlen( s ) - 1;
150     while ( p > s ) {  // reverse string
151       *s ^= *p; *p ^= *s; *s++ ^= *p--;
152     }
153     return outstr;
154   }
155
156   vli vli::operator+( vli &addend ) // define addition
157   {
158     unsigned long x, y;
159     unsigned carry = 0;
160     int i;
161     vli SUM;
162
163     SUM = 0;
164     for ( i=0; i<8; ++i ) {
165       x = vdata[i]; y=addend.vdata[i];
166       x += y + carry; // add with carry
167       SUM.vdata[i] = x & 0x0000FFFF; // partial result
168       carry = (unsigned)( x >> 16 ); // save the carry
169     }
170     if ( carry ) SUM.vlioflow = 1; else SUM.vlioflow = 0;
171     return SUM;
172   }
173
174   vli vli::operator+( long addend ) // define addition
175   {
176     vli SUML;
177
178     SUML = addend;
179     return *this + SUML;
180   }
181
182   vli vli::operator+( int addend ) // define addition
183   {
184     vli SUMI;
185
186     SUMI = addend;
187     return *this + SUMI;
188   }
189
190   vli &vli::operator+=( vli &addend ) // comp.addition
191   {              // compound assign needs assign back to this
```

```
192     return *this = *this + addend;
193   }
194
195   vli &vli::operator+=( long addend ) // comp.addition
196   {
197     return *this = *this + addend;
198   }
199
200   vli &vli::operator+=( int addend ) // comp.addition
201   {
202     return *this = *this + addend;
203   }
204
205   vli vli::operator-( vli &subt )    // subtraction
206   {
207     int i;
208     vli DIFF;
209
210     for (i=0; i<8; ++i) subt.vdata[i] = ~subt.vdata[i];
211     subt += 1;              // complete 2's complementation
212     DIFF = *this + subt;  // perform subtraction
213     for (i=0; i<8; ++i) subt.vdata[i] = ~subt.vdata[i];
214     subt += 1;              // complete 2's complementation
215     return DIFF;
216   }
217
218   vli vli::operator-( long subt )    // subtraction
219   {
220     vli DIFFL;
221
222     DIFFL = subt;
223     return *this - DIFFL;
224   }
225
226   vli vli::operator-( int subt )    // subtraction
227   {
228     vli DIFFI;
229
230     DIFFI = subt;
231     return *this - DIFFI;
232   }
233
234   vli &vli::operator-=( vli &subt )    // subtraction
235   {
236     int i;
237                     // careful about complementing arguments
238     for ( i=0; i<8; ++i ) subt.vdata[i] = ~subt.vdata[i];
239     subt += 1;              // complete 2's complementation
240     *this = *this + subt;   // perform subtraction
241     for ( i=0; i<8; ++i ) subt.vdata[i] = ~subt.vdata[i];
242     subt += 1;              // complete 2's complementation
```

Listing 21.4. continues

Listing 21.4. continued

```
243     return *this;
244  }
245
246  vli &vli::operator-=( long subt )    // subtraction
247  {
248     return *this = *this - subt;
249  }
250
251  vli &vli::operator-=( int subt )     // subtraction
252  {
253     return *this = *this - subt;
254  }
255
256  void vli::shiftleft()                // shift left 1 bit
257  {
258     int i, carry;
259
260     for ( i=15; i>=0; --i ) {
261        if ( vdata[i] & 0x8000 ) carry = 1;
262        else carry = 0;
263        vdata[i] <<= 1;
264        if ( i < 15 ) vdata[i+1] |= carry;
265     }
266  }
267
268  void vli::shiftright()               // shift right 1 bit
269  {
270     int i;
271     unsigned carry;
272
273     for ( i=0; i<16; ++i ) {
274        if ( vdata[i] & 0x0001 ) carry = 0x8000;
275        else carry = 0;
276        vdata[i] >>= 1;
277        if ( i > 0 ) vdata[i-1] |= carry;
278     }
279  }
280
281  vli vli::operator<<( int dist )    // left shift
282  {
283     int numbytes, numbits, i;
284     long hold;
285     char *s;
286     vli SLEFT;
287
288     SLEFT = *this;
289     dist =  ( dist > 256 ) ? 256 : dist;
290     numbytes = dist / 8; numbits = dist % 8 ;
291     s = (char *)SLEFT.vdata;
```

```
292     if ( numbytes < 32 && numbytes > 0 )
293       memmove( &s[numbytes], &s[0],
294                 32 - numbytes );
295     for ( i=0; i<numbytes; ++i ) s[i] = 0;
296     for ( i=0; i<numbits; ++i ) SLEFT.shiftleft();
297     return SLEFT;
298   }
299
300   vli vli::operator>>( int dist )    // right shift
301   {
302     int numbytes, numbits, i;
303     long hold;
304     char *s;
305     vli SRIGHT;
306
307     SRIGHT = *this;
308     dist = ( dist > 256 ) ? 256 : dist;
309     numbytes = dist / 8; numbits = dist % 8 ;
310     s = (char *)SRIGHT.vdata;
311     if ( numbytes < 32 && numbytes > 0 )
312       memmove( &s[0], &s[numbytes],
313                 32 - numbytes );
314     for ( i=32-numbytes; i<32; ++i ) s[i] = 0;
315     for ( i=0; i<numbits; ++i ) SRIGHT.shiftright();
316     return SRIGHT;
317   }
318
319   vli vli::operator *( vli &mcand ) // multiplication
320   {
321     unsigned char mask;
322     unsigned char *m1;
323     int loop, inloop;
324     vli MUX;
325
326     MUX = 0; // init running total
327     m1 = (unsigned char *)vdata;
328     for ( loop=15; loop>=0; --loop )
329       if ( m1[loop] != 0 ) break; //skip leading 0's
330     if ( loop < 0 ) return MUX;
331     for ( ; loop>=0; --loop ) { // process every byte
332       mask = 0x80;
333       for ( inloop=0; inloop<8; ++inloop ) { // every bit
334         if ( m1[loop] & mask ) MUX += mcand;
335         mask >>= 1;              // shift mask for next bit
336         MUX.shiftleft();              // adjust running sum
337       }
338     }
339     MUX.shiftright(); // put last shift back
340     return MUX;
341   }
342
```

Listing 21.4. continues

Listing 21.4. *continued*

```
343   vli vli::operator *( long mcand ) // multiplication
344   {
345     vli MUXL;
346
347     MUXL = mcand;
348     return MUXL * *this;
349   }
350
351   vli vli::operator *( int mcand ) // multiplication
352   {
353     vli MUXI;
354
355     MUXI = mcand;
356     return MUXI * *this;
357   }
358
359   vli vli::operator/( vli &div )    // define division
360   {
361     int i, aneg = 0, bneg = 0;
362     vli DIVIDEND;
363     vli DIVISOR;
364     vli FRAG;
365
366     DIVIDEND = *this;          // working copy of dividend
367     DIVISOR = div;             // working copy of divisor
368     DIVISOR -= 1;
369     if ( DIVISOR.vdata[7] & 0x8000 ) // it was 0
370       return DIVIDEND;
371     DIVISOR += 1;
372     if ( DIVIDEND.vdata[7] & 0x8000 ) {      // any neg.?
373       aneg = 1; // dividend was negative
374       for (i=0;i<8;++i) DIVIDEND.vdata[i]=~DIVIDEND.vdata[i];
375       DIVIDEND += 1;            // complete 2's complementation
376     }
377     if ( DIVISOR.vdata[7] & 0x8000 ) {
378       bneg = 1; // dividend was negative
379       for (i=0;i<8;++i) DIVISOR.vdata[i]=~DIVISOR.vdata[i];
380       DIVISOR += 1;             // complete 2's complementation
381     }
382
383     for ( i=0; i<128; i+=16 ) { // skip 0's in dividend
384       if ( DIVIDEND.vdata[7] != 0 )
385         break;
386       else DIVIDEND = DIVIDEND << 16;
387     }
388     if ( i == 128 ) return DIVIDEND;
389
390                     // the gyrations with FRAG are necessary
```

```
391                        // to allow arithmetic with the high order
392                        // part of DIVIDEND
393
394     for ( ; i<128; ++i ) {                     // do division
395       DIVIDEND.shiftleft();     // shift dividend left one bit
396       memmove( (void *)&FRAG.vdata[0],   // set up subtraction
397                (void *)&DIVIDEND.vdata[8], 16 );
398       FRAG -= DIVISOR;                          // trial subtraction
399       if ( FRAG.vdata[7] & 0x8000 ) FRAG += DIVISOR;
400       else DIVIDEND.vdata[0] |= 0x0001;   // clock in quot bit
401       memmove( (void *)&DIVIDEND.vdata[8],       // restore it
402                (void *)&FRAG.vdata[0], 16 );
403     }
404
405     if ( aneg ^ bneg ) {        // make it negative if necessary
406       for (i=0;i<8;++i) DIVIDEND.vdata[i]=~DIVIDEND.vdata[i];
407       DIVIDEND += 1;             // complete 2's complementation
408     }
409     return DIVIDEND;
410   }
411
412   vli vli::operator/( long div ) // define division
413   {
414     vli DIVL;
415
416     DIVL = div;
417     return *this / DIVL;
418   }
419
420   vli vli::operator/( int div ) // define division
421   {
422     vli DIVI;
423
424     DIVI = div;
425     return *this / DIVI;
426   }
427
428   vli vli::operator%( int div )    // define modulus
429   {
430     int i;
431     vli MODULUS, FRAG;
432
433     MODULUS = div;
434     MODULUS = *this / MODULUS;
435                 // use this memmove to do the 128-bit
436                 // shift quickly
437     memmove( (void *)&FRAG.vdata[0],
438       (void *)&MODULUS.vdata[8], 16 );
439     return FRAG;
440   }
```

The numeric values of `vli` objects are stored in arrays of integers containing 16 entries (32 bytes). For most operations, only the first 8 entries (16 bytes) are significant. Thus, you can test for a negative number as follows:

```
if ( vdata[7] & 0x8000 ) ... // if true, is negative
```

Further, the array entries are stored with the low-order bytes beginning in subscript 0, thus allowing most arithmetic to proceed from left to right.

The first task is to get values in and out of `vli` objects. `operator=(int)` and `operator=(long)` assignments are fairly obvious — just place the `int` or `long` in the first one or two array positions, and extend the sign.

`operator=(char *)` assignment and the cast operator `char *()` may be less obvious. Both require repeated multiplication or division, and are quite slow in this implementation. The basic trick is to understand that the numeric values of the numeric characters can be turned into true numbers by adding or subtracting a character `'0'`. You don't have to know where these characters are in the collating sequence, because the ANSI standard guarantees that they are together, wherever they are. Thus you can scale, multiply, and sum to convert strings to `vli` objects, and take the remainder after dividing by 10, scale, and place it in a string to convert from `vli` to string. Because the cast to string proceeds from low to high order, you are faced with the additional task of reversing the resultant string.

Addition of `vli` objects proceeds by adding the eight integers that store the number. Before addition, however, each addend is moved to a `long,` thus allowing any carries to appear in the high-order part of the `long`, from which the carry can be retrieved and applied to the next iteration.

Subtraction is even easier, in a way. First the two's complement is taken for the second (righthand) operand by using the ˜ (one's complement operator) on every element, and then adding one to that result. Subtraction is then accomplished by simply adding the complemented operands.

Multiplication and division of such long numbers, implemented as an array, is fairly complex. First consider the following simple 4-bit binary multiplication problem:

```
    1101
X   1001
-------
    1101
1101
-------
1110101
```

If you look closely, you can see that the result can be formed by processing the multiplier (bottom number) *from left to right*, and keeping a running total that "slides over" to the left for every bit tested in the multiplier. If the bit in the multiplier is on, the multiplicand is added to the running total. Knuth has complete details on this algorithm (see the bibliography).

Division is even trickier. It requires the use of all 32 bytes of the dividend (including the temporary extended range), considered as a stream of 256 bits. The first step is to make both operands positive, if necessary (noting which was which, so that the result can be given the correct sign).

Next, the dividend (the top number) is right-justified in the 32-byte field. This amounts to little more than ensuring that the high-order positions are zero (and that was taken care of by converting operands to positive numbers).

At this point, you *conceptually* have a dividend composed of both high-order and low-order parts, each of which is the same size as an ordinary vli number. The algorithm develops the *quotient* in the low-order part, and leaves the *remainder* in the high-order part, by looping 256 times (once for every bit in the extended range) and doing the following:

❑ *Shifting the entire 256-bit dividend one bit left, and discarding the high-order bit shifted out.*

❑ *Subtracting the divisor from the high-order part of the dividend.* Because subtraction involves only half the extended range, the high-order part is moved temporarily to a working object FRAG, where the subtraction is carried out.

❑ *If the trial subtraction overborrows (the result was negative), add the divisor back to the high-order part.* (It didn't fit, so put it back the way it was.)

❑ *If the trial subtraction is all right (did not overborrow) leave the high part reduced, and OR in a 1-bit in the low-order part, least significant bit.* This builds up the quotient.

If you study this method carefully, you see that it is nothing more nor less than an electronic version of longhand binary division. It is, in fact, an emulation of the shift-register technique used by IBM 370 hardware for fixed-point division. Because operations on vli objects frequently are forced to return objects, not references, this method is a little slow. The lack of speed really shows up clearly in casting vli to string, because that involves repeated division. For very large values, there could be millions of discrete operations involved in the cast. Performance varies from moderate (on an 80386), to sluggish (on an 80286), to unacceptable (on an original 4.7 MHz PC).

Slow or not, it works — and illustrates something about overloading operators. As is illustrated by the program in listing 21.5, the vli operators can handle both compound expressions and extremely large numbers successfully.

Listing 21.5. usevli.cpp (Test driver for very large integer object definition).
Turbo C++, Zortech C++

```
 1   #include <conio.h>
 2   #include "vli.hpp"
 3
 4   main()
 5   {
 6     vli X, Y, Z;
 7
 8     clrscr();
 9     X = 2; Y = 3; Z = 4;   // evaluate complex expression
10     X = ( X * Y - Z ) / 2;
11     printf( "%ld\n", (long)X );
12     X = "-99999999999";     // show range capability
13     printf( "%s\n", (char *)X ); // this takes a while!
14     X = ( X / 2 ) * 3;
15     printf( "%s\n", (char *)X ); // this takes a while!
16   }
```

When you run this program, the first expression should result in a value of 1. The second expression results in an answer of –149,999,999,997. If you run this on a slower machine, be prepared to wait several seconds for the second answer!

User-defined Type Conversions

The vli also illustrates another important technique: user-defined casts. You can cast your class objects to any kind of object you want. For instance, the cast operator function for converting vli to long is as follows:

```
vli::operator long()            // cast to long
{
   return *(long *)vdata;
}
```

Using the conversion operator function can be implicit or by explicit cast operator. The following code fragment illustrates both uses:

```
vli X = 4194304L; // get something in it
long hold;
...
```

```
hold = (long)X;    // explicit conversion
hold = X;          // implicit conversion
```

As you may have noticed in listing 21.5, the cast invoked by the `printf()` is an explicit one. A cast in that context must be explicit; if it is not, you receive a compile-time error.

Recent Changes to C++

Bjarne Stroustrup first published *The C++ Programming Language* in 1986; it was reprinted in 1987, with some corrections. Since that time, C++ has undergone a number of changes, some of which are quite important. We conclude this whirlwind tour of C++ with a few comments about some of those changes.

Multiple Inheritance and Virtual Base Classes

Some OOPS pundits outside the C++ world formerly down-graded C++ as not being truly object-oriented, because it did not originally support multiple inheritance. It does now! You declare a class to be multiply dependent on several base classes, as follows:

```
class A {...};
class B {...};
class C : public A, public B {...};
...
C::C( int x, int y ) : A(x), B(y) {...}
```

Note that both the base dependency and the base constructor call have been expanded to a list. It's as simple as that.

The order of calls to constructors is a little more complicated now, however. The base class constructor is still called first, but there may be several to call. It gets even worse if there is some ambiguity as to *which* base class constructor to call. Consider the following example — a case in which a class inherits from two other classes, each of which inherits from the *same* superclass:

```
class A {...};
class B : public A {...};
class C : public A {...};
...
class D : public B, public C {...};
```

Even though the base class name is now prepended to the constructor call, there is still a problem. The B and C constructors, for example, invoke their base class constructor like this:

```
B( args ) : A( args ) {...}
C( args ) : A( args ) {...}
```

but D invokes *each* of its direct base class constructors. This implies that the superclass A constructor is called twice.

Because that could prove disastrous, the concept of *virtual base classes* has been introduced. With virtual base classes, the declarations can now be rewritten as follows:

```
class A {...};
class B : virtual public A {...};
class C : virtual public A {...};
...
class D : public B, public C {...};
```

The presence of the virtual keyword informs the compiler that the indirect base class constructor may be mentioned several times, but is to be called only once.

When virtual base classes are present, their constructors are called first, followed by ordinary base class constructors, followed by the constructors for derived and other class objects.

Overloaded Functions and Type-Safe Linkage

Version 2.0-compatible compilers support a feature called *type-safe linkage*, which has made the overload keyword obsolete (by making it unnecessary). What is type-safe linkage? Type-safe linkage is a process used by the C++ compiler (internally) to guarantee that a call to an overloaded function is matched to the correct version of the function.

The newer C++ compilers *assume* that there is function overloading in the program. Therefore, they perform a process called *mangling* on every function name, without exception. *Mangling* is the process of adding (internally and invisibly) to the function name sufficient information (based on argument matching and return types) so that there is no possibility of ambiguity in identifying which function is meant for a given call. Thus, mangling is the underlying process that permits the compiler to select the correct function — to guarantee type-safe linkage.

With some compilers, this causes a problem when plain C headers are included — mangling the function names can prevent the linker from successfully locating a plain C function in the library. For such compilers, you can "turn off" mangling like this:

```
extern "C" {
#include <stdio.h>
}
```

where the `extern "C"` declaration indicates *alternate linkage* to the plain C libraries. With other compilers, such as Turbo C++, this is not necessary (because the header files already have the `extern "C"` declaration where needed).

Using *const, volatile*, and *static* Member Functions

Class member functions can now be specified as `const`, `volatile`, or `static`. As you can see from the following example, the `const` and `volatile` keywords *follow* the argument list in the function definition:

```
#include <iostream.h>

class OC {
  int A;
public:
  OC() { A = 37; }
  int query() const;
};

int OC::query() const{
  return A;
}

main()
{
  const OC X;
  cout << X.query() << '\n';
}
```

You can mix `const` and *nonconst* functions in the class declaration. If you do, then only `const` member functions can be called when the instance object is a `const` (as in the preceding short program), and only `const` member functions can be called by other `const` member functions. You need not specify `const` for constructor and destructor functions. `volatile` member functions are analogous to `const` member functions.

The static key word appears *before* the declaration part of the function prototype, as in:

```
#include <iostream.h>

class SC {
   static int A;
public:
   SC() { A = 37; }
   static int query() const;
   static void set_it( int );
};

int SC::query() const
{
   return A;
}

void SC::set_it( int val )
{
   A = val;
}

main()
{
   SC::set_it( 64 );       // no instance obj yet !
   cout << SC::query() << '\n';
   SC X;                   // declare an instance
   cout << X.query() << '\n';
   X.set_it( 128 );   // access via normal means
   cout << X.query() << '\n';
}
```

Declaring a member function static means that it "belongs" to the class in general, and is not a specific instance object. It therefore exists before any object of that class is declared. The preceding short program shows how to use the scope resolution operation to access a static member function before an instance object is created. It also demonstrates that you can access the function in the normal way, after an instance is created.

Summary

This is the last chapter about C++ — and the last chapter of the book! This chapter acquainted you with the following four major topics:

❑   *C++ pointers and references*. Pointers and references in C++ are closely related and serve complementary functions: referencing and dereferencing objects. References are designed to remove much of the drudgery of pointer manipulation. Most important of all: *references bind to objects*!

❑ *C++ overloaded functions*. You can overload (define multiple times) any function in a C++ program: ordinary, member, or friend function. The compiler detects which one is to be called by matching arguments to parameter lists and possibly return types if needed.

❑ *C++ overloaded operators*. Overloading operators is one of the more powerful features of C++. You can assign meaning to almost all of the standard C operators for your classes. The trade-off is that, if you don't overload an operator for a class, it isn't defined at all.

❑ *AT&T C++ 2.0 compatibility*. Recent changes to C++ compilers compatible with the AT&T 2.0 compiler have in some ways drastically affected the look and operation of C++ programs. We have only touched on the surface of those changes here. If you have already been programing in C++, prior to current releases, you should carefully consult your new compiler's manuals to determine what effects these changes will have on existing code.

This concludes *Using C*! If you have made it this far, you have accomplished something substantial. Take a break, rest your mind a bit, and then — go write some C code!

APPENDIX

ASCII Character Set

Dec Val	Char	Ctl Name	Dec Val	Char	Ctl Name	Dec Val	Char	Ctl Name	Dec Val	Char	Ctl Name
000		NUL	016	►	DLE	032			048	0	
001	☺	SOH	017	◄	DC1	033	!		049	1	
002	●	STX	018	↕	DC2	034	"		050	2	
003	♥	ETX	019	‼	DC3	035	#		051	3	
004	♦	EOT	020	¶	DC4	036	$		052	4	
005	♣	ENQ	021	§	NAK	037	%		053	5	
006	♠	ACK	022	▬	SYN	038	&		054	6	
007	•	BEL	023	↨	ETB	039	'		055	7	
008	◘	BS	024	↑	CAN	040	(		056	8	
009	○	HT	025	↓	EM	041	)		057	9	
010	◙	LF	026	→	SUB	042	*		058	:	
011	♂	VT	027	←	ESC	043	+		059	;	
012	♀	FF	028	∟	FS	044	,		060	<	
013	♪	CR	029	↔	GS	045	-		061	=	
014	♫	SO	030	▲	RS	046	.		062	>	
015	☼	SI	031	▼	US	047	/		063	?	

Dec Val	Char	Ctl Name	Dec Val	Char	Ctl Name	Dec Val	Char	Ctl Name	Dec Val	Char	Ctl Name
064	@		080	P		096	`		112	p	
065	A		081	Q		097	a		113	q	
066	B		082	R		098	b		114	r	
067	C		083	S		099	c		115	s	
068	D		084	T		100	d		116	t	
069	E		085	U		101	e		117	u	
070	F		086	V		102	f		118	v	
071	G		087	W		103	g		119	w	
072	H		088	X		104	h		120	x	
073	I		089	Y		105	i		121	y	
074	J		090	Z		106	j		122	z	
075	K		091	[		107	k		123	{	
076	L		092	\		108	l		124	¦	
077	M		093	]		109	m		125	}	
078	N		094	^		110	n		126	~	
079	O		095	_		111	o		127	Δ	DEL

Dec Val	Char	Ctl Name	Dec Val	Char	Ctl Name	Dec Val	Char	Ctl Name	Dec Val	Char	Ctl Name
128	Ç		144	É		160	á		176	▒	
129	ü		145	æ		161	í		177	▓	
130	é		146	Æ		162	ó		178	█	
131	â		147	ô		163	ú		179	│	
132	ä		148	ö		164	ñ		180	┤	
133	à		149	ò		165	Ñ		181	╡	
134	å		150	û		166	ª		182	╢	
135	ç		151	ù		167	º		183	╖	
136	ê		152	ÿ		168	¿		184	╕	
137	ë		153	Ö		169	⌐		185	╣	
138	è		154	Ü		170	¬		186	║	
139	ï		155	¢		171	½		187	╗	
140	î		156	£		172	¼		188	╝	
141	ì		157	¥		173	¡		189	╜	
142	Ä		158	₧		174	«		190	╛	
143	Å		159	ƒ		175	»		191	┐	

Dec Val	Char	Ctl Name	Dec Val	Char	Ctl Name	Dec Val	Char	Ctl Name	Dec Val	Char	Ctl Name
192	└		208	╨		224	α		240		
193	⊥		209	╤		225	ß		241	±	
194	┬		210	╥		226	Γ		242	≥	
195	├		211	╙		227	π		243	≤	
196	–		212	╘		228	Σ		244	⌠	
197	┼		213	╒		229	σ		245	⌡	
198	╞		214	╓		230	μ		246	÷	
199	╟		215	╫		231	τ		247	≈	
200	╚		216	╪		232	Φ		248	°	
201	╔		217	┘		233	θ		249	•	
202	╩		218	┌		234	Ω		250	·	
203	╦		219	█		235	δ		251	√	
204	╠		220	▄		236	∞		252	ⁿ	
205	=		221	▌		237	ø		253	²	
206	╬		222	▐		238	∈		254	■	
207	╧		223	▀		239	∩		255		

B

ANSI C
Predefined Macros

This appendix contains a list of the macros defined in each header file. Any values in parentheses to the right of a description represent ANSI minimum values.

#include <assert.h>

```
void assert(int expression);
```

When this function-like macro is invoked, information—including __FILE__ and __LINE__—is displayed on stderr and abort() is called.

#include <float.h>

Table B.1. *Floating-point manifest constants.*

Macro Name	Description	(Minimum Required Value)
FLT_ROUNDS	Rounding behavior	(−1,0,1,2,3)
FLT_RADIX	Radix of exponent representation	(2)
FLT_MANT_DIG	Digits in mantissa	
DBL_MANT_DIG		
LDBL_MANT_DIG		
FLT_DIG	Decimal digits	(6)
DBL_DIG	of precision	(10)
LDBL_DIG		(10)
FLT_MIN_EXP	Minimum exponent of FLT_RADIX	
DBL_MIN_EXP		
LDBL_MIN_EXP		
FLT_MIN_10_EXP	Minimum exponent	(−37)
DBL_MIN_10_EXP	of 10	(−37)
LDBL_MIN_10_EXP		(−37)
FLT_MAX_EXP	Maximum exponent of FLT_RADIX	
DBL_MAX_EXP		
LDBL_MAX_EXP		
FLT_MAX_10_EXP	Maximum exponent	(+37)
DBL_MAX_10_EXP	of 10	(+37)
LDBL_MAX_10_EXP		(+37)
FLT_MAX	Maximum representable	(1E+37)
DBL_MAX	finite value	(1E+37)
LDBL_MAX		(1E+37)
FLT_MIN	Minimum normalized	(1E−37)
DBL_MIN	value	(1E−37)
LDBL_MIN		(1E−37)
FLT_EPSILON	Minimum significant	(1E−5)
DBL_EPSILON	change	(1E−9)
LDBL_EPSILON		(1E−9)

#include <limits.h>

Table B.2. *Manifest constants for limiting values.*

Macro Name	Description	(Minimum Required Value)
CHAR_BIT	Bits per byte	(8)
SCHAR_MIN	Minimum value signed char	(–127)
SCHAR_MAX	Maximum value signed char	(+127)
UCHAR_MAX	Maximum value unsigned char	(255)
CHAR_MIN	Minimum value char	
CHAR_MAX	Maximum value char	
MB_LEN_MAX	Max bytes multibyte character	(1)
SHRT_MIN	Min value short	(–32767)
SHRT_MAX	Max value short	(+32767)
USHRT_MAX	Max value unsigned short	(65535)
INT_MIN	Min value int	(–32767)
INT_MAX	Max value int	(+32767)
UINT_MAX	Max value unsigned int	(65535)
LONG_MIN	Min value long	(–2147483647)
LONG_MAX	Max value long	(+2147483647)
ULONG_MAX	Max value unsigned long	(429499667295)

#include <locale.h>

Table B.3. *Manifest constants for locale-dependent values.*

Macro Name	Description	(Minimum Required Value)
LC_ALL	Values implementation defined	
LC_COLLATE		
LC_CTYPE		
LC_MONETARY		
LC_NUMERIC		
LC_TIME		

#include <math.h>

Table B.4. *Manifest constants for arithmetic errors.*

Macro Name	Description	(Minimum Required Value)
HUGE_VAL	Returned on range error	

#include <setjmp.h>

```
int setjmp( jmp_buf env );
```

#include <signal.h>

Table B.5. *Manifest constants for signal types.*

Macro Name	Description	(Minimum Required Value)
SIG_DFL	Signal default	
SIG_IGN	Signal ignore	
SIG_ERR	Signal error (when defining handler)	
SIGABRT	Abort signal	
SIGFPE	Arithmetic error signal	
SIGILL	Illegal-instruction signal	
SIGINT	Interactive-attention signal	
SIGSEGV	Invalid storage-access signal	
SIGTERM	Program-termination request signal	

#include <stdarg.h>

Table B.6. *Function-like macros for processing variable-length argument lists (variadic lists).*

Macro Prototype

```
void va_start( va_list ap, parmN );
type va_arg( va_list ap, type );
void va_end( va_list ap );
```

#include <stddef.h>

Table B.7. *Miscellaneous manifest constants and function-like macros.*

Macro	Description
wchar_t	Type for wide characters
NULL	Empty pointer, 0
offsetof(type, member-designator)	

#include <stdio.h>

Table B.8. *Manifest constants for I/O control and stream names.*

Macro	Description
_IOFBF	Full buffering
_IOLBF	Line buffering
_IONBF	No buffering
BUFSIZ	Default buffer size
EOF	End-of-file (−1)
FOPEN_MAX	Max files open
FILENAME_MAX	Max file name length
L_tmpnam	Array size required to hold *tmpname*
SEEK_CUR	Seek from current position
SEEK_END	Seek from end-of-file
SEEK_SET	Seek from beginning-of-file
TMP_MAX	Max names generated by tmpnam()
stderr	pointer to FILE, standard error device
stdin	pointer to FILE, standard input device
stdout	pointer to file, standard output device

#include <stdlib.h>

Table B.9. *Manifest constants for exit( ), random numbers, and multibyte character size.*

Macro	Description
EXIT_FAILURE	Arg to exit(), successful execution
EXIT_SUCCESS	Arg to exit(), execution failed
RAND_MAX	Max value pseudo-random number
MB_CUR_MAX	Max bytes multibyte char, current locale

#include time.h

Table B.10. *Manifest constants for time and clock functions.*

Macro	Description
CLK_TCK	Number of clock ticks per second

APPENDIX ___ C

ANSI C Function Library

This appendix contains a list of the functions declared in each of the ANSI standard header files.

#include <ctype.h>

Table C.1. *Character detection and conversion functions.*

Function Prototype	Description
`int isalnum( int c );`	Test for alphanumeric character
`int isalpha( int c );`	Test for alphabetic characters
`int iscntrl( int c );`	Test for control character
`int isdigit( int c );`	Test for digit character
`int isgraph( int c );`	Test for graphic character
`int islower( int c );`	Test for lowercase character
`int isprint( int c );`	Test for printable character
`int ispunct( int c );`	Test for punctuation character
`int isspace( int c );`	Test for whitespace character
`int isupper( int c );`	Test for uppercase character
`int isxdigit( int c );`	Test for hexadecimal digit character
`int tolower( int c );`	Translate to lowercase character
`int toupper( int c );`	Translate to uppercase character

#include <locale.h>

Table C.2. *Locale-dependent functions.*

Function Prototype	Description
`char *setlocale( int category, const char *locale );`	Select the appropriate portion of the program's locale
`struct lconv *localeconv( void );`	Prepare an object with type `struct lconv` with the appropriate values for formatting numeric quantities

#include <math.h>

Table C.3. *Advanced math functions.*

Function Prototype	Description
`double acos( double x );`	Compute the arccosine of x
`double asin(double x );`	Compute the arcsine of x
`double atan( double x );`	Compute the arctangent of x
`double atan2( double y, double x );`	Compute the arctangent of y/x, using the sines of the arguments to determine the quadrant of the result
`double cos( double x );`	Compute the cosine of x
`double sin( double x );`	Compute the sine of x
`double tan( double x );`	Compute the tangent of x
`double cosh( double x );`	Compute the hyperbolic cosine of x
`double sinh( double x );`	Compute the hyperbolic sine of x
`double tanh( double x );`	Compute the hyperbolic tangent of x
`double exp( double x );`	Compute e^x
`double frexp( double arg_val, int *exp );`	Break `arg_val` into a normalized fraction (returned) and an integral power of 2 (stored in `*exp`)
`double ldexp( double x, int exp );`	Multiply x by 2^{exp}
`double log( double x );`	Compute the *natural* logarithm (base *e*) of x

Function Prototype	Description
`double log10( double x );`	Compute the base-10 logarithm of x
`double modf( double x, double *ptr );`	Break x into integral (stored in `*ptr`) and fraction (returned) parts
`double pow( double x, double y );`	Compute x^y
`double sqrt( double x );`	Compute the square-root of x
`double ceil( double x );`	Compute the smallest integral value not less than x (the next highest whole number).
`double fabs( double x );`	Compute the absolute value of x
`double floor( double x );`	Compute the largest integral value not greater than x (the next smaller whole number).
`double fmod( double x, double y );`	Compute the remainder of x/y

#include <setjmp.h>

Table C.4. *Direct jump functions.*

Function Prototype	Description
`void longjmp( jmp_buf env, int val );`	Restore the `jmp_buf` environment env. This causes a return to the point immediately after the `setjmp()` invocation that created it, as if with return code `val`
`int setjmp( jmp_buf env );`	Establish the jump buffer environment env. A direct, initial invocation yields a 0 return

#include <signal.h>

Table C.5. *Signal-handling functions.*

Function Prototype	Description
```void (*signal(int sig, void (*func) (int))) (int);```	Establish a signal-handler function for `sig`, pointed to by `func`
```int raise(int sig);```	Force the signal `sig`

#include <stdio.h>

Table C.6. *Standard Input/Output functions.*

Function Prototype	Description
```int remove(const char *filename);```	Remove the physical file *filename*
```int rename(const char *old, const char *new);```	Rename the physical file `old` with the name `new`
```FILE *tmpfile(void);```	Create a temporary file
```char *tmpnam(char *s);```	Create a temporary file name
```int fclose(FILE *stream);```	Close the stream
```int fflush(FILE *stream);```	Flush the buffers for `stream`
```FILE *fopen(const char *filename, const char *mode);```	Open the stream for `filename` with `mode`
```FILE *freopen(const char *filename, const char *mode, FILE *stream);```	Reopen the stream for `filename`
```void setbuf(FILE *stream, char *buf);```	Equivalent to `setvbuf()` with arguments of `_IOFBF` and `BUFSIZE`; or with `_IONBF` of `buf == NULL`. For many but not all compilers, you can turn off line buffering for `stdin` using the second call configuration

Function Prototype	Description
`int setvbuf( FILE *stream, char *buf, int mode, size_t size );`	Set the buffer for `stream` to `size` bytes, located by `buf`, using `mode` (`_IONBF,_IOLBF, _IOFBF`)
`int fprintf( FILE *stream, const char *format, ... );`	Convert the arguments specified in the variable argument list (variadic list) according to the conversion string `format` and send the text to `stream`
`int fscanf( FILE *stream, const char *format, ... );`	Retrieve successive text tokens from `stream`, convert them according to the conversion string `format`, and place the results in successive arguments from the variable list
`int printf( const char *format, ... );`	See `fprintf()`; output is to `stdout`
`int scanf( const char *format, ... );`	See `fscanf()`; input is from `stdin`
`int sprintf( char *s, const char *format, ... );`	See `fprintf()`; output is to string `s`
`int sscanf( const char *s, const char *format, ... );`	See `fscanf()`; input is from string `s`
`int vfprintf( FILE *stream, const char *format, va_list argptr );`	See `fprintf()`; the last argument is an argument pointer, `argptr`
`int vprintf( const char *format, va_list arg );`	See `vfprintf()`; output is to `stdout`
`int vsprintf( char *s, const char *format, va_list arg );`	See `vfprintf()`; output is to string `s`
`int fgetc( FILE *stream );`	Get a character from `stream`
`char *fgets( char *s, int n, FILE *stream );`	Get a string from `stream`, at most n-1 characters, including the newline character
`int fputc( int c, FILE *stream );`	Put a character to `stream`
`int fputs( const char *s, FILE *stream );`	Put a string to `stream`
`int getc( FILE *stream );`	Get a character from `stream`

Table C.6. continues

Table C.6. *continued*

Function Prototype	Description
`int getchar( void );`	Get a character from `stdin`
`char *gets( char *s );`	Get a string from `stdin`
`int putc( int c, FILE *stream );`	Put a character to `stream`
`int putchar( int c );`	Put a character to `stdout`
`int puts( const char *s );`	Put a string to `stdout`; newline appended automatically
`int ungetc( int c, FILE *stream );`	Push a character back onto `stream`
`size_t fread( void *ptr, size_t size, size_t nmemb, FILE *stream );`	Direct read a block of data from `stream`
`size_t fwrite( const void *ptr, size_t size, size_t nmemb, FILE *stream );`	Direct write a block of data to `stream`
`int fgetpos( FILE *stream, fpos_t *pos );`	Get the current file position of `stream` and record information in `*pos`
`int fseek( FILE *stream, long int offset, int whence );`	Set the new file position for `stream` a number of bytes `offset` from location `whence` (`SEEK_SET`, `SEEK_CUR`, `SEEK_END`)
`int fsetpos( FILE *stream, const fpos_t *pos );`	Set the new file position for `stream` based on the information recorded in `*pos`
`long int ftell( FILE *stream );`	Report the current file position as a long integer
`void rewind( FILE *stream );`	Set the current file position to the beginning of the file
`void clearerr( FILE *stream );`	Clear end-of-file and error conditions for `stream`
`int feof( FILE *stream );`	Test for end-of-file on `stream`
`int ferror( FILE *stream );`	Test for error indicator on `stream`
`void perror( const char *s );`	Convert `errno` to a text message and prepend it to your message in string `s`. Display it on `stderr`

#include <stdlib.h>

Table C.7. *Miscellaneous control and conversion functions.*

Function Prototype	Description
NOTE: The ato...( ) functions do not *report errors*	
```double atof(const char *nptr);```	Convert the text token in `nptr` to a `double` float
```int atoi(const char *nptr);```	Convert the text token in `nptr` to an `int`
```long int atol(const char *nptr);```	Convert the text token in `nptr` to a `long`
NOTE: The stro...( ) functions do *report errors*	
```double strtod(const char *nptr, char **endptr);```	Convert the initial segment of string `nptr` to a `double`. Skips whitespace and reports errors
```long int strtol(const char *nptr, char **endptr, int base);```	Convert the initial segment of string `*nptr` to a `long`. Skips whitespace and reports errors
```unsigned long int strtoul (const char *nptr, char **endptr, int base);```	Convert the initial segment of string `*nptr` to an `unsigned long`. Skips whitespace and reports errors
```int rand(void);```	Generate a pseudorandom number
```void srand(unsigned int seed);```	Initialize the pseudorandom number generator using the seed value `seed`
```void *calloc(size_t nmemb, size_t size);```	Allocate `nmemb` contiguous blocks of memory, each `size` bytes long, from the heap. The whole area is initialized to nulls
```void free(void *ptr);```	Release memory acquired by `calloc()`, `malloc()`, or `realloc()`
```void *malloc(size_t size);```	Allocate a contiguous area of memory from the heap `size` bytes long
```void *realloc(void *ptr, size_t size);```	Resize the area pointed to by `ptr` to `size` bytes. If `ptr` is NULL, `realloc()` acquires new area

Table C.7. *continues*

Table C.7. *continued*

Function Prototype	Description
`void abort( void );`	Terminate the program abnormally— immediately
`int atexit( void` `( *func ) ( void ) );`	Register functions to be executed just before normal program termination
`void exit( int status );`	Terminate the program normally, reporting execution condition `status`. If any functions have been registered by `atexit()`, they are executed first, in LIFO (last in, first out) order
`char *getenv( const char` `*name );`	Get the system environment variable identified by the contents of string `name`
`int system( const char` `*string );`	Invoke the system command processor (shell), passing command line arguments in `string`

`void *bsearch( const`
`void *key, const void`
`*base, size_t nmemb,`
`size_t size, int`
`( *compar ) ( const void`
`*, const void * ) );`
	Search an array of `nmemb` objects, the first of which is pointed to by `base`, for a member that contains the value pointed to by `key`. Use the comparison function pointed to by `compar`

`void qsort( void *base,`
`size_t nmemb, size_t`
`size, int ( *compar )`
`( const void *, const`
`void * ) );`
	See `bsearch()` for argument logistics; Quicksort the array

`int abs( int j );`	Compute the absolute value of `j`
`div_t div( int numer,` `int denom );`	Compute the remainder of `numer` and `denom` and return them both in an object with type `div_t`
`long int labs( long` `int j );`	Compute the `long` absolute value of `j`
`ldiv_t ldiv(long int` `numer, long int denom );`	See `div()`; except types are `long`
`int mblen( const char` `*s, size_t n );`	Compute the number of bytes in the multibyte character `s`. Does not affect the shift state

Function Prototype	Description
int mbtowc(wchar_t *pwc, const char *s, size_t n);	Convert the multibyte character in s to a wide character code if possible and store it in pwc
int wctomb(char *s, wchar_t wchar);	The reverse of mbtowc()
size_t mbstowcs(wchar_t *pwcs, const char *s, size_t n);	Convert a multibyte string to a wide character string
size_t wcstombs(char *s, const wchar_t *pwcs, size_t n);	The reverse of mbstowcs()

#include <string.h>

Table C.8. *String manipulation functions.*

Function Prototype	Description
void *memcpy(void *s1, const void *s2, size_t n);	Always copy n byte from s2 to s1; overlapped operands are not accounted for
void *memmove(void *s1, const void *s2, size_t n);	Always copy n bytes from s2 to s1; overlapped operands are handled correctly
char *strcpy(char *s1, const char *s2);	Copy string s2 to s1, including null terminator
char *strncpy(char *s1, const char *s2, size_t n);	Copy *at most* n characters from s2 to s1
char *strcat(char *s1, const char *s2);	Concatenate string s2 on the end of s1; handle the null terminator characters accordingly
char *strncat(char *s1, const char *s2, size_t n);	Same as strcat(), but processes at most n characters

Table C.8. continues

Table C.8. *continued*

Function Prototype	Description
`int memcmp( const void *s1, const void *s2, size_t n );`	Compare n characters in the `char` arrays s1 and s2; these may be strings but a null terminator does not stop the comparison
`int strcmp( const char *s1, const char *s2 );`	Compare the two strings s1 and s2. A null terminator character *stops* the comparison
`int strcoll( const char *s1, const char *s2 );`	Works like `strcmp()`, but the comparison is controlled by the current locale
`int strncmp( const char *s1, const char *s2, size_t n );`	Works like `strcmp()`, but compares *at most* n characters
`size_t strxfrm( char *s1, const char *s2, size_t n );`	Transform s2 according to the current locale and copy *at most* n transformed characters to s1
`void *memchr( const void *s, int c, size_t n );`	Set n bytes, pointed to by s, to the value of c
`char *strchr( const char *s, int c );`	Find the first occurrence of a character in a string
`size_t strcspn( const char *s1, const char *s2 );`	Compute the length of the initial segment of s1, which consists entirely of characters *not* found in s2
`char *strpbrk( const char *s1, const char *s2 );`	Point to the first occurrence in s1 of any character, which is in s2;
`char *strrchr( const *s, int c );`	Search s in reverse for the first occurrence of c
`size_t strspn( const char *s1, const char *s2 );`	Compute the length of the initial segment of s1, which *consists entirely* of characters found in s2. The order of characters in s2 does not matter
`char *strstr( const char *s1, const char *s2 );`	Locate the string s2 in s1; point to that substring in s1

Function Prototype	Description
`char *strtok( char *s1, const char *s2 );`	Extract the next text token from `s1`. The token is delimited by the characters in `s2`, which may vary from call to call, even when scanning the same target string
`void *memset( void *s, int c, size_t n );`	Initialize every byte of `n` bytes pointed to by `s` with the value of `c`
`char *strerror( int errnum );`	Generate a text message based on `errnum`
`bsize_t strlen( const char *s );`	Compute the length of the string `s`. The length reported does *not* include the null terminator character, but it *is* a 1-origin *count, not* the 0-origin subscript of the last character in the string

#include <time.b>

Table C.9. *Date, time, and clock functions.*

Function Prototype	Description
`clock_t clock( void );`	Compute the amount of processor time used by the program
`double difftime( time_t time1, time_t time0 );`	Compute the difference between the *ending time* `time1` and *beginning time* `time0` and report as a `double`
`time_t mktime( struct tm *timeptr );`	Convert the broken-down time in the structure pointed to by `timeptr` into a calendar time with type `time_t`
`time_t time( time_t *timer );`	Compute the best approximation to the implementation's calendar time. Return it as `time_t-1`, and store it in `*timer`, if that pointer is not null
`char *asctime( const struct tm *timeptr );`	Convert the broken-down time into a string

Table C.9. *continues*

Table C.9. *continued*

Function Prototype	Description
`char *ctime( const time_t *timer );`	Convert the calendar time into a string
`struct tm *gmtime( const time_t *timer );`	Convert a calendar time to Coordinated Universal Time (UTC has replaced GMT), in broken-down format
`struct tm *localtime ( const time_t *timer );`	Convert the local calendar time to local broken-down time
`size_t strftime( char *s, size_t maxsize, const char *format, const struct tm *timeptr );`	This function works something like `sprintf()`. It converts a calendar time pointed to by `timeptr` into a string, pointed to by s, under control of a format string `format`. `strftime()` format strings have conversion specifiers that are similar in appearance to, but different in content from, `printf()` conversion specifiers

The *finance.c* Program

When you first look at this program, it may seem long and complex. It is fairly long, but it is surprisingly simple. All the I/O is done with either the simple or formatted I/O library functions introduced in Chapter 2.

The only real sophistication in the program is in the time value of money formulas implemented here, and those you can take at face value. They work, but the mathematical derivation is a little more involved than there is space for here.

The point of the program is to demonstrate what can be done with just simple I/O. This is done through the vehicle of a series of financial calculations that are of interest to anyone who likes money, owns a home, or both. finance.c can calculate percent change and markup, equivalent interest rates for periodic and continuous compounding methods, savings strategies, and complete mortgage-amortization information. Listing D.1 contains the source for finance.c.

Listing D.1. finance.c *(Financial calculations).*   *Turbo C 2.0*

```
1   #include <stdlib.h>
2   #include <stdio.h>
3   #include <io.h>
4   #include <conio.h>
5   #include <math.h>
6
7   #define FALSE 0
```

Listing D.1. continues

Listing D.1. *continued*

```
 8  #define TRUE 1
 9
10  char usermsg[160] =
11          "       Use the Up and Down ARROW keys to move the "
12          "bullet beside the item\n"
13          "\t\t   to select. Then Strike RETURN (ENTER)." ;
14
15  int rc,endjob;
16  double amtmort,levelpay,payno,prinpay,intpay;
17  double apr,freq,numpay,bal;
18
19  /* +---------------------------------------------------+
20     +              S E R V I C E    R O U T I N E S
21     +---------------------------------------------------+
22  */
23
24  int wait_key()
25  {
26    int ch;
27    ch = getch();
28    if ( ch == 27 ) return( 255 ); else return( 0 );
29  }
30
31
32  /* +---------------------------------------------------+
33     +   SINGLE PAYMENT FUTURE VALUE. Future value of a
34     +   single $1.00 payment.
35     +---------------------------------------------------+
36  */
37
38  double SPFV( double apr, double freq, double periods )
39  {
40    return( pow(1.0+(apr/freq)/100.0,periods) );
41  }
42
43  /* +---------------------------------------------------+
44     +   SINGLE PAYMENT PRESENT VALUE. Present value of a
45     +   single $1.00 payment.
46     +---------------------------------------------------+
47  */
48
49  double SPPV( double apr, double freq, double periods )
50  {
51    return( 1.0 / SPFV(apr,freq,periods) );
52  }
53
```

```
54   /* +----------------------------------------------------+
55      + UNIFORM SERIES PRESENT VALUE. Present value of a
56      + $1.00 Annuity.
57      +----------------------------------------------------+
58   */
59
60   double USPV( double apr, double freq, double periods )
61   {
62     return( ( 1.0 - 1.0
63              / SPFV(apr,freq,periods))
64              / (apr/freq/100.0) );
65   }
66
67   /* +----------------------------------------------------+
68      +  UNIFORM SERIES FUTURE VALUE. Future value of a
69      +  $1.00 Annuity.
70      +----------------------------------------------------+
71   */
72
73   double USFV( double apr, double freq, double periods )
74   {
75     return( ( SPFV(apr,freq,periods)- 1.0) / (apr/freq/100.0) );
76   }
77
78   /* +----------------------------------------------------+
79      +  BULLET controls the "bullet" (karet-cursor) for
80      +  all menus. The VARIABLE parameter RC returns the
81      +  relative item number, numbering from 1, that the
82      +  bullet was positioned next to at exit. The
83      +  VALUE parameters are used as follows:
84      +
85      +  XCOL    :The x-position for bullet.
86      +  LINE1   :Top y-position in Turbo Coordinates.
87      +  LINE2   :Bottom y-position.
88      +----------------------------------------------------+
89   */
90
91   int bullet( int xcol, int line1, int line2 )
92   {
93     char ch;
94     int  fine;
95
96     fine=FALSE;
97     gotoxy(xcol,line1); printf( "%c",0x10 );
98     while ( !fine ) {
99       ch = getch(); if ( ch == 0 ) ch = getch();
100      switch (ch) {
101        case 13:  fine=TRUE; break;
102        case 72:  gotoxy(xcol,wherey()); printf( " " );
103             if ( wherey()==line1 ) gotoxy(xcol,line2);
```

Listing D.1. continues

Listing D.1. *continued*

```
104                  else gotoxy(xcol,wherey()-1);
105              printf( "%c",0x10 ); break;
106          case 80:  gotoxy(xcol,wherey()); printf( " " );
107              if ( wherey()==line2 ) gotoxy(xcol,line1);
108                  else gotoxy(xcol,wherey()+1);
109              printf( "%c",0x10 ); break;
110      }
111    }
112    return( wherey()-line1+1 );
113  }
114
115  /* +----------------------------------------------------+
116     +           C A L C U L A T I O N     R O U T I N E S
117        +----------------------------------------------------+
118  */
119
120  void calc_SPPV()
121  {
122    double amount,apr,freq,periods;
123
124    clrscr();
125    puts(
126      "Finance/PC                                          "
127      "Present Value of an Amount");
128    gotoxy(1,6);
129    puts("PV of What Amount?: ");
130    puts("Annual Per Centage Rate: ");
131    puts("Number of Payments Per Year: ");
132    puts("Number of Years: ");
133    gotoxy(32,6); scanf("%lf",&amount);
134    gotoxy(32,7); scanf("%lf",&apr);
135    gotoxy(32,8); scanf("%lf",&freq);
136    gotoxy(32,9); scanf("%lf",&periods);
137    periods *= freq;
138    printf("Present Value = %12.2f",
139      (amount*SPPV(apr,freq,periods)) );
140    wait_key();
141  }
142
143  void calc_SPFV()
144  {
145    double amount,apr,freq,periods;
146
147    clrscr();
148    puts(
149      "Finance/PC                                          "
150      "Future Value of an Amount");
151    gotoxy(1,6);
152    puts("FV of What Amount?: ");
```

```
153    puts("Annual Per Centage Rate: ");
154    puts("Number of Payments Per Year: ");
155    puts("Number Years: ");
156    gotoxy(32,6); scanf("%lf",&amount);
157    gotoxy(32,7); scanf("%lf",&apr);
158    gotoxy(32,8); scanf("%lf",&freq);
159    gotoxy(32,9); scanf("%lf",&periods);
160    periods *= freq;
161    puts( "\n");
162    printf("Future Value = %12.2f",
163      (amount*SPFV(apr,freq,periods)) );
164    wait_key();
165  }
166
167  void calc_USPV()
168  {
169    double amount,apr,freq,periods ;
170
171    clrscr();
172    puts(
173      "Finance/PC                                    "
174      "Present Value of an Annuity");
175    gotoxy(1,6);
176    puts("Regular Payment Amount: ");
177    puts("Annual Per Centage Rate: ");
178    puts("Number of Payments Per Year: ");
179    puts("Number of Years: ");
180    gotoxy(32,6); scanf("%lf",&amount);
181    gotoxy(32,7); scanf("%lf",&apr);
182    gotoxy(32,8); scanf("%lf",&freq);
183    gotoxy(32,9); scanf("%lf",&periods);
184    periods *= freq;
185    printf("Present Value of Annuity = %12.2f",
186      (amount*USPV(apr,freq,periods)) );
187    wait_key();
188  }
189
190  void calc_USFV()
191  {
192    double amount,apr,freq,periods ;
193
194    clrscr();
195    puts(
196      "Finance/PC                                    "
197      "Future Value of an Annuity");
198    gotoxy(1,6);
199    puts("Regular Payment Amount: ");
200    puts("Annual Per Centage Rate: ");
201    puts("Number of Payments Per Year: ");
202    puts("Number of Years: ");
203    gotoxy(32,6); scanf("%lf",&amount);
```

Listing D.1. continues

```
204    gotoxy(32,7); scanf("%lf",&apr);
205    gotoxy(32,8); scanf("%lf",&freq);
206    gotoxy(32,9); scanf("%lf",&periods);
207    periods *= freq;
208    printf("Future Value of Annuity = %12.2f",
209       (amount*USFV(apr,freq,periods)) );
210    wait_key();
211  }
212
213  void calc_eff_period()
214  {
215    double apr,periods;
216    clrscr();
217    puts(
218       "Finance/PC                          "
219       "Effective Interest, Periodic Compounding");
220    gotoxy(1,6);
221    puts("Annual Per Centage Rate: ");
222    puts("Number of Compounding Periods: ");
223    gotoxy(32,6); scanf("%lf",&apr);
224    gotoxy(32,7); scanf("%lf",&periods);
225    printf("Effective Rate, Periodic Compounding = %12.2f",
226       (pow(1.0+apr/(100.0*periods),periods)-1)*100.0 );
227    wait_key();
228  }
229
230  void calc_eff_contin()
231  {
232    double apr ;
233
234    clrscr();
235    puts(
236       "Finance/PC                          "
237       "Effective Interest, Continuous Compounding");
238    gotoxy(1,6);
239    puts("Annual Per Centage Rate: ");
240    gotoxy(32,6); scanf("%lf",&apr);
241    printf("Effective Rate, Continuous Compounding = %12.2f",
242       (exp(apr/100.0)-1)*100.0 );
243    wait_key();
244  }
245
246  void get_mortgage_data()
247  {
248    char scratch[12];
249
250    clrscr();
251    puts(
```

```
252        "Finance/PC                                            "
253         "Input Mortgage Data");
254     gotoxy(1,6);
255     puts("Mortgage Amount: ");
256     puts("Annual Per Centage Rate: ");
257     puts("Number of Payments Per Year: ");
258     puts("Number of Years: ");
259     puts("Detail of Payment # ");
260
261     gotoxy(50,6); printf("(%12.2f)\n",amtmort);
262     gotoxy(50,7); printf("(%12.2f)\n",apr);
263     gotoxy(50,8); printf("(%12.2f)\n",freq);
264     gotoxy(50,9); printf("(%12.0f)\n",numpay/12);
265     gotoxy(50,10); printf("(%12.0f)\n",payno);
266
267     gotoxy(32,6); scanf("%lf",&amtmort);
268     gotoxy(32,7); scanf("%lf",&apr);
269     gotoxy(32,8); scanf("%lf",&freq);
270     gotoxy(32,9); scanf("%lf",&numpay); numpay *= freq;
271     gotoxy(32,10); scanf("%lf",&payno);
272
273     if ( payno>numpay ) payno=1;
274     puts("Calculating Amortization Constants.");
275     levelpay=1/USPV(apr,freq,numpay)*amtmort;
276     intpay=levelpay * USPV(apr,freq,numpay-payno+1.0)
277         * (apr/freq/100);
278     prinpay=levelpay-intpay;
279  }
280
281  void display_payout()
282  {
283    clrscr();
284    puts(
285      "Finance/PC                                          "
286       "Amortization Payout");
287    gotoxy(1,6);
288    puts("Mortgage Amount: ");
289    puts("Annual Per Centage Rate: ");
290    puts("Number of Payments Per Year: ");
291    puts("Number of Years: ");
292    gotoxy(32,6); printf("%12.2f",amtmort);
293    gotoxy(32,7); printf("%12.2f",apr);
294    gotoxy(32,8); printf("%12.0f",freq);
295    gotoxy(32,9); printf("%12.0f\n",numpay/freq);
296    puts("==========================================");
297    gotoxy(1,12);
298    puts("Level Payment: ");
299    puts("Total Payout: ");
300    puts("Total Interest Paid: ");
301    puts("Payment # ");
```

Listing D.1. continues

```
302    puts("  Principal Amt: ");
303    puts("  Interest  Amt: ");
304    gotoxy(32,12); printf("%12.2f",levelpay);
305    gotoxy(32,13); printf("%12.2f",levelpay*numpay);
306    gotoxy(32,14); printf("%12.2f",levelpay*numpay-amtmort);
307    gotoxy(32,15); printf("%12.0f",payno);
308    gotoxy(32,16); printf("%12.2f",prinpay);
309    gotoxy(32,17); printf("%12.2f",intpay);
310    wait_key();
311  }
312
313  void display_12tab()
314  {
315    char ch;
316
317    rc = TRUE;
318    gotoxy(1,6);
319    puts("     Paymnt #    Pay Amt      "
320       "Interest    Principal    Balance   ");
321    puts("=============================="
322       "==============================");
323    while ( payno<numpay ) {
324      payno=payno+1;
325      intpay=levelpay * USPV(apr,freq,numpay-payno+1.0)
326          * (apr/freq/100);
327      prinpay=levelpay-intpay;
328      bal=levelpay*USPV(apr,freq,numpay-payno);
329      if ( bal<0 ) bal=0;
330      printf( "%12.0f%12.2f%12.2f%12.2f%12.2f\n",
331          payno,levelpay,intpay,prinpay,bal
332        );
333      if ( ((int)payno % 12) == 0 ) return;
334      if ( kbhit() ) {
335        ch = getch(); if ( ch == 0 ) ch = getch();
336        rc=FALSE; return;
337      }
338    }
339  }
340
341  void print_48tab()
342  {
343    char ch;
344    char pline[81];
345
346    rc = TRUE;
347    sprintf(pline,"\n");
348    write( 4,pline,(unsigned)strlen(pline) );
349    sprintf(pline,"     Paymnt #    Pay Amt      "
```

```
350        "Interest     Principal      Balance    \n");
351     write( 4,pline,(unsigned)strlen(pline) );
352     sprintf(pline,"=============================="
353        "==================================\n");
354     write( 4,pline,(unsigned)strlen(pline) );
355     while ( payno<numpay )
356        {
357        payno=payno+1;
358        intpay=levelpay * USPV(apr,freq,numpay-payno+1.0)
359          * (apr/freq/100);
360        prinpay=levelpay-intpay;
361        bal=levelpay*USPV(apr,freq,numpay-payno);
362        if ( bal<0 ) bal=0;
363        sprintf( pline, "%12.0f%12.2f%12.2f%12.2f%12.2f\n",
364             payno,levelpay,intpay,prinpay,bal
365          );
366        write( 4,pline,(unsigned)strlen(pline) );
367        if ( ((int)payno % 48 ) == 0 ) return;
368        if ( kbhit() ) {
369          ch = getch(); if ( ch == 0 ) ch = getch();
370          rc=FALSE; return;
371        }
372     }
373  }
374
375  void display_table()
376  {
377     payno=payno-1;
378     if ( payno<0 ) payno=0;
379     if ( payno>numpay-1 ) payno=numpay-1;
380     bal=amtmort;
381     while ( payno < numpay) {
382       clrscr();
383       puts(
384         "Finance/PC                                      "
385         "Amortization Schedule");
386       printf(
387         "Amortizing %12.2f at %5.2f %% for %5.2f years.\n",
388         amtmort,apr,numpay/freq );
389       display_12tab();
390       if ( !rc ) return;
391       if ( wait_key() ) return;
392     }
393  }
394
395  void print_table()
396  {
397     char pline[81];
398
```

Listing D.1. continues

```
399     payno = 1;
400     bal=amtmort;
401     while ( payno < numpay ) {
402       *pline = '\0';
403       sprintf(pline,
404         "Finance/PC
405         "Amortization Schedule\n");
406       write( 4,pline,(unsigned)strlen(pline) );
407       sprintf(pline,"\n");
408       write( 4,pline,(unsigned)strlen(pline) );
409       sprintf(pline,
410         "Amortizing %12.2f at %5.2f %% for %5.2f years.\n",
411         amtmort,apr,numpay/freq );
412       write( 4,pline,(unsigned)strlen(pline) );
413       print_48tab();
414       if ( !rc ) return;
415       fprintf(stdout,"%c",12);
416     }
417   }
418
419   void calc_percent_change()
420   {
421     double oamt,namt ;
422
423     clrscr();
424     puts(
425       "Finance/PC
426       "Calculate Per Cent Change");
427     gotoxy(1,6);
428     puts("Old Amount: ");
429     puts("New Amount: ");
430     gotoxy(32,6); scanf("%lf",&oamt);
431     gotoxy(32,7); scanf("%lf",&namt);
432     printf("Per Cent Change = %12.2f%%\n",
433       ((namt-oamt)/oamt)*100.0 );
434     wait_key();
435   }
436
437   void calc_percent_total()
438   {
439     double part,total ;
440
441     clrscr();
442     puts(
443       "Finance/PC
444       "Calculate Per Cent of Total");
445     gotoxy(1,6);
446     puts("Partial Amount: ");
```

```
447     puts("Total Amount: ");
448     gotoxy(32,6); scanf("%lf",&part);
449     gotoxy(32,7); scanf("%lf",&total);
450     printf("Per Cent of Total = %12.2f%%\n",
451        (part/total)*100.0 );
452     wait_key();
453  }
454
455  void calc_markup_cost()
456  {
457     double price,cost ;
458
459     clrscr();
460     puts(
461       "Finance/PC                                    "
462       "Calculate Markup as Per Cent of Cost");
463     gotoxy(1,6);
464     puts("Price of Item: ");
465     puts("Cost of Item: ");
466     gotoxy(32,6); scanf("%lf",&price);
467     gotoxy(32,7); scanf("%lf",&cost);
468     printf("Markup %% of Cost = %12.2f%%\n",
469        ((price-cost)/cost)*100.0 );
470     wait_key();
471  }
472
473  void calc_markup_price()
474  {
475     double price,cost ;
476
477     clrscr();
478     puts(
479       "Finance/PC                                   "
480       "Calculate Markup as Per Cent of Price");
481     gotoxy(1,6);
482     puts("Price of Item: ");
483     puts("Cost of Item: ");
484     gotoxy(32,6); scanf("%lf",&price);
485     gotoxy(32,7); scanf("%lf",&cost);
486     printf("Markup %% of Price = %12.2f %%\n",
487        ((price-cost)/price)*100.0 );
488     wait_key();
489  }
490
491  /* +----------------------------------------------------+
492     +              F U N C T I O N   M E N U S           
493     +----------------------------------------------------+
494  */
495
496  void menu_GENBUS()
```

Listing D.1. continues

```
497  {
498    while ( !endjob ) {
499      clrscr();
500      printf("%55s\n","Finance/PC General Business Menu");
501      gotoxy(1,8);
502      puts(
503        "\t\t\t    Per cent (%) Change\n"
504        "\t\t\t    Per cent (%) of Total\n"
505        "\t\t\t    Markup as Per cent (%) of Cost\n"
506        "\t\t\t    Markup as Per cent (%) of Price\n"
507        "\t\t\t    QUIT THIS MENU\n\n" );
508      puts( usermsg );
509      switch ( bullet( 26,8,12 ) ) {
510        case 1: calc_percent_change(); break;
511        case 2: calc_percent_total(); break;
512        case 3: calc_markup_cost(); break;
513        case 4: calc_markup_price(); break;
514        case 5: return;
515      }
516    }
517  }
518
519  void menu_INTEREST()
520  {
521    while ( !endjob ) {
522      clrscr();
523      printf("%60s\n","Finance/PC Interest Rate Conversion Menu");
524      gotoxy(1,8);
525      puts(
526        "\t\t\t    Effective Rate, Periodic Compounding\n"
527        "\t\t\t    Effective Rate, Continuous Compounding\n"
528        "\t\t\t    QUIT THIS MENU\n\n" );
529      puts( usermsg );
530      switch ( bullet( 26,8,10 ) ) {
531        case 1: calc_eff_period(); break;
532        case 2: calc_eff_contin(); break;
533        case 3: return;
534      }
535    }
536  }
537
538  void menu_AMORTIZE()
539  {
540    while ( !endjob ) {
541      clrscr();
542      printf("%53s\n","Finance/PC Amortization Data");
543      gotoxy(1,8);
544      puts(
```

```
545            "\t\t\t    INPUT Basic Data Items\n"
546            "\t\t\t    Display Payment/Payout Data\n"
547            "\t\t\t    Display Amortization Table\n"
548            "\t\t\t    Print Amortization Table\n"
549            "\t\t\t    QUIT THIS MENU\n\n" );
550       puts( usermsg );
551       switch ( bullet( 26,8,12 ) ) {
552         case 1: get_mortgage_data(); break;
553         case 2: if ( amtmort>0 ) display_payout(); break;
554         case 3: if ( amtmort>0 ) display_table(); break;
555         case 4: if ( amtmort>0 ) print_table(); break;
556         case 5: return;
557       }
558     }
559   }
560
561   void menu_ACTUARIAL()
562   {
563     while ( !endjob ) {
564       clrscr();
565       printf("%53s\n","Finance/PC Time Value of Money");
566       gotoxy(1,8);
567       puts(
568         "\t\t\t    Future Value of an Amount\n"
569         "\t\t\t    Present Value of an Amount\n"
570         "\t\t\t    Future Value of a Regular Annuity\n"
571         "\t\t\t    Present Value of a Regular Annuity\n"
572         "\t\t\t    QUIT THIS MENU\n\n" );
573       puts( usermsg );
574       switch ( bullet( 26,8,12 ) ) {
575         case 1: calc_SPFV(); break;
576         case 2: calc_SPPV(); break;
577         case 3: calc_USFV(); break;
578         case 4: calc_USPV(); break;
579         case 5: return;
580       }
581     }
582   }
583
584   void menu_0() /* MASTER MENU (0) */
585   {
586     while ( !endjob ) {
587       clrscr();
588       printf("%48s\n","Finance/PC Master Menu");
589       gotoxy(1,8);
590       puts(
591         "\t\t\t    General Business\n"
592         "\t\t\t    Interest Rate Conversions\n"
593         "\t\t\t    Time Value of Money\n"
594         "\t\t\t    Amortization\n"
```

Listing D.1. continues

Listing D.1. *continued*

```
595          "\t\t\t   QUIT FINANCE/PC\n\n" );
596       puts( usermsg );
597       switch ( bullet( 26,8,12 ) ) {
598         case 1: menu_GENBUS(); break;
599         case 2: menu_INTEREST(); break;
600         case 3: menu_ACTUARIAL(); break;
601         case 4: menu_AMORTIZE(); break;
602         case 5: return;
603       }
604    }
605  }
606
607  main()
608  {
609    amtmort = 0; levelpay = 0; payno = 1; prinpay = 0;
610    intpay = 0; apr = 0; freq = 0; numpay = 0;
611    textbackground(BLUE); textcolor(LIGHTGRAY);
612    clrscr(); endjob = FALSE; menu_0(); clrscr();
613  }
```

Program Structure and Operation

finance.c presents the user with a hierarchy of menus, as shown in figure D.1. The menus are built in a simple way, and items are selected from them under control of the bullet() function (lines 91–113 of listing D.1). bullet() moves the bullet cursor up and down the menu in response to input from the arrow keys.

It is up to the calling function to place the menu items on the screen in the correct location and invoke bullet(), passing to it as parameters the top- and bottom-line numbers of the menu, and the horizontal coordinate (or just *x value*) for the bullet character. This character is a decimal 16 (0x10), which appears on the screen as a right-pointing triangle.

bullet() uses two Turbo C functions that are extensions to the ANSI standard library, and may not be found in every compiler. The first of these, gotoxy(int x, int y), moves the display cursor to a new location.

The other is getch(), which receives a single keystroke from the keyboard, waiting for it if necessary, *without* echoing the character to the screen. Its use in line 99 shows a way to handle IBM's extended ASCII-character and scan codes (which the arrow keys produce).

Fig. D.1. `finance.c` *(Menu structure).*

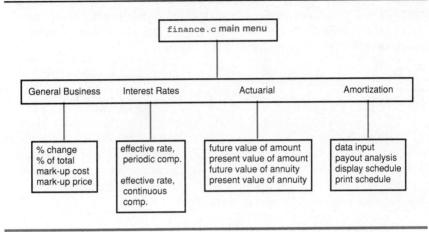

IBM and compatible PCs send back not one but two bytes of data for every key pressed—a *character code* and a *scan code*. If the keystroke was for an ordinary ASCII character, the character and scan codes are the same. But if it was for a key that produces an extended ASCII code, the character code is zero, and the scan code identifies the key that was pressed. For example, the up-arrow produces an extended ASCII code with scan code 72 decimal, and the down-arrow, an 80. You can see in line 99 how the `if` and second `getch()` capture an extended ASCII scan code.

The `switch` statement in lines 100–110 handles the logic of moving the bullet up and down the menu items. This code allows the bullet to "wrap" from top-to-bottom and bottom-to-top of the menu list. Line 112 finally computes an integer indicating which item was selected when the Enter key (character code 13 decimal) was pressed. It does this by computing the distance from the bullet's current location to the first line of the menu list.

The menu item number must now be processed by the calling routine's logic to determine what to do. This can be handled by another `switch` statement. If the call to `bullet()` was placed as the `switch` expression to evaluate, very clean, readable code results, as illustrated by the following excerpt from `menu_0()`, the master menu driver:

```
switch ( bullet( 26,8,12 ) ) {
   case 1: menu_GENBUS();  break;
   case 2: menu_INTEREST(); break;
   case 3: menu_ACTUARIAL(); break;
   case 4: menu_AMORTIZE(); break;
   case 5: return;
}
```

For each `case` statement within the `switch`, another menu-driver routine is invoked. At the lowest level of the menu structure, of course, the calculation routines are invoked. For all of its seeming complexity, this just about exhausts the tricky code in `finance.c`. All that remains is to understand what the calculations actually accomplish.

Using *finance.c* Computations

The main menu of `finance.c` presents the user with four classes of computations that can be performed. These are *general business* functions, *interest rate* conversions, actuarial or *time value of money* calculations, and *mortgage analysis and amortization*. The functions supported by each of these classes will be discussed in turn.

General Business Functions

This group contains the simplest functions in the program. They calculate simple ratios and percentages of interest to the business person.

- ❏ `calc_percent_change()` Calculates the percent change from one amount to another.

- ❏ `calc_percent_total()` Calculates the ratio of two amounts as a percentage.

- ❏ `calc_markup_cost()` The user inputs two amounts: the price and cost of an item. The markup is computed as a percentage of wholesale cost.

- ❏ `calc_markup_price()` The user inputs the price and cost of an item. The markup is computed as a percentage of retail price.

Interest-Rate Conversion

Effective interest-rate conversions are based on the fundamental time value of money formula:

```
Future value of 1 = ( 1 + r )ⁿ
```

where r is the *periodic* interest rate (APR divided by the number of compounding periods per year) and n is the number of compounding periods for which money draws interest (for example, 12 per year). The "future value of 1" refers to the amount to which one dollar will grow over the computed period.

❑ `calc_eff_contin()` The user is asked to input only the APR (Annual Percentage Rate). The algorithm assumes that earnings *are* reinvested and computes an equivalent rate that would be required if they *were not*, but would still generate the same total income over time. No compounding frequency is needed as input, because continuous compounding presumes that interest is earned continuously (such as with money market instruments). Interest on such accounts is usually *computed* on a daily basis, however. This sort of account earns more than one with periodic compounding.

❑ `calc_eff_period()` This function performs the same task as `calc_eff_contin()`, except that compounding is presumed to be monthly, not daily. The user is prompted for the APR and the number of compounding periods (that is, the number of months the money will draw interest).

Time Value of Money

The time value of money functions can be used to analyze your savings strategy. You can project what a regular savings plan will earn over the years, which lump-sum deposit will do the same work as a regular savings plan, or what a lump sum will grow to, given a rate and compounding frequency. When you understand these formulas, you can compute what you must do to reach a goal or how available funds will perform over time.

One of the terms is used here in an uncommon sense. An *annuity* in the present context is a *series of equal and regular deposits you make* into an account. These deposits are presumed to be made at the same frequency and time as interest is compounded for the account.

❑ `SPFV()` *[Single Payment Future Value]*

Computes the final value of an account into which you deposit a lump sum of money, and do nothing else but wait.

❑ `USFV()` *[Uniform Series Future Value]*

Computes the final value of an annuity. This is the function you want to analyze the outcome of a regular savings plan.

❑   SPPV() [Single Payment Present Value]

Suppose that you know how much you want an account to be worth later, and that you want to know the required size of a lump sum to open the account in order to achieve that goal. This function computes that amount. Among other things, the user is prompted for "the number of payments per year." In this function, that refers to the interest payments *received* per year.

❑   USPV() [Uniform Series Present Value]

This function effectively computes the *input* to SPFV(). Given the parameters for a regular annuity (savings deposits), a lump-sum amount is computed which is equivalent to an initial lump-sum deposit and no additional deposits.

This is also the selection you want if you want to know what size loan you can afford to amortize. For example, suppose that you are in the fortunate position of being able to put $50,000.00 down on a house, and your budget can tolerate a $100.00 per month note. If the note is for 30 years, at 10% interest, the present value of an annuity function tells you that you can finance $11,395.08. Thus you can afford a home costing $61,395.08.

Mortgage Analysis and Amortization

This group of functions should be useful to the home owner. You can generate an amortization schedule for your mortgage and either display or print it. You can also perform a payout analysis, which tells you just how badly the lender got to you.

❑   get_mortgage_data()

Displays a formatted data-entry screen for mortgage details. Because scanf() is used in a primitive way, you *must* enter something in every field; failure to do so causes unpredictable behavior on-screen. You would come back to this screen later if you wanted to specify another particular payment number— unfortunately, you must reenter everything with it. Making this more flexible would be a good practice project. You must come to this screen at least once before selecting any of the other amortization screens or options.

❏ `display_table()`

Displays the amortization schedule on the terminal, 12 payments at a time. Press Enter to get the next page; press Esc to leave the display and return to the menu. The first payment number displayed is the one entered in the data-entry screen, or the one just after the last one previously displayed. The amortization schedule includes the payment number, the level payment amount, the amount of principal, and the amount of interest for each payment.

❏ `print_table()`

Sends the entire amortization schedule to the system printer. This routine uses the nonstandard low-level `write()` function with a DOS handle to access the printer. As you may recall, you can also use `fprintf(stdprn,...)` to do this, although this too is nonstandard.

❏ `display_payout()`

Do an analysis of the loan payout. Use the data-entry screen first, being sure to indicate a specific payment for extra analysis. The output display includes the level payment required to amortize the loan, the total principal and total interest paid over the life of the loan, and details for the specific payment requested.

A payout analysis tells you some astounding things. For example, lenders do not like to make home loans for less than 30 years. For a typical home, with a 30 year mortgage, *interest paid alone equals two to three times the entire value of the house*, depending on the interest rate. Look at the following comparison, for instance:

Years	Interest Paid Out	Level Payment
30	107,962.88	438.79
20	65,802.60	482.51

If you can stand an extra $50.00 per month on your note, you can put $41,890.28 back in your pocket later!

`finance.c` demonstrates that some pretty amazing things can be done in C with just the basic I/O functions and a little patience. With this program you can plan the impact of various savings strategies on your financial future, completely analyze and report mortgage-loan data, and do a number of computations of value to business planning. We hope that you enjoy it and find it useful.

E

IBM PC Communications Programming

The program in listing E.1 `ccom.c`, is a "dumb" terminal program. It doesn't support file-transfer protocols, user commands, configuration changes, or any number of other things that would make it a full-blown communications package. It does provide built-in VT52 terminal emulation (at least enough to get formatted screens on CompuServe), and a limited command and scripting facility. Before we launch into the source listing for `ccom.c`, some explanation of the program's purpose and construction is necessary.

The program's purpose is to give you a skeleton program, with the most difficult parts already written, that you can use to build your own communications program that has all the features you want. It also amply illustrates what it costs you, the programmer, to write I/O support code without the benefit of the C function library (there are no library functions for communications I/O). The fact that this "dumb" program requires 436 lines of code is perhaps the best indication of what that cost is.

`ccom.c` provides interrupt-driven I/O support for communications port COM1 on an IBM PC or true compatible, running at 1200 Baud, with 7 data bits, even parity, and 1 stop bit (written as 7E1). A 2K (2,048 byte) recirculating buffer `hold_buf` is used to hold incoming data bytes until the program is ready to deal with them.

Lines 18–36 in listing E.1 provide `#define` macros for the character values of many of the ASCII-based communications control characters. Not all of them are used in `ccom.c`, but many are provided for your future use.

The purpose and operation of the 18 functions in listing E.1, other than `main()`, are described briefly as follows:

❑   `void interrupt int_svc( void );`

This is the interrupt-handler routine for COM1. When the interrupt controller chip raises IRQ4 (Interrupt Request 4), interrupt vector 12 is used to route control to the handler—this is set up by `hook_com()`, discussed next. `int_svc()` reads the byte from the communications port and places it in the recirculating buffer. Because the buffer has a wrap-around design, any bytes "in the way" are overwritten and lost. Data loss can be controlled by limiting the amount of work the PC is allowed to do before fetching the next byte, and also by providing a large enough buffer. A 2K buffer is large enough for most purposes, even on slower machines.

Because the interrupt triggering this function is a hardware interrupt, the interrupt condition must be cleared before leaving the function.

❑   `void hook_com( void );`

`hook_com()` programs the 8259 Interrupt Controller chip to associate IRQ4 with interrupt vector 12. This is not an arbitrary choice. A close inspection of `hook_com()` shows that all the code does is *enable* IRQ4; it is assumed that the hardware is arranged so that this corresponds to vector 12.

❑   `void unhook_com( void );`

This disables interrupts before terminating the program.

❑   `void init_com( void );`

This function does two things. First, it clears any pending hardware interrupts that may have been left by previous executions of the communications program. Don't tinker with this code unless you are an expert on PC hardware programming. Second, it programs the asynchronous communications chip, via I/O ports, for 1200 Baud and 7E1 bit configuration.

❑   `void near send_comm_byte( void );`

Wait until the communications line is ready, and then send the byte in `key_in`. This object usually contains the last input keystroke, but you could place anything you want in it, from any source, to implement a macro key facility.

Notice that this and all following functions have the near type qualifier. This is a PC-specific memory-model control keyword, not part of standard C. It is used to reduce the overhead of linkage to the functions, saving time, and perhaps preventing the loss of incoming data traffic.

❏   `void near get_comm_byte( void );`

Receive any number of bytes from the communications line, and display them on the screen. If parity is on (it is—by default—in this program), the high-order bit of the incoming byte may be on; it is set off by using bitwise AND in line 231.

❏   `void near wait_for_tx( void );`

Wait for one byte only from the communications line. This function is used when an escape character has been detected in the incoming traffic stream, indicating that some special VT52 (the basis of CompuServe's Vidtex mode) screen-formatting characters are about to appear. Those characters must be waited for and processed separately.

❏   `void near ch_out( unsigned char data );`

Display a single character on-screen. A combination of Turbo C's windowing capabilities and direct screen-RAM access are used for extremely high-speed display. This is pleasing to the user, and also reduces the time not spent processing communications traffic (this may be much more important at higher baud rates).

❏   `int near test_key( void );`

Uses the system BIOS services to determine whether a character from the keyboard is available. This function is called by the `main()` function to check on user keyboard input for transmission, and also by `wait_for_tx()`, where it is used to abort the wait for a received data byte.

Aborting a wait may be necessary if a transmission error occurred during the receipt of a VT52 formatting sequence. You generally are able to tell that something is wrong because your screen stops at what appears to be the wrong time. Press any key to break in and continue communications processing.

❑   `unsigned char near get_key( void );`

Use the system BIOS services to get the next keystroke from the keyboard.

❑   `void near scroll_up( void );`

Scroll the display window up one line, clearing the bottom line of the screen.

❑   `void near vidtex( void );`

This function handles all the VT52 escape sequences. It is called by the `ch_out()` function, which has detected that formatting is needed, rather than display service (that is, it has received an ESC character to process). `vidtex()` waits for the next incoming data byte and positions or formats the display accordingly.

❑   `void near vidtex_sba( void );`

`vidtex_sba()` handles the special positioning request for a random placement of the screen cursor. The acronym *sba* means *set buffer address*, and is borrowed from the IBM mainframe communications environment.

❑   `void near overlay( char *string );`

`overlay()` is used only to place part of the banner line at the top of the screen with different color attributes. When `overlay()` encounters a blank in the argument string, it *does not* write a blank to the screen; it merely spaces over, presuming that another function—`string_out()`—has already put something on the screen. This is how the banner line is built with both red and black characters on a gray background.

❑   `void near string_out( char *string );`

Display the argument string on-screen. All characters are output exactly as received. It is assumed that the cursor has already been positioned to the place where output is to occur.

❑   `void near kbd_command( void );`

When the Esc key is pressed, this function inputs a command from the user and routes it to the command handler, `exe_command()`.

❏　`int near exe_command( char *s );`

Interprets and executes the command in `s`. The command may be the `run` command, which invokes script processing. The script processor in turn calls `exe_command()`—these two functions are mutually recursive. Note that this means that a script may contain a `run` command to start an embedded script.

❏　`int run_script( char *sname );`

Load the script file `sname` into dynamically acquired memory and run the script. A script may contain any valid command, plus the special verbs `ifkey` and `goto`. (Script processing is illustrated after the program listing has been presented.)

Listing E.1. `ccom.c` (*Asynchronous communications program with VT52 support and scripting*).　　　　　　　　　　　　　　　　　　　　　*Turbo C 2.0*

```
 1   /* +---------------------------------------------------+
 2       + CCOM.C
 3       +    Compile this program with the LARGE MEMORY MODEL.
 4       +    If you do not, you receive warnings for suspicious
 5       +    pointer conversion for the memcpy() function, and
 6       +    the program may not function correctly.
 7       +---------------------------------------------------+
 8   */
 9   #include <stdio.h>
10   #include <stdlib.h>
11   #include <string.h>
12   #include <mem.h>
13   #include <conio.h>
14   #include <ctype.h>
15   #include <dos.h>
16   #include <bios.h>
17
18   #define TRUE   1
19   #define FALSE  0
20   #define FF     12
21   #define LF     10
22   #define CR     13
23   #define BEL    7
24   #define BS     8
25   #define HT     9
26   #define ESC    27
27   #define XON    17
28   #define XOFF   27
29   #define ACK    6
```

Listing E.1. continues

```
30   #define NAK   21
31   #define SYN   22
32   #define CAN   24
33   #define SOH   1
34   #define EOT   4
35   #define ENQ   5
36   #define DEL   127
37
38   struct {
39     int x, y;
40     size_t sizebuf;
41     unsigned char far *savebuf;
42   } hscreen;
43
44
45   union REGS reg;
46   void interrupt (*old_12)();
47   int pad_lcr = 0x03fb;      /* Line Control Reg, COM1 */
48   int pad_dll = 0x03f8;      /* Divisor Latch, Low, DLAB=1 */
49   int pad_dlm = 0x03f9;      /* Divisor Latch, Hi Byte */
50   int pad_mcr = 0x03fc;      /* MODEM Control Reg. */
51   int pad_lsr = 0x03fd;      /* Line Status Reg */
52   int pad_msr = 0x03fe;      /* Modem Status Reg */
53   int pad_rbr = 0x03f8;      /* Receive Buf Reg, DLAB=0 */
54   int pad_thr = 0x03f8;      /* Tx Hold Reg, DLAB=0 */
55   int pad_ier = 0x03f9;      /* Intr Enable Reg, DLAB=0 */
56   int pad_iir = 0x03fa;      /* Intr Ident Reg, R/O */
57   unsigned char port_data;
58   unsigned char tx_in;
59   unsigned char hwi_level;
60   unsigned key_in;
61   unsigned char hold_buf[2048];
62   volatile int headq;
63   volatile int endq;
64   int ext_ascii = FALSE;
65   int echo = 0;
66   int orphan = FALSE;
67   int strip = TRUE;
68   struct text_info screen;
69   int x,y;
70   unsigned char far *vram;
71
72   void interrupt int_svc( void );
73   void hook_com( void );
74   void unhook_com( void );
75   void init_com( void );
76   void near send_comm_byte( void );
77   void near send_string( char *s );
78   void near get_comm_byte( void );
```

```
79   void near wait_for_tx( void );
80   int near wait_for_string( char *s );
81   void near ch_out( unsigned char data );
82   int near test_key( void );
83   unsigned char near get_key( void );
84   void near scroll_up( void );
85   void near vidtex( void );
86   void near vidtex_sba( void );
87   void near overlay( char *string );
88   void near string_out( char *string );
89   void near kbd_command( void );
90   int near exe_command( char *s );
91   int run_script( char *sname );
92
93   main()
94   {
95     textmode( 3 );
96     textbackground( BLUE );
97     textcolor( LIGHTGRAY );
98     clrscr();
99     x = y = 1;
100    gettextinfo( &screen );
101    switch ( screen.currmode ) {
102      case 1:
103      case 2:
104      case 3:
105      case 4:
106      case 5:
107      case 6: vram = MK_FP( 0xB800, 0 ); break;
108      case 7: vram = MK_FP( 0xB000, 0 ); break;
109      default: vram = MK_FP( 0xA000, 0 ); break;
110    }
111    window( 1, 1, 80, 1 );
112    textbackground( LIGHTGRAY );
113    textcolor( BLACK );
114    clrscr();
115    gotoxy( 2, 1 );
116    gettextinfo( &screen );
117    string_out( "  -Command    -Duplex    -Orphan       -Quit" );
118
119    textbackground( LIGHTGRAY );
120    textcolor( RED );
121    gotoxy( 2, 1 );
122    gettextinfo( &screen );
123    overlay( "F1-          F2-          F3-          F10-     " );
124
125    window( 1, 2, 80, 25 );
126    textbackground( BLUE );
127    textcolor( LIGHTGRAY );
128    gettextinfo( &screen );
```

Listing E.1. continues

```
129     hscreen.sizebuf = 4000U;
130     if ( NULL == ( hscreen.savebuf =
131           malloc( hscreen.sizebuf ) ) ) {
132       window( 1, 1, 80, 25 );
133       clrscr();
134       printf( "Allocate for screen save memory failed.\n" );
135       exit( 8 );
136     }
137     x = y = 1;
138     gotoxy( x, y );
139     init_com();
140     hook_com();
141     while ( 1 ) {
142       get_comm_byte();
143       if ( test_key() ) {
144         key_in = get_key();
145         if ( ext_ascii ) {
146           switch ( key_in ) {
147             case 59: kbd_command(); break;
148             case 60: echo = !echo; break;
149             case 61: orphan = !orphan; break;
150             case 68: window( 1, 1, 80, 25 ); clrscr();
151                     unhook_com(); exit( 0 ) ;
152           }
153         }
154         else { /* not ext_ascii */
155           send_comm_byte();
156           if ( echo ) {
157             ch_out( key_in );
158             gotoxy( x, y );
159           }
160         }
161       } /* if (test_key()) */
162     } /* while */
163   }
164   /* +----------------------------------------------------+
165      + Interrupt Service Routine ...
166      +    Get a byte from the Receive Buffer Register
167      +    (RBR) when interrupt 12 occurs, and place it
168      +    in the circulating buffer.
169      +----------------------------------------------------+
170   */
171   void interrupt int_svc( void )
172   {
173     disable();
174     if ( ++endq == 2048 ) endq = 0;
175     hold_buf[endq] = inp( pad_rbr );
176     outp( 0x20,0x64 ); /* Signal End of Interrupt to 8259 */
```

```
177    enable();
178  }
179
180  /* +---------------------------------------------------+
181     + Install Communications Interrupt Service
182     +     Hook ISR int_svc to interrupt vector 12
183     +     Latch IRQ 4 signal to ISR 12
184     +---------------------------------------------------+
185  */
186  void hook_com( void )
187  {
188    old_12 = getvect( 12 );
189    setvect( 12,int_svc );
190    headq = endq = 0;
191    disable();
192    port_data = inp( 0x21 );      /* Read 8259 Intr. Ctlr. */
193    outp( 0x21,port_data & 0xef );    /* Set up 8259 IRQ4 */
194    port_data = inp( pad_lcr );
195    outp( pad_lcr, port_data & 0x7f ); /* DLAB=0 for IER */
196    outp( pad_ier, 0x01 );   /* Enable DATA READY Intrpts */
197    outp( pad_mcr, 0x0B );                /* Modem Ctl Reg */
198    enable();
199  }
200
201  /* +---------------------------------------------------+
202     + De-Install Communications Interrupt Service
203     +     Unhook ISR int_svc from interrupt vector 12
204     +     Unlatch IRQ 4 signal from ISR 12
205     +---------------------------------------------------+
206  */
207  void unhook_com( void )
208  {
209    port_data = inp( pad_lcr );
210    outp( pad_lcr, port_data & 0x7f );
211    outp( pad_ier, 0 );              /* Turn IER Intrpts OFF */
212    outp( pad_mcr, 0 );                   /* Modem Ctl Reg */
213    disable();
214    port_data = inp( 0x21 );      /* Read 8259 Intr. Ctlr. */
215    outp( 0x21, port_data | 0x10 );   /* 8259 DISAB lvl 4 */
216    enable();
217    setvect( 12, old_12 );
218  }
219
220  /* +---------------------------------------------------+
221     + Initialize Communications Parameters
222     +---------------------------------------------------+
223  */
224  void init_com( void )
225  {
```

Listing E.1. continues

```
226    /* Clear any outstanding hardware interrupts first */
227    outp( 0x20, 0x0B );              /* read 8259 serv reg */
228    delay(1);                             /* let it settle */
229    hwi_level = inp( 0x20 );       /* read hw level pending */
230    if ( hwi_level ) {                /* interrupt exists */
231      port_data = inp( 0x21 );              /* get masks */
232      outp( 0x21, port_data | hwi_level ); /* mask off hwi */
233      outp( 0x20, 0x64 );        /* and send End-Of-Intrpt */
234    }
235    unhook_com();                  /* attempt to init port */
236    outp( pad_lcr, 0x9A ); /* DLAB=1, 8 DATA, NO/P, 1 STOP */
237    outp( pad_dlm, 0 ); outp( pad_dll, 0x60 ); /* 1200 BAUD */
238    port_data = inp( pad_lcr );
239    outp( pad_lcr, port_data & 0x7f );           /* DLAB=0 */
240  }
241
242  /* +---------------------------------------------------+
243     + Transmit a Character Over the Comm Line
244     +---------------------------------------------------+
245  */
246  void near send_comm_byte( void )
247  {
248    port_data = 0;
249    while ( port_data != 32 ) {
250      port_data = inp( pad_lsr );  /* Get Line Status Reg */
251      port_data = port_data & 0x20;  /* See if THRE is on */
252    }
253    outp( pad_thr, key_in );         /* XMIT byte to THR */
254  }
255
256  /* +---------------------------------------------------+
257     + Send a String of Characters Over the Comm Line
258     +---------------------------------------------------+
259  */
260  void near send_string( char *s )
261  {
262    while ( *s ) {
263      key_in = *s++;
264      send_comm_byte();
265      if ( echo ) {
266        ch_out( key_in );
267        gotoxy( x, y );
268      }
269    }
270  }
271
272  /* +---------------------------------------------------+
```

```
273        + Receive a Character From Transmission Line
274        +    As long as there are bytes in the circulating
275        +    buffer, get and process them.
276        +-------------------------------------------------+
277   */
278   void near get_comm_byte( void )
279   {
280     while ( headq != endq ) {
281       headq += 1;
282       if ( headq == 2048 ) headq = 0;
283       tx_in = hold_buf[headq];
284       if ( strip ) tx_in &= 0x7F;
285       ch_out( tx_in );
286     }
287     gotoxy( x, y );
288   }
289
290   /* +-------------------------------------------------+
291      + Receive One Character From Transmission Line
292      +    Wait for it if not ready.
293      +    Break out if user strikes any key.
294      +-------------------------------------------------+
295   */
296   void near wait_for_tx( void )
297   {
298     while ( headq == endq ) {
299       if ( test_key() ) {
300         get_key();
301         tx_in = 255;
302         return;
303       }
304     }
305     headq += 1;
306     if ( headq == 2048 ) headq = 0;
307     tx_in = hold_buf[headq];
308     if ( strip ) tx_in &= 0x7F;
309   }
310
311   /* +-------------------------------------------------+
312      + Wait For a String Pattern in Incoming Traffic
313      +-------------------------------------------------+
314   */
315   int near wait_for_string( char *s )
316   {
317     char *p = s;
318
319     while ( *p ) {
320       wait_for_tx();
321       if ( tx_in == 255 ) return 0;
```

Listing E.1. continues

```
322        ch_out( tx_in );
323        gotoxy( x, y );
324        if ( *p == tx_in ) p++;
325        else p = s;
326     }
327     return 1; /* Found whole pattern */
328  }
329
330  /* +----------------------------------------------------+
331     + Display a Character on the Screen
332     +----------------------------------------------------+
333  */
334  void near ch_out( unsigned char data )
335  {
336     switch ( data ) {
337       case ESC: vidtex(); break;
338       case LF:  ++y; break;
339       case CR:  x = 1;
340                 if ( orphan ) ++y; break;
341       case FF:  clrscr();
342                 x = y = 1;
343                 break;
344       case BEL: break;
345       case BS:  if ( --x < 1 ) {
346                    x = screen.winright - screen.winleft + 1;
347                    if ( --y < 1 ) y = 1;
348                 }
349                 break;
350       default: *(vram + (screen.winleft+x-2)*2
351                    + (screen.wintop+y-2)*160) = data;
352                 ++x;
353     }
354     if ( x > screen.winright - screen.winleft + 1 ) {
355       x = 1;
356       ++y;
357     }
358     if ( y > screen.winbottom - screen.wintop + 1 ) {
359       scroll_up();
360       y = screen.winbottom - screen.wintop + 1;
361     }
362  }
363
364  /* +----------------------------------------------------+
365     + Test for Keystroke Availability
366     +----------------------------------------------------+
367  */
368  int near test_key( void )
369  {
```

```
370      reg.x.ax = 0x0100;
371      int86( 0x16, &reg, &reg );
372      if ( reg.x.flags & 0x0040 ) return( 0 );
373      else return( 1 );
374  }
375
376  /* +-----------------------------------------------------+
377       + Get the Next Available Keystroke
378       +-----------------------------------------------------+
379  */
380  unsigned char near get_key( void )
381  {
382      reg.x.ax = 0x0000;
383      int86( 0x16, &reg, &reg );
384      if ( reg.h.al ) {
385        ext_ascii = FALSE;
386        return ( reg.h.al );
387      }
388      else {
389        ext_ascii = TRUE;
390        return( reg.h.ah );
391      }
392  }
393
394  /* +-----------------------------------------------------+
395       + Scroll the Display Screen One Line Up
396       +-----------------------------------------------------+
397  */
398  void near scroll_up( void )
399  {
400      reg.x.ax = 0x0601;              /* Scroll up 1 line */
401      reg.h.bh = screen.attribute;     /* Use attribute */
402      reg.h.ch = screen.wintop - 1;      /* Area to use */
403      reg.h.cl = screen.winleft - 1;
404      reg.h.dh = screen.winbottom - 1;
405      reg.h.dl = screen.winright - 1;
406      int86( 0x10, &reg, &reg );
407  }
408
409  /* +-----------------------------------------------------+
410       + Handle CompuServe's VIDTEX Escape Sequences
411       +-----------------------------------------------------+
412  */
413  void near vidtex( void )
414  {
415      static int i;
416
417      wait_for_tx();
418      if (tx_in == 255 ) return;
```

Listing E.1. continues

Listing E.1. *continued*

```
419    switch ( tx_in ) {
420      case 'A': --y;
421              if ( y < 1 )
422                  y = screen.winbottom - screen.wintop + 1;
423              break;
424      case 'B': ++y;
425              if ( y > screen.winbottom - screen.wintop + 1 )
426                  y = 1;
427              break;
428      case 'C': ++x;
429              if ( x > screen.winright - screen.winleft +1 ) {
430                  x = 1;
431                  ++y;
432                  if ( y > screen.winbottom - screen.wintop + 1 )
433                      y = screen.wintop;
434              }
435              break;
436      case 'D': --x;
437              if ( x < 1 ) {
438                  x = screen.winright - screen.winleft + 1;
439                  --y;
440                  if ( y < 1 )
441                      y = screen.winbottom - screen.wintop + 1;
442              }
443              break;
444      case 'H': x = y = 1;
445              break;
446      case 'K': clreol();
447              brcak;
448      case 'J': clreol();
449              for ( i=y+1; i<=screen.winbottom-y+1; i++ ) {
450                  gotoxy( 1, i ); clreol();
451              }
452              break;
453      case 'j': clrscr();
454              x = 1;
455              y = 1;
456              break;
457      case 'Y': vidtex_sba(); break;
458    }
459  }
460
461  /* +----------------------------------------------------+
462     + VIDTEX Set-Cursor-Address Sequence
463     +----------------------------------------------------+
464  */
465  void near vidtex_sba( void )
466  {
```

```
467    wait_for_tx();
468    if ( tx_in == 255 ) return;
469    y = tx_in - 31;
470    if ( y < 1 ) y = 1;
471    if ( y > screen.winbottom - screen.wintop + 1 )
472      y = screen.winbottom - screen.wintop + 1;
473    wait_for_tx();
474    if ( tx_in == 255 ) return;
475    x = tx_in - 31;
476    if ( x < 1 ) y = 1;
477    if ( x > screen.winright - screen.winleft + 1 )
478      y = screen.winright;
479  }
480
481  void near overlay( char *string )
482  {
483    x = wherex();
484    y = wherey();
485    while ( *string ) {
486      if ( *string != ' ' ) *(vram + ( screen.winleft + x - 2 ) * 2
487        + ( screen.wintop + y - 2 ) * 160 ) = *string;
488      if ( *string != ' ' ) *(vram + ( screen.winleft + x - 2 ) * 2
489        + ( screen.wintop + y - 2 ) * 160  + 1 ) = screen.attribute;
490      x++; string++;
491      if ( x > screen.winright ) { x = screen.winleft; ++y; }
492      if ( y > screen.winbottom ) {
493        scroll_up();
494        y = screen.winbottom;
495      }
496    }
497    gotoxy( x, y );
498  }
499
500  void near string_out( char *string )
501  {
502    x = wherex();
503    y = wherey();
504    while ( *string ) {
505      *(vram + ( screen.winleft + x++ - 2 ) * 2
506        + ( screen.wintop + y - 2 ) * 160 ) = *string++;
507      if ( x > screen.winright ) { x = screen.winleft; ++y; }
508      if ( y > screen.winbottom ) {
509        scroll_up();
510        y = screen.winbottom;
511      }
512    }
513    gotoxy( x, y );
514  }
515
516  void near kbd_command( void )
```

Listing E.1. continues

```
517  {
518    char cmdline[41];
519
520    ch_out( CR ); ch_out( LF ); gotoxy( x, y );
521    string_out( "<Enter Command>: " );
522    gets( cmdline );
523    ch_out( CR ); ch_out( LF ); gotoxy( x, y );
524    exe_command( cmdline );
525  }
526
527  int near exe_command( char *s )
528  {
529    char *p = s;
530
531    while ( *p ) {                        /* replace ~ with CR */
532      if ( *p == '~' ) *p = '\r';
533      p++;
534    }
535    if ( !strncmp( s, "send", 4 ) ) {
536      while ( *s && *s != ' ' ) s++; /* get beyond verb */
537      while ( *s && *s == ' ' ) s++; /* get to object */
538      send_string( s );              /* put it on the line */
539      return 1;
540    }
541    if ( !strncmp( s, "wait", 4  ) ) {
542      while ( *s && *s != ' ' ) s++; /* get beyond verb */
543      while ( *s && *s == ' ' ) s++; /* get to object */
544      return wait_for_string( s );   /* see if we got it */
545    }
546    it ( !strncmp( s, "run", 3  ) ) {
547      while ( *s && *s != ' ' ) s++;
548      while ( *s && *s == ' ' ) s++;
549      return run_script( s );
550    }
551    if ( !strncmp( s, "display", 7  ) ) {
552      while ( *s && *s != ' ' ) s++;
553      s++;
554      while ( *s ) ch_out( *s++ );
555      ch_out( CR ); ch_out( LF );
556      gotoxy( x, y );
557      return 1;
558    }
559    if ( !strncmp( s, "push", 4  ) ) {
560      if ( !hscreen.savebuf ) return 0;
561      memcpy( hscreen.savebuf, vram, hscreen.sizebuf );
562      hscreen.x = wherex();
563      hscreen.y = wherey();
564      return 1;
```

```
565      }
566      if ( !strncmp( s, "pop", 3 ) ) {
567        if ( !hscreen.savebuf ) return 0;
568        memcpy( vram, hscreen.savebuf, hscreen.sizebuf );
569        x = hscreen.x;
570        y = hscreen.y;
571        gotoxy( x, y );
572        return 1;
573      }
574      if ( !strncmp( s, "getkey", 6 ) ) {
575        key_in = get_key();
576        return 1;
577      }
578      if ( !strncmp( s, "system", 6 ) ) {
579        while ( *s && *s != ' ' ) s++;
580        while ( *s && *s == ' ' ) s++;
581        return system( s );
582      }
583      if ( !strncmp( s, "help", 4 ) ) {
584        return run_script( "help.scr" );
585      }
586    }
587
588    int run_script( char *sname )
589    {
590      FILE *sfile;
591      char *cmdbuf;
592      char *cmd;
593      char label[9];
594
595      if ( NULL == ( cmdbuf = (char *)malloc( 16384 ) ) ) {
596        ch_out( CR ); ch_out( LF );
597        string_out( "Not Enough Memory." );
598        ch_out( CR ); ch_out( LF );
599        return 0;
600      }
601      *cmdbuf = '\0';
602      cmd = cmdbuf;
603      if ( NULL == ( sfile = fopen( sname, "r" ) ) ) {
604        ch_out( CR ); ch_out( LF );
605        string_out( "Can't find script: " );
606        string_out( sname );
607        ch_out( CR ); ch_out( LF );
608        return 0;
609      }
610      while ( NULL != fgets( cmd, 255, sfile ) ) {
611        while ( *cmd && *cmd != '\n' ) cmd++;
612        if ( *cmd == '\n' ) *cmd++ = '\0';
613        else cmd++;
```

Listing E.1. continues

Listing E.1. continued

```
614      }
615      *cmd = '\0';              /* terminate command list with a null */
616      fclose( sfile );
617      cmd = cmdbuf;                     /* reset the command pointer */
618
619      while ( *cmd ) {                 /* and EXECUTE THE COMMANDS */
620        if ( !strncmp( cmd, "ifkey", 5 ) ) {
621          while ( *cmd && *cmd != ' ' ) cmd++;
622          while ( *cmd && *cmd == ' ' ) cmd++;
623          if ( key_in == *cmd ) {
624            while ( *cmd && *cmd != ' ' ) cmd++;
625            while ( *cmd && *cmd == ' ' ) cmd++;
626          }
627        }
628        if ( !strncmp( cmd, "goto", 4 ) ) {    /* do JUMPS here */
629          while ( *cmd && *cmd != ' ' ) cmd++;
630          while ( *cmd && *cmd == ' ' ) cmd++;
631          strcpy( label, cmd );
632          cmd = cmdbuf;                 /* goto top to start search */
633          while ( *cmd ) {                      /* search for label */
634            if ( !strncmp( cmd, label, strlen( label ) ) )
635              break;
636            while ( *cmd++ ) ;                      /* next string */
637          }
638        }
639        if ( !exe_command( cmd ) ) {        /* if execution error */
640          ch_out( CR ); ch_out( LF );
641          string_out( "Failing Command: " );
642          string_out( cmd );
643          ch_out( CR ); ch_out( LF );
644          free( cmdbuf );                       /* release the buffer */
645          return 0;                             /* and get out dirty */
646        }
647        while ( *cmd++ ) ;                        /* next string */
648      }
649      free( cmdbuf );                  /* release the command buffer */
650      return 1;             /* finished the script with no errors */
651    }
```

Writing a script for ccom.c is easy. Just use your favorite text editor to create a text file containing ccom commands and script directives. A command verb must begin in the first character of each line, and it must be in lowercase letters. The following are three of the most commonly used commands:

❏ *display*

Code exactly one blank after the verb. Everything after that, to the end of the line, is displayed on your screen, but not sent over the communications line.

❏ *send*

Code a blank as with *display*. Everything following the blank is transmitted over the communications line. To send a carriage return (CR) character, code a tilde (˜). It is converted internally to CR, and then sent.

❏ *Everything after the single blank is used as a string pattern for matching against incoming bytes.* The program loops until all bytes in the pattern have been received. You can strike any key on the keyboard to break out of the wait, which also terminates the script.

A script to dial up CompuServe and automatically supply your user identification and password (in other words, to log you on automatically) is easy to write with just these three commands, as you can see from the following example:

```
display ---- Dialing CompuServe ----
send atdtnnnnnnnn,,,˜ ( ˜ means send CR )
wait CONNECT 1200
send         ( sends Control-C character )
wait User ID: ( wait on string pattern )
send nnnnn,nnnn˜      ( send CR here too )
wait word:
send your.password˜ ( CR one more time )
```

If this script file resides in a text file named cis, to run it, you just press F1 to get the command prompt, and then enter the following:

```
run cis
```

and press Enter. The script runs without further input from you. More complicated scripts, using other commands, are possible. For example, you could write scripts to provide a complete on-line help facility. The first script file, help.scr, might contain something like this:

```
push
display                       CCOM Master Help Menu
display ---------------------------------------------------------
display ˜ ( this leaves a blank line on the screen )
display                       a - help on commands
display                       b - help on scripts
```

```
display                              c - help on communications parms
display                              d - help on upload / download
display                              x - QUIT HELP
display     ~ ( this leaves a blank line on the screen )
display                     Strike a key for help on the topic listed,
display                          or strike x to quit help.
getkey
ifkey a run cmd.scr
ifkey b run scr.scr
ifkey x goto pop
goto display
pop
```

The push command saves a copy of the current screen so that it can be restored later. After the screen is painted, the getkey command collects a keystroke from the user, corresponding to one of the menu items. The ifkey script directive then selects which additional script file to run in order to get more detailed information.

The goto script directive is a little unusual. The argument for goto is not quite like a C label statement (although you can make it look like that, if you want). When a goto is encountered, the script is positioned at the top, and the *first characters of every* line are compared against the search string until a line containing them is found. *It doesn't matter what those first characters are*—they can be a command verb, or any label you make up.

As an exercise, we suggest that you examine the program thoroughly, and then devise the succeeding help scripts.

F

B-Spline Derivation

The B-spline interpolation procedure for curve smoothing is based on the parametric cubic representation of an *n*-dimensional curve. In this representation, the variable names x_1, x_2, and x_3 are used rather than x, y, and z. The general position variable is then x_i, where i = 1, 2, 3. Furthermore, a given x_i is computed using a parameter variable *t*. The point of the B-spline interpolation is to find a suitable value for *t* so that a cubic function of *t* both smooths the curve and controls the end points of each segment sufficiently.

The derivation is carried out using matrix algebra. In general the matrix equation for the parameteric cubic form of a curve is as follows:

```
x  = TMG       i = 1, 2, 3
 i       i
```

In this equation, because the matrix product TM remains constant for all x_i, it is derived first. The matrix T is the row matrix of the cubic polynomial in *t*:

```
T = Ü t3 t2 t 1ᶠ Ü
```

The matrix M is known as the *Hermite matrix*. You might think of it as a set of characteristic equations that transform the original points into a smooth curve. For the B-spline, the value of the Hermite matrix is

$$M = 1/6 * \begin{bmatrix} -1 & 3 & -3 & 1 \\ 3 & -6 & 3 & 0 \\ -3 & 0 & 3 & 0 \\ 1 & 4 & 1 & 0 \end{bmatrix}$$

The product of these two matrices is a row matrix:

$$1/6 * [(-t^3+3t^2-3t+1) \quad (3t^3-6t^2+4) \quad (-3t^3+3t^2+3t+1) \quad (t^3)]$$

Finally, for each of the x_i variables, the G matrix is a column matrix called the *Hermite geometry matrix*. Its function is to provide a set of original points that acts as boundary markers for the smooth curve. The B-spline formulation considers four points at a time: the current point being processed, one point preceding, and two points following. If we let P_i stand for the current point, then:

$$G_i = \begin{bmatrix} P_{i-1} \\ P_i \\ P_{i+1} \\ P_{i+2} \end{bmatrix}$$

This particular selection of geometry points is why the B-spline interpolation does not pass through the end points of the curve being smoothed.

When the geometry matrix G_i is applied (using a post-multiplication procedure) an equation results that can be used to calculate the interpolated points:

$$\begin{aligned} x_i = \; & 1/6(-t^3+3t^2-3t+1)P_{i-1} \\ + \; & 1/6(3t^3-6t^2+4)P_i \\ + \; & 1/6(-3t^3+3t^2+3t+1)P_{i+1} \\ + \; & 1/6(t^3)P_{i+2} \end{aligned}$$

To understand how to implement this algorithm, go back to thinking of the curve in Cartesian coordinates—x, y, and z. At each point on the curve, you must calculate previous, current, and next values of x, apply the formula, calculate previous, current, and next values of y, apply the formula, and so on. The algorithm can be speeded up by premultiplying the 1/6 across each expression and hard-coding the fractional values that result.

G

Performance-Measurement Software

P recision measurement of the performance of a computer algorithm is somewhat problematic on the IBM PC, because the system clock ticks just 18.2 times per second. This is true whether you are running the original 8088-based PC or the latest 80386 with a 33 MHz CPU clock frequency. The best resolution you can get at 18.2 ticks per second is about 0.055 sec., or a little better than one-twentieth of a second.

Clearly, a fast computer can do a lot of work in that time. Something better is needed to compare the speeds and performance of functions under development. Fortunately, the timer chip supplied on all PCs and good clones can be programmed to tick faster or slower, as desired. In this case, we want faster—much faster—ticks. All you have to do is reprogram the timer chip temporarily. A word of caution: a high tick rate on a slow processor can eat up too much of the machine's processing capability.

The actual chip used in your machine may vary, depending on the model you own. On the original 8088 machines, the Intel 8253-5 was used. On PC/ AT-class machines (including 80286 and most 80386 clones), the Intel 8254-2 chip was used, whereas PS/2 models implement timing in custom integrated circuits.

Because the programming interface is the same in every case, no matter which chip is used, the routines given here should work just about universally—although you may have to vary the tick rate on some machines. These routines have been tested on machines from a plain "blue" IBM PC (4.77 MHz; 1,000 ticks per second) to an AT-class clone with an 80386 running at 20 MHz (10,000 ticks per second).

In order to reprogram the timer chip successfully, you must control three things. Each of them is as important as the other two—you must get them all right, or you probably will have to power-on reset your machine. These three things are as follows:

❑ *The 8259A Programmable Interrupt Controller (PIC).* For each timer tick, the ordinary operation of the CPU is interrupted and control is given to a special routine that does whatever the software designer wants it to. In this case, you are the designer. You must know how to inform the PIC that you are finished servicing the timer-tick interrupt.

❑ *The 8253/4 timer.* The timer is driven by an oscillator with a frequency of 1.19318 MHz, and controlled by a count-down or *divisor* register (within the chip) that determines how often the timer signals the PIC to interrupt the system. You must know how to program the divisor register with a new value, and—just as important—set it back the way you found it.

❑ *The IRQ0 (level 0) Interrupt Service Routine (ISR).* You must supply a replacement ISR in place of the original. The object is to update your own tick counter "clock," but not to prevent the original ISR from servicing system requirements.

From the programmer's point of view, the main thing is the ISR code. Such a routine is provided in `timer.c` (see listing G.1). This source file is not a complete program—it is meant to be compiled separately and linked with other `.OBJ` files to form a complete program. `timer.c` contains functions to start and reset a higher clock rate, to handle time-tick interrupts while in that mode, and to calculate the precise amount of time spent in that mode.

As is often the case, the best way to explain the theory of an operation is found in the program that implements it. Look over the program in listing G.1, which implements the routines for an 80386, 10,000 ticks per second, and familiarize yourself with its major features. Then we analyze its parts and bring it all together.

Listing G.1. `timer.c` *(Performance-measurement routine).*

Microsoft QuickC 2.5

```
1   /* +----------------------------------------------------+
2       +                    T I M E R . C
3       +    Benchmark and performance measurement routines
4       +    supplying 100 microsecond precision.
5       +----------------------------------------------------+
6   */
```

```
 7   #include <stdlib.h>
 8   #include <stdio.h>
 9   #include <dos.h>
10   #include <conio.h>
11
12   #define ICR 0x20
13   #define EOI 0x20
14
15   unsigned long ticks;
16   unsigned long begin_time;
17   unsigned long end_time;
18   unsigned long far *clock = (unsigned long far *)0x0040006CUL;
19   unsigned long far *oflow = (unsigned long far *)0x00400070UL;
20   unsigned long save_clock;
21   unsigned long save_oflow;
22
23   void (interrupt far *oldint8)();
24
25   /* +---------------------------------------------------+
26      + void interrupt newint8()
27      +    Handle 10,000 clock ticks per second.
28      +---------------------------------------------------+
29   */
30   void interrupt far newint8()
31   {
32     static unsigned int count = 551;
33
34     ++ticks;
35     if ( --count == 0 ) {
36       (*oldint8)();
37       count = 551;
38     }
39     else outp( ICR, EOI );
40   }
41
42   /* +---------------------------------------------------+
43      + hires_clock()
44      +    Place Timer0 in high resolution, 100 microsecond
45      +    mode. Save previous status of clock.
46      +---------------------------------------------------+
47   */
48   static void hires_clock( void )
49   {
50     _disable();
51     save_clock = *clock;
52     save_oflow = *oflow;
53     ticks = 0;
54     oldint8 = _dos_getvect( 8 );
55     _dos_setvect( 8, newint8 );
```

Listing G.1. continues

```
56      outp( 0x43, 0x36 ); /* 119 ( 0x0077 ) for divisor */
57      outp( 0x40, 0x77 );
58      outp( 0x40, 0x00 );
59      _enable();
60   }
61
62   /* +---------------------------------------------------+
63      + lores_clock()
64      +    Place Timer0 in low resolution, 18.2 ticks/sec.
65      +    Correct system clock for true elapsed time.
66      +---------------------------------------------------+
67   */
68   static void lores_clock( void )
69   {
70     _disable();
71     outp( 0x43, 0x36 );
72     outp( 0x40, 0 );
73     outp( 0x40, 0 );
74     _dos_setvect( 8, oldint8 );
75     *oflow = save_oflow;
76     *clock = save_clock + ( end_time - begin_time ) / 551UL;
77     _enable();
78   }
79
80   void start_bench( void )
81   {
82     hires_clock();
83     begin_time = ticks;
84   }
85
86   void stop_bench( void )
87   {
88     end_time = ticks;
89     lores_clock();
90   }
91
92   double duration( void )
93   {
94     return( ( (double)( end_time - begin_time ) / 10000.0 ) );
95   }
```

Data Areas Used in *timer.c*

Seven unsigned long int variables, lines 15–21, constitute the main
data areas in timer.c. The first of these, ticks, is to be the temporary
replacement clock while the timer is in what we call *high-resolution mode*.

Very simply, `ticks` are incremented at each timer tick. This does not mean that the original system clock is no longer to be updated—just that we do not want to update it at the new, higher rate. That oversight would alter the true system clock drastically. One consequence would be that files accessed after using these functions would no longer be correctly date- and time-stamped.

The next two areas, `begin_time` and `end_time`, are copies of the high-resolution clock at the beginning and end of a performance benchmark and timing run. They will be used by one of the support functions to calculate the elapsed interval in high-resolution mode.

The far pointers to `*clock` and `*oflow` give access to the real system clock and clock overflow flag (which indicates that midnight has rolled around). The program needs to know where these are in order to ensure that they are set back (to a close approximation) to what they would have been if high-resolution mode had never been entered. Normally, this action is redundant, because our routine invokes the original ISR at very close to the normal frequency, allowing the system clock to be updated as before.

However, if you tinker with the count-down values, you may cause interrupts faster than they can realistically be serviced. To cover that eventuality, the correct value of the clock is recalculated from the high-resolution clock and restored, and the overflow flag is set to its original value.

Theoretically, you can set the count-down value to 1 and get 1,193,180 ticks per second. In practice, that doesn't work. The interrupt service routines can't do everything they need to do in eight-tenths of a microsecond. The highest reasonable tick rate was found (through experimentation) to be about 10,000 ticks per second. This yields a high-resolution precision of about 100 microseconds per tick, or a time value accurate to four decimal places.

The last two variables, `save_clock` and `save_oflow`, simply save the values of the true clock and overflow flag before high-resolution timing begins.

Reprogramming the Timer Chip

It is not intended that routines external to the `timer.c` source file initiate high-resolution timing directly. They should instead call `start_bench()`, lines 80–84, primarily to ensure that `begin_time` is noted correctly. `start_bench()` then calls `hires_clock()` to actually start high-resolution timing.

`hires_clock()` is in lines 48–60. The function is executed with interrupts disabled (`_disable()`) while the system clock is being saved and the timer chip reprogrammed, after interrupts are again allowed (`_enable()`).

The address of the original ISR for interrupt vector 8 (the timer interrupt) is saved in line 54, and the new ISR is hooked in line 55. Interrupt vector 8 is the one used for timer-tick interrupts because of the way the 8259A is implemented on the PC.

The 8259A can control eight levels of hardware interrupt, numbered 0 through 7. On the PC, Interrupt Request 0 (IRQ0) is used for the timer. The PC's circuitry is further arranged so that a hardware interrupt level triggers a software interrupt vector that is 8 greater than its own value. Hence, IRQ0 invokes interrupt vector 8—which points to the system's timer-tick ISR.

Having preserved the original interrupt address, line 55 now hooks in the new interrupt handler—`newint8()`. We discuss that routine shortly.

Reprogramming of the timer chip occurs in lines 56–58. This is done using two byte ports. Port 0x43 is a *control port* for the timer. A value of 0x36 is output to the port, telling the timer that (1) the system timer (not the speaker timer or memory-refresh timer) is about to be reprogrammed with a new divisor value; and, (2) that the least significant byte appears first, followed by the most significant byte. Thus the divisor is basically an unsigned integer. The divisor is output to the timer through byte port 0x40, one byte at a time.

Now, why do we keep calling the count-down value a *divisor*, and how do you pick values for it? Remember that the timer chip is being driven by a 1.19318 MHz oscillator. Each cycle from the oscillator causes the divisor value *first* to be decremented by one, and *second* checked for zero. If it is zero, the timer signals a timer interrupt to the PIC.

Normally, the divisor is set to a value of 0. Because it is decremented before being checked, its value wraps around to 0xFFFF, and so on down to zero. It therefore is decremented 65,536 times before reaching zero again. But because it is being decremented at 1,193,180 times a second, interrupts are triggered 1193180 / 65536 = 18.2 per second, approximately. Thus the count-down value *is* properly a divisor—of the oscillator frequency.

You can turn the formula around to compute the divisor for a desired interrupt rate. Because we want 10,000 interrupts a second, 1193180 / 10000 is about 119, or 0x0077. Notice in line 57 that the 0x77 is sent to port 0x40 first, followed by the 0x00.

Reprogramming of the timer is now complete. It runs at the higher rate behind the scenes, so that your program can now execute whatever it is you want precise timing for, without paying further attention to the timer (for the time being). But the routine behind the scenes is `newint8()`, the very one that was just hooked in by `hires_clock()`.

Handling the Timer-Tick Interrupts

`newint8()` is executed every time a timer tick occurs, now that high-resolution timing has begun. In a very real sense it is running at the same time as the other functions in the program, although only one routine has control of the CPU at any given moment. This situation is called *multitasking*. What does this multitasking interrupt service routine accomplish?

It does exactly two things: it updates the high-resolution mode clock that was defined earlier in the program, and it invokes the original ISR at the right times. This is all done in lines 30–40 of `timer.c`. Updating `ticks` is simple— the `++` prefix operator is used.

Determining when to pass control to the original ISR is not so simple. How many ticks at the higher rate must occur to reach the equivalent of 18.2 ticks per second? It's probably best to look at it from the perspective of the divisor values. At 18.2 ticks per second, the divisor was the equivalent of 65,536. Now, the divisor is 119 for 10,000 ticks per second. The old rate is 65536 / 119, or about 551 times slower. Therefore, every 551 ticks, the code should invoke the old ISR. For any new timer-tick rate, the ratio of the original to the new divisor (truncated to an integer) is the number of ticks to count before invoking `oldint8()`.

It is important that `newint8()` actually invokes the old ISR, and that it does it at the right rate. There are two reasons for doing it at all. First, the old ISR chains to the *user timer-tick interrupt*, which may be being used by pop-up software or some other application that would be disabled without this interrupt. Second, the old ISR is responsible also for checking the diskette drive motor and turning it off after an appropriate time. This is also the reason for invoking the old ISR at the right rate, because drive motor control is a time-dependent function.

Last, it is important to notice the last statement in `newint8()`. It is as follows:

```
else outp( ICR, EOI );
```

As the else implies, this statement is executed only when the old ISR is *not* invoked. (This operation is taken care of by the old ISR when it does execute.) But what is this output for?

Look at the #defines in lines 12 and 13. Both ICR and EOI are defined to be 0x20, but the fact that they are the same is only incidental. The ICR is the Interrupt Control Register, through which you read and write control information for the 8259A PIC. In this case we want to send EOI (End Of Interrupt) to it.

The reason for doing this is quite simple—if you don't, the system hangs up completely! Timer-tick interrupts are not quite like normal software interrupts, because they are mediated by the PIC. When the PIC causes an interrupt, it *disables any further interrupts* until you send it this byte indicating that interrupt processing is complete.

This, incidentally, is why it is possible to either make interrupts too frequent, or what amounts to the same thing, write so much code in newint8() that it can't finish by the next interrupt. If you haven't sent the EOI code when the next interrupt arrives, it never happens. The PIC prevents it. The result can be quite unpredictable—but never desirable.

Cleaning Up after High Resolution Timing

Terminating high-resolution timing is mostly a matter of reprogramming the timer with its original divisor value. Only a couple of points need mentioning here.

High-resolution mode is terminated by calling stop_bench(). This function stores the ending value of the high-resolution clock, and calls lores_clock() to reprogram the timer. This is just a mirror-image process, so far.

lores_clock(), however, does one extra thing. It uses the elapsed time from the high-resolution clock to compute the equivalent number of ticks at 18.2 per second, and refreshes the system clock in low storage with that computed value. This is done in line 76. Notice that the conversion factor is the same one used to detect timing for invoking the old ISR, as described earlier.

This particular clean-up function is, as we have mentioned, normally redundant—ordinarily, invoking the old ISR at the proper rate keeps the real system clock straight. If, however, you find yourself tempted to experiment with the divisor value, this function may prove its worth in making it unnecessary to reset the system date and clock through DOS commands after each attempt.

A more realistic rate for an 8088, 4.77 MHz machine, would be 1,000 ticks per second. In this case, the count-down value would be 1193180 / 1000 = 1193, or 0x04A9. Because this is 10 times slower than the rate shown in the program, `newint8()` need only invoke the old clock interrupt every 55 counts, rather than 551; this value also needs to be substituted in `lore_clock()`, where the original clock value is being computed. Finally, the divisor in `duration()` should be made 1,000 rather than 10,000.

Separate Compilation of *timer.c*

`timer.c` should be compiled separately to an `.OBJ` file. You can bring it into your application programs by including it in the appropriate make list, project file, or linker response file. Whatever the method, get it linked into the main executable file.

Only certain data objects and functions are meant to be visible to the main source file (or other program modules). You can gain access to them from other files by writing the following include:

```
#include "timer.h"
```

The contents of the timer header file are shown below, in listing G.2.

Listing G.2. *Header file for timer routine.*

```
 1   /* +--------------------------------------------------+
 2       +                    T I M E R . H
 3       +  Benchmark and performance measurement routines
 4       +  supplying 100 microsecond precision.
 5       +--------------------------------------------------+
 6   */
 7   #include <stdlib.h>
 8   #include <stdio.h>
 9   #include <dos.h>
10   #include <conio.h>
11
```

Listing G.2. continues

Listing G.2. *continued*

```
12   #define ICR 0x20
13   #define EOI 0x20
14
15   extern unsigned long ticks;
16   extern unsigned long begin_time;
17   extern unsigned long end_time;
18   extern unsigned long far *clock;
19
20   extern void (interrupt far *oldint8)();
21
22   void start_bench( void );
23   void stop_bench( void );
24   double duration( void );
```

Converting *timer.c* to Turbo C

The version of `timer.c` shown in listing G.1 was written in Microsoft QuickC. Converting the code to Turbo C is easy. Just make the indicated changes at the following line numbers:

Line 23	Change the QC `void (interrupt far *oldint8)()` to the TC notation `void interrupt far (*oldint8)()`. Actually, the QC notation here makes more intuitive sense, because this object is a far pointer to an interrupt function (all in parentheses), which returns nothing (`void` outside the parentheses). In fact, Turbo C accepts either notation, whereas QuickC accepts only the first.
Line 30	You *can* change the QC `void interrupt far newint8( void )` to the TC `void interrupt newint8( void )`, but you don't need to. Turbo C assumes that an interrupt function has the far attribute, but QuickC flags the statement at compile time, informing you that it *must* have the far attribute.
et al	You should change the following forms of several function names:

QC Name	TC Name
`_disable`	`disable`
`_enable`	`enable`
`_dos_getvect`	`getvect`
`_dos_setvect`	`setvect`

These are all the changes to the source you need to make in order to use the code with either compiler. If you plan to use it much with both, it would be worth the trouble to package a single source file using `#define` and `#ifdef` macros so that only one line need be modified to compile correctly. See Chapter 4 for details on these macros.

Using the *timer.c* Functions

You can use the facilities provided in `timer.c` in two ways: you can use the functions to time in high-resolution mode, or you can just use the data areas to time in low-resolution mode. Both methods are illustrated in `testtime.c`, shown in listing G.3.

Listing G.3. *Using the* `timer.c` *facilities.*   *Turbo C 2.0*

```
1   #include "timer.h"
2
3   main()
4   {
5     unsigned long i;
6
7     start_bench();
8     for ( i=0; i<367000; ++i ) i = i;
9     stop_bench();
10    printf( " Elapsed time at 10,000 ticks/sec = %.4f\n",
11        duration() );
12
13    begin_time = *clock;
14    for ( i=0; i<367000; ++i ) i = i;
15    end_time = *clock;
16    printf( " Elapsed time at 18.2 ticks/sec = %.4f\n",
17        ( (double)( end_time - begin_time ) ) / 18.2 );
18  }
```

You can inspect the code and see how to handle the two timing methods. Just remember that when you use high-resolution timing, you should be sure to terminate it.

This Turbo C program was compiled and linked in the interactive editor environment. To do this, a project file was necessary to name all the parts for the compiler and linker. The project file is simple, and is composed of the following two lines:

```
testtime.c (timer.h)
timer.obj
```

testtime.c performs benchmark timings on exactly the same code—a loop that should last very close to one second on an 80386, 20 MHz. The program produces the following output on-screen:

```
Elapsed time at 10,000 ticks/sec = 1.1985
Elapsed time at 18.2 ticks/sec = 0.9890
```

Notice that during high-resolution mode, it appears to take about 21 percent longer to run the same loop. Why are the timings different at the different tick rates? First, because the slower tick rate is accurate only to plus or minus 0.05 seconds. This means that the time actually elapsed is in the range 1.0390 >= 0.9890 >= 0.9390, but it cannot be known precisely. The high-resolution elapsed time is between 1.1984 and 1.1986—much more accurate.

The second reason for the differing results is the extra overhead of executing the ISR instructions almost 10,000 extra times per second. The difference between the closest extreme values for the two speeds is 1.1984 − 1.0390 = 0.1594 seconds. This is not accounted for by inaccuracies, and must be due to the added overhead during high-resolution timing. Thus there is a 0.1594 / 1.1984 * 100 = 13.3 percent added overhead.

This raises another question: does this overhead destroy the accuracy of the timer routines? If you think about it for a moment, you will see that this overhead is present also at the normal tick rate—it is just less noticeable. Further, in comparing *two* routines, the overhead is *consistently present*, so that the *relative* durations of alternative methods have real significance.

That is the true point of benchmark timing: whether one method or routine is *relatively faster* than another. If it is, it is preferred. In addition, you can get a close idea of what the normal elapsed time will be by simply reducing the high-resolution timing by about 13.3 percent. This will, in fact, be more accurate, because high-resolution timing at 18.2 ticks per second is two orders of magnitude more precise.

Bibliography

The following volumes do not exhaust the library of references on C programming and related subjects. They are listed as representative of the literature and should give you a good start toward building your library.

You may also wish to read magazine material on C programming. Two publications in particular are excellent and generally available. They are *Dr. Dobb's Journal* and *The C User's Journal.*

From time to time, some of the magazines specific to certain machines also feature interesting material on C—more and more as the language gains popularity.

UNIX System V Programmer's Guide. Englewood Cliffs: Prentice-Hall, Inc., 1987.

Description of the UNIX programming environment, including C.

ANSI (American National Standards Institute). *American National Standard for Information Systems—Programming Language C.* 1988.

This is the X3J11 committee document containing the formal specifications for ANSI standard C.

ANSI (American National Standards Institute). *Rationale for Draft Proposed American National Standard for Information Systems—Programming Language C.* 1988.

This is the X3J11 committee document containing the rationale used to decide what should be standard C.

Davis, William S. *Operating Systems: A Systematic Overview*. Reading: Addison-Wesley Publishing Company, 1987.

A conceptual, non-technical overview of operating systems, including MS-DOS and UNIX.

Dettmann, Terry. *DOS Programmer's Reference*, 2nd ed. Carmel, IN: Que Corporation, 1989.

A remarkable compilation of PC and DOS internals for the systems programmer.

Eckel, Bruce. *Using C++*. Berkeley: Osborne/McGraw-Hill, 1989.

An excellent tutorial on C++, covering lots of ground.

Fischer, Charles N.; LeBlanc, Richard J. *Crafting a Compiler*. Menlo Park: The Benjamin/Cummings Publishing Company, 1988.

A good introduction to the technical aspects of scanning, parsing, and compiler theory.

Hunter, Bruce H. *Understanding C*. Berkeley: Sybex Inc., 1984.

A very good introductory book, even if somewhat older. Does not cover ANSI C (too early), but has a good approach to learning C.

Iacobucci, Ed. *OS/2 Programmer's Guide*. Berkeley: Osborne/McGraw-Hill, 1988.

A technical reference for programming in the OS/2 environment. Not for the novice.

Kernighan, Brian W.; Ritchie, Dennis M. *The C Programming Language*. Englewood Cliffs: Prentice-Hall, Inc.

The first edition of this book (1978) is considered the *base document* for the C language and is worth having for its historical value. The second edition (1988) has been updated to reflect the ANSI standard for C.

Knuth, Donald E. *The Art of Computer Programming*, 2nd ed., 7 vols. Reading: Addison-Wesley Publishing Company, 1973.

This is *the* standard reference on programming algorithms.

Mueller, Scott. *Upgrading and Repairing PCs*. Carmel, IN: Que Corporation, 1988.

The industry-standard book for this topic, it contains a gold mine of information on PC and compatible hardware.

Norton, Peter; Wilton, Richard. *The New Peter Norton Programmer's Guide to the IBM PC and PS/2*. Redmond: Microsoft Press, 1988.

A good introduction to IBM PC internals.

Plantz, Alan; Brown, William M.; Yester, Michael; Atkinson, Lee. *Turbo C Programming*. Carmle, IN: Que Corporation, 1989.

Lots of material here on program development in the Turbo C specific environment. Includes program design, assembler interfacing, and debugging procedures.

Plauger, P. J.; Brodie, Jim. *Standard C: Programmer's Quick Reference*. Redmond: Microsoft Press, 1989.

Concise summary of ANSI C by two members of the ANSI X3J11 committee. A reference for the experienced, this is not a learning tool.

Schildt, Herbert. *ANSI C Made Easy*. Berkeley: Osborne/McGraw-Hill, 1989.

A very basic introduction to C for the novice programmer.

Sedgewick, Robert. *Algorithms*. Reading: Addison-Wesley Publishing Company, 1983.

An excellent shorter work on programming algorithms, but you need to be familiar with Pascal to follow the sample programs.

Stroustrup, Bjarne. *The C++ Programming Language*. Reading: Addison-Wesley Publishing Company, 1986.

This book is considered by the C++ world to be the base document for C++, as K & R is for C.

Waite, Mitchell; Prata, Stephen; Martin, Donald. *C Primer Plus*, Revised Edition. Carmel, IN: Howard W. Sams & Company, 1987.

A primer, as the title implies, for the beginner.

Index

#if preprocessing directive, 548
#include preprocessing directive, 20-25
% conversion specification, 603, 609
& bitwise AND operator, 110
& address-of operator, 465
& reference operator, 719
* indirection operator, 327
+= add assign operator, 111
-> structure pointer operator, 464-465
. dot operator, structure, 464
[conversion specification, 608
[] postfix operator, 346-348, 464
::operator new(), dynamic objects, 762, 767
<< inserter operator, 788-791
== equality operator, 142
>> shift-right operator, 110
>> extractor operator, 788-791
80x86 CPU, segmented addresses, 338-339
8253/4 timer, 900
8259A programmable interrupt controller, 900
86-DOS, 11

A

abort() function, 321, 647-648
   destructors, 726
abs() function, 654
absolute value functions, 568, 654-655
   program listing, 569

abstract data type, 688-691, 692-693, 703
accessing external data objects, 200-202, 204-210
accessing external functions, 200-202, 204-210
acos() function, 560
add assign operator (+ =), 111
address
   object, 326
   offset, 328, 338-339, 465-466
   RAM, 326
   segment, 328, 338-339
address values, 328, 332
address-of operator (&), 465
addressing, indirect, 326
advanced project make facilities, 38
aggregate initializer, classes, 724-725
alert character, mnemonic escape sequences, 159
algebraic expressions, parsing, 396, 401-403
algorithms
   Horner's method, 291
   measurement, 899-910
aligning braces/parentheses in C language programs, 35
allocating memory, 26, 644-645
American National Standards Institute see ANSI
AND (&) bitwise operator, 110
angle brackets (<>), C language punctuation, 24
annuity, 873
ANSI C standard, 11
   character set, 165
   codes, 131-132

conditional directives, 184-186
converting from K&R standard, 524-529
differences from K&R standard, 523-528
extensions, 322-323, 455-456
    asm keyword, 531
    environment arguments, 530
    external definitions, 531
    file modes, 532
    file-position indicator, 532
    fortran keyword, 531
    function pointer casts, 531
    identifiers, 530-531
    macro arguments, 532
    macro names, 532
    signal handlers, 532
    stream types, 532
    string literals, 531
file modes, 429-434
full conformity, 39-41
functions, 173-174
header files, 845-856
include directives, 175-177
keywords, 172-173
macros, 173
mnemonic escape sequences, 158-162
multibyte characters, 165-166
numeric escape sequences, 162-163
portability, 505-523
    implementation-defined behavior, 507, 518-523
    undefined behavior, 510-517
    unspecified behavior, 508-510
predefined macro names, 188-189
required character set, 152-156, 166
translation limitations for compilers, 528-529
trigraph escape sequences, 163-164
append mode, file mode parameter, 70
argc parameter, 256-257
argument lists
    control, 571-582
    variable, 254, 571-572, 575-582
    variable length, 249
arguments
    environment, extensions to ANSI standard, 530
    function, 247
    macro, 180
        extensions to ANSI standard, 532
    passing to functions, 247-249
    precision, 601
    promoting, 247-249
arguments lists, variable, 573-574

argv[] parameter, 256-257
arithmetic, integer, 654-655
arithmetic errors, manifest constants, 840
array data type, 131-132
array identifier, 120
array of structures, 470-471
array type derivation, 457
array.cpp program listing, 710-713
arraycl2.cpp program listing, 755-757
arraycla.cpp program listing, 754
arrays, 18
    character, 26
    combining with structures, 469-472
    declaring, 341-342, 344-345
    elements, 340, 343
    fencing, 347
    function parameters, 376-377
    multidimensional, 344-346
    of pointers, 76, 403-405
    one-dimensional, 341
    output polygon, 354-355
    pointers to arrays, 405-406
    pointers to structures, 471-472
    referencing, 343-346
    representing shapes, 349-355
    searching, 651-652
    smoothing curves, 348-355
    solving equations, 356-359
    sorting, 653
ASCII character set, 833-835
ascii.c program listing, 299-301
asctime() function, 678-679
asin() function, 561
asm keyword, extensions to ANSI standard, 531
assembly language compared to C, 13-14
assert() macro, 537-538, 837
assert.h header file, 837
assignment operators
    compound, 233-234
    simple, 233-234
associativity of operators, 221
asterisk (*), indirection operator, 67-69
asterisk slash (*/) marking comments in C language
    programs, 17
asynchronous communications program, 881-896
asynchronous events, 271
atan() function, 561
atan2() function, 561
atexit() function, 319-321, 648
    destructors, 726

atexit.c program listing, 320-321, 649
atof() function, 84-85, 637
atoi() function, 84-85, 637-638
atol() function, 84-85, 638
attributes, 771, 774
auto keyword, 194
auto storage class, 122-123, 125-126, 192-194, 720
    defining, 193-194
    register keyword, 194
automatic data type conversions, 237-238
automatic duration, 123, 125, 130
autonomous objects, 705

B

B-Spline derivation, 897-898
back substitution, 358-359
back-end condition checking, 283-284, 292-297
backspace character, mnemonic escape sequences, 159
backward chaining, linked lists, 498-501
bar.c program listing, 581-582
base class, 778-786
based pointer, 338-339
BCPL language, 10
beginning of file, accessing, 418-420
Bezier curve-smoothing method, 349-355
bezier() function, 355
bibliography, C programming, 911-913
binary digit (bit), 152-153
binary expressions, 228-232
binary file mode, 109, 431-434
binary files, 594-595
    whence, 627
binary operators, 228-232
binary search, 651-652
binary streams, 61, 432-433
BIOS (Basic I/O System), 55
bit (binary digit), 152
    least significant, 153
    most significant, 153
bit-fields
    unnamed, 469
    within structures, 467-469
bits per char, constant range, 113
block scope, 195-196
block statements, 17, 27, 125-126
    see also compound statements
braces ({})
    aligning in C language programs, 35

C language punctuation, 17
break statement, 142, 303, 317-318
    versus goto, 304-305
bsearch function, 650-652
buffer.c program listing, 599
buffered I/O, 421-422
buffers
    changing size, 422-423
    flushing, 70-71, 431
    I/O, 57, 421-425
    releasing, 454
BUFSIZ macro, 587-588
BUFSIZE macro, 452
buildmsg() function, 342
bullet() function, 870
business functions, 872-875
byte, 152
    least significant bit, 153
    most significant bit, 153
bytes per multibyte character, 113
b_spline() function, 355

C

c conversion specification, 603, 608
C language, 9
    ANSI, 11-13
    C++, 12-13
    bibliography, 911-913
    character set, 152-154
        extended, 165-166
        minimal, 155-156
    compared to assembly, 14
    compared to C, 13
    compared to COBOL, 14
    compared to FORTRAN, 15
    compared to Pascal, 14
    compatibility with other languages, 44-45
    compilers, features, 38-43
    conventions, 152-166
    environment
        text editor, 36-38
        writing programs, 36-44
    extensions, 95-97
    history, 10
    programs, 15-17
        defining data, 26-27
        design, 32-33
        punctuation, 16-17, 24

writing, 31-44
source program, 166-167
C++ constructor, 691
C++ language, 12-13
  classes, 707-711
  free store, 752-753
  stream I/O, 787-791
  stream objects cin/cout, 787-791
  support, 41-42
calc_crc16() function, 145
calc_eff_contain() function, 873
calc_eff_contin() function, 873
calc_eff_period() function, 873
calc_markup_cost() function, 872
calc_markup_price() function, 872
calc_percent_change() function, 872
calc_percent_total() function, 872
calling functions, 243-280
calloc() function, 454, 478-481, 643-644
carriage-return character, mnemonic escape
  sequences, 160
cascading, 788-789
case, labeled statement, 144
case: labels, 313-318
cast expressions, 228
cast operators, 228
casts, user-defined, 826-827
ccom.c program listing, 877-896
cdelete() function, 365-366
ceil() function, 568
center.c program listing, 90
center_text function, 90
chaining forward/backward in linked lists, 498-501
channel I/O, 53
char keyword, 119
character, 113, 152
  error, 542
  handling, 537-541, 543-544
character (char) data type, 105, 107, 247
  constant range, 113
character arrays, 26
character detection functions, 845
character I/O, 615-623
  functions, 432
character set
  ASCII, 833-835
  C language, 152-154
  extended, 165-166
  minimal, 155-156
character string, 157-158

characters
  control, 18, 153-156
  display, 18, 153-154
  multibyte, 165-166, 655-657
  null, 18
CHAR_BIT macro, 551
CHAR_MAX macro, 552
CHAR_MIN macro, 552
checking, type, 132
ch_out() function, 879
cin stream object, 787-791
cinout.cpp program listing, 789
cinsdel.c program listing, 365-367
cinsert() function, 365-366
cipher.c program listing, 72-79
class declaration, 698-699
class inheritance, 702, 778-783
class objects, 726-729
  initializing, 720-725
  new operator, 753
  pointers, 795-799
    defining, 797-799
    referencing, 801-803
    vli (very large integer), 797-799, 824-826
classes, 691-693
  base class, 778-786
  C++, 707-711
  constructors, 767-768
  defining, 708-716
  derived class, 771, 778-786
  versus structures, 718-719
  virtual screens, 729-749
clear.c program listing, 632
clearerr() function, 83, 631-632
clip.c program listing, 255
CLK_TCK macro, 673
clock() function, 674
clock.c program listing, 675
clock_t() function, 673
closest integer functions, 568
  program listing, 569
closing files, 70-72
cmem.c program listing, 644
cminus.c program listing, 689-691
COBOL language, 11
  compared to C, 14
coding
  reusing, 702, 771-788
  state-dependent, 165
  top down, 32-33

collating sequence, 154
comma operator, 234-235, 332
command tail, 256
command-line
    argument, 259-260
    environment, 45-46
    formats
        designing, 258-260
    option, 259-260
    parameters see execution parameters
comments, MAKE utility, 212-213
comments in C language programs, 17, 34
commonality, 703
communications programming, 877-896
compare.c program listing, 663
compares() function, 270-271
compares.c program listing, 269-270, 407-409
compatibility of C language with other languages,
    44-45
compiler directives, 20, 174
    see also preprocessing directives
compilers
    ANSI standards, 528-529
    C language, 38-42
    one-pass, 168
    syntax directed, 167
    two-pass, 168
    see also program translation
compiling programs separately, 202
    external data objects, 208-209
    header files, 207-209
    linking modules, 210-213
    MAKE utility, 211-213
compose.cpp program listing, 772-778
composition method, reusing code, 771-778
compound assignment operators, 233-234
compound statements, 144-145
compounds, 125-126
computer languages
    assembly, 13-14
    BCPL, 10
    C, 10, 13-14
        C++, 12-13
        programs, 15-17
    COBOL, 11, 14
    FORTRAN, 15
    Pascal, 14
concatenating string objects, 362
concatenating strings, 661-662
condition checking
    back-end, 283-284, 292-297

front-end, 284, 289-292
    loops, 283
conditional
    compilation directives, 184-186
    expressions, 232-233
    inclusion directives, 184-186
    logic, 282-284, 308-318
    operators, 111, 232-233
conio.h header file, 364
connecting files to streams, 66-67
const keyword, 829-830
const type qualifier, 111
constants, 112, 157-158
    enumeration, 501-503
    limits, 113
    manifest, 342, 838-843
    minimum range, 113
    ordinary tokens, 170
    primary expressions, 217
    ranges
        bits per char, 113
        data types, 113
constructor member functions, 696
constructors, 720-721,756
    class objects, 767-768
    copy, 726-729
    defining, 722-725
    new operator, 757
    screen(), 741, 743
continue statement, 303-308
continue.c program listing, 307-308
continuous values, collating sequence, 154
control argument lists, 571-582
control characters, 18, 153-156
    motion-control, 154
control functions, 851-853
conversion functions, 845, 851-853
conversion specifications, 607, 609
conversion specifiers, 86-92, 602, 604
    %, 603, 609
    c, 603, 608
    d, 602, 607
    e, 602, 608
    f, 602-603, 608
    g, 603, 608
    h, 601
    i, 602, 607
    l, 601
    n, 601, 603
    o, 602, 607

p, 603, 608-609
s, 603, 608
strftime() functions, 681
u, 602, 607
x, 602, 607
X, 607
[, 608
conversions
date, 130
interest-rate, 872-873
converting data formats, 83-85
converting data types, 236-238
automatic conversions, 237-238
explicit conversion, 238-240
implicit conversion, 238
type casts, 238-240
type promotion, 237-238
converting programs from K&R standard to ANSI
standard, 524-529
copy constructors, 726-729
copy initializer, 726-729
copy of a variable, 127
_copy.c program listing, 617-618
cos() function, 561
cosh() function, 563
cout stream object, 787-791
CP/M operating system, 10-11
cprint.c program listing, 96-97
crc16.c program listing, 146
ctime() function, 678-679
ctype.h header file, 540
functions, 845
currency_symbol, lconv data structure, 557
current file position, reporting, 439-441
curse.h library header file, 364
curses library functions, 364
curve-smoothing, 349-355
cvtdtos() function, 205
cvtitos() function, 205
cvtjul.c program listing, 128-130
cvtltos() function, 205
cvtstr.c program listing, 202-206

D

d, conversion specifier, 602, 607
damfile.c program listing, 441-448
__DATE__ macro, 189
data
displaying, 87-91

hiding, 686, 688
managing, 104
within memory, 478-482
text, 156-157
variable, 115-116
data abstraction, 686-693
data files, 60
data formats, converting, 83-85
data objects
accessing external, 200-210
class objects, 795-803
declaring, 66-67
defining classes, 713-716
external definitions
extensions to ANSI standard, 531
identifiers, 171-172
initializing, 199-200
linkage, 195-196
effect of storage class, 198-199
external, 196-209
internal, 196-198
no, 196-198
passing to functions, 799-801
references, 795-799
scope, 195-196
block, 195-196
effect on linkage of objects, 198-199
file, 195-196
function, 195-196
prototype, 195-196
surrounding, 196
structured
defining, 458-459
visibility see linkage
data structures, lconv, 557-559
data types, 103-105
array, 131-132
bit-fields, 467-468
char (character), 105, 107, 247
converting, 236-238
automatic conversions, 237-238
explicit conversion, 238-240
implicit conversion, 238
type casts, 238-240
type promotion, 237-238
double, 106-107, 112, 548
double floating-point, 92
float, 106-107, 112, 548
floating-point, 105, 548
int, 106, 247

long double, 106-107, 112-113, 548
long int, 106
short, 247
short int, 106-107, 247
signed, 105
signed char, 106-107
struct, 131
union, 131
unsigned, 106, 247
unsigned char, 106-107
unsigned int, 105
unsigned long, 106
unsigned short, 106
void, 131
date conversion, 130
date functions, 855-856
date values structure, 673-674
DBL_DIG macro, 549
DBL_EPSILON macro, 550-551
DBL_MANT_DIG macro, 548-549
DBL_MAX macro, 550
DBL_MAX_10_EXP macro, 550
DBL_MAX_EXP macro, 549
DBL_MIN macro, 550
DBL_MIN_10_EXP macro, 549
DBL_MIN_EXP macro, 549
debugger
    features, 48-49
    uses, 49
    visual, 46-48
debugging, 537-544
DEC PDP-11, 10
decimal_point,lconv data structure, 557
declaration type-specifiers, 119
declarations, 15, 23
    class, 698-699
    inner, 125-126
    member-function prototype, 713-716
    outer, 124-126
    outer declaration, 123
    struct {...}, 459-462
    structure, 458-472
    type, 572
    typedef, 698-699
declarators, 116-118
    function definition, 134
    lists, 116-118
    parameter, 137

declaring
    arrays
        multidimensional, 344-345
        one-dimensional, 341-342
    bit-field structure members, 468-469
    classes, 710-716
        copy constructor, 726-729
    derived class, 778-783
    functions, 131-132
    pointers, 329
    stream data object, 66-67
    string variables, 359-361
    structures
        with tags, 463-464
        without tags, 461
    unions, 474-476
    user-defined types, 476-477
    variables, 27
decode_file() function, 78
default: label code, 317-318
defaults
    int, 131, 135
    value, 244
defining data, C language programs, 26-27
defining functions, 243-280
definition
    function, 138
    type, 575, 579-580
delete operator, 751-757
    redefining, 758-765
deleting files, 416-417
demo.cpp program listing, 745-746
dependency condition, MAKE utility, 212-213
dereferencing pointers, 67-69, 329, 381, 794
    multiple indirection, 381
derivation
    B-spline, 897-898
    type, 699-700, 703
derived class, declaring, 778-783
derived types
    array type, 457
    function type, 457
    pointer type, 457-458
    structure type, 458
    union type, 458, 473-476
deriving classes, 771
description blocks, MAKE utility, 212-213
design C language programs, 32-33
designing command-line formats, 258-260

destructors, 720-722
  calling, 725-726
  class objects, 767-768
detab.c program listing, 293-297
device control port, 54
device controller circuitry, 55
devices, interactive, 58-60
digraph notation, 163
difft.c program listing, 675-676
difftime() function, 674-676
direct branching statements, 303-308
direct I/O, 623-631
  functions, 432-433
direct memory access (DMA), 53
direct recursion, 260-261
direct-access file programming, 434-441, 449
  hashed keys, 442-448
directives
  compiler, 17, 20
  conditional inclusion, 184-186
  #error, 186-188
  #include, 175-177
  #line, line control, 186-187
  macro substitution, 177-183
  multibyte character, 607
  # (null), 186, 188
  #pragma, 186, 188
  preprocessor, 17, 20-25, 174
  whitespace character, 606-607
directory mask, 499-501
dir_io.c program listing, 624
dir_wrt.c program listing, 625-626
disk rotation timing, 55
display characters, 18, 153-154
display command, script file, 895-896
DISPLAY macro, 262
displaying data, 87-91
display_payout() function, 875
display_table() function, 875
disp_box() function, 741
disp_move() function, 740
disp_open() function, 740
disp_printf() function, 741
disp_scroll() function, 741
div() function, 205
division, integer, 654-655
div_t function, 654
div_t type declaration, 636
DMA see direct memory access, 53

do-while() statement, 288, 292-297
DOS (disk operating system)
  handles, 64-65
  operating system, 10-11
  streams, extended, 95-97
double data type, 106-107, 112-113, 548
  constant range, 113
double keyword, 119
double question marks character (??), 162
double-floating point data types, scanf(), 92
doubly linked lists, 484-501
draw() function, 784
draw_polygon() function, 355
dumb terminal program, 877
dump program, 107
duration
  object, 122
  storage classes, 192-194
dynamic memory
  managing data in, 478-482
  pointer to arrays, 480
dynamic objects, 765-767
  on the stack, 766
d_addrec() function, 446
d_create() function, 446
d_delrec() function, 446-447
d_getrec() function, 446

E

e conversion specifier, 602, 608
editor, linkage, 41-42
edit_environment() function, 375
edit_text() function, 364-366, 368-373, 375
EDOM macro, 539, 560
elements of an array, 340, 343
elimination
  forward, 358
  Gaussian, 356-358
ellipsis, 250
encapsulation, 686-688, 699
encode_() function, 78
end-of-file, 83
end-recursion removal, 266
enum {} enumeration constants, 501-503
enum, specifier keyword, 119
environment arguments, extensions to ANSI standard, 530
environmental variables, 373-375

environments
    freestanding, 256
    hosted, 256
EOF macro, 71-72, 588
equality operator (==), 142
equations, solving with arrays, 356-359
equivalence, pointer and subscript, 346-348
eraeol() function, 367-372
ERANGE macro, 539, 560
errno macro, 538-539
#error directive, 186-188
error conditions
    handling, 537-544
    I/O, 83
    undefined behavior (ANSI standard), 510-511, 513
error location facilities, 38
error-handling functions, 631-634
escape sequence, 156-157
    mnemonic, 158-162
    numeric, 162-163
    trigraph, 163-164
escape.c program listing, 157
euclid.c program listing, 261-262
euclid2.c program listing, 265-266
exchange.c program listing, 147
execution parameters, 256-258
exe_command() function, 881
exit() function, 318-321, 648-650
    destructors, 726
exit() manifest constants, 843
EXIT_FAILURE macro, 636
EXIT_SUCCESS macro, 636
exp() function, 564
explicit data type conversion, 238-240
exponential functions, 564-565
exponentiation functions program listing, 565
expression operator, 396
expressions
    binary, 228-232
    cast, 228
    conditional, 232-233
    function designator, 219-220
    lvalue, 218-219
    postfix, 221-224
    primary, 217-218
    rvalue, 218-219
    sequence points, 214-217
    side effects, 214-217
    statements, 140-141
    subexpressions, 214-217

ternary, 232-233
unary, 224-228
void, 220
extensions to ANSI standards, 322-323, 455-456
    asm keyword, 531
    environment arguments, 530
    external definitions, 531
    file modes, 532
    file-position indicator, 532
    fortran keyword, 531
    function pointer casts, 531
    identifiers, 530-531
    macro arguments, 532
    macro names, 532
    signal handlers, 532
    stream types, 532
    string literals, 531
extern keyword, 135, 194-195
external definitions, extensions to ANSI standard, 531
external identifiers, 171-172
external linkage, 196-206, 208-209
    functions, 135
extractor (>>) operator, 788-789, 791
Exxxxxxx macro, 539-540

F

f conversion specification, 602-603, 608
fabs() function, 568
factor operator, 397
factorials, 264
far pointer, 338-339
fclose() function, 70-72, 592-593
fcloseall() function, 78
fencing arrays, 347
feof() function, 83, 632-633
ferror() function, 83, 633
fflush() function, 431, 593
fgetc() function, 65, 78-79, 615-616
fgetpos() function, 439-441, 626
fgets() function, 65, 79-80, 616
fget_str.c program listing, 616-617
field-width specifiers, 468, 601
__FILE__ macro, 189
file-position indicator
    extensions to ANSI standard, 532
FILENAME_MAX macro, 588
files
    accessing, 592-599

beginning of file, 418-420
binary, 594-595
closing, 70-72
connecting to streams, 66-67
data, 60
deleting, 416-417
direct-access, 435-438, 449
extensions
    .COM, 61
    .EXE, 61
    .MAK, 38
    .MIX, 42
    .OBJ, 42
    .PRJ, 38
fully buffered, 60
handles, 64-65
header, 206-209, 548-559, 561-569, 635, 658,
    693-694, 837-856
I/O programming, 415-434
management functions, 416-421
mode parameter, 69-70
modes
    binary, 431-434
    choosing, 450
    extensions to ANSI standard, 532
    text, 431-434
multiple source, 25
names, 66-67
opening, 68-70
position, current, reporting, 439-441
positioning functions, 432-434
processing, sequential, 418-420
random-access, 435-438
renaming, 417
searching for named, 24-25
scope, 195-196
temporary, 420-421
unbuffered, 58-59
utilities, 589-592
finance.c program listing, 94, 857-876
financial calculations program, 857-876
first.c program listing, 19-20
fixed duration, 123
flags, 600
float data type, 107, 112, 548
    constant range, 113
float keyword, 119
float.h header file, 548-551
    macros, 838
floating-point manifest constants, 838

floating-point data type, 105-106, 602, 311
floating-point numbers, 112-114, 547-551, 602-603
floor() function, 568
flow control statements, writing, 141-142
flow of program execution, 281-284
fltcnvrt.c program listing, 639
FLT_DIG macro, 549
FLT_EPSILON macro, 550-551
FLT_MANT_DIG macro, 548-549
FLT_MAX macro, 550
FLT_MAX_10_EXP macro, 550
FLT_MAX_EXP macro, 549
FLT_MIN macro, 550
FLT_MIN_10_EXP macro, 549
FLT_MIN_EXP macro, 549
FLT_RADIX macro, 548-550
FLT_ROUNDS macro, 548
flush.c program listing, 594
flushing buffers, 70-71, 431
fmod() function, 568
fmore.c program listing, 98-100
fopen() function, 66-70, 143, 593-596
    I/O modes, 426-429
FOPEN_MAX macro, 588
for() statement, 288, 297-301
formal argument list, 178-180
formal parameter list, 136-137
format string, 86-87, 606
formatted I/O, 83-93, 432, 599-615
formfeed character, mnemonic escape sequences, 159
formula.c program listing, 397-403
fortran keyword, extensions to ANSI standard, 531
FORTRAN language compared to C, 15
forward chaining, linked lists, 498-501
forward declare, 138
forward elimination, 358
fpos_t type definition, 587
fprintf() function, 90-91, 599-600
fputc() function, 65, 78-79, 617
fputs() function, 65, 79-80, 618
fput_str.c program listing, 618-619
fractional number, floating-point number, 113
fread() function, 623-624
free store, 752-753
    static objects, 770-771
free() function, 454, 478, 481-482, 644-645
freestanding environments, 256
freopen() function, 596
frexp() function, 564
friend functions, 800-801

overloading, 806
frmtime.c program listing, 682
front-end condition checking, 284, 289-292
fscanf() function, 605-606, 609-611
fseek() function, 440-441, 627
fsetpos() function, 440-441, 628-630
ftell() function, 439, 630
function arguments, 247
function declarations, 133-134, 138
function default type, int, 131
function definition, 138
function designator expressions, 219-220
function identifier, 120
function parameters
    arrays, 376-377
    strings, 376
    structures, 482-483
    unions, 482-483
function pointer casts, extensions to ANSI standard, 531
function prototypes, 20, 132, 135, 139
    incomplete type, 248
    scope, 195-196
    variable-length argument lists, 250-253
function scope, 195-196
function syntax, 134
function type derivation, 457
function type-specifiers, 134-135
function types, 105
function-like macro, 177-180
functional objects, 705
functions, 16, 20, 22
    abort(), 321, 647-648, 726
    abs(), 654
    absolute value, 568-569
    accessing external, 200-210
    acos(), 560
    advanced math, 846-847
    ANSI C standard, 173-174
    asctime(), 678-679
    asin(), 561
    atan(), 561
    atan2(), 561
    atexit(), 319-321, 648, 726
    atof(), 84-85, 637
    atoi(), 84-85, 637-638
    atol(), 84-85, 638
    bezier(), 355
    bsearch(), 650-652
    building, 139

bullet(), 870
b_spline(), 355
calc_crc16(), 145
calc_eff_contain(), 873
calc_eff_contin(), 873
calc_eff_period(), 873
calc_markup_cost(), 872
calc_markup_price(), 872
calc_percent_change(), 872
calc_percent_total(), 872
calling, 243-280
calloc(), 454, 478-481, 643-644
cdelete(), 365-366
ceil(), 568
center_text(), 90
character detection, 845
character I/O, 432
ch_out(), 879
cinsert(), 365-366
clearerr(), 83, 631-632
clock(), 674, 855-856
clock_t, 673
closest integer, 568-569
compares(), 270-271
control, 851-853
conversion, 845, 851-853
cos(), 561
cosh(), 563
ctime(), 678-679
ctype.h(), 540
cvtdtos(), 205
cvtitos(), 205
cvtltos(), 205
date(), 855-856
declaring, 131-132
decode_file(), 78
defining, 243-280
difftime(), 674-676
direct I/O, 432-433
direct jump, 847
display_payout(), 875
display_table(), 875
disp_box(), 741
disp_move(), 740
disp_open(), 740
disp_printf(), 741
disp_scroll(), 741
div(), 205
div_t(), 654
draw(), 784

draw_polygon(), 355
d_addrec(), 446
d_create(), 446
d_delrec(), 446-447
d_getrec(), 446
edit_environment(), 375
edit_text(), 364-366, 372-373, 375
encode_file(), 78
eraeol(), 367-372
error-handling, 631-634
exe_command(), 881
exit(), 318-321, 648-650, 726
exp(), 564
exponential, 564-565
external linkage, 135
fabs(), 568
fclose(), 70-72, 592-593
fcloseall(), 78
feof(), 83, 632-633
ferror(), 83, 633
fflush(), 431, 593
fgetc(), 65, 78-79, 615-616
fgetpos(), 439-441, 626
fgets(), 65, 79-80, 616
file management, 416-421
file positioning, 432-434
floor(), 568
fmod(), 568
fopen(), 66-70, 143, 426-428, 594-596
formatted I/O, 83-93, 432
fprintf(), 90-91, 599-600
fputc(), 65, 78-79, 617
fputs(), 65, 79-80, 618
fread(), 623-624
free(), 454, 478, 481-482, 644-645
freopen(), 596
frexp(), 564
friend function, 800-801
fscanf(), 605-606, 609-611
fseek(), 440-441, 627
fsetpos(), 440-441, 628-630
ftell(), 439, 630
fwrite(), 624-625
gauss(), 358
general business, 872-875
generate_key(), 78
getc(), 63-65
getch(), 101, 368-372
getchar(), 63-65, 619-620
getenv(), 650

gets(), 65, 79-80, 620
get_comm_byte(), 879
get_entries(), 499-501
get_key(), 880
get_mortgage_data(), 874
_gettextpostion(), 367
_getvideoconfig(), 100
gmtime(), 679
hex_char(), 109-110
hook_com(), 878
hyperbolic, 563
I/O, 55
init_com(), 878
inline, 718-719
input/output, 848-850
internal linkage, 136
int_svc(), 878
invoking, 266
is...(), 540
isalnum(), 540
isalpha(), 540-541
iscntrl(), 541
isdigit(), 541
isgraph(), 541
islower(), 541
isprint(), 542
ispunct(), 542
isspace(), 542
isupper(), 542
isxdigit(), 542
jump, nonlocal, 267
kbd_command(), 880
labs(), 654-655
ldexp(), 564
ldiv(), 205
ldiv_t(), 655
library, 31
locale-dependent, 846
localeconv(), 557-559
localtime(), 679-680
log(), 565
log10(), 565
logarithmic, 565-566
longjmp(), 274-280, 572-575
lores_clock(), 906
main(), 28-29, 115
malloc(), 454, 472, 478, 481, 645
mblen(), 655-656
mbstowcs(), 657-658
mbtowc(), 656-657

member, 801-802, 829-830
memchr(), 666-667
memcmp(), 662
memcpy(), 659-660
memmove(), 659-660
memory management, 478-482
memset(), 107, 671-672
mktime(), 676-677
modf(), 206, 566
mortgage analysis/amortization, 874-875
naming, 136-137, 148
newint8(), 905
nonlocal, 266
overlay(), 880
overloading, 722, 804-806, 828-829
parser(), 393
passing objects to, 799-801
perror(), 83, 633-634
placement, 30-31
pointers to, 266
poly(), 290
polynomial, 290
pop(), 744
popold(), 744
pow(), 567
power, 567
print(), 784
printf(), 87-91, 612
print_table(), 875
process(), 132
push(), 744
pushold(), 744
putc(), 63-65
putchar(), 63-65, 620-621
putenv(), 373
puts(), 65, 79-80, 621
qsort(), 413, 652-653
raise(), 271-274
rand(), 642-643
realloc(), 478, 481, 645-647
registering, 649-650
remainder, 568-569
remove(), 416-417, 589-590
rename(), 590
reset_it(), 245-246
rewind(), 418-420, 630-631
run_script(), 881
scanf(), 91-93, 612
scanner(), 384-385, 391-393

scroll_up(), 880
send_comm_byte(), 878-879
setbuf(), 451-452, 597
setjmp(), 274-280, 574-575
setlocale(), 556
setvbuf(), 422-423, 451-454, 598
set_new_handler(), 758-761
_settextpostion(), 367
shell_sort(), 413
show_line(), 101
signal(), 266, 271-274, 577-578
signal-handling, 848
sin(), 561
sinh(), 563
sizeof(), 644
sltrtok(), 670-671
SPFV(), 873
SPPV(), 874
sprintf(), 90, 612
sqrt(), 567
sscanf(), 612-613
stop_bench(), 906
strcat(), 82, 362, 661
strchr(), 82, 667
strcmp(), 663
strcoll(), 664
strcpy(), 82, 361-362, 660
strcspn(), 667-668
strerror(), 672
strftime(), 680-682
string I/O, 79-82
string manipulation, 853-855
string_out(), 880
strlen(), 90, 336-337, 362, 672
strncat(), 661-662
strncmp(), 664-665
strncpy(), 660-661
strol(), 84-85
stroul(), 84-85, 640-642
strpbrk(), 668
strrchr(), 668-669
strspn(), 669
strstr(), 669-670
strtod(), 84-85, 638-639
strtok(), 383-384
strtol(), 639-640
strxfrm(), 665-666
str_invert(), 205-206, 332
system(), 321-323, 650

tan(), 562
tanh(), 563
test_key(), 879
time(), 676-677
time/clock, 855-856
time_t, 673
tmpfile(), 420-421, 590
tmpnam(), 420-421, 591-592
tolower(), 543
toupper(), 543
trigonometric, 560-562
ungetc(), 621-622
unhook_com(), 878
user-defined, 29-31
USFV(), 873
USPV(), 874
vfprintf(), 613
vidtex(), 880
vidtex_sba(), 880
vprintf(), 613-614
vsprintf(), 255, 615
wait_for_tx(), 879
wcstombs(), 658
wctomb(), 657
writing, 140
fwrite() function, 624-625

G

g conversion specification, 603, 608
gauss() function, 358
gauss.c program listings, 356-358
Gaussian elimination, 356-358
generate_key() function, 78
getc() function, 63-65
getch() function, 101, 368-372
getchar() function, 63-65, 619-620
getenv() function, 650
gets() function, 65, 79-80, 620
_gettextpostion() function, 367
_getvideoconfig() function, 100
get_comm_byte() function, 879
get_data.c program listing, 610
get_entries() function, 499-501
get_key() function, 880
get_mortgage_data() function, 874
get_name.c program listing, 604

glass teletype, 98-101
glblnew.cpp program listing, 760-761
global operators
    delete, 753-765
    new, 753-765
global scope, 122
global static object, 768-770
global variable, 27, 122-127, 130
gmtime() function, 679
goloop.c program listing, 304-305
goto statement, 142-143, 285, 288, 303, 305
    versus break, 304-305
graph.h header file, 364
grouping, lconv data structure, 557

H

h conversion specification, 601
handles
    DOS, 64-65
    file, 64-65
handling end-of-file, 83
handling I/O errors, 83
hardware/system dependencies, 94
    C language extensions, 95-97
hashing, 435
    modulus method, 436-438
hashkey, 436-438, 441-448
header files, 20, 23, 206-209, 585-634
    assert.h, 837
    compiling programs separately, 207-209
    conio.h, 364
    ctype.h, 845
    float.h, 548-551, 838
    graph.h, 364
    include directives, 175-176
    iostream.h, 787-788
    keyboard, 693-694
    limits.h, 551-553, 839
    locale.h, 554-559, 840, 846
    math.h, 559-569, 840, 846-847
    scanner.h, 390
    setjmp.h, 840, 847
    signal.h, 841, 848
    stdarg.h, 841
    stddef.h, 585-634, 842
    stdio.h, 585-634, 842, 848-850
    stdlib.h, 635, 843, 851-853

stream.hpp, 787-788
stredit.h, 372
string.h, 658, 853-855
time.h, 672, 843, 855-856
timer.h, 907-908
typical uses, 22-23
Hermite matrix, 897
hexadecimal numeric escape sequences, 162-163
hex_char() function, 109-110
high-resolution
    mode, 902
    timing, 904-906
hook_com() function, 878
horizontal tab character, mnemonic escape
    sequences, 161
Horner's method algorithm, 291
hosted environments, 256
HUGE_VAL macro, 559-560
hyperbolic functions, 563

I

i conversion specifier, 602, 607
I/O (input/output)
    buffered, 421-422
    control manifest constants, 842
    events, reducing, 453-454
    functions, 55, 62-63
    modes, 425
        input, 426-427
        output, 427
        update, 428-431
    device, 52
    overhead, 450-454
    stream, 421-425
    ports, 97
    programming, 51-55, 73-82
        buffering, 57
        error handling, 83
        file, 415-434, 455-456
        hardware/system dependencies, 94
        interactive devices, 58-60
        network environment, 455-456
        setup-overhead time, 57-58
        stream I/O, 56-57
        text streams, 61-72
    redirection, 62-63, 791
identifiers
    conventions, 171-172

data object, 171-172
    extensions to ANSI standard, 530-531
    external, 171-172
    internal, 171-172
    ordinary tokens, 170
    primary expressions, 217
    simple, 118
    user-defined function, 171-172
identifiers in primary expressions, 217
ideograms, 165
if() statement, 308-311
if-else() statements, 308-312
    nested, 311-312
implementation-defined
    behavior (ANSI standard), 507, 518-523
    search, 24-25
implementation-dependent extensions, 12
implicit data type conversion, 238
#include directives
    header files, 175-176
    macro names, 175-176
incomplete type function prototypes, 105, 248
increment postfix operator, 78
incremental modification, 702
indentation in C language programs, 33-35
indirect recursion, 260-261
indirection (*) operator, 67-69, 327
    multiple indirection, 380-381
inherit.cpp program listing, 780-783
inheritance, 700-701, 752-753, 771
    class, 702
    multiple, 704-705, 783
    reusing code, 778-788
initializer list, 77-78
    constructor definition, 723-725
initializers, optional, 118
initializing
    data objects, 199-200
    loops, 283
    pointers, 327, 329
    string variables, 361
    structures
        with tags, 463-464
        without tags, 461
    variables, 121
init_com() function, 878
inline functions, 718-719
inner declaration, 125-126
input, 91-93

input item, 609
input mode, 426-427
input operations, 52
input/output functions, 848-850
inserter (<<) operator, 788-791
int data type, 106, 247
    constant range, 113
    function default type, 131
int keyword, 119
integers
    arithmetic, 654-655
    division, 654-655
    leapyear, 130
    signed, 112
integral types, 311
integrated development environment (IDE), 38,
    45-46
interactive devices, 58-60
interest-rate conversions, 872-873
intermediate representation, C language program
    translation, 168
internal identifiers, 171-172
internal linkage, 136, 196-198
int_curr_symbol, lconv data structure, 557
int_frac_digits, lconv data structure, 558
INT_MAX macro, 553
INT_MIN macro, 553
int_svc() function, 878
inverse trig functions program listing, 562
invoking functions, 266
_IOFBF macro, 451-452, 587
_IOLBF macro, 451-452, 587
_IONBF macro, 451-452, 587
iostream.h header file, 787-788
IRQ0 interrupt service routine (ISR), 900
isalnum() function, 540
isalpha() function, 540-541
iscntrl() function, 541
isdigit() function, 541
isfunct.c program listing, 543-544
isgraph() function, 541
islower() function, 541
isprint() function, 542
ispunct() function, 542
isspace() function, 542
isupper() function, 542
isxdigit() function, 542
iterations, loop, 283

J

jmperr.c program listing, 276-277
jmpsig.c program listing, 278-280
jmp_buf type declaration, 572
jump buffer, 275
jump functions, direct, 847
jump statements
    break, 303
    continue, 303, 306-308
    goto, 303, 305
    return, 303
jump.c program listing, 573-574

K

K&R standard
    converting to ANSI standard, 524-529
    differences from ANSI standard, 523-528
kbd_command() function, 880
Kernighan, Brian W, 10
keyboard.h header file, 693-694
keyboard.cpp program listing, 694-696
keyboard.hpp program listing, 693
keyio.c program listing, 424-425
keywords
    asm, 531
    auto, 194
    char, 119
    const, 829-830
    double, 119
    enum-specifier, 119
    extern, 135, 194-195
    float, 119
    fortran, 531
    int, 119
    long, 119
    ordinary tokens, 170
    quick reference, 172-173
    register, 194
    signed, 119
    static, 135, 194-195, 829-830
    struct-or-union-specifier, 119
    this, 716-720
    type-def name, 119
    typedef, 195
    unsigned, 119

void, 119
virtual, 784
volatile, 829-830

L

l conversion specification, 601
labels/labeled statements, 143-144
    case:, 313-318
    default:, 317-318
labs() function, 654-655
language convention, 152-166
languages (computer)
    assembly language, 13-14
    BCPL, 10
    C, 10
        C+, 13
        C++, 12
        compared to assembly language, 13-14
        compared to COBOL, 14
        compared to FORTRAN, 15
        compared to Pascal, 14
        programs, 15-17
    COBOL, 11, 14
    FORTRAN, 15
    Pascal, 14
lcnvrt.c program listing, 641
lconv data structure
    currency_symbol, 557
    decimal_point, 557
    grouping, 557
    int_curr_symbol, 557
    int_frac_digits, 558
    mon_decimal_point, 557
    mon_grouping, 558
    mon_thousands_sep, 558
    negative_sign, 558
    n_cs_precedes, 558
    n_sep_by_space, 558
    n_sign_posn, 559
    positive_sign, 558
    p_cs_precedes, 558
    p_sep_by_space, 558
    p_sign_posn, 559
    thousands_sep, 557
LC_ALL macro, 554-555
LC_COLLATE macro, 555
LC_CTYPE macro, 555
LC_MONETARY macro, 555

LC_NUMERIC macro, 555
LC_TIME macro, 555-556
LDBL_DIG macro, 549
LDBL_EPSILON macro, 550-551
LDBL_MANT_DIG macro, 548-549
LDBL_MAX macro, 550
LDBL_MAX_10_EXP macro, 550
LDBL_MAX_EXP macro, 549
LDBL_MIN macro, 550
LDBL_MIN_10_EXP macro, 549
LDBL_MIN_EXP macro, 549
ldexp() function, 564
ldisplay.c program listing, 254
ldiv() function, 205
ldiv_t type declaration, 636
ldiv_t() function, 655
leading characters, 116
least significant bit, 153
lexical scanners *see* scanners
library functions, 31
    curses, 364
limit values manifest constants, 839
limits, constants, 113
limits.h header file, 551-553
    macros, 839
__LINE__ macro, 189
line buffered I/O, 57, 60, 64-65
line control (#line) directive, 186-187
line feed/newline character, 159-160
linkage editor, 41-42
linkage of data objects, 195-196
    effect of scope, 198-199
    effect of storage class, 198-199
    external, 196-206, 208-209
    internal, 196-198
    no, 196-198
linked lists, 466
    anchor, 466
    building with structures, 483-501
    chaining, 498-501
    doubly, 467, 484-501
    singly, 466-467, 498-501
listings *see* program listings
lists
    declarator, 116-118
    formal parameter, 136-137
    initializer, 723-725
    linked, 466-467
    variable argument, 841

literal.c program listing, 114-115
literals *see* constants
load modules, 41-42
local scope, 122
local variables, 27, 122, 125-127, 131
locale-dependent
    functions, 846
    values, manifest constants, 840
locale.h header file, 554-559
    functions, 846
    macros, 840
localeconv() function, 557-559
localtime() function, 679-680
log() function, 565
log10() function, 565
logarithmic functions, 565-566
    program listing, 566
logic, conditional, 308-318
logic flow
    altering in a loop, 301-314
    program, 281-284
long double data type, 106-107, 112-113, 548
    constant range, 113
long int data type, 106
    constant range, 113
long keyword, 119
longjmp() function, 274-280, 572-575
LONG_MAX macro, 553
LONG_MIN macro, 553
loops, 282
    altering logic flow, 301-314
    coding, 284-288
    condition checking, 283-284
    controlling, 288
    goto vs. break, 304-305
    initializing, 283
    iteration, 283
    nesting, 298-301
lores_clock() function, 906
lvalue expressions, 218-219
L_tmpnam macro, 588

M

macros
    ANSI C standard, 173-174
    arguments, 180
        extension to ANSI standard, 532

assert(), 537-538, 837
BUFSIZ, 587-588
BUFSIZE, 452
buildmsg(), 342
CHAR_BIT, 551
CHAR_MAX, 552
CHAR_MIN, 552
CLK_TCK, 673
__DATE__, 189
DBL_DIG, 549
DBL_EPSILON, 550-551
DBL_MANT_DIG, 548-549
DBL_MAX, 550
DBL_MAX_10_EXP, 550
DBL_MAX_EXP, 549
DBL_MIN, 550
DBL_MIN_10_EXP, 549
DBL_MIN_EXP, 549
DISPLAY, 262
EDOM, 539, 560
EOF, 71-72, 588
ERANGE, 539, 560
errno, 538-539
EXIT_FAILURE, 636
EXIT_SUCCESS, 636
expansion, 181-183
Exxxxxx, 539-540
__FILE__, 189
FILENAME_MAX, 588
float.h header file, 838
FLT_DIG, 549
FLT_EPSILON, 550-551
FLT_MANT_DIG, 548-549
FLT_MAX, 550
FLT_MAX_10_EXP, 550
FLT_MAX_EXP, 549
FLT_MIN, 550
FLT_MIN_10_EXP, 549
FLT_MIN_EXP, 549
FLT_RADIX, 548-550
FLT_ROUNDS, 548
FOPEN_MAX, 588
function-like, 177-180
HUGE_VAL, 559-560
INT_MAX, 553
INT_MIN, 553
_IOFBF, 451-452, 587
_IOLBF, 451-452, 587
_IONBF, 451-452, 587

LC_ALL, 554-555
LC_COLLATE, 555
LC_CTYPE, 555
LC_MONETARY, 555
LC_NUMERIC, 555
LC_TIME, 555-556
LDBL_DIG, 549
LDBL_EPSILON, 550-551
LDBL_MANT_DIG, 548-549
LDBL_MAX, 550
LDBL_MAX_10_EXP, 550
LDBL_MAX_EXP, 549
LDBL_MIN, 550
LDBL_MIN_10_EXP, 549
LDBL_MIN_EXP, 549
limits.h header file, 839
__LINE__, 189
locale.h header file, 840
LONG_MAX, 553
LONG_MIN, 553
L_tmpnam, 588
math.h header file, 840
MB_CUR_MAX, 637
MB_LEN_MAX, 552
names
    extensions to ANSI standard, 532
    #include directives, 175-176
    predefined, 188-189
NULL, 68-69, 586
object-like, 177-178
offsetof(), 465-466, 586
raise(), 577-578
RAND_MAX, 636
SCHAR_MAX, 551
SCHAR_MIN, 551
SEEK_CUR, 440-441, 588-589
SEEK_END, 440-441, 588-589
SEEK_SET, 440-441, 588-589
setjmp(), 572
SHRT_MAX, 552
SHRT_MIN, 552
SIGABRT, 272, 576
SIGFPE, 272, 274, 576
SIGILL, 272, 576
SIGINT, 272, 576
signal.h header file, 575, 841
SIGSEGV, 272, 576-577
SIGTERM, 272, 274, 577
SIG_DFL, 575

SIG_ERR, 576
SIG_IGN, 575
__STDC__, 189
stddef.h header file, 579, 842
stderr, 589
stdin, 589
stdout, 589
substitution, 174, 177-178
__TIME__, 189
TMP_MAX, 589
UCHAR_MAX, 551
UINT_MAX, 553
ULONG_MAX, 553
USHRT_MAX, 552-553
va_arg(), 252-253, 580-581
va_end(), 253, 582
va_start(), 251-252, 580
wchar_t, 586
main storage, 52
main() function, 115
    program termination, 29
    purpose, 28
MAKE project-management utility, 43, 211
    comments, 212-213
    dependency condition, 212-213
    description blocks, 212-213
    target fields, 212-213
malloc() function, 454, 472, 478, 481, 645
manifest constants, 178-180, 342, 842
    arithmetic errors, 840
    exit(), 843
    floating-point, 838
    I/O control, 842
    limiting values, 839
    locale-dependent values, 840
    multibyte character size, 843
    random numbers, 843
    signal types, 841
    stream names, 842
    time/clock functions, 843
mantissa, 106, 113
math functions, 846-847
math.h header file, 559-569
    functions, 846-847
    macros, 840
matrix, Hermite, 897
matrix algebra, b-spline derivation, 897-898
mblen() function, 655-656
mbstowcs() function, 657-658

mbtowc() function, 656-657
MB_CUR_MAX macro, 637
MB_LEN_MAX macro, 552
measurement of algorithms, 899-910
member elements
    private:, 715-716
    protected:, 715-716
    public:, 715-716
member functions, 801-802
    calling, 727-729
    const keyword, 829-830
    overloading, 806
    prototype declarations, 713-716
    static keyword, 829-830
    volatile keyword, 829-830
members
    structure, 464-469
    union, 474-476
memchr() function, 666-667
memcmp() function, 662
memcpy() function, 659-660
memmove() function, 659-660
memory
    allocating, 26, 644-645
    allocating at run-time, 478-482
    dynamic, 478-482
    managing, 643-644
        management functions, 478-482
    memory models, 328
    reallocating, 646-647
memory address pointer, 67-69
memory-mapped I/O, 53
memset() function, 107, 671-672
menus.cpp program listing, 746-749
Microsoft QuickC editor, 37-38
minimal character set, C language, 155-156
minimum range for constants, 113
mixstr.cpp program listing, 791
mktime() function, 676-677
mktime.c program listing, 677-678
mmem.c program listing, 646
mnemonic escape sequences, 158
    alert character, 159
    backspace character, 159
    carriage-return character, 160
    double question marks character, 162
    formfeed character, 159
    horizontal tab character, 161
    newline character, 159-160

single quotation marks, 161
    vertical tab character, 161
modes
    file, 431-434, 450
    I/O, 425-431
    video, 101
modf() function, 206, 566
modulus method, key hashing, 436-438
mon_decimal_point, lconv data structure, 557
mon_grouping, lconv data structure, 558
mon_thousands_sep,lconv data structure, 558
most significant bit, 153
motion-control characters, 154
MS LINK, 42
multibyte
    character directive, 607
    character size manifest constants, 843
    characters, 165-166, 655-657
    sequences, 165-166
    strings, 657-658
multidimensional arrays, 344-346
multif.cpp program listing, 805-806
multiple indirection, 380-381
    dereferencing pointers, 381
    indirection operator, 380-381
    referencing pointers, 381
multiple inheritance, 704-705, 783
    virtual base classes, 827-828
multiple source files, 25
multitasking, 905

N

n conversion specification, 601, 603
names
    file, 66-67
    stream, 66-67
    variables, 115-116
near pointer, 338-339
negative_sign, lconv data structure, 558
nested if-else() statements, 311-312
nesting loops, 298-301
networking, I/O programming, 455-456
new operator, 751-757
    constructor function, 757
    redefining, 758-765
newcp.cpp program listing, 762-763
newcp2.cpp program listing, 764-765
newint8() function, 905

newline character, mnemonic escape sequences, 159-160
NMAKE project-management utility, 43
no linkage, 196-198
nonlocal jump functions, 266-267
normal program termination, 29
notation
    digraph, 163
    trigraph, 163
null (#) directive, 186, 188
null character, 18
    multibyte encoding, 166
NULL macro, 68-69, 586
null pointers, 68-69
null statements, 144
null strings, 77-78
number.c program listings, 81-82
numbers
    floating-point, 112, 547-548, 549-551
    pseudorandom, 642-643
numeric escape sequences
    hexadecimal, 162-163
    octal, 162
nybble, 110
n_cs_precedes,lconv data structure, 558
n_sep_by_space,lconv data structure, 558
n_sign_posn, lconv data structure, 559

O

o conversion specifier, 602, 607
object-like macros, 177-178
object-oriented programming (OOP), 13, 685-699, 705
    Stroustrup's comments, 703-704
    Wegner's definition, 700-702
    Zortech's definition, 702-703
objects, 686-688
    address, 326
    class, 720-729
    concatenating strings, 362
    constructors, 767-768
    creating dynamically, 765-766
    data, 458-459
    dynamic, 765-767
    implementations
        autonomous, 705
        functional, 705

    server, 705
    slot-based, 705
    modules, 41-42
    new operator, 753
    static, 765-766, 768-771
    stream, 787-791
    typing, 105, 692-693
octal numeric escape sequences, 162
offset parameter, 255
offset address, 328, 338-339, 465-466
offsetof() macro, 465-466, 586
one-dimensional array, 341
one-pass compiler, 168
OOP see object-oriented programming
open addressing, 436-438
open-ended recursion, 262-264
opening files, 68-70
operating systems, 55
    CP/M, 10-11
    DOS, 10-11
    UNIX, 10
operations, input/output, 52
operators
    * indirection, 327
    add assign (+=), 111
    address of (&), 465
    associativity, 221
    binary, 228-232
    bitwise AND (&), 110
    cast, 228
    comma, 234-235
    compound assignment, 233-234
    conditional, 111, 232-233
    delete, 751-765
    equality (==), 142
    expression, 396
    extractor (>>), 788-789, 791
    factor, 397
    formula, 396
    indirection (*), 67-69, 380-381
    inserter (<<), 788-789, 791
    new, 751-765
    ordinary tokens, 170
    overloading, 807-813, 824-826
    postfix, 78, 221-224, 333, 346-348, 464
    power, 397
    precedence, 221, 235-236
    reference (&), 719, 794-797
    shift-right (>>), 110

signed factor, 397
simple assignment, 233-234
simple expression, 396
structure dot (.), 464
structure pointer (->), 465
term, 397
ternary, 111, 232-233
unary, 224-228
optional initializer, 118
order of precedence of operators, 221, 235-236
ordinary tokens
constants, 170
identifiers, 170
keywords, 170
operators, 170
punctuators, 170
string literals, 170
outer declaration, 123-125
output
mode, 427
operations, 52
polygon array, 354-355
overlay() function, 880
overloading
functions, 722, 804-806, 828-829
new/delete operators, 758-765
other operators, 807-813, 824-826
ovloadf.cpp program listing, 804-805

P

p conversion specification, 603, 608-609
parameter declarators, 137
parameters
argc, 256-257
argv[], 256-257
file mode, 69-70
offset, 255
passing, 131-132, 139
by reference, 244-249
by value, 244-249
main(), 256-258
parentheses, aligning in C language programs, 35
parenthesized expressions in primary expressions, 218
parser, C language program translation, 167
parser() function, 393
parsing routines, 394-397, 401-403
algebraic expressions, 396, 401-403

recursive descent, 394-397, 401-403
Pascal language compared to C, 14
passing objects to functions, 799-801
passing parameters, 131-132, 139
Paterson, Tim, 11
performance-measurement software, 899-910
peripheral device, 52
perror() function, 83, 633-634
phases of C language program translation, 168-169
placing functions in a program, 30-31
pointer difference type see ptrdiff_t
pointers, 326-337, 340, 472, 794-797
arithmetic, 338-340
array, 76
arrays of pointers, 403-405
based, 338-339
casts, extensions to ANSI standard, 531
class objects, 795-799
comparisons, 331-337
declaring, 329
dereferencing, 67-69, 329, 381, 794
far, 338-339
if-else() statements, 311
increasing program flexibility, 406-407
initializing, 327, 329
memory address, 67-69
multiple indirection, 380-381
near, 338-339
null, 68-69
pointer to structures, 403
pointers to arrays, 405-406
reference operator, 794-797
referencing, 381
sorting, 407-413
subscript equivalence, 346-348
to functions, 121, 266-270
to identifiers, 120
to pointers see multiple indirection
to self, 716-719
to types, 327
type derivation, 457-458
use in scanners, 384-385, 391-393
pointers to pointers see multiple indirection
poly() function, 290
poly.c program listing, 289-292
polymorphism, 702-703, 783-784
polynomial() function, 290
pop() function, 744
popold() function, 744
portability (ANSI standards), 12, 505-523

differences from K&R standard, 523-528
    implementation-defined behavior, 507, 518-523
    translation limitations for compilers, 528-529
    undefined behavior, 510-517
    unspecified behavior, 508-510
ports
    device control, 54
    I/O, 53-54, 97
positive_sign, lconv data structure, 558
postfix expressions, 221-224
postfix operators, 78, 221-224, 333, 346-348, 464
pow() function, 567
power() function, 567
power operator, 397
#pragma (#error) directive, 186, 188
precedence of operators, 221, 235-236
precision argument, 601
preprocessing tokens, 170
preprocessor directives, 17, 20-23, 25, 174, 548
primary expressions, 217-218
    constants, 217
    identifiers, 217
    parenthesized expressions, 218
    string literals, 217-218
prime.c program listing, 285-287, 438
print() function, 784
printf() function, 87-91, 612
printit.c program listing, 89
print_it.c program listing, 605
print_table() function, 875
private: member elements, 715-716
process() function, 132
program listings, 653
    array.cpp, 710-713
    arraycl2.cpp, 755-757
    arraycla.cpp, 754
    ascii.c, 299-301
    atexit.c, 320-321, 649
    bar.c, 581-582
    buffer.c, 599
    ccom.c, 97, 877-896
    center.c, 90
    cinout.cpp, 789
    cinsdel.c, 365-367
    cipher.c, 72-79
    clear.c, 632
    clip.c, 255
    clock.c, 675
    cmem.c, 644

cminus.c, 689-691
compare.c, 663
compares.c, 269-270, 407-409
compose.cpp, 772-778
continue.c, 307-308
_copy.c, 617-618
cprint.c, 96-97
crc16.c, 146
cvtjul.c, 128-130
cvtstr.c, 202-206
damfile.c, 441-448
demo.cpp, 745-746
detab.c, 293-297
difft.c, 675-676
dir_io.c, 624
dir_wrt.c, 625-626
escape.c, 157
euclid.c, 261-262
euclid2.c, 265-266
exchange.c, 147
fget_str.c, 616-617
finance.c, 94, 857-876
first.c, 19-20
fltcnvrt.c, 639
flush.c, 594
fmore.c, 98-100
formula.c, 397-403
fput_str.c, 618-619
frmtime.c, 682
gauss.c, 356-358
get_data.c, 610
get_name.c, 604
glblnew.cpp, 760-761
goloop.c, 304-305
inherit.cpp, 780-783
isfunct.c, 543-544
jmperr.c, 276-278
jmpsig.c, 278-280
jump.c, 573-574
keyboard.cpp, 694-696
keyboard.hpp, 693
keyio.c, 424-425
lcnvrt.c, 641
ldisplay.c, 254
literal.c, 114-115
menus.cpp, 746-749
mixstr.cpp, 791
mktime.c, 677-678
mmem.c, 646

`multif.cpp`, 805-806
`newcp.cpp`, 762-763
`newcp2.cpp`, 764-765
`number.c`, 81-82
`ovloadf.cpp`, 804-805
`poly.c`, 289-292
`power()` function, 567
`prime.c`, 285-287, 438
`printit.c`, 89
`print_it.c`, 605
`readit.c`, 93
`reopen.c`, 597
`rewind.c`, 631
`rmem.c`, 647
`scanner.c`, 386-393
`screen.cpp`, 733-744, 746, 748
`screen.hpp`, 731-732
`sdump.c`, 107-109
`search.c`, 652
`seek.c`, 628
`select.c`, 314-318
`set_pos.c`, 629
`shellsrt.c`, 409-413
`showarg.c`, 257-258
`showsig.c`, 273-274
`sigdemo.c`, 578-579
`speedbuf.c`, 422-423
`spline.c`, 349-355
`srand()`, 643
`stream.c`, 63
`stredit.c`, 368-372
`strtox.c`, 85-86
`struct.c`, 461
`struct2.c`, 463-464
`struct3.c`, 468
`struct4.c`, 469-470
`struct5.c`, 470-471
`struct6.c`, 471-472
`struct7.c`, 480
`sysenv.c`, 373-375
`temp.c`, 591
`testcstr.c`, 201-202
`testkey.cpp`, 696-699
`testtime.c`, 909-910
`this1.cpp`, 717-718
`this2.cpp`, 719-720
`timer.c`, 900-909
`token.c`, 671
`uctouch.c`, 44

`ulcnvrt.c`, 642
`un_read.c`, 622-623
`usevli.cpp`, 826
`versions.c`, 417-419
`vinherit.cpp`, 785-788
`vli.cpp`, 815-823
`vli.hpp`, 814
`vprint.c`, 614-615
`xdir.c`, 484-497
`xfrm.c`, 666
program stub, 28
program termination, 29, 318-321
program translation
    C language, 167-169
        parser, 167
        scanner, 167
        tokens, 167, 170
    phases, 168-169
project-management facilities, 42
    MAKE utility, 43
    NMAKE utility, 43
    TOUCH utility, 43-44
promotion of arguments, 247-249
`protected`: member elements, 715-716
prototypes, function, 132
pseudorandom numbers, 642-643
`ptrdiff_t` type definition, 585
`public`: member elements, 715-716
punctuating C language programs, 16-17, 24
punctuators, ordinary tokens, 170
`push()` function, 744
`pushold()` function, 744
`putc()` function, 63-65, 620
`putchar()` function, 63-65, 620-621
`putenv()` function, 373
`puts()` function, 65, 79-80, 621
`p_cs_precedes`, `lconv` data structure, 558
`p_sep_by_space`, `lconv` data structure, 558
`p_sign_posn`, `lconv` data structure, 559

Q

`qsort()` function, 413, 652-653
QuickC editor, 37-38

R

raise() function, 271-272, 274
raise() macro, 577-578
RAM (random access memory), 52
    address, 326
    video I/O, 98-101
rand() function, 642-643
random numbers manifest constants, 843
random-access files, direct-access, 435-438
RAND_MAX macro, 636
read operations *see* input
read-only mode, file mode parameter, 69-70
read/write heads, 55
readit.c program listing, 93
realloc() function, 478, 481, 645-647
reallocating memory, 646-647
recursion
    direct, 260-261
    eliminating, 264-266
    indirect, 260-261
    open-ended, 262-264
    recursive descent, 394-397, 401-403
recursive function call *see* recursion
redirecting I/O, 62-63, 791
reference (&) operator, 719, 794-797
referencing, 794-796
    arrays
        multidimensional, 345-346
        one-dimensional, 343
    class objects, 801-803
    pointers, 381
        multiple indirection, 381
        dereferencing pointers, 794
register keyword, 194
registers, 194
regular trig functions program listing, 562
remainder functions, program listing, 568-569
remove() function, 589
rename() function, 590
renaming files, 417
reopen.c program listing, 597
replacement list, 177
required significant digits, 112
reset_it function, 245-246
return statement, 142 145-146, 274, 303
reusing code, 771
    composition method, 772-778

inheritance method, 778-788
rewind() function, 418-420, 630-631
rewind.c program listing, 631
Richards, Martin, 10
Ritchie, Dennis M, 10
rmem.c program listing, 647
routines, high-performance, 450-454
running the chain, 467
run_script() function, 881
rvalue expressions, 218-219

S

s conversion specification, 603, 608
scalar type, 311
scanf() function, 91-93, 612
scanlist, 608
scanner, C language program translation, 167
scanner() function, 384-385, 391-393
scanner.c program listing, 386-393
scanner.h header file, 390
scanners
    parsing routines, 394-397, 401-403
        recursive descent, 394-397, 401-403
    purpose, 382-384
    searching for tokens, 383-384
    use of pointers, 384-385, 391-393
SCHAR_MAX macro, 551
SCHAR_MIN macro, 551
scope of data objects, 195-196
    block, 195-196
    effect on linkage of objects, 198-199
    file, 195-196
    function, 195-196
    function prototype, 195-196
    global, 122
    local, 122
    surrounding, 196
    variable, 122
screen() constructor, 741, 743
screen.cpp program listing, 733-744, 746, 748
screen.hpp program listing, 731-732
script file, 894-896
scroll_up() function, 880
sdump.c program listing, 107-109
search functions, 650-652
search.c program listing, 652
secondary storage, 52

seek.c program listing, 628
SEEK_CUR macro, 440-441, 588-589
SEEK_END macro, 440-441, 588-589
SEEK_SET macro, 440-441, 588-589
segment address, 328
    80x86 CPU, 338-339
select.c program listing, 314-318
self-referential structures, 466-467
semantic routines, C language program translation,
    168
send command, script file, 895
send_comm_byte() function, 878-879
separate compilation, 202
    external data objects, 208-209
    header files, 207-209
    linking modules, 210-213
    MAKE utility, 211-213
sequence points, 214-217
sequential file processing, 418-420
sequential logic flow, 281-283
server objects, 705
set-up overhead time, 57-58
setbuf() function, 451-452, 597
setjmp() function, 274-280, 574-575
setjmp() macro, 572
setjmp.h header file, 571-572
    functions, 847
    macros, 840
setlocale() function, 556
_settextpostion() function, 367
setvbuf() function, 422-423, 451-454, 598
set_new_handler() function, 758-761
set_pos.c program listing, 629
shellsrt.c program listing, 409-413
shell_sort() function, 413
shift states, 165
shift-right operator (>>), 110
short data type, 247
short int data type, 106-107, 247
    constant range, 113
showarg.c program listing, 257-258
showsig.c program listing, 273-274
show_line() function, 101
SHRT_MAX macro, 552
SHRT_MIN macro, 552
side effects of expressions, 214-217
SIGABRT macro, 272, 576
sigdemo.c program listing, 578-579
SIGFPE macro, 272, 274, 576

SIGILL macro, 272, 576
SIGINT macro, 272, 576
sign bit, 112
signal types, manifest constants, 841
signal() function, 266, 271-274, 577-578
signal-handling functions, 848
    extensions to ANSI standard, 532
signal.h header file, 575
    functions, 848
    macros, 841
signed char data type, 106-107
    constant range, 113
signed data type, 105
signed factor operator, 397
signed integer data type, 106
signed keyword, 119
SIGSEGV macro, 272, 576-577
SIGTERM macro, 272, 274, 577
sig_atomic_t type definition, 575
SIG_DFL macro, 575
SIG_ERR macro, 576
SIG_IGN macro, 575
simple assignment operators, 233-234
simple expression operator, 396
simple identifiers, 118
sin() function, 561
single payment future value (SPFV), 873
single payment present value (SPPV), 874
single quotation marks, escape sequences, 161
singly linked lists, 466, 498-501
sinh() function, 563
size_t type definition, 586
sizeof() function, 644
slash asterisk (/*) marking comments in C language
    programs, 17
slot-based objects, 705
SMALL memory model, 26
sort() function, 653
sort.c program listing, 653
sorting with pointers, 407-413
source files, 166-167
    including, 21
    multiple, 25
specifiers
    field-width, 468
    typedef, 476-477
speed matching, 57, 421-422
speedbuf.c program listing, 422-423
SPFV() function, 873

spline.c program listings, 349-355
SPPV() function, 874
sprintf() function, 90, 612
sqrt() function, 567
srand() program listing, 643
sscanf() function, 612-613
stack, dynamic objects, 766
stack oriented machines, 244
standard auxiliary (stdaux) stream, 65
standard error (stderr) stream, 61-65, 423-425
standard input (stdin) stream, 61-65, 423-425
standard output (stdout) stream, 61-65, 423-425
standard printer (stdprn) stream, 65
standards
    ANSI
        extensions, 530-532
        portability, 505-529
    K&R, 523-528
state-dependent coding, 165
statements, 16
    block, 17
    break, 142, 303, 317-318
    compound, 144-145
    continue, 303, 306-308
    direct branching, 303, 305-308
    do-while(), 288, 292-297
    expression, 140-141
    flow control, 141-142
    for(), 288, 297-301
    goto, 142-143, 285, 288, 303, 305
    if(), 308-311
    if-else(), 308-312
    labeled, 143
    null, 144
    return, 142, 145-146, 274, 303
    switch(), 296, 308-309, 311-318
    while(), 288-292
static storage class, 122, 192, 194-195, 332, 720
    defining, 194-195
    duration, 125, 135
    extern keyword, 194-195
    specifier, 124-126
    storage type-specifier, 130-131
static keyword, 135, 194-195, 829-830
static objects, 765-766
    free store, 770-771
    global, 768-770
stdarg.h header file, 579, 841
stdaux (standard auxiliary) stream, 65

__STDC__ macro, 189
stddef.h header file, 585-634
    macros, 842
stderr (standard error) stream, 65
stderr macro, 589
stdin (standard input) stream, 61-65, 423-425
stdin macro, 589
stdio.h header file, 585-634
    functions, 848-850
    macros, 842
stdlib.h header file, 635
    functions, 851-853
    macros, 843
stdout (standard output) stream, 61-65, 423-425
stdout macro, 589
stdprn (standard printer) stream, 65
stop_bench() function, 906
storage classes, 171-172, 192-195
    auto , 122, 192-194, 720
    duration, 192-195
    effect on linkage of objects, 198-199
    static, 122, 124-126, 130-131, 192, 194-195, 332, 720
strcat() function, 82, 362, 661
strchr() function, 82, 667
strcmp() function, 663
strcoll() function, 664
strcpy() function, 82, 361-362, 660
strcspn() function, 667-668
stream I/O, 56, 57, 421-423, 425, 787-791
stream.c program listing, 63
stream.hpp header file, 787-788
streams, 57, 60
    binary, 61, 432-433
    buffering, 451-452
    connecting to files, 66-67
    DOS, 95-97
    manipulators, 790
    names, 66-67
        manifest constants, 842
    objects, 787-789, 791
    standard auxiliary (stdaux), 65
    standard error (stderr), 61-63, 65, 423-425
    standard input (stdin), 61-65, 423-425
    standard output (stdout), 61-65, 423-425
    standard printer (stdprn), 65
    text, 61-72, 432-433
    types, extensions to ANSI standards, 532
stredit.c program listing, 368-372

stredit.h header file, 372
strerror() function, 672
strftime() function, 680-682
string literals
    extensions to ANSI standard, 531
    primary expressions, 217-218
    ordinary tokens, 170
    transformation function, 665-666
string.h header file, 658
    functions, 853-855
strings, 18
    arrays of characters, 359
    comparing, 662-666
    concatenating, 661-662
    concatenating objects, 362
    converting to numbers, 637-642
    copying, 659-661
    function parameters, 376
    internal representation, 359-360
    I/O functions, 79
    manipulation functions, 361-363, 853-855
    multibyte, 657-658
    screen I/O, 367
    searching, 666-671
    text, editing, 363-367
    transformation functions, 665-666
    variables
        declaring, 359-361
        initializing, 361
string_out() function, 880
strlen() function, 90, 336-337, 362, 672
strncat() function, 661-662
strncmp() function, 664-665
strncpy() function, 660-661
strol() function, 84-85
stroul() function, 84-85, 640-642
Stroustrup, Bjarne, 13
    comments on C++ language programming,
        703-704
strpbrk() function, 668
strrchr() function, 668-669
strspn() function, 669
strstr() function, 669-670
strtod() function, 84-85, 638-639
strtok() function, 383-384, 670-671
    searching for tokens, 383-384
strtol() function, 639-640
strtox.c program listing, 85-86
struct data type, 131

struct {...} declaration, 459-462
struct-or-union-specifier keyword, 119
struct.c program listing, 461
struct2.c program listing, 463-464
struct3.c program listing, 468
struct4.c program listing, 469-470
struct5.c program listing, 470-471
struct6.c program listing, 471-472
struct7.c program listing, 480
structure dot operator (.), 464
structure pointer operator (->), 465
structure tags, 462-464
structure type derivation, 458
structured programming, 687
structures, 457, 692-693
    accessing members, 464-467
    array of, 470-471
    array of pointers to, 471-472
    bit-fields within, 467-469
    building linked lists, 483-501
    combining with arrays, 469-472
    declaration list, 459-461
    defining, 458-472
    function parameters, 482-483
    pointers to structures, 403
    self-referential, 466-467
    tm {}, 673-, 674
    unions, 473-476
strxfrm() function, 665-666
str_invert() function, 205-206, 332
stub, 28
subclass, 704, 778
subexpressions, 214-217
superclass, 704, 778
surrounding scope, 196
switch() statement, 296, 308-309, 311-318
symbol table, C language program translation, 168
symmetric matrices, 359
syntax directed compiler, 167
sysenv.c program listing, 373-375
system() function, 321-323, 650

T

tags, structure, 462-464
tan() function, 562
tanh() function, 563
target fields, MAKE utility, 212-213

target machine code, C language program translation, 168
temp.c program listing, 591
temporary files, 420-421
term operator, 397
terminal, dumb, 877
terminating programs, 29, 318-321
ternary expressions, 232-233
ternary operators, 111, 232-233
testcstr.c program listing, 201-202
testkey.cpp program listing, 696-699
testtime.c program listing, 909-910
test_key() function, 879
text, editing with strings, 363-367
text data, 156-157
text editor
    C environment, 36-38
    QuickC, 37-38
text file mode, 431-434
text streams, 61-72, 432-433
    stdaux (standard printer), 65
    stderr (standard error), 61-63, 65
    stdin (standard input), 61-65
    stdout (standard output), 61-65
this keyword, 716-720
this1.cpp program listing, 717-718
this2.cpp program listing, 719-720
Thompson, Ken, 10
thousands_sep, lconv data structure, 557
__TIME__ macro, 189
time
    converting, 678-682
    functions, 855-856
    manipulating, 674-678
    time value of money, 873
    values, 672-674
time() function, 676-677
time.h header file, 672
    functions, 855-856
    macros, 843
time/clock functions manifest constants, 843
timer, high-resolution mode, 902
timer chip, reprogramming, 900, 903-905
timer.c program listing, 900-906
    convert to Turbo C, 908-909
    header file, 907-908
timer.h header file, 907-908
time_t function, 673
TLINK, 42

tm{} structure, 673-674
tmpfile() function, 420-421, 590-591
tmpnam() function, 420-421, 591-592
TMP_MAX macro, 589
tokens
    C language program translation, 167, 170
    ordinary, 170
    preprocessing, 170
    searching for, 383-384
        strtok() function, 383-384
tokens.c program listing, 671
tolower() function, 543
top-down tree structure, 32-33
TOUCH project-management utility, 43-44
toupper() function, 543
transfer of control, 281-284
translation limitations for compilers (ANSI standards), 528-529
translation see source program
triangulation, 358
trigonometric functions, 560-562
trigraph escape sequences, 163-164
trigraph notation, 163
two-pass compiler, 168
type casts, data type conversion, 238-240
type checking, 132
type declarations
    div_t, 636
    jmp_buf, 572
    ldiv_t, 636
type definitions
    FILE, 587
    fpos_t, 587
    ptrdiff_t, 585
    sig_atomic_t, 575
    size_t, 586
    va_list, 251-252, 579-580
type derivation, 699-700, 703
type promotion (data types), 237-238
type safe linkage, 828
type-def name keyword, 119
type-specifiers, 117-118
typedef declaration, 698-699
typedef keyword, 195
typedef specifier, 476-477
types of data see data types

U

u conversion specifier, 602, 607
UCHAR_MAX macro, 551
uctouch.c program listing, 44
UINT_MAX macro, 553
ulcnvrt.c program listing, 642
ULONG_MAX macro, 553
unary operators, 224-228
unbuffered files, 58-59
unbuffered I/O, 57
undefined behavior (ANSI standard), 510-517
ungetc() function, 621-622
unhook_com() function, 878
uniform series future value (USFV), 873
uniform series present value (USPV), 874
union data type, 131
union type derivation, 458, 473-476
unions
    accessing members, 474-476
    declaring, 474-476
    function parameters, 482-483
    members, 474-476
UNIX operating system, 10
unnamed bit-fields, 469
unsigned char data type, 106-107
    constant range, 113
unsigned data type, 106
unsigned int data type, 105-106, 247
    constant range, 113
unsigned keyword, 119
unsigned long data type, 106
    constant range, 113
unsigned short int data type, 106
    constant range, 113
unspecified behavior (ANSI standard), 508-510
un_read.c program listing, 622-623
update mode, 428-431
user-defined casts, 826-827
user-defined functions, 29-31
    identifiers, 172
usevli.cpp program listing, 826
    USFV() function, 873
USHRT_MAX macro, 552-553
USPV() function, 874
utilities, project management
    MAKE, 43, 211-213
    NMAKE, 43
    TOUCH, 43-44

V

value, default, 244
variable-length argument lists, 249, 254, 571-579, 580-581
    function prototypes, 250-253
    processing, 841
variables
    auto, 123, 125-126
    copy, 127
    declaring, 27
    environmental, 373-375
    global, 27, 122-126, 130
    initializing, 121
    local, 27, 122, 125-127, 131
    naming, 115-116
    scope, 122
    static, 123
    string
        declaring, 359-361
        initializing, 361
va_arg() macro, 252-253, 580-581
va_end() macro, 253, 582
va_list() type definition, 251-252, 579-580
va_start() macro, 251-252, 580
versions.c program listing, 417-419
vertical tab character, mnemonic escape sequences, 161
vfprintf() function, 613
video I/O, 98-101
video mode, 101
vidtex() function, 880
vidtex_sba() function, 880
vinherit.cpp program listing, 785-788
virtual base classes, multiple inheritance, 827-828
virtual functions, 783-788
virtual keyword, 784
virtual screens, 729-749
    manager, 731-732
    member functions, 733-749
visibility of data objects see linkage of data objects
visual debugger, 46-49
vli (very large integer) class objects, 797-799, 824-826
vli.cpp program listing, 815-823
vli.hpp program listing, 814
void data type, 131
void expressions, 220
void keyword, 119

volatile keyword, 111-112, 829-830
vprint.c program listing, 614-615
vprintf() function, 613-614
vsprintf() function, 255, 615

W

wait_for_tx() function, 879
wchar_t macro, 586
wcstombs() function, 658
wctomb() function, 657
Wegner, object-based languages, 700-702
whence binary file, 627
while() statement, 288-292
white space in C language programs, 33-34, 609

whitespace character directive, 606-607
wide characters, multibyte sequences, 166
write operations *see* output
write-only mode, file mode parameter, 69-70

X-Z

x conversion specifier, 602, 607
X3J11 standard committee, 11-12
X3J16 standard committee, 13
xdir.c program listing, 484-497
xfrm.c program listing, 666
Zortech
    compiler, 729, 732
    display-management facilities, 740-741
    object-oriented programming, 702-703

ORDER YOUR PROGRAM DISK TODAY!

You can save yourself hours of tedious, error-prone typing by ordering the companion disk to **Using C**. The disk contains the source code for all complete programs, for many shorter samples in the book, plus MAKE files or Project file samples for multiple source-file programs.

Disks are only available in 5-1/4" format. The cost is $20 per set of disk(s). (Foreign orders, add $5 for shipping and handling.)

Simply complete the blanks on this page, make a copy of it, enclose payment, and send to

> **Using C Diskette**
> **Atkinson, Campbell Development**
> **P.O. Box 8292**
> **Jackson, MS 39284**

Payment method:

*Check: _____ Money Order: _____

Date: _____

Signature: _____

*Checks require 10 days to clear

Checks and money orders should be made payable to Atkinson, Campbell Development. This offer is made by Atkinson, Campbell Development, not by Que Corporation.